ACCA

S
T
U
D
Y

T
E
X
T

PAPER F5

PERFORMANCE MANAGEMENT

BPP Learning Media is **an ACCA Approved Learning Partner – content. This means we work closely with** ACCA to ensure this Study Text contains the information you need to pass your exam.

In this Study Text which has been reviewed by the **ACCA examination team** we:

- Highlight the **most important elements** in the syllabus and the **key skills** you will need
- Signpost how each chapter links to the syllabus and the study guide
- Provide lots of **exam focus points** demonstrating what is expected of you in the exam
- Emphasise key points in regular **fast forward summaries**
- Test your knowledge in quick quizzes
- Examine your understanding in our practice question bank
- Reference all the important topics in our full index

BPP's **Practice & Revision Kit** and **i-Pass** products also support this paper.

FOR EXAMS IN DECEMBER 2014 AND JUNE 2015

BPP
LEARNING MEDIA

First edition 2007
Seventh edition June 2014

ISBN 9781 4727 1080 2
(Previous ISBN 9781 4453 9647 7)

e-ISBN 9781 4453 6734 7

British Library Cataloguing-in-Publication Data

A catalogue record for this book
is available from the British Library

Published by

BPP Learning Media Ltd
BPP House, Aldine Place
London W12 8AA

www.bpp.com/learningmedia

Printed in the United Kingdom by

Polestar Wheatons
Hennock Road
Marsh Barton
Exeter
EX2 8RP

We are grateful to the Association of Chartered Certified
Accountants for permission to reproduce past
examination questions. The suggested solutions in the
practice answer bank have been prepared by BPP
Learning Media Ltd, unless otherwise stated.

Your learning materials, published by BPP Learning
Media Ltd, are printed on paper obtained from
traceable sustainable sources.

Contents

A note about copyright

Dear Customer

What does the little © mean and why does it matter?

Your market-leading BPP books, course materials and e-learning materials do not write and update themselves. People write them: on their own behalf or as employees of an organisation that invests in this activity. Copyright law protects their livelihoods. It does so by creating rights over the use of the content.

Breach of copyright is a form of theft – as well as being a criminal offence in some jurisdictions, it is potentially a serious breach of professional ethics.

With current technology, things might seem a bit hazy but, basically, without the express permission of BPP Learning Media:

- Photocopying our materials is a breach of copyright
- Scanning, ripcasting or conversion of our digital materials into different file formats, uploading them to Facebook or e-mailing them to your friends is a breach of copyright

You can, of course, sell your books, in the form in which you have bought them – once you have finished with them. (Is this fair to your fellow students? We update for a reason.) Please note the e-products are sold on a single user licence basis: we do not supply 'unlock' codes to people who have bought them second-hand.

And what about outside the UK? BPP Learning Media strives to make our materials available at prices students can afford by local printing arrangements, pricing policies and partnerships which are clearly listed on our website. A tiny minority ignore this and indulge in criminal activity by illegally photocopying our material or supporting organisations that do. If they act illegally and unethically in one area, can you really trust them?

Helping you to pass

BPP Learning Media – Approved Learning Partner - content

As ACCA's **Approved Learning Partner – content**, BPP Learning Media gives you the **opportunity** to use study materials reviewed by the ACCA examination team. By incorporating the examination team's comments and suggestions regarding the depth and breadth of syllabus coverage, the BPP Learning Media Study Text provides excellent, **ACCA-approved** support for your studies.

The PER alert

Before you can qualify as an ACCA member, you not only have to pass all your exams but also fulfil a three year **practical experience requirement** (PER). To help you to recognise areas of the syllabus that you might be able to apply in the workplace to achieve different performance objectives, we have introduced the '**PER alert**' feature. You will find this feature throughout the Study Text to remind you that what you are **learning to pass** your ACCA exams is **equally useful to the fulfilment of the PER requirement**.

Your achievement of the PER should now be recorded in your on-line *My Experience* record.

Tackling studying

Studying can be a daunting prospect, particularly when you have lots of other commitments. The **different features** of the text, the **purposes** of which are explained fully on the **Chapter features** page, will help you whilst studying and improve your chances of **exam success**.

Developing exam awareness

Our Texts are completely **focused** on helping you pass your exam.

Our advice on **Studying F5** outlines the **content** of the paper, the **necessary skills** you are expected to be able to demonstrate and any **brought forward knowledge** you are expected to have.

Exam focus points are included within the chapters to highlight when and how specific topics were examined, or how they might be examined in the future.

Using the Syllabus and Study Guide

You can find the syllabus and Study Guide on pages x – xviii of this Study Text

Testing what you can do

Testing yourself helps you develop the skills you need to pass the exam and also confirms that you can recall what you have learnt.

We include **Questions** – lots of them – both within chapters and in the **Practice Question Bank**, as well as **Quick Quizzes** at the end of each chapter to test your knowledge of the chapter content.

Chapter features

Each chapter contains a number of helpful features to guide you through each topic.

Topic list

Topic list	Syllabus reference

What you will be studying in this chapter and the relevant section numbers, together with ACCA syllabus references.

Introduction

Puts the chapter content in the context of the syllabus as a whole.

Study Guide

Links the chapter content with ACCA guidance.

Exam Guide

Highlights how examinable the chapter content is likely to be and the ways in which it could be examined.

> Knowledge brought forward from earlier studies

What you are assumed to know from previous studies/exams.

> FAST FORWARD

Summarises the content of main chapter headings, allowing you to preview and review each section easily.

Examples

Demonstrate how to apply key knowledge and techniques.

Key terms

Definitions of important concepts that can often earn you easy marks in exams.

Exam focus points

When and how specific topics were examined, or how they may be examined in the future.

Formula to learn

Formulae that are not given in the exam but which have to be learnt.

Gives you a useful indication of syllabus areas that closely relate to performance objectives in your Practical Experience Requirement (PER).

 Question

Gives you essential practice of techniques covered in the chapter.

 Case Study

Real world examples of theories and techniques.

Chapter Roundup

A full list of the Fast Forwards included in the chapter, providing an easy source of review.

Quick Quiz

A quick test of your knowledge of the main topics in the chapter.

Practice Question Bank

Found at the back of the Study Text with more comprehensive chapter questions. Cross referenced for easy navigation.

Studying F5

The F5 exam requires candidates to be able to apply management accounting techniques in business environments. The key question you need to be able to answer is 'what does it all actually mean?' Modern technology is capable of producing vast amounts of management accounting information but it has to be used to help managers to make good decisions and manage effectively. The emphasis in this paper is therefore on practical elements and application to the real world. The exam does not set out to trick you: the paper will be fair.

1 What F5 is about

The aim of this syllabus is to develop knowledge and skills in the application of management accounting techniques. It covers a number of specialist techniques, decision making, budgeting and standard costing, concluding with how business performance should be managed and controlled.

F5 is the middle paper in the management accounting section of the qualification structure. F2 concerns just techniques and P5 thinks strategically and considers environmental factors. F5 requires you to be able to apply techniques and think about their impact on the organisation.

2 What skills are required?

- You are expected to have a core of management accounting knowledge from Paper F2

- To deal with the multiple choice questions, you will need to demonstrate understanding of the subject across the entire syllabus

- For the longer questions, you will be required to carry out calculations, with **clear workings** and a logical structure

- You will be required to **interpret** data

- You will be required to **explain** management accounting techniques and **discuss** whether they are appropriate for a particular organisation

- You must be able to **apply** your skills in a practical context

3 How to improve your chances of passing

- There is no choice in this paper, all questions have to be answered. You must therefore study the **entire syllabus**, there are no short-cuts

- You should then practise extensively on examination-style questions. Practice will improve your ability to answer questions well, and should enable you to answer them more quickly. BPP's Practice and Revision Kit contains questions on all areas of the syllabus.

- Keep an eye out for **articles** as the **examination team** will use **Student Accountant** to communicate with students

- Read journals etc to pick up on ways in which real organisations apply management accounting and think about your own organisation if that is relevant

4 Brought forward knowledge

You will need a good working knowledge of basic management accounting from Paper F2. Chapter 1 of this Study Text revises elements of costing, and further revision material is provided in other chapters, such as those on CVP analysis and variance analysis. If you struggle with the examples and questions used to revise this knowledge, you should go back and revisit your previous work. The examination team will assume you know this material and it may form part of an exam question.

The exam paper and exam formulae

Format of the paper

From December 2014, the exam is a three-hour paper divided into two sections. Section A consists of 20 multiple choice questions of two marks each.

Section B consists of three questions of 10 marks each and two questions of 15 marks each. All questions are compulsory. In Section B, answers to the questions will require a mixture of calculations and discussion.

You also have 15 minutes for reading and planning.

The exam will cover as much of the syllabus as possible.

Exam formulae

Set out below are the **formulae you will be given in the exam**. If you are not sure what the symbols mean, or how the formulae are used, you should refer to the appropriate chapter in this Study Text.

Chapter in Study Text

Demand curve

5

$P = a - bQ$

$b = \dfrac{\text{change in price}}{\text{change in quantity}}$

a = price when $Q = 0$

$MR = a - 2bQ$

Learning curve

9

$Y = ax^b$

Where Y = cumulative average time per unit to produce x units
a = the time taken for the first unit of output
x = the cumulative number of units
b = the index of learning (log LR/log 2)
LR = the learning rate as a decimal

Syllabus and Study Guide

The F5 syllabus and study guide can be found below.

Syllabus

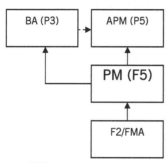

AIM

To develop knowledge and skills in the application of management accounting techniques to quantitative and qualitative information for planning, decision-making, performance evaluation, and control

MAIN CAPABILITIES

On successful completion of this paper, candidates should be able to:

A   Explain and apply cost accounting techniques

B   Select and appropriately apply decision-making techniques to facilitate business decisions and promote efficient and effective use of scarce business resources, appreciating the risks and uncertainty inherent in business and controlling those risks

C   Identify and apply appropriate budgeting techniques and methods for planning and control

D   Use standard costing systems to measure and control business performance and to identify remedial action

E   Identify and discuss performance management information and measurement systems and assess the performance of an organisation from both a financial and non-financial viewpoint, appreciating the problems of controlling divisionalised businesses and the importance of allowing for external aspects

RELATIONAL DIAGRAM OF MAIN CAPABILITIES

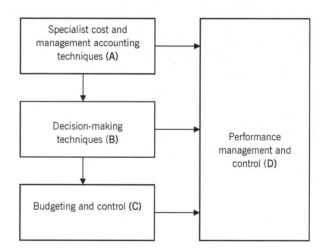

RATIONALE

The syllabus for Paper F5, *Performance Management*, builds on the knowledge gained in Paper F2, *Management Accounting*. and seek to examine candidates' understanding of how to manage the performance of a business. It also prepares candidates for more specialist capabilities which are covered in P5 *Advanced Performance Management*.

The syllabus begins by introducing more specialised management accounting topics. There is some knowledge assumed from Paper F2 – primarily overhead treatments. The objective here is to ensure candidates have a broader background in management accounting techniques.

The syllabus then considers decision-making. Candidates need to appreciate the problems surrounding scarce resource, pricing and make-or-buy decisions, and how this relates to the assessment of performance. Risk and uncertainty are a factor of real-life decisions and candidates need to understand risk and be able to apply some basic methods to help resolve the risks inherent in decision-making.

Budgeting is an important aspect of many accountants' lives. The syllabus explores different budgeting techniques and the problems inherent in them. The behavioural aspects of budgeting are important for accountants to understand, and the syllabus includes consideration of the way individuals react to a budget. The preparation of fixed, flexible and incremental budgets is assumed knowledge from F2.

Standard costing and variances are then built on. All the variances examined in Paper F2 are assumed knowledge in F5. Mix and yield variances, and planning and operational variances are explored here and the link is made to performance management. It is important for accountants to be able to interpret the numbers that they calculate and ask what they mean in the context of performance.

The syllabus concludes with performance management systems, measurement and control. This is a major area of the syllabus. Accountants need to understand how a business should be managed and controlled and how information

systems can be used to facilitate this. They should appreciate the importance of both financial and non-financial performance measures in management. Accountants should also appreciate the difficulties in assessing performance in divisionalised businesses and the problems caused by failing to consider external influences on performance. This section leads directly to Paper P5.

All of the subject areas covered in this syllabus could be examined in either a public sector or private sector context.

DETAILED SYLLABUS

A Specialist cost and management accounting techniques

1. Activity-based costing

2. Target costing

3. Life-cycle costing

4. Throughput accounting

5. Environmental accounting

B Decision-making techniques

1. Relevant cost analysis

2. Cost volume analysis

3. Limiting factors

4. Pricing decisions

5. Make-or-buy and other short-term decisions

6. Dealing with risk and uncertainty in decision-making

C Budgeting and control

1 Budgetary systems

2. Types of budget

3. Quantitative analysis in budgeting

4 Standard costing

5 Material mix and yield variances

6 Sales mix and quantity variances

7. Planning and operational variances

8 Performance analysis and Behavioural aspects

D Performance measurement and control

1. Performance management information systems

2. Sources of management information

3. Management reports

4. Performance analysis in private sector organisations

5. Divisional performance and transfer pricing

6. Performance analysis in not-for-profit organisations and the public sector

7. External considerations and behavioural aspects

APPROACH TO EXAMINING THE SYLLABUS

The syllabus is assessed by a three-hour paper-based examination.

All questions are compulsory. It will contain both computational and discursive elements.
Some questions will adopt a scenario/case study approach.

Section A of the exam comprises 20 multiple choice questions of 2 marks each.

Section B of the exam comprises three 10 mark questions and two 15 mark questions.

The two 15 mark questions will come from decision making techniques, budgeting and control and or performance measurement and control areas of the syllabus. The section A questions and the other questions in section B can cover any areas of the syllabus.

Candidates are provided with a formulae sheet

Study Guide

A   SPECIALIST COST AND MANAGEMENT ACCOUNTING TECHNIQUES

1. Activity based costing

a) Identify appropriate cost drivers under ABC.[1]

b) Calculate costs per driver and per unit using ABC.[2]

c) Compare ABC and traditional methods of overhead absorption based on production units, labour hours or machine hours.[2]

2. Target costing

a) Derive a target cost in manufacturing and service industries.[2]

b) Explain the difficulties of using target costing in service industries.[2]

c) Suggest how a target cost gap might be closed.[2]

3. Life-cycle costing

a) Identify the costs involved at different stages of the life-cycle.[2]

b) Derive a life cycle cost in manufacturing and service industries.[2]

c) Identify the benefits of life cycle costing.[2]

4. Throughput accounting

a) Discuss and apply the theory of constraints.[2]

b) Calculate and interpret a throughput accounting ratio (TPAR).[2]

c) Suggest how a TPAR could be improved.[2]

d) Apply throughput accounting to a multi-product decision-making problem.[2]

5. Environmental accounting

a) Discuss the issues business face in the management of environmental costs.[1]

b) Describe the different methods a business may use to account for its environmental costs.[1]

B   DECISION-MAKING TECHNIQUES

1   Relevant cost analysis

a) Explain the concept of relevant costing.[2].

b) Identify and calculate relevant costs for a specific decision situations from given data.[2]

c) Explain and apply the concept of opportunity costs.[2]

2. Cost volume profit analysis

a)   Explain the nature of CVP analysis.[2]

b) Calculate and interpret break even point and margin of safety.[2]

c) Calculate the contribution to sales ratio, in single and multi-product situations, and demonstrate an understanding of its use.[2].

d) Calculate target profit or revenue in single and multi-product situations, and demonstrate an understanding of its use.[2]

e) Prepare break even charts and profit volume charts and interpret the information contained within each, including multi-product situations.[2]

f) Discuss the limitations of CVP analysis for planning and decision making.[2]

3. Limiting factors

a) Identify limiting factors in a scarce resource situation and select an appropriate technique.[2]

b) Determine the optimal production plan where an organisation is restricted by a single limiting factor, including within the context of "make" or "buy" decisions.[2].

c) Formulate and solve multiple scarce resource problem both graphically and using simultaneous equations as appropriate.[2]

d) Explain and calculate shadow prices (dual prices) and discuss their implications on decision-making and performance management. [2]

e) Calculate slack and explain the implications of the existence of slack for decision-making and performance management.[2]
(Excluding simplex and sensitivity to changes in objective functions)

4. Pricing decisions

a) Explain the factors that influence the pricing of a product or service.[2]

b) Explain the price elasticity of demand.[1]

c) Derive and manipulate a straight line demand equation. Derive an equation for the total cost function(including volume-based discounts).[2]

d) Calculate the optimum selling price and quantity for an organisation, equating marginal cost and marginal revenue[2]

e) Evaluate a decision to increase production and sales levels, considering incremental costs, incremental revenues and other factors.[2]

f) Determine prices and output levels for profit maximisation using the demand based approach to pricing (both tabular and algebraic methods) .[1]

g) Explain different price strategies, including: [2]
   i) All forms of cost-plus
   ii) Skimming
   iii) Penetration
   iv) Complementary product
   v) Product-line
   vi) Volume discounting
   vii) Discrimination
   viii) Relevant cost

h) Calculate a price from a given strategy using cost-plus and relevant cost.[2]

5. Make-or-buy and other short-term decisions

a) Explain the issues surrounding make vs. buy and outsourcing decisions.[2]

b) Calculate and compare "make" costs with "buy-in" costs.[2]

c) Compare in-house costs and outsource costs of completing tasks and consider other issues surrounding this decision.[2]

d) Apply relevant costing principles in situations involving shut down, one-off contracts and the further processing of joint products.[2]

6. Dealing with risk and uncertainty in decision-making

a) Suggest research techniques to reduce uncertainty e.g. Focus groups, market research.[2]

b) Explain the use of simulation, expected values and sensitivity.[1]

c) Apply expected values and sensitivity to decision-making problems.[2]

d) Apply the techniques of maximax, maximin, and minimax regret to decision-making problems including the production of profit tables.[2]

e) Draw a decision tree and use it to solve a multi-stage decision problem

f) Calculate the value of perfect and imperfect information.

C   BUDGETING AND CONTROL

1. Budgetary systems

a) Explain how budgetary systems fit within the performance hierarchy.[2]

b) Select and explain appropriate budgetary systems for an organisation, including top-down, bottom-up, rolling, zero-base, activity-base, incremental and feed-forward control.[2]

c) Describe the information used in budget systems and the sources of the information needed.[2]

d) Explain the difficulties of changing a budgetary system.[2]

e) Explain how budget systems can deal with uncertainty in the environment.[2]

2. **Types of Budget**

a) Prepare rolling budgets and activity based budgets.[2]

b) Indicate the usefulness and problems with different budget types (including fixed, flexible, zero-based, activity- based, incremental, rolling, top-down, bottom up, master, functional).[2]

c) Explain the difficulties of changing the type of budget used.[2]

3. **Quantitative analysis in budgeting**

a) Analyse fixed and variable cost elements from total cost data using high/low method.

b) Estimate the learning rate and learning effect[2]

c) Apply the learning curve to a budgetary problem, including calculations on steady states [2]

c) Discuss the reservations with the learning curve.[2]

d) Apply expected values and explain the problems and benefits.[2]

e) Explain the benefits and dangers inherent in using spreadsheets in budgeting. [2]

4. **Standard costing**

a) Explain the use of standard costs.[2]

b) Outline the methods used to derive standard costs and discuss the different types of cost possible.[2]

c) Explain and illustrate the importance of flexing budgets in performance management.[2]

d) Explain and apply the principle of controllability in the performance management system.[2]

5. **Material mix and yield variances**

a) Calculate, identify the cause of, and explain material mix and yield variances.[2]

b) Explain the wider issues involved in changing material mix e.g. cost, quality and performance measurement issues.[2]

c) Identify and explain the relationship of the material usage variance with the material mix and yield variances.[2]

d) Suggest and justify alternative methods of controlling production processes.[2]

6. **Sales mix and quantity variances**

a) Calculate, identify the cause of, and explain sales mix and quantity variances.[2]

b) Identify and explain the relationship of the sales volume variances with the sales mix and quantity variances.[2]

7. **Planning and operational variances**

a) Calculate a revised budget.[2]

b) Identify and explain those factors that could and could not be allowed to revise an original budget.[2]

c) Calculate, identify the cause of and explain planning and operational variances for:
   i) sales, including market size and market share;
   ii) materials;
   iii) labour, including the effect of the learning curve.[2]

d) Explain and discuss the manipulation issues involved in revising budgets.[2]

8. **Performance analysis and behavioural aspects**

a) Analyse and evaluate past performance using the results of variance analysis.[2]

b) Use variance analysis to assess how future performance of an organisation or business can be improved.[2]

c) Identify the factors which influence behaviour.[2]

d) Discuss the issues surrounding setting the difficulty level for a budget.[2]

e) Discuss the effect that variances have on staff motivation and action.[2]

f) Explain the benefits and difficulties of the participation of employees in the negotiation of targets.[2]

g) Describe the dysfunctional nature of some variances in the modern environment of JIT and TQM.[2]

h) Discuss the behavioural problems resulting from using standard costs in rapidly changing environments.[2]

D PERFORMANCE MEASUREMENT AND CONTROL

1. Performance management information systems

a) Identify the accounting information requirements and describe the different types of information systems used for strategic planning, management control and operational control and decision-making. [2]

b) Define and identify the main characteristics of transaction processing systems; management information systems; executive information systems; and enterprise resource planning systems.[2]

c) Define and discuss the merits of, and potential problems with, open and closed systems with regard to the needs of performance management. [2]

2. Sources of management information

a) Identify the principal internal and external sources of management accounting information. [2]

b) Demonstrate how these principal sources of management information might be used for control purposes. [2]

c) Identify and discuss the direct data capture and process costs of management accounting information. [2]

d) Identify and discuss the indirect costs of producing information.[2]

e) Discuss the limitations of using externally generated information.[2]

3. Management reports

a) Discuss the principal controls required in generating and distributing internal information.[2]

b) Discuss the procedures that may be necessary to ensure security of highly confidential information that is not for external consumption.[2]

4. Performance analysis in private sector organisations

a) Describe, calculate and interpret financial performance indicators (FPIs) for profitability, liquidity and risk in both manufacturing and service businesses. Suggest methods to improve these measures.[2]

b) Describe, calculate and interpret non-financial performance indicators (NFPIs) and suggest method to improve the performance indicated.[2]

c) Analyse past performance and suggest ways for improving financial and non-financial performance.[2]

d) Explain the causes and problems created by short-termism and financial manipulation of results and suggest methods to encourage a long term view.[2]

e) Explain and interpret the Balanced Scorecard, and the Building Block model proposed by Fitzgerald and Moon.[2]

f) Discuss the difficulties of target setting in qualitative areas.[2]

5. **Divisional performance and transfer pricing**

a) Explain and illustrate the basis for setting a transfer price using variable cost, full cost and the principles behind allowing for intermediate markets.[2]

b) Explain how transfer prices can distort the performance assessment of divisions and decisions made.[2]

c) Explain the meaning of, and calculate, Return on Investment (ROI) and Residual Income (RI), and discuss their shortcomings.[2]

d) Compare divisional performance and recognise the problems of doing so.[2]

6. **Performance analysis in not for profit organisations and the public sector**

a) Comment on the problems of having non-quantifiable objectives in performance management.[2]

b) Explain how performance could be measured in this sector.[2]

c) Comment on the problems of having multiple objectives in this sector.[2]

d) Outline Value for Money (VFM) as a public sector objective.[1]

7. **External considerations and behavioural aspects**

a) Explain the need to allow for external considerations in performance management, including stakeholders, market conditions and allowance for competitors.[2]

b) Suggest ways in which external considerations could be allowed for in performance management.[2]

c) Interpret performance in the light of external considerations.[2]

d) Identify and explain the behaviour aspects of performance management [2]

SUMMARY OF CHANGES TO F5

ACCA periodically reviews its qualification syllabuses so that they fully meet the needs of stakeholders such as employers, students, regulatory and advisory bodies and learning providers.

There were no deletions but a few additions to clarify what was already assumed in the syllabus as detailed below

Section and subject area	Syllabus content
A4 Throughput accounting	a) Discuss and apply the theory of constraints'
C3. Quantitative analysis in budgeting	b) Estimate the learning rate and learning effect[2]
C8 Performance analysis and behaviour aspects	a) Analyse and evaluate past performance using the results of variance analysis. b) Use variance analysis to assess how future performance of an organisation or business can be improved..
D4 Performance analysis in private sector organisations	c) Analyse past performance and suggest ways for improving for improving financial and non-financial performance.
Note that budgeting and standard costing are now merged into one syllabus area- budgeting and control.	

Specialist cost and management accounting techniques

Costing

1

Introduction

Part A of this Study Text looks at specialist cost and management accounting techniques. This chapter serves as a revision of concepts you should have covered in your previous studies.

In the following chapter we will be looking at more complex techniques, so it is important that you are familiar with the key concepts and terminology in this chapter.

Exam guide

This chapter serves as an introduction to your study of cost and management accounting techniques, as knowledge is assumed from Paper F2 Management Accounting and is still examinable at this level. Questions in this paper will focus on interpretation rather than doing complex calculations.

1 Costing

Costing is the process of determining the costs of products, services or activities.

Cost accounting is used to determine the cost of products, jobs or services (whatever the organisation happens to be involved in). Such costs have to be built up using a process known as **cost accumulation.**

In your earlier studies you will have learnt how to accumulate the various cost elements which make up total cost.

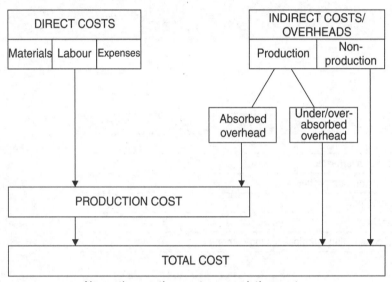

Absorption costing cost accumulation system

2 The problem of overheads

Indirect costs, or **overheads**, are costs incurred in making a product or providing a service, but which cannot be traced directly to products or services. **Absorption costing** is a means of incorporating a fair share of these costs into the cost of each unit of product manufactured or each service provided.

If a company manufactures a product, the cost of the product will include the cost of the raw materials and components used in it and cost of the labour effort required to make it. These are **direct costs** of the product. The company would, however, incur many other costs in making the product which are not directly attributable to a single product, but which are incurred generally in the process of manufacturing a large number of product units. These are **indirect costs** or **overheads**. Such costs include the following.

- Factory rent and rates
- Machine depreciation
- Supervision costs
- Heating and lighting

Key terms

A **direct cost** is a cost that can be traced in full to the product, service or department that is being costed.

An **indirect cost** or **overhead** is a cost that is incurred in the course of making a product, providing a service or running a department, but which cannot be traced directly and in full to the product, service or department.

In some companies, total overhead costs may be substantially greater than the total of direct production costs.

It might seem unreasonable to ignore indirect costs entirely when accumulating the costs of making a product, and yet there **cannot be a completely satisfactory way of sharing out indirect costs** between the many different items of production which benefit from them.

2.1 Using absorption costing to deal with the problem of overheads

Traditionally, the view has been that a fair share of overheads should be added to the cost of units produced to obtain a full unit cost of production and sales. This fair share should **include a portion of production overhead expenditure** and possibly administration and marketing overheads too. This is the view embodied in the principles of **absorption costing.**

2.1.1 Theoretical justification for using absorption costing

In a manufacturing organisation, production overheads are incurred in making the output, so each unit of product receives some benefit from these costs. Each unit of output should therefore be charged with some of the overhead costs.

2.1.2 Practical reasons for using absorption costing

(a) **Inventory valuations**

Inventory in hand must be valued for two reasons.

(i) For the closing inventory figure in the statement of financial position
(ii) To calculate the cost of sales figure in the income statement

The valuation of inventories will affect profitability during a period because of the way in which the cost of sales is calculated.

Cost of goods sold = cost of goods produced + the value of opening inventories – the value of closing inventories

(b) **Pricing decisions**

Many companies attempt to set selling prices **by calculating the full cost of production or sales** of each product, and then adding a margin for profit. 'Full cost plus pricing' can be particularly useful for companies which do jobbing or contract work, where each job or contract is different, so that a standard unit sales price cannot be fixed. Without using absorption costing, it may be difficult to decide what the price should be to earn a satisfactory profit.

(c) **Establishing the profitability of different products**

This argument in favour of absorption costing states that if a company sells more than one product, it will be difficult to judge **how profitable each individual product is**, unless overhead costs are shared on a fair basis and charged to the cost of sales of each product.

2.2 Using marginal costing to deal with the problem of overheads

For many planning and decision-making purposes, absorption costing is less useful as a costing method than marginal costing. In some situations, **absorption costing can actually be misleading** in the information it supplies.

Advocates of **marginal costing** take the view that only the variable costs of making and selling a product or service should be identified. **Fixed costs should be dealt with separately** and treated as a cost of the accounting period rather than shared out somehow between units produced. However, some overhead costs are variable costs, which increase as the total level of activity rises; so the marginal cost of production and sales should include an amount for variable overheads.

3 Revision of absorption costing

Absorption costing is a traditional approach to dealing with overheads, involving three stages: allocation, apportionment and absorption.

Apportionment has two stages, general overhead apportionment and service department cost apportionment.

Key term

> **Absorption costing** is a method of product costing which aims to include in the total cost of a product (unit, job and so on) an appropriate share of an organisation's total overhead, which is generally taken to mean an amount which reflects the amount of time and effort that has gone into producing the product.

You should have covered absorption costing in your earlier studies. We will therefore summarise the simpler points of the topic but will go into some detail on the more complex areas to refresh your memory.

Knowledge brought forward from earlier studies

> *Absorption costing*
>
> - Product costs are built up using absorption costing by a process of **allocation**, **apportionment** and **overhead absorption**.
>
> - **Allocation** is the process by which whole cost items are charged directly to a cost unit or cost centre. **Direct costs** are allocated directly to cost units. **Overheads** clearly identifiable with cost centres are allocated to those cost centres but costs which cannot be identified with one particular cost centre are allocated to general overhead cost centres. The cost of a warehouse security guard would therefore be charged to the warehouse cost centre but heating and lighting costs would be charged to a general overhead cost centre.
>
> - The **first stage of overhead apportionment** involves sharing out (or apportioning) the overheads within **general overhead cost centres** between the other cost centres using a fair basis of apportionment (such as floor area occupied by each cost centre for heating and lighting costs).
>
> - The **second stage of overhead apportionment** is to apportion the costs of **service cost centres** (both directly allocated and apportioned costs) to production cost centres.
>
> - After the apportionment of production overheads, all the overhead costs have been divided or shared between the production departments. The final stage in absorption costing is the **absorption** into product costs (using overhead absorption rates) of the overheads that have been allocated and apportioned to the production cost centres.
>
> - An overhead absorption rate is calculated for each production department (or for production activity as a whole). Typically, this is an absorption rate per direct labour hour worked or an absorption rate per machine hour worked.

Question   **Cost apportionment**

Briefly discuss the factors which could affect the choice of the bases an organisation may use to apportion service department costs.

Answer

(a) The type of service being provided by the service department
(b) The amount of overhead expenditure involved
(c) The number of departments benefiting from the service
(d) The ability to be able to produce realistic estimates of the usage of the service by these departments
(e) The resulting costs and benefits

Question   **More cost apportionment**

A company is preparing its production overhead budgets and determining the apportionment of those overheads to products. Cost centre expenses and related information have been budgeted as follows.

	Total $	Machine shop A $	Machine shop B $	Assembly $	Canteen $	Mainten- ance $
Indirect wages	78,560	8,586	9,190	15,674	29,650	15,460
Consumable materials	16,900	6,400	8,700	1,200	600	–
Rent and rates	16,700					
Buildings insurance	2,400					
Power	8,600					
Heat and light	3,400					
Depreciation (machinery)	40,200					
Value of machinery	402,000	201,000	179,000	22,000	–	–
Power usage (%)	100	55	40	3	–	2
Direct labour (hours)	35,000	8,000	6,200	20,800	–	–
Machine usage (hours)	25,200	7,200	18,000	–	–	–
Area (sq ft)	45,000	10,000	12,000	15,000	6,000	2,000

Required

Using the direct apportionment to production departments method and bases of apportionment which you consider most appropriate from the information provided, calculate overhead totals for the three production departments.

Answer

	Total $	A $	B $	Assembly $	Canteen $	Main- tenance $	Basis of apportionment
Indirect wages	78,560	8,586	9,190	15,674	29,650	15,460	Actual
Consumable materials	16,900	6,400	8,700	1,200	600	–	Actual
Rent and rates	16,700	3,711	4,453	5,567	2,227	742	Area
Insurance	2,400	533	640	800	320	107	Area
Power	8,600	4,730	3,440	258	–	172	Usage
Heat and light	3,400	756	907	1,133	453	151	Area
Depreciation	40,200	20,100	17,900	2,200	–	–	Val of mach
	166,760	44,816	45,230	26,832	33,250	16,632	
Reallocate	–	7,600	5,890	19,760	(33,250)	–	Direct labour
Reallocate	–	4,752	11,880	–	–	(16,632)	Mach usage
Totals	166,760	57,168	63,000	46,592	–	–	

4 Overhead absorption

After apportionment, overheads are **absorbed** into products using an appropriate **absorption rate** based on budgeted costs and budgeted activity levels.

Having allocated and/or apportioned all **overheads**, the next stage in absorption costing is to **add them to, or absorb them into**, the cost of production or sales.

Overhead costs are absorbed using a predetermined rate based on budgeted figures.

4.1 Use of a predetermined absorption rate

Knowledge brought forward from earlier studies

Step 1   The overhead likely to be incurred during the coming year is estimated.

Step 2   The total hours, units or direct costs on which the overhead absorption rates are based (activity levels) are estimated.

Step 3   Absorption rate = Estimated overhead ÷ Budgeted activity level

4.2 Choosing the appropriate absorption base

Question

Absorption bases

List as many possible bases of absorption (or 'overhead recovery rates') as you can think of.

Answer

(a)   A percentage of direct materials cost
(b)   A percentage of direct labour cost
(c)   A percentage of prime cost
(d)   A percentage of factory cost (for administration overhead)
(e)   A percentage of sales or factory cost (for selling and distribution overhead)
(f)   A rate per machine hour
(g)   A rate per direct labour hour
(h)   A rate per unit

The choice of an absorption basis is a **matter of judgement and common sense**. There are no strict rules or formulae involved. But the basis should realistically reflect the characteristics of a given production centre, avoid undue anomalies and be 'fair'. The **choice will be significant in determining the cost of individual products, but the total cost of production overheads is the budgeted overhead expenditure, no matter what basis of absorption is selected**. It is the relative share of overhead costs borne by individual products and jobs which is affected.

Question

Absorption rates

Using the information in and the results of the question on page 7, determine budgeted overhead absorption rates for each of the production departments using appropriate bases of absorption.

Machine shop A: $57,168/7,200   = $7.94 per machine hour
Machine shop B: $63,000/18,000   = $3.50 per machine hour
Assembly: $46,592/20,800   = $2.24 per direct labour hour

4.3 Over- and under-absorption of overheads

Under- or over-absorbed overhead occurs when overheads incurred do not equal overheads absorbed.

The rate of overhead absorption is based on estimates in the budget, of both the numerator (budgeted expenditure) and denominator (budgeted activity level), and it is quite likely that what actually occurs will differ from either one or both of these estimates. As a consequence, actual overheads incurred will probably be either greater than or less than overheads absorbed into the cost of production, and so it is almost inevitable that at the end of the accounting year there will have been an over-absorption or under-absorption of the overhead actually incurred.

- **Over–absorption** means that the **overheads charged to the cost of production or sales are greater than the overheads actually incurred**.

- **Under-absorption** means that **insufficient overheads have been included in the cost of production or sales**.

Under-absorption may also be called under-recovery of overheads; over-absorption may be called over-recovery.

Suppose that the budgeted overhead in a production department is $80,000 and the budgeted activity is 40,000 direct labour hours. The overhead recovery rate (using a direct labour hour basis) would be $2 per direct labour hour.

Suppose that actual overheads in the period are $84,000 and 45,000 direct labour hours are worked.

	$
Overhead incurred (actual)	84,000
Overhead absorbed (45,000 × $2)	90,000
Over-absorption of overhead	6,000

In this example, the cost of production has been charged with $6,000 more than was actually spent and so the recorded cost of production will be too high. The over-absorbed overhead will be an adjustment to profit at the end of the accounting period to reconcile the overheads charged to the actual overhead.

Question

Under and over-absorption

The total production overhead expenditure of the company in the questions above was $176,533 and its actual activity was as follows.

	Machine shop A	Machine shop B	Assembly
Direct labour hours	8,200	6,500	21,900
Machine usage hours	7,300	18,700	–

Required

Using the information in and results of the previous questions, calculate the under- or over-absorption of overheads.

Answer

		$	$
Actual expenditure			176,533
Overhead absorbed			
Machine shop A	7,300 hrs × $7.94	57,962	
Machine shop B	18,700 hrs × $3.50	65,450	
Assembly	21,900 hrs × $2.24	49,056	
			172,468
Under-absorbed overhead			4,065

4.4 The reasons for under-/over-absorbed overhead

The overhead absorption rate is predetermined from budget estimates of overhead cost and activity level. Under or over recovery of overhead will occur in the following circumstances.

- Actual overhead costs are different from budgeted overheads.
- The actual activity level is different from the budgeted activity level.
- Actual overhead costs **and** actual activity level differ from those budgeted.

Question   Over and under-absorption

A production department has a budgeted production overheads of $180,000 and budgeted activity of 45,000 machine hours. Overheads are absorbed on a machine hour basis.

Required

Calculate the under-/over-absorbed overhead, and note the reasons for the under-/over-absorption in the following circumstances.

(a) Actual overheads cost $170,000 and 45,000 machine hours were worked.
(b) Actual overheads cost $180,000 and 40,000 machine hours were worked.
(c) Actual overheads cost $170,000 and 40,000 machine hours were worked.

Answer

The overhead recovery rate is $180,000/45,000 = $4 per machine hour.

		$
(a)	Actual overhead	170,000
	Absorbed overhead (45,000 × $4)	180,000
	Over-absorbed overhead	10,000

Reason: Actual and budgeted machine hours are the same but actual overheads cost less than expected.

		$
(b)	Actual overhead	180,000
	Absorbed overhead (40,000 × $4)	160,000
	Under-absorbed overhead	20,000

Reason: Budgeted and actual overhead costs were the same but fewer machine hours were worked than expected.

		$
(c)	Actual overhead	170,000
	Absorbed overhead (40,000 × $4)	160,000
	Under-absorbed overhead	10,000

Reason: A combination of the reasons in (a) and (b).

5 Marginal costing

In **marginal costing**, inventories are valued at variable production cost whereas in absorption costing they are valued at their full production cost. Profit is calculated by deducting variable costs of sales from sales revenue to obtain contribution, and then deducting fixed costs to obtain a figure for profit.

Key terms

Marginal cost is the cost of one unit of a product/service which could be avoided if that unit were not produced/provided.

Contribution is the difference between sales revenue and variable (marginal) cost of sales.

Marginal costing is an alternative to absorption costing. Only variable costs (marginal costs) are charged as a cost of sales. Fixed costs are treated as period costs and are charged in full against the profit of the period in which they are incurred.

Knowledge brought forward from earlier studies

Marginal costing

- In **marginal costing**, closing **inventories are valued at marginal (variable) production cost** whereas, in **absorption costing**, inventories are **valued at their full production cost** which includes absorbed fixed production overhead.

- If the opening and closing inventory levels differ in an accounting period, the **profit reported** for the period will **differ between absorption costing and marginal costing**.

- But **in the long run, total profit for a company will be the same** whichever costing method is used, because in the long run total costs will be the same by either method of accounting. The different costing methods merely affect the reported profit for individual accounting periods.

Question

Absorption and marginal costing

A company makes and sells a single product. At the beginning of period 1, there are no opening inventories of the product, for which the variable production cost is $4 and the sales price $6 per unit. There are no variable selling costs. Fixed costs are $2,000 per period, of which $1,500 are fixed production costs. Normal output is 1,500 units per period. In period 1, sales were 1,200 units, production was 1,500 units. In period 2, sales were 1,700 units, production was 1,400 units.

Required

Prepare profit statements for each period and for the two periods in total using both absorption costing and marginal costing.

Answer

It is important to notice that although production and sales volumes in each period are different, over the **full period, total production volume equals sales volume**. The total cost of sales is the same and therefore the **total profit is the same by either method** of accounting. **There are differences** in the reported profit in Period 1 and in Period 2, but these are merely **timing differences** which cancel out over a longer period of time (in this example over the two periods).

(a) **Absorption costing.** The absorption rate for fixed production overhead is $1,500/1,500 units = $1 per unit. The fully absorbed cost per unit = $(4+1) = $5.

	Period 1		Period 2		Total	
	$	$	$	$	$	$
Sales		7,200		10,200		17,400
Production costs						
Variable	6,000		5,600		11,600	
Fixed	1,500		1,400		2,900	
	7,500		7,000		14,500	
Add opening inventory b/f (300×$5)	–		1,500		1,500	
	7,500		8,500		16,000	
Less closing inventory c/f (300×$5)	1,500		–		1,500	
Production cost of sales	6,000		8,500		14,500	
Under-absorbed o/hd	–		100		100	
Total costs		6,000		8,600		14,600
Gross profit		1,200		1,600		2,800
Other costs		(500)		(500)		(1,000)
Net profit		700		1,100		1,800

(b) **Marginal costing**

The marginal cost per unit = $4.

	Period 1		Period 2		Total	
	$	$	$	$	$	$
Sales		7,200		10,200		17,400
Variable production cost	6,000		5,600		11,600	
Add opening inventory b/f (300×$4)	–		1,200		1,200	
	6,000		6,800		12,800	
Less closing inventory c/f (300×$4)	1,200		–		1,200	
Variable prod. cost of sales		4,800		6,800		11,600
Contribution		2,400		3,400		5,800
Fixed costs		2,000		2,000		4,000
Profit		400		1,400		1,800

Question	Marginal and absorption costing

RH makes and sells one product, which has the following standard production cost.

		$
Direct labour	3 hours at $6 per hour	18
Direct materials	4 kilograms at $7 per kg	28
Variable production overhead		3
Fixed production overhead		20
Standard production cost per unit		69

Normal output is 16,000 units per annum. Variable selling, distribution and administration costs are 20 per cent of sales value. Fixed selling, distribution and administration costs are $180,000 per annum. There are no units in finished goods inventory at 1 October 20X2. The fixed overhead expenditure is spread evenly throughout the year. The selling price per unit is $140. Production and sales budgets are as follows.

	Six months ending 31 March 20X3	Six months ending 30 September 20X3
Production	8,500	7,000
Sales	7,000	8,000

Required

Prepare profit statements for each of the six-monthly periods, using the following methods of costing.

(a) Marginal costing
(b) Absorption costing

Answer

(a) **Profit statements for the year ending 30 September 20X3**
Marginal costing basis

	Six months ending 31 March 20X3		Six months ending 30 September 20X3	
	$'000	$'000	$'000	$'000
Sales at $140 per unit		980		1,120
Opening inventory			73.5	
Std. variable prod. cost (at $49 per unit)	416.5		343.0	
	416.5		416.5	
Closing inventory (W1)	73.5		24.5	
		343		392
		637		728
Variable selling and so on costs		196		224
Contribution		441		504
Fixed costs: production (W2)	160		160	
selling and so on	90		90	
		250		250
Net profit		191		254

(b) **Profit statements for the year ending 30 September 20X3**
Absorption costing basis

	Six months ending 31 March 20X3		Six months ending 30 September 20X3	
	$'000	$'000	$'000	$'000
Sales at $140 per unit		980		1,120
Opening inventory			103.5	
Std. cost of prod. (at $69 per unit)	586.5		483.0	
	586.5		586.5	
Closing inventory (W1)	103.5		34.5	
	483.0		552.0	
(Over-)/under-absorbed overhead (W3)	(10.0)		20.0	
		473		572
Gross profit		507		548
Selling and so on costs				
Variable	196		224	
Fixed	90		90	
		286		314
Net profit		221		234

Workings

1

	Six months ending 31 March 20X3	Six months ending 30 September 20X3
	Units	Units
Opening inventory		1,500
Production	8,500	7,000
	8,500	8,500
Sales	7,000	8,000
Closing inventory	1,500	500
Marginal cost valuation (× $49)	$73,500	$24,500
Absorption cost valuation (× $69)	$103,500	$34,500

2   Budgeted fixed production o/hd = 16,000 units × $20 = $320,000 pa = $160,000 per six months

3

	Six months ending 31 March 20X3		Six months ending 30 September 20X3	
Normal output (16,000 ÷ 2)	8,000	units	8,000	units
Budgeted output	8,500	units	7,000	units
Difference	500	units	1,000	units
× std. fixed prod. o/hd per unit	× $20		× $20	
(Over-)/under-absorbed overhead	($10,000)		$20,000	

6 Absorption costing and marginal costing compared

If opening and closing inventory levels differ, the profit reported under the two methods will be different. In the long run, total profit will be the same whichever method is used.

6.1 Reconciling the profit figures given by the two methods

The **difference in profits** reported under the two costing systems is due to the **different inventory valuation methods** used.

(a)   **If inventory levels increase** between the beginning and end of a period, **absorption costing will report the higher profit** because some of the fixed production overhead incurred during the period will be carried forward in closing inventory (which reduces cost of sales) to be set against sales revenue in the following period, instead of being written off in full against profit in the period concerned.

(b)   **If inventory levels decrease, absorption costing will report the lower profit** because as well as the fixed overhead incurred, fixed production overhead which had been carried forward in opening inventory is released and is also included in cost of sales.

6.2 Example: Reconciling profits

The profits reported for period 1 in the question on page 12 would be reconciled as follows.

	$
Marginal costing profit	400
Adjust for fixed overhead in inventory (inventory increase of 300 units × $1 per unit)	300
Absorption costing profit	700

Exam focus point

Remember that if opening inventory values are greater than closing inventory values, marginal costing shows a bigger profit than absorption costing. If opening inventory values are lower than closing inventory values, absorption costing shows a bigger profit than marginal costing.

6.3 Marginal versus absorption costing: reporting to management

Marginal costing is more **useful** for **decision-making** purposes, but absorption costing is needed for **financial reporting** purposes to comply with accounting standards.

We know that the reported profit in any period is likely to differ according to the costing method used, but does one method provide a more reliable guide to management about the organisation's profit position?

With marginal costing, contribution varies in direct proportion to the volume of units sold. Profits will increase as sales volume rises, by the amount of extra contribution earned. Since fixed cost expenditure does not alter, marginal costing gives an accurate picture of how a firm's cash flows and profits are affected by changes in sales volumes.

With absorption costing, in contrast, **there is no clear relationship between profit and sales volume**, and as sales volume rises the total profit will rise by the sum of the gross profit per unit plus the amount of overhead absorbed per unit. Arguably this is a confusing and unsatisfactory method of monitoring profitability.

If sales volumes are the same from period to period, marginal costing reports the same profit each period (given no change in prices or costs). In contrast, using absorption costing, profits can vary with the volume of production, even when the volume of sales is constant. **Using absorption costing there is therefore the possibility of manipulating profit, simply by changing output and inventory levels.**

6.4 Example: Manipulating profits

Gloom Co budgeted to make and sell 10,000 units of its product in 20X1. The selling price is $10 per unit and the variable cost $4 per unit. Fixed production costs were budgeted at $50,000 for the year. The company uses absorption costing and budgeted an absorption rate of $5 per unit. During 20X1, it became apparent that sales demand would only be 8,000 units. The management, concerned about the apparent effect of the low volume of sales on profits, decided to increase production for the year to 15,000 units. Actual fixed costs were still expected to be $50,000 in spite of the significant increase in production volume.

Required

Calculate the profit at an actual sales volume of 8,000 units, using the following methods.

(a)   Absorption costing
(b)   Marginal costing

Explain the difference in profits calculated.

Solution

(a)   **Absorption costing**

	$	$
Sales (8,000 × $10)		80,000
Full cost of production (15,000 × $9)	135,000	
Closing inventory (7,000 × $9)	(63,000)	
Production cost of sales	72,000	
Less: over-absorbed overhead (5,000 × $5)	(25,000)	
Cost of sales		(47,000)
Profit		33,000

(b) **Marginal costing**

	$	$
Sales		80,000
Variable cost of production (15,000 × $4)	60,000	
Closing inventory (7,000 × $4)	(28,000)	
Variable cost of sales		32,000
Contribution		48,000
Fixed costs		50,000
Loss		(2,000)

The difference in profits of $35,000 is explained by the **difference in the increase in inventory values** (7,000 units × $5 of fixed overhead per unit). With absorption costing, the expected profit will be higher than the original budget of $10,000 (10,000 units × ($10 – 9)) simply because $35,000 of fixed overheads will be carried forward in closing inventory values. By producing to absorb overhead rather than to satisfy customers, inventory levels will, of course, increase. Unless this inventory is sold, however, there may come a point when production has to stop and the inventory has to be sold off at lower prices. Marginal costing reports a contribution of $6 per unit, or $48,000 in total for 8,000 units, which fails to cover the fixed costs of $50,000 by $2,000.

Chapter Roundup

- **Costing** is the process of determining the costs of products, services or activities.

- **Indirect costs**, or **overheads**, are costs incurred in making a product or providing a service, but which cannot be traced directly to products or services. **Absorption costing** is a means of incorporating a fair share of these costs into the cost of each unit of product manufactured or each service provided.

- **Absorption costing** is a traditional approach to dealing with overheads, involving three stages: allocation, apportionment and absorption.

- **Apportionment** has two stages, general overhead apportionment and service department cost apportionment.

- After apportionment, overheads are **absorbed** into products using an appropriate **absorption rate** based on budgeted costs and budgeted activity levels.

- **Under- or over-absorbed overhead** occurs when overheads incurred do not equal overheads absorbed.

- In **marginal costing**, inventories are valued at variable production cost whereas in absorption costing they are valued at their full production cost. Profit is calculated by deducting variable costs of sales from sales revenue to obtain contribution, and then deducting fixed costs to obtain a figure for profit.

- If opening and closing inventory levels differ, the profit reported under the two methods will be different.

  In the long run, total profit will be the same whichever method is used.

- Marginal costing is more **useful** for **decision-making** purposes, but absorption costing is needed for **financial reporting** purposes to comply with accounting standards.

1   Here are some terms you should have encountered in your earlier studies. *Match the term to the definition.*

Terms	Definitions
Direct cost	(a) Specific costs of, say, an activity, which would not be incurred if the activity did not exist
Prime cost	
Overhead	(b) Total of direct costs
Classification by function	(c) Future cash flow which will be changed as the result of a decision
	(d) Product produced by an organisation
Fixed cost	(e) Dividing costs into production, administration, selling and distribution, research and development and financing costs
Variable cost	
Product cost	(f) Cost that can be traced in full to whatever is being costed
Avoidable cost	(g) Organisation's departments
Controllable cost	(h) A cost that varies with the level of output
Relevant cost	(i) A cost that is incurred in the course of making a product but which cannot be traced directly and in full to the product
Cost centre	
Cost unit	(j) Cost that is incurred for a particular period of time and which, within certain activity levels, is unaffected by changes in the level of activity
	(k) Cost identified with goods produced or purchased for resale and initially included in the value of inventory
	(l) Cost which can be influenced by management decisions and actions

2   .... is the process of determining the costs of products, activities or services.

3   How is an overhead absorption rate calculated?

A   Estimated overhead ÷ actual activity level
B   Estimated overhead ÷ budgeted activity level
C   Actual overhead ÷ actual activity level
D   Actual overhead ÷ budgeted activity level

4   Over-absorption means that the overheads charged to the cost of sales are greater than the overheads actually incurred.

☐ True   ☐ False

5   *Fill in the blanks in the statements about marginal costing and absorption costing below.*

(a)   If inventory levels .... between the beginning and end of a period, absorption costing will report the higher profit.

(b)   If inventory levels decrease, ... costing will report the lower profit.

6   *Fill in the following blanks with either 'marginal' or 'absorption'.*

(a)   Using .... costing, profits can be manipulated simply by changing output and inventory levels.

(b)   Fixed costs are charged in full against the profit of the period in which they are incurred when .... costing is used.

(c)   .... costing fails to recognise the importance of working to full capacity.

(d)   .... costing could be argued to be preferable to .... costing in management accounting in order to be consistent with the requirements of accounting standards.

(e)   .... costing should not be used when decision-making information is required.

Answers to Quick Quiz

1. | Direct cost | (f) |
   |---|---|
   | Prime cost | (b) |
   | Overhead | (i) |
   | Classification by function | (e) |
   | Fixed cost | (j) |
   | Variable cost | (h) |
   | Product cost | (k) |
   | Avoidable cost | (a) |
   | Controllable cost | (l) |
   | Relevant cost | (c) |
   | Cost centre | (g) |
   | Cost unit | (d) |

2. Costing

3. B

4. True

5. (a) Increase
   (b) Absorption

6. (a) absorption
   (b) marginal
   (c) marginal
   (d) absorption, marginal
   (e) absorption

Now try the question below from the Practice Question Bank

Number	Level	Marks	Time
Q1	Introductory	10	18 mins

Activity based costing

2a

Topic list	Syllabus reference
1 Activity based costing	A1 (a), (b)
2 Absorption costing versus ABC	A1 (c)
3 Merits and criticisms of ABC	A1 (c)

Introduction

Chapter 2 covers Part A of the syllabus, specialist cost and management accounting techniques. It has been divided into five sub-chapters to reflect the examiner's emphasis that all five techniques are equally important and equally examinable.

In this chapter we will be looking at a method of cost accumulation, **activity based costing (ABC)**, which is an alternative to traditional absorption costing. ABC attempts to overcome the problems of costing in a modern manufacturing environment, where a very large proportion of total production costs are overhead costs.

Study guide

		Intellectual level
A1	**Activity based costing**	
(a)	Identify appropriate cost drivers under ABC	1
(b)	Calculate costs per driver and per unit using ABC	2
(c)	Compare ABC and traditional methods of overhead absorption based on production units, labour hours or machine hours	2

Exam guide

There was a part-question on ABC in Section B of the Specimen Paper for F5. It was also examined in June 2008, June 2010, December 2011 and December 2012. It is therefore an important topic to understand.

1 Activity based costing   6/08, 6/10, 12/11, 12/12, Specimen paper

FAST FORWARD

Activity based costing (ABC) is an alternative to traditional absorption costing as a method of costing.

ABC involves the identification of the factors **(cost drivers)** which 'cause' or 'drive' the costs of an organisation's major activities. Overheads are allocated and apportioned to activity cost centres or 'cost pools'. From these activity cost centres, the overhead costs are then absorbed into the product costs on the basis of their usage of the activity. The absorption rate for each activity is a rate per unit of the relevant cost driver.

- For activity costs that seem to relate to the volume of production, the cost driver will be volume-related (labour or machine hours).

- For activity costs that do not seem to relate to production volume, a different cost driver is identified, such as the number of production runs or number of orders received.

1.1 Reasons for the development of ABC

Traditional **absorption costing** was developed in a time when most manufacturers produced only a **narrow range of products**, so that products underwent **similar operations** and consumed **similar proportions of overheads**. In addition, **overhead costs were only a very small fraction of total production costs**: direct labour and direct material costs accounted for the largest proportion of the costs.

With the **dramatic fall** in the costs of processing information, and with the advent of **advanced manufacturing technology (AMT)**, overhead costs have become a much larger proportion of total production costs, and direct labour has become much less important. Direct labour may now account for as little as 5% of production costs. It is therefore now difficult to justify the use of direct labour hours as the basis for absorbing overheads, to produce 'realistic' product costs.

The **falling costs of information processing** have also made it possible to switch to a different and more complex system for accumulating and analysing overhead costs. ABC may now be cost-effective whereas in the past its high costs could have made it difficult to justify.

Many resources are used in **non-volume related support activities**, which have increased due to AMT. Non-volume-related support activities are activities that support production, but where the level of support activity (and so the level of cost) depends on something other than production volume – such as setting-up production runs, production scheduling and inspection. These support activities assist the efficient manufacture of a wide range of products and are **not, in general, affected by changes in production**

volume. They tend to **vary in the long term according to the range and complexity** of the products manufactured, rather than the volume of output.

The wider the range and the more complex the products, the more support services are required. Consider, for example, Factory X which produces 10,000 units of one product, the Alpha, and Factory Y which produces 1,000 units each of ten slightly different versions of the Alpha. Support activity costs in the Factory Y are likely to be a lot higher than in Factory X, even though the factories produce an identical number of units. For example, Factory X will need to set-up only a single production run, whereas Factory Y will have to set-up a production run at least ten times, for each of the ten different products. Factory Y will therefore incur more set-up costs for the same volume of production.

Traditional absorption costing systems, which assume that all products consume all support resources in proportion to production volumes, tend to **allocate:**

(a) **too great a proportion of overheads to high volume products**, which cause relatively little diversity and hence use fewer support services, and

(b) **too small a proportion of overheads to low volume products** (which cause greater diversity and therefore use more support services).

Activity based costing (ABC) attempts to overcome this problem.

1.2 Definition of ABC

Key term

> **Activity based costing (ABC)** is a method of costing which involves identifying the costs of the main support activities and the factors that 'drive' the costs of each activity. Support overheads are charged to products by absorbing cost on the basis of the product's usage of the factor driving the overheads.

The major ideas behind activity based costing are as follows.

(a) **Activities cause costs**. Activities include ordering, materials handling, machining, assembly, production scheduling and despatching.

(b) **Manufacturing products creates demand for the support activities.**

(c) Costs are assigned to a product **on the basis of the product's consumption of these activities.**

1.3 Outline of an ABC system

An ABC system operates as follows.

Step 1 Identify an organisation's major activities that support the manufacture of the organisation's products or the provision of its services.

Step 2 Use cost allocation and apportionment methods to charge overhead costs to each of these activities. The costs that accumulate for each activity cost centre is called a **cost pool**.

Step 3 Identify the factors which determine the size of the costs of an activity/affect the costs of an activity. These are known as **cost drivers.**

Key term

> A **cost driver** is a factor which has most influence on the cost of an activity.

Look at the following examples.

Cost pool	Possible cost driver
Ordering costs: handling customer orders	Number of orders
Materials handling costs	Number of production runs
Machine set-up costs	Number of machine set-ups
Machine operating costs	Number of machine hours
Production scheduling costs	Number of production runs
Despatching costs	Number of orders despatched

Step 4	For each cost pool/activity cost centre, calculate an absorption rate per unit of cost driver.
Step 5	Charge overhead costs to products for each activity, on the basis of their usage of the activity (the number of cost drivers they use). Overheads are charged by absorbing them into product costs at a rate per unit of cost driver.

Question
Cost driver

Which of the following definitions best describes a cost driver?

A   Any activity which causes an increase in costs
B   A collection of costs associated with a particular activity
C   A cost that varies with production levels
D   Any factor which causes a change in the cost of an activity

Answer

D   Any factor which causes a change in the cost of an activity.

Exam focus point

Questions on activity based costing may require a comparison with more traditional absorption costing methods.

2 Absorption costing versus ABC
6/08, 6/10, 12/10, 12/12

The following example illustrates the point that traditional absorption costing techniques result in a misleading and inequitable division of costs between low-volume and high-volume products, and that ABC can provide a more meaningful way of charging overhead costs to products.

2.1 Example: Activity based costing

Suppose that Cooplan manufactures four products, W, X, Y and Z. Output and cost data for the period just ended are as follows.

	Output units	Number of production runs in the period	Material cost per unit $	Direct labour hours per unit	Machine hours per unit
W	10	2	20	1	1
X	10	2	80	3	3
Y	100	5	20	1	1
Z	100	5	80	3	3
		14			

Direct labour cost per hour: **$5**

Overhead costs	$
Short run variable costs	3,080
Set-up costs	10,920
Expediting and scheduling costs	9,100
Materials handling costs	7,700
	30,800

Required

Prepare unit costs for each product using:

(a)   conventional absorption costing, and
(b)   ABC.

Assume that in the traditional absorption costing system, overheads are absorbed at a direct labour hour rate.

Solution

(a)   Using a **conventional absorption costing approach** the absorption rate for overheads based on direct labour hours or machine hours is:

$30,800 ÷ 440 hours = $70 per direct labour.

The product costs would be as follows.

	W	X	Y	Z	Total
	$	$	$	$	$
Direct material	200	800	2,000	8,000	
Direct labour	50	150	500	1,500	
Overheads	700	2,100	7,000	21,000	
	950	3,050	9,500	30,500	44,000
Units produced	10	10	100	100	
Cost per unit	$95	$305	$95	$305	

(b)   Using **activity based costing**, it will be assumed that the number of production runs is the cost driver for set-up costs, expediting and scheduling costs and materials handling costs; and that machine hours are the cost driver for short-run variable costs. Product costs per unit are as follows.

	W	X	Y	Z	Total
	$	$	$	$	$
Direct material (no change)	200	800	2,000	8,000	
Direct labour (no change)	50	150	500	1,500	
Short-run variable overheads (W1)	70	210	700	2,100	
Set-up costs (W2)	1,560	1,560	3,900	3,900	
Expediting, scheduling costs (W3)	1,300	1,300	3,250	3,250	
Materials handling costs (W4)	1,100	1,100	2,750	2,750	
	4,280	5,120	13,100	21,500	44,000
Units produced	10	10	100	100	
Cost per unit	$428	$512	$131	$215	

Workings

1	$3,080 ÷ 440 machine hours =	$7 per machine hour
2	$10,920 ÷ 14 production runs =	$780 per production run
3	$9,100 ÷ 14 production runs =	$650 per production run
4	$7,700 ÷ 14 production runs =	$550 per production run

Summary

Product	Conventional absorption costing unit cost	ABC unit cost	Difference per unit	Difference in total
	$	$	$	$
W	95	428	+ 333	+3,330
X	305	512	+ 207	+2,070
Y	95	131	+ 36	+3,600
Z	305	215	− 90	−9,000

These figures might suggest that the traditional volume-based absorption costing system is flawed, because the low-volume products W and X are not being charged with a 'fair share' of the costs of overhead support activities.

More specifically, **traditional absorption costing may be unsatisfactory** for two main reasons.

(a) It **under-allocates overhead costs to low-volume products** (here, W and X) and **over-allocates overheads to higher-volume products** (here Z in particular).

(b) It **under-allocates overhead costs to smaller-sized products** (here W and Y with just one hour of work needed per unit) and **over allocates overheads to larger products** (here X and particularly Z).

ABC addresses these problems, and arguably produces a more 'realistic' or 'satisfactory' cost.

2.2 Cost drivers

ABC focuses attention on **what** factors are most influential in determining the level of support activity costs, ie the cost drivers. However it is important to understand that activity-based costs should **not be regarded as variable costs** that vary with the volume of the cost driver. Some activity costs may be variable, but many are not. Cost drivers affect or influence total costs of the activity, but not in a direct 'variable cost' relationship between activity level and cost.

(a) **Activity costs that relate to production volume**, such as power costs, should be traced to products using production **volume-related cost drivers**, such as direct labour hours or direct machine hours worked.

Overheads which do not relate to production volume, but to **some other activity** should be traced to products using **transaction-based cost drivers**, such as number of production runs and number of orders received.

(b) Traditional absorption costing charges overhead costs to products in a way that ignores the costs of support activities and their cost drivers. As a consequence it produces less satisfactory or 'reliable' product costs.

Question	Traditional costing (v) ABC

A company manufactures two products, L and M, using the same equipment and similar processes. An extract of the production data for these products in one period is shown below.

	L	*M*
Quantity produced (units)	5,000	7,000
Direct labour hours per unit	1	2
Machine hours per unit	3	1
Set-ups in the period	10	40
Orders handled in the period	15	60

Overhead costs	$
Relating to machine activity	220,000
Relating to production run set-ups	20,000
Relating to handling of orders	45,000
	285,000

Required

Calculate the production overheads to be absorbed by one unit of each of the products using the following costing methods.

(a) A traditional costing approach using a direct labour hour rate to absorb overheads
(b) An activity based costing approach, using suitable cost drivers to trace overheads to products

(a) **Traditional costing approach**

	Direct labour hours
Product L = 5,000 units × 1 hour	5,000
Product M = 7,000 units × 2 hours	14,000
	19,000

$$\therefore \text{ Overhead absorption rate } = \frac{\$285,000}{19,000}$$

$$= \$15 \text{ per hour}$$

Overhead absorbed would be as follows.

Product L	1 hour × $15 =	$15 per unit
Product M	2 hours × $15 =	$30 per unit

(b) **ABC approach**

		Machine hours
Product L	= 5,000 units × 3 hours	15,000
Product M	= 7,000 units × 1 hour	7,000
		22,000

Using ABC the overhead costs are absorbed according to the cost drivers. The absorption rate for each cost pool is as follows.

	$			Absorption rate, ABC
Machine-hour driven costs	220,000	÷	22,000 m/c hours	= $10 per m/c hour
Set-up driven costs	20,000	÷	50 set-ups	= $400 per set-up
Order driven costs	45,000	÷	75 orders	= $600 per order

Overhead costs are therefore as follows.

		Product L $		Product M $
Machine-driven costs	(15,000 hrs × $10)	150,000	(7,000 hrs × $10)	70,000
Set-up costs	(10 × $400)	4,000	(40 × $400)	16,000
Order handling costs	(15 × $600)	9,000	(60 × $600)	36,000
		163,000		122,000
Units produced		5,000		7,000
Overhead cost per unit		$32.60		$17.43

These figures suggest that with traditional absorption costing, Product M absorbs an 'unfair' amount of overhead costs using a direct labour hour absorption rate. If overhead costs are absorbed accordingly for each activity, based on the cost drivers for the activity, the resulting costs are more 'fair'.

ABC has both advantages and disadvantages, and tends to be more widely used by larger organisations and the service sector.

As you will have discovered when you attempted the question above, there is nothing difficult about ABC. Once the necessary information has been obtained it is similar to traditional absorption costing. This simplicity is part of its appeal. Further merits of ABC are as follows.

(a)   The **complexity of manufacturing has increased**, with wider product ranges, shorter product life cycles and more complex production processes. **ABC recognises this complexity with its multiple cost drivers.**

(b)   In a more competitive environment, companies must be able to assess product profitability realistically. **ABC facilitates a good understanding of what drives overhead costs**.

(c)   In modern manufacturing systems, overhead functions include a lot of non-factory-floor activities such as product design, quality control, production planning and customer services. **ABC is concerned with all overhead costs** and so it can take management accounting beyond its 'traditional' factory floor boundaries.

3.1 ABC and decision making   12/10

Many of ABC's supporters claim that it can assist with decision making in a number of ways.

- It provides accurate and reliable cost information
- It establishes a long-run product cost
- It provides cost data which may be used to evaluate different ways of delivering business.

It is particularly suited to the following types of decision:

- Pricing, where selling prices are derived by adding a profit mark-up to cost

- Promoting or discontinuing products or parts of the business, since ABC may help management to identify activity costs that may be either incurred or saved

- Developing new products or new ways to do business, because ABC focuses attention on the support activities that would be required for the new product or business procedure.

Note, however, that an ABC cost is **not a variable cost**. ABC is a form of absorption costing that seeks to charge overheads to products on a more 'fair' basis than traditional absorption costing. An ABC cost is therefore **not a relevant cost** for decision-making purposes.

ABC attempts to **relate the incidence of costs to the level of activities undertaken**. A **hierarchy of activities** has been suggested.

Classification level	Cause of cost	Types of cost	Cost driver
Unit level	Production/acquisition of a single unit of product or delivery of single unit of service	Direct materials Direct labour	Units produced
Batch level	A group of things being made, handled or processed	Purchase orders Set-ups Inspection	Batches produced
Product level	Development, production or acquisition of different items	Equipment maintenance Product development	Product lines produced

Classification level	Cause of cost	Types of cost	Cost driver
Facility sustaining level	Some costs cannot be related to a particular product line, instead they are related to maintaining the buildings and facilities. These costs cannot be related to cost objects with any degree of accuracy and are often excluded from ABC calculations for this reason.	Building depreciation Organisational advertising	None - supports the overall production or service process

3.2 Criticisms of ABC

It has been suggested by critics that **activity based costing has some weaknesses.**

(a) Cost apportionment may still be required at the cost pooling stage for shared items of cost such as rent, rates and building depreciation. Apportionment can be an arbitrary way of sharing costs.

(b) A single cost driver may not explain the cost behaviour of all items in a cost pool. An activity may have two or more cost drivers.

(c) Unless costs are 'driven' by an activity that is measurable in quantitative terms, cost drivers cannot be used. What drives the cost of the annual external audit, for example?

(d) There must be a reason for using a system of ABC. ABC must provide meaningful product costs or extra information that management will use. If management is not going to use ABC information for any practical purpose, a traditional absorption costing system would be simpler to operate and just as good.

(e) The cost of implementing and maintaining an ABC system can exceed the benefits of 'improved accuracy' in product costs.

(f) **Implementing** ABC is often problematic, due to problems with understanding activities and their costs.

(g) ABC is an absorption costing system. Absorption costing has only limited value for management accounting purposes.

Chapter Roundup

Activity based costing (ABC) is an alternative to traditional absorption costing as a method of costing.

ABC involves the identification of the factors **(cost drivers)** which 'cause' or 'drive' the costs of an organisation's major activities. Overheads are allocated and apportioned to activity cost centres or 'cost pools'. From these activity cost centres, the overhead costs are then absorbed into the product costs on the basis of their usage of the activity. The absorption rate for each activity is a rate per unit of the relevant cost driver.

- For activity costs that seem to relate to the volume of production, the cost driver will be volume-related (labour or machine hours).

- For activity costs that do not seem to relate to production volume, a different cost driver is identified, such as the number of production runs or number of orders received.

- ABC has both advantages and disadvantages, and tends to be more widely used by larger organisations and the service sector.

Quick Quiz

1   *Choose the correct phrases.*

    Traditional costing systems tend to charge **too great/too small** a proportion of overheads to high volume products and **too great/too small** a proportion of overheads to low volume products.

2   *Fill in the blanks.*

    The major ideas behind ABC are as follows.

    (a)   Activities cause ....
    (b)   Producing products creates demand for the ....
    (c)   Costs are assigned to a product on the basis of the product's consumption of the ....

3   *Match the most appropriate cost driver to each cost.*

Costs	*Cost driver*
(a) Machine set-up costs	Number of machine hours
(b) Machine operating costs	Number of set-ups
(c) Materials handling and despatch	Number of orders executed

4   ABC recognises the complexity of modern manufacturing by the use of multiple cost pools. **True or false?**

5   Direct labour hours or direct machine hours are used to trace costs to products occurs with absorption costing, but not with ABC. **True or false?**

6   The cost driver for quality inspection is likely to be batch size. **True or false?**

7   ABC is not a system that is suitable for use by service organisations. **True or false?**

1   Too great
     Too small

2   (a)   Costs
     (b)   Activities
     (c)   Activities

3   (a)   Number of set-ups
     (b)   Number of machine hours
     (c)   Number of orders executed

4   True. There is a separate cost pool for each significant activity that incurs costs.

5   False. The use of volume-related cost drivers should be used for costs that do vary with production volume.

6   False. It is more likely to be the number of production runs.

7   False. It is more suitable for manufacturing but can be used to cost services in some service industries.

Now try the questions below from the Practice Question Bank

Number	Level	Marks	Time
Q2	Introductory	15	27 mins
Q3	Examination	15	27 mins

Target costing

Introduction

Target costing is the second specialist cost accounting technique we will consider. It is a process which involves setting a target cost for a product by subtracting a desired profit margin from a target selling price.

In a competitive market where organisations are continually redesigning products and developing new products, target costing can be an invaluable technique for helping the organisation to make a satisfactory profit on the items that it sells.

Study guide

		Intellectual level
A2	**Target costing**	
(a)	Derive a target cost in manufacturing and service industries	2
(b)	Explain the difficulties of using target costing in service industries	2
(c)	Suggest how a target cost gap might be closed	2

Exam guide

Target costing may form part of a Section B question comparing its use to other costing techniques (such as life cycle costing) or it may form an entire question including calculation of a target cost.

1 What is target costing? 12/07

FAST FORWARD

Target costing involves setting a target cost for a product, having identified a target selling price and a required profit margin. The target cost is the target sales price minus the required profit.

In a competitive market, selling prices must be competitive. In order to sell at a competitive price and make a required amount of profit, the cost of production and sales must be kept at a level that will provide the required profit at the chosen selling price.

Target costing is concerned with designing a product and its production process so that it can be made and sold at a cost that delivers the required profit at the chosen price. It focuses on getting the expected cost of a product down to a target cost amount. Achieving a target cost will usually require some re-designing of the product and the removal of unnecessary costs.

In many markets, new product innovation and the re-designing of existing products is a continual process. Target costing is most effective at the product design stage, rand is less effective for established products that are made in established processes. At the design stage, it is easier and cheaper to make changes that reduce costs.

Here are some examples of **decisions made at the design stage** which **impact on the cost of a product.**

- The number of different components in a product, that have to be assembled in the production process
- Whether the components are standard or not: using standard components can reduce costs
- Deciding to exclude design features on the product that do not add any value for the customer
- Using cheaper materials to make the product, where this does not affect product quality
- Simplifying the production process, for example to make it easier and quicker to change over tools.

Key terms

Target costing involves setting a target cost by subtracting a desired profit margin from a target selling price.

Target cost is the cost at which a product must be produced and sold in order to achieve the required amount of profit at the target selling price. When a product is first planned, its estimated cost will often be higher than its target cost. The aim of target costing is then to find ways of closing this target cost gap, and producing and selling the product at the target cost.

2 Implementing target costing

In an article 'Product costing/pricing strategy' (*ACCA Students Newsletter*, August 1999), a previous examiner provided a useful summary of the steps in the implementation of the target costing process.

Step 1   Determine a product specification of which an adequate sales volume is estimated.

Step 2   Decide a target selling price at which the organisation will be able to sell the product successfully and achieve a desired market share.

Step 3   Estimate the required profit, based on required profit margin or return on investment.

Step 4   Calculate: Target cost = Target selling price − Target profit.

Step 5   Prepare an estimated cost for the product, based on the initial design specification and current cost levels.

Step 6   Calculate: Target cost gap = Estimated cost − Target cost.

Step 7   Make efforts to close the gap. This is more likely to be successful if efforts are made to 'design out' costs prior to production, rather than to 'control out' costs after 'live' production has started.

It is usual for estimates of target cost to be based not only on a target selling price per unit, but also on the expected volume of sales.

Case Study

Swedish retailer IKEA dominates the home furniture market in many countries. The "IKEA concept" as defined on the company website www.ikea.com is "based on offering a wide range of well designed functional home furnishing products at prices so low as many people as possible will be able to afford them."

IKEA is widely known for pricing products at 30-50% below the price charged by competitors. Extracts from the website outline how the company has successfully employed a strategy of target pricing:

"While most retailers use design to justify a higher price, IKEA designers work in exactly the opposite way. Instead they use design to secure the lowest possible price. IKEA designers design every IKEA product starting with a functional need and a price. Then they use their vast knowledge of innovative, low-cost manufacturing processes to create functional products, often co-ordinated in style. Then large volumes are purchased to push prices down even further.

Most IKEA products are also designed to be transported in flat packs and assembled at the customer's home. This lowers the price by minimising transportation and storage costs. In this way, the IKEA Concept uses design to ensure that IKEA products can be purchased and enjoyed by as many people as possible."

3 Deriving a target cost

The target cost is calculated by starting with a market-based target selling price and subtracting a desired profit margin. The target cost is simply the target price minus the required profit.

3.1 Example: Target costing

A car manufacturer wants to calculate a target cost for a new car, the price of which will be set at $17,950. The company requires an 8% profit margin on sales.

Required

What is the target cost?

Solution

Profit required = 8% × $17,950 = $1,436
Target cost = $(17,950 – 1,436) = $16,514

The car manufacturer will then need to carefully compile an estimated cost for the new car. ABC will help to ensure that costs allocated to the new model are more accurate.

3.2 Example: Target costing and the target cost gap

Great Games, a manufacturer of computer games, is in the process of introducing a new game to the market and has undertaken market research to find out about customers' views on the value of the product and also to obtain a comparison with competitors' products. The results of this research have been used to establish a target selling price of $60. This is the price that the company thinks it will have to sell the product to achieve the required sales volume.

Cost estimates have been prepared based on the proposed product specification.

Manufacturing cost	$
Direct material	3.21
Direct labour	24.03
Direct machinery costs	1.12
Ordering and receiving	0.23
Quality assurance	4.60
Non-manufacturing costs	
Marketing	8.15
Distribution	3.25
After-sales service	1.30

The target profit margin for the game is 30% of the target selling price.

Required

Calculate the target cost of the new game and the target cost gap.

Solution

	$
Target selling price	60.00
Target profit margin (30% of selling price)	18.00
Target cost (60.00 – 18.00)	42.00
Projected cost	45.89

The projected cost exceeds the target cost by $3.89. This is the target cost gap. Great Games will therefore have to investigate ways to reduce the cost from the current estimated amount down to the target cost.

4 Closing a target cost gap   12/07

The **target cost gap** is the estimated cost less the target cost. When a product is first manufactured, its currently-attainable cost may be higher than the target cost. Management can then set **benchmarks for improvement** towards the target cost, by improving production technologies and processes. Various techniques can be employed.

- Reducing the **number of components**
- Using **cheaper staff**
- Using **standard components** wherever possible
- Acquiring new, more efficient **technology**
- **Training** staff in more efficient techniques
- Cutting out **non-value-added activities**
- Using **different materials** (identified using **activity analysis** etc)

However, as stated earlier, the most effective time to eliminate unnecessary cost and reduce the expected cost to the target cost level is during the product design and development phase, not after 'live' production has begun.

Exam focus point

When answering a question on closing a target cost gap, you may be expected to refer to the specific circumstances of the business in the question.

5 Target costing in service industries 6/12

Target costing is difficult to use in service industries due to the **characteristics** and **information requirements** of service businesses.

5.1 Characteristics of services

FAST FORWARD

Unlike manufacturing companies, services are characterised by **intangibility, inseparability, variability, perishability** and no **transfer of ownership.**

Examples of service businesses include:

(a) **Mass service** eg the banking sector, transportation (rail, air), mass entertainment
(b) **Either / or** eg fast food, teaching, hotels and holidays, psychotherapy
(c) **Personal service** eg pensions and financial advice, car maintenance

Key term

"**Services** are any activity of benefit that one party can offer to another that is essentially intangible and does not result in the ownership of anything. Its production may or may not be tied to a physical product."

(P Kotler, *Social Marketing*)

There are **five major characteristics** of services that distinguish services from products.

(a) **Intangibility**. This refers to the lack of substance which is involved with service delivery. Unlike goods (physical products such as confectionery), there is no substantial material or physical aspects to a service: no taste, feel, visible presence and so on.

(b) **Inseparability/simultaneity**. Many services are created at the same time as they are consumed. (Think of dental treatment.) No service exists until it is actually being experienced or consumed by the person who has bought it.

(c) **Variability/heterogeneity**. Many services face the problem of maintaining consistency in the standard of output. It may be hard to attain precise standardisation of the service offered, but customers expect it (such as with fast food). When services are delivered by humans, it is very difficult to ensure that the same service is provided in exactly the same way every time.

(d) **Perishability.** Services are innately perishable. The services of a beautician, for example, are purchased for a period of time.

(e) **No transfer of ownership.** Services do not result in the transfer of property. The purchase of a service only confers on the customer access to or a right to use a facility.

Services also vary widely in nature. For example, services include banking, transport, parcel delivery, energy supply, entertainment, education, hotels and holidays, car repairs and maintenance, professional services such as law and accountancy, cleaning, security services, and so on. The list is virtually endless. A feature of many services, however, is that although the labour content may be high, the materials content is often quite low. With products, the material content is higher and the labour element may be lower.

5.2 Problems with target costing for services

FAST FORWARD

> Some of the characteristics of services make it difficult to use target costing, and identify a target cost for a service having established a target selling price.

A target cost for a product is a cost for an item whose design and make-up is specified in exact detail in a product specification. A target cost is the cost for this detailed specification.

Services are much more difficult to specify exactly. This is due to some of the characteristics of a service.

(a)   Intangibility. Some of the features of a service cannot be properly specified because they are intangible. What exactly does a customer receive, for example, when he or she goes to a cinema? When services are provided by a human, the quality of the personal service can be critically important for the customer, but this is difficult or impossible to specify.

When services do not have any material content, it is not possible to reduce costs to a target level by reducing material costs. In comparison, reducing material costs can be an effective approach to target costing for products.

(b)   Variability/homogeneity. A service can differ every time it is provided, and a standard service may not exist. For example, repairing a motor car, providing an accountancy service, or driving a delivery truck from London to Paris are never exactly the same each time. When services are variable, it is possible to calculate an estimated average cost, but this is not specific and so not ideal for target costing.

Chapter Roundup

- **Target costing** involves setting a target cost for a product, having identified a target selling price and a required profit margin. The target cost is the target sales price minus the required profit.

- Unlike manufacturing companies, services are characterised by **intangibility, inseparability, variability, perishability** and no **transfer of ownership**.

- Some of the characteristics of services make it difficult to use target costing, and identify a target cost for a service having established a target selling price.

Quick Quiz

1   *Fill in the blanks using words from the list (a) to (h).*

    Target cost   = ... − ....
    Cost gap   = ... − ....

    (a)   target cost   (e)   target selling price
    (b)   cost gap   (f)   estimated cost
    (c)   budgeted selling price   (g)   target profit
    (d)   production cost

2   What might be effective ways of reducing the labour cost element in a product, in order to lower expected cost towards a target cost?

3   Which two of the following characteristics of services make it difficult to establish target costs for services?

    (a)   Intangibility   (d)   Variability
    (b)   Perishability   (e)   Simultaneity
    (c)   No transfer of ownership

1   Target cost = Target selling price – Target profit
     Cost gap = Estimated cost – Target cost

2   Replace labour activities with automated activities: alter production methods or processes so as to improve labour efficiency

3   Intangibility and Variability.

Life cycle costing

Introduction

Life cycle costing is the third specialist cost accounting technique we will consider. It is an approach that accumulates costs over a **product's entire life**, rather than calculating them for each accounting period through the product's life. It is used to determine the **total expected profitability** of a product over its entire life, from its design and development stage, through its market introduction, to its eventual withdrawal from the market.

It is a costing technique used primarily for planning lifetime costs and profitability. It is not a technique for recording and reporting historical costs of production and sales.

Study guide

		Intellectual level
A3	**Life cycle costing**	
(a)	Identify the costs involved at different stages of the life cycle	2
(b)	Derive a life cycle cost in manufacturing and service industries	2
(c)	Identify the benefits of life cycle costing	2

Exam guide

Life cycle costing may form part of a 10-mark Section B question on costing techniques but it could form an entire question.

1 The product life cycle

FAST FORWARD

A **product life cycle** can be divided into five phases.

- Development
- Introduction
- Growth

- Maturity
- Decline

The 'classical' life cycle of a product has five phases or stages.

(a) **Development**. The product has a research or design and development stage. Costs are incurred but the product is not yet on the market and there are no sales revenues.

(b) **Introduction**. The product is introduced to the market. Potential customers are initially unaware of the product or service, and the organisation may have to spend heavily on advertising to bring the product or service to the attention of the market. In addition, capital expenditure costs may be incurred in order to increase the production capacity as sales demand grows.

(c) **Growth**. The product gains a bigger market as demand builds up. Sales revenues increase and the product begins to make a profit.

(d) **Maturity**. Eventually, the growth in demand for the product will slow down and it will enter a period of relative maturity, when sales have reached a peak and are fairly stable. This should be the most profitable phase of the product's life. The product may be modified or improved, as a means of sustaining its demand and making this phase of the life cycle as long as possible.

(e) **Decline**. At some stage, the market will have bought enough of the product and it will therefore reach 'saturation point'. Demand will start to fall. Eventually it will become a loss-maker and this is the time when the organisation should decide to stop selling the product or service.

The level of sales and profits earned over a life cycle can be illustrated diagrammatically as follows.

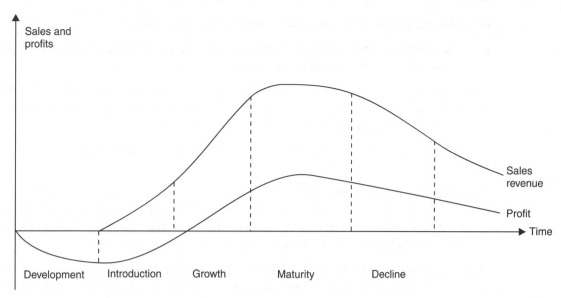

The horizontal axis measures the **duration of the life cycle**, which can last from several months to several hundred years. Children's crazes or fad products have very short lives while some products, such as binoculars (invented in the eighteenth century) can last a very long time.

'Generic' products have a longer life cycle than specific types of the product, which in turn have a longer life cycle than specific models of the product. For example, television continues to have a long life cycle, but global sales of black-and-white televisions have declined. Product models have an even shorter life: for example, Mark II may replace Mark I.

2 Life cycle costs   12/08, 12/11, 6/13

Life cycle costing estimates the costs and revenues attributable to a product over its entire expected life cycle.

The **life cycle costs** of a product are all the costs attributable to the product over its entire life, from product concept and design to eventual withdrawal from the market.

A product's life cycle costs are incurred **from its design stage through development to market launch, production and sales, and finally to its eventual decline and withdrawal from the market**.

The component elements of a product's cost over its life cycle could therefore include the following.

- **Research & development costs**

    – Design costs
    – Cost of making a prototype
    – Testing costs
    – Production process and equipment: development and investment

- The **cost of purchasing any technical data** required (for example purchasing the right from another organisation to use a patent)

- **Training costs** (including initial operator training and skills updating)

- **Production costs,** when the product is eventually launched in the market

- **Distribution costs**. Transportation and handling costs

- **Marketing and advertising costs**

    – Customer service
    – Field maintenance
    – Brand promotion

- **Inventory costs** (holding spare parts, warehousing and so on)
- **Retirement and disposal costs**. Costs occurring at the end of a product's life. These may include the costs of cleaning up a contaminated site

Some of these costs such as design costs are 'once-only costs'. Others are incurred regularly throughout the product's life, but vary with production and sales volumes. Production costs for example will vary each year with changes in annual production volumes through the product's life.

Life cycle costs can also be estimated for **services**, customers and projects as well as to physical products.

Traditional cost accumulation systems are based on the financial accounting year and tend to dissect a product's life cycle into a series of 12-month periods. This means that traditional management accounting systems **do not accumulate costs over a product's entire life cycle** and **do not** therefore **assess a product's profitability over its entire life.** Instead they do it on a periodic basis.

Life cycle costing, on the other hand, **tracks and accumulates actual costs and revenues** attributable to each product **over the entire product life cycle.** Hence the total profitability of any given product can be determined.

Key term

> **Life cycle costing** is the accumulation of costs over a product's entire life.

2.1 Why calculate life cycle costs?

Life cycle costing has a different purpose from cost accumulation systems that measure actual costs of production and sales. Traditional costing systems are intended to measure the cost of a product in each accounting period, and the profit or loss that should be reported for the product for that period.

The **purpose of life cycle costing** is to assess the total costs of a product over its entire life, to assess the expected profitability from the product over its full life. Products that are not expected to be profitable after allowing for design and development costs, or clean-up costs, should not be considered for commercial development.

2.2 The benefits of life cycle costing 12/11

There are a number of benefits associated with life cycle costing.

(a) It helps management to assess profitability over the full life of a product, which in turn helps management to decide whether to develop the product, or to continue making the product.

(b) It can be very useful for organisations that continually develop products with a relatively short life, where it may be possible to estimate sales volumes and prices can with reasonable accuracy.

(c) The life cycle concept results in earlier actions to generate more revenue or to lower costs than otherwise might be considered.

(d) Better decisions should follow from a more accurate and realistic assessment of revenues and costs, at least within a particular life cycle stage.

(e) It encourages longer-term thinking and forward planning, and may provide more useful information than traditional reports of historical costs and profits in each accounting period.

3 Life cycle costing in manufacturing and service industries

FAST FORWARD

Both manufacturing and service organisations can use life cycle costing, to estimate returns over a product/service life cycle.

With life cycle costing, all costs are traced to individual products or services over their complete life cycles. This encourages management to think of the life cycle, and ways in which this may perhaps be managed.

It has been reported that some organisations operating with an **advanced manufacturing technology** environment find that approximately 90% of a product's life cycle costs are determined by decisions made early within the cycle, at the design stage. Life cycle costing is therefore particularly useful for these organisations, to monitoring spending during the early stages of a product's life cycle.

Another feature of many competitive markets is that product life cycles are getting shorter, and organisations must continually re-design existing products and develop new ones. The **planning, design and development stages of a product's cycle** are therefore **critical** to an organisation's costs and profits. Cost reduction at this stage of a product's life cycle, rather than during the production process, is one of the most important ways of reducing product cost.

Note: The techniques of life cycle costing and target costing can be combined, to plan for achieving certain levels of cost at different stages of the product's life cycle. Both are essentially forward-looking techniques of costing.

3.1 Maximising return over the product life cycle

3.1.1 Design costs out of products

Between 70% to 90% of a product's life cycle costs are determined by decisions made early in the life cycle, at the design or development stage. Careful design of the product and manufacturing and other processes will keep cost to a minimum over the life cycle.

3.1.2 Minimise the time to market

'Time to market' is the time from the conception of the product to its introduction to the market. Competitors watch each other very carefully to determine what types of product their rivals are developing. If an organisation is launching a new product it is vital to get it to the market place as soon as possible. This will give the product as long a period as possible without a rival in the market place, and should mean increased market share in the long run. Furthermore, the life span of a product may be affected by delay in its the market introduction. It is not unusual for the product's overall profitability to fall by 25% if the launch is delayed by six months. This means that it is usually worthwhile incurring extra costs to keep the launch on schedule or to speed up the launch.

3.1.3 Minimise breakeven time (BET)

A short BET is very important in keeping an organisation liquid. The sooner the product is launched the quicker the research and development costs will be repaid, providing the organisation with funds to develop further products. In life cycle costing, break even occurs when revenue from the product has covered all the costs incurred to date, including design and development costs.

3.1.4 Maximise the length of the life span

Product life cycles are not predetermined; they can be influenced by the actions of management and competitors. For example some products lend themselves to a number of different uses; this is especially true of materials, such as plastic, PVC, nylon and other synthetic materials. The life cycle of these materials can be extended by finding new uses for them. The life cycle of the material is then a series of individual product curves nesting on top of each other as shown below.

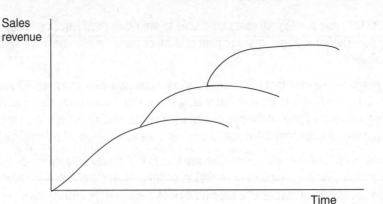

Sales revenue

Time

By entering different national or regional markets one after another an organisation may be able to extend the growth phase of a product's life. On the other hand, in today's fast moving world, an organisation could lose out to a competitor if it failed to establish an early presence in a particular market.

3.2 Service and project life cycles

Services have life cycles. The only difference with the life cycle of a product is that the **R & D stages** will not usually exist in the same way. The **different processes** that go to form the complete service are important, however, and consideration should be given in advance as to how to carry them out and arrange them so as to minimise cost.

Products that take years to produce or come to fruition are usually called **projects**, and **discounted cash flow calculations** are invariably used to cost them over their life cycle in advance. The projects need to be **monitored** very carefully over their life to make sure that they **remain on schedule** and that **cost overruns** are not being incurred.

3.3 Customer life cycles

Customers also have life cycles, and an organisation will wish to **maximise the return from a customer over their life cycle**. The aim is to **extend the life cycle of a particular customer** or decrease the 'churn' rate, as the Americans say. This means **encouraging customer loyalty**. For example, some supermarkets and other retail outlets issue **loyalty cards** that offer discounts to loyal customers who return to the shop and spend a certain amount with the organisation. As existing customers tend to be more profitable than new ones they should be retained wherever possible.

Customers become more profitable over their life cycle. The profit can go on increasing for a period of between approximately four and 20 years. For example, if you open a bank account, take out insurance or invest in a pension, the company involved has to set up the account, run checks and so on. The initial cost is high and the company will be keen to retain your business so that it can recoup this cost. Once customers get used to their supplier they tend to use them more frequently, and so there is a double benefit in holding on to customers.

| Question | Life cycle costing |

Solaris specialises in the manufacture of solar panels. It is planning to introduce a new slimline solar panel specially designed for small houses. Development of the new panel is to begin shortly and Solaris is in the process of determining the price of the panel. It expects the new product to have the following costs.

	Year 1	Year 2	Year 3	Year 4
Units manufactured and sold	2,000	15,000	20,000	5,000
	$	$	$	$
R&D costs	1,900,000	100,000	-	-
Marketing costs	100,000	75,000	50,000	10,000
Production cost per unit	500	450	400	450
Customer service costs per unit	50	40	40	40
Disposal of specialist equipment				300,000

The Marketing Director believes that customers will be prepared to pay $500 for a solar panel but the Financial Director believes this will not cover all of the costs throughout the lifecycle.

Required

Calculate the cost per unit looking at the whole life cycle and comment on the suggested price.

Answer

Life cycle costs

	$'000
R&D (1,900 + 100)	2,000
Marketing (100 + 75 + 50 + 10)	235
Production (1,000 + 6,750 + 8,000 + 2,250)	18,000
Customer service (100 + 600 + 800 + 200)	1,700
Disposal	300
Total lifecycle costs	22,235
Total production ('000 units)	42
Cost per unit	529.40

The total life cycle costs are $529.40 per solar panel which is higher than the price proposed by the marketing director. Solaris will either have to charge a higher price or look at ways to reduce costs.

It may be difficult to increase the price if customers are price sensitive and are not prepared to pay more. Costs could be reduced by analysing each part of the costs throughout the life cycle and actively seeking cost savings. For example, using different materials, using cheaper staff or acquiring more efficient technology.

Chapter Roundup

- A **product life cycle** can be divided into five phases.

    - Development   – Maturity
    - Introduction   – Decline
    - Growth

- Life **cycle costing** estimates the costs and revenues attributable to a product over its entire expected life cycle.

    The **life cycle costs** of a product are all the costs attributable to the product over its entire life, from product concept and design to eventual withdrawal from the market.

- Both manufacturing and service organisations can use life cycle costing, to estimate returns over a product/service life cycle.

Quick Quiz

1   *Match the following costs to the appropriate life cycle cost classification.*

Costs	Classifications
Design	Inventory costs
Energy costs	Acquisition costs
Warehousing	Maintenance costs
Transportation	Operation costs
Customer service	Product distribution costs

2   Life cycle costing is the profiling of cost over a product's production life. **True or false?**

3   Life cycle costing is particularly useful for products with a short expected life cycle. **True or false?**

Answers to Quick Quiz

1   *Cost*   *Classification*
    Design   Acquisition costs
    Energy costs   Operation costs
    Warehousing   Inventory costs
    Transportation   Product distribution costs
    Customer service   Maintenance costs

2   False. It also looks at development costs and so on which are incurred prior to production, and any dismantling costs, which are incurred once production ceases.

3   True. When the life cycle is short, estimates of life cycle costs and revenues are likely to be easier, and life cycle costs should also be easier to monitor.

Now try the question below from the Practice Question Bank

Number	Level	Marks	Time
Q4	Examination	15	27 mins

2d

Throughput accounting

Topic list	Syllabus reference
1 Theory of constraints	A4
2 Throughput accounting	A4
3 Performance measures in throughput accounting	A4
4 Throughput accounting ratio	A4

Introduction

Throughput accounting is the fourth management accounting technique in Section A of the syllabus. It is based on the theory of constraints and is consistent with the use of just-in-time (JIT) production methods. The basic concept in throughput accounting is that an organisation should seek to **maximise throughput** by identifying and eliminating **bottlenecks**.

Study guide

		Intellectual level
A4	**Throughput accounting**	
(a)	Discuss and apply the theory of constraints	2
(b)	Calculate and interpret a throughput accounting ratio (TPAR)	2
(c)	Suggest how a TPAR could be improved	2
(d)	Apply throughput accounting to a multi-product decision-making problem	2

Exam guide

Questions in Section B on this topic will be for 10 marks and are likely to be a mixture of calculation and discussion. You may be required to use your knowledge of limiting factors from previous studies. You can also expect multiple choice questions on both the theory of constraints and throughput accounting calculations in Section A.

1 Theory of constraints   12/13

FAST FORWARD

> **Throughput accounting** supports a production management system which aims to maximise throughput, and therefore cash generation from sales. It is not concerned with 'traditional' measurements of profit, or maximisation of this profit. A **just in time (JIT) production system** is operated, with some buffer inventory kept only when there is a **bottleneck resource**.

Exam focus point

The October and November 2011 editions of *Student Accountant* contain a two-part article on **throughput accounting** and the **theory of constraints**, written by the **examiner**.

The first article summarises the story contained in *The Goal*, a book by Eli Goldratt and Jeff Cox that presents the theory of constraints and throughput accounting within the context of a novel. The second article talks through a practical **approach to questions on throughput accounting**.

The theory of constraints (TOC) is an **approach to production management** and optimising production performance. It was formulated by Goldratt and Cox in the USA in 1986. Its key financial concept is to turn materials into sales as quickly as possible, thereby maximising the net cash generated from sales.

1.1 Throughput: sales, inventory and operational expenses

In the theory of constraints and throughput accounting, **throughput** is the money generated by a system through the sales that it makes.

Inventory is the amount of money the system has invested in purchasing things that it intends to re-sell within its finished products. You can think of 'inventory' in its normal sense, as stocks of materials or finished goods waiting to be used. 'Inventory' should also be considered as costs of materials purchased. **Inventory has no value** because it does not create throughput until it is used to sell products.

Throughput is the money obtained from sales minus the cost of materials that have gone into making them. In conventional cost accounting terms, the materials are the direct materials used in production. (Indirect materials are part of the fixed factory costs.)

Throughput = Sales – Material costs

Operational expenses, also known as factory expenses, are all the other costs of operations. They include what in traditional costing would be both direct labour costs and overhead costs.

In throughput accounting, all operational expenses or factory expenses are assumed to be 'fixed' costs.

1.2 Bottleneck factor: the constraint

The objective should be to maximise throughput.

The theory of constraints also states that at any time there will always be a **bottleneck resource** or factor that sets a limit on the amount of throughput that is possible. This bottleneck resource could in theory be sales demand for the organisation's output, but it is more likely to be a resource that the organisation uses. This 'bottleneck resource' which prevents output and throughput from getting any higher, could be:

(a)   A production resource, such as time available on a type of machine, or the available amount of skilled employee time

(b)   A selling resource, such as the number of sales representatives

(c)   The existence of an uncompetitive selling price

(d)   A need to deliver on time to particular customers

(e)   A lack of product quality and reliability

(f)   The lack of reliable material suppliers

In the exam, the bottleneck resource is likely to be a production factor, such as machine time or labour time. You may be familiar with the concept of 'limiting factor' in production. A bottleneck resource is a limiting factor. In the theory of constraints and throughput accounting, a bottleneck resource is also known as the **binding constraint**.

The objective of an organisation should therefore be to maximise total throughput, given the existence of a bottleneck resource.

> **Theory of constraints (TOC)** is an approach to production management which aims to maximise sales revenue less material cost. It focuses on bottlenecks which act as constraints to the maximisation of throughput.
>
> **Throughput** is the money generated from sales minus the cost of the materials used in making the items sold.
>
> **Bottleneck resource** or **binding constraint** – an activity which has a lower capacity than preceding or subsequent activities, thereby limiting throughput.

1.3 Production scheduling and the bottleneck resource

Taking the theory of constraints a stage further, since there is one bottleneck resource, it follows that all the other resources in production and elsewhere are not bottlenecks. Since production and throughput are limited by the bottleneck resource, it follows that there will be idle capacity for all the other resources.

Idle time should be accepted. Since all operational costs are fixed, idle time is not costing any money.

Resources that are not the bottleneck resource should not be used beyond the amount required for the maximum achievable throughput, given the bottleneck resource. Using non-binding constraints beyond this amount will simply result in a build-up of inventories.

(a)   In traditional cost accounting, improving efficiency and creating more inventory will increase profits. Higher inventories reduce the cost of sales and increase reported profits.

(b)   In the theory of constraints using non-bottleneck resources above the amount required for maximum throughput is wasteful. It does not increase throughput, it only increases unused inventory levels.

To avoid the build-up of work in progress, **production must be limited to the capacity of the bottleneck resource** but this capacity must be **fully utilised.**

There will be idle resources in non-bottleneck areas, but this does not matter. The focus should be on maximising throughput, given the limitation of the bottleneck.

Output through the binding constraint should never be delayed or held up otherwise sales will be lost. To avoid this happening a small **buffer inventory** should be built up immediately prior to the bottleneck

constraint. This is the only inventory that the business should hold, with the exception of possibly a very small amount of finished goods inventory and raw materials, which is consistent with a just-in-time (JIT) approach.

Operations in the production line prior to the binding constraint should operate at the same speed as the binding constraint; otherwise excess and unwanted work in progress (other than the buffer inventory) will be built up. According to TOC, inventory costs money in terms of storage space and interest costs, and so **inventory is not desirable**.

1.4 Increasing throughput: elevating the bottleneck

The theory of constraints states that the aim should be to maximise total throughput. The only way to increase throughput is to increase the capacity of the bottleneck constraint. All the focus of management attention should be on increasing the capacity of the bottleneck resource, or 'elevating the bottleneck'.

For example, time on Machine Type X may be a bottleneck resource. The only way to increase throughput is to increase the output capacity of Machine Type X. Ways in which this might be done, without buying a new Type X machine, could include:

- Moving from working 5 days a week to working 6 or 7 days a week

- Moving from working a 12-hour production day to an 18-hour or 24-hour production day

- Carrying out routine maintenance work on the machine outside normal working hours, so that it does not disrupt production.

If the capacity of a bottleneck resource is elevated (increased) sufficiently it will eventually cease to be a bottleneck resource. Another resource in the system will become the new bottleneck resource.

The same approach is now used for the new bottleneck resource. Maximise total throughput given the restriction of this resource, and seek to increase total throughput by increasing the capacity of the bottleneck resource.

1.5 Example: elevating the constraint

A company manufactures a single product, which is processed in turn through three machines, Machine type A, Machine type B and Machine type C. The current maximum output capacity per week on the existing machinery is as follows:

Machine type A: 1,800 units

Machine type B: 1,600 units

Machine type C: 1,500 units.

The company could purchase an additional machine type C for $8 million which would increase output capacity on Machines C by 600 units per week. It could also purchase an additional Machine type B that would cost $5 million and increase output capacity by 300 units per week.

An increase in weekly output capacity is worth (in present value terms) $50,000 per unit of additional output.

What should the company do? Should it buy either or both of the additional machines?

(1)   The current bottleneck resource is Machine Type C and output is restricted to 1,500 units per week. There is no point in buying an additional Machine Type B unless a new Machine type C is purchased first, to elevate the bottleneck resource.

If an additional Machine Type C is purchased, output capacity will increase as follows:

Machine type A: 1,800 units
Machine type B: 1,600 units
Machine type C: 2,100 units

By elevating the capacity of Machine type C, Machine type C is no longer the bottleneck resource. The new bottleneck resource is Machine type B and output is restricted to 1,600 units per week, which is 100 units per week more than the current output limit.

The benefit will be (100 units × $50,000) – $8 million = –$3,000,000 (= net loss).

(2)   If an additional Machine Type C and an additional Machine type B are purchased, output capacity will increase as follows:

Machine type A: 1,800 units
Machine type B: 1,900 units
Machine type C: 2,100 units

The new bottleneck resource is Machine Type A and output is restricted to 1,800 units per week, which is 300 units more than the current limit.

The benefit will be (300 units × $50,000) – $8 million – $5 million = + $2,000,000.

Conclusion. By purchasing an additional Machine type C and Machine type B output would be increased by 300 units per week. The new bottleneck constraint would be Machine type A. The company would benefit from this by $2,000,000.

1.6 Theory of constraints: summary

Goldratt devised a **five-step approach** to summarise the key stages of **TOC**.

Step 1   **Identify** the constraint (bottleneck resource).

Step 2   Decide how to **exploit** the constraint in order to maximise throughput.

Step 3   **Subordinate** and **synchronise** everything else to the decisions made in **step 2**.

Step 4   **Elevate** the performance of the constraint.

Step 5   If the **constraint has shifted** during any of the above steps, go back to **step 1**. Do not allow inertia to cause a new constraint.

The overall aim of TOC is to **maximise throughput**. This may be called '**throughput contribution**' (sales revenue – material cost) while keeping **operational costs** (all operating costs except material costs) and **investment costs** (inventory, equipment and so on) to the **minimum.**

1.7 Example: An illustration of the theory of constraints

Machine X can process 1,000 kg of raw material per hour, machine Y 800 kg. Of an input of 900 kg, 100 kg of processed material must wait on the bottleneck machine (machine Y) at the end of an hour of processing because machine Y does not have the capacity to produce it.

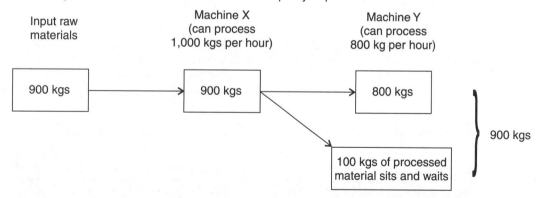

The **traditional view** is that **machines should be working, not sitting idle**. So if the desired output from the above process were 8,100 kgs, **machine X would be kept in continual use** and all 8,100 kgs would be processed through the machine in nine hours. There would be a **backlog** of 900 kgs [8,100 – (9 hrs × 800)] of processed material in front of machine Y, however. All this material **would require handling** and

storage space and **create the additional costs related to these non-value added activities**. Its **processing would not increase throughput** and would not earn any money for the organisation.

2 Throughput accounting   12/13

The concept of throughput accounting has been developed from the theory of constraints (TOC) as an alternative system of cost and management accounting in a **JIT production** environment.

> **Throughput accounting (TA)** is an approach to production management which aims to maximise sales revenue less materials cost, whilst also reducing inventory and operational expenses.

Throughput accounting is based on the following concepts, all derived from the TOC.

(a) **Concept 1**

In the short run, all costs in the factory (with the exception of materials costs) are **fixed costs**. These fixed costs include direct labour costs. It is useful to group all these costs together and call them **Total Factory Costs (TFC).**

(b) **Concept 2**

In a JIT environment, all inventory is a 'bad thing' and the **ideal inventory level is zero.** Products should not be made unless a customer has ordered them. When goods are made, the factory effectively operates at the rate of the slowest process, and there will be unavoidable idle capacity in other operations.

Work in progress should be **valued at material cost only** until the output is eventually sold, so that no value will be added and no profit earned until the sale takes place. Working on output just to add to work in progress or finished goods inventory creates no profit, and so should not be encouraged.

(c) **Concept 3**

Profitability is determined by the rate at which 'money comes in at the door' (that is, sales are made) and, in a JIT environment, this depends on **how quickly** goods can be produced to satisfy customer orders. Since the goal of a profit-orientated organisation is to make money, inventory must be sold for that goal to be achieved. The bottleneck resource slows the process of making money. Making money means maximising throughput.

Question   Throughput accounting

How are these concepts a direct contrast to the fundamental principles of conventional cost accounting?

Answer

Conventional cost accounting	Throughput accounting
Inventory is an asset.	Inventory is not an asset. It is a result of unsynchronised manufacturing and is a barrier to making profit.
Costs can be classified either as direct or indirect.	Such classifications are no longer useful.
Direct labour is a variable cost	All labour costs are part of TFC, which are fixed costs.
Product profitability can be determined by deducting a product cost from selling price.	Profitability is determined by the rate at which money is and throughput is earned.
Profit can be increased by reducing cost elements.	Profit is a function of material cost, total factory cost and throughput. Profit = Throughput minus TFC

2.1 Example: Throughput accounting in a service industry

Throughput accounting can be applied is a service industry as well as in production.

A not-for-profit organisation performs a medical screening service in three sequential stages.

1. Take an X-ray.
2. Interpret the result.
3. Recall patients who require further investigation / inform others that all is fine.

The 'goal unit' of this organisation will be to progress a patient through all three stages. The number of patients who complete all three stages is the organisation's throughput, and the organisation should seek to maximise its throughput. The duration of each stage and the weekly resource available is as follows.

Process	Time per patient (hours)	Total hours available per week
Take an X-ray (stage 1)	0.50	80
Interpret the result (stage 2)	0.20	40
Recall patients (stage 3)	0.40	60

The maximum number of patients (goal units) who can be dealt with in each process is as follows.

X-rays	80/0.5 = 160
Interpret results	40/0.20 = 200
Recall patients	60/0.40 = 150

The recall procedure (stage 3) is the bottleneck resource (constraint), because there are sufficient resources for the recall of only 150 patients. Throughput, and therefore the organisation's performance, cannot be improved until stage 3 can deal with more patients. There are a number of actions that the organisation could take to improve throughput.

(a) Investigate whether less time could be spent on the bottleneck activity.

(b) Ensure there is no idle time in the bottleneck resource as this will be detrimental to overall performance.

(c) Increase the bottleneck resource available.

There is little point in improving stage 1 and stage 2 if the process grinds to a halt at stage 3. Patients are only helped when the whole process is completed and they are recalled if necessary. Increasing the bottleneck resource, or the efficiency with which it is used may be relatively cheap and easy to do as stage 3 is a relatively simple piece of administration in comparison to the first two stages that use expensive machinery and highly skilled personnel.

3 Performance measures in throughput accounting
6/09, 6/11, 12/13

In a throughput accounting environment, **production priority** is given to the products best able to generate throughput. Performance measures in throughput accounting are based around the concept that the aim is to maximise throughput. This is achieved by maximising the **throughput per unit of bottleneck resource**.

When an organisation makes more than one product, total throughput is maximised by **giving priority to those products that earn the largest throughput per unit of bottleneck resource**. Products should be ranked in order of priority according to their throughput per unit of bottleneck resource.

In throughput accounting, the aim is to maximise throughput. Many organisations make more than one product, and each product uses a different amount of the bottleneck resource and earns a different amount of throughput per unit.

Throughput is maximised by ranking products in order for production and sales according to the throughput that they earn per unit of bottleneck resource they consume.

The top-ranking product should be manufactured up to the limit of maximum sales demand. The second-ranking product should be made next up to the limit of maximum sales demand, then the third, and so on.

The ratio for ranking products is therefore:

Throughput return per factory hour:

$$\frac{\text{Sales} - \text{direct material costs}}{\text{Usage of bottleneck resource in hours (factory hours)}}$$

3.1 Example: Maximising throughput and multiple products

WR Co manufactures three products, A, B and C. Product details are as follows:

	Product A	Product B	Product C
	$	$	$
Sales price	2.80	1.60	2.40
Materials cost	1.20	0.60	1.20
Direct labour cost	1.00	0.80	0.80
Weekly sales demand	4,000 units	4,000 units	5,000 units
Machine hours per unit	0.5 hours	0.2 hours	0.3 hours

Machine time is a bottleneck resource and maximum capacity is 4,000 machine hours per week. Operating costs including direct labour costs are $10,880 per week. Direct labour workers are not paid overtime and work a standard 38 hour week.

Required

Determine the optimum production plan for WR Co and calculate the weekly profit that would arise from the plan.

Solution

Step 1 Determine the bottleneck resource

The bottleneck resource is machine time (4,000 machine hours available each week).

Step 2 Calculate the throughput per unit for each product

	Product A	Product B	Product C
	$	$	$
Sales price	2.80	1.60	2.40
Materials cost	1.20	0.60	1.20
Throughput/unit	1.60	1.00	1.20

Step 3 Calculate throughput per unit of limiting factor (machine hours)

	Product A	Product B	Product C
Machine hours per unit	0.5 hours	0.2 hours	0.3 hours
Throughput per machine hour	$3.20*	$5.00	$4.00

* $1.60 / 0.5 hours = $3.20

Step 4 Rank products

	Product A	Product B	Product C
	3rd	1st	2nd

Step 5 Allocate resources to arrive at optimum production plan

The profit-maximising weekly output and sales volumes are as follows.

Product	Units	Bottleneck resource hours/unit	Total hours	Throughput per hour $	Total throughput $
B	4,000	0.2 hours	800	5.00	4,000
C	5,000	0.3 hours	1,500	4.00	6,000
			2,300		
A (balance)	3,400	0.5 hours	1,700	3.20	5,440
			4,000		15,440

Less: operating expenses	(10,880)
Profit per week	4,560

4 Throughput accounting ratio

The **throughput accounting ratio** (TA ratio) is the ratio of the throughput per unit of bottleneck resource to the factory cost per unit of bottleneck resource. This ratio should be as high as possible, and certainly more than 1.0.

The throughput accounting ratio (TA ratio) is a useful ratio, which you need to learn for your examination.

$$\text{Throughput accounting ratio} = \frac{\text{Throughput per unit of bottleneck resource}}{\text{Factory cost per unit of bottleneck resource}}$$

(Note: Instead of 'per unit of bottleneck resource', you may come across the term 'per factory hour'. This means the same thing in this context.)

The throughput per unit of bottleneck resource has been described above.

$$\text{Factory cost per unit of bottleneck resource} = \frac{\text{Total factory costs}}{\text{Total units of bottleneck resource}}$$

(Note: Total factory costs' are also described as 'Total operating costs'. They are all the costs other than material costs, and are regarded as a fixed cost per period.)

For example, suppose that a factory manufactures a single product. Each unit of product takes 2 hours to make on Machine X and output capacity is restricted by the available time on Machine X, which is restricted to 500 hours per week. The product has a material cost of $20 per unit and sells for $160 per unit. Total operating costs are $30,000 per week.

Throughput per Machine X hour = $(160 – 20)/2 hours = $70

Factory cost per Machine X hour = $30,000/500 hours = $60

TA ratio = $70/$60 = 1.17

4.1 Interpreting the TA ratio

Total throughput should exceed total factory costs; otherwise the organisation will make a loss. This means that **the TA ratio should exceed 1.0**.

A TA ratio that is not much higher than 1.0 is barely profitable. The aim should be to achieve as high a TA ratio as possible.

TA ratios can also be used to assess the **relative earning capabilities** of different products. Products can be ranked in order of priority for manufacture and sale in order of their TA ratios. (Higher TA ratios should be given priority over lower TA ratios).

However ranking products in order of priority according to their TA ratio will always give the same ranking as putting them in order of throughput per unit of bottleneck resource.

4.2 Example: TA ratios and ranking products

Corrie Company produces three products, X, Y and Z. The capacity of Corrie's plant is restricted by process Alpha. Process Alpha is expected to be operational for eight hours per day and can produce 1,200 units of X per hour, 1,500 units of Y per hour, and 600 units of Z per hour.

Selling prices and material costs for each product are as follows.

Product	Selling price $ per unit	Material cost $ per unit	Throughput $ per unit
X	150	80	70
Y	130	40	90
Z	300	100	200

Operating costs are $720,000 per day.

Required

(a) Calculate the profit per day if daily output achieved is 6,000 units of X, 4,500 units of Y and 1,200 units of Z.

(b) Calculate the TA ratio for each product.

(c) In the absence of demand restrictions for the three products, advise Corrie's management on the optimal production plan.

Solution

(a) Profit per day = Throughput contribution – Operating costs

$$= [(\$70 \times 6,000) + (\$80 \times 4,500) + (\$200 \times 1,200)] - \$720,000$$
$$= \$300,000$$

(b) TA ratio = Throughput per factory hour/ Operating costs per factory hour

Operating costs per factory hour = $720,000/8 = $90,000

Product	Throughput per factory hour	Cost per factory hour	TA ratio
X	$70 × 1,200 = $84,000	$90,000	0.93
Y	$90 × 1,500 = $135,000	$90,000	1.50
Z	$200 × 600 = $120,000	$90,000	1.33

(c) If it is not possible to increase the number of factory hours available, priority should be given to making and selling Product Y, since it has the highest TA ratio. If only Product Y is made and sold (since there is no restriction on sales demand), total output per day would be (1,500 × 8 hours) = 12,000 units of Product Y. Total throughput would be $1,080,000 (= 12,000 units × $90) per day. Total profit per day would be $1,080,000 - $720,000 = $360,000.

This is $60,000 more per day than the profit from the production mix in the answer to part (a).

The TA ratio of Product X is 0.93, which is less than 1.0. Product X makes less throughput per hour than its factory cost per hour.

Management should consider ways of raising the TA ratio above 1.0, or should give consideration to ceasing production of Product X entirely.

Question

Performance measurement in throughput accounting

Growler manufactures computer components. Health and safety regulations mean that one of its processes can only be operated 8 hours a day. The hourly capacity of this process is 500 units per hour. The selling price of each component is $100 and the unit material cost is $40. The daily total of all factory costs (conversion costs) is $144,000, excluding materials. Expected production is 3,600 units per day.

Required

Calculate

(a) Total profit per day
(b) Return per factory hour
(c) Throughput accounting ratio

Answer

(a) Total profit per day

$=$ Throughput contribution – Conversion costs
$=$ $(3,600 \times (100 - 40) - 144,000)$
$=$ $72,000

(b) Return per factory hour

$$= \frac{\text{Sales} - \text{direct material costs}}{\text{Usage of bottleneck resource in hours (factory hours)}}$$

$$= \frac{100 - 40}{1/500}$$

$=$ $30,000

(c) Throughput accounting ratio

$$= \frac{\text{Return per factory hour}}{\text{Total conversion cost per factory hour}}$$

$$= \frac{30,000}{144,000/8}$$

$=$ 1.67

4.3 How can a business improve a throughput accounting ratio?

In an exam question on throughput accounting, you may be asked about ways in which the TA ratio for a product might be increased. The ratio is increased by either:

(a) increasing the throughput per bottleneck hour, or
(b) reducing the operating cost per bottleneck hour,

The TA ratio could be increased in any of the following ways.

(a) Increase the selling price for the product. This will increase the throughput per unit, and so will increase the throughput per unit of bottleneck resource.

(b) Reducing the material cost per unit. This will increase the throughput per unit, and so will increase the throughput per unit of bottleneck resource.

(c) Reduce expenditure on operating costs/factory costs. This will reduce the operating cost per unit of bottleneck resource.

(d) Improve efficiency, and increase the number of units or product that are made in each bottleneck hour. This would increase total throughput per hour. The operating costs per hour would be unaffected; therefore the TA ratio would increase.

(e) Elevate the bottleneck, so that there are more hours available of the bottleneck resource. Throughput per unit of bottleneck resource would be unaffected, but since operating costs are all fixed costs and there are more bottleneck hours available, the operating cost per bottleneck hour would fall, and the TA ratio would increase.

However there may be adverse consequences from some of these measures.

Measures	Consequences
• Increase sales price per unit	• Demand for the product may fall
• Reduce material costs per unit, e.g. change materials and/or suppliers	• Quality may fall and bulk discounts may be lost
• Reduce operating expenses	• Quality may fall and/or errors increase

4.4 Throughput and limiting factor analysis

The throughput accounting approach to prioritising products for manufacture and sale is very similar to the approach of **maximising contribution per unit of scarce resource**, which you should have covered in your earlier studies.

Knowledge brought forward from earlier studies

Limiting factor analysis

- An organisation might be faced with just one limiting factor (other than maximum sales demand) but there might also be several scarce resources, with two or more of them putting an effective limit on the level of activity that can be achieved.

- Examples of limiting factors include sales demand and production constraints.

  - Labour. The limit may be either in terms of total quantity or of particular skills.
  - Materials. There may be insufficient available materials to produce enough units to satisfy sales demand.
  - Manufacturing capacity. There may not be sufficient machine capacity for the production required to meet sales demand.

- It is assumed in limiting factor analysis that management would make a product mix decision or service mix decision based on the option that would maximise profit and that profit is maximised when contribution is maximised (given no change in fixed cost expenditure incurred). In other words, marginal costing ideas are applied.

  - Contribution will be maximised by earning the biggest possible contribution per unit of limiting factor. For example if grade A labour is the limiting factor, contribution will be maximised by earning the biggest contribution per hour of grade A labour worked.
  - The limiting factor decision therefore involves the determination of the contribution earned per unit of limiting factor by each different product.
  - If the sales demand is limited, the profit-maximising decision will be to produce the top-ranked product(s) up to the sales demand limit.

- In limiting factor decisions, we generally assume that fixed costs are the same whatever product or service mix is selected, so that the only relevant costs are variable costs.

- When there is just one limiting factor, the technique for establishing the contribution-maximising product mix or service mix is to rank the products or services in order of contribution-earning ability per unit of limiting factor.

Attention! Throughput is defined as sales less material costs whereas contribution is defined as sales less **all** variable costs, including direct labour and variable overheads. Throughput assumes that all costs except direct materials are fixed in the short run.

Chapter Roundup

- **Throughput accounting** supports a production management system which aims to maximise throughput, and therefore cash generation from sales. It is not concerned with 'traditional' measurements of profit of maximisation of this profit. A **just in time (JIT) production system** is operated, with some buffer inventory kept only when there is a **bottleneck resource**.

- In a throughput accounting environment, **production priority** is given to the products best able to generate throughput. Performance measures in throughput accounting are based around the concept that the aim is to maximise throughput. This is achieved by maximising the **throughput per unit of bottleneck resource**.

- When an organisation makes more than one product, total throughput is maximised by **giving priority to those products that earn the largest throughput per unit of bottleneck resource**. Products should be ranked in order of priority according to their throughput per unit of bottleneck resource.

- The **throughput accounting ratio** (TA ratio) is the ratio of the throughput per unit of bottleneck resource to the factory cost per unit of bottleneck resource. This ratio should be as high as possible, and certainly more than 1.0.

Quick Quiz

1   Fill in the blanks in the statements below, using the words in the box. Some words may be used twice.

(a)   The theory of constraints is an approach to production management which aims to maximise (1)...................................... less (2)...................................... . It focuses on factors such as (3)...................................... which act as (4)......................................

(b)   Throughput contribution = (5)...................................... minus (6)......................................

(c)   TA ratio = (7) .... per factory hour ÷ (8) .... per factory hour

• bottlenecks	• throughput
• material costs	• constraints
• sales revenue	• factory cost

2   Fill in the right hand side of the table below, which looks at the differences between throughput accounting and traditional product costing.

Traditional product costing	Throughput accounting
Labour costs and 'traditional' variable overheads are treated as variable costs.	
Inventory is valued in the income statement and statement of financial position at total production cost.	
Variance analysis is employed to determine whether standards were achieved.	
Efficiency is based on labour and machines working to full capacity.	
Value is added when an item is produced.	

BPP
LEARNING MEDIA

3   The following details relate to three services offered by DSF.

	V	A	L
	$ per service	$ per service	$ per service
Selling price of service	120	170	176
Direct labour	20	30	20
Variable overhead	40	56	80
Fixed overhead	20	32	40
	80	118	140
Profit	40	52	36

All three services use the same direct labour, but in different quantities.

In a period when the labour used on these services is in short supply, the most and least profitable use of the labour is:

	Most profitable	Least profitable
A	L	V
B	L	A
C	V	A
D	A	L

1   1   sales revenue
    2   material costs
    3   bottlenecks
    4   constraints
    5   sales revenue
    6   material costs
    7   throughput
    8   factory cost

2

Traditional product costing	Throughput accounting
Labour costs and 'traditional' variable overheads are treated as variable costs.	They are not normally treated as variable costs.
Inventory is valued in the income statement and balance sheet at total production cost.	It is valued at material cost only.
Variance analysis is employed to determine whether standards were achieved.	It is used to determine why the planned product mix was not produced.
Efficiency is based on labour and machines working to full capacity.	Efficiency requires schedule adherence and meeting delivery dates.
Value is added when an item is produced.	It is added when an item is sold.

3   B

	V	A	L
	$	$	$
Selling price per service	120	170	176
Variable cost per service	60	86	100
Contribution per service	60	84	76
Labour cost per service	$20	$30	$20
Contribution per $ of labour	$3	$2.80	$3.80
Ranking	2	3	1

Now try the question below from the Practice Question Bank

Number	Level	Marks	Time
Q5	Examination	20	36 mins

Environmental accounting

Topic list	Syllabus reference
1 Managing environmental costs	A5 (a)
2 Accounting for environmental costs	A5 (b)

Introduction

Environmental accounting is the fifth and final management accounting technique in Section A of the syllabus.

Environmental issues are becoming increasingly important in the business world. Businesses are responsible for the environmental impact of their operations and are becoming increasingly aware of problems such as carbon emissions.

The growth of environmental issues and regulations has also brought greater focus on how businesses **manage** and **account** for environmental costs.

The focus of this chapter is on methods of providing information to management on environmental costs. It does not deal with environmental reporting to shareholders and other stakeholders.

Study guide

		Intellectual level
A5	**Environmental accounting**	
(a)	Discuss the issues businesses face in the management of environmental costs	1
(b)	Describe the different methods a business may use to account for its environmental costs	1

Exam guide

Environmental accounting is becoming increasingly topical in the modern business environment. The July 2010 edition of *Student Accountant*, contains an article on environmental management accounting written by the **examiner**.

For your examination, you should try to understand the nature of environmental costs, and you should be able to describe briefly the four methods of environmental management accounting that are described in this chapter.

1 Managing environmental costs

FAST FORWARD

Environmental costs are important to businesses for a number of reasons.

- Identifying environmental costs associated with individual products and services can assist with **pricing** decisions.
- Ensuring compliance with **regulatory standards.**
- Potential for **cost savings**.

Key term

Environmental management accounting (EMA) is the generation and analysis of both financial and non-financial information in order to support internal environmental management processes.

1.1 Environmental concern and performance

Martin Bennett and Peter James ('The green bottom line: management accounting for environmental improvement and business benefit', *Management Accounting*, November 1998) looked at the **ways in which a company's concern for the environment can impact on its performance.**

(a) **Short-term savings** through waste minimisation and energy efficiency schemes can be substantial.

(b) Companies with poor environmental performance may face **increased cost of capital** because investors and lenders demand a higher risk premium.

(c) There are a number of **energy and environmental taxes**, such as the UK's landfill tax on waste disposal.

(d) **Pressure group campaigns** can cause damage to reputation and/or additional costs.

(e) Environmental legislation may cause the **'sunsetting'** of products and opportunities for **'sunrise' replacements**.

(f) The cost of processing input which becomes **waste** is equivalent to 5-10% of some organisations' revenue.

On 20 April 2010, multinational oil company BP's Deepwater Horizon rig exploded off the coast of the US state of Louisiana, killing 11 workers. BP chairman, Carl-Henric Svanberg was invited to meet US President Barack Obama amid concerns that the company did not have enough cash to pay for the clean-up operation and compensation for those affected – estimated at $32.2 billion. The reputation of the global BP brand was seriously damaged.

1.1.1 Achieving business and environmental benefits

Bennett and James went on to suggest six main **ways in which business and environmental benefits can be achieved**.

(a) **Integrating the environment into capital expenditure decisions** (by considering environmental opposition to projects which could affect cash flows, for example)

(b) **Understanding and managing environmental costs.** Environmental costs are often 'hidden' in overheads and environmental and energy costs are often not allocated to the relevant budgets.

(c) **Introducing waste minimisation schemes**

(d) **Understanding and managing life cycle costs.** For many products, the greatest environmental impact occurs upstream (such as mining raw materials) or downstream from production (such as energy to operate equipment). This has led to producers being made responsible for dealing with the disposal of products such as cars, and government and third party measures to influence raw material choices. Organisations therefore need to identify, control and make provision for environmental life cycle costs and work with suppliers and customers to identify environmental cost reduction opportunities.

(e) **Measuring environmental performance.** Business is under increasing pressure to measure all aspects of environmental performance, both for statutory disclosure reasons and due to demands for more environmental data from customers.

(f) **Involving management accountants in a strategic approach to environment-related management accounting and performance evaluation.** A 'green accounting team' incorporating the key functions should analyse the strategic picture and identify opportunities for practical initiatives. It should analyse the short-, medium- and long-term impact of possible changes in the following.

    (i) **Government policies**, such as on transport
    (ii) **Legislation and regulation**
    (iii) **Supply conditions**, such as fewer landfill sites
    (iv) **Market conditions**, such as changing customer views
    (v) **Social attitudes**, such as to factory farming
    (vi) **Competitor strategies**

Possible action includes the following.

    (i) Designating an **'environmental champion'** within the strategic planning or accounting function to ensure that environmental considerations are fully considered.

    (ii) Assessing whether **new data sources** are needed to collect more and better data

    (iii) Making **comparisons** between sites/offices to highlight poor performance and generate peer pressure for action

    (iv) Developing **checklists** for internal auditors

Such analysis and action should help organisations to better understand present and future environmental costs and benefits.

1.2 Defining environmental costs

There are many varied definitions of environmental costs. The US Environmental Protection Agency make a distinction between four types of cost.

(a) **Conventional costs** such as raw materials and energy costs that have an impact on the environment.

(b) **Potentially hidden costs** are relevant costs that are captured within accounting systems but may be 'hidden' within 'general overheads'.

(c) **Contingent costs** are costs that will be incurred at a future date as a result of discharging waste into the environment such as **clean-up** costs.

(d) **Image and relationship costs** are costs incurred to preserve the reputation of the business, for example, the costs of preparing environmental reports to ensure compliance with regulatory standards.

Environmental costs are internal or external. Internal costs are environmental costs that an organisation incurs. **External environmental costs** are costs that an organisation causes, but which are suffered by others - for example the general public. For example unless an organisation is punished for causing environmental damage, such as pollution from toxic air emissions, society as a whole may bear the cost of the pollution and any clean-up operation.

The **internal environmental costs** for an organisation may be associated with itself which are related to an environmental include the costs of preventing environmental damage (such as air filters and water treatment equipment); the costs of detecting environmental damage or emissions; the costs of correcting environmental damage that is caused; and the costs of disposal of any waste.

Yet another way of looking at environmental cost is to say that an organisation incurs environmental costs when it **consumes a valuable environmental resource**, such as oil and petrol, and other forms of energy.

1.3 Identifying environmental costs

Many environmental costs are already captured within accounting systems. The difficulty lies in **pinpointing** them and **allocating** them to a specific product or service. Typical environmental costs are listed below.

- Consumables and raw materials
- Transport and travel
- Waste
- Waste and effluent disposal
- Water consumption
- Energy

You may be familiar with process costing. This is a method of costing for a system where output is produced in a process, and there may be some loss or wastage in the process. A principle of process costing is that if waste or loss is expected in production, it should not be given a cost.

For example, suppose that 1,000 kilos of materials are input to a process in which 10% of input is normally lost, and the total costs of the process are $180,000. In 'traditional' process costing, the costing system would allow for normal loss and process and would not give it a cost. So if 10% loss is expected, input of 1,000 kilos will produce only 900 kilos of output, and the cost per kilo of output is therefore $200 (= $180,000/900).

The normal waste in the process is ignored for costing purposes. Waste is an environmental cost, but in this example the reported cost of loss or waste is $0.

For the purpose of environmental management accounting, this is unsatisfactory. Management should be given better information about environmental costs.

1.4 Controlling environmental costs

Once a business has **defined**, **identified** and **allocated** environmental costs, it can begin the task of trying to control them through **environmental management systems**.

1.4.1 ISO 14000

ISO 14000 was first published in 1996 and based on earlier quality management standards. It provides a general framework on which a number of specific standards have been based (the ISO family of standards). ISO 14001 prescribes that an environmental management system must comprise:

* An **environmental policy statement**
* An assessment of environmental aspects and legal and voluntary obligations
* A management system
* Internal audits and reports to senior management
* A public declaration that ISO 14001 is being complied with

Critics of ISO 14000 claim that its emphasis on management systems rather than performance is misplaced, and that it does not include rigorous verification and disclosure requirements.

1.4.2 Management systems

In *Accounting for the Environment* Gray and Bebbington listed the functions that environmental management systems should cover.

Function	Description
Environmental review and policy development	A first review of environmental impacts of materials, issues and products and of business issues arising, also the development of a tailored in-house policy or measures to ensure adherence to external standards
Objectives and target development	As with all business objectives and targets, it is preferable that those set be unambiguous and achievable. Targets should be quantified within a specified time period eg reducing carbon dioxide emissions by X% within a specified time period
Life-cycle assessment	This aims to identify all interactions between a product and its environment during its lifetime, including energy and material usage and environmental releases. • Raw materials used have to be traced back to the biosphere and the company recognise impact on habitat, gas balance, the energy used in the extraction and transportation and the energy used to produce the means of extraction • For intermediate stages, emissions, discharges and co-products • At the consumer purchase stage, the impact of manufacture and disposal of packaging, transport to shops and ultimately impacts of consumers using and disposing of the product
Establishment and maintenance of environmental management systems	Key features of environmental management systems (as with other management systems) including information systems, budgeting, forecasting and management accounting systems, structure of responsibilities, establishment of an environmentally-friendly culture, considering impact on human resource issues such as education and performance appraisal
Regulatory compliance	Making sure that current legal requirements are being fulfilled and keeping up-to-date with practical implications of likely changes in legislation
Environmental impact assessment	A regular review of interactions with the environment, the degree of impact and also the impact of forthcoming major investments
Eco-label applications	Eco-labelling allows organisations to identify publicly products and services that meet the highest environmental standards. To be awarded an eco-label requires the product to be the result of a reliable quality management system

Function	Description
Waste minimisation	Whether waste can be minimised (or better still eliminated), possibility of recycling or selling waste
Pollution prevention programmes	Deciding what to target
Research, development and investment in cleaner technologies	How to bring desirable features into product development, bearing in mind product development may take several years, and opinion and legal requirements may change during that period. Desirable features may include minimum resource usage, waste, emissions, packaging and transport, recycling, disassembly and longer product life
Environmental performance and issues reporting	Consideration of the benefits and costs of reporting, how to report and what to include (policies, plans, financial data, activities undertaken, sustainability)

2 Accounting for environmental costs 12/13

FAST FORWARD The UNDSD (2003) identified a number of management accounting techniques to account for environmental costs. They include **input/output analysis**, **(material) flow cost accounting**, **environmental activity-based costing** and **environmental life-cycle costing**.

The United Nations Division for Sustainable Development (UNDSD, 2003) identified management accounting techniques which are useful for the identification and allocation of environmental costs. They are **input/output analysis**, **flow cost accounting**, **environmental activity-based accounting** and **life-cycle costing**.

You need to have a basic understanding of what these techniques are.

2.1 Input/output analysis

Input/output analysis operates on the principal that what comes in must go out. Process flow charts can help to trace inputs and outputs, in particular waste. They effectively demonstrate the details of the processes so that the relevant information can be allocated to the main activities.

Input/output analysis may involve some fairly complex modelling, but at a simple level, it measures the input to a production process or system, and the output from the system. Any difference between the amount input and the amount input is 'residual', which is called 'waste'.

Input and output quantities are measured first, and these can then be given a cost.

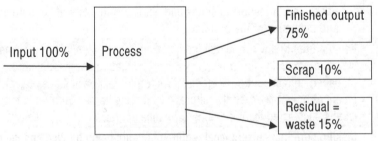

As shown in the diagram above, the input is regarded as 100% and split across the outputs which are **sold and stored goods** and **residual** (regarded as waste).

By accounting for process outputs in this way both in physical quantities and in monetary terms, businesses are forced to focus on environmental costs.

2.2 Flow cost accounting

Flow cost accounting (also known as Material Flow Cost Accounting or MFCA) is a development from input/output analysis, that was originally developed in Germany in the 1990s.

With this technique, inputs and outputs are measured through each individual process of production.. A distinction is made between:

(a)   positive products: this is good output
(b)   negative products: this is the measurement of waste.

Positive products + Negative products = Total input

Positive and negative products are measured in both physical and cost terms.

Under this technique, material flows through an organisation are divided into three categories, and the cost of each category is measured separately.

• Material
• System: this is the in-house handling that is required (including labour) and its cost
• Delivery and disposal: this is the cost of transport and the cost of disposal of waste

An important focus of management attention with flow cost accounting should be to reduce the proportion of negative products in total output and increasing the proportion of positive products.

This approach is applied to each individual process within the overall production system.

2.3 Environmental activity-based costing

Activity-based costing (ABC) '…represents a method of managerial cost accounting that allocates all internal costs to the cost centres and cost drivers on the basis of the activities that caused the costs,' (UNDSD, 2003).

Environmental activity-based costing combined elements of environmental costing with an activity-based costing system. Environment costs can be divided into two categories:

(a)   environment-related costs, such as an incinerator or a sewage treatment plant, for which costs can be directly traced

(b)   environment-driven costs, which are normally hidden within total overheads in a conventional costing system.

The main challenge with environmental activity-based costing is to:

(a)   identify the hidden environmental costs and link them to 'environmental activities'

(b)   charge the costs of each environmental activity to individual product costs according the amount that each product is responsible for the environmental activity.

Environmental activities and environment-driven will vary between different organisations, but they may include activities and costs relating to:

(a)   prevention work
(b)   detection
(c)   corrective action
(d)   disposal of waste.

Suitable environmental activities should be identified and an activity cost centre created for it. It should be possible to trace environment-driven costs to these cost centres.

Environment costs that have been allocated and apportioned to environmental activity cost centres can then be absorbed into product costs on a suitable basis.

For example, if an environmental activity is prevention of air pollution, costs will include the costs of equipment, the cost of labour time and so on. These costs may be absorbed into products costs using the volume of waste emissions as a cost driver. Each product will then be charged a share of the costs according to the volume of waste emitted in their manufacture.

Other environmental activities may be disposal of industrial waste, treating contaminated ground, and so on.

The general principle should be reasonably familiar to you if you understand the basics of activity-based costing (ABC).

To decide on the environmental cost drivers, the production processes involved in making a product or providing a service need to be carefully analysed. The **levels** of environmental **hazards** and **costs** need to be **established**. This may mean installing **tracking systems** to track environmental waste. Tracking waste may itself be regarded as an environmental activity, for which costs are measured.

Schaltegger and Muller (1998) stated 'the choice of an adequate allocation key (cost driver) is crucial for obtaining correct information'. The four main allocations are listed below.

- Volume of emissions or waste
- Toxicity of emissions and waste treated
- Environmental impact added (volume x input per unit of volume)
- The relative costs of treating different kinds of emissions

2.4 Environmental life-cycle costing

Under this method of environmental cost accounting, environmental costs for a product are considered from the **design stage** of the product right up to the **end-of-life costs** such as decommissioning and removal.

As with 'normal' life-cycle costing, this approach makes an assessment of expected environmental costs over the entire life of a product. These costs will include 'internal' costs that the organisation will incur. There is an argument that they should also include external environmental costs, which are costs that others in society will incur, rather than the organisation itself.

By identifying the environmental costs of a product over its entire expected life, including the costs of clean-up and disposal at the end of the product's life, management can make a decision about whether the environmental costs or acceptable, or they can consider ways of reducing the costs to a more acceptable level.

These decisions can be made before the product is actually brought into production.

Chapter Roundup

- **Environmental costs** are important to businesses for a number of reasons.

  - Identifying environmental costs associated with individual products and services can assist with **pricing** decisions.

  - Ensuring compliance with **regulatory standards**.

  - Potential for **cost savings**.

- The UNDSD (2003) identified a number of management accounting techniques to account for environmental costs. They include **input/output analysis, (material) flow cost accounting**, **environmental activity-based costing** and **environmental life-cycle costing**.

Quick Quiz

1   What are the main elements of an environmental management system per ISO 14001?

2   *Choose the appropriate words from those highlighted.*

    Costs that will be incurred at a future date such as clean up costs are known as **contingent/image and relationship** costs.

    Raw materials and energy are examples of **potentially hidden/conventional** costs

3   List the three categories of material flows under a system of (material) flow cost accounting.

Answers to Quick Quiz

1
- An environmental policy
- An assessment of environmental aspects and legal and voluntary obligations
- A management system
- Internal audits and reports to senior management
- A public declaration that ISO 14001 is being complied with

2   contingent
conventional

3
- Material
- System
- Delivery and disposal

P
A
R
T

B

Decision-making techniques

Cost volume profit (CVP) analysis

Topic list	Syllabus reference
1 A recap of basic CVP analysis	B2 (a), (b)
2 Preparing a basic breakeven chart	B2 (a)
3 Breakeven analysis in a multi-product environment	B2 (b), (e)
4 Breakeven point for multiple products	B2 (b)
5 Contribution to sales (C/S) ratio for multiple products	B2 (c)
6 Margin of safety for multiple products	B2 (b)
7 Target profits for multiple products	B2 (d)
8 Multi-product breakeven charts	B2 (e)
9 Further aspects of CVP analysis	B2 (f)

Introduction

You will have **already encountered CVP (or breakeven) analysis** in your earlier studies, so you should be reasonably familiar with the terminology or basic techniques that you will meet in this chapter. But a brief revision of the topic is provided, before the chapter moves on to more high-level material such as multi-product CVP analysis.

Study guide

		Intellectual level
B2	**Cost volume profit analysis**	
(a)	Explain the nature of CVP analysis	2
(b)	Calculate and interpret break even point and margin of safety	2
(c)	Calculate the contribution to sales ratio, in single and multi-product situations, and demonstrate an understanding of its use	2
(d)	Calculate target profit or revenue in single and multi-product situations, and demonstrate an understanding of its use	2
(e)	Prepare break even charts and profit volume charts and interpret the information contained within each, including multi-product situations	2
(f)	Discuss the limitations of CVP analysis for planning and decision making	2

Exam guide

The July 2010 issue of *Student Accountant* contains an article on CVP analysis written by the **examiner**. Ensure that you are familiar with this article.

1 A recap of basic CVP analysis

1.1 Knowledge brought forward from earlier studies

FAST FORWARD

Cost volume profit (CVP)/breakeven analysis is the study of the interrelationships between costs, volume and profit at various levels of activity.

1.1.1 Breakeven analysis

Key terms

- **Contribution per unit** = unit selling price – unit variable costs
- **Profit** = (sales volume × contribution per unit) – fixed costs
- **Breakeven point** = activity level at which there is neither profit nor loss

$$= \frac{\text{total fixed costs}}{\text{contribution per unit}} = \frac{\text{contribution required to breakeven}}{\text{contribution per unit}}$$

- **Contribution/sales (C/S) ratio** = profit/volume (P/V) ratio = (contribution/sales) × 100%
- **Sales revenue at breakeven point** = fixed costs ÷ C/S ratio
- **Margin of safety (in units)** = budgeted sales units – breakeven sales units
- **Margin of safety (as %)** $= \dfrac{\text{budgeted sales} - \text{breakeven sales}}{\text{budgeted sales}} \times 100\%$

- **Sales volume to achieve a target profit** $= \dfrac{\text{fixed cost} + \text{target profit}}{\text{contribution per unit}}$

1.1.2 Assumptions

(a) CVP analysis can apply to one product only, or to more than one product only if they are sold in a fixed sales mix (fixed proportions)

(b) Fixed costs per period are same in total, and unit variable costs are a constant amount at all levels of output and sales

(c) Sales prices are constant at all levels of activity

(d) Production volume = sales volume.

BPP
LEARNING MEDIA

1.1.3 Example: Breakeven point and margin of safety

A company makes and sells a single product. The selling price is $12 per unit. The variable cost of making and selling the product is $9 per unit and fixed costs per month are $240,000.

The company budgets to sell 90,000 units of the product a month.

Required

(a)   What is the budgeted profit per month and what is the breakeven point in sales?

(b)   What is the margin of safety?

(c)   What must sales be to achieve a monthly profit of $120,000?

Answer

(a)   Contribution per unit = $(12 – 9) = $3. The C/S ratio is 3/12 = 0.25

       Budgeted profit = (90,000 × $3) – $240,000 = $30,000

       Breakeven point in units of sale = $240,000/$3 pr unit = 80,000 units per month

       (Breakeven point in sales revenue = Fixed costs/C/S ratio = $240,000/0.25 = $960,000)

(b)   Margin of safety = (90,000 – 80,000)/90,000 = 11.1%

(c)   To achieve a profit of $120,000, total contribution must be $(240,000 + 120,000) = $360,000.

       Sales must be $360,000/$3 per unit = 120,000 units (or $360,000/0.25 = $1,440,000 in sales revenue).

1.1.4 Breakeven, contribution and P/V charts

- Breakeven chart

- Contribution (contribution breakeven) chart

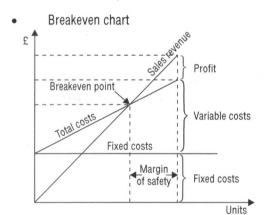

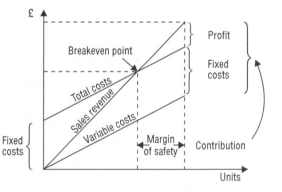

- Profit/volume (P/V) chart

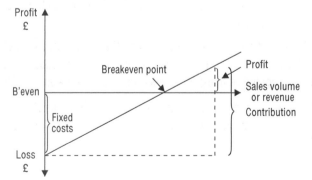

The gradient of the straight line is the contribution per unit (if the horizontal axis is measured in sales value).

2 Preparing a basic breakeven chart

FAST FORWARD

In a breakeven chart, the x axis is the volume of production and sales and the y axis represents money value (revenue and cost). The chart is prepared by drawing a line to show total revenue at all levels of sales, and a total cost line to show total costs at all levels of production and sales. The **breakeven point** is where the **sales revenue** line and **total cost** line intersect.

Key term

> **Breakeven point** is the level of sales at which there is neither profit nor loss.

2.1 Example: Basic breakeven chart

A new product has the following sales and cost data.

Selling price $60 per unit

Variable cost $40 per unit

Fixed costs $25,000 per month

Forecast sales 1,800 units per month

Required

Prepare a breakeven chart using the above data.

Solution

Step 1   Draw the axes and label them. Your graph should fill as much of the page as possible, this will make it clearer and easier to read.

The highest value on the vertical axis will be the monthly sales revenue.

1,800 units × $60 = $108,000

Step 2   Draw the fixed cost line and label it. This will be a straight line parallel to the horizontal axis at the $25,000 level. The $25,000 fixed costs are incurred even with zero activity.

Step 3   Draw the total cost line and label it. The best way to do this is to calculate the total costs for the maximum sales level (1,800 units). Mark this point on the graph and join it to the cost incurred at zero activity, that is, $25,000.

	$
Variable costs for 1,800 units (1,800 × $40)	72,000
Fixed costs	25,000
Total cost for 1,800 units	97,000

Step 4   Draw the revenue line and label it. Once again, start by plotting the revenue at the maximum activity level. 1,800 units × $60 = $108,000. This point can be joined to the origin, since at zero activity there will be no sales revenue.

Step 5   Mark any required information on the chart and read off solutions as required. Check that your chart is accurate by reading off the measures that we have already covered in this chapter: the breakeven point, the margin of safety, the profit for sales of 1,800 units.

Step 6   Check the accuracy of your readings using arithmetic. If you have time, it is good examination technique to check your answer and make adjustments for any errors in your chart.

The completed graph is shown below.

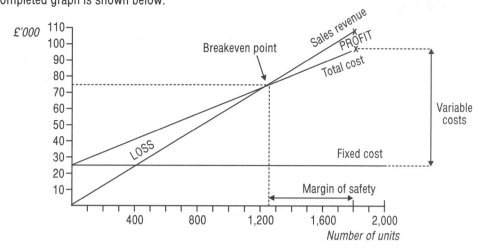

3 Breakeven analysis in a multi-product environment

FAST FORWARD

To perform breakeven analysis for a multi-product organisation, either a **constant sales mix** must be assumed, or all products must have the **same C/S ratio**.

3.1 A major assumption

Organisations typically produce and sell a number of different products or services. This makes breakeven analysis difficult. To perform breakeven analysis in a multi-product organisation, a constant product sales mix must be assumed. In other words, we have to assume that whenever x units of product A are sold, y units of product B and z units of product C are also sold.

By assuming a constant sales mix for the products, we can calculate a weighted average contribution per unit sold. The weighting is based on the quantities or proportions of each product in the constant sales mix. This means that the unit contribution of the product that makes up the largest proportion of the mix has the greatest impact on the average contribution per mix.

As an alternative to calculating a weighted average contribution per unit of sale, we can calculate a weighted average C/S ratio.

The only situation when the mix of products does not affect the analysis is when all of the products have the same ratio of contribution to sales (C/S ratio). This is unlikely to happen in most businesses, but may occasionally occur in, say, retailing when all products are re-sold at the same percentage mark-up on cost.

4 Breakeven point for multiple products   12/12

FAST FORWARD

The **breakeven point** for a standard sales mix of products is calculated by dividing the total fixed costs by the weighted average contribution per unit, or by the weighted average C/S ratio.

4.1 Example: Breakeven point for multiple products

PL produces and sells two products, M and N. Product M sells for $7 per unit and has a total variable cost of $2.94 per unit, while Product N sells for $15 per unit and has a total variable cost of $4.40 per unit. The marketing department has estimated that for every five units of M sold, one unit of N will be sold. The organisation's fixed costs per period total $123,600.

Required

Calculate the breakeven point for PL.

Solution

We calculate the breakeven point as follows.

Step 1   Calculate the contribution per unit and the weighted average contribution per unit.

	M	N
	$ per unit	$ per unit
Sales price	7.00	15.00
Variable cost	2.94	4.40
Contribution	4.06	10.60

	$
Contribution from sale of 5 units of M (× $4.06)	20.30
Contribution from sale of 1 unit of N	10.60
Contribution from sale of 6 units in standard sales mix	30.90

Weighted average contribution per unit = $30.90/6 = $5.15 per unit.

Step 2   Calculate the **breakeven point in units**.

Fixed costs/Weighted average contribution per unit = $123,600/$5.15 = 24,000 units.

These are in the ratio 5:1; therefore breakeven is at the point where 20,000 units of M are sold (= 24,000 × 5/6) and 4,000 units of N are sold (= 24,000 × 1/6).

Step 3   Calculate the **breakeven point in sales revenue**.

20,000 units of M at $7 + 4,000 units of N at $15

= $140,000 + $60,000 = $200,000

It is important to note that the breakeven point is not $200,000 regardless of the sales mix of products. The breakeven point is $200,000 provided that the sales mix remains 5:1. Likewise the breakeven point is not at a production/sales level of 24,000 units regardless of the sales mix. Rather, it is when 20,000 units of M and 4,000 units of N are sold, assuming a sales mix of 5:1.

Question

Breakeven point for multiple products

Alpha manufactures and sells three products, the Beta, the Gamma and the Delta. Relevant information is as follows.

	Beta	Gamma	Delta
	$ per unit	$ per unit	$ per unit
Selling price	135.00	165.00	220.00
Variable cost	72.80	57.90	146.20

Total fixed costs are $1,025,000.

An analysis of past trading patterns indicates that the products Beta, Gamma and Delta are sold in the ratio 3:4:5 respectively.

Required

Fill in the blanks in the sentence below.

Alpha's breakeven point in terms of revenue of the three products is ………………............. of Beta, ……………............. of Gamma and ………........……..... of Delta, making ……….……….…..... in total.

The correct answer is $421,875 of Beta, $687,501 of Gamma and $1,145,833 of Delta, making $2,255,209 in total.

Step 1 Calculate weighted average **contribution per unit**.

	Beta	Gamma	Delta
	$ per unit	$ per unit	$ per unit
Selling price	135.00	165.00	220.00
Variable cost	72.80	57.90	146.20
Contribution per unit	62.20	107.10	73.80

	$
Contribution from sale of 3 units of Beta (× $62.20)	186.60
Contribution from sale of 4 units of Gamma (× $107.10)	428.40
Contribution from sale of 5 units of Delta (× $73.80)	369.00
Contribution from sale of 12 units in standard sales mix	984.00

Weighted average contribution per unit = $984/12 = $82 per unit

Step 2 Calculate the **breakeven point** in units in the standard sales mix.

= Fixed costs/Weighted average contribution per unit

= $1,025,000/$82 = 12,500 units

Step 3 Calculate the breakeven sales for each product.

Beta: 12,500 × 3/12 = 3,125 units. (Revenue × $135 = $421,875)

Gamma: 12,500 × 4/12 = 4,166.67 units (Revenue × $165 = $687,501)

Delta: 12,500 × 5/12 = 5,208.33 units (Revenue × $220 = $1,145,833)

Step 4 Calculate the **breakeven point** in terms of **revenue**.

Beta: 3,125 units × $135 = $421,875

Gamma: 4,166.67 units × $165 = $687,501

Delta: 5,208.33 units × $220 = $1,145,833

= $2,255,209 in total

5 Contribution to sales (C/S) ratio for multiple products

FAST FORWARD

The **breakeven point in terms of sales revenue** can be calculated by dividing the fixed costs (= required contribution) by the weighted average C/S ratio.

Formula to learn

The **breakeven point in terms of sales revenue** = fixed costs/average C/S ratio.

5.1 Calculating the ratio

An alternative way of **calculating the breakeven point** is to use the weighted **average contribution to sales (C/S) ratio** for the standard mix.

As you should already know, the C/S ratio is sometimes called the **profit/volume ratio** or **P/V ratio**.

We can calculate the breakeven point of PL (see Section 4.1) as follows.

Step 1   Calculate **revenue and contribution per mix** of 5 units of M and 1 unit of N.

	Contribution		Revenue	
	Per unit	Total	Per unit	Total
	$	$	$	$
Product M (5 units)	4.06	20.30	7	35
Product N (1 unit)	10.60	10.60	15	15
		30.90		50

Weighted average C/S ratio = $30.90/$50 = 61.8% or 0.618

Step 2   Calculate **breakeven point** (total).

= Fixed costs ÷ Weighted average C/S ratio

Fixed costs/Weighted average contribution per unit = $123,600/0.618 = $200,000 in sales revenue.

Step 3   Calculate **breakeven sales for each product**.

M = $200,000 × (35/50) = $140,000

Sales price per unit = $7

Therefore breakeven point in units = $140,000/$7 = 20,000 units.

N = $200,000 × (15/50) = $60,000

Sales price per unit = $15

Therefore breakeven point in units = $60,000/$15 = 4,000 units.

Question	C/S ratio for multiple products

Required

Calculate the breakeven sales revenue of product Beta, Gamma and Delta (see Question under 4.1 above) using the approach shown in Section 5.1.

Answer

Step 1   Calculate **revenue and contribution per mix** of 3 units of Beta, 4 units of Gamma and 5 units of Delta.

	Beta	Gamma	Delta	Total
Sales mix	3	4	5	
Revenue per unit	$135	$165	$220	
Contribution per unit	$62.20	$107.10	$73.80	
	$	$	$	$
Revenue per mix 3:4:5	405.00	660.00	1,100.00	2,165
Contribution per mix 3:4:5	186.60	428.40	369.00	984

Weighted average C/S ratio = 984/2,165 = 0.4545035

Step 2   Calculate breakeven point (total)

= Fixed costs ÷ Weighted average C/S ratio
= $1,025,000/0.4545035

= $2,255,208

Step 3   Calculate breakeven sales

Breakeven sales of Beta   = 405/2,165 × $2,255,208 = $421,875

Breakeven sales of Gamma = 660/2,165 × $2,255,208 = $687,500

Breakeven sales of Delta   = 1,100/2,165 × $2,255,208 = $1,145,833

Alternatively you might be provided with the individual C/S ratios of a number of products. For example if an organisation sells two products (A and B) in the ratio 2:5 and if the C/S ratio of A is 10% whereas that of B is 50%, the average C/S ratio is calculated as follows.

$$\text{Average C/S ratio} = \frac{(2 \times 10\%) + (5 \times 50\%)}{2 + 5} = 38.6\%$$

Question
Average C/S ratio

TIM produces and sells two products, the MK and the KL. The organisation expects to sell 1 MK for every 2 KLs and have monthly sales revenue of $150,000. The MK has a C/S ratio of 20% whereas the KL has a C/S ratio of 40%. Budgeted monthly fixed costs are $30,000.

Required

What is the budgeted breakeven sales revenue?

Answer

$$\text{Average C/S ratio} = \frac{(20\% \times 1) + (40\% \times 2)}{3} = 33\tfrac{1}{3}\%$$

$$\text{Sales revenue at the breakeven point} = \frac{\text{fixed costs}}{\text{C/S ratio}} = \frac{\$30,000}{0.333} = \$90,000$$

The C/S ratio is a measure of how much contribution is earned from each $1 of sales of the standard mix. The C/S ratio of 33⅓% in the question above means that for every $1 of sales of the standard mix of products, a contribution of 33.33c is earned. To earn a total contribution of, say, $20,000, sales revenue from the standard mix must therefore be

$$\frac{\$1}{33.33c} \times \$20,000 = \$60,006$$

Question
Using the C/S ratio

Refer back to the information in the paragraph following Question: C/S ratio for multiple products. Suppose the organisation in question has fixed costs of $100,000, and wishes to earn total contribution of $200,000.

Required

What level of revenue must be achieved?

Answer

$$\text{Sales revenue must be } \frac{\$1}{38.6c} \times \$200,000 = \$518,135$$

5.2 Points to bear in mind

Any change in the proportions of products in the sales mix will change the contribution per mix and the weighted average C/S ratio. This will change the breakeven point.

(a) If the mix shifts towards products with lower contribution margins, the breakeven point (in units) will increase and profits will fall unless there is a corresponding increase in total revenue.

(b) A shift towards products with higher contribution margins without a corresponding decrease in revenues will cause an increase in profits and a lower breakeven point.

(c) If sales are at the specified level but not in the specified mix, there will be either a profit or a loss depending on whether the mix shifts towards products with higher or lower contribution margins.

6 Margin of safety for multiple products

The **margin of safety** for a multi-product organisation is equal to the budgeted sales in the standard mix less the breakeven sales in the standard mix. It should be expressed as a percentage of the budgeted sales.

It should not surprise you to learn that the calculation of the margin of safety for multiple products is exactly the same as for single products, but we use the standard sales mix.

6.1 Example: Margin of safety for multiple products

BA produces and sells two products. The W sells for $8 per unit and has a total variable cost of $3.80 per unit, while the R sells for $14 per unit and has a total variable cost of $4.30. For every five units of W sold, six units of R are sold. BA's expected fixed costs are $83,160 for the per period.

Budgeted sales revenue for next period is $150,040, in the standard sales mix.

Required

Calculate the margin of safety in terms of sales revenue and also as a percentage of budgeted sales revenue.

Solution

To calculate the margin of safety we must first determine the breakeven point.

Step 1   Calculate the weighted average **contribution per unit**

	W	R
	$ per unit	$ per unit
Selling price	8.00	14.00
Variable cost	3.80	4.30
Contribution	4.20	9.70

	$
Contribution from sale of 5 units of W	21.00
Contribution from sale of 6 units of R	58.20
Contribution from sale of 11 units	79.20

Weighted average contribution per unit = $72.80/11 = $7.20

Step 2   Calculate the **breakeven point** in terms of the **number of shares (total)**

= Fixed costs/Weighted average contribution per unit = $83,160/$7.20

= 11,550 units

Step 3   Calculate the **breakeven point** in terms of the **number of units of the products**

Product W: 11,550 × (5/11) = 5,250 units

Product R: 11,550 × (6/11)= 6,300 units

Step 4   Calculate the **breakeven point** in terms of **revenue**

= (5,250 × $8) + (6,300 × $14)

= $42,000 of W revenue and $88,200 of R revenue= $130,200 in total

Step 5   Calculate the **margin of safety**

= Budgeted sales − Breakeven sales

= $150,040 − $130,200 = $19,840, in the standard sales mix

As a percentage: $19,840/$150,040 = 13.2% of budgeted sales

7 Target profits for multiple products

FAST FORWARD

> The sales mix required to achieve a **target profit** is the sales mix that will earn a contribution equal to the fixed costs plus the target profit.

You should already be familiar with the problem of target profits for single products in a CVP context from your earlier studies. This section expands the concept to multiple products, illustrating the calculations in several examples.

7.1 A reminder of the formula for target profits

At **breakeven point** there is no profit – that is:

Contribution = Fixed costs

Suppose an organisation wishes to achieve a certain level of profit during a period. To achieve this profit, contribution must cover fixed costs and leave the required profit:

So **Total contribution required = Fixed costs + Required profit**

Once we know the total contribution required we can calculate the sales revenue of each product needed to achieve a target profit. The method is the same as the method used to calculate the breakeven point.

Formula to learn

> The total number of units to be sold to achieve a **target profit** is calculated as (Fixed costs + Required profit)/Weighted average contribution per unit, on the assumption that products are sold in a constant sales mix.

7.2 Example: Target profits for multiple products

An organisation makes and sells three products, F, G and H. The products are sold in the proportions F:G:H = 2:1:3. The organisation's fixed costs are $80,000 per month and details of the products are as follows.

Product	Selling price $ per unit	Variable cost $ per unit
F	22	16
G	15	12
H	19	13

The organisation wishes to earn a profit of $52,000 next month. Calculate the required sales value of each product in order to achieve this target profit.

Solution

Step 1   Calculate the **weighted average contribution per unit**

	F	G	H
	$ per unit	$ per unit	$ per unit
Selling price	22	15	19
Variable cost	16	12	13
Contribution	6	3	6

	$
Contribution from 2 units of F	12
Contribution from 1 unit of G	3
Contribution from 3 units of H	18
Total contribution from sale of 6 units	33

Weighted average contribution per unit = $33/6 = $5.50

Step 3   Calculate the **required number of sales units**

= (Fixed costs + Required profit)/Weighted average contribution per unit
= ($80,000 + $52,000)/$5.50
= 24,000 units

Step 4   Calculate the required sales in terms of the number of units of the products and sales revenue of each product

Product		Units	Selling price $ per unit	Sales revenue required $
F	24,000 × 2/6	8,000	22	176,000
G	24,000 × 1/6	4,000	15	60,000
H	24,000 × 3/6	12,000	19	228,000
Total				464,000

The sales revenue of $464,000 will generate a profit of $52,000 if the products are sold in the mix 2:1:3.

Alternatively the C/S ratio could be used to determine the required sales revenue for a profit of $52,000. The method is again similar to that demonstrated earlier when calculating the breakeven point.

7.3 Example: Using the C/S ratio to determine the required sales

We'll use the data from the example above.

Step 1   **Calculate revenue per mix of 2 units of F, 1 unit of G and 3 units of H**
= (2 × $22) + (1 × $15) + (3 × $19)
= $44 + $15 + $57
= $116

Step 2   **Calculate contribution per mix of 2 units of F, 1 unit of G and 3 units of H**
= $33 (from See solution in Section 7.2)

Step 3   **Calculate weighted average C/S ratio**
= ($33/$116) × 100%
= 28.45%

Step 4   **Calculate required total revenue**
= Required contribution ÷ C/S ratio
= ($80,000 + $52,000) ÷ 0.2845
= $463,972

BPP
LEARNING MEDIA

Step 6   **Calculate required sales from each product**: see Step 1 for proportions

Required sales of F = 44/116 × $463,972 = $175,989
Required sales of G = 15/116 × $463,972 = $59,996
Required sales of H = 57/116 × $463,972 = $227,986

Which, allowing for rounding differences, this is the same answer as calculated in the first example.

8 Multi-product breakeven charts   12/12

FAST FORWARD

Breakeven charts for multiple products can be drawn if a constant product sales mix is assumed.

The **P/V chart** can show information about each product individually.

Exam focus point

As well as being able to ca[...]ulations you may be asked to produce a breakeven chart in a multiple product situation. [...] re involved in producing multi-product breakeven charts and prof[...]

8.1 Breakeven ch[...]

Key term

A **breakeven chart** is a [...]fit or loss at different levels of sales volume within a limited range. [...]

A very serious limitatio[...] show the costs, revenues, profits and margins of safety for a[...] single 'sales mix' of products.

Breakeven charts for [...] onstant product sales mix is assumed.

For example suppos[...] Z which have variable unit costs of $3, $4 and $5 respectively. The [...] $6 and the price of Z is $6. Fixed costs per annum are $10,000[...]

A breakeven chart c[...] ow the proportions of X, Y and Z in the sales mix.

Exam focus point

If you are not sure [...] w a breakeven chart with the information given. It should not be pos[...]

There are a numb[...] this problem, however.

8.1.1 Approa[...] nstant product mix

Assume that bu[...] 0 units of Y and 3,000 units of Z. A breakeven chart would make th[...], Y and Z are in the proportions 2,000: 4,000: 3,000 at all levels of [...] x is 'fixed' in these proportions.

We begin by c[...]

Budgeted co[...]

	Costs		Revenue
	$		$
Variable cos[...]	6,000	X (2,000 × $8)	16,000
Variable cos[...]	16,000	Y (4,000 × $6)	24,000
Variable co[...]	15,000	Z (3,000 × $6)	18,000
Total varia[...]	37,000	Budgeted revenue	58,000
Fixed cost[...]	10,000		
Total bud[...]	47,000		

The **breakeven chart** can now be drawn.

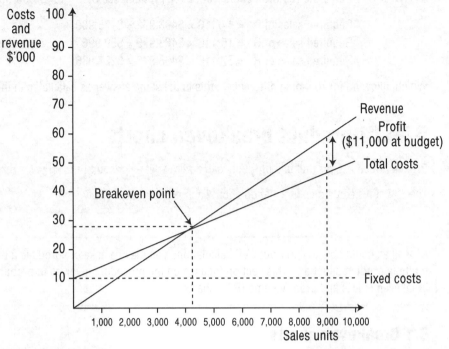

The **breakeven point** is approximately $27,500 of sales revenue. This may either be **read from the chart or computed mathematically**.

(a)   The budgeted C/S ratio for all three products together is contribution/sales = $(58,000 – 37,000)/$58,000 = 36.21%.

(b)   The required contribution to break even is $10,000, the amount of fixed costs. The breakeven point is $10,000/36.21% = $27,500 (approx) in sales revenue.

The margin of safety is approximately $(58,000 – 27,500) = $30,500.

8.1.2 Approach 2: products in sequence

The products could be plotted in a particular sequence (say X first, then Y, then Z). Using the data from Approach 1, we can calculate cumulative costs and revenues as follows.

Product	Cumulative units	Cumulative costs $	Cumulative revenue $
	Nil	10,000	Nil
X (2,000 units)	2,000	16,000	16,000
Y (4,000 units)	6,000	32,000	40,000
Z (3,000 units)	9,000	47,000	58,000

In this case the breakeven point occurs at 2,000 units of sales (2,000 units of product X). The margin of safety is roughly 4,000 units of Y and 3,000 units of Z.

8.1.3 Approach 3: output in terms of % of forecast sales and a constant product mix

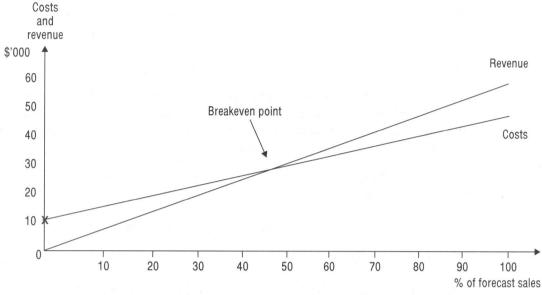

The breakeven point can be read from the graph as approximately 48% of forecast sales ($30,000 of revenue).

Alternatively, with contribution of $(58,000 – 37,000) = $21,000, one percent of forecast sales is associated with $21,000/100 = $210 contribution.

Breakeven point (%)   = fixed costs/contribution per 1%
                                     = $10,000/$210 = 47.62%
∴ Margin of safety   = (100 – 47.62) = 52.38%

> The general point of setting out these three approaches is to demonstrate that output can be viewed in several different ways.

8.2 Multi-product P/V charts

The same information could be shown on a **P/V chart**, as follows.

Multi-product P/V chart

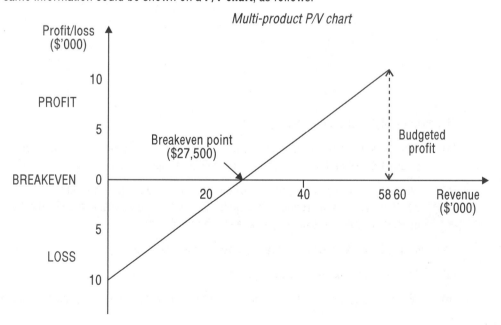

An **addition** to the chart would **show further information about the contribution earned by each product individually**, so that their performance and profitability can be compared.

	Contribution $	Sales $	C/S ratio %
Product X	10,000	16,000	62.50
Product Y	8,000	24,000	33.33
Product Z	3,000	18,000	16.67
Total	21,000	58,000	36.21

By convention, the **products are shown individually** on a P/V chart from **left to right**, in **order of the size of their C/S ratio**. In this example, product X will be plotted first, then product Y and finally product Z. A **dotted line** is used to show the **cumulative profit/loss and the cumulative sales** as each product's sales and contribution in turn are added to the sales mix.

Product	Cumulative sales $		Cumulative profit $
X	16,000	($10,000 contribution – $10,000 fixed costs)	–
X and Y	40,000		8,000
X, Y and Z	58,000		11,000

You will see on the graph which follows that these three pairs of data are used to plot the dotted line, to indicate the contribution from each product. The **solid line** which joins the two ends of this dotted line **indicates the average profit** which will be earned from sales of the three products in this mix.

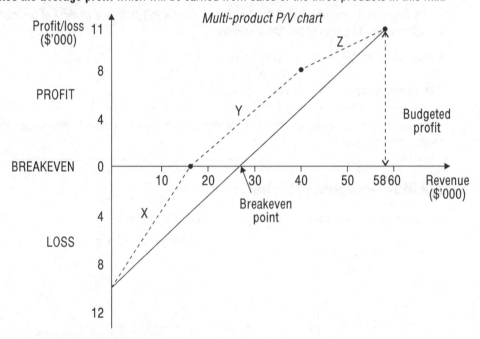

The diagram **highlights** the following points.

(a)   Since X is the most profitable in terms of C/S ratio, it might be worth considering an increase in the sales of X, even if there is a consequent fall in the sales of Z.

(b)   Alternatively, the pricing structure of the products should be reviewed and a decision made as to whether the price of product Z should be raised so as to increase its C/S ratio (although an increase is likely to result in some fall in sales volume).

The **multi-product P/V chart** therefore helps to **identify** the following.

(a)   The overall company breakeven point.

(b)   Which products should be expanded in output and which, if any, should be discontinued.

(c)   What effect changes in selling price and sales volume will have on the company's breakeven point and profit.

A company sells three products, X, Y and Z. Cost and sales data for one period are as follows.

	X	Y	Z
Sales volume	2,000 units	2,000 units	5,000 units
Sales price per unit	$3	$4	$2
Variable cost per unit	$2.25	$3.50	$1.25
Total fixed costs	$3,250		

Required

Construct a multi-product P/V chart based on the above information on the axes below.

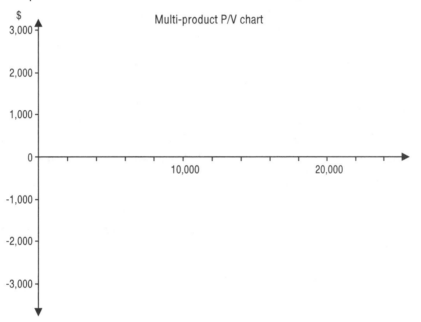

Answer

	X	Y	Z	Total
Contribution per unit	$0.75	$0.50	$0.75	$
Budgeted contribution (total)	$1,500	$1,000	$3,750	6,250
Fixed costs				3,250
Budgeted profit				3,000

Product	Cumulative sales $		Cumulative profit $
Z	10,000	($3,750 – $3,250)	500
Z and X	16,000		2,000
Z, X and Y	24,000		3,000

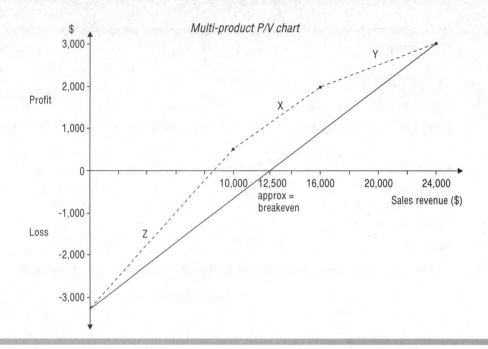

Multi-product P/V chart

Breakeven point and sales value constraints

Sutton produces four products. Relevant data is shown below for period 2.

	Product M	Product A	Product R	Product P
C/S ratio	5%	10%	15%	20%
Maximum sales value	$200,000	$120,000	$200,000	$180,000
Minimum sales value	$50,000	$50,000	$20,000	$10,000

The fixed costs for period 2 are budgeted at $60,000.

Required

Fill in the blank in the sentence below.

The lowest breakeven sales value, subject to meeting the minimum sales value constraints, is $............

Answer

The correct answer is $390,000

Breakeven point occurs when contribution = fixed costs

∴ Minimum breakeven point occurs when contribution is $60,000.

Contribution achieved from minimum sales value

			$
M	5% × $50,000		2,500
A	10% × $50,000		5,000
R	15% × $20,000		3,000
P	20% × $10,000		2,000
			12,500

Product P has the highest C/S ratio and so should be produced first (as it earns more contribution per $ of revenue than the others).

Contribution from sales of P between minimum and maximum points = $170,000 × 20% = $34,000

∴ Required contribution from Product R (which has the next highest C/S ratio)

   = $(60,000 − 12,500 − 34,000)
   = $13,500

Revenue from Product R of $13,500/0.15 = $90,000 will produce $13,500 of contribution.

∴ Lowest breakeven sales

   = $130,000 (minimum sales) + $170,000 (from P) + $90,000 (from R)
   = $390,000

9 Further aspects of CVP analysis

FAST FORWARD

The usefulness of CVP analysis is restricted by its **unrealistic assumptions**, such as constant sales price at all levels of activity. However CVP has the advantage of being more **easily understood** by non-financial managers due to its graphical depiction of cost and revenue data.

Exam focus point

As well as being able to carry out CVP calculations, you may be asked to criticise the CVP approach to short-term decision-making. This does not only mean giving the limitations of CVP but also being aware of the advantages as well.

9.1 Limitations and advantages

9.1.1 Limitations

(a) It is assumed that fixed costs are the same in total and variable costs are the same per unit at all levels of output. This assumption is a great simplification.

   (i) Fixed costs will change if output falls or increases substantially (most fixed costs are step costs).

   (ii) The variable cost per unit will decrease where economies of scale are made at higher output volumes, but the variable cost per unit will also eventually rise when diseconomies of scale begin to appear at even higher volumes of output (for example the extra cost of labour in overtime working).

   The assumption is only correct within a normal range or relevant range of output. It is generally assumed that both the budgeted output and the breakeven point lie within this relevant range.

(b) It is assumed that sales prices will be constant at all levels of activity. This may not be true, especially at higher volumes of output, where the price may have to be reduced to win the extra sales.

(c) Production and sales are assumed to be the same, so that the consequences of any increase in inventory levels or of 'de-stocking' are ignored.

(d) Uncertainty in the estimates of fixed costs and unit variable costs is often ignored.

9.1.2 Advantages

(a) Graphical representation of cost and revenue data (breakeven charts) can be more easily understood by non-financial managers.

(b) A breakeven model enables profit or loss at any level of activity within the range for which the model is valid to be determined, and the C/S ratio can indicate the relative profitability of different products.

(c) Highlighting the breakeven point and the margin of safety gives managers some indication of the level of risk involved.

Chapter Roundup

- **Cost volume profit (CVP)/breakeven analysis** is the study of the interrelationships between costs, volume and profit at various levels of activity.

- In a breakeven chart, the x axis is the volume of production and sales and the y axis represents money value (revenue and cost). The chart is prepared by drawing a line to show total revenue at all levels of sales, and a total cost line to show total costs at all levels of production and sales The **breakeven point** is where the **sales revenue** line and **total cost** line intersect.

- To perform breakeven analysis for a multi-product organisation, either a **constant sales mix** must be assumed, or all products must have the **same C/S ratio**.

- The **breakeven point** for a standard sales mix of products is calculated by dividing the total fixed costs by the weighted average contribution per unit, or by the weighted average C/S ratio.

- The **breakeven point in terms of sales revenue** can be calculated by dividing the fixed costs (= required contribution) by the weighted average C/S ratio.

- The **margin of safety** for a multi-product organisation is equal to the budgeted sales in the standard mix less the breakeven sales in the standard mix. It should be expressed as a percentage of the budgeted sales.

- The sales mix required to achieve a **target profit** is the sales mix that will earn a contribution equal to the fixed costs plus the target profit.

- **Breakeven charts** for multiple products can be drawn if a constant product sales mix is assumed.

  The **P/V chart** can show information about each product individually.

- The usefulness of CVP analysis is restricted by its **unrealistic assumptions**, such as constant sales price at all levels of activity. However CVP has the advantage of being more **easily understood** by non-financial managers due to its graphical depiction of cost and revenue data.

Quick Quiz

1   *Fill in the blanks.*

    Breakeven point in units for a multi-product organisation = Total fixed costs divided by
    _____ .

    Breakeven point in sales revenue for a multi-product organisation = Total fixed costs divided by
    _____ .

2   C/S ratio = P/V ratio × 100. **True or false?**

3   *Fill in the blanks.*

$$\text{Margin of safety (as \%)} = \left(\frac{\text{.................... sales} - \text{.................... sales}}{\text{.................... sales}} \right) \times 100\%$$

4   Mark the following on the breakeven chart below.

- Profit
- Sales revenue
- Total costs
- Margin of safety

- Variable costs
- Fixed costs
- Breakeven point

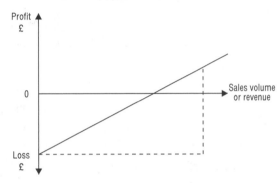

5   Mark the following on the P/V chart below.

- Breakeven point
- Fixed costs

- Contribution
- Profit

6   Which of the following is not a major assumption of breakeven analysis?

A   It can only apply to one product or a constant sales mix.
B   Fixed costs are the same in total and unit variable costs are the same at all levels of output.
C   Sales prices vary in line with levels of activity.
D   Production level is equal to sales level.

7   *Choose the appropriate words from those highlighted and fill in the blanks.*

When showing multiple products individually on a P/V chart, the products are shown from **left to right/right to left**, in order of **increasing/decreasing** size of C/S ratio. The line joining the two ends of the dotted line (which shows ....) indicates

....

8   *Choose the appropriate words from those highlighted.*

The assumption in breakeven analysis that variable cost is the same per unit at all levels of output is a great simplification. The variable cost per unit will decrease where (1) **economies/diseconomies** of scale are made at higher volumes of output, but will also eventually rise where (2) **economies/diseconomies** of scale begin to appear at even (3) **higher/lower** volumes of output.

1   Weighted average contribution per unit

     Weighted average C/S ratio

2   False. The C/S ratio is another name for the P/V ratio.

3   Margin of safety (as %) = $\left(\dfrac{\text{Budgeted sales} - \text{breakeven sales}}{\text{Budgeted sales}} \right) \times 100\%$

4

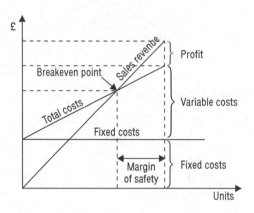

5

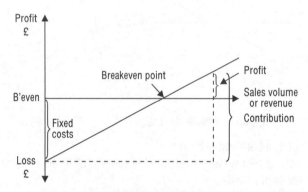

The gradient of the straight line is the contribution per unit (if the horizontal axis is measured in sales units) or the C/S ratio (if the horizontal axis is measured in sales value).

6   C. Sales prices *are constant* at all levels of activity.

7   When showing multiple products individually on a P/V chart, the products are shown from left to right, in order of decreasing size of C/S ratio. The line joining the two ends of the dotted line (which shows the cumulative profit/loss and the cumulative sales) indicates the average profit which will be earned from sales of the products in the mix.

8   (1)   economies
     (2)   diseconomies
     (3)   higher

Now try the question below from the Practice Question Bank

Number	Level	Marks	Time
Q6	Examination	15	27 mins

Limiting factor analysis

Introduction

We have looked at **limiting factor analysis** in connection with throughput accounting in Chapter 2d and you will have encountered it in your earlier studies.

When there is more than one resource constraint, the technique of **linear programming** can be used. A multiple scarce resource problem can be solved using a **graphical method** and **simultaneous equations.**

We also look at the meaning and calculation of **shadow prices** and **slack.**

Study guide

		Intellectual level
B3	**Limiting factors**	
(a)	Identify limiting factors in a scarce resource situation and select an appropriate technique	2
(b)	Determine the optimal production plan where an organisation is restricted by a single limiting factor, including within the context of "make" or "buy" decisions	2
(c)	Formulate and solve a multiple scarce resource problem both graphically and using simultaneous equations as appropriate	2
(d)	Explain and calculate shadow prices (dual prices) and discuss their implications on decision-making and performance management	2
(e)	Calculate slack and explain the implications of the existence of slack for decision-making and performance management (Excluding simplex and sensitivity to changes in objective functions)	2

Exam guide

Linear programming is a popular topic in management accounting exams and is likely to be examined as a mixture of calculations and discussion. There is an article on linear programming in *Student Accountant*, March 2008.

1 Limiting factors

FAST FORWARD

All companies have a maximum capacity for producing goods or providing services, because there is a limit to the amount of resources available. There is always at least one resource that is more restrictive than others: this is known as a **limiting factor**.

Key term

A **limiting factor** is any factor that is in scarce supply and that stops the organisation from expanding its activities further, so that there is a maximum level of activity at which the organisaiton can operate.

Knowledge brought forward from earlier studies

- An organisation might be faced with just one limiting factor (other than maximum sales demand) but there might also be several scarce resources, with two or more of them putting an effective limit on the level of activity that can be achieved.

- Examples of limiting factors include sales demand and production constraints.

  - **Labour**. The limit may be either in terms of total quantity of labour or a limit to the availability of employees with particular skills.

  - **Materials**. There may be insufficient available materials to produce enough units to satisfy sales demand.

  - **Machine capacity**. There may not be sufficient machine capacity for the production required to meet sales demand.

- It is assumed in limiting factor analysis that management will decide to use its scarce resources in such a way as to maximise total contribution (and so profit). **In other words, marginal costing ideas are applied.**
    - If there is just one limiting factor, total contribution will be maximised by earning the biggest possible contribution per unit of limiting factor. For example if grade A labour is the limiting factor, contribution will be maximised by earning the biggest contribution per hour of grade A labour worked.
    - The limiting factor decision therefore involves the determination of the contribution earned per unit of limiting factor by each different product.
    - If the sales demand is limited, the profit-maximising decision will be to produce the top-ranked product(s) up to the sales demand limit.
- In limiting factor decisions, we generally assume that fixed costs are the same whatever product or service mix is selected, so that the only relevant costs are variable costs.
- When there is just one limiting factor, the technique for establishing the contribution-maximising product mix or service mix is to rank the products or services in order of the contribution they earn per unit of limiting factor.

1.1 Example: Limiting factor decision

Sausage makes two products, the Mash and the Sauce. Unit variable costs are as follows.

	Mash	Sauce
	$	$
Direct materials	1	3
Direct labour ($3 per hour)	6	3
Variable overhead	1	1
	8	7

The sales price per unit is $14 per Mash and $11 per Sauce. During July the available direct labour is limited to 8,000 hours. Sales demand in July is expected to be as follows.

Mash	3,000 units
Sauce	5,000 units

Required

Determine the production budget that will maximise profit, assuming that fixed costs per month are $20,000 and that there is no opening inventory of finished goods or work in progress.

Solution

Step 1   Confirm that the limiting factor is something other than sales demand.

	Mash	Sauces	Total
Labour hours per unit	2 hrs	1 hr	
Sales demand	3,000 units	5,000 units	
Labour hours needed	6,000 hrs	5,000 hrs	11,000 hrs
Labour hours available			8,000 hrs
Shortfall			3,000 hrs

Labour is a limiting factor on production.

Step 2   Identify the contribution earned by each product per unit of scarce resource, that is, per labour hour worked.

	Mash	Sauce
	$	$
Sales price	14	11
Variable cost	8	7
Unit contribution	6	4
Labour hours per unit	2 hrs	1 hr
Contribution per labour hour (= per unit of limiting factor)	$3	$4

Although the Mash earns a higher unit contribution than the Sauce, two units of Sauce can be made in the time it takes to make one unit of Mash. Because labour is in short supply it is therefore more profitable to make Sauces than Mashes.

Step 3   Determine the budgeted production and sales. Sufficient Sauces will be made to meet the full sales demand, and the remaining labour hours available will then be used to make Mashes.

(a)

Product	Demand	Hours required	Hours available	Priority for manufacture
Sauces	5,000	5,000	5,000	1st
Mashes	3,000	6,000	3,000 (bal)	2nd
		11,000	8,000	

(b)

Product	Units	Hours needed	Contribution per unit	Total
			$	$
Sauces	5,000	5,000	4	20,000
Mashes (balance)	1,500	3,000	6	9,000
		8,000		29,000
Less fixed costs				20,000
Profit				9,000

Conclusion

(a)   Unit contribution is *not* the correct way to decide priorities for production and sales.

(b)   Labour hours are the scarce resource in this example, therefore **contribution per labour hour** is the correct way to decide priorities for production and sales.

(c)   The Sauce earns $4 contribution per labour hour, and the Mash earns $3 contribution per labour hour. Sauces therefore make more profitable use of the scarce resource, and should be manufactured first.

(d)   Sauces should be made only up to the limit of sales demand. If there is any unused labour time after this quantity of Sauces has been produced, the remaining time should be used to make the product that earns the next-highest contribution per labour hour, which in this example is the Mash.

1.2 Two potentially limiting factors

You may be asked to deal with situations where two factors are potentially the limiting factor (and there are also sales demand limitations). The approach in these situations is to find out which factor (if any) prevents the business from fulfilling maximum sales demand.

Exam focus point

Where there is a **maximum potential sales demand** for an organisation's products, they should be ranked in order of contribution-earning ability per unit of the limiting factor. The contribution-maximising decision will be to produce the top-ranked products (or to provide the top-ranked services) up to the sales demand limit.

1.3 Example: Two potentially limiting factors

Lucky manufactures and sells three products, X, Y and Z, for which budgeted sales demand, unit selling prices and unit variable costs are as follows.

		X		Y		Z	
Budgeted sales demand		550 units		500 units		400 units	
		$	$	$	$	$	$
Unit sales price			16		18		14
Variable costs:	materials	8		6		2	
	labour	4		6		9	
			12		12		11
Unit contribution			4		6		3

The organisation has existing inventory of 250 units of X and 200 units of Z, which it is quite willing to use up to meet sales demand. All three products use the same direct materials and the same type of direct labour. In the next year, the available supply of materials will be restricted to $4,800 (at cost) and the available supply of labour to $6,600 (at cost).

Required

Determine what product mix and sales mix would maximise the organisation's profits in the next year.

Solution

There are **two scarce resources** that may be a limiting factor, direct materials and direct labour. However this is not certain. Because there is a limit to sales demand, either of the following may apply.

- There is **no limiting factor at all**, except sales demand.
- There is **only one scarce resource** that prevents the full potential sales demand being achieved.

Step 1 Establish which of the resources, if any, is scarce.

	X Units	Y Units	Z Units
Budgeted sales	550	500	400
Inventory in hand	250	0	200
Minimum production to meet demand	300	500	200

	Minimum production to meet sales demand Units	Required materials at cost $	Required labour at cost $
X	300	2,400	1,200
Y	500	3,000	3,000
Z	200	400	1,800
Total required		5,800	6,000
Total available		4,800	6,600
(Shortfall)/Surplus		(1,000)	600

Materials are a limiting factor, but labour is not.

Step 2 Rank X, Y and Z in order of contribution earned per $1 of direct materials consumed.

	X $	Y $	Z $
Unit contribution	4	6	3
Cost of materials	8	6	2
Contribution per $1 materials	$0.50	$1.00	$1.50
Ranking	3rd	2nd	1st

Step 3   **Determine a production plan.** Z should be manufactured up to the limit where units produced plus units held in inventory will meet sales demand; then Y should be produced second and X third, until all the available materials are used up.

Ranking	Product	Sales demand less units held Units	Production quantity Units		Materials cost $
1st	Z	200	200	(× $2)	400
2nd	Y	500	500	(× $6)	3,000
3rd	X	300	175	(× $8)	*1,400
		Total available			4,800

* Balancing amount using up total available.

Step 4   **Draw up a budget.** The profit-maximising budget is as follows.

Product	Units	Material cost / unit $	Total material cost $	Contribution per $1 of material $	Total contribution $
Z opening inventory	200				
Z production	200				
	400	$2	800	$1.50	1,200
Y production	500	$6	3,000	$1.00	3,000
X opening inventory	250				
X production	175				
	425	$8	3,400	$0.50	1,700
				Total contribution	5,900

2 Limiting factor analysis – make or buy decisions and scarce resources
6/11, 6/12

In a situation where a company is able to **sub-contract work to make up a shortfall in its own in-house production capabilities**, its total costs will be minimised if those units bought from the sub-contractor have the lowest extra variable cost per unit of scarce resource saved by buying. Extra variable cost is the difference between the variable cost of in-house production and the cost of buying from the sub-contractor.

2.1 Combining internal and external production

An organisation might **want to do more things than it has the resources for**, and so its alternatives would be as follows.

(a)   Make the best use of the available resources and ignore the opportunities to buy help from outside by sub-contracting some of the work

(b)   Combine internal resources with buying externally so as to produce (and sell) more and so increase profitability

3 The principles of linear programming   6/08

FAST FORWARD

Linear programming is a technique for solving problems of profit maximisation or cost minimisation and resource allocation. 'Programming' has nothing to do with computers: the word is simply used to denote a series of events. If a scenario contains **two or more limiting factors**, linear programming should be used to determine the contribution-maximising or cost-minimising solution.

Linear programming is a technique that may be used to determine the contribution-maximising or cost-minimising solution to a problem when there are two (or more) limiting factors, not just one.

Ranking products in order of the contribution they earn per unit of limiting factor is not possible, because there is more than one limiting factor, and the ranking of products is likely to be different for each of the limiting factors.

Linear programming can be used to identify the contribution-maximising (or cost-minimising) solution, that makes the best use of all the limiting factors.

When an organisation makes and sells just two products, a graphical method can be used to formulate the linear programming problem and then solve it.

4 The graphical method   6/08, 6/10

FAST FORWARD

The graphical method of linear programming can be used when there are just two products (or services). The steps involved are as follows.

1   Define the problem:

     (a)   Define variables
     (b)   Establish constraints
     (c)   Construct objective function

2   Draw the constraints on a graph
3   Establish the feasible region for the optimal solution
4   Determine the optimal solution

4.1 Example: WX Co

The following example will be used throughout the chapter to illustrate the graphical method of linear programming.

WX Co manufactures two products, A and B. Both products pass through two production departments, mixing and shaping. The organisation's objective is to maximise contribution to fixed costs.

Product A is sold for $1.50 whereas product B is priced at $2.00. There is unlimited demand for product A but demand for B is limited to 13,000 units per annum. The machine hours available in each department are restricted to 2,400 per annum. Other relevant data are as follows.

Machine hours required	Mixing Hrs	Shaping Hrs
Product A	0.06	0.04
Product B	0.08	0.12

Variable cost per unit	$
Product A	1.30
Product B	1.70

What are the constraints in the situation facing WX Co?

Answer

These are the constraints that will prevent WX from producing and selling as much of each product as it chooses.

The constraints are machine hours in each department and sales demand for product B. There is no restriction on the availability of labour hours. Selling price cannot be a constraint.

4.2 Formulating the problem

Let's formulate the linear programming problem for WX.

Step 1 **Define the variables**

The variables are the items whose value we are trying to decide. In this problem, the variables are the two products that WX can make and sell; we want to decide the quantities of Product A and Product B that should be made in order to maximise contribution (and profit).

For the graphical method of linear programming to be possible, there can be only two variables. The variables in this problem will therefore be stated as follows.

Let x = number of units of Product A produced and sold.

Let y = number of units of Product B produced and sold.

Step 2 **Establish the constraints**

Constraints are anything that sets a maximum or a minimum limit on the solution. Typically, there may be a maximum limit to the sales demand for each product, or a maximum limit to the amount of a production resource available, such as the quantity of a material, labour time or machine time.

In this problem there are constraints for the maximum sales demand for Product B, the maximum machine hours in the Mixing Department and the maximum machine hours in the Shaping Department.

In a linear programming problem there may also be a minimum constraint, such as a minimum quantity of a product that must be made and sold to meet a confirmed customer order.

There are also non-negativity constraints. In this example, the values of x and y cannot be negative. (You cannot produce a negative quantity of a product.)

Each constraint must now be stated as a formula or 'inequality'. An inequality is similar to an equation except that the symbol 'less than or equal to) ($\leq$) or 'greater than or equal to ($\geq$) is used instead of the equation sign (=).

(a)   Consider the Mixing Department machine hours constraint.

    (i)   **Each unit of product A** requires 0.06 hours of machine time. Producing five units therefore requires 5 × 0.06 hours of machine time and, more generally, **producing x units will require 0.06x hours**.

    (ii)   Likewise producing **y units of product B will require 0.08y hours**.

(iii) The total machine hours needed in the mixing department to make x units of product A and y units of product B is 0.06x + 0.08y.

(iv) We know that this **cannot be greater in total than 2,400 hours** and so we arrive at the following inequality.

0.06x + 0.08y ≤ 2,400

How can the constraint facing the **Shaping Department** be written as an inequality?

Answer

The constraint facing the Shaping Department can be written as follows:

0.04x + 0.12y ≤ 2,400

The constraint has to be a 'less than or equal to' inequality, because the amount of resource used (0.04x + 0.12y) has to be 'less than or equal to' the amount available of 2,400 hours.

(b) The final inequality is easier to obtain. The **number of units of product B produced and sold is y** but this has to be **less than or equal to 13,000**. Our inequality is therefore as follows.

y ≤ 13,000.

(c) We also need to add **non-negativity constraints (x ≥ 0, y ≥ 0)** since negative numbers of products cannot be produced. (Linear programming is simply a mathematical tool and so there is nothing in this method which guarantees that the answer will 'make sense'. An unprofitable product may produce an answer which is negative. This is mathematically correct but nonsense in operational terms. Always remember to include the non-negativity constraints. The examiner will not appreciate 'impossible' solutions.)

Step 3 **Construct the objective function**

The objective function is a formula that states what we are trying to achieve as a solution to the problem. The objective function is always an objective of wanting to maximise something or minimise something. Typically, the objective function will be to maximise total contribution or to minimise total cost.

In the problem we are looking at here, the objective function is to maximise total contribution. We must put this into a formula.

We know that the **contribution on each type of product** is as follows.

		$ per unit
Product A	$(1.50 – 1.30) =	0.20
Product B	$(2.00 – 1.70) =	0.30

The **objective of the company is to maximise contribution** and so the **objective function to be maximised** is as follows.

Maximise contribution (C): 0.2x + 0.3y

The problem has now been reduced to the following four inequalities and one equation.

Maximise contribution (C) = 0.2x + 0.3y, subject to the following constraints:

$$0.06x + 0.08y \leq 2,400$$

$$0.04x + 0.12y \leq 2,400$$

$$y \leq 13,000$$

$$x, y \geq 0$$

4.3 Graphing the problem

Having identified the linear programme constraints, the next step is to draw these constraints on a graph. **The constraints are all drawn as straight lines**.

Remember that a **graphical solution** is **only possible** when there are **two variables** in the problem. One variable is represented by the **x axis** of the graph and one by the **y axis**. Since non-negative values are not usually allowed, the graph shows **only zero and positive values of x and y**.

4.3.1 Rules for drawing a constraint as a straight line on a graph

There are three types of constraint that you may need to draw as lines on a graph.

(a)   A constraint 'x is less than or equal to a given amount'.

For example, $x \leq 12$

This constraint is drawn by drawing the boundary limit of this constraint. The boundary is where $x = 12$. In other words, we turn the inequality into an equation and draw a line of the equation.

To draw $x = 12$, we need to plot any two points on the graph and join them up. For example:

When $y = 0$, $x = 12$

When $y = 10$, $x = 12$

The value of x is 12 whatever the value of y.

The equation $x = 12$ is drawn as a vertical line on a graph at the point where $x = 12$.

(b)   A constraint 'y is less than or equal to a given amount'.

For example, $y \leq 15$

We turn the inequality into an equation and draw a line of the equation. Here the equation is $y = 15$.

To draw $y = 15$, we need to plot any two points on the graph and join them up. For example:

When $x = 0$, $y = 15$

When $x = 10$, $y = 15$

The value of y is 15 whatever the value of x.

The equation $y = 15$ is drawn as a horizontal line on a graph at the point where $y = 15$.

(c)   The most common type of constraint is where there is a value for both x and y; for example:

$$3x + 5y \leq 45$$

Once again we turn the inequality into an equation and draw a line of the equation. Here the equation is $3x + 5y = 45$.

To draw this line on a graph, we need to identify two points and join them up as a straight line. The two points that are easiest to plot on the graph, are:

$3x + 5y = 45$ when $x = 0$. When $x = 0$, $y = 9$, so plot $x = 0$, $y = 9$ on the graph.

$3x + 5y = 45$ when $y = 0$. When $y = 0$, $x = 15$, so plot $x = 15$, $y = 0$ on the graph.

Join up these two points, and you have drawn the equation on the graph for any combination of values of x and y (where x and y are not negative values).

Let's apply these rules to the linear programming problem of WX Co.

4.3.2 Drawing the constraints in the WX Co problem

In addition to the non-negativity constraints for x and y, there are three constraints in the problem.

(a)   Mixing Department hours: **0.06x + 0.08y ≤ 2,400**

Draw a line for the equation 0.06x + 0.08y = 2,400

If x = 0, y = 30,000

If y = 0, x = 40,000

Plot these two points on the graph and join them up to shown the boundary line of the constraint.

(b)   Shaping Department hours: **0.04x + 0.12y ≤ 2,400**

Draw a line for the equation 0.04x + 0.12y = 2,400

If x = 0, y = 20,000

If y = 0, x = 60,000

Plot these two points on the graph and join them up to shown the boundary line of the constraint.

(c)   Maximum sales demand for Product B: **y ≤ 13,000**

Draw the line y = 13,000.

This is a horizontal line on the graph at the point where y = 13,000, and for all value of x.

The graph should look like this.

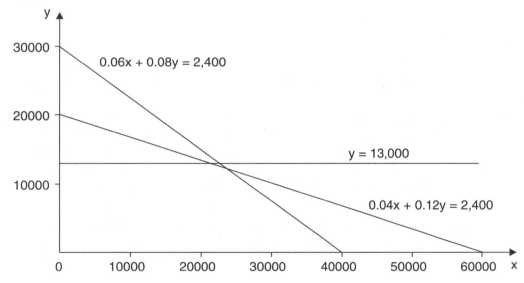

4.3.3 Establishing the feasible region

The feasible region in a linear programming problem is the area in the graph where the combinations of x and are all 'feasible'. In other words, any combination of the values of x and y within the feasible region comply with the constraints in the linear programming problem.

When a constraint is a 'less than or equal to' (≤) constraint, all the feasible combinations of x and y are either on the boundary line (the equation line) or below it, where values of x and y are lower.

When a constraint is a 'more than or equal to' (≤) constraint, all the feasible combinations of x and y are either on the boundary line (the equation line) or above it, where values of x and y are higher.

When the constraint is a vertical line 'x ≤ a given amount', the feasible values of x cannot exceed this amount, and so are either on the equation line or to the left of it.

The feasible region for the solution of a linear programming problem is the various combinations of x and y that comply with all the constraints in the linear programming problem.

In the example of WX Co, the feasible region is identified as the shaded area on the graph.

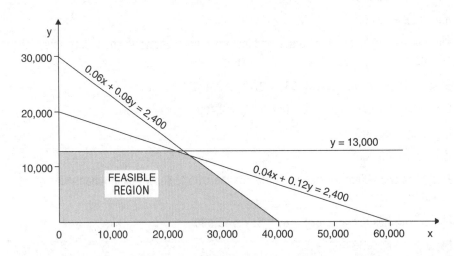

4.4 Finding the optimum allocation of resources　　6/08, 6/10, 12/10

FAST FORWARD

The **optimum solution** to a linear programming problem can be found by 'sliding the iso-contribution line out'.

Having found the feasible region (which includes all the possible solutions to the problem) we need to **find which of these possible solutions is 'best'** or **optimal** in the sense that it yields the best value for the objective function – in this example, the maximum possible contribution.

Look at the feasible region of the problem faced by WX. Even in such a simple problem as this, there are a **great many possible solution points within the feasible region.** Even to write them all down would be a time-consuming process and also an unnecessary one, as we shall see.

Here is the graph of WX's problem.

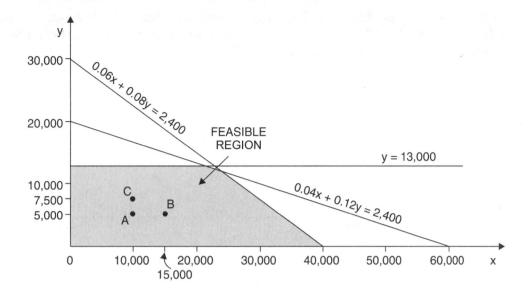

(a) Consider point A at which 10,000 units of product A and 5,000 units of product B are being manufactured. This will yield a contribution of (10,000 × $0.20) + (5,000 × $0.30) = $3,500.

(b) We would clearly get more contribution at point B, where the same number of units of product B are being produced but where the number of units of product A has increased by 5,000.

(c) We would also get more contribution at point C where the number of units of product A is the same but 2,500 more units of product B are being produced.

This argument suggests that the **'best' solution** is going to be at a **point on the edge of the feasible region**, on one or more of the equation lines, rather than in the middle of it.

This still leaves us with quite a few points to look at but there is a way in which we can **narrow down still further the likely points at which the best solution will be found.** Suppose that WX wishes to earn contribution of $3,000. Given that the contribution per unit of Product A is $0.2 and the contribution per unit of Product B is $0.3, the company could sell the following combinations of the two products.

(a) 15,000 units of A, no B (x = 15,000, y = 0)
(b) No A, 10,000 units of B (x = 0, y = 10,000).
(c) A suitable mix of the two, such as 7,500 A and 5,000 B.

The **possible combinations required to earn contribution of $3,000** could be **shown by the straight line 0.2x + 0.3y = 3,000.**

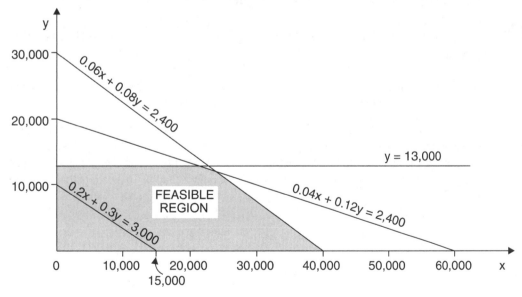

Likewise to earn total contribution of $6,000 and to earn total contribution of $1,500, lines of 0.2x + 0.3y = 6,000 and 0.2x + 0.3y = 1,500 could be drawn **showing the combination of the two products** which would **achieve contribution of $6,000 or $1,500.**

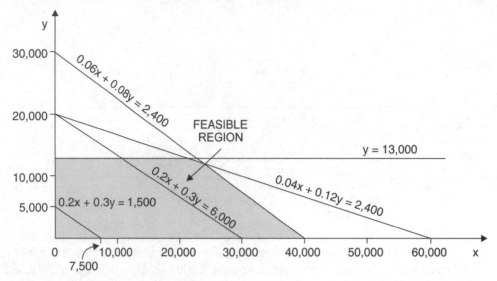

The **contribution lines are all parallel to each other.** (They are called **iso-contribution lines,** 'iso' meaning equal.) A similar line drawn for any other total contribution would also be parallel to the lines shown here. **Bigger contribution is shown by lines further from the origin** (0.2x + 0.3y = 6,000), smaller contribution by lines closer to the origin (0.2x + 0.3y = 1,500). As WX tries to increase possible contribution, we need to 'slide' any contribution line outwards from the origin, while always keeping it parallel to the other contribution lines.

As we do this there will come a point at which, if we were to move the contribution line out any further, it would cease to lie in the feasible region. Greater contribution could not be achieved, because of the constraints. In our example concerning WX this will happen, as you should test for yourself, where the contribution line just passes through the intersection of 0.06x + 0.08y = 2,400 and 0.04x + 0.12y = 2,400 (at coordinates (24,000, 12,000)).

The point (24,000, 12,000) will therefore give us the optimal allocation of resources (**to produce 24,000 units of A and 12,000 units of B**).

5 Using simultaneous equations 6/08

FAST FORWARD ›

The optimal solution to a linear programming problem can also be found using **simultaneous equations**.

You might think that a lot of time could be saved if we started by solving the simultaneous equations in a linear programming problem and did not bother to draw the graph.

Certainly, this procedure may give the right answer, but in general, it is *not* recommended until you have shown graphically which constraints are effective in determining the optimal solution, and you have identified the feasible region. Some constraints may not affect the feasible region at all. (In particular, if a question requires 'the graphical method', you *must* draw a graph). To illustrate this point, consider the following graph.

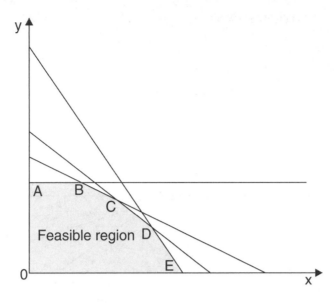

No figures have been given on the graph but the feasible region is OABCDE. When solving this problem, we would know that the optimum solution would be at one of the corners of the feasible area. We need to work out the profit at each of the corners of the feasible area and pick the one where the profit is greatest.

Once the optimum point has been determined graphically, simultaneous equations can be applied to find the exact values of x and y at this point.

Instead of a 'sliding the contribution line out' approach, **simultaneous equations** can be used to determine the optimal allocation of resources, as shown in the following example.

5.1 Example: Using simultaneous equations

The process for solving the linear programming problem for WX Co is summarised below. Let's focus the final step to illustrate how simultaneous equations can be used to establish the contribution-maximising product mix.

Step 1

(a) **Define variables**

x = number of units of product A produced
y = number of units of product B produced

(b) **Establish the constraints**

The constraints are as follows.

$$0.06x + 0.08y \leq 2,400 \qquad \text{(mixing department)}$$
$$0.04x + 0.12y \leq 2,400 \qquad \text{(shaping department)}$$
$$y \leq 13,000 \qquad \text{(demand for product B)}$$
$$x, y \geq 0 \qquad \text{(non-negativity)}$$

(c) **Construct the objective function**

Product A yields a contribution of $0.20 per unit $(1.50 − 1.30).

Product B yields a contribution of $0.30 per unit $(2.00 − 1.70).

Therefore the objective is to maximise contribution (C) = 0.2x + 0.3y subject to the above constraints.

Step 2   Graph the problem

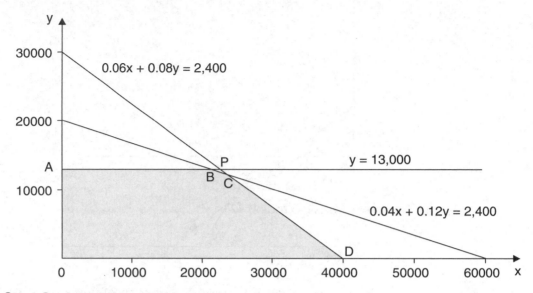

Step 3   Establish feasible region

The combinations of x and y that satisfy all three constraints are represented by the area OABCD.

Step 4   Determine optimal solution

Which combination will maximise contribution? Obviously, the more units of x and y, the bigger the contribution will be, and the optimal solution will be at point B, C or D. It will not be at A, since at A, y = 13,000 and x = 0, whereas at B, y = 13,000 (the same) and x is greater than zero.

Using simultaneous equations to calculate the value of x and y at each of points B, C and D, and then working out total contribution at each point from this, we can establish the contribution-maximising product mix.

Point B

(1)	y	=	13,000
(2)	0.04x + 0.12y	=	2,400
Substitute (1) into (2)	0.04x + 0.12 (13,000)	=	2,400
	0.04x + 1,560	=	2,400
	0.04x	=	840
	x	=	21,000

When x = 21,000 and y = 13,000, total contribution = $(21,000 × 0.2) + $(13,000 × 0.3) = $4,200 + $3,900 = $8,100.

Point C

(1)	0.06x + 0.08y	=	2,400
(2)	0.04x + 0.12y	=	2,400
Multiply (1) by 2			
(3)	0.12x + 0.16y	=	4,800
Multiply (2) by 3			
(4)	0.12x + 0.36y	=	7,200
Subtract (3) from (4)	0.20y	=	2,400
	=	=	12,000
Substitute in (1)	0.06x + 0.08 (12,000)	=	2,400
	0.06x	=	1,440
	x	=	24,000

When x = 24,000 and y = 12,000, total contribution = $(24,000 × 0.2) + $(12,000 × 0.3) = $4,800 + $3,600 = $8,400.

Point D

Total contribution = 40,000 × $0.20 = $8,000.

Comparing B, C and D, we can see that contribution is maximised at C, by making 24,000 units of product A and 12,000 units of product B, to earn a contribution of $8,400.

6 Slack and surplus   6/08

FAST FORWARD

Slack occurs when maximum availability of a resource is not used: slack is the amount of the unused resource or other constraint, were the constraint is a 'less than or equal to' constraint

Surplus occurs when more than a minimum requirement is used: surplus is the excess over the minimum amount of constraint, were the constraint is a 'more than or equal to' constraint

Key term

> **Slack** occurs when maximum availability of a resource or other constraining factor is not used.

If, at the optimal solution, the amount of the resource used equals the amount of the resource available, there is **no spare capacity** of a resource and so there is **no slack.**

If, at the optimal solution, the amount of the resource used is less than the amount of the resource available, there is **spare capacity** for the resource and so there is **slack.**

For example, a machine shop makes boxes (B) and tins (T). Contribution per box is $5 and per tin is $7. A box requires 3 hours of machine processing time, 16kg of raw materials and 6 labour hours. A tin requires 10 hours of machine processing time, 4kg of raw materials and 6 labour hours. In a given month, 330 hours of machine processing time are available, 400kg of raw material and 240 labour hours. The manufacturing technology used means that at least 12 tins must be made every month. The constraints are:

$3B + 10T \leq 330$
$16B + 4T \leq 400$
$6B + 6T \leq 240$
$\qquad T \geq 12$
$\qquad B \geq 0$

The solution is not shown in detail here, but the optimal solution is found to be to manufacture and sell 10 boxes and 30 tins.

If we substitute these values into the inequalities representing the constraints, we can determine whether the constraints are binding or whether there is slack.

Machine time:	$(3 \times 10) + (10 \times 30) = 330$ = availability Constraint is **binding**.
Raw materials:	$(16 \times 10) + (4 \times 30) = 280 < 400$ There is **slack** of 120kg of raw materials.
Labour:	$(6 \times 10) + (6 \times 30) = 240$ = availability Constraint is **binding**.

If a minimum quantity of a resource must be used and, at the optimal solution, **more than that quantity is used**, there is a **surplus** on the minimum requirement. This is shown here in the production of tins where the optimal production is 30 tins but $T \geq 12$. There is therefore a **surplus** of 18 tins over the minimum production requirement.

You can see from this that slack is associated with $\leq$ constraints and surplus with $\geq$ constraints. Machine time and labour are **binding constraints** so they have been used to their full capacity. It can be

argued that if more machine time and labour could be obtained, more boxes and tins could be produced and contribution increased.

7 Shadow prices

FAST FORWARD

> The **shadow price** or **dual price** of a limiting factor is the increase in value which would be created by having one additional unit of the limiting factor at its original cost.

Key term

> The **shadow price** or dual price of a constraint factor is the amount of change in the value of the objective function (for example, the increase in contribution) created by the availability of one extra unit of the limited resource at its original cost.

7.1 Limiting factors and shadow prices

Whenever there are limiting factors, there are **opportunity costs**. These are the **benefits forgone** by using a limiting factor in one way instead of in the next most profitable way.

For example, suppose that an organisation provides two services X and Y, which earn a contribution of $24 and $18 per unit respectively. Service X requires 4 labour hours, and service Y 2 hours. Only 5,000 labour hours are available, and potential demand is for 1,000 of each of X and Y.

Labour hours are a limiting factor, and with X earning $6 per hour and Y earning $9 per hour, the profit-maximising decision would be as follows.

	Services	Hours	Contribution $
Y	1,000	2,000	18,000
X (balance)	750	3,000	18,000
		5,000	36,000

Priority is given to Y because the **opportunity cost** of providing Y instead of more of X is $6 per hour (X's contribution per labour hour), and since Y earns $9 per hour, the incremental benefit of providing Y instead of X would be $3 per hour.

If extra labour hours could be made available, more X (up to 1,000) would be provided, and an extra contribution of $6 per hour could be earned. Similarly, if fewer labour hours were available, the decision would be to provide fewer X and to keep provision of Y at 1,000, and so the loss of labour hours would cost the organisation $6 per hour in lost contribution. This $6 per hour, the **marginal contribution-earning potential of the limiting factor at the profit-maximising output level**, is referred to as the **shadow price** (or **dual price**) of the limiting factor.

Note that the shadow price only applies on the assumption that the extra unit of resource can be obtained at its **normal variable cost**. The shadow price also indicates the amount by which contribution could fall if an organisation is deprived of one unit of the scarce resource.

The shadow price of a resource is its **internal opportunity cost.** This is the marginal contribution towards fixed costs and profit that can be earned for each unit of the limiting factor that is available.

Depending on the resource in question, shadow prices enable management to make **better informed decisions** about the payment of overtime premiums, bonuses, premiums on small orders of raw materials and so on, in order to obtain additional units of a limiting resource.

7.2 Linear programming and shadow prices

In terms of linear programming, the **shadow price** is the **extra contribution (and so profit) that may be earned by obtaining one extra unit of a binding resource constraint**.

Suppose the availability of materials is a binding constraint. If one extra kilogram becomes available so that an alternative production mix becomes optimal, with a resulting increase over the original production mix contribution of $2, the shadow price of a kilogram of material is $2.

Note, however, that this increase in contribution of $2 per extra kilogram of material made available is calculated on the **assumption** that the **extra kilogram would cost the normal variable amount**.

Note the following points.

(a) The shadow price therefore represents the maximum **premium** above the basic rate that an organisation should be **willing to pay for one extra unit** of a resource.

(b) Since shadow prices indicate the effect of a one unit change in a constraint, they provide a measure of the **sensitivity** of the result.

(c) The **shadow price** of a constraint that is **not binding** at the optimal solution is **zero**. In other words if there is slack for a constraining resource, the shadow price (dual price) of the resource is $0.

(d) Shadow prices are **only valid for up to a limited number of additional units,** because if additional quantities of a binding constraint are obtained, another constraint will eventually become a binding constraint instead.

7.3 Example: Calculating shadow prices

This example re-visits the scenario faced by WX Co which was used to demonstrate the graphical method of linear programming earlier in the chapter. The key points are re-capped below.

WX manufactures two products, A and B. Both products pass through two production departments, mixing and shaping. The organisation's objective is to maximise contribution to fixed costs.

Product A is sold for $1.50 whereas product B is priced at $2.00. There is unlimited demand for product A but demand for B is limited to 13,000 units per annum. The machine hours available in each department are restricted to 2,400 per annum. Other relevant data are as follows.

Machine hours required	Mixing	Shaping
	Hrs	Hrs
Product A	0.06	0.04
Product B	0.08	0.12

Variable cost per unit	$
Product A	1.30
Product B	1.70

The constraints are:

$$0.06x + 0.08y \leq 2,400$$
$$0.04x + 0.12y \leq 2,400$$
$$y \leq 13,000$$
$$x,y \geq 0$$

The objective function is:

Contribution (C) = 0.2x + 0.3y

The optimal solution is where x = 24,000 and y = 12,000, and total contribution = $(24,000 × 0.2) + $(12,000 × 0.3) = $4,800 + $3,600 = $8,400.

The availability of time in both departments are limiting factors because both are used up fully in the optimal product mix. Machine time in both departments are a limiting resource, which means that machine time in the Mixing Department and machine time in the Shaping Department both have a shadow price greater than $0.

Let us therefore calculate the effect if **one extra hour of Shaping Department machine time** was made available so that 2,401 hours were available.

The new optimal product mix would be at the intersection of the two constraint lines 0.06x + 0.08y = 2,400 and 0.04x + 0.12y = 2,401.

Solution by simultaneous equations (workings not shown) gives x = 23,980 and y = 12,015.

(You should solve the problem yourself if you are doubtful about the derivation of the solution.)

Product	Units	Contribution per unit $	Total contribution $
A	23,980	0.20	4,796.0
B	12,015	0.30	3,604.5
			8,400.5
Contribution in original problem			8,400.0
Increase in contribution from one extra hour of shaping time			0.5

The **shadow price** of an hour of machining time in the Shaping Department is therefore $0.50. It would add to total contribution if additional machine hours could be made available in the department for less than $0.5 per hour on top of the normal variable cost of the machine time.

This means that extra machine capacity could be rented, for example, provided the cost premium is less than $0.50 per hour.

This value of machine time only applies as long as shaping machine time is a limiting factor. If more and more machine hours become available, there will eventually be so much machine time that it is no longer a limiting factor.

Question

Shadow prices

What is the shadow price of one hour of machine time in the Mixing Department?

A	$3		C	$10.50
B	$7		D	$1,193

Answer

The correct answer is A.

If we assume one more hour of machine time in the Mixing Department is available, the new optimal solution is at the intersection of $0.06x + 0.08y = 2,401$ and $0.04x + 0.12y = 2,400$

Solution by simultaneous equations gives x = 24,030, y = 11,990

Product	Units	Contribution per unit $	Total contribution $
A	24,030	0.20	4,806
B	11,990	0.30	3,597
			8,403
Contribution in original problem			8,400
Reduction in contribution			3

∴ Shadow price of one hour of machine time in the mixing department is $3.

Chapter Roundup

- All companies have a maximum capacity for producing goods or providing services, because there is a limit to the amount of resources available. There is always at least one resource that is more restrictive than others: this is known as a **limiting factor**.

- In a situation where a company is able to **sub-contract work to make up a shortfall in its own in-house production capabilities**, its total costs will be minimised if those units bought from the sub-contractor have the lowest extra variable cost per unit of scarce resource saved by buying. Extra variable cost is the difference between the variable cost of in-house production and the cost of buying from the sub-contractor.

- **Linear programming** is a technique for solving problems of profit maximisation or cost minimisation and resource allocation. 'Programming' has nothing to do with computers: the word is simply used to denote a series of events. If a scenario contains **two or more limiting factors**, linear programming should be used to determine the contribution-maximising or cost-minimising solution.

- The graphical method of linear programming can be used when there are just two products (or services). The steps involved are as follows.

  1 Define the problem:

      (a) Define variables
      (b) Establish constraints
      (c) Construct objective function

  2 Draw the constraints on a graph
  3 Establish the feasible region for the optimal solution
  4 Determine the optimal solution

- The **optimum solution** to a linear programming problem can be found by 'sliding the iso-contribution line out'.

- The optimal solution to a linear programming problem can also be found using **simultaneous equations**

- **Slack** occurs when maximum availability of a resource is not used. **Surplus** occurs when more than a minimum requirement is used.

- The **shadow price** or **dual price** of a limiting factor is the increase in value which would be created by having one additional unit of the limiting factor at its original cost.

Quick Quiz

1   *Fill in the blanks.*

    The shadow price of a scarce resource indicates the amount by which contribution would
    .... if an organisation were deprived of one unit of the resource. The shadow
    price only applies while the extra unit of resource can be obtained at its .... cost.

2   *Put the following steps in the graphical approach to linear programming in the correct order.*

    Draw a graph of the constraints   Establish constraints
    Define variables   Construct objective function
    Establish the feasible region   Determine optimal product mix

3   In what circumstances does slack arise?

    A   At the optimal solution, when the resource used equals the resource available
    B   At the optimal solution, when a minimum quantity of a resource must be used, and more than that quantity is used
    C   At the optimal solution, when the resource used is less than the resource available
    D   At the optimal solution, when a minimum quantity of resource is used

Answers to Quick Quiz

1   fall
    normal variable

2   Define variables   Draw a graph of the constraints
    Establish constraints   Establish the feasible region
    Construct objective function   Determine optimal product mix

3   C. If a resource has a maximum availability and it's not binding at the optimal solution, there will be slack.

Now try the question below from the Practice Question Bank

Number	Level	Marks	Time
Q7	Examination	20	36 mins

5

Pricing decisions

Topic list	Syllabus reference
1 Pricing policy and the market	B4 (a)
2 Demand	B4 (b), (c)
3 The profit-maximising price/output level	B4 (d), (f)
4 Decisions to increase production and sales	B4 (e)
5 Price strategies	B4 (g), (h)

Introduction

All profit organisations and many non-profit organisations face the task of setting a price for their products or services.

In this chapter we will begin by looking at the **factors which influence pricing** policy. Perhaps the most important of these are the prices charged by competitors, and the **level of demand** for the organisation's products or services. In a market that Is not so competitive, pricing should still be set at a level that customers will pay but which also provides a satisfactory profit.

This chapter also considers the **profit-maximising price/output level** and a range of different **pricing strategies.**

Study guide

		Intellectual level
B4	**Pricing decisions**	
(a)	Explain the factors that influence the pricing of a product or service	2
(b)	Explain the price elasticity of demand	1
(c)	Derive and manipulate a straight line demand equation. Derive an equation for the total cost function (including volume-based discounts)	2
(d)	Calculate the optimum selling price and quantity for an organisation, equating marginal cost and marginal revenue	2
(e)	Evaluate a decision to increase production and sales levels, considering incremental costs, incremental revenues and other factors	2
(f)	Determine prices and output levels for profit maximisation using the demand based approach to pricing (both tabular and algebraic methods)	1
(g)	Explain different price strategies, including: (i) All forms of cost-plus (ii) Skimming (iii) Penetration (iv) Complementary product (v) Product-line (vi) Volume discounting (vii) Discrimination (viii) Relevant cost	2
(h)	Calculate a price from a given strategy using cost-plus and relevant cost	2

Exam guide

Exam questions on pricing in Section B are likely to be a mixture of calculation and discussion and the examiner will expect a **practical application** of pricing theories.

1 Pricing policy and the market

FAST FORWARD

> In the modern world there are many more **influences on price** than cost (eg competitors, product range, quality).

1.1 Influences on price

6/13

Influence	Explanation/Example
Price sensitivity	Sensitivity to price levels will vary amongst purchasers. Those that can pass on the cost of purchases will be the least sensitive and will therefore respond more to other elements of perceived value. For example, a business traveller will be more concerned about the level of service in looking for an hotel than price, provided that it fits the corporate budget. In contrast, a family on holiday are likely to be very price sensitive when choosing an overnight stay.
Price perception	Price perception is the way customers react to prices. For example, customers may react to a price increase by buying more. This could be because they expect further price increases to follow (they are 'stocking up').

Influence	Explanation/Example
Quality	This is an aspect of price perception. In the absence of other information, customers tend to judge quality by price. Thus a price rise may indicate improvements in quality, a price reduction may signal reduced quality.
Intermediaries	If an organisation distributes products or services to the market through independent intermediaries, such intermediaries are likely to deal with a range of suppliers and their aims concern their own profits rather than those of suppliers.
Competitors	In some industries (such as petrol retailing) pricing moves in unison; in others, price changes by one supplier may initiate a price war. Competition is discussed in more detail below.
Suppliers	If an organisation's suppliers notice a price rise for the organisation's products, they may seek a rise in the price for their supplies to the organisation.
Inflation	In periods of inflation the organisation may need to change prices to reflect increases in the prices of supplies, labour, rent and so on.
Newness	When a new product is introduced for the first time there are no existing reference points such as customer or competitor behaviour; pricing decisions are most difficult to make in such circumstances. It may be possible to seek alternative reference points, such as the price in another market where the new product has already been launched, or the price set by a competitor.
Incomes	If incomes are rising, price may be a less important marketing variable than product quality and convenience of access (distribution). When income levels are falling and/or unemployment levels rising, price will be more important.
Product range	Products are often interrelated, being complements to each other or substitutes for one another. The management of the pricing function is likely to focus on the profit from the whole range rather than the profit on each single product. For example, a very low price is charged for a loss leader to make consumers buy additional products in the range which carry higher profit margins (eg selling razors at very low prices whilst selling the blades for them at a higher profit margin).
Ethics	Ethical considerations may be a further factor, for example whether or not to exploit short-term shortages through higher prices.

1.2 Markets

FAST FORWARD

The price that an organisation can charge for its products will be determined to a greater or lesser degree by the **market** in which it operates.

Here are some familiar economic terms that might feature as background for a question or that you might want to use in a written answer.

Key terms

Perfect competition: many buyers and many sellers all dealing in an identical product. Neither producer nor user has any market power and both must accept the prevailing market price.

Monopoly: one seller who dominates many buyers. The monopolist can use his market power to set a profit-maximising price.

Monopolistic competition: a large number of suppliers offer similar, but not identical, products. The similarities ensure elastic demand whereas the slight differences give some monopolistic power to the supplier.

Oligopoly: where relatively few competitive companies dominate the market. Whilst each large firm has the ability to influence market prices, the unpredictable reaction from the other giants makes the final industry price indeterminate. Cartels are often formed.

1.3 Competition

In **established industries** dominated by a few major firms, it is generally accepted that a price initiative by one firm will be countered by a price reaction by competitors. In these circumstances, prices tend to be **fairly stable**, unless pushed upwards by inflation or strong growth in demand.

If a rival **cuts its prices** in the expectation of increasing its market share, a firm has several options.

(a) It will **maintain its existing prices** if the expectation is that only a small market share would be lost, so that it is more profitable to keep prices at their existing level. Eventually, the rival firm may drop out of the market or be forced to raise its prices.

(b) It may maintain its prices but respond with a **non-price counter-attack**. This is a more positive response, because the firm will be securing or justifying its current prices with a product change, advertising, or better back-up services.

(c) It may **reduce its prices**. This should protect the firm's market share so that the main beneficiary from the price reduction will be the consumer.

(d) It may **raise its prices** *and respond with a* **non-price counter-attack**. The extra revenue from the higher prices might be used to finance an advertising campaign or product design changes. A price increase would be based on a campaign to emphasise the quality difference between the firm's and the rival's products.

Question
Pricing in the modern business environment

What approach may be used to achieve a satisfactory profit when the selling price is determined by competition in the market?

Answer

The answer is **target costing,** which is explained in Chapter 2b. Price is determined by the market. Costs have to come below this price.

2 Demand (Specimen paper)

FAST FORWARD **Economic theory** argues that the **higher the price of a good**, the **lower** will be the **quantity demanded**.

2.1 The economic analysis of demand

You will probably agree from your personal experience as a consumer that the theory of demand is essentially true: the higher the price of a good, the less will be quantity demanded. We have already seen that in practice it is by no means as straightforward as this (some goods are bought *because* they are expensive, for example, because the customer enjoys the status value of a high-priced item).

There are two extremes in the relationship between price and demand. A supplier can either **sell a certain quantity, Q, at any price** (as in graph (a)). Demand is totally unresponsive to changes in price and is said to be **completely inelastic**. Alternatively, **demand might be limitless at a certain price** P (as in graph (b)), but there would be no demand above price P and there would be little point in dropping the price below P. In such circumstances demand is said to be **completely elastic**. This situation may be faced by organisations in a highly competitive market, where they must sell at the prevailing market price. If they ⁀ their price any higher, they will not get any customers.

127

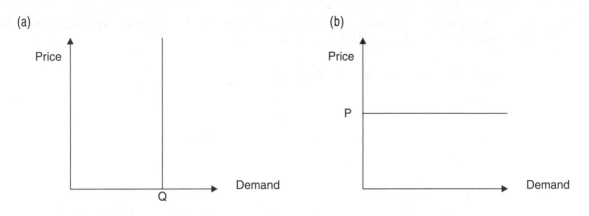

(a)

(b)

A more **normal situation** for companies that sell a unique product or service is shown below. The **downward-sloping** demand curve shows that demand will increase as prices are lowered, or demand will fall if the selling price is raised. There is 'elasticity' in demand, because sales demand responds to changes in the selling price.

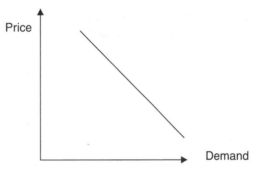

2.1.1 Price elasticity of demand (η)

The **price elasticity of demand (PED)** is a measure of the extent of change in demand for a good in response to a change in its price.

Key term

Price elasticity of demand (η) is a measure of the extent of change in market demand for a good in response to a change in its price. It is measured as:

$$\frac{\text{The change in quantity demanded, as a \% of demand}}{\text{The change in price, as a \% of the price}}$$

Since the demand goes up when the price falls, and goes down when the price rises, the elasticity has a negative value. However, it is usual to ignore the minus sign.

2.1.2 Example: Price elasticity of demand

The price of a good is $1.20 per unit and annual demand is 800,000 units. Market research indicates that an increase in price of 10 cents per unit will result in a fall in annual demand of 75,000 units. What is the price elasticity of demand between prices of $1.20 and $1.20 per unit?

Solution

Annual demand at $1.20 per unit is 800,000 units.

Annual demand at $1.30 per unit is 725,000 units.

% change in demand	=	(75,000/800,000) × 100% = 9.375%
% change in price	=	(0.10/1.20) × 100% = 8.333%
Price elasticity of demand	=	(−9.375/8.333) = −1.125

Ignoring the minus sign, price elasticity is 1.125.

The demand for this good, at a price of $1.20 per unit, would be referred to as **elastic** because the **price elasticity of demand is greater than 1**.

2.1.3 Elastic and inelastic demand

The value of demand elasticity may be anything from zero to infinity.

Demand is referred to as **inelastic** if the absolute value is less than 1 and **elastic** if the absolute value is greater than 1.

Think about what this means.

(a)   Where demand is **inelastic**, the **quantity demanded falls by a smaller percentage than the percentage increase in price**.

(b)   Where demand is **elastic, demand falls** by a **larger percentage than the percentage rise in price**.

2.1.4 Price elasticity and the slope of the demand curve

Generally, **demand curves slope downwards**. Consumers are willing to buy more at lower prices than at higher prices. In general, **elasticity** will **vary** in value **along the length of a demand curve**.

(a)   If a downward sloping demand curve becomes **steeper** over a particular range of quantity, then demand is becoming **more inelastic**.

(b)   A **shallower** demand curve over a particular range indicates **more elastic** demand.

The ranges of price elasticity at different points on a downward sloping straight line demand curve are illustrated in the diagram below.

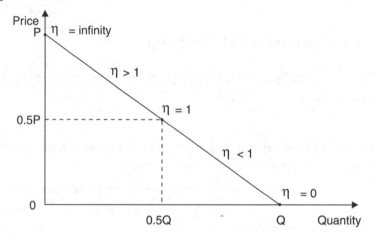

(a)   At **higher prices** on a straight line demand curve (the **top** of the demand curve), **small percentage price reductions** can bring **large percentage increases in the quantity** demanded. This means that **demand is elastic** over these ranges, and **price reductions** bring **increases in total expenditure** by consumers on the commodity in question.

(b)   At **lower prices** on a straight line demand curve (the **bottom** of the demand curve), **large percentage price reductions** can bring **small percentage increases in quantity**. This means that **demand is inelastic** over these price ranges, and **price increases** result in **increases in total expenditure**.

2.1.5 Special values of price elasticity

There are two special values of price elasticity of demand.

(a)   **Demand is perfectly inelastic ($\eta = 0$).** There is **no change in quantity** demanded, **regardless of the change in price**. The demand curve is **a vertical straight line** (as in graph (a) in Section 2.1).

(b) **Perfectly elastic demand ($\eta = \infty$).** Consumers will want to **buy an infinite amount**, but **only up to a particular price** level. Any price increase above this level will reduce demand to zero. The demand curve is a **horizontal straight line** (as in graph (b) in Section 2.1).

2.1.6 Elasticity and the pricing decision

In practice, organisations will have only a rough idea of the shape of their demand curve. There will only be a limited amount of data about quantities sold at certain prices over a period of time *and*, of course, factors other than price might affect demand. Because any conclusions drawn from such data can only give an indication of likely future behaviour, management skill and expertise are also needed. Despite this limitation, an **awareness of the concept of elasticity can assist management with pricing decisions**.

(a) (i) In circumstances of **inelastic demand**, **prices should be increased** because revenues will increase and total costs will reduce (because quantities sold will reduce).

(ii) In circumstances of **elastic demand**, increases in prices will bring decreases in revenue and decreases in price will bring increases in revenue. Management therefore have to **decide** whether the **increase/decrease in costs will be less than/greater than the increases/decreases in revenue**.

(b) In situations of **very elastic demand**, overpricing can lead to a massive drop in quantity sold and hence a massive drop in profits whereas underpricing can lead to costly stock outs and, again, a significant drop in profits. **Elasticity must therefore be reduced by creating a customer preference which is unrelated to price** (through advertising and promotional activities).

(c) In situations of **very inelastic demand**, customers are **not sensitive to price**. **Quality, service, product mix and location** are therefore **more important** to a firm's pricing strategy.

Question	Elasticity

Read the four statements below. Where the statement is expressed in layman's terms, rephrase it using the appropriate variant of the term *elasticity*. Where it is already phrased in terms of elasticity, translate it into layman's terms.

(a) We doubled sales of product A by dropping the price from $1.99 to $1.75.
(b) Price elasticity of product B is low.
(c) Demand for product C is highly inelastic.
(d) A large reduction in price will be necessary to stimulate further demand for product D.

Answer

Situation (a) is an example of elastic demand; (b) is a case of *inelasticity* and should be appropriately worded; (c) is the same as (b); (d) is also an example of inelasticity.

Question	Elasticity

A sales director believes that the price elasticity of demand for Product X is greater than 1, and he proposes to take advantage of this by reducing the selling price for Product X. What will happen to sales revenue and profit if the price is reduced?

Answer

If price elasticity of demand is greater than 1, a reduction in the selling price will result in an increase in the sales demand, so that total sales revenue increases.

However we do not know what will happen to total costs. Total costs will inevitably rise because more units of product will be made and sold. Without knowing more about the product's costs, we do not know by how much costs will rise.

Total profit may well increase, but there is also a possibility that profits will fall because the increase in costs will exceed the increase in revenue following the price rise.

2.2 Variables which influence demand

Here are some **variables which determine both the degree of elasticity and the volume of demand for a good in the market as a whole.**

Variable	Detail
Price of other goods	For some goods the market demand is connected to the price of other goods Such goods are of two types.
	(a) Substitutes, so that an increase in demand for one version of a good is likely to cause a decrease in demand for others. Common examples are rival brands of the same commodity (like Coca-Cola and Pepsi-Cola), bus journeys versus car journeys, or different forms of entertainment.
	(b) Complements, so that an increase in demand for one is likely to cause an increase in demand for the other. Examples are cups and saucers, cars and components, audits and tax consultancy.
Income	A rise in income gives households more to spend and they will want to buy more goods. However this phenomenon does not affect all goods in the same way.
	(a) Normal goods are those for which a rise in income increases the demand.
	(b) Inferior goods are those for which demand falls as income rises, such as cheap wine.
	(c) For some goods demand rises up to a certain point and then remains unchanged, because there is a limit to what consumers can or want to consume. Examples are basic foodstuffs such as salt and bread.
Tastes or fashion	A change in tastes or fashion will alter the demand for a good, or a particular variety of a good. Changes in taste may stem from psychological, social or economic causes. There is an argument that tastes and fashions are created by the producers of products and services. There is undeniably some truth in this, but the modern focus on responding to customers' needs and wants suggests otherwise.
Expectations	If consumers have expectations that prices will rise or that shortages will occur they will attempt to stock up on the product, thereby creating excess demand in the short term.
Obsolescence	Many products and services have to be replaced periodically because of obsolescence.
	(a) In early 2011 there will be substantial demand for audits for the year ended 31 December 2010. Demand will dry up once the statutory time limit for filing audited accounts is passed. In other words many services need to be bought repeatedly for reasons beyond the control of the consumer. A haircut is another example.
	(b) Physical goods are literally 'consumed'. Carpets become threadbare, glasses get broken, foodstuffs get eaten, children grow out of clothes.
	(c) Technological developments render some goods obsolete. Manual office equipment has been replaced by electronic equipment, because it does a better job, more quickly, quietly, efficiently and effectively.

2.3 Demand and the individual firm

We have looked at demand in the market as a whole. We also need to consider **factors that influence demand for one organisation's goods rather than another's.**

2.3.1 Product life cycle

FAST FORWARD

Most products pass through the five stages of the **product life cycle.**

The product life cycle was explained in the chapter on life cycle costing. A typical product goes through several phases in its commercial life: introduction, growth, maturity and decline.

(a) During the introduction phase of the life cycle, when the market is new, price is not affected by competition. There is little or no competition, so an organisation could (in theory) charge whatever price it wanted, and hope that customers will buy at that price. A choice of pricing strategies is possible at this stage, ranging from market skimming prices to market penetration prices. These pricing strategies are explained in more detail later.

(b) During the growth stage, prices may start to fall as competition increases. Price reductions are possible because sales demand is increasing, and as production and sales increase, unit costs fall.

(c) In the maturity stage of the life cycle, the price may be fairly stable, but some organisations may occasionally try to win market share with price reduction offers.

(d) In the decline stage of the life cycle, prices will change again. Prices may fall as fewer customers want to buy the product. Alternatively, prices may rise because when most suppliers withdraw from the market, the few remaining producers may be able to charge a higher price for a product that is now difficult to get hold of.

2.3.2 Quality

One firm's product may be perceived to be better quality than another's, and may in some cases actually be so, if it uses sturdier materials, goes faster or does whatever it is meant to do in a 'better' way. Other things being equal, the **better quality good** will be **more in demand** than other versions. Quality in a product gives the customer a sense of 'value' or benefit received, and they are prepared to pay more for extra value.

2.3.3 Marketing

You may be familiar with the 'four Ps' of the marketing mix, all of which influence demand for a firm's goods.

(a) **Price**

(b) **Product**

(c) **Place** refers to the place **where a good can be purchased**, or is likely to be purchased.

    (i) If potential buyers find that a particular version of a good is difficult to obtain, they will turn to substitutes.

    (ii) Some goods have no more than local appeal.

(d) **Promotion** refers to the various means by which firms draw attention to their products and services.

    (i) A good **brand name** is a strong and relatively permanent influence on demand.

    (ii) Demand can be stimulated by a variety of **promotional tools**, such as free gifts, money off, shop displays, direct mail and media advertising.

In recent years, emphasis has been placed, especially in marketing, on the **importance of non-profit factors** in demand. Thus the roles of product quality, promotion, personal selling and distribution and, in overall terms, brands, have grown. Whilst it can be relatively easy for a competitor to copy a price cut, at

least in the short term, it is much **more difficult to copy a successful brand image based on a unique selling proposition.** Successful branding can even imply premium pricing.

2.4 Deriving the demand equation

> You need to be able to derive the **demand equation** $P = a - bQ$.

An examination question may indicate that the demand curve for a product can be stated as a straight line equation: $P = a - bQ$.

In practice this is most unlikely to happen, but it is an aspect of pricing theory that you need to understand. You may be given sufficient information in a question to enable you to derive the demand curve.

Exam formulae

When demand is linear the equation for the demand curve is:

$P = a - bQ$

where
P = the price
Q = the quantity demanded
a = the price at which demand would be nil
b = $\dfrac{\text{change in price}}{\text{change in quantity}}$

The constant a is calculated as follows.

$a = \$(\text{current price}) + \left(\dfrac{\text{Current quantity at current price}}{\text{Change in quantity when price is changed by \$b}} \times \$b \right)$

This may look rather complicated in words, but it is very easy to use once you have learned the technique.

2.4.1 Example: Deriving the demand equation

The current price of a product is $12. At this price the company sells 60 items a month. One month the company decides to raise the price to $15, but only 45 items are sold at this price. Determine the demand equation, which is assumed to be a straight line equation.

Solution

Step 1 **Find the price at which demand would be nil**

Assuming demand is linear, each increase of $3 (from $12 to $15) in the price would result in a fall in demand of 15 units (from 60 to 45). For demand to fall to nil, the price needs to rise from its current level $12 by as many times as there are 15 units in 60 units (60/15 = 4) ie to $12 + (4 × $3) = $24.

$a = \$(\text{current price}) + \left(\dfrac{\text{Current quantity at current price}}{\text{Change in quantity when price is changed by \$b}} \times \$b \right)$

$a = \$12 + [(60/15) \times \$3)] = \$24$.

Step 2 **Calculate b**

$b = \dfrac{\text{change in price}}{\text{change in quantity}} = \dfrac{\$15 - \$12}{60 - 45} = \dfrac{3}{15} = 0.2$

The demand equation is therefore $P = 24 - 0.2Q$

Step 3 **Check your equation**

We can check this by finding Q when P is $12.

$P = 24 - 0.2Q$

$$12 = 24 - (0.2Q)$$
$$0.2Q = 24 - 12$$
$$0.2Q = 12$$
$$Q = \frac{12}{0.2} = 60$$

An alternative approach is to find 'b' first, then substitute the known value for 'b' into the demand function.

Step 1   Calculate b

$$b = \frac{\text{change in price}}{\text{change in quantity}} = \frac{\$15 - \$12}{60 - 45} = \frac{3}{15} = 0.2$$

Step 2   Substitute the known value for 'b' into the demand function to find 'a'

$$P = a - (0.2Q)$$

$$12 = a - (0.2 \times 60)$$

$$12 = a - 12$$

$$a = 24$$

The demand equation is therefore P = 24 − 0.2Q

Step 3   Check your equation

We can check this by finding Q when P is $12.

$$12 = 24 - (0.2Q)$$
$$0.2Q = 24 - 12$$
$$0.2Q = 12$$
$$Q = \frac{12}{0.2} = 60$$

Question   Deriving the demand equation

The current price of a product is $30 and its the producers sell 100 items a week at this price. One week the price is dropped by $3 as a special offer and the producers sell 150 items. Find an expression for the demand curve, assuming that this is a linear equation.

Answer

a	$= \$30 + (100/50 \times \$3)$ $= \$36$
b	$= \dfrac{\$3}{150 - 100} = 0.06$
P	$= 36 - 0.06Q$

Check

$$27 = 36 - 0.06Q$$
$$0.06Q = 36 - 27$$
$$Q = \frac{9}{0.06} = 150$$

2.5 The total cost function

Cost behaviour can be **modelled** using equations.

In order to decide a profit-maximising price and sales quantity, we need to consider costs as well as revenue.

Determining the optimum (profit-maximising) price and output level requires that both **cost and revenue behaviour** can be **modelled using equations**. These equations can range from simple to complex, although those you encounter in the exam will tend towards the 'simple' end of the range.

The cost function is likely to be expressed in terms of total costs = fixed costs plus variable costs.

For example, an organisation's total costs (TC) might be modelled by the equation $TC = 6,500 + 0.75Q$, where Q is the number of units sold.

Here the cost model is a simple linear equation of the form $y = a + bx$, where a ($6,500) represents the fixed costs and b ($0.75) represents the unit variable cost.

In your earlier studies, you will have covered how this equation can be derived using **linear regression analysis.** As you will remember, 'a' is the intercept of the line on the y axis and 'b' is the slope of the line.

The following graph demonstrates the total cost function.

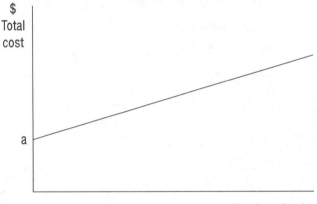

There are a number of **problems** associated with using such models.

(a) The cost model assumes fixed costs remain unchanged over all ranges of output. (Think about the possibility of step costs, say.)

(b) The cost model assumes a constant unit variable cost over all ranges of output. (Think about the implications of economies and diseconomies of scale.)

3 The profit-maximising price/output level

If we assume that there is a demand curve with the equation $P = a - bQ$, and a total cost function $C = F + vQ$, we can determine the profit-maximising price for the product.

Profits are maximised where **marginal cost (MC) = marginal revenue (MR)**. The **optimal selling price** can be determined by deriving equations for MC and MR. Alternatively, the **optimum selling price** can be determined using tabulation.

The overall objective of an organisation should be **profit maximisation**. In this section we look at how the profit-maximising price and output levels can be derived. In microeconomic theory, profits are maximised when marginal revenue = marginal cost.

If we have a demand curve $P = a - bQ$ and a total cost curve that states costs as fixed costs plus variable costs ($C = F + vQ$), we can calculate the selling price that will maximise profit. This is the price at which marginal cost equals marginal revenue (MC = MR).

3.1 Microeconomic theory and profit maximisation

In economics, **profit maximisation** is the process by which a firm determines the price and output level that returns the greatest profit. There are two common approaches to this problem.

(a) The **Total revenue (TR) – Total cost (TC)** method is based on the fact that profit equals revenue minus cost.

(b) The **Marginal revenue (MR) – Marginal cost (MC)** method is based on the fact that total profit in a perfect market reaches its maximum point where marginal revenue equals marginal cost.

To obtain the profit maximising output quantity under the TR – TC method, we start by recognising that profit is equal to total revenue minus total cost.

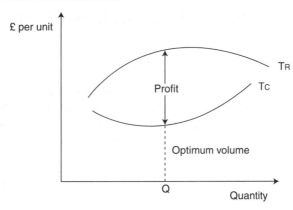

From the graph above it is evident that the difference between **total costs** and **total revenue** is greatest at point Q. This is the profit maximising output quantity.

3.2 MC = MR   6/11

Microeconomic theory suggests that as output increases, the marginal cost per unit may rise (due to the law of diminishing returns) as the quantity produced and sold increases. However when costs are the sum of fixed costs and variable costs, the marginal MC is the variable cost per unit for each additional unit that is made and sold.

Whenever a firm is faced with a downward sloping demand curve, the **marginal revenue per unit will decline**. By raising the sales price, total revenue may increase, but by an ever-decreasing amount.

Eventually, a level of output will be reached where the **extra cost** of making one extra unit of output is greater than the **extra revenue** obtained from its sale. It would then be unprofitable to make and sell that extra unit.

Profits will continue to be maximised only up to the output level where marginal cost has risen to be exactly equal to the marginal revenue.

Profits are maximised using marginalist theory when **marginal cost (MC) = marginal revenue (MR)**.

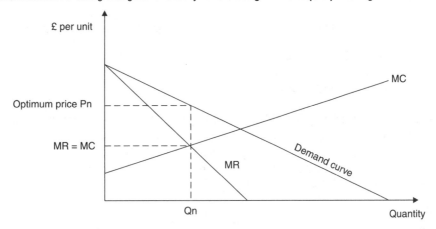

Profits are **maximised** at the point where **MC = MR**, ie at a volume of Qn units. If we add a demand curve to the graph, we can see that at an output level of Qn, the sales price per unit would be Pn.

It is important to make a clear distinction in your mind between the **sales price** and **marginal revenue**. In this example, the optimum price is Pn, but the marginal revenue is much less. This is because the 'additional' sales unit to reach output Qn has only been achieved by reducing the unit sales **price** from an amount higher than Pn for all the units to be sold, not just the marginal extra one. The increase in sales volume is therefore partly offset by a reduction in unit price; hence MR is lower than Pn.

<table>
<tr><td>**Exam focus point**</td><td>The examiner has noted that many candidates struggle to equate marginal cost and marginal revenue in order to calculate optimum price and quality.</td></tr>
</table>

3.3 Determining the profit-maximising selling price: using equations

The **optimal selling price** can be determined by deriving equations for MC and MR (and profits are maximised where **MC = MR**).

In your exam, you may be **provided with the equations for marginal cost and marginal revenue** or you may have to **devise them from information** in the question. Remember, **marginal cost** is the **extra cost of producing one extra unit**, **marginal revenue** is the **extra revenue from selling one extra unit**. **Marginal revenue may not be the same as** the **price** charged for all units up to that demand level, as to increase volumes the price may have to be reduced.

Section 2.4 explained how to derive an equation for the demand curve. The marginal revenue curve is derived from the demand curve.

When $P = a - bQ$

$MR = a - 2bQ$

where P = the price
  Q = the quantity demanded
  a = the price at which demand would be nil
  $b = \dfrac{\text{change in price}}{\text{change in quantity}}$

The following step-by-step approach can be applied to most questions involving algebra and pricing.

Step 1   Establish the demand function (find the values for 'a' and 'b')

Step 2   Obtain a value for MR from the demand curve. $MR = a - 2bQ$

Step 2   Establish MC (the marginal cost). This will simply be the variable cost per unit

Step 4   To maximise profit, equate MC and MR to find Q

Step 5   Substitute Q into the demand function and solve to find P (the optimum price)

You will need to be able to solve simple examples like those that follow.

3.3.1 Example: MC = MR

MOC makes and sells a copyrighted, executive game for two distinct markets, in which it has a monopoly. The fixed costs of production per month are $20,000 and variable costs per unit produced, and sold, are $40. (The monthly sales can be thought of as X, where $X = X_1 + X_2$, with X_1 and X_2 denoting monthly sales in their respective markets.) Detailed market research has revealed the demand functions in the markets to be as follows, with prices shown as P_1, P_2.

Market 1: $P_1 = 55 - 0.05X_1$
Market 2: $P_2 = 200 - 0.2X_2$

(Note. These formulae are simply **linear equations**. They show how the price (P) can be determined for a given level of demand (X). So in market 1, at a level of demand of 100, the price (P) will be 55 − (0.05 × 100) = 50.)

From these, the management accountant has derived that the marginal revenue functions in the two markets are as follows.

Market 1: $MR_1 = 55 − 0.1X_1$
Market 2: $MR_2 = 200 − 0.4X_2$

(Note. In market 1, the marginal revenue if 100 units are sold is 55 − (0.1 × 100) = 45.)

The management accountant believes there should be price discrimination; the price is currently $50 per game in either market.

Required

Analyse the information for the executive game and, given the management accountant's belief, do the following.

(a)   Calculate the price to charge in each market, and the quantity to produce (and sell) each month, to maximise profit.

(b)   Determine the revenue function for each market and the maximum monthly profit in total.

(c)   Calculate and comment on the change in total profitability and prices.

Solution

(a)   In both markets, **marginal cost = variable cost per unit** = $40

Profit is maximised when **marginal revenue = marginal cost**.

Market 1
$55 − 0.1X_1$ $= 40$
$0.1X_1$ $= 15$
X_1 $= 15/0.1 = 150$
and price $P_1 = 55 − (0.05 × 150) = 47.5.

Hence the price in market 1 should be $47.50 per unit and 150 units should be produced.

Market 2
$200 − 0.4X_2$ $= 40$
$0.4X_2$ $= 160$
X_2 $= 160/0.4 = 400$
and price $P_2 = 200 − (0.2 × 400) = 120.

Hence the price in market 2 should be $120 per unit and 400 units should be produced.

Total number of items to be produced per month is 550.

(b)   **Revenue = unit price × number of units sold**

Market 1

Revenue $= P_1X_1 = 55X_1 − 0.05X_1^2$

Market 2

Revenue $= P_2X_2 = 200X_2 − 0.2X_2^2$

From (a), profit is maximised when

$X_1 = 150$ and $X_2 = 400$

$P_1 = 47.5$ and $P_2 = 120$

At maximum profit:

Total revenue $= (47.5 × 150) + (120 × 400) = $55,125$

Total costs = 20,000 + (40 × 550) = $42,000

Total maximum monthly profit = $13,125

(c)　Currently the price is $50 in both markets.

Market 1　　$50 = 55 - 0.05X_1$

$0.05X_1 = 55 - 50 = 5$

$X_1 = 5/0.05 = 100$

Market 2　　$50 = 200 - 0.2X_2$

$0.2X_2 = 200 - 50 = 150$

$X_2 = 150/0.2 = 750$

Therefore the **total number of units** = 100 + 750 = 850.

Total revenue = $50 × 850 = $42,500.

Total cost = 20,000 + (40 × 850) = $54,000.

So the game **currently makes a loss** of $11,500.

Hence, if the prices are changed to $47.50 in market 1 and $120 in market 2, the company can expect to turn a monthly loss of $11,500 into a profit of $13,125.

You will be provided with equations representing MC and MR if they are needed. Note, however, that if a question states that the extra cost of producing one extra item is $20, say, you will be expected to realise that the MC is $20. Likewise, if you are told that **100 units are sold for $10 each**, but **101 can only be sold for $9.99**, the **MR of the 101st item is (101 × $9.99) – (100 × $10) = $8.99**.

Question

Deriving a MR equation from the demand curve

AB has used market research to determine that if a price of $250 is charged for product G, demand will be 12,000 units. It has also been established that demand will rise or fall by 5 units for every $1 fall/rise in the selling price. The marginal cost of product G is $80.

Required

If marginal revenue = a –2bQ when the selling price (P) = a – bQ, calculate the profit-maximising selling price for product G.

Answer

$b = \dfrac{\text{change in price}}{\text{change in quantity}} = \dfrac{\$1}{5} = 0.2$

$a = \$250 + ((12,000/5) \times \$1) = \$2,650$

$MR = 2,650 - (2 \times 0.2)Q \quad = 2,650 - 0.4Q$

Profits are maximised when MC = MR, i.e. when $80 = 2,650 - 0.4Q$

$2,650 - 80 = 2,570 \times \dfrac{10}{4} = 6,425$

Profit-maximising demand　= 6,425

Now, substitute the values into the demand curve equation to find the profit-maximising selling price

$P = a - bQ$

$P = 2,650 - (0.2 \times 6,425)$

∴ Profit-maximising price　= $(2,650 - 1,285)

　　　　　　　　　　　　= $1,365

3.4 Determining the profit-maximising selling price: visual inspection of a tabulation of data

The **optimum selling price** can also be determined using tabulation.

To determine the profit-maximising selling price:

(a) Work out the **demand curve** and hence the **price** and the **total revenue** (PQ) at various levels of demand.

(b) Calculate **total cost** and hence **marginal cost** at each level of demand.

(c) Finally calculate **profit** at each level of demand, thereby determining the price and level of demand at which profits are maximised.

Question   Tabulation approach to find profit-maximising price

An organisation operates in a market where there is imperfect competition, so that to sell more units of output, it must reduce the sales price of all the units it sells. The following data is available for prices and costs.

Total output Units	Sales price per unit (AR) $	Average cost of output (AC) $ per unit
0	–	–
1	504	720
2	471	402
3	439	288
4	407	231
5	377	201
6	346	189
7	317	182
8	288	180
9	259	186
10	232	198

The total cost of zero output is $600.

Required

Complete the table below to determine the output level and price at which the organisation would maximise its profits, assuming that fractions of units cannot be made.

Units	Price $	Total revenue $	Marginal revenue $	Total cost $	Marginal cost $	Profit $
0						
1						
2						
3						
4						
5						
6						
7						
8						
9						
10						

The correct answer is that profit is maximised at seven units of output and a price of $317, when MR is most nearly equal to MC.

Units	Price $	Total revenue $	Marginal revenue $	Total cost $	Marginal cost $	Profit $
0	0	0	0	600	–	(600)
1	504	504	504	720	120	(216)
2	471	942	438	804	84	138
3	439	1,317	375	864	60	453
4	407	1,628	311	924	60	704
5	377	1,885	257	1,005	81	880
6	346	2,076	191	1,134	129	942
7	317	2,219	143	1,274	140	945
8	288	2,304	85	1,440	166	864
9	259	2,331	27	1,674	234	657
10	232	2,320	(11)	1,980	306	340

4 Decisions to increase production and sales   12/07

FAST FORWARD

> If you are required to evaluate a decision to increase production and sales levels, you will need to consider **incremental costs**, **incremental revenues** and other factors.

Key term

> **Incremental costs and revenues** are the difference between costs and revenues for the corresponding items under each alternative being considered.   *Drury*

The **incremental cost** of increasing production from 500 to 600 units per month is the additional cost of producing an extra 100 units each month. If fixed costs increase as a result of the decision, they are an incremental cost together with the increased variable costs of production.

4.1 Example: A decision to increase production

George manufactures a product which uses two types of material, A and B. Each unit of production currently sells for $10. A local trader has expressed an interest in buying 5,000 units but is only prepared to pay $9 per unit.

Current costs and revenues are as follows.

	$'000	$'000
Sales		350
Less production costs		
Material A – 1 kg per unit	25	
Material B – 1 litre per unit	50	
Labour – 1 hour per unit	75	
Variable overhead	50	
Fixed overhead	25	
Non-production costs	25	
Total cost		250
Budgeted profit		100

The following additional information has also been made available.

(a)   There is minimal inventory of material available and prices for new material are expected to be 5% higher for Material A and 3% higher for Material B.

(b)   George has been having problems with his workforce and is short of labour hours. He currently has the capacity to produce 36,000 units but would have to employ contract labour at $3.50 per hour to make any additional units.

(c)   Included in the fixed production overhead is the salary of the production manager. He is stressed and exhausted and has threatened to leave unless he receives a pay rise of $5,000. George would not be able to fulfil any new orders without him.

Required

Evaluate whether George should accept the new order.

Solution

Workings

Current production = 350,000/10 = 35,000 units

Current cost per unit of Material A $= \dfrac{\$25,000}{35,000} = \$0.71$

Current cost per unit of Material B $= \dfrac{\$50,000}{35,000} = \$1.43$

Current cost of labour $= \dfrac{\$75,000}{35,000} = \$2.14$

	$	$
Incremental revenue (5,000 × $9)		45,000
Incremental costs		
Material A (1.05 × $0.71 × 5,000)	3,728	
Material B (1.03 × $1.43 × 5,000)	7,365	
Labour [(1,000 × $2.14) + (4,000 × $3.50)]	16,140	
Fixed overhead	5,000	
		32,233
Incremental profit		12,767

The new order would produce an additional $12,767 so is probably worthwhile but other factors may need to be considered. For example, the effect of a price cut on existing customer expectations and whether the workforce and production manager will be able to fulfil the new order with the same labour efficiency.

4.1.1 Offering volume based discounts

Key term

> A **volume-based discount** is a discount given for buying in bulk.

An organisation may wish to consider offering a volume-based discount to customers for purchases above a certain quantity. The intention may be that by offering the sale price discount, customers will buy more of the product.

To decide whether a volume-based discount on selling prices is financially worthwhile, the following calculation is needed:

By reducing the selling price with a volume based discount and reducing the price from P_1 to P_2, sales volume may be expected to increase from Q_1 to Q_2. Assume that the variable cost of sale is $V per unit, and fixed costs will be unaffected by a change in sales volume.

	$
Total sales revenue at discounted price	(Q2 × P2)
Total sales revenue at non-discounted price	(Q1 × P1)
Increase in sales revenue	Difference
Increase in costs	(Q2 – Q1) × V

Change in profit = (Q2 × P2) – (Q1 × P1) – [(Q2 – Q1) × V]

For example, suppose that a company sells a product at a price of $10 per unit. The unit variable cost is $4. The sales manager believes that by offering a customer a discount of 5% for buying at least 5,000 units a year, the customer will increase purchases from his current level of 4,000 units to a level of 5,000 units per year.

The effect on profits each year would be calculated as follows.

	$
Total sales revenue at discounted price: 5,000 × $10 × 95%	47,500
Total sales revenue at non-discounted price: 4,000 × $10	40,000
Increase in sales revenue	7,500
Increase in costs (1,000 units × $4)	4,000
Increase in annual profit from volume –based price discounting	3,500

5 Price strategies

FAST FORWARD

> The price to be charged for a product or service is often one of the most important decisions made by business organisations. There are a number of alternative pricing strategies.

5.1 Cost-plus pricing

FAST FORWARD

> **Full cost-plus pricing** is a method of deciding the sales price by adding a percentage mark-up for profit to the full cost of the product.

In practice cost is one of the most important influences on price. Many firms base price on simple **cost-plus rules** (costs are estimated and then a profit margin is added in order to set the price).

The 'full cost' may be a fully absorbed production cost only, or it may include some absorbed administration, selling and distribution overhead.

A business might have an idea of the percentage profit margin it would like to earn, and so might **decide on an average profit mark-up** as a general guideline for pricing decisions.

Businesses that carry out a large amount of **contract work or jobbing work**, for which individual job or contract prices must be quoted regularly would find this a useful method to adopt. Since every job or contract is different, there are no market prices; and in the absence of a market price, adding a profit mark-up to cost provides a logical way to decide the selling price. The percentage profit **mark-up**, however, **does not have to be rigid and fixed**, but can be varied to suit different circumstances.

5.1.1 Example: Full cost-plus pricing

Markup Co has begun to produce a new product, Product X, for which the following cost estimates have been made.

	$
Direct materials	27
Direct labour: 4 hrs at $5 per hour	20
Variable production overheads: machining, ½ hr at $6 per hour	3
	50

Production fixed overheads are budgeted at $300,000 per month and because of the shortage of available machining capacity, the company will be restricted to 10,000 hours of machine time per month. The absorption rate will be a direct labour rate, however, and budgeted direct labour hours are 25,000 per month. It is estimated that the company could obtain a minimum contribution of $10 per machine hour on producing items other than product X.

The direct cost estimates are not certain as to material usage rates and direct labour productivity, and it is recognised that the estimates of direct materials and direct labour costs may be subject to an error of ± 15%. Machine time estimates are similarly subject to an error of ± 10%.

The company wishes to make a profit of 20% on full production cost from product X.

Required

Ascertain the full cost-plus based price.

Solution

Even for a relatively 'simple' cost-plus pricing estimate, some problems can arise, and certain assumptions must be made and stated. In this example, we can identify two problems.

- Should the opportunity cost of machine time be included in cost or not?
- What allowance, if any, should be made for the possible errors in cost estimates?

Different assumptions could be made.

(a) **Exclude machine time opportunity costs: ignore possible costing errors**

	$
Direct materials	27.00
Direct labour (4 hours)	20.00
Variable production overheads	3.00
Fixed production overheads	48.00
(at $\dfrac{\$300,000}{25,000}$ = $12 per direct labour hour)	
Full production cost	98.00
Profit mark-up (20%)	19.60
Selling price per unit of product X	117.60

(b) **Include machine time opportunity costs: ignore possible costing errors**

	$
Full production cost as in (a)	98.00
Opportunity cost of machine time:	
contribution forgone (½ hr × $10)	5.00
Adjusted full cost	103.00
Profit mark-up (20%)	20.60
Selling price per unit of product X	123.60

A problem with this approach is that since the opportunity cost of machine is contribution forgone, it must include some element for profit. Adding a profit margin to a figure that already includes profit is arguably being 'greedy'. This may set the price at a high level that the customer may refuse to accept.

(c) **Exclude machine time opportunity costs but make full allowance for possible under-estimates of cost**

	$	$
Direct materials	27.00	
Direct labour	20.00	
	47.00	
Possible error (15%)	7.05	
		54.05
Variable production overheads	3.00	
Possible error (10%)	0.30	
		3.30

	$	$
Fixed production overheads (4 hrs × $12)	48.00	
Possible error (labour time) (15%)	7.20	
		55.20
Potential full production cost		112.55
Profit mark-up (20%)		22.51
Selling price per unit of product X		135.06

(d)   **Include machine time opportunity costs and make a full allowance for possible under-estimates of cost**

	$
Potential full production cost as in (c)	112.55
Opportunity cost of machine time:	
Potential contribution forgone (½ hr × $10 × 110%)	5.50
Adjusted potential full cost	118.05
Profit mark-up (20%)	23.61
Selling price per unit of product X	141.66

Using different assumptions, we could arrive at any of four different unit prices in the range $117.60 to $141.66.

5.1.2 Disadvantages of full cost-plus pricing

There are several disadvantages with cost-plus pricing.

(a)   It fails to recognise that since demand may be determining price, there will be a profit-maximising combination of price and demand.

(b)   There may be a need to **adjust prices to market and demand conditions**. When there is an existing market price for the product, that competitors are charging, prices based on 'cost plus' may be uncompetitive.

(c)   **Budgeted output volume** needs to be established. Output volume is a key factor in the overhead absorption rate and so in the calculation of full cost. If there is over- or under-absorption due to incorrect estimates of production capacity, measures of full cost will be too high or too low.

(d)   A **suitable basis for overhead absorption** must be selected, where a business produces more than one product. Some products may be charged with too much overhead, so that the full cost and selling price are too high (at a price that customers may be unwilling to pay); and other products may be charged with too little overhead, so that the selling price is too low.

5.1.3 Advantages of full cost-plus pricing

Full cost plus pricing has some advantages.

(a)   It is a **quick, simple and cheap** method of pricing which can be delegated to junior managers.

(b)   Since the size of the profit margin can be varied, a decision based on a price in excess of full cost should ensure that a company working at normal capacity will **cover all of its fixed costs and make a profit**.

(c)   When there is no market price for the product, deciding a price by adding a profit margin to cost is a logical approach, which seeks to ensure that the organisation makes a profit.

Question	Full cost-plus method

A company budgets to make 20,000 units which have a variable cost of production of $4 per unit. Fixed production costs are $60,000 per annum. If the selling price is to be 40% higher than full cost, what is the selling price of the product using the full cost-plus method?

Answer

Full cost per unit = variable cost + fixed cost

Variable cost = $4 per unit

Fixed cost = $\frac{\$60,000}{20,000}$ = $3 per unit

Full cost per unit = $(4 + 3) = $7

∴ Selling price using full cost-plus pricing method = $7.00 × $\frac{140\%}{100}$

= $9.80

5.2 Marginal cost-plus pricing

5.2.1 Introduction

FAST FORWARD

> **Marginal cost-plus pricing, also called mark-up pricing,** involves adding a profit margin to the marginal cost of the product.

Whereas a full cost-plus approach to pricing draws attention to net profit and the net profit margin, a variable cost-plus approach to pricing **draws attention to gross profit** and the **gross profit margin**, or **contribution**.

Question   Profit margin

A product has the following costs.

	$
Direct materials	5
Direct labour	3
Variable overheads	7

Fixed overheads are $10,000 per month. Budgeted sales per month are 400 units to allow the product to break even.

Required

Determine the profit margin which needs to be added to *marginal* cost to allow the product to break even.

Answer

Breakeven point is when total contribution equals fixed costs.

At breakeven point, $10,000 = 400 (price – $15)

∴ $25 = price – $15
∴ $40 = price
∴ Profit margin = (40 – 15) / 15 × 100% = 166%

5.2.2 Advantages of marginal cost-plus pricing

Marginal cost pricing has several advantages.

(a) It is a **simple and easy** method to use.

(b) The **mark-up percentage can be varied**, and so mark-up pricing can be adjusted to reflect demand conditions.

(c) It **draws management attention to contribution**, and the effects of higher or lower sales volumes on profit. For example, if a product costs $10 per unit and a mark-up of 150% ($15) is added to reach a price of $25 per unit, management should be clearly aware that every additional $1 of sales revenue would add 60 cents to contribution and profit ($15 ÷ $25 = $0.60).

(d) In practice, mark-up pricing is **used** in businesses **where there is a readily-identifiable basic variable cost**. **Retail industries** are the most obvious example, and it is quite common for the prices of goods in shops to be fixed by adding a mark-up (20% or 33.3%, say) to the purchase cost.

5.2.3 Disadvantages of marginal cost-plus pricing

There are also disadvantages with marginal cost plus pricing.

(a) Although the size of the mark-up can be varied in accordance with demand conditions, it does not ensure that sufficient attention is paid to demand conditions, competitors' prices and profit maximisation.

(b) It **ignores fixed overheads and sales volumes** in the pricing decision, but the sales price must be sufficiently high to ensure that a profit is made after covering fixed costs.

5.3 Full cost pricing versus marginal cost pricing

Perhaps the most important **criticism** of full cost pricing is that it **fails to recognise** that since sales demand may be determined by the sales price, there will be a **profit-maximising combination** of price and demand. A full cost based approach to pricing will be most unlikely, except by coincidence or 'luck', to arrive at the profit-maximising price. In contrast, a marginal costing approach to looking at costs and prices would be more likely to help with identifying a profit-maximising price.

5.3.1 Example: Full cost versus profit-maximising prices

Tigger has budgeted to make 50,000 units of its product, timm. The variable cost of a timm is $5 and annual fixed costs are expected to be $150,000.

The financial director of Tigger has suggested that a profit margin of 25% on full cost should be charged for every product sold.

The marketing director has challenged the wisdom of this suggestion, and has produced the following estimates of sales demand for timms.

Price per unit	Demand
$	Units
9	42,000
10	38,000
11	35,000
12	32,000
13	27,000

Required

(a) Calculate the profit for the year if a full cost price is charged.
(b) Calculate the profit-maximising price.

Assume in both (a) and (b) that 50,000 units of timm are produced regardless of sales volume.

Solution

(a) (i) The full cost per unit is $5 variable cost plus $3 fixed costs, ie $8 in total. A 25% mark-up on this cost gives a selling price of $10 per unit so that sales demand would be 38,000 units. (Production is given as 50,000 units.)

	$	$
Profit (absorption costing)		
Sales		380,000
Costs of production (50,000 units)		
Variable (50,000 × $5)	250,000	
Fixed (50,000 × $3)	150,000	
	400,000	
Less increase in inventory (12,000 units × 8)	(96,000)	
Cost of sales		304,000
Profit		76,000

(ii) **Profit using marginal costing** instead of absorption costing, so that fixed overhead costs are written off in the period they occur, would be as follows. (The 38,000 unit demand level is chosen for comparison.)

	$
Contribution (38,000 × $(10 – 5))	190,000
Fixed costs	150,000
Profit	40,000

Since the company cannot go on indefinitely producing an output volume in excess of sales volume, this profit figure is more indicative of the profitability of timms in the longer term.

(b) A **profit-maximising price** is one which gives the greatest net (relevant) cash flow, which in this case is the **contribution-maximising price**.

Price	Unit contribution	Demand	Total contribution
$	$	Units	$
9	4	42,000	168,000
10	5	38,000	190,000
11	6	35,000	210,000
12	7	32,000	224,000
13	8	27,000	216,000

The profit maximising price is $12, with annual sales demand of 32,000 units.

This example shows that a **cost based price** is **unlikely to be the profit-maximising** price, and that a **marginal costing approach**, calculating the total contribution at a variety of different selling prices, will be **more helpful** for establishing what the profit-maximising price ought to be.

5.3.2 Cost plus pricing versus target costing

As you should remember from Chapter 2b on target costing, **target prices** are set in order to achieve a desired market share. Deduction of a desired profit margin produces the cost that has to be achieved. Design specifications and production methods are examined to establish ways in which the target cost can be met without reducing the value of the product to the customer.

Such an approach is likely to **offer greater competitive advantage** than cost plus pricing, being far more **strategically orientated** as it **takes account of the external environment**.

However target prices are probably more relevant to new product design and development, when the organisation identifies a selling price that will be needed if the product is to be competitive in the market place.

5.4 Market skimming pricing

> Pricing strategies for new products include **market skimming** and **market penetration pricing**.

Key term

> **Price skimming** involves charging high prices when a new product is first launched on the market, in order to maximise short-term profitability. Initially there is heavy spending on advertising and sales promotion to encourage sales demand. As the product moves into the later stages of its life cycle (growth, maturity and decline) progressively lower prices are charged. The profitable 'cream' is thus skimmed off in stages until sales can only be sustained at lower prices.

The aim of market skimming is to gain **high unit profits** early in the product's life, in the hope of recovering the costs of investment quickly. High unit prices make it more likely that **competitors** will enter the market than if lower prices were to be charged.

A price skimming policy may be appropriate in the cases below.

(a) The product is **new and different**, so that customers are prepared to pay high prices so as to be one up on other people who do not own it.

(b) The strength of **demand** and the sensitivity of demand to price are **unknown**. It is better from the point of view of marketing to start by charging high prices and then reduce them if the demand for the product turns out to be price elastic than to start by charging low prices and then attempt to raise them substantially if demand appears to be insensitive to higher prices.

(c) High prices in the early stages of a product's life might generate **high initial cash flows**. A firm with liquidity problems may prefer market-skimming for this reason.

(d) The firm can identify **different market segments** for the product, each prepared to pay progressively lower prices. It may therefore be possible to continue to sell at higher prices to some market segments when lower prices are charged in others. This is discussed further below.

(e) Products may have a **short life cycle**, and so need to recover their development costs and make a profit relatively quickly.

Products to which the policy has been applied include:

- Calculators
- Video recorders
- Desktop computers

5.5 Market penetration pricing

Key term

> **Penetration pricing** is a policy of low prices when a product is first launched in order to obtain strong demand for the product as soon as it is launched on the market. Low prices should encourage bigger demand.

A penetration pricing policy may be appropriate in the cases below.

(a) The firm wishes to **discourage new entrants** into the market.

(b) The firm wishes to **shorten the initial period** of the product's life cycle in order to enter the growth and maturity stages as quickly as possible.

(c) There are significant **economies of scale** to be achieved from a high volume of output.

(d) Demand is **highly elastic** and so would respond well to low prices.

Penetration prices are prices which aim to secure a substantial share in a substantial total market. A firm might therefore deliberately build **excess production capacity** and set its prices very low. As demand builds up the spare capacity will be used up gradually and unit costs will fall; the firm might even reduce prices further as unit costs fall. In this way, early losses will enable the firm to dominate the market and have the lowest costs.

150   **5: Pricing decisions** | Part B Decision-making techniques

BPP
LEARNING MEDIA

5.6 Complementary product pricing

Complementary products are goods that tend to be bought and used together. If an organisation makes and sells complementary products, it may wish to decide the selling prices for the products in a single pricing policy decision.

Complementary products are sold separately but are **connected** and dependent on each other for sales, for example, an electric toothbrush and replacement toothbrush heads. The electric toothbrush may be priced competitively to attract demand but the replacement heads can be relatively expensive.

On the other hand, the decision could be to set low prices for all the complementary products (or high prices for all complementary products) so that the expected sales demand for each is consistent. For example a company selling digital book readers may also sell digital books. The prices of both may be set low in order to win sufficient sales demand for all the products. (This would be a different policy from, say, charging low prices for digital books but a high price for the reader.)

A **loss leader** is when a company sets a very low price for one product intending to make consumers buy other products in the range which carry higher profit margins. Another example is selling razors at very low prices whilst selling the blades for them at a higher profit margin. People will buy many of the high profit items but only one of the low profit items – yet they are 'locked in' to the former by the latter. This can also be described as **captive product pricing**.

Loss leaders are common in retailing, where stores may advertise very low prices for selected products, hoping that this will attract customers into the store where they will also buy other products that are 'normally' priced.

5.7 Product line pricing

A **product line** is a group of products that are related to one another. A product line may be a range of branded products, and a consistent pricing policy should be applied to all the products in the range.

A **product line** is the marketing strategy of offering for sale several related products. A line can comprise related products of various sizes, types, colours, qualities, or prices. Demand for and costs of the products are likely to be **inter-related.** For example a company may manufacture a range of hygiene and skin care products, such as soaps, shower gels, bath oils and so on, under the same brand name. With product line pricing, there will be a consistent pricing policy for all the products in the range.

There is a range of product line pricing strategies.

(a)   Set prices proportional to full or marginal cost with the same percentage profit margin for all products. This means that prices are dependent on cost and ignore demand.

(b)   Set prices reflecting the demand relationships between the products so that an overall required rate of return is achieved.

(c)   Set prices that reflect customer opinion about the quality of the products, and how they compare with similar products of competitor organisations.

5.8 Volume discounting

A **volume discount** is a reduction in price given for larger than average purchases.

The aim of a volume discount is to increase sales from large customers. The discount acts as a form of **differentiation** between types of customer (wholesale, retail and so on).

The reduced costs of a large order will hopefully compensate for the loss of revenue from offering the discount.

5.9 Price discrimination

FAST FORWARD With **price discrimination**, the same product or service is sold at different prices to different customers. This can be very difficult to implement in practice because it relies for success upon the continued existence of certain market conditions.

In certain circumstances the **same product** can be sold at different prices to **different customers**.

Key term

> **Price discrimination** is the practice of charging different prices for the same product to different groups of buyers when these prices are not reflective of cost differences.

There are a number of bases on which such discriminating prices can be set.

(a) **By market segment**. A cross-channel ferry company would market its services at different prices in England and France, for example. Items such as cinema tickets and hairdressing services are often available at lower prices to old age pensioners, students or juveniles.

(b) **By product version**. Many car models have 'add on' extras which enable one brand to appeal to a wider cross-section of customers. The final price need not reflect the cost price of the add on extras directly. Usually the top-of-the-range model carries a price much in excess of the cost of provision of the extras, as a prestige appeal.

(c) **By place**. Theatre seats are usually sold according to their location so that patrons pay different prices for the same performance according to the type of seat and its location in the theatre auditorium.

(d) **By time**. This is perhaps the most popular type of price discrimination. Off-peak travel bargains, hotel prices and telephone charges are all attempts to increase sales revenue by covering variable but not necessarily average cost of provision. Railway companies are successful price discriminators, charging more to rush hour rail commuters whose demand is inelastic at certain times of the day.

Price discrimination can only be effective if a number of **conditions** hold.

(a) The market must be **segmentable** in price terms, and different sectors must show different intensities of demand. Each of the sectors must be identifiable, distinct and separate from the others, and be accessible to the firm's marketing communications.

(b) There must be little or **no** chance of a **black market** developing (this would allow those in the lower priced segment to resell to those in the higher priced segment).

(c) There must be little or **no** chance that **competitors** can and will undercut the firm's prices in the higher priced (and/or most profitable) market segments.

(d) The cost of segmenting and **administering** the arrangements should not exceed the extra revenue derived from the price discrimination strategy.

Try the following question which, although it has a few 'tricks', **looks more daunting than it is** if you keep your head and take care.

Question	Differential pricing

Curltown Cinemas operates a chain of 30 cinemas. Standard admission price is $7 per person, but this is subject to certain discounts. Average attendance at a cinema per month on normal price days is 5,000 people, but this is expected to be subject to seasonal variation, as follows.

Month	J	F	M	A	M	J	J	A	S	O	N	D
%	+10	−2	0	+5	−5	−5	+10	+7	−4	−4	0	+12

In December, January, July and August audiences are made up of 60% under-14s, who pay half-price admission. For the rest of the year under 14s represent only 10% of the audience. One day per month all tickets are sold at a special offer price of $1, irrespective of the age of the customer. This invariably guarantees a full house of 200 customers.

Required

(a) What is Curltown Cinemas' total revenue from cinema admissions for a year?

(b) If Curltown puts up prices for over-14s (other than the $1 special offer price) to $8 what will its total revenue from cinema admissions be for the year?

(c) Should the special offer be continued?

Answer

(a) This is simply a matter of reading the question carefully and patiently tabulating the data using a **different layout** to the one given in the question. Note that you save yourself potential error if you convert percentages into decimals as you transfer the question information into your own table. Don't forget that there are 30 cinemas.

Month	Variation	Average no	Adjusted no	Full price	Revenue @ $7.00 $	Half price	Revenue @ $3.50 $
Jan	+0.10	5,000	5,500	0.4	15,400.00	0.6	11,550.00
Feb	-0.02	5,000	4,900	0.9	30,870.00	0.1	1,715.00
Mar	+0.00	5,000	5,000	0.9	31,500.00	0.1	1,750.00
Apr	+0.05	5,000	5,250	0.9	33,075.00	0.1	1,837.50
May	-0.05	5,000	4,750	0.9	29,925.00	0.1	1,662.50
Jun	-0.05	5,000	4,750	0.9	29,925.00	0.1	1,662.50
Jul	+0.10	5,000	5,500	0.4	15,400.00	0.6	11,550.00
Aug	+0.07	5,000	5,350	0.4	14,980.00	0.6	11,235.00
Sept	-0.04	5,000	4,800	0.9	30,240.00	0.1	1,680.00
Oct	-0.04	5,000	4,800	0.9	30,240.00	0.1	1,680.00
Nov	0.00	5,000	5,000	0.9	31,500.00	0.1	1,750.00
Dec	+0.12	5,000	5,600	0.4	15,680.00	0.6	11,760.00
					308,735.00		59,832.50

	$
Total normal price ($308,735.00 + $59,832.50)	368,567.50
Special offer (12 × $1 × 200)	2,400.00
Total per cinema	370,967.50
Total per 30 cinemas	11,129,025.00

(b) **There is no need to work out all the numbers again at the new prices.**

	$
Total as calculated above	11,129,025.00
Less: current adult normal price ($308,735 × 30)	(9,262,050.00)
Add: revised adult normal price ($308,735 × 30 × 8/7)	10,585,200.00
	12,452,175.00

(c) If the income of $200 per cinema on the twelve special offer days is compared with an average of, say, $368,567.50/(365 – 12 days) = over $1,000, then it is clearly not worthwhile. The cinemas get average attendances of (5000 × 12)/365 = about 164 people in any case, even without special offers. (You could do **rough calculations** to estimate the overall loss of revenue per annum. Try it, making any **assumptions** you need, if you haven't done so, but not at the expense of written comments.)

However, the offer is a **loss-leader** which probably has other benefits. Customers will like it, and if the film they see is a good one they will recommend it to their friends. It may help to encourage the

cinema-going habit amongst potential new customers. You may have thought of other relevant comments, either in favour of the policy or against it.

Exam focus point

> A Section B exam question on this topic may have fewer calculations and more interpretation/analysis, so make sure you really think about the implications of price discrimination.

5.10 Relevant cost pricing

FAST FORWARD

> Special orders may require a **relevant cost** approach to the calculation of the price. A relevant cost approach is to identify a price at which the organisation will be no better off, but no worse off, if it sells the item at that price. Any price in excess of this minimum price will add to net profit.

A special order is a **one-off** revenue earning opportunity. These may arise in the following situations.

(a)   When a business has a regular source of income but also has some **spare capacity**, allowing it to take on extra work if demanded. For example a brewery might have a capacity of 500,000 barrels per month but only be producing and selling 300,000 barrels per month. It could therefore consider special orders to use up some of its spare capacity.

(b)   When a business has **no regular source of income** and relies exclusively on its ability to respond to demand. A building firm is a typical example as are many types of sub-contractors. In the service sector, consultants often work on this basis.

The reason for making the distinction is that in the case of (a), a firm would normally attempt to cover its longer-term running costs in its prices for its regular product. Pricing for special orders therefore does not need to consider unavoidable fixed costs, which will be incurred anyway. This is clearly not the case for a firm in (b)'s position, where special orders are the only source of income for the foreseeable future.

Exam focus point

> Examination questions featuring pricing for special orders could present a scenario in which a firm has to decide whether to bid for a contract. The term 'minimum price' should be a clear indication that an incremental cost price is required.

5.10.1 Minimum pricing

The basic approach in both situations is to determine the price at which the firm would break even if it undertook the work, that is, the **minimum price** that it could afford to charge without a reduction in profit. To make a profit on the product or the order, the actual price charged should be higher than the minimum price.

A minimum price is the minimum price that would have to be charged so as to cover the following two groups of cost.

(a)   The **incremental costs** of producing and selling the item
(b)   The **opportunity costs** of the resources consumed in making and selling the item

A minimum price would leave the business no better or worse off than if it did not sell the item.

Two essential points to understand immediately about a minimum price are as follows.

(a)   It is based on **relevant** costs, that is the incremental costs plus the opportunity costs of making and selling the product or providing the service. You have covered this in your earlier studies and we will look at this aspect again in Chapter 6.

(b)   It is **unlikely that a minimum price would actually be charged**, because if it were it would not provide the business with any incremental profit. However, the minimum price for an item shows the following.

  (i)   An **absolute minimum** below which the price should not be set.

(ii) The **incremental profit** that would be obtained from any price that is actually charged in excess of the minimum. For example, if the minimum price is $200 and the actual price charged is $240, the incremental profit on the sale would be $40.

If there are no **scarce resources**, and a company has **spare capacity**, the **minimum price** of a product would be an amount which equals the **incremental cost of making it**. Any price in excess of this minimum would provide an incremental contribution towards profit.

If there are scarce resources and a company makes more than one product, minimum prices would include an allowance for the **opportunity cost** of using the scarce resources to make and sell the product (instead of using the resources on the next most profitable product).

Where a firm also has to consider its **long-term costs** in the decision because it has no other way of recovering them it would have to **add a proportion of estimated unattributable costs to the price of each order**. This could be calculated on a time basis (if the job is expected to take one month, one twelfth of unavoidable costs would be included). However this may lead to inconsistencies if, say, the unavoidable costs are borne in full by one customer in one month, but shared between several customers in another month.

Question	Relevant cost pricing

Ennerdale has been asked to quote a price for a one-off contract. The following information is available:

Materials

The contract requires 3,000 kg of material K, which is a material used regularly by the company in other production. The company has 2,000 kg of material K currently in stock which had been purchased last month for a total cost of $19,600. Since then the price per kilogram for material K has increased by 5%.

The contract also requires 200 kg of material L. There are 250 kg of material L in stock which are not required for normal production. This material originally cost a total of $3,125. If not used on this contract, the stock of material L would be sold for $11 per kg.

Labour

The contract requires 800 hours of skilled labour. Skilled labour is paid $9.50 per hour. There is a shortage of skilled labour and all the available skilled labour is fully employed in the company in the manufacture of product P. The following information relates to product P:

	$ per unit	$ per unit
Selling price		100
Less:		
Skilled labour	38	
Other variable costs	22	
		(60)
		40

Required

Prepare on a relevant cost basis, the lowest cost estimate that could be used as the basis for a quotation.

Relevant cost – Material K

Since the material is regularly used by the company, the relevant cost of material K is the current price of the material.

Cost last month $= \dfrac{\$19,600}{2,000\,kg}$

$= \$9.80$

Revised cost (+5%) $= \$9.80 \times 1.05$

$= \$10.29$

∴ Relevant cost of Material K $= 3,000\,kg \times \$10.29$ per kg

$= \$30,870$

Relevant cost – Material L

Since the material is not required for normal production, the relevant cost of this material is its net realisable value if it were sold.

∴ Relevant cost of Material L $= 200\,kg \times \$11$ per kg

$= \$2,200$

Relevant cost – Skilled labour

Skilled labour is in short supply and therefore the relevant cost of this labour will include both the actual cost and the opportunity cost of the labour employed.

	$
Cost of skilled labour (800 hours × $9.50)	7,600
Opportunity cost of skilled labour (see working)	8,000
Relevant cost – skilled labour	15,600

Working

Skilled labour cost per unit of Product P = $38

Cost per skilled labour hour = $9.50

∴ Number of hours required per unit of Product P $= \dfrac{\$38}{\$9.50}$

$= 4$ hours

Contribution per unit of Product P $= \$40$

∴ Contribution per skilled labour hour $= \dfrac{\$40}{4\,hours}$

$= \$10$ per hour

∴ Opportunity cost of skilled labour $= 800$ hours $\times \$10$ per hour

$= \$8,000$

The total relevant costs of this contract are therefore $(30,870 + 2,200 + 15,600) = \$48,670$

Chapter Roundup

- In the modern world there are many more **influences on price** than cost (eg competitors, product range, quality).

- The price that an organisation can charge for its products will be determined to a greater or lesser degree by the **market** in which it operates

- **Economic theory** argues that the **higher the price of a good**, the **lower** will be the **quantity demanded**.

- The **price elasticity of demand (PED)** is a measure of the extent of change in demand for a good in response to a change in its price.

- Most products pass through the five stages of the **product life cycle.**

- You need to be able to derive the **demand equation** $P = a - bQ$.

- Cost behaviour can be **modelled** using equations.

- If we assume that there is a demand curve with the equation $P = a - bQ$, and a total cost function $C = F + vQ$, we can determine the profit-maximising price for the product.

  Profits are maximised where **marginal cost (MC) = marginal revenue (MR)**. The **optimal selling price** can be determined by deriving equations for MC and MR. alternatively, the **optimum selling price** can be determined using tabulation.

- If you are required to evaluate a decision to increase production and sales levels, you will need to consider **incremental costs**, **incremental revenues** and other factors.

- The price to be charged for a product or service is often one of the most important decisions made by business organisations. There are a number of alternative pricing strategies.

- **Full cost-plus pricing** is a method of deciding the sales price by adding a percentage mark-up for profit to the full cost of the product.

- **Marginal cost-plus pricing, also called mark-up pricing**, involves adding a profit margin to the marginal cost of the product.

- Pricing strategies for new products include **market skimming and market penetration pricing**.

- With **price discrimination**, the same product or service is sold at different prices to different customers. This can be very difficult to implement in practice because it relies for success upon the continued existence of certain market conditions.

- Special orders may require a **relevant cost** approach to the calculation of the price. A relevant cost approach is to identify a price at which the organisation will be no better off, but no worse off, if it sells the item at that price. Any price in excess of this minimum price will add to net profit.

1   *Fill in the blanks.*

Demand is said to be elastic when a .... change in price produces a ....
change in quantity demanded. PED is .... than 1.

Demand is said to be inelastic when a .... change in price produces a ....
change in quantity demanded. PED is .... than 1.

2   Fill in the blanks in the formula below for the variable 'a' in the equation for a demand curve.

$$a = \$(\text{............…................}) + \left(\frac{\text{...}}{\text{...}} \times \$...... \right)$$

3   Cost-based approaches to pricing take more account of the external environment than target costing.
    True or false?

4   *Fill in the blanks.*

(a)   One of the problems with relying on a full cost-plus approach to pricing is that it fails to recognise
      that since price may be determining demand, there will be a .... combination of
      .... and ....

(b)   An advantage of the full cost-plus approach is that, because the size of the profit margin can be
      varied, a decision based on a price in excess of full cost should ensure that a company working at
      .... capacity will cover .... and make a ....

5   Pricing based on mark-up per unit of limiting factor is particularly useful if an organisation is not working
    to full capacity. **True or false?**

6   *Fill in the blank.*

The .... price is the price at which an organisation will break even if it undertakes particular
work.

7   *Choose the correct word from those highlighted.*

Market **skimming/penetration** pricing should be used if an organisation wishes to discourage new
entrants into a market.

1   (a)   Demand is said to be elastic when a **small change** in the price produces a **large change** in the quantity demanded. PED is **greater** than 1.

   (b)   Demand is said to be **inelastic** when a small change in the price produces only a **small change in the quantity** demanded. **PED is less than 1**.

2   $a = (\text{current price}) + \left(\dfrac{\text{Current quantity at current price}}{\text{Change in quantity when price is changed by \$b}} \times \$b \right)$

3   False

4   (a)   profit-maximising combination of price and demand

   (b)   working at normal capacity will cover all of its fixed costs and make a profit

5   False. It is useful if the organisation is working at full capacity.

6   Minimum

7   Market penetration

Now try the question below from the Practice Question Bank

Number	Level	Marks	Time
Q8	Examination	15	27 mins

Short-term decisions

Topic list	Syllabus reference
1 Identifying relevant costs	B1 (a), (b), (c)
2 Make or buy decisions	B5 (a), (b), (c)
3 Outsourcing	B5 (a), (b), (c)
4 Further processing decisions	B5 (d)
5 Shut down decisions	B5 (d)

Introduction

The concept of **relevant costs** has already been re-visited in this study text and their use in one-off contracts to identify a minimum price was explained in the previous chapter.

In this chapter we look in greater depth at relevant costs and at how they should be applied in **decision-making situations**.

We look at a variety of common short-run business decisions and consider how they can be dealt with using relevant costs as appropriate.

Study guide

		Intellectual level
B1	**Relevant cost analysis**	
(a)	Explain the concept of relevant costing	2
(b)	Identify and calculate relevant costs for specific decision situations from given data	2
(c)	Explain and apply the concept of opportunity costs	2
B5	**Make-or-buy and other short-term decisions**	
(a)	Explain the issues surrounding make vs buy and outsourcing decisions	2
(b)	Calculate and compare 'make' costs with 'buy-in' costs	2
(c)	Compare in-house costs and outsource costs of completing tasks and consider other issues surrounding this decision	2
(d)	Apply relevant costing principles in situations involving shut down, one-off contracts and the further processing of joint products	2

Exam guide

The ability to recognise relevant costs and revenues is a key skill for the F5 exam and is highly examinable. Questions will be based on practical scenarios.

One of the competencies you require to fulfil performance objective 12 of the PER is the ability to prepare management information to assist in decision making. You can apply the knowledge you obtain from this section of the text to help to demonstrate this competence.

1 Identifying relevant costs   12/11

FAST FORWARD

Relevant costs are future cash flows arising as a direct consequence of a decision.

- Relevant costs are **future costs**
- Relevant costs are **cash flows**
- Relevant costs are **incremental costs**, arising as a direct consequence of the decision

1.1 When are relevant costs used?

Relevant costs are used when a decision has to be taken and the concern is whether the decision will increase profits or not, or which decision will increase profits the most. Examples of decisions where relevant costs (and benefits) are used include:

(a) Deciding whether to agree to accept a job or undertake some work at a stated price that the customer will pay.

(b) Whether to sell joint products from a common process at the point where they are output from the common process, or whether they should be processed further before selling them at a higher price.

(c) Whether to make products 'in house' or whether to sub-contract or outsource the work to an external supplier.

There are two basic types of decision where relevant costs are used:

(a) Decisions about whether to do something or whether not to do it.
(b) Decisions that involve selecting between two or more different options about what to do.

1.2 The approach to identifying relevant costs and benefits

To identify the relevant costs and benefits that will be affected by a decision, the approach should be to look at each item of cost or benefit in turn. (Benefits may be additional revenue or savings in costs as a result of the decision.) For each item of cost (or benefit), it is necessary to specify the relevant cost (or benefit). This is the cost (or benefit) that should be taken into account when reaching the decision.

Each item of cost or benefit should be considered in turn. In your exam, you may be required not only to identify the correct relevant cost for each item, but also to explain the logic or reasoning – in other words, explain why the cost (or benefit) that you have identified is the relevant cost.

In this section we explain the approach to identifying the relevant costs for different types of cost.

Exam focus point

Question 1 of the December 2011 exam asked candidates to prepare a cost statement using relevant costing principles, with detailed notes to support each number included in the statement.

The examiner noted that many candidates 'just wrote down that a cost was included because it was relevant, but didn't say why'. Ensure you are able to explain **why** a cost is relevant / not relevant to a decision.

1.3 Definition of relevant costs

A relevant cost is a future cash flow arising as a direct consequence of a decision.

(a) It must be a cost that will occur in the future. Any cost that has already been incurred in the past cannot be a relevant cost.

(b) It must be a cost (or benefit) that results in cash flow. Depreciation charges and overhead absorption costs cannot be relevant costs.

(c) It must arise as a direct consequence of the decision. Any costs (or benefits) that will happen anyway, regardless of the decision, cannot be a relevant cost.

It follows from this definition that:

(a) **Sunk costs cannot be relevant costs**. Sunk costs are costs that have already been incurred.

(b) **Committed costs cannot be relevant costs**. These are costs that will be incurred in the future, but they cannot be avoided because they have already been committed by a previous decision.

In the rest of this section, we explain the approach to identifying the relevant costs for different types of cost.

1.4 Machinery user costs

A decision may involve having to use an item of machinery to do some additional work.

Once a machine has been bought its purchase cost is a **sunk** cost. **Depreciation** is not a relevant cost, because it is not a cash flow.

However, **using** machinery may involve some incremental costs. These costs may be referred to as **user costs**. They include hire charges where machinery will have to be hired or rented as a result of the decision. They also include any fall in the resale value of machinery or other assets that the organisation owns, where the fall in value will be caused by using the asset as a consequence of the decision.

1.4.1 Example: Machine user costs

Bronty Co is considering whether to undertake some contract work for a customer. The machinery required for the contract would be as follows.

(a) A special cutting machine will have to be hired for three months for the work (the length of the contract). Hire charges for this machine are $75 per month, with a minimum hire charge of $300.

(b) All other machinery required in the production for the contract has already been purchased by the organisation on hire purchase terms. The monthly hire purchase payments for this machinery are $500. This consists of $450 for capital repayment and $50 as an interest charge. The last hire purchase payment is to be made in two months time. The cash price of this machinery was $9,000 two years ago. It is being depreciated on a straight line basis at the rate of $200 per month. However, it still has a useful life which will enable it to be operated for another 36 months.

The machinery is highly specialised and is unlikely to be required for other, more profitable jobs over the period during which the contract work would be carried out. Although there is no immediate market for selling this machine, it is expected that a customer might be found in the future. It is further estimated that the machine would lose $200 in its eventual sale value if it is used for the contract work.

What is the relevant cost of machinery for the contract?

Solution

(a) The **cutting machine** will incur an incremental cost of $300, the minimum hire charge.

(b) The historical cost of the **other machinery** is irrelevant as a past cost; depreciation is irrelevant as a non-cash cost; and future hire purchase repayments are irrelevant because they are committed costs. The only relevant cost is the loss of resale value of the machinery, estimated at $200 through use. This 'user cost' will not arise until the machinery is eventually resold and the $200 should be discounted to allow for the time value of money. However, discounting is ignored here, and will be discussed in a later chapter.

(c) **Summary of relevant costs**

	$
Incremental hire costs	300
User cost of other machinery	200
	500

1.5 Relevant cost of labour

Often the labour force will be paid irrespective of the decision made and the costs are therefore **not incremental**. Take care, however, if the labour force could be put to an **alternative use**, in which case the relevant costs are the **variable costs** of the labour and associated variable overheads **plus** the **contribution forgone** from not being able to put it to its alternative use.

For example, suppose that a special job would require 50 hours of labour time. Employees are paid $10 per hour. There is sufficient idle capacity among the work force for 40 hours of the work. The extra ten hours would be worked in overtime, for which the additional pay is $12.50 per hour.

In this example, the relevant cost of labour is the incremental cost. Of the 50 hours required for the work, 40 hours would be paid anyway, so the cost is a committed cost that will be incurred anyway, and it is not relevant. However there will be additional costs of $125 (10 hours at $12.50 per hour) for the overtime working, which will be an additional 'cash' cost.

Suppose that another special job will require 20 hours of skilled labour. The skilled work force is paid $15 per hour and is working at full capacity. If the special job is undertaken, the skilled labour would be taken off other work that earns a contribution of $12 per hour, after deducting the costs of the labour and variable overheads of $1.5 per hour. In this situation the relevant cost of labour must include the variable cost of the labour plus any associated variable overhead, and the contribution that would be lost by taking the skilled workers off the other work.

	$
Labour cost of 20 hours (× $15 per hour)	300
Variable overhead costs (× $1.50 per hour)	30
Contribution forgone (× $12 per hour)	240
Total relevant cost of labour time	570

1.6 Relevant cost of materials

The relevant cost of raw materials is generally their current **replacement** cost, unless the materials have already been purchased and would not be replaced once used.

If materials have already been purchased but will not be replaced, then the relevant cost of using them is **either** (a) their current **resale** value **or** (b) the value they would obtain if they were put to an **alternative use**, if this is greater than their current resale value.

The **higher** of (a) or (b) is then the opportunity cost of the materials. If the materials have no resale value and no other possible use, then the relevant cost of using them for the opportunity under consideration would be nil.

The flowchart below shows how the relevant costs of materials can be identified, **provided that** the materials are **not in short supply**, and so have **no internal opportunity cost**.

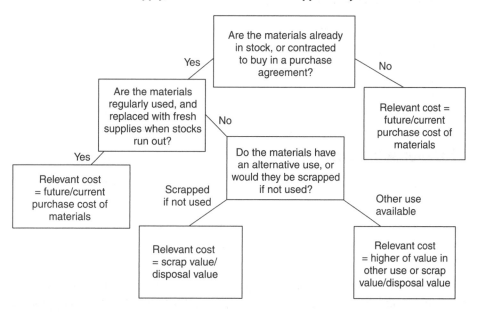

Question

O'Reilly Co has been approached by a customer who would like a special job to be done for him, and who is willing to pay $22,000 for it. The job would require the following materials:

Material	Total units required	Units already in inventory	Book value of units in inventory $/unit	Realisable value $/unit	Replacement cost $/unit
A	1,000	0	–	–	6
B	1,000	600	2	2.5	5
C	1,000	700	3	2.5	4
D	200	200	4	6.0	9

(a) Material B is used regularly by O'Reilly Ltd, and if units of B are required for this job, they would need to be replaced to meet other production demand.

(b) Materials C and D are in inventory as the result of previous over-buying, and they have a restricted use. No other use could be found for material C, but the units of material D could be used in another job as substitute for 300 units of material E, which currently costs $5 per unit (of which the company has no units in inventory at the moment).

What are the relevant costs of material, in deciding whether or not to accept the contract?

Answer

(a) **Material A** is not owned and would have to be bought in full at the replacement cost of $6 per unit.

(b) **Material B** is used regularly by the company. There is existing inventory (600 units) but if these are used on the contract under review a further 600 units would be bought to replace them. Relevant costs are therefore 1,000 units at the replacement cost of $5 per unit.

(c) **Material C:** 1,000 units are needed and 700 are already in inventory. If used for the contract, a further 300 units must be bought at $4 each. The existing inventory of 700 will not be replaced. If they are used for the contract, they could not be sold at $2.50 each. The realisable value of these 700 units is an opportunity cost of sales revenue forgone.

(d) **Material D:** these are already in inventory and will not be replaced. There is an opportunity cost of using D in the contract because there are alternative opportunities either to sell the existing inventory for $6 per unit ($1,200 in total) or avoid other purchases (of material E), which would cost 300 × $5 = $1,500. Since substitution for E is more beneficial, $1,500 is the opportunity cost.

(e) **Summary of relevant costs**

	$
Material A (1,000 × $6)	6,000
Material B (1,000 × $5)	5,000
Material C (300 × $4) plus (700 × $2.50)	2,950
Material D	1,500
Total	15,450

1.7 Opportunity costs

Other potential relevant costs include **opportunity costs**. These have been mentioned already in the context of relevant labour costs.

Opportunity cost is the **benefit sacrificed** by choosing one opportunity rather than the next best alternative. You will often encounter opportunity costs when there are several possible uses for a scarce resource.

For example, if a material is in short supply, it may be transferred from the production of one product to that of another product. The opportunity cost is the **contribution lost** from ceasing production of the original product.

Key term

> **Opportunity cost** is the value of a benefit sacrificed when one course of action is chosen, in preference to an alternative. The opportunity cost is represented by the forgone potential benefit from the best rejected course of action.

Question

Opportunity costs

An information technology consultancy firm has been asked to do an urgent job by a client, for which a price of $2,500 has been offered. The job would require the following.

(a) 30 hours' work from one member of staff, who is paid on an hourly basis, at a rate of $20 per hour, but who would normally be employed on work for clients where the charge-out rate is $45 per hour. No other member of staff is able to do the member of staff in question's work.

(b) The use of 5 hours of mainframe computer time, which the firm normally charges out to external users at a rate of $50 per hour. Mainframe computer time is currently used 24 hours a day, 7 days a week.

(c) Supplies and incidental expenses of $200.

Required

Fill in the blank in the sentence below.

The relevant cost or opportunity cost of the job is $........

Answer

The correct answer is $1,800.

The relevant cost or opportunity cost of the job would be calculated as follows.

	$
Labour (30 hours × $45)	1,350
Computer time opportunity cost (5 hours × $50)	250
Supplies and expenses	200
	1,800

2 Make or buy decisions 6/12

FAST FORWARD

In a **make or buy decision**, the choice is between making items in-house or purchasing them from an external supplier. When there are no limiting factors restricting the in-house production capacity, the relevant costs are the differential costs between the two options.

Exam focus point

In the exam, you may be required to apply the principles of relevant costs to a specific decision that is described in the quesiton.

There are different types of decision where relevant costs are required to evaluate the decision choices. One type of decision is the so-called 'make-or-buy' decision, where the choice is between making products internally, or sub-contracting production to an external supplier.

Here are some examples of make or buy decisions.

(a) Whether a company should manufacture its own components, or else buy the components from an outside supplier

(b) Whether a construction company should do some work with its own employees, or whether it should sub-contract the work to another company

(c) Whether a service should be carried out by an internal department or whether an external organisation should be employed.

The **'make'** option should give **management more direct control** over the work, but the **'buy'** option often has the benefit that the **external organisation** has a **specialist skill** and expertise in the work. Make or buy decisions should certainly **not be based exclusively on cost considerations.** Issues such as control, quality, flexibility, reliability of delivery, and speed of delivery may all affect the decision to make or buy.

From the point of view of identifying relevant costs, a very important issue is whether the organisation has sufficient capacity to manufacture all the products in –house. If an organisation has the freedom of choice about whether to make internally or buy externally, it has no scarce resources that put a restriction on what it can do itself. In other words, there is no limiting factor that restricts the output capacity of in-house operations. In this situation, the **relevant costs** for the make or buy decision are the **differential costs** between the two options.

2.1 Example: Make or buy decision

Shellfish Co makes four components, W, X, Y and Z, for which costs in the forthcoming year are expected to be as follows.

	W	X	Y	Z
Production (units)	1,000	2,000	4,000	3,000
Unit marginal costs	$	$	$	$
Direct materials	4	5	2	4
Direct labour	8	9	4	6
Variable production overheads	2	3	1	2
	14	17	7	12

Directly attributable fixed costs per annum and committed fixed costs:

	$
Incurred as a direct consequence of making W	1,000
Incurred as a direct consequence of making X	5,000
Incurred as a direct consequence of making Y	6,000
Incurred as a direct consequence of making Z	8,000
Other fixed costs (committed)	30,000
	50,000

Directly attributable fixed costs are all items of cash expenditure that are incurred as a direct consequence of making the product in-house.

A sub-contractor has offered to supply units of W, X, Y and Z for $12, $21, $10 and $14 respectively. Should Shellfish make or buy the components?

Solution

(a) The **relevant costs** are the differential costs between making and buying, and they consist of **differences in unit variable costs plus differences in directly attributable fixed costs**. Sub-contracting will result in some **fixed cost savings.**

	W	X	Y	Z
	$	$	$	$
Unit variable cost of making	14	17	7	12
Unit variable cost of buying	12	21	10	14
	(2)	4	3	2
Annual requirements (units)	1,000	2,000	4,000	3,000
	$	$	$	$
Extra variable cost of buying (per annum)	(2,000)	8,000	12,000	6,000
Fixed costs saved by buying	(1,000)	(5,000)	(6,000)	(8,000)
Extra total cost of buying	(3,000)	3,000	6,000	(2,000)

(b) The company would save $3,000 pa by sub-contracting component W (where the purchase cost would be less than the marginal cost per unit to make internally) and would save $2,000 pa by sub-contracting component Z (because of the saving in fixed costs of $8,000).

(c) In this example, relevant costs are the variable costs of in-house manufacture, the variable costs of sub-contracted units, and the saving in fixed costs.

(d) **Further considerations**

  (i) If components W and Z are sub-contracted, the company will have **spare capacity**. How should that spare capacity be profitably used? Are there hidden benefits to be obtained from sub-contracting? Would the company's workforce resent the loss of work to an outside sub-contractor, and might such a decision cause an industrial dispute?

  (ii) Would the sub-contractor be **reliable** with delivery times, and would he supply components of the same **quality** as those manufactured internally?

(iii)   Does the company wish to be **flexible** and maintain better **control** over operations by making everything itself?

(iv)   Are the **estimates** of fixed cost savings reliable? In the case of Product W, buying is clearly cheaper than making in-house. In the case of product Z, the decision to buy rather than make would only be financially beneficial if it is feasible that the fixed cost savings of $8,000 will really be 'delivered' by management. All too often in practice, promised savings fail to materialise!

2.2 Make or buy decisions with a limiting factor

A manufacturing organisation may want to produce items in-house but does not have sufficient capacity to produce everything that it needs, due to a limiting factor on production, such as a shortage of machine time or labour time.

In this situation, the decision is not whether to make internally or purchase externally. The decision is about which items to make internally and which to purchase externally. The optimal decision, based on financial considerations alone, is to arrange internal production and external purchasing g in a way that minimises total costs.

Make or buy decisions involving limiting factors are described in Chapter 4.

3 Outsourcing   12/07, 6/12

FAST FORWARD

The relevant costs/revenues in decisions relating to the **operating of internal service departments or the use of external services** are the differential costs between the two options.

3.1 The trend in outsourcing

A significant trend in the 1990s was for companies and government bodies to **concentrate on their core competences** – what they are really good at (or set up to achieve) – and turn other functions over to **specialist contractors.** A company that earns its profits from, say, manufacturing bicycles, does not also need to have expertise in, say, mass catering or office cleaning. **Facilities management** companies such as Serco and G4S have grown in response to this.

Key term

> **Outsourcing** is the use of external suppliers for finished products, components or services. This is also known as **contract manufacturing** or **sub-contracting.**

Basically, decisions about outsourcing activities or using internal staff to do the work is a form of 'make or buy' decision, and the basic principles are the same.

Reasons for the trend towards outsourcing activities include the following:

(a)   Frequently the decision is made on the grounds that **specialist contractors** can offer **superior quality** and **efficiency**. If a contractor's main business is making a specific component it can invest in the specialist machinery and labour and knowledge skills needed to make that component. However, this component may be only one of many needed by the contractor's customer, and the complexity of components is now such that attempting to keep internal facilities up to the standard of specialists detracts from the main business of the customer.

(b)   Contracting out manufacturing **frees capital** that can then be invested in core activities such as market research, product definition, product planning, marketing and sales.

(c)   **Contractors** have the **capacity** and **flexibility** to start production very quickly to meet sudden **variations in demand**. In-house facilities may not be able to respond as quickly, because of the need to redirect resources from elsewhere.

(d)   There is not enough work to keep internal staff fully occupied, so it is cheaper to outsource the work. For example many organisations outsource payroll administration because it is not worthwhile employing staff with knowledge of payroll work.

3.2 Internal and external services

Companies will often use specialist companies for administrative and support functions. Decisions such as the following are now common.

(a) Whether the **design and development of a new computer system** should be entrusted to in-house data processing staff or whether an external software house should be hired to do the work.

(b) Whether **maintenance and repairs** of certain items of equipment should be dealt with by in-house engineers, or whether a maintenance contract should be made with a specialist organisation.

(c) Office cleaning is often outsourced to external contractors. The management of the organisation do not want to have their time consumed by management problems relating to office cleaning, so they are happy to pay another firm to do the work and take on the operational problems.

(d) Security services are often outsourced to specialist companies. In the UK, some prison management services are outsourced by the government to private sector contractors.

The costs **relevant** to decisions about whether or not to outsource activities are little different (if at all) to those that are taken into account in a 'conventional' make or buy situation. The relevant costs are the **differential costs** between performing the service internally or using an external provider.

Exam focus point

The major problem in examination questions is likely to be identifying whether existing staff will be made redundant or whether they will be redeployed, and whether there are alternative uses for the other resources made available by ceasing to perform the service internally. These, it hardly needs stating, are also likely to be the major problems in practice.

3.3 Performance of outsourcers

An 'outsourcer' here means the organisation to which work is outsourced.

Once a decision has been made to outsource, it is essential that the **performance** of the outsourcer is monitored and **measured**.

Measures could include cost savings, service improvement and employee satisfaction. It is important to have **realistic goals** and expectations and to have **objective ways** to measure success.

The performance of the outsourcer, whether good or bad, can interfere with the performance assessment of an **internal function**. For example:

- Maintenance of equipment could be carried out badly by an outsourcer and this may result in increased breakdowns and reduced labour efficiency of a production team

- If information arrives late or is incorrect, the wrong decision may be made

3.4 Example: Outsourcing

Stunnaz is considering a proposal to use the services of a press cuttings agency. At the moment, press cuttings are collected by a junior member of the marketing department, who is also responsible for office administration (including filing), travel bookings, a small amount of proof reading and making the tea. The total annual cost of employing this person is $15,000 pa.

There is concern that the ability of this person to produce a comprehensive file of cuttings is limited by the time available. She has calculated that she needs to spend about two hours of her seven and a half hour day simply reading the national and trade press, but usually only has about five hours a week for this job.

Press subscriptions currently cost $850 pa and are paid annually in advance.

The assistant makes use of a small micro-fiche device for storing cuttings. The cuttings are sent to a specialist firm once a month to be put onto fiche. Stunnaz pays $45 each month for this service. The micro-fiche reader is leased at a cost of $76 per calendar month. This lease has another 27 months to run.

The cuttings service bureau has proposed an annual contract at a cost of $1,250. Several existing users have confirmed their satisfaction with the service they receive.

Should Stunnaz outsource its press cuttings work?

Solution

Current annual costs amount to:

	$
Micro fiche service	$45 × 12 = 540
Subscriptions	850
	1,390

The monthly leasing charge is a **committed cost** that must be paid whatever the decision. It is not therefore a decision-relevant cost.

Engaging the services of the press cuttings agency therefore has the *potential* to save Stunnaz $140 pa. However, this is not the final word: there are other considerations.

(a) The **'in-house' option** should give management **more direct control** over the work, but the **'outsource' option** often has the benefit that the external organisation has a **specialist skill and expertise** in the work. Decisions should certainly not be based exclusively on cost considerations.

(b) Will outsourcing create **spare capacity**? How should that spare capacity be profitably used?

(c) Are there **hidden benefits** to be obtained from subcontracting?

(d) Would the company's workforce resent the loss of work to an outside subcontractor, and might such a decision cause an **industrial dispute**?

(e) Would the subcontractor be **reliable with delivery times** and **quality**?

(f) Does the company wish to be **flexible** and **maintain better control** over operations by doing everything itself?

4 Further processing decisions   12/07, 12/13

FAST FORWARD

> A further processing decision often involves joint products from a common manufacturing process. The decision is whether to sell the products at the split-off point, as soon as they emerge from the common process, or whether they should be processed further before selling them.
>
> A joint product should be **processed further** past the split-off point if the additional sales revenue exceeds the relevant post-separation (further processing) costs.

4.1 Joint products

You should have covered joint products in your earlier studies and the following will act as a brief reminder.

Knowledge brought forward from earlier studies

- **Joint products** are two or more products which are output from the same processing operation, but which are indistinguishable from each other up to their point of separation.

- Joint products (unlike by-products from a process) have a **substantial sales value**. Often they require further processing before they are ready for sale. Joint products arise, for example, in the oil refining industry where diesel fuel, petrol, paraffin and lubricants are all produced from the same process.

- A joint product is regarded as an important saleable item, and so it should be **separately costed**. The profitability of each joint product should be assessed in the cost accounts.

- The point at which joint products become separately identifiable is known as the **split-off point** or **separation point**.

- Costs incurred prior to this point of separation are **common** or **joint costs**.

- Problems in **accounting** for joint products are basically of two different sorts.

(a) How common costs should be apportioned between the joint products, in order to put a value to closing inventory and to the cost of sale (and profit) for each product. This may be necessary for financial reporting and preparing profit statements, but it has no relevance to decision making.

(b) Whether it is more profitable to sell a joint product at one stage of processing, usually at the split-off point, or whether to process the product further and sell it at a later stage. This is a decision for which relevant costs and benefits should be considered.

Suppose a manufacturing company carries out process operations in which two or more joint products are made from a common process. If the joint products can be sold either in their existing condition at the 'split-off' point at the end of common processing or after further separate processing, **a decision should be taken about whether to sell each joint product at the split-off point or after further processing.**

Attention!

> Note that **joint (pre-separation) costs** are incurred regardless of the decision and they are therefore **irrelevant to the further processing decision.**

4.2 Example: Further processing decision

The Poison Chemical Company produces two joint products, Alash and Pottum from the same process. Joint processing costs of $150,000 are incurred up to split-off point, when 100,000 units of Alash and 50,000 units of Pottum are produced. The selling prices at split-off point are $1.25 per unit for Alash and $2.00 per unit for Pottum.

The units of Alash could be processed further to produce 60,000 units of a new chemical, Alashplus, but at an extra fixed cost of $20,000 and variable cost of 30c per unit of input. The selling price of Alashplus would be $3.25 per unit. Should the company sell Alash or Alashplus?

Solution

The only relevant costs/incomes are those which compare selling Alash against selling Alashplus. Every other cost is irrelevant: they will be incurred regardless of what the decision is.

	Alash			Alashplus
Selling price per unit	$1.25			$3.25
	$		$	$
Total sales	125,000			195,000
Incremental post-separation processing costs	–	Fixed	20,000	
	–	Variable	30,000	50,000
Sales minus post-separation (further processing) costs	125,000			145,000

It is $20,000 more profitable to convert Alash into Alashplus.

 Question

Further processing decision

A company manufactures four products from an input of a raw material to Process 1. Following this process, product A is processed in Process 2, product B in Process 3, product C in Process 4 and product D in Process 5.

The normal loss in Process 1 is 10% of input, and there are no expected losses in the other processes. Scrap value in Process 1 is $0.50 per litre. The costs incurred in Process 1 are apportioned to each product according to the volume of output of each product. Production overhead is absorbed as a percentage of direct wages.

Data in respect of the month of October

	Process					
	1	2	3	4	5	Total
	$'000	$'000	$'000	$'000	$'000	$'000
Direct materials at $1.25 per litre	100					100
Direct wages	48	12	8	4	16	88
Production overhead						66

	Product			
	A	B	C	D
	litres	litres	litres	litres
Output	22,000	20,000	10,000	18,000
	$	$	$	$
Selling price	4.00	3.00	2.00	5.00
Estimated sales value at end of Process 1	2.50	2.80	1.20	3.00

Required

Suggest and evaluate an alternative production strategy which would optimise profit for the month. It should not be assumed that the output of Process 1 can be changed.

Answer

During the month, the quantity of input to Process 1 was 80,000 litres. Normal loss is 10% = 8,000 litres, and so total output should have been 72,000 litres of A, B, C and D. Instead, it was only 70,000 litres. In an 'average' month, output would have been higher, and this might have some bearing on the optimal production and selling strategy.

The **central question** is whether or not the output from Process 1 should be **processed further** in processes 2, 3, 4 and 5, or whether it should be **sold at the 'split-off' point**, at the end of Process 1. Each joint product can be looked at **individually**.

A further question is whether the **wages costs** in process 2, 3, 4 and 5 would be avoided if the joint products were sold at the end of process 1 and not processed further. It will be assumed that all the wages costs would be **avoidable**, but none of the **production overhead** costs would be. This assumption can be challenged, and in practice would have to be investigated.

	A	B	C	D
	$	$	$	$
Selling price, per litre	4.00	3.00	2.00	5.00
Selling price at end of process 1	2.50	2.80	1.20	3.00
Incremental selling price, per litre	1.50	0.20	0.80	2.00
Litres output	22,000	20,000	10,000	18,000
	$'000	$'000	$'000	$'000
Total incremental revenue from further processing	33	4	8	36
Avoidable costs from selling at split-off point (wages saved)	12	8	4	16
Incremental benefit/(cost) of further processing	21	(4)	4	20

This analysis would seem to indicate that **products A, C and D should be further processed** in processes 2, 4 and 5 respectively, but that **product B should be sold at the end of process 1**, without further processing in process 3. The saving would be at least $4,000 per month.

If **some production overhead** (which is 75% of direct wages) were also **avoidable**, this would mean that:

(a)   Selling product B at the end of process 1 would offer further savings of up to (75% of $8,000) $6,000 in overheads, and so $10,000 in total.

(b)   The incremental benefit from further processing product C might fall by up to (75% of $4,000) $3,000 to $1,000, meaning that it is only just profitable to process C beyond the split-off point.

5 Shut down decisions   12/09

Shutdown/discontinuance problems may sometimes be simplified into short-run relevant cost decisions. A shutdown decision is whether to close down an operation or stop making and selling a particular product or service.

5.1 The nature of shutdown decisions

Discontinuance or shutdown problems involve the following decisions.

(a)   **Whether or not to close down** a product line, department or other activity, either because it is making losses or because it is too expensive to run

(b)   If the decision is to shut down, **whether the closure should be permanent or temporary**

In practice, shutdown decisions may often involve **longer-term considerations,** and **capital expenditures and revenues.**

(a)   A shutdown should result in savings in **annual operating costs** for a number of years into the future.

(b)   Closure will probably release **unwanted non-current assets for sale**. Some assets might have a small scrap value, but other assets, in particular property, might have a substantial sale value.

(c)   **Employees** affected by the closure must be made redundant or relocated, perhaps after retraining, or else offered early retirement. There will be lump sum payments involved which must be taken into account in the financial arithmetic. For example, suppose that the closure of a regional office would result in annual savings of $100,000, non-current assets could be sold off to earn income of $2 million, but redundancy payments would be $3 million. The shutdown decision would involve an assessment of the net capital cost of closure ($1 million) against the annual benefits ($100,000 pa).

It is possible, however, for shutdown problems to be **simplified into short-run decisions**, by making one of the following assumptions.

(a)   Non-current asset sales and redundancy costs would be negligible.

(b)   Income from non-current asset sales would match redundancy costs and so these capital items would be self-cancelling.

In such circumstances the financial aspect of shutdown decisions would be based on **short-run relevant costs.**

5.2 Example: Adding or deleting products (or departments)

A company manufactures three products, Pawns, Rooks and Bishops. The present net annual income from these is as follows.

	Pawns $	Rooks $	Bishops $	Total $
Sales	50,000	40,000	60,000	150,000
Variable costs	30,000	25,000	35,000	90,000
Contribution	20,000	15,000	25,000	60,000
Fixed costs	17,000	18,000	20,000	55,000
Profit/loss	3,000	(3,000)	5,000	5,000

The company is concerned about its poor profit performance, and is considering whether or not to cease selling Rooks. It is felt that selling prices cannot be raised or lowered without adversely affecting net income. $5,000 of the fixed costs of Rooks are direct fixed costs which would be saved if production ceased (ie there are some attributable fixed costs). All other fixed costs, it is considered, would remain the same.

By **stopping production of Rooks**, the **consequences** would be a $10,000 fall in profits.

	$
Loss of contribution	(15,000)
Savings in fixed costs	5,000
Incremental loss	(10,000)

Suppose, however, it were possible to use the resources realised by stopping production of Rooks and **switch to producing a new item**, Crowners, which would sell for $50,000 and incur variable costs of $30,000 and extra direct fixed costs of $6,000. A new decision is now required.

	Rooks $	Crowners $
Sales	40,000	50,000
Less variable costs	25,000	30,000
	15,000	20,000
Less direct fixed costs	5,000	6,000
Contribution to shared fixed costs and profit	10,000	14,000

It would be **more profitable to shut down production of Rooks and switch** resources to making Crowners, in order to boost profits by $4,000 to $9,000.

5.3 Timing of shutdown

An organisation may also need to consider the most appropriate **timing** for a shutdown. Some costs may be avoidable in the long run but not in the short run. For example, office space may have been rented and three months' notice is required to terminate the rental agreement. This cost during the three-month notice period is therefore **unavoidable** for the three months. In the same way supply contracts may require notice of cancellation. A month-by-month analysis of when notice should be given and savings will be made may be needed for the relevant costing and decision making process.

5.4 Qualitative factors

With shutdown decisions, as with many other decisions involving relevant costs, the decision is not merely a matter of choosing the best financial option. **Qualitative** factors may be significant and may influence the final decision. For example:

(a)   What impact will a shutdown decision have on the morale of employees who remain?

(b)   What signal will the decision give to competitors? How will they react?

(c)   How will customers react? Will they lose confidence in the company's products?

(d)   How will suppliers be affected? If one supplier suffers disproportionately there may be a loss of goodwill and damage to future relations.

Question

How would the above decision change if Pawns, Rooks and Bishops were manufactured in different departments, variable costs could be split down into the costs of direct materials, labour and overheads, and fixed costs could be analysed into the costs of administrative staff and equipment and premises costs?

Answer

The decision would not change at all – unless perhaps activity based analysis of overheads were undertaken and unexpected cost patterns were revealed. The point of this exercise is to make you realise that problems that look complicated are sometimes very simple in essence even if the amount of calculations seems daunting.

Chapter Roundup

- **Relevant costs** are future cash flows arising as a direct consequence of a decision.
    - Relevant costs are **future costs**
    - Relevant costs are **cash flows**
    - Relevant costs are **incremental costs**, arising as a direct consequence of the decision

- In a **make or buy decision**, the choice is between making items in-house or purchasing them from an external supplier. When there are no limiting factors restricting the in-house production capacity, the relevant costs are the differential costs between the two options.

- The relevant costs/revenues in decisions relating to the **operating of internal service departments or the use of external services** are the differential costs between the two options.

- A further processing decision often involves joint products from a common manufacturing process. The decision is whether to sell the products at the split-off point, as soon as they emerge from the common process, or whether they should be processed further before selling them.

- A joint product should be **processed further** past the split-off point if the additional sales revenue exceeds the relevant post-separation (further processing) costs.

- **Shutdown/discontinuance problems** may sometimes be simplified into short-run relevant cost decisions. A shutdown decision is whether to close down an operation or stop making and selling a particular product or service.

Quick Quiz

1   *Fill in the relevant costs in the four boxes in the diagram below.*

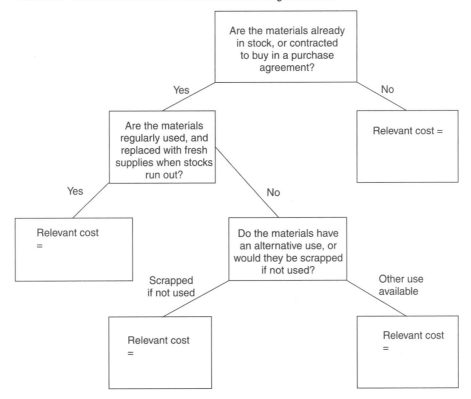

2   *Choose the correct word(s) from those highlighted.*

In a situation where a company must subcontract work to make up a shortfall in its own in-house capabilities, its total cost will be minimised if those units **bought out from a sub-contractor/made in-house** have the **lowest/highest** extra **variable/fixed** cost of **buying out/making in-house** per unit of **scarce resource/material**.

3   In a decision about whether or not to sell a joint product at the split-off point or after further processing, joint costs are relevant. **True or false?**

4   *Fill in the blanks.*

Most of the decisions considered in this chapter involve calculating .... obtained from various options after identifying .... They always involve ....
issues, which depend upon the precise situation described.

1

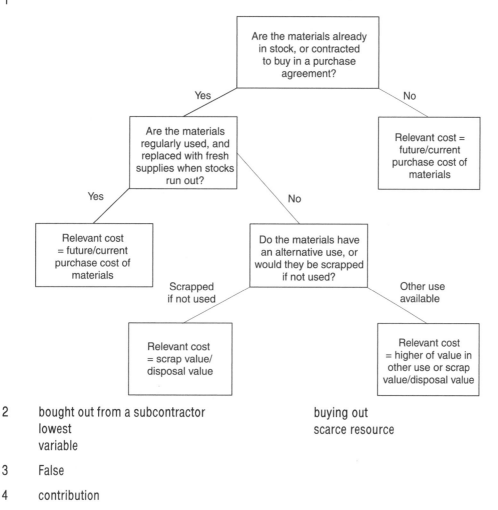

2   bought out from a subcontractor   buying out
    lowest   scarce resource
    variable

3   False

4   contribution

    relevant costs

    qualitative

Now try the question below from the Practice Question Bank

Number	Level	Marks	Time
Q9	Examination	15	27 mins

7

Risk and uncertainty

Topic list	Syllabus reference
1 Risk and uncertainty	B6 (a)
2 Allowing for uncertainty	B6 (a)
3 Probabilities and expected values	B6 (b), (c)
4 Decision rules	B6 (d)
5 Decision trees	B6 (e)
6 The value of information	B6 (f)
7 Sensitivity analysis	B6 (b), (c)
8 Simulation models	B6 (b)

Introduction

Decision making involves making decisions now about what will happen in the future. Obviously, decisions can turn out badly, or actual results can prove to be very different from the estimates on which the original decision was made. **Ideally** the decision maker would **know with certainty** what the future consequences will be for each choice facing him. But the real world is not normally so helpful, and decisions must be made in the knowledge that their expected **consequences**, although probable perhaps, are **rarely 100% certain**.

Various **methods of bringing uncertainty and risk** into the analysis and evaluation of decisions will be described in this chapter. You may well think that some methods are more sensible or practical than others, but you should **judge** each method on its merits. You should also be prepared to apply or show an understanding of a number of different decision-making rules in your examination.

Study guide

		Intellectual level
B6	**Dealing with risk and uncertainty in decision-making**	
(a)	Suggest research techniques to reduce uncertainty, eg focus groups, market research	2
(b)	Explain the use of simulation, expected values and sensitivity	1
(c)	Apply expected values and sensitivity to decision-making problems	2
(d)	Apply the techniques of maximax, maximin, and minimax regret to decision-making problems including the production of profit tables	2
(e)	Draw a decision tree and use it to solve a multi-stage decision problem	1
(f)	Calculate the value of perfect and imperfect information	2

Exam guide

Management accounting exams have increasingly expected candidates to have a good understanding of risk in decision-making. The principles of relevant costing apply to the decision-making, but in addition an element of risk or uncertainty may affect the decision. Section B questions are likely to be a mixture of calculations and explanation.

1 Risk and uncertainty

FAST FORWARD

> When there is a strong element of risk or uncertainty in a decision, the decision that is taken may be affected by the extent of the risk or uncertainty.
>
> 'Risk' and 'uncertainty' are often used to mean the same thing. However, to be more exact, 'risk' in decision making exists when the future outcome cannot be predicted for certain, but probabilities can be estimated for each possible outcome. Uncertainty, in contrast, is when there is insufficient information to make a reliable prediction about what will happen and there are no probability estimates of different possible outcomes.

Key terms

> **Risk** involves situations or events which may or may not occur, but whose probability of occurrence can be estimated statistically.
>
> **Uncertain events** are events where the outcome cannot be estimated with a statistical probability.

In everyday usage the terms risk and uncertainty are not clearly distinguished. If you are asked to explain the difference, risk exists when probabilities of different outcomes can be estimated and uncertainty exists when there is insufficient information to assess probabilities. As a general rule, however, the terms are used interchangeably.

In the previous chapters on decision-making, the problem of risk and uncertainty has not been considered. In practice, however, risk or uncertainty can have a significant influence on decision-making This chapter looks at different methods of assessing risk or uncertainty in order to assist decision-making.

1.1 Risk preference

FAST FORWARD

> People may be **risk seekers**, **risk neutral** or **risk averse**. A person's attitude to risk and uncertainty may affect the decision that is taken.

A **risk seeker** is a decision maker who is interested in the best outcomes no matter how small the chance that they may occur.

A decision maker is **risk neutral** if he is prepared to make a decision that balances risk and return. He is willing take on more risk, but only if the expected profit or return is higher. He will also accept a lower return for lower risk.

A **risk averse** decision maker acts on the assumption that the worst outcome might occur and will make a decision that limits or minimises the risk.

Attitudes to risk have clear implications for managers and organisations. A **risk seeking manager** working for an **organisation** that is characteristically **risk averse** is likely to make decisions that are **not consistent with the goals of the organisation**. There may be a role for the management accountant here, who could be instructed to present decision-making information in such a way as to ensure that the manager considers *all* the possibilities, including the worst.

2 Allowing for uncertainty

Management accounting directs its attention towards the **future** and the future is **uncertain**. For this reason a number of methods of taking **uncertainty** into consideration have evolved.

One approach to dealing with uncertainty is to obtain more information, in order to reduce the amount of uncertainty about what will happen. Reliable information reduces uncertainty.

2.1 Research techniques to reduce uncertainty

Market research into customer habits, attitudes or intentions can be used to reduce uncertainty.

Market research is the systematic process of gathering, analysing and reporting data about markets to investigate, describe, measure, understand or explain a situation or problem facing a company or organisation.

Market research involves **tackling problems**. The assumption is that these problems can be solved, no matter how complex the issues are, if the researcher follows a line of enquiry in a **systematic** way, without losing sight of the main objectives. Gathering and analysing all the facts will ultimately lead to **better decision making.**

2.1.1 The role of market research

In the last 20 years or so market research has become a much more widespread activity. Organisations – in the private sector, the public sector and the not-for-profit sector – rely on research to inform and improve their **planning and decision making**.

Market research enables organisations to understand the needs and opinions of their customers and other stakeholders. Armed with this knowledge they are able to make better quality decisions and provide better products and better services.

Thus, research influences what is provided and the way it is provided. It **reduces uncertainty and monitors performance.** A management team which possesses accurate information relating to the marketplace will be in a strong position to make the best decisions in an increasingly competitive world.

Decision-makers need data to reduce **uncertainty** and **risk** when planning for the future and to monitor business performance. Market researchers provide the data that helps them to do this.

An organisation wanting market research information will typically hire the services of a firm that specialises in market research. This firm will plan the market research exercise so as to gather information or opinions from a selected sample of individuals (or organisations). The information obtained can then be analysed **both qualitatively and statistically**.

2.1.2 Focus groups

A focus group may be used to obtain **qualitative views and opinions** from a small group of individuals. The group is asked about their opinions and attitudes towards a product or service, and members of the group are encouraged to share their views with each other as well as with the person leading the group.

Focus groups are used in marketing to obtain qualitative data about customer or consumer attitudes. They are used for example to obtain marketing information about attitudes to a new product, or to a new advertisement for a product. They may be used in the early stages of product development, when an organisation is trying to assess the strength of consumer attitudes and to find out in detail what they think of it.

Participants in a focus group are recruited on the basis of similar demographics, life styles, buying attitudes, or other behaviour, so that the views the group provides may be regarded as typical of the target market for the product.

Like market research, focus groups reduce uncertainty by providing information, and the information will influence decisions about designing and marketing a product.

2.1.3 Types of data collected

Data can be analysed to provide information that reduces uncertainty or enables an organisation to estimate probabilities.

The sources of data may be primary or secondary. Data may also be either qualitative or quantitative in nature.

Primary data is data that is obtained for a specific purpose and collected at first hand, typically from a sample of respondents. Market research and focus groups are sources of primary data. **Secondary data** is data that has been collected by someone else, and not for the specific purpose for which it is now being used. Secondary research is also known as **desk research**, because it can be carried out in an office by researching files or archives. Government statistics, published by the government's statistics department or bureau, are widely-used by business organisations as a source of secondary data.

Data can be either quantitative or qualitative.

(a)   **Quantitative** data is in the form of numbers and measurements. For example, quantitative data may provide a decision maker with information about **how many** customers or competitors act in a certain way. Quantitative data can, for example, tell the researcher the numbers or percentages of consumers who are likely to buy a product and may give numerical measurements about **where**, **when** and **how** people buy goods or consumer services.

(b)   **Qualitative** data tells us **why** consumers think/buy or act the way they do. Qualitative data is used in **consumer insight** (eg understanding what makes consumers prefer one brand to another), **media awareness** (eg how much of an advertisement is noticed by the public), **new product development** studies and for many other reasons.

Qualitative research has as its specific purpose the uncovering and understanding of thought and opinion. It is carried out on relatively small samples and unstructured or semi-structured techniques, such as individual in depth interviews and focus group discussions.

2.2 Worst/most likely/best outcome estimates

A fairly simple approach to assessing the uncertainty in a decision is to consider the range of possible outcomes for different decision options, and to identify:

(a)   the most likely outcome

(b)   the worst possible outcome (where 'worst possible' is an estimate of what, within reason, may happen. It is not an extreme and unlikely possibility.)

(c)   the best possible outcome (where 'best possible' is a 'within reason' estimate).

This will show the **full range of possible outcomes** from a decision, and may be used to reach a decision. For example assessing the worst possible outcomes may help managers to reject Option A in favour of Option B because the worst possible outcome with Option A would involve an unacceptable amount of loss.

When comparing the worst possible, most likely and best possible outcomes for different decision choices (decision options) it often helps to construct a **pay-off table**.

2.2.1 Pay-off tables
(Specimen paper)

Pay-off tables **identify and record all possible outcomes (or pay-offs)** in situations where there are two or more decision options and the outcome from each decision depends on the eventual circumstances that arise ('worst possible', 'most likely' or 'best possible').

A pay-off table is a table or matrix where:

(a)   one side of the table has a different row (or column0 for each decision option
(b)   the other side of the table has a column (or row) for the eventual circumstances that may arise

The boxes in the middle of the table record the outcome given the decision option and the circumstances that arise.

An example will help to demonstrate how a pay-off table is constructed.

2.2.2 Example: Worst/best possible outcomes

Omelette Co is trying to set the sales price for one of its products. Three prices are under consideration, and expected sales volumes and costs are as follows.

Pricing choices	Sales demand (units)	
$4	Best possible	16,000
	Most likely	14,000
	Worst possible	10,000
$4.30	Best possible	14,000
	Most likely	12,500
	Worst possible	8,000
$4.40	Best possible	12,500
	Most likely	12,000
	Worst possible	6,000

Fixed costs are $20,000 and variable costs of sales are $2 per unit.

Prepare a pay-off table for the different possible outcomes for each decision option.

Solution

Here we need to prepare a pay-off table showing **pay-offs** (contribution) **dependent on different levels of demand and different selling prices**.

In the table below, there is a column for each of the three possible pricing options, and there is a row for each of the three possible outcomes: best possible, most likely and worst possible.

The table is completed by entering the total contribution (or it could be profit, if you prefer) for each different price, given each possible outcome. The workings are not shown here.

Pay-off table

Price per unit	$4	$4.30	$4.40
Contribution per unit	$2	$2.30	$2.40
Total contribution towards fixed costs	$	$	$
Best possible	32,000	32,200	30,000
Most likely	28,000	28,750	28,800
Worst possible	20,000	18,400	14,400

So how does a pay-off table help with reaching a decision?

(a) The highest contribution based on **most likely** sales volume would be at a price of $4.40. However it may be argued that $4.30 would be a much better choice for price than $4.40, since the most likely profit is almost as good, the worst possible profit is not as bad, and the best possible profit is better.

(b) However, given fixed costs of $20,000, only a price of $4 guarantees that the company would **not make a loss,** even if the worst possible outcome occurs. (The fixed costs of $20,000 would just be covered.) A risk averse management might therefore prefer a price of $4 to either of the other two prices.

To use a pay-off table to reach a decision, we need to establish the 'rule' or 'criterion' for making the decision. There are different possible decision criteria or rules, such as expected value (EV) rule, the maximin rule the minimax regret rule, and so on. These are explained in the following sections.

3 Probabilities and expected values 6/11, 6/13

FAST FORWARD ⟩⟩

An expected value is a weighted average value of the different possible outcomes from a decision, where weightings are based on the probability of each possible outcome.

Expected values indicate what an outcome is likely to be in the long term, if the decision can be repeated many times over. Fortunately, many business transactions do occur over and over again.

Although the outcome of a decision may not be certain, the probabilities of different possible outcomes may possibly be estimated, for example on the basis of historical experience of similar circumstances.

3.1 Expected values

Where probabilities are assigned to different outcomes we can measure the weighted average value of the different possible outcomes. Each possible outcome is given a weighting equal to the probability that it will occur.

The expected value (EV) decision rule is that the decision option with the highest EV of benefit or the lowest EV of cost should be selected.

3.1.1 Example: Expected values

Suppose a manager has to choose between mutually exclusive options A and B, and the probable outcomes of each option are as follows.

Option A		Option B	
Probability	Profit $	Probability	Profit $
0.8	5,000	0.1	(2,000)
0.2	6,000	0.2	5,000
		0.6	7,000
		0.1	8,000

The expected value (EV) of profit of each option would be measured as follows.

Option A				Option B			
Prob p		Profit x $	EV of profit px $	Prob p		Profit x $	EV of profit px $
0.8	×	5,000 =	4,000	0.1	×	(2,000) =	(200)
0.2	×	6,000 =	1,200	0.2	×	5,000 =	1,000
		EV =	5,200	0.6	×	7,000 =	4,200
				0.1	×	8,000 =	800
						EV	5,800

In this example, since it offers a higher EV of profit, option B would be selected in preference to A, unless further risk analysis is carried out.

3.1.2 Example: Expected values and pay-off tables

IB Newsagents stocks a weekly lifestyle magazine. The owner buys the magazines at the beginning of each week for $0.30 each and sells them at the retail price of $0.50 each.

At the end of the week unsold magazines are obsolete and have no value, so they are discarded as recycled waste. The estimated probability distribution for weekly demand is shown below.

Weekly demand in units	Probability
20	0.20
30	0.55
40	0.25
	1.00

The actual demand in each week does not affect the actual demand in the following week.

Required

If the owner is to order a fixed quantity of magazines per week how many should that be? Since the outcomes occur every week, many times over, the EV decision rule is considered appropriate here.

Assume no seasonal variations in demand.

Solution

Start by identifying the different decision options. These are assumed here to be the different buying decisions, with three options: buy 20 per week, buy 30 per week or buy 40 per week.

The different possible outcomes are the three possibilities for actual demand: 20 units, 30 units or 40 units.

The next step is to set up a decision matrix of possible strategies (numbers bought) and possible demand.

The 'pay-off' from each combination of action and outcome is then computed.

No sale = cost of $0.30 per magazine

Sale = profit of $0.20 per magazine ($0.50 − $0.30)

Probability	Outcome (number demanded)	Decision (number bought)		
		20	30	40
		$	$	$
0.20	20	4.00	1.00*	(2.00) **
0.55	30	4.00	6.00	3.00 ***
0.25	40	4.00	6.00	8.00

* Buy 30 and sell only 20 gives a profit of (20 × $0.5) − (30 × $0.3) = $1

** Buy 40 and sell only 20 gives a loss of (20 × $0.5) − (40 × $0.3) = $(2)

*** Buy 40 and sell 30 gives a profit of (30 × $0.5) − (40 × $0.3) = $3

We can now calculate the EV of each decision option, as the weighted average value of the different possible outcomes for each option.

Decision option		EV of weekly profit
Buy 20	($4 × 0.20) + ($4 × 0.55) + ($4 × 0.25) =	$4.00
Buy 30	($1 × 0.20) + ($6 × 0.55) + ($6 × 0.25) =	$5.00
Buy 40	($(2) × 0.20) + ($3 × 0.55) + ($8 × 0.25) =	$3.25

The strategy which gives the highest expected value of pay-off is to stock 30 magazines each week.

(Note: The expected value of weekly demand in this example is (20 × 0.20) + (30 × 0.55) + (40 × 0.25) = 30.5 copies, but this does not help with the calculation of the expected value of profit, because the profit is dependent on the purchase quantity as well as the sales demand quantity.)

<table>
<tr><td>**Exam focus point**</td><td>The examiner has noted in that candidates often struggle to construct an accurate pay-off table. Make sure that you understand the above example which demonstrates this technique.</td></tr>
</table>

Question

EVs

A manager has to choose between mutually exclusive options C and D and the probable outcomes of each option are as follows.

	Option C			Option D	
Probability		Cost	Probability		Cost
		$			$
0.29		15,000	0.03		14,000
0.54		20,000	0.30		17,000
0.17		30,000	0.35		21,000
			0.32		24,000

Both options will produce an income of $30,000. Which should be chosen, on the basis of the expected value decision rule?

Answer

Option C. Do the workings yourself in the way illustrated above. Note that the probabilities are for *costs* not profits.

3.1.3 Limitations of expected values

Making a decision between different options on the basis of expected value has some significant limitations.

(a) An expected value is a weighted average outcome that will occur in the long run if events occur many times over. It is a long run average.

(b) The expected value of a decision may be a value that will never occur. For example if there is a 0.7 probability of a profit of $10,000 and a 0.3 probability of a loss of $5,000, the expected value is (0.7 × $10,000) − (0.3 × $5,000) = + $5,500. The EV is a profit of $5,500, but this value cannot actually occur.

(c) Because an EV is an average value, it ignores the extreme outcomes. For example if there is a 0.7 probability of a profit of $10,000 and a 0.3 probability of a loss of $5,000, the expected value is a profit of $5,500. However if the organisation cannot afford to incur a loss, making the decision on the basis of EV would be too risky.

Expected values are used to support a **risk-neutral attitude**. A risk-neutral decision maker will ignore any variability in the range of possible outcomes and be concerned only with the expected value of outcomes.

Expected values are more valuable as a guide to decision making where they refer to outcomes which will occur **many times over**. Examples would include the probability that so many customers per day will buy a can of baked beans, the probability that a customer services assistant will receive so many phone calls per hour, and so on.

4 Other decision rules   12/08, 6/11, Specimen paper

The 'play it safe' basis for decision making is referred to as the **maximin basis**. This is short for **'maximise the minimum achievable profit'**.

A basis for making decisions by looking for the best outcome is known as the **maximax basis**, short for **'maximise the maximum achievable profit'**.

The 'opportunity loss' basis for decision making is known as **minimax regret**.

The expected value rule is just one possible 'rule' or criterion on which to base a decision. There are other rules that a decision-maker may prefer to use. In using these alternative decision rules, it is often useful to compare the different possible outcomes of all the decision options in a **pay-off table**.

4.1 Maximin decision rule

Key term

The **maximin decision rule** is that a decision maker should select the alternative that offers the least unattractive worst outcome. This would mean choosing the alternative that *maximises* the *minimum* profits.

Suppose a businessman is trying to decide which of three **mutually exclusive** projects to undertake. Since they are mutually exclusive, only one of the projects can be selected. Each of the projects could lead to varying net profit under three possible scenarios or outcomes. (The figures in the pay-off table are figures for profit, in $000.)

Pay-off table		Project choice		
		D	E	F
	I	100	80	60
Scenarios	II	90	120	85
	III	(20)	10	85

The maximin decision rule is to select the option that offers the best minimum profit – the best 'worst possible result' that could happen.

In this example, the worst possible is a loss of $20,000 with Project D, a profit of $10,000 with Project E and a profit of $60,000 with Project F. The best worst outcome is 60 and project F would therefore be selected (because this is a better 'worst possible' than either D or E).

4.1.1 Criticisms of the maximin rule

(a) It is **defensive** and **conservative**, being a safety first principle of avoiding the worst outcomes without taking into account opportunities for maximising profits.

(b) It ignores the **probability** of each different outcome taking place.

4.2 Maximax decision rule

Key term

The **maximax criterion** looks at the best possible results. Maximax means 'maximise the maximum profit'. The decision with this rule is to choose the option that could provide the maximum possible profit.

Using the example in Section 4.1 above, the maximum profit for Project D is $100,000; for Project E it is $120,000; and and for Project F it is $85,000.

Project E would be chosen if the maximax rule is followed, because it offers the prospect of the biggest profit.

4.2.1 Criticisms of the maximax rule

(a) It ignores the probabilities of different outcomes.

(b) It ignores the outcomes that are less than the best possible. For some decision options, the worst possible may be more than the organisation can afford. It is a decision rule for the **risk-seeker.**

Question

A company is considering which one of three alternative courses of action, A, B and C to take. The profit or loss from each choice depends on which one of four economic circumstances, I, II, III or IV will apply. The possible profits and losses, in thousands of pounds, are given in the following payoff table. Losses are shown as negative figures.

		Decision option		
		A	B	C
	I	70	60	70
Circumstance/outcome	II	−10	20	−5
	III	80	0	50
	IV	60	100	115

Required

State which option would be selected using

(a) the maximax decision rule
(b) the maximin decision rule.

Answer

(a) The **best possible outcomes** are as follows.

A (circumstance III):   80
B (circumstance IV):   100
C (circumstance IV):   115

As 115 is the highest of these three figures, action C would be chosen using the maximax criterion.

(b) The **worst possible outcomes** are as follows.

A (circumstance II):   −10
B (circumstance III):   0
C (circumstance II):   −5

The best of these figures is 0 (neither a profit nor a loss), so action B would be chosen using the maximin criterion.

4.3 Minimax regret rule

Key term

> The **minimax regret rule** aims to minimise the regret from making the wrong decision. **Regret** is the opportunity lost through making the wrong decision.

The 'minimax regret' decision rule is another possible decision rule for choosing between different decision options. It is a bit more complicated than the maximin rule or the maximax rule.

With this decision rule, for each of the possible outcome situations, we compare the different values of profit (or cost) for each of the decision options.

For each outcome situation, we measure the amount of the 'regret' for each decision option.

Regret for the decision option	=	Profit from the best decision option, given the outcome circumstances or situation	−	Profit from the decision option, given the outcome circumstances or situation

For the decision option with the best outcome, given the circumstances or situation, the regret = $0. For the other decision options, the regret always has a positive value. It is the amount by which the profit is worse than if the best decision option had been taken, in view of the outcome circumstances.

The regret is calculated for all the decision options in each of the possible outcome circumstances, and these are recorded in a pay-off table.

The decision rule is to select the decision option that has the lowest value of regret (= the minimum regret).

The minimax regret decision rule is that the decision option selected should be the one which **minimises the maximum potential regret** for any of the possible outcomes.

This may seem complicated, but an example should help to clarify the rule.

Using the example in Section 4.1, a table of regrets can be compiled as follows.

The pay-off table (in $000s) is as follows:

Pay-off table		Project choice		
		D	E	F
	I	100	80	60
Scenarios	II	90	120	85
	III	(20)	10	85

The regret for each decision option in each outcome situation is shown in the pay-off table below.

		Project option		
		D	E	F
	I *	0	20	40
Scenario/outcome situation	II **	30	0	35
	III ***	105	75	0
Maximum regret		105	75	40

* With outcome situation I, the best possible result is obtained from Project D, so the regret with Project D is $0. The result with Option E would be 20 worse and the result from Option F would be 40 worse. So 20 and 40 are the amounts of the regret for Options D and F respectively.

** With outcome situation II, the best possible result is obtained from Project E, so the regret with Project E is $0. The result with Option D would be 30 worse and the result from Option F would be 35 worse. So 30 and 735 are the amounts of the regret for Options D and F respectively.

*** With outcome situation III, the best possible result is obtained from Project F, so the regret with Project F is $0. The result with Option D would be 105 worse and the result from Option E would be 75 worse. So 105 and 75 are the amounts of the regret for Options D and E respectively.

The **lowest** of maximum regrets is 40 with project Option F so Option F would be selected, if the minimax regret rule is used as the basis for making the decision.

4.4 Contribution tables

Questions requiring application of the decision rules often incorporate a **number of variables, each with a range of possible values**. For example these variables might be:

- Unit price and associated level of demand
- Unit variable cost

Each variable might have, for example, three possible values.

Before being asked to use the decision rules, exam questions could ask you to **work out** the **contribution** for each of the possible outcomes, and record these in a contribution table. (Alternatively profit figures could be required if you are given information about fixed costs.)

The **number of possible outcomes** = number of values of variable 1 × number of values of variable 2 × number of values of variable 3 etc

So, for example, if there are **two** variables, each with **three** possible values, there are **3 × 3 = 9 outcomes.**

Perhaps the easiest way to see how to draw up contribution tables is to look at an example.

4.4.1 Example: Contribution tables and the decision rules

Suppose the budgeted demand for product X will be 11,500 units if the price is $10, 8,500 units if the price is $12 and 5,000 units if the price is $14. Variable costs are estimated at either $4, $5, or $6 per unit. A decision needs to be made on the **price** to be charged.

Here is a contribution table showing the budgeted contribution for each of the nine possible outcomes.

Demand	Price	Variable cost	Unit contribution	Total contribution
	$	$	$	$'000
11,500	10	4	6	69.0
11,500	10	5	5	57.5
11,500	10	6	4	46.0
8,500	12	4	8	68.0
8,500	12	5	7	59.5
8,500	12	6	6	51.0
5,000	14	4	10	50.0
5,000	14	5	9	45.0
5,000	14	6	8	40.0

Once the table has been drawn up, the decision rules can be applied.

The decision is the selection of the selling price.

Solution

Maximin decision rule

If the maximin decision rule is used, we should select the price that provides the highest possible total contribution, given the different possible amounts of variable cost per unit. We need to maximise the minimum contribution.

Demand/price	Minimum contribution
11,500/$10	$46,000
8,500/$12	$51,000
5,000/$14	$40,000

Set a price of $12.

Maximax decision rule

With the maximax rule, we select the option that offers the highest possible total contribution.

Demand/price	Maximum possible contribution
11,500/$10	$69,000
8,000/$12	$68,000
5,000/$14	$50,000

Set a price of $10.

Minimax regret decision rule

We need to minimise the maximum regret (lost contribution) of making the wrong decision. The regret with each decision option, given the possible amounts for variable cost per unit, are set out in the following pay-off table.

Variable cost (= outcome) $	$10	Price (option) $12	$14
4	$0	$1,000	$19,000
5	$2,000	$0	$14,500
6	$5,000	$0	$11,000
Minimax regret	$5,000	$1,000	$19,000

Using the minimax regret decision rule, a price of $12 would be charged, because this has the minimum 'worst possible value' for regret. **(price of $12, maximum regret = $1,000).**

Sample working

At a variable cost of $4, the best strategy would be a price of $10. Choosing a price of $12 would mean lost contribution of $69,000 – $68,000 = $1,000, while choosing a price of $14 would mean lost contribution of $69,000 – $50,000 = $19,000.

Exam focus point

Decision rules are a popular exam topic. The examiner has commented that candidates struggle to justify decisions with supporting calculations.

5 Decision trees   6/13

FAST FORWARD

Decision trees are diagrams which illustrate the choices and possible outcomes of a decision. The possible outcomes are usually given associated probabilities of occurrence.

Rollback analysis evaluates the EV of each decision option. You have to work from right to left and calculate EVs at each outcome point.

Exam focus point

There has been an article in *Student Accountant* on decision trees. This is available on the ACCA web site and you are strongly recommended to read it.

A probability problem such as 'what is the probability of throwing a six with one throw of a die?' is fairly straightforward and can be solved using the basic principles of probability.

More complex probability questions, although solvable using the basic principles, require a clear logical approach to ensure that all possible choices and outcomes of a decision are taken into consideration. **Decision trees** are a useful means of analysing a probability problem.

Key term

A **decision tree** is a pictorial method of showing the different decision options in a given situation, and the possible outcomes from each decision option. a sequence of interrelated decisions and their expected outcomes. Decision trees can incorporate both the probabilities the expected outcomes and the EV of each decision option. Decision tress can also show both initial decisions and subsequent decisions, where a decision is taken in two stages, a two different times.

Exactly how does the use of a decision tree help to provide a clear and logical approach to decision making?

- All the possible **choices** that can be made are shown as **branches** on the tree.
- All the possible **outcomes** of each choice are shown as **subsidiary branches** on the tree.

5.1 Constructing a decision tree

There are two stages in preparing a decision tree.

- Drawing the tree itself to show all the decision options or choices, and the different possible outcomes from each decision

- Putting in the numbers (the probabilities, outcome values and EVs)

Every **decision tree starts** from a **decision point** with the **decision options** that are currently being considered, and the decision that must be made 'now'.

(a) It helps to identify the **decision point**, and any subsequent decision points in the tree, with a symbol. Here, we shall use a **square shape** to indicate that a decision must be made at this point.

(b) There should be a **line**, or **branch**, for each **option** or **alternative**.

It is conventional to draw decision trees from left to right, and so a decision tree will start as follows.

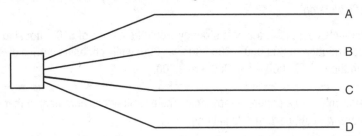

In this example, the **square** is the **decision point**, and A, B, C and D represent **four alternatives** from which a choice must be made (such as buy a new machine with cash, hire a machine, continue to use existing machine, raise a loan to buy a machine).

If the outcome from any choice is certain, the branch of the decision tree for that decision option is complete.

If the outcome of a particular choice is uncertain, the various possible outcomes must be shown.

We show the various possible outcomes on a decision tree by inserting an **outcome point** on the **branch** of the tree. Each possible outcome is then shown as a **subsidiary branch**, coming out from the outcome point. The probability of each outcome occurring should be written on to the branch of the tree which represents that outcome.

To distinguish decision points from outcome points, **a circle will be used as the symbol for an outcome point**.

In the example above, there are two choices facing the decision-maker, A and B. The outcome if A is chosen is known with certainty, but if B is chosen, there are two possible outcomes, high sales (0.6 probability) or low sales (0.4 probability).

When several outcomes are possible, it may be simpler to show two or more stages of outcome points on the decision tree.

5.2 Example: Several possible outcomes

A company can choose to launch a new product XYZ or not. If the product is launched, expected sales and expected unit costs might be as follows.

Sales		Unit costs	
Units	Probability	£	Probability
10,000	0.8	6	0.7
15,000	0.2	8	0.3

(a) The decision tree could be drawn as follows.

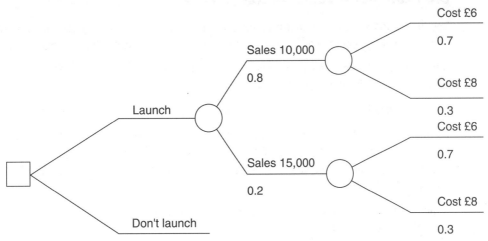

(b) The layout shown above will usually be easier to use than the alternative way of drawing the tree, which is as follows.

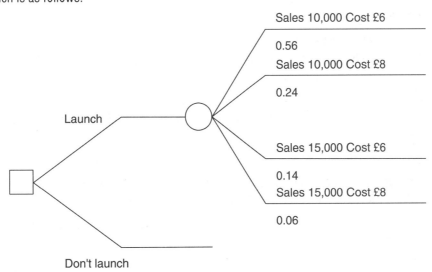

However, both decision trees are 'correct'. You can draw whichever you prefer.

Sometimes, a **decision taken now** will lead to **other decisions to be taken in the future**. When this situation arises, the decision tree can be drawn as a **two-stage tree**, as follows.

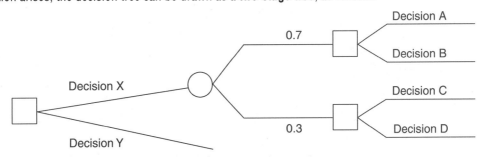

In this decision tree, if the initial decision is to select Decision X a subsequent cdecsion will have to be made. This subsequent decision is either a choice between A and B or else a choice between C and D will be made, depending on the outcome which occurs after choosing X.

The decision tree should be in **chronological order** from **left to right**. When there are two-stage decision trees, the first decision in time should be drawn on the left.

5.3 Example: A decision tree

Beethoven Co has a new wonder product, the vylin, of which it expects great things. At the moment the company has two courses of action open to it, to test market the product or abandon it.

If the company test markets it, the cost will be $100,000 and the market response could be positive or negative with probabilities of 0.60 and 0.40.

If the response is positive the company could either abandon the product or market it full scale.

If it markets the vylin full scale, the outcome might be low, medium or high demand, and the respective net gains/(losses) would be (200), 200 or 1,000 in units of $1,000 (the result could range from a net loss of $200,000 to a gain of $1,000,000). These outcomes have probabilities of 0.20, 0.50 and 0.30 respectively.

If the result of the test marketing is negative and the company goes ahead and markets the product, estimated losses would be $600,000.

If, at any point, the company abandons the product, there would be a net gain of $50,000 from the sale of scrap. All the financial values have been discounted to the present.

Required

(a)   Draw a decision tree.
(b)   Include figures for cost, loss or profit on the appropriate branches of the tree.

Solution

The starting point for the tree is to **establish what decision has to be made now**. What are the options?

(a)   To test market
(b)   To abandon

The outcome of the 'abandon' option is known with certainty. There are two possible outcomes of the option to test market, positive response and negative response.

Depending on the outcome of the test marketing, another decision will then be made, to abandon the product or to go ahead.

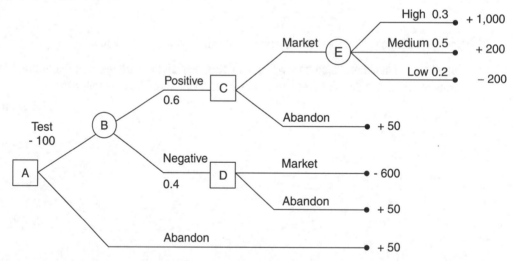

Exam focus point

In an examination, remember to draw decision trees (and *all* diagrams) neatly, using a pen and ruler. Remember also to label decision points and branches as clearly as possible.

5.4 Evaluating the decision with a decision tree: rollback analysis

Rollback analysis evaluates the EV of each decision option. You have to **work from right to left** and calculate EVs at each outcome point.

The EV of each decision option can be evaluated, using the decision tree to help with keeping the logic on track. The basic rules are as follows.

(a) We start on the **right hand side** of the tree and **work back** towards the left hand side and the current decision under consideration. This is sometimes known as the **'rollback' technique** or **'rollback analysis'**.

(b) Working from **right to left**, we calculate the **EV of revenue, cost, contribution or profit** at each outcome point on the tree.

In the above example, the right-hand-most outcome point is point E, and the EV is as follows.

	Profit	Probability	
	x	p	px
	$'000		$'000
High	1,000	0.3	300
Medium	200	0.5	100
Low	(200)	0.2	(40)
		EV	360

This is the EV of the decision to market the product if the test shows positive response. It may help you to write the EV on the decision tree itself, at the appropriate outcome point (point E).

(a) **At decision point C**, the **choice** is to select the option with the highest EV of profit (or lowest EV of cost). Here the EV of the two decision options, 'market' or 'abandon' are as follows.

  (i) Market, EV = + 360 (the EV at point E)
  (ii) Abandon, value = + 50

  The choice would be to market the product, and so the EV at decision point C is +360.

(b) **At decision point D**, the **choice** is again to select the option with the highest EV of profit (or lowest EV of cost). The two decision options and their associated EVs are as follows.

  (i) Market, value = – 600
  (ii) Abandon, value = +50

  The choice would be to abandon, and so the EV at decision point D is +50.

The second stage decisions have therefore been made. If the original decision is to test market, the company will market the product if the test shows positive customer response, and will abandon the product if the test results are negative.

The evaluation of the decision tree is completed as follows.

(a) **Calculate the EV at outcome point B.**

  $$
  \begin{array}{rll}
  & 0.6 \times 360 & \text{(EV at C)} \\
  + & 0.4 \times \ 50 & \text{(EV at D)} \\
  = & 216 + \ 20 = 236.
  \end{array}
  $$

(b) **Compare the options at point A**, which are as follows.

  (i) Test: EV = EV at B minus test marketing cost = 236 – 100 = 136
  (ii) Abandon: Value = 50

The choice would be to test market the product, because it has a **higher EV of profit**.

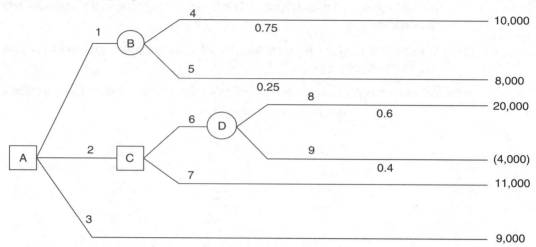

Consider the following diagram.

If a decision maker wished to maximise the value of the outcome, which options should be selected?

A   Option 2 and option 7
B   Option 3
C   Option 1 and option 4
D   Option 2, option 6 and option 8

Answer

The correct answer is A.

The various outcomes must be evaluated using expected values.

EV at point B: $(0.75 \times 10,000) + (0.25 \times 8,000) = 9,500$

EV at point D: $(0.6 \times 20,000) + (0.4 \times (4,000)) = 10,400$

EV at point C: Choice between 10,400 and 11,000

EV at point A: Choice between B (9,500), C (10,400 or 11,000) and choice 3 (9,000).

If we are trying to maximise the figure, option 2 and then option 7 are chosen to give 11,000.

Evaluating decisions by using **decision trees has a number of limitations**.

(a)   Decision trees are not very suitable for use with complex decisions because the decision tree becomes too big and complicated to follow.

(b)   Decision trees are just a graphical way of making a decision based on the expected value rule. So the decision tree method has all the benefits and limitations of EV as a decision rule.

(c)   The probabilities associated with different branches of the 'tree' are likely to be estimates, and possibly unreliable or inaccurate. (In the same way, estimates of probabilities with the EV decision rule method may be unreliable.)

6 The value of information

Perfect information is guaranteed to predict the future with 100% accuracy. **Imperfect information** is better than no information at all but could be wrong in its prediction of the future.

The **value of perfect information** is the difference between the EV of profit with perfect information and the EV of profit without perfect information.

The risk or uncertainty in a decision can be reduced by obtaining information about the likely outcome situation. Information about the likely outcome has value, because it improves the likelihood of making the best possible decision when faced with a number of different options.

The **value of information** can be calculated on the assumption that the EV decision criterion is used. The value of information is the difference between the EV of a decision if no information is available and the EV of the decision if the information is made available.

Information may be either perfect or imperfect.

Perfect information is information that predicts with 100% accuracy what the outcome situation will be. Having perfect information removes all doubt and uncertainty from a decision, and enables managers to make decisions with complete confidence that they have selected the best decision option.

6.1 The value of perfect information   6/13

Step 1   If we **do not have perfect information** and we must choose between two or more decision options, we would **select** the decision option which offers the **highest EV** of profit (or lowest EV of cost). This option will not be the best decision under all circumstances. There will be some probability that what was really the best option will not have been selected, given the way actual events turn out.

Step 2   With **perfect information**, the **best decision option will always be selected**. The decision option that is selected will differ according to what the outcome situation will be. The choice will be the outcome that gives the highest profit (or lowest cost) in the circumstances that we know will occur. We can calculate an EV of profit, given the different possible outcomes and their associated probabilities. The EV of profit with perfect information should be higher than the EV of profit without the information.

Step 3   The **value of perfect information** is **the difference between the E of profit with perfect information and the EV of profit with the information**.

6.2 Example: The value of perfect information

The management of Ivor Ore must choose whether to go ahead with either of two **mutually exclusive** projects, A and B. The expected profits are as follows.

	Profit if there is strong demand	Profit if there is moderate demand	Profit/(loss) if there is weak demand
Option A	$4,000	$1,200	$(1,000)
Option B	$1,500	$1,000	$500
Probability of demand	0.2	0.3	0.5

Required

(a)   Ascertain what the decision would be, based on expected values, if no information about demand were available.

(b)   Calculate the value of perfect information about demand.

Solution

Step 1   If there is **no information** to help with the decision, the project with the higher EV of profit would be selected.

Probability	Project A		Project B	
	Profit	EV	Profit	EV
	$	$	$	$
0.2	4,000	800	1,500	300
0.3	1,200	360	1,000	300
0.5	(1,000)	(500)	500	250
		660		850

Project B would be selected and the EV of the decision is + $850.

This is clearly the better option if demand turns out to be weak. However, if demand were to turn out to be moderate or strong, project A would be more profitable. There is a 50% chance that this could happen (30% + 20%).

Step 2   **Perfect information** will indicate for certain whether demand will be weak, moderate or strong. If demand is forecast 'weak' project B would be selected. If demand if forecast as 'moderate' project A would be selected, and perfect information would improve the profit from $1,000, which would have been earned by selecting B, to $1,200.

If demand is forecast as 'strong', project A would again be selected, and perfect information would improve the profit from $1,500, which would have been earned by selecting B, to $4,000.

Forecast demand	Probability	Project chosen	Profit	EV of profit
			$	$
Weak	0.5	B	500	250
Moderate	0.3	A	1,200	360
Strong	0.2	A	4,000	800
		EV of profit with perfect information		1,410

Step 3

	$
EV of profit without perfect information (ie if project B is always chosen)	850
EV of profit with perfect information	1,410
Value of perfect information	560

Provided that the information does not cost more than $560 to collect, it would be worth having, on the assumption that the EV decision rule is applied.

 Question   **Decision based on EV of profit**

WL must decide at what level to market a new product, the urk. The urk can be sold nationally, within a single sales region (where demand is likely to be relatively strong) or within a single area. The decision is complicated by uncertainty about the general strength of consumer demand for the product, and the following conditional profit table has been constructed.

		Demand		
		Weak	Moderate	Strong
		$	$	$
Market	nationally (A)	(4,000)	2,000	10,000
	in one region (B)	0	3,500	4,000
	in one area (C)	1,000	1,500	2,000
Probability		0.3	0.5	0.2

Required

Option B should be selected, based on EVs of profit. True or false?

Answer

The correct answer is option B and so the statement is true.

Without perfect information, the option with the highest EV of profit will be chosen.

Probability	Option A (National) Profit $	EV $	Option B (Regional) Profit $	EV $	Option C (Area) Profit $	EV $
0.3	(4,000)	(1,200)	0	0	1,000	300
0.5	2,000	1,000	3,500	1,750	1,500	750
0.2	10,000	2,000	4,000	800	2,000	400
		1,800		2,550		1,450

Marketing regionally (option B) has the highest EV of profit, and would be selected.

Question   Perfect information

Required

Using the information in your answer to the question above (decision based on EV of profit) calculate the value of perfect information about the state of demand.

Answer

The correct answer is $1,500. It would be worth paying up to $1,500 to obtain perfect information.

If perfect information about the state of consumer demand is available, option A would be preferred if the forecast demand is strong and option C would be preferred if the forecast demand is weak.

Demand	Probability	Choice	Profit $	EV of profit $
Weak	0.3	C	1,000	300
Moderate	0.5	B	3,500	1,750
Strong	0.2	A	10,000	2,000
EV of profit with perfect information				4,050
EV of profit, selecting option B				2,550
Value of perfect information				1,500

6.3 Perfect information and decision trees

When the option exists to obtain information, the decision can be shown, like any other decision, in the form of a decision tree, as follows. We will suppose, for illustration, that the cost of obtaining perfect information is $400.

					Profit
		Demand strong	0.2	Choose A	10,000
EV 4,050 → (1)		Demand moderate	0.5	Choose B	3,500
Obtain information (400)		Demand weak	0.3	Choose C	1,000
	No information Choose A (2)	Demand strong	0.2		10,000
		Demand moderate	0.5		2,000
	EV 1,800	Demand weak	0.3		(4,000)
	No information Choose B (3)	Demand strong	0.2		4,000
		Demand moderate	0.5		3,500
	EV 2,550	Demand weak	0.3		0
	No information Choose C (4)	Demand strong	0.2		2,000
		Demand moderate	0.5		1,500
	EV 1,450	Demand weak	0.3		1,000

The decision would be to obtain perfect information, since the EV of profit is $4,050 – $400 = $3,650.

You should check carefully that you understand the logic of this decision tree and that you can identify how the EVs at outcome boxes 1, 2, 3 and 4 have been calculated.

6.4 The value of imperfect information

The **value of imperfect information** is the difference between the EV of profit with imperfect information and the EV of profit without the information.

There is one serious drawback to the 'perfect information' technique we have just looked at. In practice, **information is never perfect**. Market research findings or information from pilot tests and so on are likely to be reasonably accurate, but they can still be wrong: they provide imperfect information. It is possible, however, to arrive at an assessment of **how much it would be worth paying for such imperfect information, given that we have a rough indication of how right or wrong it is likely to be**. In other words, we can calculate the value of imperfect information provided that we have an estimate of probabilities that the information will be correct or incorrect.

Suppose that a company want to make a decision between two mutually exclusive options, Option A and Option B. the profits from each option will depend on the state of the economy in the next 12 months. Current estimates are that there is a 60% probability that the economy will be weak and a 40% probability that the economy will be strong.

The profitability with each decision option would be as follows.

	Option A	Option B
Weak economy	+ $50,000	+ $20,000
Strong economy	+ $60,000	+ $100,000

Research could be carried out into the state of the economy in the next 12 months. It has been estimated that if the true state of the economy will be weak, there is an 80% probability that the research would predict this correctly. It is also estimated that if the true state of the economy will be strong, there is an 90% probability that the research would predict this correctly.

What is the value of this imperfect information?

The value of the imperfect information is the difference between the EV of profit if no information is available and the EV of profit if the information is obtained.

(a) *Value of decision without information*

The EV of the decision if no information is available is based on the **'prior probabilities'** of the state of the economy.

Option A: (0.6 × $50,000) + (0.4 × $60,000) $54,000

Option B: (0.6 × $20,000) + (0.4 × $100,000) $52,000

The decision would be to select Option A and the EV of profit would be $54,000.

(b) *Value of decision with imperfect information*

If research information is obtained, the decision will be to select Option A if the research indicates a weak economy and to select Option B if the research indicates a strong economy. The different possible outcomes, and their associated probabilities, are as follows.

Actual state of economy	Research prediction	Decision	Profit	Probability		EV of profit
Weak	Weak	Option A	$50,000	(0.6 × 0.8)	0.48	24,000
Weak	Strong	Option B	$20,000	(0.6 × 0.2)	0.12	2,400
Strong	Strong	Option B	$100,000	(0.4 × 0.9)	0.36	36,000
Strong	Weak	Option A	$60,000	(0.4 × 0.1)	0.04	2,400
						64,800

The EV of profit when the decision is based on the imperfect information is $64,800. (The probabilities of the different possible outcomes with the information are called 'posterior probabilities.)

The information is imperfect because it is not 100% certain to be correct, which means that there is a possibility that the best decision option will not be selected, in spite of obtaining the information.

The **value of the imperfect information** = EV of profit with the information minus EV of profit without the information

= $64,800 – $54,000 = **$10,800**

6.4.1 Example: The value of imperfect information

Suppose that the Small Oil Company (SOC) is trying to decide whether or not to drill on a particular site. The chief engineer has assessed the probability that there will be oil, based on past experience, as 20%, and the probability that there won't be oil as 80%.

It is possible for SOC to hire a firm of international consultants to carry out a complete survey of the site. SOC has used the firm many times before and has estimated that if there really is oil, there is a 95% chance that the report will be favourable, but if there is no oil, there is only a 10% chance that the report will indicate that there is oil.

Required

Determine whether drilling should occur.

Solution

Read the information given carefully. We are given *three* sets of probabilities.

(a) The probability that there will be oil (0.2) or there will not be (0.8). These outcomes are mutually exclusive.

(b) The probability that, if there is oil, the report will say there is oil (0.95) or say there is no oil (0.05).

(c) The probability that, if there is no oil, the report will say there *is* oil (0.1) or say there is no oil (0.9).

Both (b) and (c) describe conditional events, since the existence of oil or otherwise influences the chances of the survey report being correct.

SOC, meanwhile faces a number of choices which we can show as a decision tree.

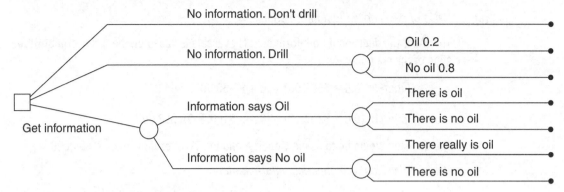

We must now calculate the probabilities of the following outcomes.

- The information will say 'oil' or 'no oil'
- The information will be right or wrong if it says 'oil'
- The information will be right or wrong if it says 'no oil'

If you check the information given in the problem, you will find that these probabilities are not given.

(a) We are told that the engineer has assessed that there is a 20% chance of oil and an 80% chance of no oil (ignoring information entirely). These are the **prior probabilities** of future possible outcomes.

(b) The **probabilities that there will be oil or no oil once the information has been obtained are posterior probabilities**.

Step 1   We can tabulate the various probabilities as percentages.

		Actual outcome					
		Oil		No oil		Total	
Survey	oil	19	(W2)	8	(W3)	27	(W4)
result:	no oil	1		72		73	
	Total	20	(W1)	80		100	

Workings

1   The engineer estimates 20% probability of oil and 80% of no oil.

2   If there is oil, ie in 20 cases out of 100, the survey will say so in 95% of these cases, ie in $20 \times 0.95 = 19$ cases. The 1 below the 19 is obtained by subtraction.

3   In the 80 per 100 cases where there is in fact no oil, the survey will wrongly say that there is oil 10% of the time; ie $80 \times 0.10 = 8$ cases. The 72 below the 8 is obtained by subtraction.

4   The horizontal totals are given by addition.

Step 2   We can now provide all the probabilities needed to complete the tree.

P (survey will say there is oil)   = 27/100   = 0.27

P (survey will say there is no oil)   = 73/100   = 0.73

If survey says oil   P (there is oil)   = 19/27 = 0.704
P (there is no oil)   = 8/27 = 0.296 (or 1–0.704)
If survey says no oil   P (there is oil)   = 1/73 = 0.014
P (there is no oil)   = 72/73 = 0.986 (or 1–0.014)

Step 3   We can now go on to complete the decision tree. Let us make the following assumptions. (In an exam question such information would have been given to you from the start.)

- The cost of drilling is $10m.
- The value of the benefits if oil is found is $70m, giving a net 'profit' of $60m.
- The cost of obtaining information from the consultants would be $3m.

An assumption is made that the decision maker will take whichever decision the information indicates is the best. If the information says 'oil', the company will drill, and if the information says 'no oil' it will not drill.

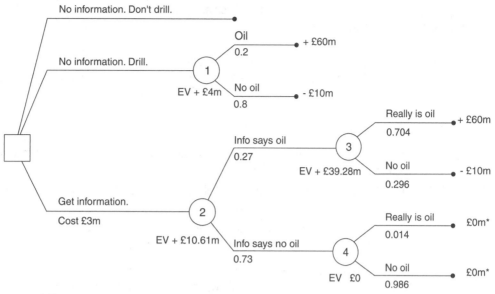

* The information is 'no oil', so the company won't drill, regardless of whether there really is oil or not.

Step 4   We can now perform rollback analysis.

		$m
EV at point 3 =	0.704 × $60m	42.24
	0.296 × ($10m)	(2.96)
		+ 39.28

		$m
EV at point 2 =	0.27 × $39.28m	10.61
	0.73 × $0	0.00
		+ 10.61

Step 5   There are three choices.   EV

(a)   Do not obtain information and do not drill $0
(b)   Do not obtain information and drill   +$4 million
(c)   Obtain information first, decide about drilling later ($(10.61m – 3m))

+$7.61 million

The decision should be to obtain the information from a survey first.

Step 6   The value of the imperfect information is the difference between (b) and (c), $3.61 million.

7 Sensitivity analysis   12/08

FAST FORWARD

Sensitivity analysis is a method of analysing the uncertainty in a situation or decision. It measures the effect of changes in the estimated value of an item ('key factor') on the future outcome. It can therefore be used to assess the sensitivity of the expected outcome to variations or changes in the value of the item ('key factor').

7.1 Approaches to sensitivity analysis

Key term

> **Sensitivity analysis** is a term used to describe any technique whereby decision options are tested for their vulnerability to changes in any 'variable' such as expected sales volume, sales price per unit, material costs, or labour costs.

Sensitivity analysis is a technique for analysing uncertainty about the outcome of a decision. The starting point is an estimate of what the outcome will be, based on estimates for key variables such as selling price, sales volume, unit variable cost fixed cot expenditures, and so on. Sensitivity analysis may be used because there is uncertainty about some of these estimates. Here are three useful approaches to sensitivity analysis.

(a) To estimate by **how much costs and revenues would need to differ** from their estimated values before the decision would change.

(b) To estimate whether a decision would change if estimated costs were **x% higher** than estimated, or estimated revenues **y% lower** than estimated.

(c) To estimate by how much costs and/or revenues would need to differ from their estimated values before the decision maker would be **indifferent** between two options.

The essence of the approach, therefore, is to carry out the calculations with one set of values for the variables and then substitute other possible values for the variables to see how this affects the overall outcome.

(a) From your studies of information technology you may recognise this as **'what if' analysis** that can be carried out using a **spreadsheet**.

(b) From your studies of **linear programming** you may remember that sensitivity analysis can be carried out to determine over which ranges the various constraints have an impact on the optimum solution.

(c) **Flexible budgeting** can also be a form of sensitivity analysis.

7.2 Example: Sensitivity analysis

Sensivite Co has estimated the following sales and profits for a new product which it may launch on to the market.

		$	$
Sales	(2,000 units)		4,000
Variable costs:	materials	2,000	
	labour	1,000	
			3,000
Contribution			1,000
Less incremental fixed costs			800
Profit			200

Required

Analyse the sensitivity of the project to changes in key variables.

Solution

(a) If incremental **fixed costs** are more than 25% above estimate (= 200/800), the project would make a loss.

(b) If **unit costs of materials** are more than 10% above estimate (200/2,000), the project would make a loss.

(c) Similarly, the project would be sensitive to an **increase in unit labour costs** of more than $200, which is 20% above estimate.

(d)   And the project would become unprofitable if the selling price is more than 5% (200/4,000) below the estimate, given no change in sales volume.

(e)   The **margin of safety**, given a breakeven point of 1,600 units, is (400/2,000) × 100% = 20%.

Management would then be able to judge more clearly whether the product is likely to be profitable, by making an assessment of the scale of the uncertainty in the estimates. The items to which profitability is most sensitive in this example are the selling price (5%) and material costs (10%). Sensitivity analysis can help to **concentrate management attention** on the most important factors.

8 Simulation models   12/08

FAST FORWARD ⟫

Simulation models can be used to deal with decision problems when there are a large number of uncertain variables in the situation. **Random numbers** are used to assign values to the variables.

One of the chief problems encountered in decision making is the uncertainty of the future. Where only a few factors are involved, probability analysis and expected value calculations can be used to find the most likely outcome of a decision. Often, however, in real life, there are so **many uncertain variables** that this approach does not give a true impression of possible variations in outcome.

To get an idea of what will happen in real life one possibility is to use a **simulation model** in which the **values and the variables are selected at random**. Obviously this is a situation **ideally suited to a computer** (large volume of data, random number generation).

The term 'simulation' model is often used more specifically to refer to modelling which **makes use of random numbers**. This is the **'Monte Carlo'** method of simulation. In the business environment it can, for example, be used to examine inventory, queuing, scheduling and forecasting problems.

Random numbers are allocated to each possible value of the uncertain variable in proportion to the probabilities, so that a probability of 0.1 gets 10% of the total numbers to be assigned. These random numbers are used to assign values to the variables.

Exam focus point

> You will **not** be required to develop a simulation model in your exam. The following example is provided so that you can **understand** how simulation models are developed.

8.1 Example: Simulation and spreadsheets

A supermarket sells a product for which the daily demand varies. An analysis of daily demand over a period of about a year shows the following probability distribution.

Demand per day Units	Probability
35	0.10
36	0.20
37	0.25
38	0.30
39	0.08
40	0.07
	1.00

To develop a simulation model in which one of the variables is daily demand, we would **assign a group of numbers to each value for daily demand**. The probabilities are stated to two decimal places, and so there must be 100 random numbers in total, 00 – 99 (we use 00-99 rather than 1-100 so that we can use two-digit random numbers.) Random numbers are assigned in proportion to the **probabilities**, so that a probability of 0.1 gets 10% of the total numbers to be assigned, that is 10 numbers: 0, 1, 2, 3, 4, 5, 6, 7, 8 and 9.

The assignments would therefore be as follows.

Demand per day Units	Probability	Numbers assigned
35	0.10	00 – 09
36	0.20	10 – 29
37	0.25	30 – 54
38	0.30	55 – 84
39	0.08	85 – 92
40	0.07	93 – 99

When the simulation model is run, random numbers will be generated to derive values for daily demand. For example, if the model is used to simulate demand over a ten day period, the random numbers generated might be as follows.

19007174604721296802

The model would then **assign values** to the demand per day as follows.

Day	Random number	Demand Units
1	19	36
2	00	35
3	71	38
4	74	38
5	60	38
6	47	37
7	21	36
8	29	36
9	68	38
10	02	35

You might notice that on none of the ten days is the demand 39 or 40 units, because the random numbers generated did not include any value in the range 85 – 99. When a simulation model is used, there must be a long enough run to give a good representation of the system and all its potential variations.

8.2 Uses of simulation

In the example above, the supermarket would use the information to minimise inventory holding without risking running out of the product. This will reduce costs but avoid lost sales and profit.

A supermarket can also use this technique to estimate queues at check-out desks, with predicted lengths of waiting time determining the number of staff required.

Chapter Roundup

- When there is a strong element of risk or uncertainty in a decision, the decision that is taken may be affected by the extent of the risk or uncertainty.

- 'Risk' and 'uncertainty' are often used to mean the same thing. However, to be more exact, 'risk' in decision making exists when the future outcome cannot be predicted for certain, but probabilities can be estimated for each possible outcome. Uncertainty, in contrast, is when there is insufficient information to make a reliable prediction about what will happen and there are no probability estimates of different possible outcomes.

- People may be **risk seekers**, **risk neutral** or **risk averse**. A person's attitude to risk and uncertainty may affect the decision that is taken.

- Management accounting directs its attention towards the **future** and the future is **uncertain**. For this reason a number of methods of taking **uncertainty** into consideration have evolved.

- One approach to dealing with uncertainty is to obtain more information, in order to reduce the amount of uncertainty about what will happen. Reliable information reduces uncertainty.

- **Market research** into customer habits, attitudes or intentions can be used to reduce uncertainty.

- An expected value is a weighted average value of the different possible outcomes from a decision, where weightings are based on the probability of each possible outcome.

- **Expected values** indicate what an outcome is likely to be in the long term, if the decision can be repeated many times over. Fortunately, many business transactions do occur over and over again.

- The 'play it safe' basis for decision making is referred to as the **maximin basis**. This is short for '**maximise the minimum achievable profit**'.

- A basis for making decisions by looking for the best outcome is known as the **maximax basis**, short for '**maximise the maximum achievable profit**'.

- The 'opportunity loss' basis for decision making is known as **minimax regret**.

- **Decision trees** are diagrams which illustrate the choices and possible outcomes of a decision. The possible outcomes are usually given associated probabilities of occurrence.

- **Rollback analysis** evaluates the EV of each decision option. You have to work from right to left and calculate EVs at each outcome point.

- **Perfect information** is guaranteed to predict the future with 100% accuracy. **Imperfect information** is better than no information at all but could be wrong in its prediction of the future.

- The **value of perfect information** is the difference between the EV of profit with perfect information and the EV of profit without perfect information.

- The **value of imperfect information** is the difference between the EV of profit with imperfect information and the EV of profit without the information.

- **Sensitivity analysis is a method of analysing the uncertainty in a situation or decision.** It measures the effect of changes in the estimated value of an item ('key factor') on the future outcome. It can therefore be used to assess the sensitivity of the expected outcome to variations or changes in the value of the item ('key factor').

- **Simulation models** can be used to deal with decision problems when there are a large number of uncertain variables in the situation. **Random numbers** are used to assign values to the variables.

Quick Quiz

1   *Match the terms to the correct definitions.*

Terms

(a)   Risk seeker   (c)   Risk averse
(b)   Risk neutral

Definitions

1   A decision maker concerned with what will be the most likely outcome

2   A decision maker interested in the best outcomes no matter how small the chance that they may occur

3   A decision maker who acts on the assumption that the worst outcome might occur

2   *Fill in the blanks.*

(a)   Maximin decision rule: choosing the alternative that ....….... the …....................……
(b)   Minimax decision rule: choosing the alternative that ....…… the …............................….
(c)   Maximax decision rule: choosing the alternative that ....…… the…............…..................
(d)   Minimin decision rule: choosing the alternative that ....…….. the…..........................…

3   How is expected value calculated?

A Σpx C $e\Sigma px$
B $p\Sigma x$ D $x\Sigma p$

4   *Tick the correct boxes to indicate the usefulness of expected values as a guide to decision making in the following decisions.*

		Most useful	Not as useful
(a)	Whether to change the logo painted on the window of 700 retail outlets		
(b)	Whether to purchase machine X or machine Y		
(c)	Whether to launch product A		
(d)	Deciding on the optimum daily purchases of a perishable item		

5   If the decision maker is trying to maximise the figure, what figure would the decision maker choose at point B in the diagram below?

A   40,000   C   13,900

B   11,800   D   22,000

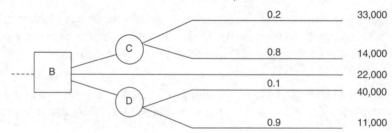

Answers to Quick Quiz

1   (a) 2; (b) 1; (c) 3

2   (a)   Maximise, minimum profits   (c)   Maximise, maximum profits
     (b)   Minimise, maximum costs/losses   (d)   Minimise, minimum costs/losses

3   A   An expected value is the sum of the different possible outcomes (x) multiplied by their associated
          probability of occurrence (p).

4   Expected values would be useful for decisions (a) and (d) because they are repeated several times.

5   D   Choice between ((0.2 × 33,000) + (0.8 × 14,000)) = 17,800 at C, 22,000, and ((0.1 × 40,000) +
          (0.9 × 11,000)) = 13,900 at D.

Now try the question below from the Practice Question Bank

Number	Level	Marks	Time
Q10	Examination	20	36 mins

Budgeting and control

Budgetary systems

Introduction

This chapter is an introduction to Part C of the Study Text and it looks at the budgeting system and methods of preparing budgets. We look at the various stages in the **planning process**, and where the annual budget fits in to this. We also see how the budget is used in the **control process**.

We then go on to look at the **traditional approach** to budget preparation, **incremental budgeting**. And alternative approaches to budget preparation: **zero based budgeting**, **rolling budgets** and **activity based budgeting**.

CARDIFF METROPOLITAN UNIVERSITY
LLANDAFF LEARNING CENTRE
WESTERN AVE
CARDIFF CF5 2YB

Study guide

		Intellectual level
C1	**Budgetary systems**	
(a)	Explain how budgetary systems fit within the performance hierarchy	2
(b)	Select and explain appropriate budgetary systems for an organisation, including top-down, bottom-up, rolling, zero base, activity-base, incremental and feed-forward control	2
(c)	Describe the information used in budget systems and the sources of the information needed	2
(d)	Explain the difficulties of changing a budgetary system	2
(e)	Explain how budget systems can deal with uncertainty in the environment	2
C2	**Types of budget**	
(a)	Prepare rolling budgets and activity based budgets	2
(b)	Indicate the usefulness and problems with different budget types (including fixed, flexible, zero-based, activity-based, incremental, rolling, top-down, bottom up, master, functional).	2
(c)	Explain the difficulties of changing the type of budget used	2

Exam guide

The examiner expects you to be aware of the problems of traditional budgeting systems and why organisations may be reluctant to change to more appropriate systems.

One of the competencies you require to fulfil performance objective 13 is the ability to contribute to budget planning and production. You can apply the knowledge you obtain from this chapter to help to demonstrate this competence.

1 Revision – Objectives of budgeting systems

> **FAST FORWARD**
>
> A budget is a **quantified plan of action** for a forthcoming accounting period.
>
> A budget can be set from the **top down** (**imposed** budget) or from the **bottom up** (**participatory** budget).

> **FAST FORWARD**
>
> Here are the objectives of a budgetary planning and control system.
>
> - Ensure the achievement of the organisation's objectives
> - Compel planning
> - Communicate ideas and plans
> - Coordinate activities
> - Provide a framework for responsibility accounting
> - Establish a system of control
> - Motivate employees to improve their performance

You should be familiar with the objectives of budgetary systems from your earlier studies. The key points are summarised below.

Knowledge brought forward from earlier studies

A budgetary planning and control system is essentially a system for ensuring **communication**, **coordination** and **control** within an organisation. Communication, coordination and control are general objectives: more information is provided by an inspection of the specific objectives of a budgetary planning and control system.

Objective	Comment
Ensure the achievement of the organisation's objectives	Objectives are set for the organisation as a whole, and for individual departments and operations within the organisation. Quantified expressions of these objectives are then drawn up as targets to be achieved within the timescale of the budget plan.
Compel planning	This is probably the most important feature of a budgetary planning and control system. Planning forces management to **look ahead**, to set out **detailed plans** for achieving the targets for each department, operation and (ideally) each manager and to anticipate problems. It thus prevents management from relying on ad hoc or uncoordinated planning which may be detrimental to the performance of the organisation.
Communicate ideas and plans	A formal system is necessary to ensure that each person affected by the plans is aware of what he or she is **supposed to be doing**. Communication might be one-way, with managers giving **orders to subordinates**, or there might be a two-way dialogue and exchange of ideas.
Coordinate activities	The activities of different departments or sub-units of the organisation need to be coordinated to ensure **maximum integration** of effort towards common goals. This concept of coordination implies, for example, that the purchasing department should base its budget on production requirements and that the production budget should in turn be based on sales expectations. Although straightforward in concept, coordination is remarkably difficult to achieve, and there is often 'sub-optimality' and conflict between departmental plans in the budget so that the efforts of each department are not fully integrated into a combined plan to achieve the company's best targets.
Provide a framework for responsibility accounting	Budgetary planning and control systems require that managers of **budget centres** are made responsible for the achievement of budget targets for the operations under their personal control.
Establish a system of control	A budget is a **yardstick** against which actual performance is measured and assessed. Control over actual performance is provided by the comparisons of actual results against the budget plan. Departures from budget can then be investigated and the reasons for the departures can be divided into **controllable** and **uncontrollable** factors.
Motivate employees to improve their performance	The interest and commitment of employees can be retained via a system of **feedback of actual results**, which lets them know how well or badly they are performing. The identification of controllable reasons for departures from budget with managers responsible provides an incentive for improving future performance.

2 The planning and control cycle

The **planning and control cycle** has seven steps.

- *Step 1*. Identify **objectives**
- *Step 2*. Identify potential **strategies**
- *Step 3*. Evaluate strategies
- *Step 4*. Choose alternative courses of action
- *Step 5*. Implement the long-term plan
- *Step 6*. Measure actual results and compare with the plan
- *Step 7*. Respond to divergences from the plan

The diagram below represents the planning and control cycle. The first five steps cover the planning process. **Planning** involves making choices between alternatives and is primarily a decision-making activity. The last two steps cover the **control** process, which involves measuring and correcting actual performance to ensure that the alternatives that are chosen and the plans for implementing them are carried out.

The planning and control cycle

Planning process	
Identify objectives	Step 1
Identify alternative courses of action (strategies) which might contribute towards achieving the objectives	Step 2
Evaluate each strategy	Step 3
Choose alternative courses of action	Step 4
Implement the long-term plan in the form of the annual budget	Step 5
Control process	
Measure actual results and compare with the plan	Step 6
Respond to divergences from plan	Step 7

Step 1   Identify objectives

Objectives establish the direction in which the management of the organisation wish it to be heading. They answer the question: 'where do we want to be?'

Step 2   Identify potential strategies

Once an organisation has decided 'where it wants to be', the next step is to identify a range of possible courses of action or **strategies** that might enable the organisation to get there. The organisation must therefore carry out an **information-gathering exercise** to ensure that it has a full **understanding of where it is now.** This is known as a **'position audit'** or **'strategic analysis'** and involves looking both inwards and outwards.

(a)   The organisation must **gather information from all of its internal parts** to find out what resources it possesses: what its manufacturing capacity and capability is, what is the state of its technical know-how, how well it is able to market itself, how much cash it has in the bank and so on.

(b)   It must also **gather information externally** so that it can assess its position in the environment. Just as it has assessed its **own strengths and weaknesses**, it must do likewise for its competitors (**threats**). Current and potential markets must be analysed to identify possible new **opportunities**. The 'state of the world' must be considered. Is it in recession or is it booming? What is likely to happen in the future?

Having carried out a strategic analysis, alternative strategies can be identified. An organisation might decide to be the lowest cost producer in the industry, perhaps by withdrawing from some markets or developing new products for sale in existing markets. This may involve internal development or a joint venture.

Step 3 **Evaluate strategies**

The strategies must then be evaluated **in terms of suitability, feasibility and acceptability**. Management should select those strategies that have the greatest potential for achieving the organisation's objectives.

Step 4 **Choose alternative courses of action**

The next step in the process is to collect the **chosen strategies** together and **co-ordinate them into a long-term financial plan.** Typically this would show the following.

- Projected cash flows
- Projected long-term profits
- A description of the long-term objectives and strategies in words
- Capital expenditure plans
- Balance sheet forecasts

Step 5 **Implement the long-term plan**

The **long-term plan** should then be **broken down into smaller parts**. It is unlikely that the different parts will fall conveniently into successive time periods. Strategy A may take two and a half years, while Strategy B may take five months, but not start until year three of the plan. It is usual, however, to break down the plan as a whole into equal time periods (usually one year). The resulting **short-term plan** is called a **budget**.

Step 6 **Measure actual results and compare with plan**

Actual results are recorded and analysed and information about actual results is fed back to the management concerned, often in the form of accounting reports. This reported information is **feedback** (see section 3.2.1 below).

Step 7 **Respond to divergences from plan**

By comparing actual and planned results, management can then do one of three things, depending on how they see the situation.

(a) They can take control action. By identifying what has gone wrong, and then finding out why, corrective measures can be taken.

(b) They can decide to do nothing. This could be the decision when actual results are going better than planned, or when poor results were caused by something which is unlikely to happen again in the future.

(c) They can alter the plan or target if actual results are different from the plan or target, and there is nothing that management can do (or nothing, perhaps, that they want to do) to correct the situation.

| Question | | Planning and control cycles |

Is your organisation's planning and control cycle similar to the one described here? If it differs, how does it differ? Why does it differ? Try to find out your organisation's objectives and the strategies being adopted to attain these objectives.

Answers to this question could be usefully employed in the exam.

3 Planning and control in the performance hierarchy

Planning and control occurs at all levels of the performance hierarchy to different degrees. The performance hierarchy refers to the system by which performance is measured and controlled at different levels of management within the organisation.

3.1 Planning

Although it implies a 'top down' approach to management, we could describe **a cascade of goals, objectives and plans** down through the layers of the organisation. The **plans** made at the **higher levels** of the performance hierarchy provide a **framework** within which the plans at the lower levels must be achieved. The **plans** at the **lower levels** are the **means** by which the plans at the higher levels are achieved.

It could therefore be argued that without the plans allied directly to the vision and corporate objective the operational-level and departmental plans have little meaning. **Planning** could therefore be deemed as **more significant** at the **higher levels** of the performance hierarchy than the lower levels.

This is not to say that planning at an operational level is not important. It is just that the nature of planning differs according to the level in the management hierarchy that it takes place.

Level	Detail
Corporate plans/strategic plans **Prepared at a strategic level by senior management**	• Focused on overall corporate performance • Environmental influence • Set overall plans and targets for units and departments • Sometimes qualitative planning (eg a programme to change the culture of the organisation)
Tactical plans **Prepared at lower management level ('management control' level), within guidelines set by senior management**	• Time horizon typically 12 months • Plans for individual departments or activities, within guidelines set by senior management • Some budgets may be prepared in non-financial terms, but all budgets are converted into money values • The overall budget is expressed in financial terms, with a budgeted income statement, budgeted end-of-year financial position and budgeted cash flow forecast • Provides a link between strategic plans at senior level and operational planning • Budget targets should be consistent with strategic objectives • Approved by senior management (board of directors)
Operational plans **Prepared by managers at a fairly junior level, at a practical operational level**	• Based on objectives about 'what' to achieve in operational terms • Specific (eg acceptable number of 'rings' before a phone is answered) • Operational targets likely to be quantitative • Detailed specifications of targets and standards • Based on 'how' something is achieved • Short time horizons • Operational plans should be prepared that enable budget targets to be achieved.

3.2 Control

Consider how the activities of **planning** and **control** are **inter-related**.

(a) **Plans** set the targets.

(b) **Control** involves two main processes.

    (i) **Measure** actual results against the plan.

    (ii) **Take action** to adjust actual performance to achieve the plan or to change the plan altogether.

Control is therefore **impossible without planning.**

The essence of control is the **measurement of results** and **comparing** them with the original **plan**. Any deviation from plan indicates that **control action** is required to make the results conform more closely with plan.

3.2.1 Feedback

> **Feedback** occurs when the results (outputs) of a system are used to control it, by adjusting the input or behaviour of the system. Feedback is information produced as output from operations; it is used to compare actual results with planned results for control purposes.

A business organisation uses feedback for control.

(a) **Negative feedback** indicates that results or activities must be brought back on course, as they are deviating from the plan.

(b) **Positive feedback** results in control action continuing the current course. You would normally assume that positive feedback means that results are going according to plan and that no corrective action is necessary: but it is best to be sure that the control system itself is not picking up the wrong information.

(c) **Feedforward control** is control based on **forecast** results: in other words if the forecast is bad, control action is taken well in advance of actual results.

There are two types of feedback.

(a) **Single loop feedback** is control, like a thermostat, which regulates the output of a system. For example, if sales targets are not reached, control action will be taken to ensure that targets will be reached soon. The plan or target itself is not changed, even though the resources needed to achieve it might have to be reviewed.

(b) **Double loop feedback** is of a different order. It is information used to **change the plan itself**. For example, if sales targets are not reached, the company may need to change the plan.

3.2.2 Control at different levels

> **Budgetary control** occurs at the middle management or **'management control'** levels of the performance hierarchy.

Control at the middle management or **'management control' level** of the performance hierarchy, such as standard costing, and budgetary control has the following features.

- It is exercised by measuring actual performance against planned performance in the budget or similar medium-term plans.

- Actual results are measured and reported to the managers responsible for the performance. There are formal feedback system for reporting, and performance reports may be produced monthly, in the form of a budgetary control repot or variance report.

- Reports are based mainly on feedback, i.e. performance information produced from within the organisation's systems. They do not make any significant use of information obtained externally, from outside the organisation.

- Comparisons of actual and budgeted performance are often expressed in financial terms.

At a more senior level control reporting, strategic performance reports may be produced periodically say every three months, six months or one year). These assess performance and the organisation's strategic position, in terms of the overall business plan (strategic plans). Information gathered from outside the organisation as well as information gathered internally may be used for strategic performance reports.

At an operational level, control measures are reported and monitored regularly, often on a day-to-day basis. Operational managers are expected to achieve performance standards that are set, and actual performance is compared with the standards. Many performance measures used for control purposes are non-financial in nature, such as standard times to complete a task and maximum rates of wastage or loss in process.

3.3 Other aspects of budget preparation

The following are other key points about budget preparation, included here as revision material.

Point	Detail
Long-term plan	The **starting point**, this will show **what the budget has to achieve** (the introduction of new production, the required return, and so on) and outline **how it is to be done**. It will also contain **general guidelines** on allowable price increases like wage rates. The **long-term policy** needs to be **communicated** to all managers responsible for preparing budgets so that they are aware of the context within which they are budgeting and how their area of responsibility is expected to contribute.
Limiting factor	This is the factor in the budget that **limits the scale of operations**. The limiting factor is often sales demand, but it may be production capacity, when sales demand is high or when a key production resource is in short supply. Budgeting cannot proceed until the budget for the limiting factor has been prepared, since this affects all the other budgets.
Budget manual	A budget manual is a guide or instruction document to **assist functional managers** with preparing their functional budgets. It shows how figures and forecasts for the budget should be calculated, and gives other practical information. It is likely to include **proformas** showing how the information is to be presented. If budgeting is done with spreadsheets, layouts and computations may be pre-programmed, requiring only the entry of the figures. It may include a **flow diagram** showing how individual budgets are interlinked and specify deadlines by which first drafts must be prepared.
Sales budget	This contains **information on the expected volume of sales** (based on estimates or market research), the **sales mix, and selling prices.** The total revenues indicated will be used to compile the cash budget, although this information needs to be adjusted to allow for the expected timing of receipts. The volume of sales indicates the level of production required and the extent of spending on distribution and administration.
Production capacity	The level of sales anticipated is matched against opening inventory and desired closing inventory to establish the level of production. From this can be calculated the need for materials (again allowing for opening and closing inventory), labour and machine hours. In other words production budgeting is **done in terms of physical resources initially and costed afterwards**. At this stage, too, it is likely that needs for new capital expenditure will be identified. This information will be used in preparing the capital budget.

Point	Detail
Functional budgets	Functional budgets are budgets for the different departments or functions within the organisation. **Budgets for production-related functions** such as purchasing, engineering and inspection and testing, maybe based on the budgeted volume of production. Budgets **for other areas of the organisation,** such as distribution and administration may take the anticipated sales level as their point of reference. Vehicle costs, carriage costs, stationery and communication costs, and above all staff costs feature in these budgets. Some budgeted, such as the budget for **R&D spending,** may be entirely discretionary and set at a level that management consider the organisation can or should afford
Discretionary costs	**Training and R&D** are known as 'discretionary costs' and have special features.
Consolidation and coordination	This can begin once all parts of the organisation have submitted their individual budgets. It is most **unlikely** that **all of the budgets will be in line with each other** at the first attempt. Areas of **incompatibility** must be identified and the **budgets modified** in consultation with individual managers. **Spreadsheets** are invaluable at this stage, both for the consolidation itself and to allow changes to be made quickly and accurately.
Cash budget	This can only be prepared at this stage because it **needs to take account of all of the plans of the organisation** and translate them into expected cash flows. Cash must be available when it is needed to enable the plans to be carried out. Overdraft facilities may need to be negotiated in advance, or some activities may need to be deferred until cash has been collected.
Master budget	The final stage, once all of the necessary modifications have been made, is to prepare a **summary** of all of the budgets in the form of a master budget, which generally comprises a **budgeted income statement, a budgeted balance sheet and a budgeted cash flow statement.**

3.3.1 Top-down and bottom-up budgeting

'Top down' and 'bottom up' are two different approaches to budget preparation.

(a) With **top-down budgeting**, budget targets are set at senior management level for the organisation as a whole and for each major department or activity within the organisation. The departmental budget targets are then given to the departmental managers, who are required to prepare a budget that conforms to the targets that have been imposed on them from above. Similarly, when budgets have been set at departmental level, targets are then given to managers lower down the organisation hierarchy; these managers are then require to prepare budgets that meet the targets for their area of operations that have been imposed on them.

(b) With **bottom-up budgeting**, the budgeting process starts at a relatively low level of management. Managers are required to draft a budget for their area of operations. These are submitted to their superior, who combines the lower-level budgets into a combined budget for the department as a whole. Departmental budgets are then submitted to senior management, where they are combined into a co-ordinated budget for the organisation as a whole.

Top-down budgeting takes much less time and planning effort than bottom-up budgeting and senior management can use top-down budgets to impose their views. Bottom-up budgeting is much more time-consuming, and draft budgets may have to be revised many times until they are properly co-ordinated.

However, bottom-up budgeting has two potential advantages.

(a) It reflects the views and expectations of managers who are closer to operations and so who may have a better understanding of what and what Is not achievable.

(b) Bottom-up budgeting is a form of participative budgeting process, which can have behavioural and motivational advantages. These are considered further in a later chapter.

4 Incremental budgeting
12/08, 12/10, 6/13

FAST FORWARD

With the 'traditional' approach to budgeting, known as **incremental budgeting**, the budget for the next financial year is based on the actual results for the current financial year. At its simplest level, a budget based on an incremental costing approach is the actual (or budgeted) performance for the current year, adjusted for expected growth and inflation. Incremental budgeting encourages slack and wasteful spending to creep into budgets.

Key term

Incremental budgeting is a method of budgeting in which next year's budget is prepared by using the current's year's actual results as a starting point, and making adjustments for expected inflation, sales growth or decline and other known changes.

The main advantage of incremental budgeting is that it is a relatively straightforward way of preparing a budget.

Incremental budgeting may also be a reasonable procedure if current operations are as effective, efficient and economical as they can be. It is also appropriate for budgeting for costs such as staff salaries, which may be estimated on the basis of current salaries plus an increment for inflation, provided that no significant changes in the work force are anticipated. and are hence administratively fairly easy to prepare.

In general, however, it is an **inefficient form of budgeting** as it **encourages slack** and **wasteful spending** to creep into budgets. Past inefficiencies are perpetuated because cost levels are rarely subjected to close scrutiny.

Advantages of incremental budgets	Disadvantages of incremental budgets
• Considered to be the quickest and easiest method of budgeting	• Builds in previous problems and inefficiencies
• Suitable for organisations that operate in a stable environment where historic figures are reliable and are not expected to change significantly	• Managers may spend for the sake of spending in order to use up their budget for the year and thus ensure that they get the same (or larger) budget next year
	• Uneconomic activities may be continued. For example, a car manufacturer may continue to make parts in-house when it may be cheaper to outsource

Question

Incremental budgeting

Can incremental budgeting be used to budget for rent? What about for advertising expenditure?

Answer

Incremental budgeting is appropriate for budgeting for rent, which may be estimated on the basis of current rent plus an increment for the annual rent increase. Advertising expenditure, on the other hand, is not so easily quantifiable and is more discretionary in nature. Using incremental budgeting for advertising expenditure could allow slack and wasteful spending to creep into the budget.

4.1 Incremental budgeting in the public sector

The traditional approach to budgeting in the public sector has been incremental and this has resulted in existing patterns of public expenditure being locked in. The public spending round in the UK established an annual cycle of year-on-year incremental bids by departments rather than an analysis of outputs and efficiency.

5 Fixed and flexible budgets

FAST FORWARD

A **fixed budget** is a financial plan that does not change throughout the budget period, regardless of any changes from the plan in the actual volume of activity. A **flexible budget** recognises cost behaviour and changes as the actual volume of activity changes.

A fixed budget is normally used for **planning purposes** and is prepared in advance of the beginning of the financial period. A flexible budget is used for **control purposes** and is normally prepared retrospectively, when the actual level of activity in a period is known.

One of the competencies you require to fulfil performance objective 13 is the ability to amend budgets to reflect changes in circumstances. You can apply the knowledge you obtain from this chapter to help to demonstrate this competence.

5.1 Fixed budgets

Key term

A **fixed budget** is a budget which remains unchanged throughout the budget period, regardless of differences between the actual and the original planned volume of output or sales.

The master budget, which is prepared and approved before the beginning of the budget period, is normally a **fixed budget**. The term 'fixed' means the following.

(a)   The budget is **prepared on the basis of an estimated volume of production** and an **estimated volume of sales**, but no plans are made for the event that actual volumes of production and sales may differ from budgeted volumes.

(b)   When actual volumes of production and sales during a control period (month or four weeks or quarter) are achieved, the budget is **not adjusted or revised (in retrospect) to the new levels of activity.**

The major purpose of a fixed budget is for planning. It is prepared at the planning stage, when it is used to define the objectives and targets of the organisation for the budget period (financial year).

5.2 Flexible budgets

Key term

A **flexible budget** is a budget which, by recognising different cost behaviour patterns, is changed as the volume of output and sales changes. It recognises cost behaviour patterns, such as changes in sales revenue and variable costs as sales volumes change, and step changes in fixed costs as activity levels rise or fall by more than a certain amount.

Flexible budgets may be used in one of two ways.

(a)   **At the planning stage**. An organisation may prepare flexible budgets at the planning stage for different levels of activity. For example, suppose that a company expects to sell 10,000 units of output during the next year. A master budget (the fixed budget) would be prepared on the basis of these expected volumes. However, if the company thinks that output and sales might be as low as 8,000 units or as high as 12,000 units, it may prepare **contingency flexible budgets**, at volumes of, say 8,000, 9,000, 11,000 and 12,000 units and then assess the possible outcomes. However,

preparing flexible budgets in advance adds to the time and effort required for preparing budget, and this is not common.

(b) **Retrospectively**. At the end of each month (control period) or year, the results that should have been achieved given the actual circumstances (the flexible budget) can be compared with the actual results. As we shall see, flexible budgets are an essential factor in **budgetary control**.

Whereas fixed budgets are prepared in advance for planning purposes, flexible budgets are usually prepared retrospectively, for planning purposes.

The preparation and use of flexible budgets will be looked at in more detail in Chapter 10.

6 Zero based budgeting   6/09, 12/10, 6/13

FAST FORWARD

The principle behind **zero based budgeting (ZBB)** is that the budget for each cost centre should be made from 'scratch' or zero. Every item of expenditure must be justified in its entirety in order to be included in the next year's budget.

ZBB rejects the assumption inherent in **incremental budgeting** that next year's budget should be based on the current financial year results (or the current year budget), with adjustments for incremental changes, such as growth and inflation. It is based on recognition that:

(a) the current year's results may include wasteful spending and inefficiencies

(b) budgeted activities should be reviewed and assessed, to establish whether they are still required or whether they should continue at the same level of activity as in the past.

The aim of zero based budgeting is to remove unnecessary and wasteful spending from the budget. It can be particularly useful in budgeting for administrative expenses and administrative departments, where there may be a tendency to tolerate unnecessary spending.

Key term

> **Zero based budgeting** involves preparing a budget for each cost centre or activity from a zero base. Every item of expenditure has then to be justified in its entirety in order to be included in the next year's budget.

In practice, however, managers do not have to budget from zero, but can **start from their current level of expenditure and work downwards**, asking what would happen if any particular aspect of current expenditure and current operations were removed from the budget. In this way, every aspect of the budget is examined in terms of its cost and the benefits it provides and the selection of better alternatives is encouraged.

6.1 Implementing zero based budgeting

FAST FORWARD

There is a three-step approach to ZBB.

- Define items or activities for which costs should be budgeted, and spending decisions should be planned: these are 'decision packages'

- Evaluate and rank the packages in order of priority: eliminate packages whose costs exceed their value

- Allocate resources to the decision packages according to their ranking. Where resources such as money are in short supply, they are allocated to the most valuable activities.

The implementation of ZBB involves a number of steps, but the success of ZBB depends on the application of **a questioning attitude** by all those involved in the budgeting process. Existing practices, activities and expenditures must be challenged and searching questions about their value should be asked.

- Does the activity need to be carried out?
- What would be the consequences if the activity was not carried out?
- Is the current level of provision sufficient?

- Are there alternative (and cheaper) ways of achieving the same objective?
- How much should the activity cost?
- Is the expenditure worth the benefits achieved?

The basic approach of ZBB has three steps.

Step 1   **Define decision packages**. Decision packages are activities or items in the budget about which a decision should be made. Should this activity be included in the budget or not? Decision packages are used to **rank** activities in order of priority or preference. This ranking can be used to allocate scarce resources in the budget.

Decision packages must be thoroughly documented.

There are two types of decision package.

(a)   **Mutually exclusive packages**. These are alternative methods of getting the same job done. The best option among the packages must be selected by comparing costs and benefits and the other packages are then discarded. If there are two mutually exclusive decision packages, the preferred package is selected and the other rejected for budgeting purposes.

(b)   **Incremental packages**. These divide an aspect of operations into different levels of activity. The 'base' package will contain the minimum amount of work that must be done to carry out the activity and the cost of this minimum level. The other incremental packages identify additional (incremental) work that could be done, at what cost and for what benefits.

Suppose that a cost centre manager is preparing a budget for maintenance costs. He might first consider two mutually exclusive packages.

- Package A might be to keep a maintenance team of two men per shift for two shifts each day at a cost of $60,000 per annum
- Package B might be to obtain a maintenance service from an outside contractor at a cost of $50,000

A **cost-benefit analysis** will be conducted because the quicker repairs obtainable from an in-house maintenance service might justify its extra cost.

If we now suppose that package A is preferred, the budget analysis must be completed by describing the incremental variations in this chosen alternative.

(a)   The 'base' package would describe the minimum requirement for the maintenance work. This might be to pay for one man per shift for two shifts each day at a cost of $30,000.

(b)   Incremental package 1 might be to pay for two men on the early shift and one man on the late shift, at a cost of $45,000. The extra cost of $15,000 would need to be justified, for example by savings in lost production time, or by more efficient machinery.

(c)   Incremental package 2 might be the original preference, for two men on each shift at a cost of $60,000. The cost-benefit analysis would compare its advantages, if any, over incremental package 1; and so on.

Step 2   **Evaluate and rank each activity (decision package)** on the basis of its benefit to the organisation. This can be a lengthy process. Minimum work requirements (those that are essential to get a job done) will be given very high priority and so too will work which must be done to meet legal obligations. In the accounting department these would be minimum requirements to operate the payroll, purchase ledger and sales ledger systems, and to maintain and publish a set of accounts. Common problems that may occur at the ranking stage are discussed in the next section.

Step 3   **Allocate resources** in the budget according to the funds available and the evaluation and ranking of the competing packages. For example, a car manufacturer may choose to allocate significantly more funds to production processes than service and administration functions, based on the ranking of each activity in step 2.

Question

Base and incremental packages

What might the base and incremental packages for a personnel department cover?

Answer

The base package might cover the recruitment and dismissal of staff. Incremental packages might cover training, pension administration, trade union liaison, staff welfare and so on.

Case Study

In July 2010, South Carolina Treasurer Converse Chellis began a study into the implementation of zero-based budgeting for all state departments and agencies. It was expected that a system of zero-based budgeting would cut down on efficiency and waste in government.

Chellis commented:

'It's time to hold every agency in state government accountable for every dollar it spends. With the implementation of zero-based budgeting, agencies and departments will have to justify every tax dollar they spend each and every year. We've seen how agencies have incrementally increased their budgets. During these remarkably tough economic times, having government examine and explain how it spends money each and every year is just common sense'.

6.2 The advantages and limitations of implementing ZBB

The **advantages** of zero based budgeting are as follows.

- It is possible to identify and **remove inefficient or obsolete operations.**
- It forces employees to **avoid wasteful expenditure**.
- It can **increase motivation** of staff by promoting a culture of efficiency.
- It **responds to changes** in the business environment.
- **ZBB documentation provides** an in-depth **appraisal of an organisation's operations.**
- It **challenges the status quo**.
- In summary, ZBB should result in a **more efficient allocation of resources**.

The major **disadvantage** of zero based budgeting is the enormous extra **volume of paperwork** created and the extra time required to prepare the budget. The assumptions about costs and benefits in each package must be continually updated and new packages developed as soon as new activities emerge. The following problems might also occur.

(a)   **Short-term benefits** might be **emphasised** to the detriment of long-term benefits.

(b)   It might give the impression **that all decisions have to be made in the budget**. Management must be able to meet unforeseen opportunities and threats at all times, however, and must not feel restricted from carrying out new ideas simply because they were not approved by a decision package, cost benefit analysis and the ranking process.

(c)   It may **call for management skills** both in constructing decision packages and in the ranking process **which the organisation does not possess**. Managers may have to be trained in ZBB techniques.

(d)   The organisation's **information systems may not be capable of providing suitable information**.

(e)   **The ranking process can be difficult**. Managers face three common problems.

     (i)   A large number of packages may have to be ranked.

BPP
LEARNING MEDIA

(ii)   It can be difficult to rank packages which appear to be equally vital, for legal or operational reasons.

(iii)   It is difficult to rank activities which have qualitative rather than quantitative benefits – such as spending on staff welfare and working conditions.

In summary, perhaps the **most serious drawback to ZBB is that it requires a lot of management time and paperwork**. One way of obtaining the benefits of ZBB but of overcoming the drawbacks is to apply it selectively on a rolling basis throughout the organisation. This year finance, next year marketing, the year after personnel and so on. In this way all activities will be thoroughly scrutinised over a period of time.

6.3 Using zero based budgeting

FAST FORWARD
ZBB is particularly useful for budgeting for discretionary costs and for rationalisation purposes, in areas of operations where efficiency standards are not properly established, such as administration work.

ZBB is not particularly suitable for direct manufacturing costs, which are usually budgeted using standard costing, work study and other management planning and control techniques. It is best applied to **support expenses**, that is expenditure incurred in departments which exist to support the essential production function. These support areas include marketing, finance, quality control, personnel, data processing, accounting, sales and distribution. In many organisations, these expenses make up a large proportion of the total expenditure. These activities are less easily quantifiable by conventional methods and are more **discretionary** in nature.

ZBB can also be successfully applied to **service industries** and **non-profit-making organisations** such as local and central government departments, educational establishments, hospitals and so on, and in any organisation where alternative levels of provision for each activity are possible and where the costs and benefits are separately identifiable.

ZBB can also be used to make **rationalisation decisions**. 'Rationalisation' is a term for cutting back on production and activity levels, and cutting costs. The need for service departments to operate above a minimum service level or the need for having a particular department at all can be questioned, and ZBB can be used to make rationalisation decisions when an organisation is forced to make spending cuts.

7 Activity based budgeting

FAST FORWARD
At its simplest, **activity based budgeting (ABB)** is merely the use of activity based costing methods as a basis for preparing budgets.

ey term
Activity based budgeting involves defining the activities that underlie the financial figures in each function and using the level of activity to decide how much resource should be allocated, how well it is being managed and to explain variances from budget.

Activity based budgeting differs from traditional budgeting in the way that budgets are prepared for overhead costs. Overhead costs are budgeted on the basis of activities, rather than on a departmental basis.

Implementing ABC (see Chapter 2a) leads to the realisation that the **business as a whole** needs to be managed with reference to **activities and the cost drivers** for those activities..

7.1 Principles of ABB

With ABB, budgeting for direct costs (direct materials, direct labour) is no different from 'traditional' budgeting. The only difference is the approach to budgeting for overhead costs.

ABB involves defining the key activities that account for overhead spending, and considering the costs of the activity. Budgeted costs will depend on the expected level of activity (volume of the cost driver). A decision is made about the planned level of activity and the resources required to sustain this activity level, and the estimated cost is included in the budget.

ABB can also be used for control purposes, comparing actual and planned costs to assess how well the activity is being **managed** and to **explain variances** from budget.

ABB is therefore based on the following **principles**.

(a) It is **activities which drive costs** and the aim is to **plan and control the causes** (drivers) of costs rather than the costs themselves, with the result that in the long term, costs will be better managed and better understood.

(b) **Not all activities add value**, so activities must be examined and split up according to their ability to add value.

(c) Most departmental activities are driven by demands and decisions **beyond the immediate control** of the manager responsible for the department's budget.

(d) Traditional financial measures of performance are unable to fulfil the objective of **continuous improvement**. Additional measures which focus on drivers of costs, the quality of activities undertaken, the responsiveness to change and so on are needed.

7.2 Example: ABB

A stores department has two main activities, receiving deliveries of raw materials from suppliers into stores and issuing raw materials to production departments. Two major cost drivers, the number of deliveries of raw materials and the number of production runs, have been identified. Although the majority of the costs of the department can be attributed to the activities, there is a small balance, termed 'department running costs', which includes general administration costs, part of the department manager's salary and so on.

Based on activity levels expected in the next control period, the following cost driver volumes have been budgeted.

250 deliveries of raw materials
120 production runs

On the basis of budgeted departmental costs and the cost analysis, the following budget has been drawn up for the next control period.

Cost	Total	Costs attributable to receiving deliveries	Costs attributable to issuing materials	Dept running costs
	$'000	$'000	$'000	$'000
Salaries – management	25	8	12	5
Salaries – store workers	27	13	12	2
Salaries – administration	15	4	5	6
Consumables	11	3	5	3
Information technology costs	14	5	8	1
Other costs	19	10	6	3
	111	43	48	20
Activity volumes		250	120	
Cost per unit of cost driver		$172	$400	$20,000

Points to note

(a) The apportionment of cost will be subjective to a certain extent. The objective of the exercise is that the resource has to be justified as supporting one or more of the activities. Costs cannot be hidden.

(b) The cost driver rates of $172 and $400 can be used to calculate product costs using ABC.

(c) Identifying activities and their costs helps to focus attention on those activities which add value and those that do not.

(d) The budget has highlighted the cost of the two activities.

7.3 Benefits of ABB

Some writers treat ABB as a complete philosophy in itself and attribute to it all the good features of strategic management accounting, zero base budgeting, total quality management, and other ideas. For example, the following claims have been made.

(a) Different **activity levels** will provide a foundation for the 'base' package and incremental packages of **ZBB**.

(b) It will ensure that the organisation's overall **strategy** and any actual or likely changes in that strategy will be taken into account, because it attempts to manage the business as the **sum of its interrelated parts**.

(c) **Critical success factors** will be identified and performance measures devised to monitor progress towards them. (A critical success factor is an activity in which a business **must** perform well if it is to succeed).

(d) Because concentration is focused on the **whole of an activity**, not just its separate parts, there is more likelihood of **getting it right first time**. For example what is the use of being able to **produce** goods in time for their despatch date if the budget provides insufficient resources for the distribution manager who has to **deliver** them?

Question

Activity based budget

The production department of SPI Co has four major activities namely receiving deliveries, material handling, production runs and quality tests.

Each of these activities has an identifiable cost driver. These are provided below along with estimated volumes for the coming period.

Number of deliveries	300
Number of movements of material	400
Number of production runs	800
Number of quality tests	600

Two other activities that occur in the department are administration and supervision. Whilst these activities are non-volume related, they are necessary functions and should not be ignored in the budgeting process.

Budgeted costs for the coming period are displayed below.

	Total $'000	Attributable to $'000
Management salary	50	Supervision: $45; Administration: $5
Basic wages	30	Receiving deliveries: $7; Production runs: $5; Administration: $6 Material handling: $7; Quality tests: $5
Overtime	15	Receiving deliveries: $6; Quality tests: $1; Production runs: $8
Factory overheads	12	Receiving deliveries: $3; Production runs: $2; Administration $1.5; Material handling $2; Quality tests: $1.5; Supervision: $2
Other costs	4	Receiving deliveries: $1; Supervision: $1; Administration: $2
	111	

Required

Produce an activity based budget for the coming period that shows

(i) total cost for each activity
(ii) total cost for the production department
(iii) cost per activity unit

Activity based budget for SPI Co

	Receiving deliveries	Material handling	Production runs	Quality tests	Admin	S'vision	Total
Cost driver	No of deliveries	No of movements of material	No of production runs	No of quality tests	–	–	
Volume	300	400	800	600			
	$'000	$'000	$'000	$'000	$'000	$'000	$'000
Management salary	–	–	–	–	5	45	50
Basic wages	7	7	5	5	6	–	30
Overtime	6	–	8	1	–	–	15
Factory o'heads	3	2	2	1.5	1.5	2	12
Other	1	–	–	–	2	1	4
Total	17	9	15	7.5	14.5	48	111
Cost per activity unit	$56.67	$22.50	$18.75	$12.50			

8 Rolling budgets

12/12

FAST FORWARD

Rolling budgets (also called **continuous budgets**) are budgets which are continuously updated throughout a financial year, by adding a further period (say a month or a quarter) and removing the corresponding period that has just ended.

8.1 Dynamic conditions

Actual conditions may differ from those anticipated when the budget was drawn up for a number of reasons.

(a) **Organisational changes** may occur.

    (i)   A change in structure, from a functional basis, say, to a process-based one

    (ii)   New agreements with the workforce about flexible working or safety procedures

    (iii)   The reallocation of responsibilities following, say, the removal of tiers of middle management and the 'empowerment' of workers further down the line

(b) Action may be needed to **combat an initiative by a competitor.**

(c) **New technology** may be introduced to improve productivity, reduce labour requirements or enhance quality.

(d) **Environmental conditions** may change: there may be a general boom or a recession, an event affecting supply or demand, or a change in government or government policy.

(e) The level of **inflation** may be higher or lower than that anticipated.

(f) The **level of activities** may be different from the levels planned.

Any of these changes **may make the original budget quite inappropriate**, either in terms of the numbers expected, or the way in which responsibility for achieving them is divided, or both.

There is a risk that in a period of rapid and continual change, budgets cease to be useful as a plan and guide for management. To deal with this risk, budgets may be reviewed and amended regularly.

If management need to revise their plans regularly, to keep them relevant and realistic, they may decide to introduce a system of **rolling budgets**.

Key term

> A **rolling budget** is a budget which is continuously updated by adding a further accounting period (a month or quarter) to the end of the budget when the corresponding period in the current budget has ended.
>
> As a result, a number of rolling budgets are prepared each year; and each rolling budget covers the next 12-month period.

Rolling budgets may be used when the pace of change in the business environment is fast and continual. They represent an attempt to prepare plans which are **more realistic**, particularly with a regard to price levels, by **shortening the period between preparing budgets.**

Instead of preparing a **periodic budget** annually for the full budget period, new **budgets are prepared every one, two, three or four months** (so that there are three, four, six, or even twelve budgets each year). **Each of these budgets would cover for the next twelve months** so that the current budget is extended by an extra period as the current period ends: hence the name rolling budgets.

Suppose, for example, that a rolling budget is prepared every three months. The first three months of the budget period would be planned in great detail, and the remaining nine months in lesser detail, because of the greater uncertainty about the longer-term future. If a first continuous budget is prepared for January to March in detail and April to December in less detail, a new budget will be prepared towards the end of March, planning April to June in detail and July to March in less detail. Four rolling budgets would be prepared every 12 months on this 3 and 9 month basis, requiring, inevitably, greater administrative effort.

8.2 Example: Preparing a rolling budget

A company uses a system of rolling budgets. The sales budget is displayed below.

	Jan - Mar $	Apr - Jun $	Jul - Sep $	Oct - Dec $	Total $
Sales	78,480	86,120	91,800	97,462	353,862

Actual sales for January – March were $74,640. The adverse variance is explained by growth being lower than anticipated and the market being more competitive than predicted.

Senior management has proposed that the revised assumption for sales growth should be 2.5% per quarter.

Required

Update the budget as appropriate.

Solution

Step 1   The revised budget should incorporate 2.5% growth starting from the actual sales figure for January – March.

$74,640 × 1.025 = $76,506

Step 2   Using the revised balance for January – March, update the budget for the next four quarters (including a figure for January – March of the following year).

Apr – Jun	= $76,506 × 1.025	= $78,419
Jul – Sep	= $78,419 × 1.025	= $80,379
Oct – Dec	= $80,379 × 1.025	= $82,388
Jan – Mar	= $82,388 × 1.025	= $84,448

Step 3 Revised budget

	Apr – Jun $	Jul – Sep $	Oct – Dec $	Jan – Mar $	Total $
Sales	78,419	80,379	82,388	84,448	325,634

8.3 The advantages and disadvantages of rolling budgets

The **advantages** are as follows.

(a) They **reduce the element of uncertainty** in budgeting because they concentrate detailed planning and control on the near-term future, where the degree of uncertainty is much smaller.

(b) They force managers to reassess the budget regularly, and to produce budgets which are **up to date** in the light of current events and expectations.

(c) **Planning and control will be based on a recent plan** which is likely to be far **more realistic** than a fixed annual budget made many months ago.

(d) Realistic budgets are likely to have a **better motivational influence** on managers.

(e) There is **always a budget which extends for several months ahead**. For example, if rolling budgets are prepared quarterly there will always be a budget extending for the next 9 to 12 months. This is not the case when fixed annual budgets are used.

The **disadvantages** of rolling budgets can be a deterrent to using them.

(a) They involve **more time, effort and money** in budget preparation.

(b) Frequent budgeting might have an **off-putting effect on managers** who doubt the value of preparing one budget after another at regular intervals.

(c) Revisions to the budget might involve revisions to standard costs too, which in turn would involve revisions to stock valuations. This could replace a large **administrative effort** from the accounts department every time a rolling budget is prepared.

(d) The benefits of rolling budgets are limited, and so not worth the extra cost, when the rate of change in the business environment is not rapid and continual.

8.4 Continuous budgets or updated annual budgets

If the expected changes are not likely to be continuous there is a strong argument that routine updating of the budget is unnecessary. **Instead the annual budget could be updated whenever changes become foreseeable,** so that a budget might be updated once or twice, and perhaps more often, during the course of the year. An updated annual budget, prepared in response to a significant change in circumstances, may simply be called a **revised budget**.

When a fixed budget is updated and revised, a 'rolling' 12-month budget would probably not be prepared. For example if a budget is updated and revised in month 8 of the year, the revised budget would relate to months 8 – 12. It would not be extended to month 7 of the following year.

9 Beyond Budgeting

Beyond Budgeting is a budgeting model which proposes that traditional budgeting should be abandoned. **Adaptive management processes** should be used rather than fixed annual budgets.

9.1 Criticisms of budgeting

There are many problems with budgets and criticisms of how they are used in organisations.

The Beyond Budgeting Round Table (BBRT), an independent research organisation, proposes that budgeting, as most organisations practise it, should be abandoned. Their website (at www.bbrt.org) lists the following ten criticisms of budgeting as put forward by Hope and Fraser *Beyond Budgeting*, 1st edition, Harvard Business School Press, 2003.

(a) **Budgets are time-consuming and expensive**. Even with the support of computer models it is estimated that the budgeting process uses up to 20 to 30 per cent of senior executives' and financial managers' time.

(b) **Budgets provide poor value to users**. Although surveys have shown that some managers feel that budgets give them control, a large majority of financial directors wish to reform the budgetary process because they feel that finance staff spend too much time on 'lower value added activities'.

(c) **Budgets fail to focus on shareholder value**. Most budgets are set on an incremental basis as an acceptable target agreed between the manager and the manager's superior. Managers may be rewarded for achieving their short term budgets and will not look to the longer term or take risks, for fear of affecting their own short term results.

(d) **Budgets are too rigid and prevent fast response**. Although most organisations do update and revise their budgets at regular intervals as the budget period proceeds the process is often too slow compared with the pace at which the external environment is changing.

(e) **Budgets protect rather than reduce costs**. Once a manager has an authorised budget he can spend that amount of resource without further authorisation. A 'use it or lose it' mentality often develops so that managers will incur cost unnecessarily. This happens especially towards the end of the budget period in the expectation that managers will not be permitted to carry forward any unused resource into the budget for next period.

(f) **Budgets stifle product and strategy innovation**. The focus on achieving the budget discourages managers from taking risks in case this has adverse effects on their short term performance. Managers do not have the freedom to respond to changing customer needs in a fast changing market because the activity they would need to undertake is not authorised in their budget.

(g) **Budgets focus on sales targets rather than customer satisfaction**. The achievement of short term sales forecasts becomes the focus of most organisations. However this does not necessarily result in customer satisfaction. The customer may be sold something **inappropriate to their needs**, as in recent years in the UK financial services industry. Alternatively if a manager has already met the sales target for a particular period they might try to **delay sales to the next period**, in order to give themselves a 'head start' towards achieving the target for the next period. Furthermore, there is an incentive towards the end of a period, if a manager feels that the sales target is not going to be achieved for the period, to **delay sales until the next period**, and thus again have a head start towards achieving the target for the next period. All of these actions, focusing on sales targets rather than customer satisfaction, will have a detrimental effect on the organisation in the longer term.

(h) **Budgets are divorced from strategy**. Most organisations monitor the monthly results against the short term budget for the month. What is needed instead is a system of monitoring the longer term progress against the organisation's strategy.

(i) **Budgets reinforce a dependency culture**. The process of planning and budgeting within a framework devolved from senior management perpetuates a culture of dependency. Traditional budgeting systems, operated on a centralised basis, do not encourage a culture of **personal responsibility**.

(j) **Budgets lead to unethical behaviour**. For example building **slack** into the budget in order to create an easier target for achievement.

9.2 Beyond Budgeting concepts

Two fundamental concepts underlie the Beyond Budgeting approach.

(a) **Use adaptive management processes for making decisions rather than tie decision making to conformity with a rigid annual budget**. Traditional annual plans tie managers to predetermined

actions which are not responsive to current situations. Managers should instead plan on a **more adaptive**, rolling basis but with the focus on cash forecasting rather than purely on cost control. Performance is monitored against world-class benchmarks, competitors and previous periods.

(b) **Move towards devolved networks rather than centralised hierarchies**. The emphasis is on encouraging a culture of personal responsibility by delegating decision making and performance accountability to line managers.

10 Information used in budget systems

FAST FORWARD

Information used in budgeting comes from a wide variety of sources.

Past data may be used as a starting point for the preparation of budgets but other information from a wide variety of sources will also be used. Each **function** of the organisation will be required to estimate revenue and expenditure for the budget period. For example, marketing, personnel and research and development.

10.1 Sales budget information

As we have seen, for many organisations, the principal budget factor is sales volume. The sales budget is therefore often the primary budget from which the majority of the other budgets are derived. Before the sales budget can be prepared a **sales forecast** has to be made. Sales forecasting is complex and difficult and involves the use of information from a variety of sources.

- Past sales patterns
- The economic environment
- Results of market research
- Anticipated advertising
- Competition
- Changing consumer taste

- New legislation
- Distribution
- Pricing policies and discounts offered
- Legislation
- Environmental factors

10.2 Production budget information

Sources of information for the production budget will include:

(a) **Labour costs** including idle time, overtime and standard output rates per hour.
(b) **Raw material costs** including allowances for losses during production.
(c) **Machine hours** including expected idle time and expected output rates per machine hour.

This information will come from the production department and a large part of the traditional work of **cost accounting** involves ascribing costs to the physical information produced.

11 Changing budgetary systems

FAST FORWARD

An organisation wishing to **change** its budgetary practices will face a number of difficulties.

The business environment has become increasingly complex, uncertain and dynamic and organisations need to be able to adapt quickly to changing conditions. It has been argued that traditional budgets are too rigid and prevent fast response to changing conditions.

However, an organisation which decides to **change** its type of budget used, or budgetary system, will face a number of **difficulties**.

(a) **Resistance by employees.** Employees will be familiar with the current system and may have built in slack so will not easily accept new targets. New control systems that threaten to alter existing power relationships may be thwarted by those affected.
(b) **Loss of control.** Senior management may take time to adapt to the new system and understand the implications of results.

(c)   **Costs of implementation.** Any new system or process requires careful implementation which will have cost implications. For example, the procedures for preparing budgets will have to be re-written in a new budget manual. Establishing a system of zero based budgeting, for example, will require the design and documentation of a large number of decision packages.

(d)   **Training.** In order to prepare and implement budgets under the new system, managers will need to be fully trained. This is time-consuming and expensive.

(e)   **Lack of accounting information**. The organisation may not have the **systems** in place to obtain and analyse the necessary information for preparing the new style budget. For example, an organisation needs a system of activity-based costing if it is to implement activity-based budgeting.

12 Budget systems and uncertainty

Uncertainty can be allowed for in budgeting by means of **flexible budgeting, rolling budgets, probabilistic budgeting** and **sensitivity analysis**.

Causes of uncertainty in the budgeting process include:

(a)   **Customers.** They may decide to buy less than forecast, or they may buy more.

(b)   **Products/services**. In the modern business environment, organisations need to respond to customers' rapidly changing requirements.

(c)   **Inflation** and movements in **interest and exchange rates.**

(d)   **Volatility** in the **cost of materials.**

(e)   **Competitors.** They may steal some of an organisation's expected customers, or some competitors' customers may change their buying allegiance.

(f)   **Employees.** They may not work as hard as was hoped, or they may work harder.

(g)   **Machines.** They may break down unexpectedly.

(h)   There may be **political unrest** (terrorist activity), **social unrest** (public transport strikes) or minor or major **natural disasters** (storms, floods).

Rolling budgets are a way of trying to **reduce the element of uncertainty** in the plan. There are **other planning methods** which try to **analyse the uncertainty** such as **probabilistic budgeting** (where probabilities are assigned to different conditions – see Chapter 7) and **sensitivity analysis**. These methods are suitable when the **degree of uncertainty is quantifiable** from the start of the budget period and actual results are not expected to go outside the range of these expectations.

- A budget is a **quantified plan of action** for a forthcoming accounting period.

- A budget can be set from the **top down** (**imposed** budget) or from the **bottom up** (**participatory** budget).

- Here are the objectives of a budgetary planning and control system.

  - Ensure the achievement of the organisation's objectives
  - Compel planning
  - Communicate ideas and plans
  - Coordinate activities
  - Provide a framework for responsibility accounting
  - Establish a system of control
  - Motivate employees to improve their performance

- The **planning and control cycle** has seven steps

  - *Step 1.* Identify **objectives**
  - *Step 2.* Identify potential **strategies**
  - *Step 3.* Evaluate strategies
  - *Step 4.* Choose alternative courses of action
  - *Step 5.* Implement the long-term plan
  - *Step 6.* Measure actual results and compare with the plan
  - *Step 7.* Respond to divergences from the plan

- **Planning and control** occurs at all levels of the **performance hierarchy** to different degrees. The performance hierarchy refers to the system by which performance is measured and controlled at different levels of management within the organisation.

- **Budgetary control** occurs at the middle management or **'management control'** levels of the performance hierarchy.

- With the 'traditional' approach to budgeting, known as **incremental budgeting**, the budget for the next financial year is based on the actual results for the current financial year. At its simplest level, a budget based on an incremental costing approach is the actual (or budgeted) performance for the current year, adjusted for expected growth and inflation. Incremental budgeting encourages slack and wasteful spending to creep into budgets.

- A **fixed budget** is a financial plan that does not change throughout the budget period, regardless of any changes from the plan in the actual volume of activity. A **flexible budget** recognises cost behaviour and changes as the actual volume of activity changes.

- A fixed budget is normally used for **planning purposes** and is prepared in advance of the beginning of the financial period. A flexible budget is used for **control purposes** and is normally prepared retrospectively, when the actual level of activity in a period is known.

- The principle behind **zero based budgeting (ZBB)** is that the budget for each cost centre should be made from 'scratch' or zero. Every item of expenditure must be justified in its entirety in order to be included in the next year's budget.

- There is a three-step approach to ZBB.

  - Define items or activities for which costs should be budgeted, and spending decisions should be planned: these are 'decision packages'

  - Evaluate and rank the packages in order of priority: eliminate packages whose costs exceed their value

  - Allocate resources to the decision packages according to their ranking. Where resources such as money are in short supply, they are allocated to the most valuable activities.

- ZBB is particularly useful for budgeting for discretionary costs and for rationalisation purposes, in areas of operations where efficiency standards are not properly established, such as administration work.

- At its simplest, **activity based budgeting (ABB)** is merely the use of activity based costing methods as a basis for preparing budgets.

- **Rolling budgets** (also called **continuous budgets**) are budgets which are continuously updated throughout a financial year, by adding a further period (say a month or a quarter) and removing the corresponding period that has just ended.

- **Beyond Budgeting** is a budgeting model which proposes that traditional budgeting should be abandoned. **Adaptive management processes** should be used rather than fixed annual budgets.

- **Information** used in budgeting comes from a wide variety of sources.

- An organisation wishing to **change** its budgetary practices will face a number of difficulties.

- Uncertainty can be allowed for in budgeting by means of **flexible budgeting, rolling budgets, probabilistic budgeting** and **sensitivity analysis**.

1   Which of the following could not be a principal budget factor?

(a)   Cash   (b)   Machine capacity
(c)   Sales demand   (d)   Selling price
(e)   Labour   (f)   Premises

2   *Fill in the gaps.*

A flexible budget is a budget which, by recognising ...., is designed to .... as the level of activity changes.

3   *Match the descriptions to the budgeting style.*

Description

(a)   Budget allowances are set without the involvement of the budget holder
(b)   All budget holders are involved in setting their own budgets

Budgeting style

Bottom-up budgeting
Top-down budgeting

4   Incremental budgeting is widely used and is a particularly efficient form of budgeting.

☐   True   ☐   False

5   What are the three steps of ZBB?

Step 1 ....

Step 2 ....

Step 3 ....

6   To which of the following can ZBB be usefully applied?

	Use ZBB	Do not use ZBB
Personnel		
Social services department of local government		
Direct material costs		
Sales department		
Schools		
An inefficient production department		
An efficient production department		

7   *Choose the appropriate word from those highlighted.*

A rolling budget is also known as a **periodic/continuous** budget.

8   If a system of a ABB is in use, how might the cost of scheduling production be flexed?

A   Number of items produced
B   Number of set-ups
C   Number of direct labour hours
D   Number of parts used in production

9   A system of zero-based budgeting forces employees to remove wasteful expenditure.

☐ True   ☐ False

10   Use of zero-based budgeting implies flexing budgets on the basis of differences between budgeted and actual cost-driving activities.

☐ True   ☐ False

1   (d)

2   cost behaviour patterns
        flex or change

3   (a)   Top-down budgeting
        (b)   Bottom-up budgeting

4   False. Incremental budgeting is inefficient.

5   Step 1.Define decision packages
        Step 2.Evaluate and rank activities (decision package)
        Step 3.Allocate resources

6

	Use ZBB	Do not use ZBB
Personnel	✓	
Social services department of local government	✓	
Direct material costs		✓
Sales department	✓	
Schools	✓	
An inefficient production department	✓	
An efficient production department		✓

7   It is also known as a continuous budget.

8   B   Number of set-ups

9   True

10   False. This is a common feature of **activity-based** budgeting.

Now try the question below from the Practice Question Bank

Number	Level	Marks	Time
Q11	Examination	15	27 mins

Quantitative analysis in budgeting

Topic list	Syllabus reference
1 Analysing fixed and variable costs: high-low method	C3 (a)
2 Learning curves	C3 (b), (c)
3 Expected values in budgeting	C3 (d)
4 Using spreadsheets in budgeting	C3 (e)

Introduction

The success of a budget is largely dependent on the degree of accuracy in estimating the revenues and costs for the budget period.

This chapter looks at the **quantitative techniques** involved in budgeting, including the **high-low method** and the concept of the **learning curve**.

We also consider how **expected values** can be used to determine the best combination of profit and risk, and the use of **spreadsheets** throughout the budgeting process.

Study guide

		Intellectual level
C3	**Quantitative analysis in budgeting**	
(a)	Analyse fixed and variable cost elements from total cost data using the high/low method	2
(b)	Estimate the learning rate and learning effect	2
(c)	Apply the learning curve to a budgetary problem, including calculations on steady states	2
(d)	Discuss the reservations with the learning curve	2
(e)	Apply expected values and explain the problems and benefits	2
(f)	Explain the benefits and dangers inherent in using spreadsheets in budgeting	2

Exam guide

The quantitative techniques covered in this chapter are likely to form the calculation part of a budgeting question in Section B. Techniques may also be examined regularly in short section A multiple choice questions. There has been an article in *Student Accountant* on the learning rate and learning effect. We recommend that you read it. It can be found on the ACCA web site.

One of the competencies you require to fulfil performance objective 13 of the PER is the ability to prepare budgets based on the best information to an appropriate level of detail. You can apply the knowledge you obtain from this chapter of the text to help to demonstrate this competence.

1 Analysing fixed and variable costs: high-low method

FAST FORWARD

The **high-low method** is a quantitative technique for analysing total costs into their fixed cost and variable cost elements.

1.1 The high-low method   12/07, 12/08

You should have encountered the high-low method in your earlier studies. It is used to separate a total cost into its fixed cost and variable cost elements. This technique is still examinable in F5. Read through the knowledge brought forward and do the question below to jog your memory.

Knowledge brought forward from earlier studies

Follow the steps below.

Step 1   Review records of costs in previous periods.

- Select the period with the **highest** activity level
- Select the period with the **lowest** activity level

Step 2   If inflation makes it difficult to compare costs, adjust by indexing up or down.

Step 3	Determine the following.

- Total costs at high activity level
- Total costs at low activity level
- Total units at high activity level
- Total units at low activity level

Step 4	The difference between total costs at the high and the low activity levels must consist entirely of variable costs, since fixed costs are the same at both activity levels. So calculate the following.

$$\frac{\text{Total cost at high activity level} - \text{total cost at low activity level}}{\text{Total units at high activity level} - \text{total units at low activity level}}$$

= Variable cost per unit (v)

Step 5	The fixed costs can be determined as follows. (Total cost at high activity level) – (total units at high activity level × variable cost per unit)

Question
High-low method

A department in a large organisation wishes to develop a method of predicting its total costs in a period. The following data have been recorded.

Month	Activity level (X) units	Cost $
January	1,600	28,200
February	2,300	29,600
March	1,900	28,800
April	1,800	28,600
May	1,500	28,000
June	1,700	28,400

The total cost model for a period could be represented by what equation?

Answer

The highest activity level is in February and the lowest in May.

Total cost at highest activity level	= $29,600
Total cost at lowest activity level	= $28,000
Total units at highest activity level	= 2,300
Total units at lowest activity level	= 1,500

$$\text{Variable cost per unit} = \frac{29,600 - 28,000}{2,300 - 1,500} = \frac{1,600}{800} = \$2$$

Fixed costs = 29,600 – (2,300 × 2) = $25,000
Total costs = 25,000 + 2x
where x is the volume of activity in units.

1.2 The usefulness of the high-low method

The high-low method is a simple and easy to use method of estimating fixed and variable costs. However there are a number of problems with it.

(a) The method **ignores** all cost information apart from costs at the highest and lowest volumes of activity and these may not be **representative** of costs at all levels of activity.

(b) **Inaccurate** cost estimates may be produced as a result of the assumption of a constant relationship between costs and volume of activity.

(c) Estimates are based on **historical** information and conditions may have changed.

2 Learning curves   12/08, 12/09, 12/11, 12/13

Learning curve theory may be useful for forecasting production time and labour costs in circumstances where a work force makes a new product and improves its efficiency with experience and learning. However the method has many limitations.

Whenever an individual starts a job which is **fairly repetitive** in nature, and provided that his speed of working is not dictated to him by the speed of machinery (as it would be on a production line), he is likely to become **more confident and knowledgeable** about the work as he gains experience, to become **more efficient**, and to do the work **more quickly**.

Eventually, however, when he has acquired enough experience, there will be nothing more for him to learn, and so **the learning process will stop**.

The same principle may **apply to a work force as a whole**, when it starts to make a new product.

Key term

Learning curve theory applies to situations where the work force as a whole improves in efficiency with experience. The **learning effect** or **learning curve effect** describes the speeding up of a job with repeated performance.

2.1 Where does learning curve theory apply?

Labour time should be expected to get shorter, with experience, in the production of items which exhibit any or all of the following features.

- Made largely **by labour effort** (rather than by a **highly mechanised** process) or where labour skill is an important factor in the production process

- Brand **new** or relatively **short-lived**. (The learning process does not continue indefinitely)

- **Complex** and made in **small quantities** for **special orders**

2.2 The learning rate and learning effect

Where a learning curve applies, there is a learning rate and a learning effect.

The **learning rate** is expressed as a percentage value, such as an 80% learning curve or a 70% learning curve.

The **learning effect** is that as the work force learns from experience how to make the new product, there is a big reduction in the time to make additional units.

Specifically, **every time that the cumulative output of the product doubles**, the average time to make all the units produced to date is a proportion of what it was before. This proportion is the learning rate.

So if a 90% learning curve applies, and the labour time to make the first unit is 100 hours:

(a) The average time to make the first two units will be 90% × 100 hours = 90 hours, and the total time for the first two units will be 180 hours. Since the first unit takes 100 hours, the second unit will take 80 hours.

(b)   The average time to make the first four units will be 90% × 90 hours = 81 hours and the total time for the first four units will be 324 hours. Since the first two units take 180 hours, the third and fourth units together will take 144 hours.

This learning process continues until the learning effect comes to an end and a 'steady state' of production is achieved.

The three approaches to learning curve problems

There are two methods that can be used to deal with a learning curve scenario. Be prepared to use either or both in the exam.

- **Method 1.** The tabular approach
- **Method 2.** The algebraic approach

The tabular approach is quicker and easier when it can be used, but it can be used only for a limited type of problem. The algebraic approach is more likely to be examined and requires the application of a formula to calculate the cumulative average time per unit produced.

2.3 Method 1 – The tabular approach: cumulative average time and the learning rate

The **tabular approach** can only be used to calculate average times when cumulative output doubles. A table can be used to calculate:

(a)   the cumulative average time per unit, and
(b)   the total time to produce all the units produced so far.

The rule to remember is that every time that cumulative output doubles, the average production time is x% of what is was before, where x is the learning rate.

The approach is best explained with a numerical example.

2.4 Example: An 80% learning curve

For example, where an 80% learning effect occurs, the cumulative average time required per unit of output is reduced to 80% of the previous cumulative average time when output is doubled.

The first unit of output of a new product requires 100 hours. An 80% learning curve applies. The production times would be as follows.

Cumulative number of units	Cumulative avge time per unit (hours)	Cumulative total time (hours)	Incremental number of units	Incremental total time (hours)
1	100.0	100.0	–	–
2*	80.0	160.0	1	60.0
4*	64.0	256.0	2	96.0
8*	51.2	409.6	4	153.6

* Output is being **doubled** each time.

The cost of the additional time can be calculated by applying the labour hour rate to the number of labour hours (and variable overhead rate, where variable overheads vary with the number of labour hours). The learning effect does not affect material costs.

2.5 Example: The learning curve

Captain Kitts has designed a new type of sailing boat, for which the cost of the first boat to be produced has been estimated as follows:

	$
Materials	5,000
Labour (800 hrs × $5 per hr)	4,000
Overhead (150% of labour cost)	6,000
	15,000
Profit mark-up (20%)	3,000
Sales price	18,000

It is planned to sell all the yachts at full cost plus 20%. An 80% learning curve is expected to apply to the production work. The management accountant has been asked to provide cost information so that decisions can be made on what price to charge.

(a)   What is the separate cost of a second yacht?

(b)   What would be the cost per unit for a third and a fourth yacht, if they are ordered separately later on?

(c)   If they were all ordered now, could Captain Kitts quote a single unit price for four yachts and eight yachts?

Solution

Cumulative number of units	Cumulative avge time per unit (hours)	Cumulative total time (hours)	Incremental number of units	Incremental total time (hours)	Incremental average time (hours)
1	800.0	800.0	–	–	–
2*	640.0	1,280.0 **	1	480.0	480.0
4*	512.0	2,048.0	2	768.0	384.0
8*	409.6	3,276.8	4	1,228.8	307.2

* Output is being **doubled** each time.

** 640 × 2 = 1,280, 512 × 4 = 2,048

(a)   **Separate cost of a second yacht**

	$
Materials	5,000
Labour (480 hrs × $5)	2,400
Overhead (150% of labour cost)	3,600
Total cost	11,000

(b)   **Cost of the third and fourth yachts**

	$
Materials cost for two yachts	10,000
Labour (768 hours × $5)	3,840
Overhead (150% of labour cost)	5,760
Total cost	19,600
Cost per yacht (÷2)	9,800

(c)   **A price for the first four yachts together and for the first eight yachts together**

		First four yachts $		First eight yachts $
Materials		20,000		40,000
Labour	(2,048 hrs)	10,240	(3,276.8 hrs)	16,384
Overhead (150% of labour cost)		15,360		24,576
Total cost		45,600		80,960
Profit (20%)		9,120		16,192
Total sales price		54,720		97,152
Price per yacht	(÷4)	13,680	(÷8)	12,144

This assumes that Captain Kitts is happy to pass on the efficiency savings to the customer in the form of a lower price.

| Question | Learning curve theory |

Bortamord anticipates that a 90% learning curve will apply to the production of a new item. The first item will cost $2,000 in materials, and will take 500 labour hours. The cost per hour for labour and variable overhead is $5.

You are required to calculate the total cost for the first unit and for the first 8 units.

Answer

Cumulative number of units	Cumulative avge time per unit (hours)	Cumulative total time (hours)	Incremental number of units	Incremental total time (hours)
1	500.0	500.0	–	–
2*	450.0	900.0	1	400.0
4*	405.0	1,620.0	2	720.0
8*	364.5	2,916.0	4	1,296.0

	Cost of 1st unit		Cost of 1st 8 units
	$		$
Materials	2,000		16,000
Labour and variable o/hd (500 hrs)	2,500	(2,916 hours)	14,580
	4,500		30,580
Average cost/unit	4,500		3,822.50

2.6 Method 2 – The algebraic approach

FAST FORWARD The formula for the learning curve is **Y = ax^b**, where b, the learning coefficient or learning index, is defined as (log of the learning rate/log of 2). The learning curve formula can be used to solve all learning curve scenarios.

Exam formula

The formula for the learning curve is **Y = ax^b**

where   **Y** is the cumulative average time per unit to produce x units
         x is the cumulative number of units
         a is the time taken for the first unit of output
         b is the index of learning (logLR/log2)
         LR is the learning rate as a decimal

Exam focus point

This formula is provided in the exam paper. It refers to time rather than labour cost. The formula can also be used to calculate the labour cost per unit. The labour **times** are calculated using the curve formula and then converted to cost.

The formula approach is more likely to be required for your exam, because it can be used to calculate the time to produce each unit.

2.6.1 Calculating the time for a specific unit

The formula approach is used to calculate the incremental time for any unit where a learning curve applies. Suppose that we want to know the time that it will take to make the third and the fifth units, where a learning curve applies.

(a)   To calculate the time to make the third unit:

–   Calculate the cumulative average time for the first three units and the total time for the first three units

–   Calculate the cumulative average time for the first two units and the total time for the first two units

–   The time for the third unit is the difference in these two totals

(b)   To calculate the time to make the fifth unit:

–   Calculate the cumulative average time for the first five units and the total time for the first five units

–   Calculate the cumulative average time for the first four units and the total time for the first four units

–   The time for the fifth unit is the difference in these two totals.

This approach can be used to calculate the time required to make any unit where a learning curve applies.

2.6.2 Logarithms and the value of b

It is essential to understand how to apply the learning curve formula. You need a calculator that includes a function for calculating logarithms. Logarithms are the value of any number to the power of 10. For example the logarithm of 3 is 0.4771213 because $10^{0.4771213} = 3$. Using a calculator, it is a simple process to obtain the log value of any number.

In the formula $Y = ax^b$, three of the items are straightforward.

•   x = the cumulative number of units produced

•   Y = the cumulative average time for the first x units

•   a = the time to make the first unit

The only problem is calculating b.

The value of **b = log of the learning rate/log of 2**. The learning rate is expressed as a proportion, so that for an 80% learning curve, the learning rate is 0.8, and for a 90% learning curve it is 0.9, and so on.

For an 80% learning curve, b = log 0.8/log 2.

Using the button on your calculator marked 'log'

$$b = \frac{-0.0969}{0.3010} = -0.322$$

So $Y = ax^{-0.322}$

Another way of stating this is: $Y = a[1/x^{0.322}]$

Exam focus point

> The examiner has stated that **you should not round 'b' to less than three decimal places**. Ideally, you should keep the long number in your calculator and use that!

2.6.3 Example: Using the formula

Suppose that an 80% learning curve applies to production of a new product item ABC. To date (the end of June) 30 units of ABC have been produced. Budgeted production in July is 5 units. The time to make the very first unit of ABC in January was 120 hours. The labour cost is $10 per hour.

Required

(a)　Calculate the time required to make the 31st unit.

(b)　Calculate the budgeted total labour cost for July.

Solution

To solve this problem, we need to calculate three things.

(a)　The cumulative total labour cost so far to produce 30 units of ABC.

(b)　The cumulative total labour cost to produce 31 units of ABC.

(c)　The cumulative total labour cost to produce 35 units of ABC, that is adding on the extra 5 units for production in July.

(d)　The time to produce the 31st unit is the difference between (b) and (a). The extra cost of production of 5 units of ABC in July, as the difference between (c) and (a).

Time to produce the first 30 units

$Y = ax^b$

$b = \log 0.8/\log 2 = - 0.09691/0.30103 = -0.3219281$

$Y = 120 \times (1/30^{-0.3219281}) = 120 \times 0.3345594 = 40.147$ hours

Total time for first 30 units = 30×40.147 hours = 1,204.41 hours

Time to produce the first 31 units

$Y = 120 \times (1/31^{-0.3219281}) = 120 \times 0.3310463 = 39.726$ hours

Total time for first 31 units = 31×39.726 hours = 1,231.51 hours

Time to produce the 31st unit = (1,231.51 – 1,204.41) = 27.1 hours

Time to produce the first 35 units

$Y = 120 \times (1/35^{-0.3219281}) = 120 \times 0.3183619 = 38.203$ hours

Total time for first 35 units = 35×38.203 hours = 1,337.11 hours

Budgeted labour cost in July = (1,337.11 – 1,204.41) hours × $10 per hour = $1,327

2.6.4 Derivation of the learning rate

The approach you should use to derive the learning rate depends on the information given in the question. If you are provided with **details about cumulative production levels of 1, 2, 4, 8 or 16 (etc) units** you can use the **first approach** shown below. If details are given about other cumulative production quantities, however, you need to use the second approach, which involves the use of logarithms.

Question　　　　　　　　　　　　　　　Calculation of the percentage learning effect

BL is planning to manufacture a new product, product A. Development tests suggest that 60% of the variable manufacturing cost of product A will be affected by a learning and experience curve. This learning effect will apply to each unit produced and continue at a constant rate of learning until cumulative production reaches 4,000 units, when learning will stop. The unit variable manufacturing cost of the first unit is estimated to be $1,200 (of which 60% will be subject to the effect of learning), while the average unit variable manufacturing cost of four units will be $405.

Required

Calculate the rate of learning that is expected to apply.

Answer

Let the rate of learning be r.

Cumulative production	Cumulative average cost
	$
1	720 (= 60% × $1,200)
2	720 × r
4	720 × r²

∴ $720r² = $405

     r²   = $405/$720 = 0.5625

     r   =   0.75

∴ The rate of learning is 75%.

2.6.5 Derivation of the learning rate using logarithms

As outlined above, the **logarithm of a number, x, is the value of x expressed in terms of '10 to the power of'**.

$10 = 10^1$	The logarithm of 10 is 1.0
$100 = 10^2$	The logarithm of 100 is 2.0
$1,000 = 10^3$	The logarithm of 1,000 is 3.0

Your **calculator** will provide you with the logarithm of any number, probably using the **button marked log 10^x**. For example, to find log of 566 using a calculator you will probably press the log button then type in 566 and the close brackets and '=', to get 2.7528, which means that $10^{2.7528} = 566$.

Logarithms are useful to us for two main reasons.

(a)   The logarithm of the product of two numbers is the sum of their logarithms: **log (c × d) = log c + log d**.

(b)   The logarithm of one number (say, f) to the power of another number (say, g), is the second number multiplied by the logarithm of the first: **log (f^g) = g log f.**

Logarithms can therefore be used to derive non-linear functions of the form **y = ax^n**.

If $y = ax^n$, the logarithm of y and the logarithm of ax^n must be the same, so **log y = log a + nlog x. This gives us a linear function similar to y = a + nx**, the only difference being that in place of y we have to use the logarithm of y and in place of x we must use the logarithm of x.

Using simultaneous equations, we can get a value for n and a value for log a, which we can convert back into a 'normal' figure using antilogarithms (the button probably marked 10^x on your calculator).

For example, suppose the relationship between x and y can be described by the function $y = ax^n$, and suppose we know that if x = 1,000, y = 80,000 and if x = 750, y = 63,750.

Substitute these value into log y = log a + n log x.

log 80,000 = log a + n log 1,000

4.9031 = log a + 3n

∴ 4.9031 – 3n = log a   (1)

log 63,750 = log a + n log 750

$4.8045 = \log a + 2.8751n$ (2)

Sub (1) into (2).

$4.8045 = 4.9031 - 3n + 2.8751n$

$\therefore 0.1249n = 0.0986$

$\therefore n = 0.7894$

Sub value of n into (1)

$4.9031 - (3 \times 0.7894) = \log a$

$2.5349 = \log a$

$\therefore 342.69 = a$

$\therefore$ Our function is $\mathbf{y = 342.69x^{0.7894}}$

This technique is useful when the details given for the cumulative production levels do not take the form 1, 2, 4, 8 or 16 (etc) units.

Question

Calculation of the percentage learning effect using logs

XX is aware that there is a learning effect for the production of one of its new products, but is unsure about the degree of learning. The following data relate to this product.

Time taken to produce the first unit   28 direct labour hours

Production to date   15 units

Cumulative time taken to date   104 direct labour hours

What is the percentage learning effect?

Answer

Average time taken per unit to date $= (104 \div 15) = 6.933$ hours

Since $Y_x = aX^b$

$6.933 = 28(15)^b$

$15^b = 6.933 \div 28 = 0.2476$

Taking logs: since $15^b = 0.2476$

$b \log 15 = \log 0.2476$

Since $\log 15 = 1.1761$ (using log 10x on your calculator)

And $\log 0.2476 = -0.6062$

$b = \dfrac{\log 0.2476}{\log 15} = \dfrac{-0.6062}{1.1761} = -0.515$

$b = \dfrac{\log \text{ of learning rate}}{\log 2}$

$-0.515 = \dfrac{\log \text{ of learning rate}}{0.3010}$

Log of learning rate $= -0.515 \times 0.3010 = -0.155$

Using the button on your calculator probably marked 10x, −0.155 converts back to a 'normal' figure of 0.70. Thus the learning rate is 70%.

2.7 Learning curves and steady state production

As long as a learning curve effect applies, the time to produce each additional unit is less than the time for the previous unit. This means that it is not possible to determine a standard time or standard labour cost for producing the item.

A time will be reached, however, when the learning effect no longer applies and 'steady state' production is reached for the product. When a steady state is reached, a standard time and standard labour cost for the product can be established.

The learning curve formula can be used to calculate the expected labour time and labour cost when a steady state is reached, using the same method as described above. The following example illustrates the approach.

2.8 Example: Learning curves and standard costs

A company needs to calculate a new standard cost for one of its products. When the product was first manufactured, the standard variable cost of the first unit was as follows.

		Cost per unit $
Direct material	10 kg @ $4 per kg	40
Direct labour	10 hours @ $9 per hour	90
Variable overhead	10 hours @ $1 per hour	10
Total		140

During the following year, a 90% learning curve was observed in making the product. The cumulative production at the end of the third quarter was 50 units. After producing 50 units, the learning effect ended, and all subsequent units took the same time to make.

Required

What is the standard cost per unit for the fourth quarter assuming the learning curve had reached a **steady state** ie peak efficiency was reached after the 50th unit was produced?

Solution

$Y = ax^b$ where $b = \log 0.9/\log 2$.

$b = -0.0457575/0.30103 = -0.1520031$

So $Y = ax^{-0.1520031}$

For **50 cumulative units** $Y = 10 \times (50^{-0.1520031}) = 10 \times 0.55176$ hours = 5.5176 hours.

Total time for first 50 units = 50 × 5.5176 hours = 275.88 hours.

For **51 cumulative units** $Y = 10 \times (51^{-0.1520031}) = 10 \times 0.550103$ hours = 5.5010 hours.

Total time for first 51 units = 51 × 5.5010 hours = 280.55 hours.

Time for 51st unit = (280.55 - 275.88) = 4.67 hours

This is the standard time for the product when the steady state has been reached.

Standard cost		Cost per unit $
Direct material	10 kg @ $4 per kg	40.00
Direct labour	4.67 hours @ $9 per hour	42.03
Variable overhead	4.67 hours @ $1 per hour	4.67
Total		86.70

In practice, the standard time may be rounded to a more convenient number, such as 4.5 hours or 5.0 hours.

2.9 The practical application of learning curve theory

What costs are affected by the learning curve?

(a) Direct labour time and costs

(b) Variable overhead costs, if they vary with direct labour hours worked.

(c) **Materials costs** are usually **unaffected** by learning among the workforce, although it is conceivable that materials handling might improve, and so wastage costs be reduced.

(d) **Fixed overhead expenditure** should be **unaffected** by the learning curve (although in an organisation that uses absorption costing, if fewer hours are worked in producing a unit of output, and the factory operates at full capacity, the **fixed overheads recovered or absorbed per unit** in the cost of the output **will decline** as more and more units are made).

2.10 The relevance of learning curve effects in management accounting

Learning curve theory can be used to:

(a) Calculate the marginal (incremental) cost of making extra units of a product.

(b) **Quote selling prices for a contract**, where prices are calculated at cost plus a percentage mark-up for profit. An awareness of the learning curve can make all the difference between winning contracts and losing them, or between making profits and selling at a loss-making price.

(c) **Prepare realistic production budgets** and more **efficient production schedules**.

(d) **Prepare realistic standard costs** for cost control purposes.

Considerations to bear in mind include:

(a) **Sales projections, advertising expenditure and delivery date commitments.** Identifying a learning curve effect should allow an organisation to plan its advertising and delivery schedules to coincide with expected production schedules. Production capacity obviously affects sales capacity and sales projections.

(b) **Budgeting with standard costs**. Companies that use standard costing for much of their production output cannot apply standard times to output where a learning effect is taking place. This problem can be overcome in practice by:

    (i) Establishing **standard times** for output, once the learning effect has worn off or become insignificant, and

    (ii) Introducing a **'launch cost'** budget for the product for the duration of the learning period.

(c) **Budgetary control**. When learning is still taking place, it would be unreasonable to compare actual times with the standard times that ought eventually to be achieved when the learning effect wears off. **Allowance should be made** accordingly when interpreting labour efficiency variances.

(d) **Cash budgets**. Since the learning effect reduces unit variable costs as more units are produced, it should be allowed for in **cash flow projections**.

(e) **Work scheduling and overtime decisions**. To take full advantage of the learning effect, **idle production time** should be avoided and work scheduling/overtime decisions should pay regard to the expected learning effect.

(f) **Pay**. Where the workforce is paid a **productivity bonus**, the time needed to learn a new production process should be allowed for in calculating the bonus for a period.

(g) **Recruiting new labour**. When a company plans to take on new labour to help with increasing production, the learning curve assumption will have to be reviewed.

(h) **Market share**. The significance of the learning curve is that by increasing its share of the market, a company can benefit from shop-floor, managerial and technological 'learning' to achieve **economies of scale**.

2.11 Limitations of learning curve theory

Learning curve theory has some limitations.

(a)   The learning curve phenomenon is **not always present**.

(b)   It assumes **stable conditions** at work which will **enable learning to take place**. This is not always practicable, for example because of **labour turnover**.

(c)   It must also assume a certain degree of **motivation** amongst employees.

(d)   Breaks between repeating production of an item must not be too long, or workers will **'forget'** and the learning process will have to begin all over again.

(e)   It may be difficult to **obtain accurate data** to decide what the learning curve is.

(f)   **Production techniques may change**, or product design alterations may be made, so that it takes a long time for a **'standard'** production method to emerge, to which a learning effect will apply.

(g)   For purposes of planning and control, production management and workers may resist attempts to plan for reductions in the average production time ,because this will put them under pressure to achieve the expected reductions. The work force may demand some form of bonus as a reward for achieving reductions in time.

3 Expected values in budgeting

> **Expected values** may be used in budgeting to determine the best combination of expected profit and risk.

Key term

> **Probabilistic budgeting** assigns probabilities to different conditions (most likely, worst possible, best possible) to derive an EV of budgeted profit.

A company, for example might make the following estimates of profitability for a given budget strategy under consideration.

	Profit/(loss) $'000	Probability
Worst possible outcome	(220)	0.3
Most likely outcome	300	0.6
Best possible outcome	770	0.1

The EV of profit would be calculated as follows.

	Probability	Profit $'000	Expected value $'000
Worst possible	0.3	(220)	(66)
Most likely	0.6	300	180
Best possible	0.1	770	77
Expected value of profits			191

3.1 Example: A probabilistic budget

PIB has recently developed a new product, and is planning a marketing strategy for it. A choice must be made between selling the product at a unit price of either $15 or $17.

Estimated sales volumes are as follows.

At price of $15 per unit		At price of $17 per unit	
Sales volume	Probability	Sales volume	Probability
Units		Units	
20,000	0.1	8,000	0.1
30,000	0.6	16,000	0.3
40,000	0.3	20,000	0.3
		24,000	0.3

(a) Sales promotion costs would be $5,000 at a price of $15 and $12,000 at a price of $17.

(b) Material costs are $8 per unit.

(c) Labour and variable production overhead costs will be $5 per unit up to 30,000 units and $5.50 per unit for additional units.

(d) Fixed production costs will be $38,000.

The management of PIB wish to allow for the risk of each pricing decision before choosing $15 or $17 as the selling price.

Required

Determine which sales price would be preferred if the management selected the alternative which did the following.

(a) Minimised the worst possible outcome of profit
(b) Maximised the best possible outcome of profit

Solution

The unit contribution will be as follows.

	Price per unit	
	$15	$17
Up to 30,000 units	$2	$4
Above 30,000 units	$1.50	N/A

Sales price $15

Units of sale	Unit contb'n	Total contb'n	Fixed costs	Profit	Probability	EV of profit
'000	$	$'000	$'000	$'000		$'000
20	2	40	43	(3)	0.1	(0.3)
30	2	60	43	17	0.6	10.2
40	30 @ $2	75	43	32	0.3	9.6
	10 @ $1.50					
						19.5

Sales price $17

Units of sale	Unit contb'n	Total contb'n	Fixed costs	Profit	Probability	EV of profit
'000	$	$'000	$'000	$'000		$'000
8	4	32	50	(18)	0.1	(1.8)
16	4	64	50	14	0.3	4.2
20	4	80	50	30	0.3	9.0
24	4	96	50	46	0.3	13.8
						25.2

(a) The price which minimises the worst possible outcome is $15 (with a worst-possible loss of $3,000).

(b) The price which maximises the best possible outcome is $17 (with a best-possible profit of $46,000).

3.2 Problems and benefits of EVs in budgeting

There are problems with preparing probabilistic budgets.

(a)   Preparing probabilistic budgets is more time-consuming than preparing a single fixed budget.

(b)   A probabilistic budget represents a weighted average of expectations, and may not reflect an outcome that is actually expected to happen.

(c)   Probabilistic budgets have little practical value for the purpose of planning or control, so the cost of preparing the budgets may exceed the benefits obtained.

Probabilistic budgets may be useful in helping management to assess the risk in the budget. However there are other ways of assessing risk ,such as sensitivity analysis, especially when spreadsheets are used for preparing budgets (see below).

4 Using spreadsheets in budgeting   12/12

FAST FORWARD

> **Spreadsheet packages** can be used to build business **models** to assist the forecasting and planning process. They are particularly useful for 'what if?' analysis.

It is quite common for managers to prepare their functional budgets using a spreadsheet. For many organisations, it is also quite common for the entire budget for the organisation as a whole to be produced on a spreadsheet.

A spreadsheet is a type of general purpose software package with **many business applications**, not just accounting ones. It **can be used to build a model**, in which data is presented in these **rows and columns**, and it is up to the model builder to determine what data or information should be presented in it, how it should be presented and how the data should be manipulated by the spreadsheet program. The most widely used spreadsheet packages are Lotus 1-2-3 and Excel.

The idea behind a spreadsheet is that the model builder should **construct a model as follows**.

(a)   Identify what data goes into each row and column and by **inserting text** (for example, column headings and row identifications).

(b)   **Specify how the numerical data in the model should be derived**. Numerical data might be derived using one of the following methods.

- **Insertion into the model via keyboard input**.

- **Calculation from other data in the model** by means of a formula specified within the model itself. The model builder must insert these formulae into the spreadsheet model when it is first constructed.

- **Retrieval from data on a disk file** from another computer application program or module.

4.1 The advantages of spreadsheets

Spreadsheets have several important advantages.

(a)   A budget model can be loaded into a manager's lap top computer, so that the manager can work on the budget when he is away from the office, say on a business trip.

(b)   The complex inter-relationships of different factors in the budget can be built into the model as spreadsheet formulae. The user simply has to change values for the input variables and a new version of the budget can be prepared immediately.

(c)   Spreadsheets therefore enable managers to consider many different budget options and also carry out sensitivity analysis on the budget figures.

(d)   Spreadsheets therefore simplify and speed up a time-consuming process.

The great value of spreadsheets derives from their **simple format** of rows, columns and worksheets of data, and the ability of the data **users to have direct access themselves** to their spreadsheet model via their own PC. For example, an accountant can construct a cash flow model with a spreadsheet package on the PC on his desk: he can **create** the model, **input** the data, **manipulate** the data and **read or print the output** direct. He will also have fairly **instant access** to the model whenever it is needed, in just the time it takes to load the model into his PC. Spreadsheets therefore bring computer modelling within the everyday reach of data users.

4.2 The disadvantages of spreadsheets

Spreadsheets have significant limitations if they are not properly used.

(a) An error in the design of the model, such as **an error in a formula**, can **affect the validity of data** throughout the spreadsheet. Such errors can be very difficult to trace.

(b) Even if it is properly designed in the first place, it is very **easy to corrupt** a model by accidentally changing a cell or inputting data in the wrong place.

(c) It is possible to **become over-dependent on them**, so that simple one-off tasks that can be done in seconds with a pen and paper are done on a spreadsheet instead.

(d) The possibility for experimentation with data is so great that it is possible to **lose sight of the original intention** of the spreadsheet.

(e) Spreadsheets **cannot take account of qualitative factors** since they are invariably difficult to quantify. Decisions should not be made on the basis of quantitative information alone.

(f) There may be security problems with risk of unauthorised access, especially if managers carry their spreadsheet around with them on a laptop.

There can be **audit trail problems**. It can be difficult to track different versions of the budget, and how the initial draft of the budget was changed over time with different assumptions and input values. There may be too many different versions of the draft budget. Some system of version control should be enforced to make sure that the current budget draft can be recognised and used by managers who are still working on it.

In summary, spreadsheets should be seen as a **tool in planning and decision making**. The user must make the decision. It should be noted that a company may choose to integrate a software package into its own database rather than use a general purpose spreadsheet package. **Integrated software packages** such as Microsoft Works combine the most commonly used functions of many productivity software programs into one application.

4.3 'What if' analysis

Once a model has been constructed the consequences of changes in any of the variables may be tested by asking **'what if' questions, a form of sensitivity analysis**. For example, a spreadsheet may be used to develop a cash flow model, such as that shown below.

	A	B	C	D
1		Month 1	Month 2	Month 3
2	Sales	1,000	1,200	1,440
3	Cost of sales	(650)	(780)	(936)
4	Gross profit	350	420	504
5				
6	Receipts:			
7	Current month	600	720	864
8	Previous month		400	480
9		–	–	–
10		600	1,120	1,344
11	Payments	(650)	(780)	(936)
12		(50)	340	408
13	Balance b/f	–	(50)	290
14	Balance c/f	(50)	290	698

Typical 'what if' questions for sensitivity analysis

(a)   What if the cost of sales is 68% of sales revenue, not 65%?

(b)   What if payment from debtors is received 40% in the month of sale, 50% one month in arrears and 10% two months in arrears, instead of 60% in the month of sale and 40% one month in arrears?

(c)   What if sales growth is only 15% per month, instead of 20% per month?

Using the spreadsheet model, the answers to such questions can be obtained simply and quickly, using the editing facility in the program. The information obtained should provide management with a **better understanding** of what the cash flow position in the future might be, and what **factors are critical** to ensuring that the cash position remains reasonable. For example, it might be found that the cost of sales must remain less than 67% of sales value to achieve a satisfactory cash position.

Chapter Roundup

- The **high-low method** is a quantitative technique for analysing total costs into their fixed cost and variable cost elements.

- **Learning curve theory** may be useful for forecasting production time and labour costs in circumstances where a work force makes a new product and improves its efficiency with experience and learning. However the method has many limitations.

- The formula for the learning curve is $Y = ax^b$, where b, the learning coefficient or learning index, is defined as (log of the learning rate/log of 2). The learning curve formula can be used to solve all learning curve scenarios.

- **Expected values** may be used in budgeting to determine the best combination of expected profit and risk.

- **Spreadsheet packages** can be used to build business **models** to assist the forecasting and planning process. They are particularly useful for 'what if?' analysis.

Quick Quiz

1   The costs of production runs consist of a mix of fixed and variable elements. The lowest number of production runs during the year was 120 during February, the highest number 150 during October. If the total costs of production runs in February were $80,000 and in October were $95,000, calculate the fixed and variable cost elements.

2   List five limitations of learning curve theory.

3   It takes 60 hours to make the first unit of a product and a 95% learning curve applies. How long will it take to make the second and third units?

4   *Calculate the EV of revenue using the following information.*

Sales volume	Probability	Selling price $	Probability
10,000	0.2	3.00	0.1
12,000	0.7	3.50	0.1
13,000	0.1	4.50	0.8

5   Which of the following could be considered a disadvantage of using spreadsheets in the budgeting process?

A   An error in spreadsheet design can affect the validity of the data.

B   It is possible to become over-dependent on spreadsheets.

C   Data may become corrupted.

D   Spreadsheets cannot take account of qualitative factors.

1

	Number of runs	Total costs $
High	150	95,000
Low	120	80,000
Difference	30	15,000

Variable costs per run = $\dfrac{15,000}{30}$ = $500

Fixed costs = 95,000 − (500 × 150) = $20,000

2

(i) The learning curve phenomenon is **not always present**.

(ii) It assumes **stable conditions** at work which will **enable learning to take place**. This is not always practicable, for example because of **labour turnover**.

(iii) It must also assume a certain degree of **motivation** amongst employees.

(iv) Breaks between repeating production of an item must not be too long, or workers will **'forget'** and the learning process will have to begin all over again.

(v) It might be difficult to **obtain accurate data** to decide what the learning curve is.

(vi) **Workers might not agree** to a gradual reduction in production times per unit.

(vii) **Production techniques might change**, or product design alterations might be made, so that it takes a long time for a **'standard'** production method to emerge, to which a learning effect will apply.

3   Average time for first 2 units = 60 × 95% = 57 hours

Total time for first two units = 57 × 2 = 114 hours

Time for 2nd unit = 114 − 60 = 54 hours.

$Y = ax^b$ and b = log 0.95/log 2 = − 0.0222764/0.30103 = −0.740006

Average time for first 3 units = 60 × $3^{-0.740006}$ = 60 × 0.9219189 = 55.315 hours

Total time for first 3 units = 3 × 55.315 hours = 165.945 hours

Time to make 3rd unit = (165.945 − 114) = 51.945 hours = 52 hours approximately.

4   EV = ((10,000 × 0.2) + (12,000 × 0.7) + (13,000 × 0.1)) × ((3 × 0.1) + (3.5 × 0.1) + (4.5 × 0.8))
= 11,700 × $4.25
= $49,725

5   All of them.

Now try the question below from the Practice Question Bank

Number	Level	Marks	Time
Q12	Examination	10	18 mins

10

Budgeting and standard costing

Topic list	Syllabus reference
1 The use of standard costs	C4 (a)
2 Deriving standards	C4 (b)
3 Budgets and standards compared	C4 (a)
4 Flexible budgets	C4 (c)
5 The principle of controllability	C4 (d)

Introduction

In this chapter we will be looking at **standard costs** and **standard costing.**

You will have studied standard costing before and have learned about the principles of standard costing and how to calculate a number of cost and sales variances. We obviously look at the topic in more depth for your studies of this syllabus.

We begin this chapter by reviewing the **main principles of standard costing** as well as looking in some detail at the **way in which standard costs are set.**

Flexible budgets are vital for both planning and control and we will look at how they are constructed and their use in the overall budgetary control process.

Study guide

		Intellectual level
C4	**Standard costing**	
(a)	Explain the use of standard costs	2
(b)	Outline the methods used to derive standard costs and discuss the different types of cost possible	2
(c)	Explain and illustrate the importance of flexing budgets in performance management	2
(d)	Explain and apply the principle of controllability in the performance management system	2

Exam guide

The contents of this chapter are likely to be examined in conjunction with variance analysis, covered in the next chapter.

1 The use of standard costs   12/08

FAST FORWARD

> A **standard cost** is an estimated unit cost built up of standards for each cost element (standard resource price and standard resource usage).
>
> **Standard costing** is used to value inventories, prepare cost budgets for production and provide control information (variances).

1.1 What is a standard cost?

Key term

> A **standard cost** is an estimated unit cost.

The standard cost of product 12345 is set out below on a **standard cost card.**

STANDARD COST CARD
Product: the Splodget, No 12345

	Cost	Requirement	$	$
Direct materials				
A	$2.00 per kg	6 kgs	12.00	
B	$3.00 per kg	2 kgs	6.00	
C	$4.00 per litre	1 litre	4.00	
Others			2.00	
				24.00
Direct labour				
Grade I	$4.00 per hour	3 hrs	12.00	
Grade II	$5.40 per hour	5 hrs	27.00	
				39.00
Variable production overheads	$1.00 per hour	8 hrs	8.00	
Fixed production overheads	$3.00 per hour	8 hrs	24.00	
Standard full cost of production			95.00	

Notice how the standard cost is **built up from standards for each cost element:** standard quantities of materials at standard prices, standard quantities of labour time at standard rates and so on. It is therefore determined by management's estimates of the following.

- The expected prices of materials, labour and expenses
- Efficiency levels in the use of materials and labour
- Budgeted overhead costs and budgeted volumes of activity

We will see how management arrives at these estimates later in the chapter.

But why should management want to prepare standard costs? Obviously to assist with standard costing, but what is the point of standard costing?

1.2 The uses of standard costing

Standard costing has three main **uses**.

- **To value inventories**. It is an alternative to FIFO and average cost as a method of inventory valuation.

- To **budget production costs**. When a standard per unit of product as been established, budgeting production costs becomes a fairly straightforward process.

- **To act as a control device** by establishing standards (expected costs) and comparing actual costs with the expected costs. Variances between actual and standard cost indicate aspects of operations which may be out of control.

Standard costs may also be used for the following purposes.

(a) To **evaluate managerial performance**.

(b) To enable the principle of **'management by exception'** to be practised. A standard cost, when established, is an average expected unit cost. Because it is only an average, actual results will vary to some extent above and below the average. Only significant differences between actual and standard should be reported.

(c) To provide a prediction of future costs, for use in some **decision-making** situations.

(d) To **motivate** staff and management by providing challenging targets.

(e) To provide guidance on possible ways of **improving efficiency**.

Although the other uses of standard costing should not be overlooked, we will be concentrating on the control aspect and variance reporting.

1.3 Standard costing as a control technique

Key terms

> **Standard costing** involves the establishment of predetermined estimates of the costs of products or services, the collection of actual costs and the comparison of the actual costs with the predetermined estimates. The predetermined costs are known as standard costs and the difference between standard and actual cost is known as a **variance**. The process by which the total difference between standard and actual results is analysed in known as **variance analysis**.

Question

What are the possible advantages for the control function of an organisation of having a standard costing system?

Answer

(a) Carefully planned standards are an aid to more accurate **budgeting**.

(b) Standard costs provide a **yardstick** against which actual costs can be measured.

(c) The setting of standards involves determining the **best** materials and methods which may lead to economies.

(d)   A **target of efficiency** is set for employees to reach and **cost-consciousness** is stimulated.

(e)   Variances can be calculated which enable the principle of **'management by exception'** to be operated. Only the variances which exceed acceptable tolerance limits need to be investigated by management with a view to control action.

(f)   Standard costs and variance analysis can provide a way of **motivation** to managers to achieve better performance. However, care must be taken to distinguish between controllable and non-controllable costs in variance reporting.

1.4 Where standard costing should be used

FAST FORWARD

Standard costing is most suited to mass production and repetitive assembly work, where large quantities of a standard product are manufactured.

Although standard costing can be used in a variety of costing situations (batch and mass production, process manufacture, jobbing manufacture (where there is standardisation of parts) and service industries (if a realistic cost unit can be established)), the **greatest benefit** from its use can be gained if there is a **large amount of repetition** in the production process so that average or expected usage of resources can be determined. It is therefore most suited to **mass production** and **repetitive assembly work**. It is not well-suited to production systems where items are manufactured to customer demand and specifications.

Question   Standard service costing

Can you think of a service organisation that could apply standard costing?

Answer

One example could be restaurants which deal with standard recipes for meals. If a large number of meals are produced, say, for conference delegates, mass production systems will apply. Standards may not be calculated with the same accuracy as in manufacturing environments, but the principles are still relevant. Other examples are equally valid.

Exam focus point

The examiner is interested in whether a standard is 'meaningful'. Standards could be set for anything, but not standards would have practical meaning or value.

2 Deriving standards

FAST FORWARD

The **responsibility for deriving standard costs** should be shared between **managers able to provide the necessary information** about levels of expected efficiency, prices and overhead costs.

2.1 Setting standards for materials costs

Direct materials costs per unit of raw material will be estimated by the purchasing department from their knowledge of the following.

•   Purchase contracts already agreed
•   Pricing discussions with regular suppliers
•   The forecast movement of prices in the market
•   The availability of bulk purchase discounts
•   The quality of material required by the production departments

The standard cost ought to include an allowance for **bulk purchase discounts**, if these are available on all or some of the purchases, and it may have to be a weighted average price of the differing prices charged for the same product by alternative suppliers.

A decision must also be taken as to how to deal with price **inflation**. Suppose that a material costs $10 per kilogram at the moment, and during the course of the next 12 months, it is expected to go up in price by 20% to $12 per kilogram. What standard price should be selected?

(a)   If the **current price** of $10 per kilogram **is used in the standard**, the reported price variance will become adverse as soon as prices go up, which could be very early in the year. If prices go up gradually rather than in one big jump, it would be difficult to select an appropriate time for revising the standard.

(b)   If an **estimated mid-year price** of, say, $11 per kilogram **is used**, price variances should be favourable in the first half of the year and adverse in the second half, again assuming that prices go up gradually. Management could only really check that in any month, the price variance did not become excessively adverse (or favourable) and that the price variance switched from being favourable to adverse around month six or seven and not sooner.

Standard costing is therefore more **difficult in times of inflation but it is still worthwhile.**

- Usage and efficiency variances will still be meaningful
- Inflation is measurable: there is no reason why its effects cannot be removed
- Standard costs can be revised, so long as this is not done too frequently

2.2 Setting standards for labour costs

Direct labour rates per hour will be set by reference to the payroll and to any agreements on pay rises with trade union representatives of the employees. A separate hourly rate or weekly wage will be set for each different labour grade/type of employee and an average hourly rate will be applied for each grade (even though individual rates of pay may vary according to age and experience).

Similar problems to those which arise when setting material standards in times of high inflation can be met when setting labour standards.

2.3 Setting standards for material usage and labour efficiency

To estimate the materials required to make each product (material usage) and also the labour hours required (labour efficiency), technical specifications must be prepared for each product by production experts (either in the production department or the work study department).

2.4 Setting standards for overheads

When standard costs are **fully absorbed** standard production costs (standard costs can be used in both marginal and absorption costing systems), the **absorption rate** of fixed production overheads will be **predetermined** and **based on budgeted** fixed production **overhead** and planned **production volume**.

Production volume will depend on two factors.

(a)   **Production capacity** (or 'volume capacity') measured perhaps in standard hours of output (a standard hour being the amount of work achievable at standard efficiency levels in an hour), which in turn reflects direct production labour hours.

(b)   **Efficiency of working**, by labour or machines, allowing for rest time and contingency allowances.

Suppose that a department has a work force of ten men, each of whom works a 36 hour week to make standard units, and each unit has a standard time of two hours to make. The expected efficiency of the work-force is 125%.

(a)   Budgeted capacity, in direct labour hours, would be 10 × 36 = 360 production hours per week.

(b)   Budgeted efficiency is 125% so that the work-force should take only 1 hour of actual production time to produce 1.25 standard hours of output.

(c)   This means in our example that budgeted output is 360 production hours × 125% = 450 standard hours of output per week. At 2 standard hours per unit, this represents production activity or volume of 225 units of output per week.

Question   Budgeted output

ABC carries out routine office work in a sales order processing department, and all tasks in the department have been given standard times. There are 40 clerks in the department who work on average 140 hours per month each. The efficiency ratio of the department is 110%.

Required

Calculate the budgeted output in the department.

Answer

Capacity   = 40 × 140 = 5,600 hours per month
Efficiency   = 110%
Budgeted output   = 5,600 × 110% = 6,160 standard hours of work per month.

2.5 Setting standards for sales price and margin

The **standard selling price** will depend on a number of factors including the following.

- Anticipated market demand   • Manufacturing costs
- Competing products   • Inflation estimates

The **standard sales margin** is the difference between the standard cost and the standard selling price.

Question   Standard setting

What problems do you think could occur when standards are being set?

Answer

The following problems can occur when setting standards.

(a)   Deciding how to incorporate **inflation** into planned unit costs

(b)   Agreeing on a **performance standard** (attainable or ideal)

(c)   Deciding on the **quality** of materials to be used (a better quality of material will cost more, but perhaps reduce material wastage)

(d)   Estimating materials prices where **seasonal price variations** or **bulk purchase discounts** may be significant

(e)   Finding sufficient **time** to construct standards as standard setting can be time consuming

(f)   Incurring the **cost** of setting up and maintaining a system for establishing standards

2.6 Types of standard

FAST FORWARD ▶

There are four **types of standard: ideal, attainable, current** and **basic**. These can have an impact on employee motivation.

How demanding should a standard be? Should the standard represent perfect performance or easily attainable performance? There are four types of standard.

An **ideal standard** is a standard which can be attained under perfect operating conditions: no wastage, no inefficiencies, no idle time, no breakdowns

An **attainable standard** is a standard which can be attained if production is carried out efficiently, machines are properly operated and/or materials are properly used. Some allowance is made for wastage and inefficiencies

A **current standard** is standard based on current working conditions (current wastage, current inefficiencies)

A **basic standard** is a long-term standard which remains unchanged over the years and is used to show trends

The **different types of standard have a number of advantages and disadvantages.**

(a) **Ideal standards** can be seen as **long-term targets** but are not very useful for day-to-day control purposes.

(b) **Ideal standards cannot be achieved**. If such standards are used for budgeting, an allowance will have to be included to make the budget realistic and attainable.

(c) **Attainable standards** can be used for **product costing**, cost control, inventory valuation, estimating and as a basis for budgeting.

(d) **Current standards** or attainable standards provide the **best basis for budgeting**, because they represent an achievable level of productivity.

(e) Current standards **do not attempt to improve** on current levels of efficiency.

(f) **Current standards** are useful during **periods when inflation is high**. They can be set on a month by month basis.

(g) **Basic standards** are used to show **changes in efficiency or performance** over a long period of time. They are perhaps the least useful and least common type of standard in use.

2.6.1 The impact on employee behaviour of the type of standard set

The type of standard set can have an impact on the behaviour of the employees trying to achieve those standards.

Type of standard	Impact on behviour
Ideal	Some say that they provide employees with an **incentive to be more efficient** even though it is highly unlikely that the standard will be achieved. Others argue that they are likely to have an unfavourable effect on employee motivation because the differences between standards and actual results will always be adverse. The **employees may feel that the goals are unattainable** and so **they will not work so hard**.
Attainable	Might be an **incentive to work harder** as they provide a **realistic but challenging target of efficiency**.
Current	**Will not motivate employees to do anything more than they are currently doing.**
Basic	May have an **unfavourable impact** on the motivation of employees. Over time they will discover that they are easily able to achieve the standards. They may become bored and lose interest in what they are doing if they have nothing to aim for.

3 Budgets and standards compared

Budgets and standards are very similar and interrelated, but there are important differences between them. A budget is an overall plan and a standard cost is a unit cost. Standard costs may be used for budgeting.

Budgets and standards are **similar** in the following ways.

(a) They both involve looking to the future and **forecasting** what is likely to happen given a certain set of circumstances.

(b) They are both **used for control purposes**. A budget aids control by setting financial targets or limits for a forthcoming period. Actual achievements or expenditures are then compared with the budgets and action is taken to correct any variances where necessary. A standard also achieves control by comparison of actual results against a predetermined target.

As well as being similar, **budgets and standards are interrelated**. For example, a standard unit production cost can act as the basis for a production cost budget. The unit cost is multiplied by the budgeted activity level to arrive at the budgeted expenditure on production costs.

There are, however, **important differences between budgets and standards**.

Budget	Standard cost
Gives planned total aggregate costs for a function or cost centre	Shows the unit resource usage for a single task, for example the standard labour hours for a single unit of production
Can be prepared for all functions, even where output cannot be measured	Limited to situations where repetitive actions are performed and output can be measured
Expressed in money terms	Need not be expressed in money terms. For example a standard rate of output does not need a financial value put on it

4 Flexible budgets   6/11

Comparison of a fixed budget with the actual results for a different level of activity is of little use for control purposes. **Flexible budgets** should be used to show what cost and revenues should have been for the actual level of activity.

Key term

A **flexible budget** is a budget which, by recognising different cost behaviour patterns, changes as volume of activity (output and sales) changes.

4.1 Preparing a flexible budget

Step 1 The first step in the preparation of a flexible budget is the **determination of cost behaviour patterns**, which means **deciding whether costs are fixed, variable or semi-variable**.

Step 2 The second step in the preparation of a flexible budget is to calculate the **budget cost allowance** for each cost item.

Budget cost allowance = budgeted fixed cost* + (number of units × variable cost per unit)**

* nil for variable cost
** nil for fixed cost

Semi-variable costs therefore need splitting into their fixed and variable components so that the budget cost allowance can be calculated. One method for splitting semi-variable costs is the high/low method, which we covered in Chapter 9.

4.2 Example: Preparing a flexible budget

(a) Prepare a budget for 20X6 for the direct labour costs and overhead expenses of a production department flexed at the activity levels of 80%, 90% and 100%, using the information listed below.

(i) The direct labour hourly rate is expected to be $3.75.

(ii) 100% activity represents 60,000 direct labour hours.

(iii) *Variable costs*

Indirect labour	$0.75 per direct labour hour
Consumable supplies	$0.375 per direct labour hour
Canteen and other welfare services	6% of direct and indirect labour costs

(iv) Semi-variable costs are expected to relate to the direct labour hours in the same manner as for the last five years.

Year	Direct labour hours	Semi-variable costs $
20X1	64,000	20,800
20X2	59,000	19,800
20X3	53,000	18,600
20X4	49,000	17,800
20X5	40,000 (estimate)	16,000 (estimate)

(v) *Fixed costs*

	$
Depreciation	18,000
Maintenance	10,000
Insurance	4,000
Rates	15,000
Management salaries	25,000

(vi) Inflation is to be ignored.

(b) Calculate the budget cost allowance (ie expected expenditure) for 20X6 assuming that 57,000 direct labour hours are worked.

Solution

(a)

	80% level 48,000 hrs $'000	90% level 54,000 hrs $'000	100% level 60,000 hrs $'000
Direct labour	180.00	202.50	225.0
Other variable costs			
Indirect labour	36.00	40.50	45.0
Consumable supplies	18.00	20.25	22.5
Canteen etc	12.96	14.58	16.2
Total variable costs ($5.145 per hour)	246.96	277.83	308.7
Semi-variable costs (W)	17.60	18.80	20.0
Fixed costs			
Depreciation	18.00	18.00	18.0
Maintenance	10.00	10.00	10.0
Insurance	4.00	4.00	4.0
Rates	15.00	15.00	15.0
Management salaries	25.00	25.00	25.0
Budgeted costs	336.56	368.63	400.7

Working

Using the high/low method:

	$
Total cost of 64,000 hours	20,800
Total cost of 40,000 hours	16,000
Variable cost of 24,000 hours	4,800
Variable cost per hour ($4,800/24,000)	$0.20

	$
Total cost of 64,000 hours	20,800
Variable cost of 64,000 hours (× $0.20)	12,800
Fixed costs	8,000

Semi-variable costs are calculated as follows.

			$
60,000 hours	(60,000 × $0.20) + $8,000	=	20,000
54,000 hours	(54,000 × $0.20) + $8,000	=	18,800
48,000 hours	(48,000 × $0.20) + $8,000	=	17,600

(b)   The budget cost allowance for 57,000 direct labour hours of work would be as follows.

		$
Variable costs	(57,000 × $5.145)	293,265
Semi-variable costs	($8,000 + (57,000 × $0.20))	19,400
Fixed costs		72,000
		384,665

4.3 Flexible budgets and performance management

Budgetary control involves drawing up budgets for the areas of responsibility for individual managers (for example production managers, purchasing managers and so on) and regularly **comparing** actual results against expected results. The differences between actual results and expected results are reported as **variances** and these are used to provide a guideline for control action by individual managers.

Note that individual managers are held responsible for investigating differences between budgeted and actual results, and are then expected to take corrective action or amend the plan in the light of actual events.

The wrong approach to budgetary control is to compare actual results against a fixed budget. Suppose that a company manufactures a single product, Z. Budgeted results and actual results for June 20X2 are shown below.

	Budget	Actual results	Variance
Production and sales of the cloud (units)	2,000	3,000	
	$	$	$
Sales revenue (a)	20,000	30,000	10,000 (F)
Direct materials	6,000	8,500	2,500 (A)
Direct labour	4,000	4,500	500 (A)
Maintenance	1,000	1,400	400 (A)
Depreciation	2,000	2,200	200 (A)
Rent and rates	1,500	1,600	100 (A)
Other costs	3,600	5,000	1,400 (A)
Total costs (b)	18,100	23,200	5,100
Profit (a) – (b)	1,900	6,800	4,900 (F)

(a)   Here the variances are **meaningless** for control purposes. Costs were higher than budget because the output volume was also higher; variable costs would be expected to increase above the costs

budgeted in the fixed budget. There is no information to show whether control action is needed for any aspect of costs or revenue.

(b) For control purposes, it is necessary to know the following.

    (i) Were actual costs higher than they should have been to produce and sell 3,000 Zs?
    (ii) Was actual revenue satisfactory from the sale of 3,000 Zs?

The **correct approach to budgetary control** is as follows.

(a) **Identify fixed and variable costs**
(b) **Produce a flexible budget using marginal costing techniques**

Let's suppose that we have the following estimates of cost behaviour for the company.

(a) Direct materials, direct labour and maintenance costs are variable.
(b) Rent and rates and depreciation are fixed costs.
(c) Other costs consist of fixed costs of $1,600 plus a variable cost of $1 per unit made and sold.

Now that the cost behaviour patterns are known, a budget cost allowance can be calculated for each item of expenditure. This allowance is shown in a **flexible budget** as the expected expenditure on each item for the relevant level of activity. The budget cost allowances are calculated as follows.

(a) Variable cost allowances   = original budgets × (3,000 units/2,000 units)

    eg material cost allowance   = $6,000 × ³/₂ = $9,000

(b) Fixed cost allowances   = as original budget

(c) Semi-fixed cost allowances = original budgeted fixed costs

                               + (3,000 units × variable cost per unit)

    eg other cost allowances   = $1,600 + (3,000 × $1) = $4,600

The budgetary control analysis should be as follows.

	Fixed budget (a)	Flexible budget (b)	Actual results (c)	Budget variance (b) – (c)
Production and sales (units)	2,000	3,000	3,000	
	$	$	$	$
Sales revenue	20,000	30,000	30,000	0
Variable costs				
Direct materials	6,000	9,000	8,500	500 (F)
Direct labour	4,000	6,000	4,500	1,500 (F)
Maintenance	1,000	1,500	1,400	100 (F)
Semi-variable costs				
Other costs	3,600	4,600	5,000	400 (A)
Fixed costs				
Depreciation	2,000	2,000	2,200	200 (A)
Rent and rates	1,500	1,500	1,600	100 (A)
Total costs	18,100	24,600	23,200	1,400 (F)
Profit	1,900	5,400	6,800	1,400 (F)

Note. **(F) denotes a favourable variance and (A) an adverse or unfavourable variance.**

We can **analyse** the above as follows.

(a) In selling 3,000 units the expected profit should have been, not the fixed budget profit of $1,900, but the flexible budget profit of $5,400. Instead, actual profit was $6,800 ie $1,400 more than we should have expected. One of the reasons for the improvement is that, **given output and sales** of 3,000 units, **costs were lower than expected** (and sales revenue exactly as expected).

		$
Direct materials cost variance		500 (F)
Direct labour cost variance		1,500 (F)
Maintenance cost variance		100 (F)
Other costs variance		400 (A)
Fixed cost variances		
Depreciation		200 (A)
Rent and rates		100 (A)
		1,400 (F)

(b) Another reason for the improvement in profit above the fixed budget profit is the **sales volume** (3,000 Zs were sold instead of 2,000).

	$	$
Sales revenue increased by		10,000
Variable costs increased by:		
Direct materials	3,000	
Direct labour	2,000	
Maintenance	500	
Variable element of other costs	1,000	
Fixed costs are unchanged		6,500
Profit increased by		3,500

Profit was therefore increased by $3,500 because sales volumes increased.

(c) A full variance analysis statement would be as follows.

	$	$
Fixed budget profit		1,900
Variances		
Sales volume	3,500 (F)	
Direct materials cost	500 (F)	
Direct labour cost	1,500 (F)	
Maintenance cost	100 (F)	
Other costs	400 (A)	
Depreciation	200 (A)	
Rent and rates	100 (A)	
		4,900 (F)
Actual profit		6,800

If management believes that any of these variances are large enough to justify it, they will investigate the reasons for them to see whether any corrective action is necessary or whether the plan needs amending in the light of actual events.

Question	Budget preparation

The budgeted and actual results of Crunch Co for September were as follows. The company uses a marginal costing system. There were no opening or closing stocks.

	Fixed budget		*Actual*	
	1,000 units		700 units	
Sales and production				
	$	$	$	$
Sales		20,000		14,200
Variable cost of sales				
Direct materials	8,000		5,200	
Direct labour	4,000		3,100	
Variable overhead	2,000		1,500	
		14,000		9,800
Contribution		6,000		4,400
Fixed costs		5,000		5,400
Profit/(loss)		1,000		(1,000)

Required

Prepare a budget that will be useful for management control purposes.

Answer

We need to prepare a **flexible budget for 700 units.**

	Budget 1,000 units	per unit	Flexed budget 700 units	Actual 700 units	Variances
	$	$	$	$	$
Sales	20,000	(20)	14,000	14,200	200 (F)
Variable costs					
Direct material	8,000	(8)	5,600	5,200	400 (F)
Direct labour	4,000	(4)	2,800	3,100	300 (A)
Variable production overhead	2,000	(2)	1,400	1,500	100 (A)
	14,000	(14)	9,800	9,800	
Contribution	6,000		4,200	4,400	
Fixed costs	5,000	(N/A)	5,000	5,400	400 (A)
Profit/(loss)	1,000		(800)	(1,000)	200 (A)

By **flexing** the budget in the question above we **removed the effect on sales revenue of the difference between budgeted sales volume and actual sales volume.** But there is still a variance of $200 (F). This means that the actual *selling price* must have been different to the budgeted selling price, resulting in a $200 (F) **selling price variance.**

4.4 Factors to consider when preparing flexible budgets

The mechanics of flexible budgeting are, in theory, fairly straightforward but in practice there are a number of points to consider before figures are simply flexed.

(a)   Splitting mixed costs is not always straightforward.

(b)   Fixed costs may behave in a step-line fashion as activity levels increase/decrease.

(c)   Account must be taken of the assumptions upon which the original fixed budget was based. Such assumptions might include the constraint posed by limiting factors, the rate of inflation, judgements about future uncertainty, the demand for the organisation's products and so on.

(d)   By flexing a budget, a manager is effectively saying "If I knew then what I know now, this is the budget I would have set". It is a useful concept but can lead to some concern as managers can become confused and frustrated if faced with continually moving targets.

4.5 The need for flexible budgets

We have seen that flexible budgets may be prepared in order to plan for variations in the level of activity above or below the level set in the fixed budget. It has been suggested, however, that since many cost items in modern industry are fixed costs, the **value** of flexible budgets in planning is dwindling.

(a)   In many manufacturing industries, plant costs (depreciation, rent and so on) are a very large proportion of total costs, and these tend to be fixed costs.

(b)   Wage costs also tend to be fixed, because employees are generally guaranteed a basic wage for a working week of an agreed number of hours.

(c)   With the growth of service industries, labour (wages or fixed salaries) and overheads will account for most of the costs of a business, and direct materials will be a relatively small proportion of total costs.

Flexible budgets are nevertheless necessary, and even if they are not used at the planning stage, they must be used for budgetary control variance analysis.

5 The principle of controllability

FAST FORWARD

> The **principle of controllability** is that managers of responsibility centres should only be held accountable for costs over which they have some influence.

5.1 Budget centres

Budgetary control is based around a system of **budget centres**. Each budget centre will have its own budget and a manager will be responsible for managing the budget centre and ensuring that the budget is met.

The selection of budget centres in an organisation is therefore a key first step in setting up a control system. What should the budget centres be? What income, expenditure and/or capital employment plans should each budget centre prepare? And how will measures of performance for each budget centre be made?

A well-organised system of control should have the following features.

Feature	Explanation
A hierarchy of budget centres	If the organisation is quite large a hierarchy is needed. Subsidiary companies, departments and work sections might be budget centres. Budgets of each section would then be consolidated into a departmental budget, departmental budgets in turn would be consolidated into the subsidiary's budget, and the budgets of each subsidiary would be **combined into a master budget** for the group as a whole.
Clearly identified responsibilities for achieving budget targets	Individual managers should be made responsible for achieving the budget targets of a particular budget centre.
Responsibilities for revenues, costs and capital employed	Budget centres should be organised so that all the revenues earned by an organisation, all the costs it incurs, and all the capital it employs are made the responsibility of someone within the organisation, at an appropriate level of authority in the management hierarchy.

Budgetary control and budget centres are therefore part of the overall system of **responsibility accounting** within an organisation.

Key term

Responsibility accounting is a system of accounting that segregates revenue and costs into areas of personal responsibility in order to monitor and assess the performance of each part of an organisation.

5.2 Controllable costs

FAST FORWARD

> **Controllable costs** are items of expenditure which can be directly influenced by a given manager within a given time span.

Care must be taken to distinguish between controllable costs and uncontrollable costs in variance reporting. The **controllability principle** is that managers of responsibility centres should only be held accountable for costs over which they have some influence. From a **motivation** point of view this is important because it can be very demoralising for managers who feel that their performance is being judged on the basis of something over which they have no influence. It is also important from a **control** point of view in that control reports should ensure that information on costs is reported to the manager who is able to take action to control them.

Responsibility accounting attempts to associate costs, revenues, assets and liabilities with the managers most capable of controlling them. As a system of accounting, it therefore distinguishes between controllable and uncontrollable costs.

Most **variable costs** within a department are thought to be **controllable in the short term** because managers can influence the efficiency with which resources are used, even if they cannot do anything to raise or lower price levels.

A cost which is not controllable by a junior manager might be controllable by a senior manager. For example, there may be high direct labour costs in a department caused by excessive overtime working. The junior manager may feel obliged to continue with the overtime to meet production schedules, but his senior may be able to reduce costs by hiring extra full-time staff, thereby reducing the requirements for overtime.

A cost which is not controllable by a manager in one department may be controllable by a manager in another department. For example, an increase in material costs may be caused by buying at higher prices than expected (controllable by the purchasing department) or by excessive wastage (controllable by the production department) or by a faulty machine producing rejects (controllable by the maintenance department).

Some costs are **non-controllable**, such as increases in expenditure items due to inflation. Other costs are **controllable, but in the long term rather than the short term**. For example, production costs might be reduced by the introduction of new machinery and technology, but in the short term, management must attempt to do the best they can with the resources and machinery at their disposal.

5.2.1 The controllability of fixed costs

It is often assumed that all fixed costs are non-controllable in the short run. This is not so.

(a) **Committed fixed costs** are those costs arising from the possession of plant, equipment, buildings and an administration department to **support the long-term needs of the business**. These costs (depreciation, rent, administration salaries) are largely **non-controllable in the short term** because they have been committed by longer-term decisions affecting longer-term needs. When a company decides to cut production drastically, the long-term committed fixed costs will be reduced, but only after redundancy terms have been settled and assets sold.

(b) **Discretionary fixed costs**, such as advertising and research and development costs, are incurred as a result of a top management decision, but could be **raised or lowered at fairly short notice** (irrespective of the actual volume of production and sales).

5.2.2 Controllability and apportioned costs

Managers should only be held accountable for costs over which they have some influence. This may seem quite straightforward in theory, but it is not always so easy in practice to distinguish controllable from uncontrollable costs. **Apportioned overhead costs provide a good example**.

Suppose that a manager of a production department in a manufacturing company is made responsible for the costs of his department. These costs include **directly attributable overhead items** such as the costs of indirect labour employed and indirect materials consumed in the department. The department's overhead costs also include an apportionment of costs from other cost centres, such as rent and rates for the building it shares with other departments and a share of the costs of the maintenance department.

Should the production manager be held accountable for any of these apportioned costs?

(a) Managers should not be held accountable for costs over which they have no control. In this example, apportioned rent and rates costs would not be controllable by the production department manager.

(b) Managers should be held accountable for costs over which they have some influence. In this example, it is the responsibility of the maintenance department manager to keep maintenance costs within budget. But their costs will be partly variable and partly fixed, and the variable cost element will depend on the volume of demand for their services. If the production department's staff treat their equipment badly we might expect higher repair costs, and the production department manager should therefore be made accountable for the repair costs that his department makes the maintenance department incur on its behalf.

(c) Charging the production department with some of the costs of the maintenance department prevents the production department from viewing the maintenance services as 'free services'. Over-use would be discouraged and the production manager is more likely to question the activities of the maintenance department possibly resulting in a reduction in maintenance costs or the provision of more efficient maintenance services.

5.2.3 Controllability and dual responsibility

Quite often a particular cost might be the **responsibility of two or more managers**. For example, raw materials costs might be the responsibility of the purchasing manager (prices) and the production manager (usage). A **reporting system must allocate responsibility appropriately**. The purchasing manager must be responsible for any increase in raw materials prices whereas the production manager should be responsible for any increase in raw materials usage.

Attention!

> You can see that there are **no clear cut rules** as to which costs are controllable and which are not. Each situation and cost must be reviewed separately and a decision taken according to the control value of the information and its behavioural impact.

BPP
LEARNING MEDIA

Chapter Roundup

- A **standard cost** is an estimated unit cost built up of standards for each cost element (standard resource price and standard resource usage).

- **Standard costing** is used to value inventories, prepare cost budgets for production and provide control information (variances).

- Standard costing is most suited to mass production and repetitive assembly work, where large quantities of a standard product are manufactured.

- The **responsibility for deriving standard costs** should be shared between **managers able to provide the necessary information** about levels of expected efficiency, prices and overhead costs.

- There are four **types of standard: ideal, attainable, current** and **basic**. These can have an impact on employee motivation.

- Budgets and standards are very similar and interrelated, but there are important differences between them. A budget is an overall plan and a standard cost is a unit cost. Standard costs may be used for budgeting.

- Comparison of a fixed budget with the actual results for a different level of activity is of little use for control purposes. **Flexible budgets** should be used to show what cost and revenues should have been for the actual level of activity.

- The **principle of controllability** is that managers of responsibility centres should only be held accountable for costs over which they have some influence.

- **Controllable costs** are items of expenditure which can be directly influenced by a given manager within a given time span.

1   Choose the appropriate words from those highlighted.

The **greatest/least** benefit from the use of standard costing can be gained if there is a degree of repetition in the production process.

Standard costing is therefore **most/less** suited to organisations which produce to customer demand and requirements and **most/less** suited to mass production.

2   *Match the type of standard with the correct definition.*

Types of standard	Definitions	
Ideal	(a)	Can be attained under perfect operating conditions
Attainable	(b)	Can be attained if production is carried out efficiently, machines are properly operated and/or materials are properly used
Basic		
Current	(c)	Based on current working conditions
	(d)	Remains unchanged over the years and is used to show trends

3   *Fill in the blanks.*

Standard costing is difficult in times of inflation but it is still worthwhile.

(a)   .... and .... variances will still be meaningful.

(b)   Inflation is .... : there is no reason why its effects cannot be removed.

(c)   Standard costs can be .... , as long as this is not done
      ....

4   Provide three reasons why standard costing conflicts with schemes of continuous improvement and cost reduction programmes.

5   With what kind of standards is practical capacity associated?

6   Ideal standards are long-term targets.

☐ True   ☐ False

7   *Fill in the gaps.*

A flexible budget is a budget which, by recognising .... , is designed to .... as the level of activity changes.

8   An extract of the costs incurred at two different activity levels is shown. Classify the costs according to their behaviour patterns and show the budget cost allowance for an activity of 1,500 units.

	1,000 units	2,000 units	Type of cost	Budget cost allowance for 1,500 units
	$	$		$
Fuel	3,000	6,000	....	....
Photocopying	9,500	11,000	....	....
Heating	2,400	2,400	....	....
Direct wages	6,000	8,000	....	....

9   *Fill in the blanks.*

A well-organised system of control should have the following features.

(a)   A hierarchy of ....

(b)   Clearly identified .... for achieving budget targets

(c)   Responsibilities for .... , ... and
      ....

10   Which of the following are not controllable by a production department manager?

(a)   Direct labour rate

(b)   Variable production overheads

(c)   Apportioned canteen costs

(d)   Increases in raw material costs due to inflation

(e)   Increases in overall material costs due to high levels of wastage caused by poor supervision of production workers

(f)   An increase in the level of idle time because of poorly-maintained machines

(g)   Depreciation

(h)   Advertising for production workers

1   greatest
    less
    most

2   Ideal   (a)   Basic   (d)
    Attainable (b)   Current   (c)

3   (a)   Usage and efficiency variances will still be meaningful.
    (b)   Inflation is measurable: there is no reason why its effects cannot be removed.
    (c)   Standard costs can be reviewed, as long as this is not done too frequently.

4   (a)   Efforts to improve the efficiency of operations or reduce costs will alter quantities of inputs, prices
          and so on whereas standard costing is best used in a stable, standardised, repetitive environment.
    (b)   Predetermined standards conflict with a philosophy of continual improvement.
    (c)   Standard costs often incorporate a planned level of scrap in material standards. This is at odds with
          the aim of 'zero defects' inherent in continuous improvement programmes.

5   Attainable standards

6   True

7   cost behaviour patterns
    flex or change

8   Variable $4,500   Fixed $2,400
    Semi-variable $10,250   Semi-variable $7,000

9   (a)   budget centres   (c)   revenues
    (b)   responsibilities   costs
                                              capital employed

10 (a)
    (c)
    (d)
    (f)   (if there is a maintenance department)
    (g)
    (h)

11

Variance analysis

Introduction

The **actual results** achieved by an organisation will usually **differ from the expected results** (the expected results being the standard costs and revenues which we looked at in the previous chapter). These differences are **variances**. You should have learned basic variances in your previous studies.

This chapter begins with revision of the **basic variances**, the reasons behind them and their presentation in **operating statements**.

It then goes on to look at more complicated variances which are more likely to be examined in F5. These are materials mix and materials yield variances, and sales mix and sales quantity variances.

283

Study guide

Exam guide

Basic variances, the reasons behind them and their presentation in operating statements are assumed knowledge for F5. The variance calculations set in this paper are likely to be the more complicated variances such as materials mix and yield variances and sales mix and quantity variances. You will be required to **explain** them and **evaluate** performance.

There has been an article in *Student Accountant* on materials mix and yield variances, which you should read. It can be found on the ACCA web site.

One of the competencies you require to fulfil performance objective 14 of the PER is the ability to prepare regular variance analysis reports. You can apply the knowledge you obtain from this section of the text to help to demonstrate this competence.

1 Basic variances

Knowledge brought forward from earlier studies

- A **variance** is the difference between an actual result and an expected result. In standard costing, cost variances are the difference between the standard costs and actual costs of units produced.
- **Variance analysis** is the process by which the *total* difference between standard and actual results is analysed.
- When actual results are better than expected results, we have a **favourable variance (F).** If actual results are worse than expected results, we have an **adverse variance (A).**
- The **selling price variance** measures the effect on expected profit of a selling price different to the standard selling price. It is calculated as the difference between what the sales revenue should have been for the actual quantity sold, and what it was.
- The **sales volume variance** measures the increase or decrease in expected profit as a result of the sales volume being higher or lower than budgeted. It is calculated as the difference between the budgeted sales volume and the actual sales volume multiplied by the standard profit per unit.
- The material **total variance** is the difference between what the output actually cost and what it should have cost, in terms of material. It can be divided into the following two sub-variances.

- The **material price variance** is the difference between what the material did cost and what it should have cost.
- The **material usage variance** is the difference between the standard cost of the material that should have been used and the standard cost of the material that was used.
- The **labour total variance** is the difference between what the output should have cost and what it did cost, in terms of labour. It can be divided into two sub-variances.
- The **labour rate variance** is the difference between what the labour did cost and what it should have cost.
- The **labour efficiency variance** is the difference between the standard cost of the hours that should have been worked and the standard cost of the hours that were worked.
- **The variable production overhead total variance** is the difference between what the output should have cost and what it did cost, in terms of variable production overhead. It can be divided into two sub-variances.
- The **variable production overhead expenditure variance** is the difference between the amount of variable production overhead that should have been incurred in the actual hours actively worked, and the actual amount of variable production overhead incurred.
- The **variable production overhead efficiency variance** is the difference between the standard cost of the hours that should have been worked for the number of units actually produced, and the standard cost of the actual number of hours worked.
- **Fixed production overhead total variance** is the difference between fixed production overhead incurred and fixed production overhead absorbed. In other words, it is the under– or over-absorbed fixed production overhead.
- **Fixed production overhead expenditure variance** is the difference between the budgeted fixed production overhead expenditure and actual fixed production overhead expenditure.
- **Fixed production overhead volume variance** is the difference between actual and budgeted production/volume multiplied by the standard absorption rate per *unit*.
- **Fixed production overhead volume efficiency variance** is the difference between the number of hours that actual production should have taken, and the number of hours actually taken (that is, worked) multiplied by the standard absorption rate per *hour*.
- **Fixed production overhead volume capacity variance** is the difference between budgeted hours of work and the actual hours worked, multiplied by the standard absorption rate per *hour*.

An example will be used to illustrate how these variances are calculated.

Question

Various variances

A company produces and sells one product only, the Thing, the standard cost for one unit being as follows.

	$
Direct material A – 10 kilograms at $20 per kg	200
Direct material B – 5 litres at $6 per litre	30
Direct wages – 5 hours at $6 per hour	30
Fixed production overhead	50
Total standard cost	310

The fixed overhead included in the standard cost is based on an expected monthly output of 900 units. Fixed production overhead is absorbed on the basis of direct labour hours.

During April the actual results were as follows.

Production	800 units
Material A	7,800 kg used, costing $159,900
Material B	4,300 litres used, costing $23,650
Direct wages	4,200 hours worked for $24,150

Fixed production overhead $47,000

Required

(a) Calculate price and usage variances for each material.

(b) Calculate labour rate and efficiency variances.

(c) Calculate fixed production overhead expenditure and volume variances and then subdivide the volume variance.

Answer

(a) **Price variance – Material A**

Take the actual quantity of materials purchased/used and compare the actual prices paid for the materials with their standard price.

	$
7,800 kgs should have cost (× $20)	156,000
but did cost	159,900
Price variance (actual cost exceeds standard cost)	3,900 (A)

Usage variance – Material A

Take the actual quantity of units produced and compare the actual quantity of materials used in their production with the standard quantity that should have been used. The variance is converted into a money value at the standard price per unit of material.

800 units should have used (× 10 kgs)	8,000 kgs
but did use	7,800 kgs
Usage variance in kgs (actual usage less than standard)	200 (F)
× standard cost per kilogram	× $20
Usage variance in $	$4,000 (F)

Price variance – Material B

	$
4,300 litres should have cost (× $6)	25,800
but did cost	23,650
Price variance	2,150 (F)

Usage variance – Material B

	$
800 units should have used (× 5 l)	4,000 l
but did use	4,300 l
Usage variance in litres	300 (A)
× standard cost per litre	× $6
Usage variance in $	$1,800 (A)

(b) **Labour rate variance**

Take the number of labour hours worked and paid for, and compare the actual amount paid with the standard rate for the hours worked.

	$
4,200 hours should have cost (× $6)	25,200
but did cost	24,150
Rate variance (actual cost less than the standard rate)	1,050 (F)

Labour efficiency variance

Take the actual quantity of units produced and compare the actual time to produce them with the standard time. The variance is converted into a money value at the standard rate per labour hour.

800 units should have taken (× 5 hrs)	4,000 hrs
but did take	4,200 hrs
Efficiency variance in hours (actual time longer than standard)	200 (A)
× standard rate per hour	× $6
Efficiency variance in $	$1,200 (A)

(c) **Fixed overhead expenditure variance**

This is the difference between budgeted and actual fixed costs.

	$
Budgeted expenditure ($50 × 900)	45,000
Actual expenditure	47,000
Expenditure variance (actual spending higher than budgeted)	2,000 (A)

Fixed overhead volume variance

This is calculated when the standard cost is a full production cost that includes absorbed fixed overhead. It is not calculated in a system of standard marginal costing. It is the difference between the budgeted and actual production volumes. It is converted into a money value at the standard production overhead cost per unit.

	units
Budgeted production at standard rate (900 × $50)	900
Actual production at standard rate (800 × $50)	800
Volume variance in units (output less than budget)	100 (A)
Standard production overhead cost per unit	$50
Volume variance in $	$5,000 (A)

The volume variance may be analysed into an efficiency and a capacity variance. Fixed overhead efficiency variance + Capacity variance = Volume variance.

Fixed overhead volume efficiency variance

This is the same as the labour efficiency variance in hours. It is converted into a money value at the standard production overhead rate per hour.

	$
800 units should have taken (× 5 hrs)	4,000 hrs
but did take	4,200 hrs
Volume efficiency variance in hours	200 (A)
× standard absorption rate per hour	× $10
Volume efficiency variance	$2,000 (A)

Fixed overhead volume capacity variance

This is the difference between the budgeted hours of work (budgeted capacity) and the actual hours worked in production. It is converted into a money value at the standard production overhead rate per hour.

Budgeted hours	4,500 hrs
Actual hours	4,200 hrs
Volume capacity variance in hours	300 (A)
× standard absorption rate per hour ($50 ÷ 5)	× $10
	$3,000 (A)

Basic variance calculations are **assumed knowledge** for F5 so it is **essential** to do more practice if you struggled with this example/question.

It is assumed that you are able to calculate a sales price variance, as this variance is not included in the question above. The sales volume variance will be revised later, in the context of sales mix and quantity variances.

However the sales price and volume variances are illustrated in the example on operating statements in Section 3.

2 The reasons for variances 6/08, 12/09, 12/10

Knowledge brought forward from earlier studies

In an examination question you should review the information given and use your imagination and common sense to suggest possible reasons for variances.

Variance	Favourable	Adverse	Calculation	
Material price	Unforeseen discounts received Greater care in purchasing Change in material standard	Price increase Careless purchasing Change in material standard	Price Based on actual purchases What should it have cost? What did it cost?	$ X (X) <u>X</u>
Material usage	Material used of higher quality than standard More effective use made of material Errors in allocating material to jobs	Defective material Excessive waste Theft Stricter quality control Errors in allocating material to jobs	Usage Based on actual production What should have been used? What was used? Difference valued at standard cost per kg	Kgs X (X) <u>X</u> $X
Labour rate	Use of workers at a rate of pay lower than standard	Wage rate increase	Rate Based on actual hours paid What should it have cost? What did it cost?	$ X (X) <u>X</u>
Idle time	Possible if idle time has been built into the budget	Machine breakdown Non-availability of material Illness or injury to worker	Idle time Hours worked Hours paid Difference valued at standard rate per hour	Hrs X (X) $X

Variance	Favourable	Adverse	Calculation	
Labour efficiency	Output produced more quickly than expected, because of work motivation, better quality of equipment or materials, better learning rate Errors in allocating time to jobs	Lost time in excess of standard allowed Output lower than standard set because of lack of training, sub-standard material etc Errors in allocating time to jobs	Efficiency Based on actual production How long should it have taken? How long did it take? Difference valued at standard rate per hour	Hrs X (X) X $X
**Overhead expenditure	Savings in costs incurred More economical use of services	Increase in cost of services Excessive use of services Change in type of services used	Based on actual hours worked What should it have cost? What did it cost?	$ X (X) X
Overhead volume	Production or level of activity greater than budgeted.	Production or level of activity less than budgeted	 Budgeted units Actual units Difference valued at OAR per unit	Units X (X) X $X
Fixed overhead capacity	Production or level of activity greater than budgeted	Production or level of activity less than budgeted	 Budgeted hrs worked Actual hrs worked Difference valued at OAR per hour	Hrs X (X) X X
Selling price	Unplanned price increase	Unplanned price reduction	 For the quantity sold What revenue should have been generated Actual revenue	$ X (X) X
Sales volume	Additional demand	Unexpected fall in demand Production difficulties	 Budgeted sales Actual sales Difference valued at standard profit per unit	Units X (X) X X

3 Operating statements

Key term

- An **operating statement** is a regular report for management which compares actual costs and revenues with budgeted figures and shows variances.

- There are several ways in which an operating statement may be presented. Perhaps the most common format is one which **reconciles budgeted profit to actual profit**. Sales variances are reported first, and the total of the budgeted profit and the two sales variances results in a figure for 'actual sales minus the standard cost of sales'. The cost variances are then reported, and an actual profit calculated.

Question

Operating statement

A company manufactures one product, and the entire product is sold as soon as it is produced. There are no opening or closing inventories and work in progress is negligible. The company operates a standard costing system and analysis of variances is made every month. The standard cost card for the product, a widget, is as follows.

STANDARD COST CARD – WIDGET

		$
Direct materials	0.5 kilos at $4 per kilo	2.00
Direct wages	2 hours at $2.00 per hour	4.00
Variable overheads	2 hours at $0.30 per hour	0.60
Fixed overhead	2 hours at $3.70 per hour	7.40
Standard cost		14.00
Standard profit		6.00
Standing selling price		20.00

Budgeted output for January was 5,100 units. Actual results for January were as follows.

Production of 4,850 units was sold for $95,600
Materials consumed in production amounted to 2,300 kilos at a total cost of $9,800
Labour hours paid for amounted to 8,500 hours at a cost of $16,800
Actual operating hours amounted to 8,000 hours
Variable overheads amounted to $2,600
Fixed overheads amounted to $42,300

Required

Calculate all variances and prepare an operating statement for January.

Answer

		$
(a)	2,300 kg of material should cost (× $4)	9,200
	but did cost	9,800
	Material price variance	600 (A)
(b)	4,850 Widgets should use (× 0.5 kgs)	2,425 kg
	but did use	2,300 kg
	Material usage variance in kgs	125 kg (F)
	× standard cost per kg	× $4
	Material usage variance in $	$ 500 (F)

(c) 8,500 hours of labour should cost (× $2)   17,000
    but did cost   16,800
    Labour rate variance   200 (F)

(d) 4,850 Widgets should take (× 2 hrs)   9,700 hrs
    but did take (active hours)   8,000 hrs
    Labour efficiency variance in hours   1,700 hrs (F)
    × standard cost per hour   × $2
    Labour efficiency variance in $ $3,400 (F)

(e) Idle time variance 500 hours (A) × $2 $1,000 (A)

(f) 8,000 hours incurring variable o/hd expenditure should cost (× $0.30)   2,400
    but did cost   2,600
    Variable overhead expenditure variance   200 (A)

(g) Variable overhead efficiency variance is the same as the
    labour efficiency variance:
    1,700 hours (F) × $0.30 per hour $ 510 (F)

(h) Budgeted fixed overhead (5,100 units × 2 hrs × $3.70)   37,740
    Actual fixed overhead   42,300
    Fixed overhead expenditure variance   4,560 (A)

(i) Actual production at standard rate (4,850 units × $7.40)   35,890
    Budgeted production at standard rate (5,100 units × $7.40)   37,740
    Fixed overhead volume variance   1,850 (A)

(j) 4,850 Widgets should have sold for (× $20)   97,000
    but did sell for   95,600
    Selling price variance   1,400 (A)

(k) Budgeted sales volume   5,100 units
    Actual sales volume   4,850 units
    Sales volume variance in units   250 units (A)
    × standard profit per unit   × $6 (A)
    Sales volume variance in $ $1,500 (A)

	$	$
Budgeted profit (5,100 units × $6 profit)		30,600
Selling price variance	1,400 (A)	
Sales volume variance	1,500 (A)	
		2,900 (A)
Actual sales ($95,600) less the standard cost of sales (4,850 × $14)		27,700

OPERATING STATEMENT FOR JANUARY

	$	$
Budgeted profit		30,600
Sales variances: price	1,400 (A)	
volume	1,500 (A)	
		2,900 (A)
Actual sales minus the standard cost of sales		27,700

Cost variances

	(F) $	(A) $	
Material price		600	
Material usage	500		
Labour rate	200		
Labour efficiency	3,400		
Labour idle time		1,000	
Variable overhead expenditure		200	
Variable overhead efficiency	510		
Fixed overhead expenditure		4,560	
Fixed overhead volume		1,850	
	4,610	8,210	3,600 (A)
Actual profit for January			24,100

Check

	$	$
Sales		95,600
Materials	9,800	
Labour	16,800	
Variable overhead	2,600	
Fixed overhead	42,300	
		71,500
Actual profit		24,100

Exam focus point

Producing operating statements and reconciling actual profit to budgeted profit is **assumed knowledge** for F5 so it is **essential** to do more question practice if you struggled with this question.

3.1 Operating statements in a marginal cost environment

Knowledge brought forward from earlier studies

- There are two main differences between the variances calculated in an absorption costing system and the **variances calculated in a marginal costing system**. In a marginal costing system the only fixed overhead variance is an expenditure variance and the sales volume variance is valued at standard contribution margin, not standard profit margin.

Question

Marginal cost operating statement

Returning to the question above, now assume that the company operates a marginal costing system.

Required

Recalculate any variances necessary and produce an operating statement.

Answer

(a) There is no fixed overhead volume variance.

(b) The standard contribution per unit is $(20 – 6.60) = $13.40, therefore the sales volume variance of 250 units (A) is valued at (× $13.40) = $3,350 (A).

The other variances are unchanged, therefore an operating statement might appear as follows.

OPERATING STATEMENT FOR JANUARY

	$	$	$
Budgeted profit		30,600	
Budgeted fixed production costs		37,740	
Budgeted contribution		68,340	
Sales variances: volume		3,350 (A)	
price		1,400 (A)	
			4,750 (A)
Actual sales ($95,600) minus the standard			
variable cost of sales (4,850 × $6.60)			63,590

	(F)	(A)	
Variable cost variances	$	$	$
Material price		600	
Material usage	500		
Labour rate	200		
Labour efficiency	3,400		
Labour idle time		1,000	
Variable overhead expenditure		200	
Variable overhead efficiency	510		
	4,610	1,800	
			2,810 (F)
Actual contribution			66,400
Budgeted fixed production overhead		37,740	
Expenditure variance		4,560 (A)	
Actual fixed production overhead			42,300
Actual profit			24,100

Note. The profit here is the same on the profit calculated by standard absorption costing because there were no changes in inventory levels. Absorption costing and marginal costing do not always produce an identical profit figure.

One of the competencies you require to fulfil performance objective 12 of the PER is the ability to summarise and present financial information in an appropriate format for management purposes. You can apply the knowledge you obtain from this section of the text to help to demonstrate this competence.

4 Investigating variances

This topic should also be familiar to you from your earlier studies. The key points are recapped below.

> Knowledge brought forward from earlier studies

The decision whether or not to investigate

- Before management decide whether or not to investigate the reasons for the occurrence of a particular variance, there are a number of **factors** which should be considered in assessing the **significance** of the variance.

- **Materiality.** Because a standard cost is really only an *average* expected cost, small variations between actual and standard are bound to occur and are unlikely to be significant. Obtaining an 'explanation' of the reasons why they occurred is likely to be time consuming and irritating for the manager concerned. For such variations **further investigation is not worthwhile** since such variances are not controllable.

- **Controllability.** Only controllable variances should be investigated. **Uncontrollable variances call for a change in plan, not an investigation into the past.**

- **The type of standard being used.** The efficiency variance reported in any control period, whether for materials or labour, will depend on the **efficiency level set**. If, for example, an ideal standard is used, variances will always be adverse. Similarly, if basic standards are used, variances are likely to be favourable.

- **Variance trend.** Although small variations in a single period are unlikely to be significant, small variations that occur consistently may need more attention. The trend **provides an indication of whether the variance is fluctuating within acceptable control limits or becoming out of control.**

- **Interdependence between variances.** One variance might be inter-related with another, and much of it might have occurred only because the other variance occurred too. **When two variances are interdependent (interrelated) one will usually be adverse and the other favourable.** For example, an adverse selling price variance might be counterbalanced by a favourable sales volume variance.

- **Costs of investigation.** The costs of an investigation should be weighed against the benefits of correcting the cause of a variance.

Variance investigation models

- The **rule-of-thumb** and **statistical significance** variance investigation models and/or statistical **control charts** can be used to determine whether a variance should be investigated.

- **The rule of thumb model.** This involves **deciding a limit** and if the size of a **variance is within the limit**, it should be considered **immaterial**. Only if it exceeds the limit is it considered materially significant, and worthy of investigation.

- **Statistical significance model.** Historical data is used to **calculate** both a standard as **an expected average** and the **expected standard deviation** around this average when the process is under control. By assuming that variances that occur are normally distributed around this average, a variance will be investigated if it is *more* than a distance from the expected average that the estimated normal distribution suggests is likely if the process is in control.

- **Statistical control charts.** By marking variances and control limits on a control chart, **investigation** is signalled not only when a particular **variance exceeds the control limit** but also when the **trend of variances shows a progressively worsening movement** in actual results (even though the variance in any single control period has not yet overstepped the control limit).

5 Materials mix and yield variances   6/10, 12/11

The **materials usage variance** can be sub-divided into a materials **mix variance** and a materials **yield variance** when more than one material is used in the product.

However, calculating a mix and yield variance is only meaningful for control purposes when management is in a position to control the mix of materials used in production.

Exam focus point

The February 2010 edition of *Student Accountant* contains an article on material **mix** and **yield** variances written by the **examiner**. Ensure that you are familiar with this article.

Manufacturing processes often require that a number of different materials are combined to make a unit of finished product. When a product requires two or more raw materials in its make-up, it is often possible to **sub-analyse the materials usage variance into a materials mix and a materials yield variance**.

Adding a greater proportion of one material (therefore a smaller proportion of a different material) might make the materials mix **cheaper or more expensive**. For example the standard mix of materials for a product might consist of the following.

		$
(²/₃) 2 kg of material A at $1.00 per kg		2.00
(¹/₃) 1 kg of material B at $0.50 per kg		0.50
		2.50

It may be possible to change the mix so that one kilogram of material A is used and two kilograms of material B. The new mix would be cheaper.

		$
(¹/₃) 1 kg of material A		1
(²/₃) 2 kg of material B		1
		2

By changing the proportions in the mix, the **efficiency** of the combined material usage may change. In our example, in making the proportions of A and B cheaper, at 1:2, the product may now require more than three kilograms of input for its manufacture, and the new materials requirement per unit of product might be 3.6 kilograms.

		$
(¹/₃) 1.2 kg of material A at $1.00 per kg		1.20
(²/₃) 2.4 kg of material B at $0.50 per kg		1.20
		2.40

In establishing a materials usage standard, management may therefore have to balance the **cost** of a particular mix of materials with the **efficiency** of the yield of the mix.

Once the standard has been established it may be possible for management to exercise control over the materials used in production by calculating and reviewing mix and yield variances.

A **mix variance** occurs when the materials are not mixed or blended in standard proportions and it is a measure of whether the actual mix is cheaper or more expensive than the standard mix.

A **yield variance** arises because there is a difference between what the input should have been for the output achieved and the actual input.

5.1 When to calculate mix and yield variances

An exam question will indicate when you are required to calculate mix and yield variances. However you should also be aware when mix and yield variances may be reported for variance analysis purposes.

(a)   **Reporting a mix and yield variance is an alternative to reporting the usage variance of each material separately**. If mix and yield variances are reported, usage variances are not reported.

(b)   A **mix variance has no practical meaning unless management is able to control the mix of materials** used in production. For example, management may be able to use a cheaper mix of materials (= favourable mix variance) by including a larger proportion of the cheapest material in the production mix.

(c)   A yield variance is a total usage variance for all the materials combined. If a mix variance is calculated, there must also be a yield variance.

It would be totally inappropriate to calculate a mix variance where the materials in the 'mix' are discrete items. A chair, for example, might consist of wood, covering material, stuffing and glue. These materials are separate components, and it would not be possible to think in terms of controlling the proportions of each material in the final product. The usage of each material must be controlled separately.

5.2 Calculating mix and yield variances

The **mix variance** is calculated as follows.

(a)   Take the **total actual quantity of materials used**.

(b)   Divide this total quantity of materials into the **standard mix** or standard proportions of the different materials used in the mix.

(c) For each item of materials, the difference between the actual quantity used and the quantity in the standard mix is a **mix variance**.

(d) Convert the mix variance for each item of material into a money value **by applying the standard price per unit** for the material.

(e) The total of the mix variance for each of the materials in the mix is the **total materials mix variance**.

The **yield variance** is calculated as follows.

(a) For the actual number of units of product manufactured, calculate the total quantity of materials that should have been used (a single total for all the materials in the mix).

(b) Compare this standard quantity of materials that should have been used with the actual total quantity of materials that was used.

(c) The difference is the yield variance in material quantities.

(d) Convert this into a money value by applying the weighted average cost per unit of material.

An **alternative method of calculating the yield variance** produces the same result.

(a) Take the actual total quantity of materials used and calculate how many units of output should have been produced with this quantity of materials. (This is the total quantity of materials actually used divided by the total quantity of materials in one standard unit of product.)

(b) Compare this with the actual number of units produced. The difference is the yield variance in units of finished product.

(c) Convert this into a money value by applying the standard material cost per unit of product.

5.3 Example: Materials usage, mix and yield variances

A company manufactures a chemical, Dynamite, using two compounds Flash and Bang. The standard materials usage and cost of one unit of Dynamite are as follows.

		$
Flash	5 kg at $2 per kg	10
Bang	10 kg at $3 per kg	30
		40

In a particular period, 80 units of Dynamite were produced from 600 kg of Flash and 750 kg of Bang.

Required

Calculate the materials usage, mix and yield variances.

Solution

(a) **Usage variance**

If we do not calculate a mix and yield variance, we would calculate a usage variance separately for each material.

	Std usage for actual output of 80 units kg	Actual usage kg	Variance kg	Standard cost per kg $	Variance $
Flash	400	600	200 (A)	2	400 (A)
Bang	800	750	50 (F)	3	150 (F)
	1,200	1,350			250 (A)

The total usage variance of $250 (A) can be analysed into a mix variance and a yield variance and these may be reported instead of the usage variance.

(b) **Mix variance**

To calculate the mix variance, it is first necessary to decide how the total quantity of materials used (600 kg + 750 kg) should have been divided between Flash and Bang. In other words, we need to **calculate the standard mix of the actual quantity of materials used.**

	Actual usage	Actual total usage in standard mix (5:10 or 1:2)	Mix variance
	kg	kg	kg
Flash	600	450	150 (A)
Bang	750	900	150 (F)
	1,350	1,350	0

The mix variance in total quantities is always 0. This must always be the case since the expected mix is based on the total quantity actually used and hence the difference between the total expected and total actual is zero.

However the actual mix uses:

(a)   more of the cheaper material Flash (= adverse variance, because actual usage of Flash in the mix is more than the standard usage; therefore the cost for Flash is more), but

(b)   less of the more expensive material Bang (= favourable variance, because actual usage of Bang in the mix is less than the standard usage; therefore the cost for Bang is lower).

Taking both materials together, the actual mix of materials is cheaper than the standard mix, and this will produce a favourable mix variance overall.

The mix variances in quantities are converted into a money value at the standard price of the materials.

	Actual usage/mix	Standard mix	Mix variance	Standard price	Mix variance
	kg	kg	kg	$ per kg	$
Flash	600	450	150 (A)	2	300 (A)
Bang	750	900	150 (F)	3	450 (F)
	1,350	1,350	0		150 (F)

The total mix variance is $150 (F).

(c) **Yield variance**

The yield variance can be calculated in total or for each individual material input.

Method 1

The weighted average cost per kilogram of materials = $40/15 kg = $2.67 per kg.

	kg
80 units of product should use in total (× 15 kg)	1,200
They did use (600 + 750)	1,350
Yield variance in kg	150 (A)
Weighted average price per kg	$2.67
Yield variance in $	$400 (A)

Method 2

	units
1,350 kg of material should produce (÷ 15)	90
They did produce	80
Yield variance in units of output	10 (A)
Standard material cost per unit	$40
Yield variance in $	$400 (A)

The mix variance $150 (F) plus the yield variance $400 (A) together add up to the usage variance $250 (A).

5.4 Inter-relationship between mix and yield variance

A favourable mix variance occurs when the actual mix of materials is cheaper than the standard mix.

As a consequence of using a cheaper mix of materials, it is possible that the output/yield will be less than the standard output. In other words, a favourable mix variance may result in an adverse yield variance.

In the previous example, it is possible that by using a bigger proportion of Flash in the production mix, the actual yield of finished products (= 80 units) was less than it should have been (= 90 units).

For similar reasons, when there is an adverse mix variance because the actual mix of materials is more expensive than the standard mix, there may possibly be an inter-related favourable yield variance

Question	Mix and yield variances

The standard materials cost of product D456 is as follows.

		$
Material X	3 kg at $2.00 per kg	6
Material Y	5 kg at $3.60 per kg	18
		24

During period 2, 2,000 kg of material X (costing $4,100) and 2,400 kg of material Y (costing $9,600) were used to produce 500 units of D456.

Required

Calculate the following variances.

(a)   Price variance
(b)   Mix variance
(c)   Yield variances – in total and for each individual material

Note: **Yield variances for the individual materials** are **meaningless variances**, but they have been examined once, so study the suggested solution carefully. They are calculated as the difference between:

- the standard quantity of each material for the units produced (so the standard quantities in the standard mix), and
- the actual total quantities of materials used in the standard mix.

These are converted into a money value at the standard price of the individual materials.

Answer

(a)

	$
2,000 kg of X should cost (× $2)	4,000
but did cost	4,100
Material X price variance	100 (A)

	$
2,400 kg of Y should cost (× $3.60)	8,640
but did cost	9,600
Material Y price variance	960 (A)

(b)

	kg
Total quantity used (2,000 + 2,400) kg	4,400

		kg
Standard mix for actual use:	3/8 X	1,650
	5/8 Y	2,750
		4,400

	Actual quantity standard mix	Actual quantity actual mix	Mix variance	Standard cost per kg	Mix variance
	kg	kg	kg	$	$
X	1,650	2,000	350 (A)	2.00	700 (A)
Y	2,750	2,400	350 (F)	3.60	1,260 (F)
	4,400	4,400	–		560 (F)

(c) Yield variance

Each unit of D456 requires

3 kg of X, costing		$6
5 kg of Y, costing		$18
8 kg		$24

4,400 kg should have yielded (÷ 8 kg)	550 units
But did yield	500 units
Yield variance in units	50 units (A)
× standard material cost per unit of output	× $24
Yield variance in $	$1,200 (A)

For individual materials

	Standard quantity standard mix	Actual quantity standard mix	Variance	Standard cost per kg	Variance
	kg	kg	kg	$	$
X	1,500	1,650	150 (A)	2.00	300 (A)
Y	2,500	2,750	250 (A)	3.60	900 (A)
	4,000	4,400	400 (A)		1,200 (A)

5.5 Example: Losses, mix and yield

Sometimes there is expected loss in the production process.

Coope and Sorcerer Co make product T42 in a continuous process, for which standard and actual quantities in month 10 were as follows.

	Quantity	Standard Price per kg	Value	Quantity	Actual price per kg	Std cost of actual usage
	kg	$	$	kg	$	$
Material P	40,000	2.50	100,000	34,000	2.50	85,000
Material Q	20,000	4.00	80,000	22,000	4.00	88,000
	60,000		180,000	56,000		173,000

Losses occur at an even rate during the processing operation and are expected to be 10% of materials input. So budgeted output for the month was 54,000 kg of T42 (= 60,000 kg × 90%). Actual output during the month was 51,300 kg of T42.

Required

Calculate total usage, mix and yield variances.

Solution

Usage variance

	Std usage for actual output of 51,300 kg	Actual usage	Variance	Standard cost per kg	Variance
	kg	kg	kg	$	$
Material P	38,000*	34,000	4,000 (F)	2.50	10,000 (F)
Material Q	19,000**	22,000	3,000 (A)	4	12,000 (A)
	57,000	56,000			2,000 (A)

* (51,300/54,000) × 40,000 = 38,000 kg

** (51,300/54,000) × 20,000 = 19,000 kg

The **total usage variance** is $2,000 (A).

Mix variance

	Actual usage/mix	Standard mix (2:1)	Mix variance	Standard price	Mix variance
	kg	kg	kg	$ per kg	$
Material P	34,000	37,333.33	3,333.33 (F)	2.50	8,333 (F)
Material Q	22,000	18,666.67	3,333.33 (A)	4	13,333 (A)
	56,000	56,000.00	0		5,000 (A)

The mix variance is $5,000 (A)

Yield variance

The weighted average cost per kg of input materials = $180,000/60,000 = $3

	kg of material
51,300 kg of T34 should use (× 100/90)	57,000
They did use in total	56,000
Yield variance in units of T34	1,000 (F)
Standard material cost per kg of input material	$3
Yield variance in $	**$3,000 (F)**

Mix variance $5,000(A) + Yield variance $3,000 (F) = Usage variance $2,000 (A).

Exam focus point

Question 5 of the December 2011 exam asked candidates to calculate materials usage, mix and yield (quantity) variances. The examiner noted that some candidates calculated the variances in kg but did not convert them into a monetary value using the standard costs for each ingredient.

Variances need to be given a value in order to be used properly within a business. It is not sufficient to simply stop at quantity!

5.6 Issues involved in changing the mix

The materials mix variance indicates the **cost** of a change in the mix of materials and the yield variance indicates the **productivity** of the manufacturing process. A change in the mix can have wider implications. For example, rising raw material prices may cause pressure to change the mix of materials. Even if the yield is not affected by the change in the mix, the **quality** of the final product may change. This can have an adverse effect on sales if customers do not accept the change in quality. The production manager's performance may be measured by mix and yield variances but these **performance measures** may fail to indicate problems with falling quality and the impact on other areas of the business. **Quality targets** may also be needed.

5.7 Alternative methods of controlling production processes

In a modern manufacturing environment with an emphasis on quality management, using mix and yield variances for control purposes may not be possible or may be inadequate. Other control methods could be more useful.

- Rates of wastage
- Average cost of input calculations
- Percentage of deliveries on time
- Customer satisfaction ratings
- Yield percentage calculations or output to input conversion rates

We will be considering performance measures in more detail in Chapter 13.

BPP
LEARNING MEDIA

6 Sales mix and quantity variances

FORWARD

The **sales volume variance** can be analysed further into a sales mix variance and a sales quantity variance. This may be useful for control purposes where management is in a position to control the sales mix, for example through the allocation of spending on advertising and sales promotion.

6.1 Sales volume variance

You should be familiar with how to calculate the sales volume variance from your earlier studies. It measures the difference between the budgeted and actual sales volumes for each product, and the effect that this has had on profit. A sales volume variance in units of sale is converted into a money value by applying either the standard profit per unit (standard absorption costing) or the standard contribution per unit (standard marginal costing).

6.2 Sales mix and quantity variances   6/11, 6/13

If a company **sells more than one product**, it is possible to analyse the overall sales volume variance into a sales mix variance and a sales quantity variance.

> The **sales mix variance** occurs when the proportions of the various products sold are different from those in the budget.
>
> The **sales:quantity variance** shows the difference in contribution/profit because of a change in sales volume from the budgeted volume of sales.

6.3 When to calculate the mix and quantity variances

A sales mix variance and a sales quantity variance are only meaningful where management can control the proportions of the products sold.

Situations where management may be able to control the sales mix are:

(a)   where management can control the allocation of the advertising and sales promotion budget between different products

(b)   where the same basic product is sold in different sizes or packaging, such as large size and small size.

6.4 The units method of calculation

The sales mix variance is calculated in a similar way to the materials mix variance.

(a)   Take the **total actual quantity of units sold**, for all the products combined.

(b)   Divide this total quantity of sales units into the **budgeted standard mix** or budgeted proportions of the different products in the mix.

(c)   For each product, the difference between the actual quantity sold and the sales quantity in the budgeted standard mix is a **mix variance**.

(d)   Convert the mix variance for each product into a money value by **applying the standard profit per unit** (or standard contribution pr unit, where standard marginal costing is used).

(e)   The total of the mix variance for each of the products in the sales mix is the **total sales mix variance**.

The **sales quantity variance** is calculated in a similar way to the materials yield variance, as follows.

(a)   Calculate the weighted average standard profit per unit (or weighted average standard contribution per unit). This is calculated from the budget, as the budgeted total profit divided by the budgeted total units of sale.

(b)   Calculate the difference between the actual total sales units and the budgeted total sales units. This difference is the sales quantity variance in units.

(c)   Convert this variance in sales units into a money value by applying the weighted average standard profit (or standard contribution) per unit of sale.

The sales mix variance plus the sales quantity variance equals the total sales volume variance for all the products.

6.5 Example: Sales mix and quantity variances

Just Desserts Limited makes and sells two products, Chocolate Crunch and Strawberry Sundae. The budgeted sales and profit are as follows.

	Sales Units	Revenue $	Costs $	Profit $	Profit per unit $
Chocolate Crunch (CC)	400	8,000	6,000	2,000	5
Strawberry Sundae (SS)	300	12,000	11,100	900	3
				2,900	

Actual sales were 280 units of Chocolate Crunch and 630 units of Strawberry Sundae. The company management is able to control the relative sales of each product through the allocation of sales effort, advertising and sales promotion expenses.

Required

Calculate the sales volume variance, the sales mix variance and the sales quantity variance.

Solution

(a)   **Sales volume variance**

	CC	SS
Budgeted sales	400 units	300 units
Actual sales	280 units	630 units
Sales volume variance in units	120 units (A)	330 units (F)
× standard profit per unit	× $5	× $3
Sales volume variance in $	$600 (A)	$990 (F)
Total **sales volume variance**		$390 (F)

The favourable sales volume variance indicates that profit was better than budget because on balance more units were sold than budgeted. However the favourable variance may be due to selling a larger proportion of the more profitable product (sales mix variance) or selling more units in total (sales quantity variance).

Now we will see how to analyse this favourable volume variance into its mix and quantity elements.

(b)   **Sales mix variance**

This is calculated in a similar way to the materials mix variance. Start with the total quantity of products sold and calculate what sales of each product would have been if they had been sold in the budgeted proportions.

	Actual sales mix	Standard sales mix (4:3)	Sales mix variance	Standard profit	Sales mix variance
	units	units	units	$ per unit	$
CC	280	520	240 (A)	5	1,200 (A)
SS	630	390	240 (F)	3	720 (F)
	910	910	0		480 (A)

The total sales mix variance is $480 (A).

(c) **Sales quantity variance**

The standard weighted average profit per unit of sale, taken from the budget, is $2,900/700 = $29/7

	units
Budgeted sales in total	700
Actual sales in total	910
Sales quantity variance in units	210 (F)
Standard weighted average profit per unit	$29/7
Sales quantity variance in $	**$870 (F)**

Sales mix variance $480 (A) + Sales quantity variance $870 (F) = Sales volume variance $390 (F).

The overall favourable sales volume variance was achieved by selling products in a cheaper sales mix, but achieving a higher total quantity of sales units than budgeted.

Exam focus point

> Try not to confuse the sales volume profit variance with the sales quantity profit variance. The examiner had noted that candidates often learn formulae to churn out calculations, but do not appreciate what variances mean to a business. Make sure you understand why sales mix and quantity variances occur.

Chapter Roundup

- The **materials usage variance** can be sub-divided into a materials **mix** variance and a materials **yield** variance when more than one material is used in the product.

- However, calculating a mix and yield variance is only meaningful for control purposes when management is in a position to control the mix of materials used in production.

- The **sales volume variance** can be analysed further into a **sales mix variance** and a **sales quantity variance**. This may be useful for control purposes where management is in a position to control the sales mix, for example through the allocation of spending on advertising and sales promotion.

Quick Quiz

1   *Fill in the blanks.*

The material price variance is the difference between .... and
....

The material usage variance is the difference between .... and
....

2   If closing inventories of raw materials are valued at standard cost, the material price variance is calculated on material purchases in the period.

True ☐   False ☐

3   Are variable production overhead variances based on hours paid or hours worked?

4   *Fill in the boxes in the diagram with the names of the variances and add the appropriate definition number from the list below.*

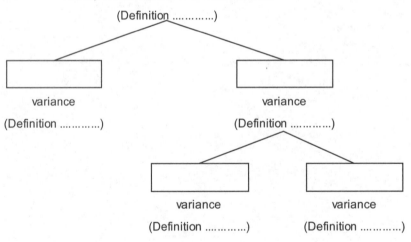

Fixed production overhead total variance
(Definition ....)

variance
(Definition ....)

variance
(Definition ....)

variance
(Definition ....)

variance
(Definition ....)

Definitions

1   The difference between actual and budgeted production, multiplied by the standard absorption rate per unit

2   The difference between budgeted hours of work and the actual hours worked, multiplied by the standard absorption rate per hour

3   The under or over absorption of fixed production overhead

4   The difference between budgeted fixed production overhead expenditure and actual fixed production overhead expenditure

5   The difference between the number of hours that actual production should have taken, and the number of hours actually taken, multiplied by the standard absorption rate per hour

5   The sales volume variance is valued at the standard selling price per unit.

    True ☐   False ☐

6   *Match the following causes of variances to the appropriate variance.*

Variances		Causes	
(a)	Favourable labour efficiency	(1)	Inexperienced staff in the purchasing department
(b)	Adverse sales volume	(2)	Materials of higher quality than standard
(c)	Adverse material price	(3)	Unexpected slump in demand
(d)	Adverse selling price	(4)	Production difficulties
(e)	Adverse fixed production overhead volume	(5)	Strike
(f)	Idle time	(6)	Poor machine maintenance

7   *Match the three pairs of interrelated variances.*

    (a)   Adverse selling price   (e)   Adverse materials price

    (b)   Favourable labour rate   (f)   Favourable materials usage

    (c)   Adverse materials usage   (g)   Adverse sales volume

    (d)   Favourable sales volume   (h)   Idle time

8   *Choose the appropriate words from those highlighted.*

    The materials mix variance is calculated as the difference between the **standard/actual** total quantity used in the **standard/actual** mix and the **standard/actual** quantities used in the **standard/actual** mix, valued at **standard/actual** costs.

9   *Choose the appropriate words from those highlighted.*

    The materials yield variance is calculated on the difference between the **standard/actual** input for **standard/actual** output, and the **standard/actual** total quantity input (in the **standard/actual** mix), valued at **standard/actual** costs.

10   The total yield variance in quantity is zero.

    True ☐   False ☐

11   *Choose the appropriate words from those highlighted*

    The sales mix variance is calculated as the difference between the **standard/actual** quantity sold in the **standard/actual** mix and the **standard/actual** quantity sold in the **standard/actual** mix, valued at **standard/actual** margin per unit.

12   *Choose the appropriate words from those highlighted*

    The sales quantity variance is calculated as the difference between the **standard/actual** sales volume in the budgeted proportions and the budgeted sales volumes, multiplied by the **standard/actual** margin.

1   The material price variance is the difference between what the material did cost and what it should have cost.

    The material usage variance is the difference between the standard cost of the material that should have been used and the standard cost of the material that was used.

2   True

3   Variable production overhead variances are based on hours worked.

4

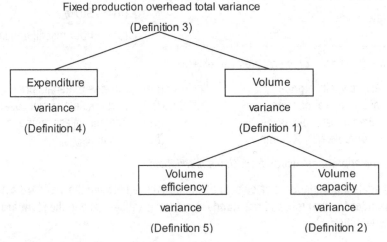

Fixed production overhead total variance
(Definition 3)

Expenditure variance (Definition 4)

Volume variance (Definition 1)

Volume efficiency variance (Definition 5)

Volume capacity variance (Definition 2)

5   False. It is valued at the standard profit margin per unit.

6   (a)   (2)   (d)   (3)
    (b)   (3) or (4) or (5)   (e)   (4) or (5) or (6)
    (c)   (1)   (f)   (5) or (6)

7   (a) and (d)
    (b) and (c)
    (e) and (f)

8   The materials mix variance is calculated as the difference between the actual total quantity used in the standard mix, and the actual quantities used in the actual mix, valued at standard costs.

9   The materials yield variance is calculated as the difference between the standard input for actual output, and the actual total quantity input (in the standard mix), valued at standard costs.

10 False. It is the total mix variance in quantity which is zero.

11 The sales mix variance is calculated as the difference between the actual quantity sold in the standard mix and the actual quantity sold in the actual mix, valued at standard margin per unit.

12 The sales quantity variance is calculated as the difference between the actual sales volume in the budgeted proportions and the budgeted sales volumes, multiplied by the standard margin.

Now try the question below from the Practice Question Bank

Number	Level	Marks	Time
Q13	Examination	15	27 mins

Planning and operational variances

Topic list	Syllabus reference
1 Revising a budget or standard cost	C7 (a), (b) (d)
2 Planning and operational variances for sales: market size and market share variances	C7 (c)
3 Planning and operational variances for materials	C7 (c)
4 Planning and operational variances for labour	C7 (c)
5 The value of planning and operational variances	C7 (b) (d)

Introduction

In this chapter we discuss the circumstances in which management may consider it appropriate to revise the budget or the standard cost.

When a budget or standard cost is revised after the budget period has begun, the reporting of variances should allow for this revision. One way of doing this is to present variances in the form of planning variances and operational variances.

We also discuss the problems of using standard costing in the modern, rapidly changing business environment.

Study guide

		Intellectual level
C7	**Planning and operational variances**	
(a)	Calculate a revised budget	2
(b)	Identify and explain those factors that could and could not be allowed to revise an original budget	2
(c)	Calculate, identify the cause of and explain planning and operational variances for: (i) sales, including market size and share (ii) materials (iii) labour, including the effect of the learning curve	2
(d)	Explain the manipulation issues in revising budgets	2

Exam guide

Planning and operational variances are likely to be a frequently-examined topic. There has been an article in *Student Accountant* on planning variances, which you are strongly advised to read. It is available on the ACCA web site.

1 Revising a budget or standard cost

FAST FORWARD

> Occasionally, it may be appropriate to **revise a budget or standard cost**. When this happens, variances should be reported in a way that distinguishes between variances caused by the revision to the budget and variances that are the responsibility of operational management.
>
> A planning and operational approach to variance analysis divides the total variance into those variances which have arisen because of inaccurate planning or faulty standards (**planning variances**) and those variances which have been caused by adverse or favourable operational performance, compared with a standard which has been revised in hindsight (**operational variances**).

1.1 Reasons for revising a budget or standard cost

When variances are reported in a system of budgetary control, it is usually assumed that:

(a) the original budget or standard cost is fairly accurate or reliable

(b) so any differences between actual results and the budget or standard, measured as variances, are attributable to the manager who is responsible for that aspect of performance.

The manager responsible will be expected to explain the reasons for any significant variances, and where appropriate take measures to rectify problems causing an adverse variance.

Occasionally however, circumstances may occur that make the original budget or standard cost invalid or inappropriate.

(a) The sales budget may have been based on expectations of the total size of the market for the organisation's product. However due to an unexpected change in economic conditions, or an unexpected technological change, or a radical change in customer attitudes, or unexpected new regulations affecting the marketability of a product, the market size may be much larger or much smaller than assumed when the sales budget was prepared.

(b) The standard cost of materials for a product may have been based on an assumption about what the market price for the materials should be. However due to a major change in the market, the available market price for the materials may become much higher or much lower than originally expected when the standard cost was prepared.

(c) The standard quantity of materials for a product may be significantly altered due to an unexpected change in the product specification, requiring much more or much less of the material in the product content.

(d) The standard labour rate may become unrealistic due to an unexpected increase in pay rates for employees.

(e) The standard time to produce a unit of product may also change for unexpected reasons.

If the budget or standard cost is not revised in these circumstances, variances reported to operational managers will be unrealistic. A large part of the **variances will be due to changes that are outside the control of the operational managers**.

In these circumstances, it may be appropriate to revise the budget or revise the standard cost.

1.2 Calculating a revised budget
12/07

The syllabus requires you to be able to calculate a revised budget, which could involve revising standards for sales, materials and/or labour so that only operational variances are highlighted when actual results are compared to the revised budget.

1.2.1 Example: Revised budget

A company produces Widgets and Splodgets which are fairly standardised products. The following information relates to period 1.

The standard selling price of Widgets is $50 each and Splodgets $100 each. In period 1, there was a special promotion on Splodgets with a 5% discount being offered. All units produced are sold and no inventory is held.

To produce a Widget they use 5 kg of X and in period 1, their plans were based on a cost of X of $3 per kg. Due to market movements the actual price changed and if they had purchased efficiently the cost would have been $4.50 per kg. Production of Widgets was 2,000 units.

A Splodget uses raw material Z but again the price of this can change rapidly. It was thought that Z would cost $30 per tonne but in fact they only paid $25 per tonne and if they had purchased correctly the cost would have been less as it was freely available at only $23 per tonne. It usually takes 1.5 tonnes of Z to produce 1 Splodget and 500 Splodgets are usually produced.

Each Widget takes 3 hours to produce and each Splodget 2 hours. Labour is paid $5 per hour. At the start of period 1, management negotiated a job security package with the workforce in exchange for a promised 5% increase in efficiency – that is, that the workers would increase output per hour by 5%.

Fixed overheads are usually $12,000 every period and variable overheads are $3 per labour hour.

Required

Produce the original budget and a revised budget allowing for controllable factors in a suitable format.

Solution

Original budget for Period 1

	$
Sales revenue ((2,000 × $50) + (500 × $100))	150,000
Material costs X (2,000 × 5kg × $3)	30,000
Material costs Z (500 × $30 × 1.5)	22,500
Labour costs ((2,000 × 3 × $5) + (500 × 2 × $5))	35,000
Variable overheads ((2,000 × 3 × $3) + (500 × 2 × $3))	21,000
Fixed overheads	12,000
Profit	29,500

Revised budget for Period 1

	$
Sales revenue ((2,000 × $50) + (500 × $100))	150,000
Material costs X (2,000 × 5kg × $4.5)	45,000
Material costs Z (500 × $23 × 1.5)	17,250
Labour costs ((2,000 × 3 × $5) + (500 × 2 × $5)) × 0.95	33,250
Variable overheads ((2,000 × 3 × $3) + (500 × 2 × $3)) × 0.95	19,950
Fixed overheads	12,000
Profit	22,550

1.2.2 When should budget revisions be allowed?

A budget revision should be allowed if something has happened which is **beyond the control** of the organisation or individual manager and which makes the original budget unsuitable for use in performance management.

Any adjustment should be **approved by senior management** who should look at the issues involved **objectively** and **independently**. **Operational issues** are the issues that a budget is attempting to control so they should **not** be subject to revision. However, it can be very **difficult to establish** what is due to operational problems (controllable) and what is due to planning (uncontrollable).

1.3 The nature of planning and operational variances

When a budget or standard cost is revised, variances are still reported as a **comparison between actual results and the original budget or standard cost**.

However, the variances should be reported that make a **clear distinction between**:

(a) variances that have been caused by the revision in the budget or standard cost, for which operational managers should not be made responsible: these are called **planning variances**

(b) variances that are caused by differences between actual performance and the revised budget or standard. For which operational managers should be made responsible and accountable. These are called **operational variances**.

Planning variances are calculated by comparing the original budget/standard cost with the revised budget/standard cost.

Operational variances are calculated in the same way as 'normal' basic variances, except that they are based on a comparison between actual results and the revised budget/standard cost.

1.4 Revising budgets: manipulation issues

When a budget or standard cost is revised, there is a potential problem. The budget or standard cost may be revised in such a way that all the reported operational variances become favourable variances, and the reason why actual results may be worse than budget is attributable entirely to planning variances, for which operational managers cannot be held responsible.

In other words, the revision to the budget or standard cost may be manipulated in such a way as to make operating results seem much better than is really the case.

To prevent manipulation, there should be strict rules about revising a budget or standard cost. In particular, the revision to the budget or standard cost should ideally be based on independent evidence (and verifiable evidence) that operational managers are not in a position to manipulate.

For example:

(a) If there is an unexpected change in the total size of the market for the company's product, there should ideally be independent evidence from an external source (such as a market research firm) about the revised expectations of the market size.

(b)   If there is an unexpected change in the market price for materials, there should ideally be an official price index or price benchmark for the material item.

(c)   If there is an unexpected change in the standard material usage for a product, this should ideally be evidenced by a documented change in the product specification.

Independent evidence may be difficult to obtain in many cases. When it is not available, the potential for manipulation of planning and operational variances should be recognised.

2 Planning and operational variances for sales: market size and market share variances   12/07, 6/13

FAST FORWARD

A sales budget may be revised when it is recognised that the original sales budget was based on expectations of the total market size that in retrospect are seen to be inappropriate and unrealistic. **When the sales budget is revised**, a **sales volume planning variance** may be reported. This is the difference in profit caused by the difference between the original sales budget and the revised sales budget. This planning variance is called a **market size variance**. **When the sales budget is revised,** a **sales volume operational variance** may be reported, for which operational sales managers should be held responsible. This is the difference in profit caused by the difference between actual sales volume and the sales volume in the revised sales budget. This operational variance is called a **market share variance**.

When the sales budget is revised it may be assumed that:

(a)   the revision to the sales budget was due to a re-assessment of the total market size for the organisation's product, but

(b)   sales management should still be expected to win the same market share (as a proportion of the total market size) as in the original budget.

On the basis of this assumption, the sales volume variance can be reported as:

(a)   a **sales volume planning variance**, or **market size variance**, which is caused by the difference between the sales volume in the original budget and the sales volume in the revised budget, and

(b)   a **sales volume operational variance**, or **market share variance**, which is caused by the difference between actual sales volume and the sales volume in the revised budget.

As there has been no change in the budgeted sales price or standard cost of products, these two variances can be converted from units into a money value by multiplying the variance is units by the standard profit (or standard contribution) per unit.

2.1 Example: market size and market share variance

Dimsek budgeted to make and sell 400 units of its product, the Role, in the four-week period no 8, as follows.

	$
Budgeted sales (100 units per week)	40,000
Variable costs (400 units × $60)	24,000
Contribution	16,000
Fixed costs	10,000
Profit	6,000

At the beginning of the second week, production came to a halt because inventories of raw materials ran out, and a new supply was not received until the beginning of week 3. As a consequence, the company lost one week's production and sales. Actual results in period 8 were as follows.

		$
Sales (320 units)		32,000
Variable costs (320 units × $60)		19,200
Contribution		12,800
Fixed costs		10,000
Actual profit		2,800

In retrospect, it is decided that the optimum budget, given the loss of production facilities in the third week, would have been to sell only 300 units in the period.

Required

Calculate appropriate planning and operational variances for sales volume.

Solution

The **sales volume planning** variance **compares the revised budget** with the **original budget**. It may be called a market size variance.

Revised sales volume, given materials shortage	300 units
Original budgeted sales volume	400 units
Sales volume planning variance in units of sales	100 units (A)
× standard contribution per unit	× $40
Sales volume planning variance in $	$4,000 (A)

Arguably, **running out of raw materials is an operational error** and so the loss of sales volume and contribution from the materials shortage is an opportunity cost that could have been avoided with better purchasing arrangements. The operational variances are variances calculated in the usual way, except that actual results are compared with the revised standard or budget. There is a sales volume variance which is an **operational variance**, as follows.

Actual sales volume	320 units
Revised sales volume	300 units
Operational sales volume variance in units	20 units (F)
(possibly due to production efficiency or marketing efficiency)	
× standard contribution per unit	× $40
Operational sales volume variance in $ contribution	$800 (F)

The operational variance for sales volume may be called a market share variance. These planning and operational variances for sales volume can be used as **control information** to reconcile budgeted and actual profit.

	$	$
Operating statement, period 8		
Budgeted profit		6,000
Planning variance: sales volume	4,000 (A)	
Operational variance: sales volume	800 (F)	
		3,200 (A)
Actual profit in period 8		2,800

You may have noticed that in this example sales volume variances were **valued at contribution forgone**. This is because it is assumed that a marginal costing system applies.

Question	Sales volumes

PG budgeted sales for 20X8 were 5,000 units. The standard contribution is $9.60 per unit. A recession in 20X8 meant that the market for PG's products declined by 5%. PG's market share also fell by 3%. Actual sales were 4,500 units.

Required

Calculate planning and operational variances for sales volume.

Planning variance

	Units
Original budgeted sales	5,000
Revised budget sales (–5%)	4,750
	250 A
@ Contribution per unit of $9.60	$2,400

Operational variance

	Units
Revised budget sales	4,750
Actual sales	4,500
	250 A
@ Contribution per unit of $9.60	$2,400

The fall in **market size** is uncontrollable by the management of PG and therefore results in a **planning** variance. The fall in **market share** is controllable and forms part of the **operational** variance.

2.2 Planning and operational variances for sales price

There may be a situation where a revision is made to the budgeted or standard selling price for a product. When this happens, a sales price planning variance and a sales price operational variance can be calculated.

The planning variance is generally outside the control of sales management, but the operational sales price variance is a sales management responsibility.

Question — Planning and operational sales variances

KSO budgeted to sell 10,000 units of a new product during 20X0. The budgeted sales price was $10 per unit, and the variable cost $3 per unit.
Actual sales in 20X0 were 12,000 units and variable costs of sales were $30,000, but sales revenue was only $5 per unit. With the benefit of hindsight, it is realised that the budgeted sales price of $10 was hopelessly optimistic, and a price of $4.50 per unit would have been much more realistic.

Required

Calculate planning and operational variances for sales price.

Answer

The only variances are selling price variances.

Planning (selling price) variance

	$ per unit
Original budgeted sales price	10.00
Revised budgeted sales price	4.50
Sales price planning variance	5.50 (A)

The planning variance is adverse because the revised sales price is lower than the sales price in the original budget. As a result, actual profit will not achieve the budgeted profit level.

The **total sales price planning variance is obtained by multiplying the planning variance per unit by the actual number of units sold** (not the budgeted number of units sold).

Sales price planning variance = $5.50 per unit (A) × 12,000 units sold

= **$66,000 (A).**

Operational (selling price) variance

The **sales price operational variance** is calculated in the same way as a 'normal' sales price variance, except that the sales price in the revised budget is used, not the original budget.

	$
12,000 units should sold for (12,000 × $5)	60,000
They should have sold for (× $4.5)	54,000
Operational (selling price) variance	**6,000 (F)**

3 Planning and operational variances for materials

12/13

> Planning and operational variances can be reported for direct materials, when the standard cost is revised for the material price, material usage per unit, or both.

The same basic principles can be applied to calculating planning and operational variances for materials, when the standard material cost per unit is changed.

However:

- Operational variances are reported as a materials price and a materials usage variance. Should these variances be calculated using the original standard cost or the revised standard cost?

- The planning variance for materials is the difference between the original standard and the revised standard. But should they be converted into a total money value using actual material quantities or standard material quantities?

An additional problem, and one that you may be expected to deal with in your exam, is that the revised standard for materials may contain a revision to both the material price and the material quantity per unit.

The calculation of planning and operational variances for materials will be explained with two examples. The first example revises just one aspect of the standard material cost. The second example revises both the standard unit price of materials and the standard material usage per unit of product.

3.1 Example 1: Planning price and usage variances

Product X had a standard direct material cost in the budget of:

4 kg of Material M at $5 per kg = $20 per unit.

Due to disruption of supply of materials to the market, the average market price for Material M during the period was $5.50 per kg, and it was decided to revise the material standard cost to allow for this.

During the period, 6,000 units of Product X were manufactured. They required 26,300 kg of Material M, which cost $139,390.

Required

Calculate:

(a)   the material price planning variance
(b)   the material price operational variance
(c)   the material usage (operational) variance

Solution

The original standard cost was 4kg × $5 = $20. The revised standard cost is 4kg × $5.50 = $22.

Material price planning variance

This is the difference between the original standard price for Material M and the revised standard price.

	$ per kg
Original standard price	5.00
Revised standard price	5.50
Material price planning variance	0.50 (A)

The planning variance is adverse because the change in the standard price increases the material cost and this will result in lower profit.

The material price planning variance is converted into a total money amount by multiplying the planning variance per kg of material by the **actual quantity of materials used**.

Material price planning variance = 26,300 kg × $0.50 (A) = $13,150 (A).

Material price operational variance

This compares the actual price per kg of material with the revised standard price. It is calculated using the actual quantity of materials used.

	$
26,300 kg of Material M should cost (revised standard $5.50)	144,650
They did cost	139,390
Material price operational variance	5,260 (F)

Material usage operational variance

This variance is calculated by comparing the actual material usage with the standard usage in the revised standard, but it is then **converted into a money value by applying the original standard price for the materials, not the revised standard price.** This is an important rule.

	kg of M
6,000 units of Product X should use (× 4kg)	24,000
They did use	26,300
Material usage (operational) variance in kg of M	2,300 (A)
Original standard price per kg of Material M	$5
Material usage (operational) variance in $	$11,500 (A)

The variances may be summarised as follows

	$	$
6,000 units of Product X at original std cost ($20)		120,000
Actual material cost		139,390
Total material cost variance		19,390 (A)
Material price planning variance	13,150 (A)	
Material price operational variance	5,260 (F)	
Material usage operational variance	11,500 (A)	
Total of variances		19,390 (A)

3.2 Example 2: Planning price and usage variances

The standard materials cost of a product is 5 kg × $7.50 per kg = $37.50. Actual production of 10,000 units used 54,400 kg at a cost of $410,000.

In retrospect it was realised that the standard materials cost should have been 5.3 kg per unit at a cost of $8 per kg. The standard cost was revised to this amount.

Required

Calculate the materials planning and operational variances in as much detail as possible.

Solution

Original standard cost: 5 kg × $7.50 per kg = $37.50 per unit of product

Revised standard cost: 5.3 kg × $8 per kg = $42.40 per unit of product

In this example, both the material price and the material usage per unit have been revised. There are planning variances for both material price and material usage.

Material price planning variance

This is the difference between the original standard price and the revised standard price.

	$ per kg
Original standard price	7.50
Revised standard price	8.00
Material price planning variance	0.50 (A)

The planning variance is adverse. The variance is converted into a total money amount by multiplying the planning variance per kg of material by the **actual quantity of materials used**.

Material price planning variance = 54,400 kg × $0.50 (A) = **$27,200 (A)**.

Material usage planning variance

This is the difference between the original standard usage and the revised standard usage for the quantity of units produced. **The usage planning variance is converted into a total money value by applying the original standard price for the material, not the revised standard price.**

	kg
10,000 units of product X should use: original standard	50,000
10,000 units of product X should use: revised standard	53,000
Material usage planning variance in kg of material	3,000 (A)
Original standard price per kg of material	$7.50
Material usage planning variance in $	$22,500 (A)

The planning variance is adverse because the revised standard is for a higher usage quantity (so higher cost and lower profit).

Material price operational variance

This is calculated using the actual quantity of materials used.

	$
54,400 kg of material should cost (revised standard $8)	435,200
They did cost	410,000
Material price operational variance	25,200 (F)

Material usage operational variance

This variance is calculated by comparing the actual material usage with the standard usage in the revised standard, and is then **converted into a money value by applying the original standard price for the materials**.

	kg
10,000 units of product X should use (× 5.3 kg)	53,000
They did use	54,400
Material usage (operational) variance in kg of material	1,400 (A)
Original standard price per kg of Material M	$7.50
Material usage (operational) variance in $	$10,500 (A)

The variances may be summarised as follows

	$	$
10,000 units of product at original std cost ($37.50)		375,000
Actual material cost		410,000
Total material cost variance		35,000 (A)
Material price planning variance	27,200 (A)	
Material usage planning variance	22,500 (A)	
Material price operational variance	25,200 (F)	
Material usage operational variance	10,500 (A)	
Total of variances		35,000 (A)

4 Planning and operational variances for labour   12/12, Specimen paper

FAST FORWARD

> Planning and operational variances can be reported for direct labour, when the standard cost is revised for the labour rate per hour, the standard labour time per unit, or both.

Precisely the same argument applies to the calculation of operational variances for labour, and the examples already given should be sufficient to enable you to do the next question. If you are not sure, check the solution carefully.

Question   Planning and operational labour variances

A company makes a single product. At the beginning of the budget year, the standard labour cost was established as $8 per unit, and each unit should take 0.5 hours to make.

However during the year the standard labour cost was revised. A new quality control procedure was introduced to the production process, adding 20% to the expected time to complete a unit. In addition, due to severe financial difficulties facing the company, the work force reluctantly agreed to reduce the rate of pay to $15 per hour.

In the first month after revision of the standard cost, budgeted production was 15,000 units but only 14,000 units were actually produced. These took 8,700 hours of labour time, which cost $130,500.

Required

Calculate the labour planning and operational variances in as much detail as possible.

Answer

Original standard cost = 0.5 hours × $16 per hour = $8 per unit

Revised standard = 0.6 hours × $15 per hour = $9 per unit

Planning and operational variances for labour are calculated in a similar way to planning and operational variances for materials. We need to look at planning and operational variances for labour rate and labour efficiency.

Labour rate planning variance

This is the difference between the original standard rate per hour and the revised standard rate per hour.

	$ per hour
Original standard rate	16
Revised standard rate	15
Labour rate planning variance	1 (F)

The planning variance for labour rate is favourable, because the revised hourly rate is lower than in the original standard. The variance is converted into a total money amount by multiplying the planning variance per hour by the **actual number of hours worked**.

Labour rate planning variance = 8,700 hours × $1 (F) = **$8,700 (F).**

Labour efficiency planning variance

This is the difference between the original standard time per unit and the revised standard time, for the quantity of units produced. **The efficiency planning variance is converted into a total money value by applying the original standard rate per hour, not the revised standard rate.**

	hours
14,000 units of product should take: original standard (× 0.5)	7,000
14,000 units of product should take: revised standard (× 0.6)	8,400
Labour efficiency planning variance in hours	1,400 (A)
Original standard rate per hour	$16
Labour efficiency planning variance in $	$22,400 (A)

The planning variance is adverse because the revised standard is for a longer time per unit (so higher cost and lower profit).

Labour rate operational variance

This is calculated using the actual number of hours worked and paid for.

	$
8,700 hours should cost (revised standard $15)	130,500
They did cost	130,500
Labour rate operational variance	0

In this example, the work force was paid exactly the revised rate of pay per hour.

Labour efficiency operational variance

This variance is calculated by comparing the actual time to make the output units with the standard time in the revised standard. It is then **converted into a money value by applying the original standard rate per hour**.

	hours
14,000 units of product should take (× 0.6 hours)	8,400
They did take	8,700
Labour efficiency (operational variance in hours	300 (A)
Original standard rate per hour	$16
Labour efficiency (operational variance in $	$4,800 (A)

The variances may be summarised as follows.

	$	$
14,000 units of product at original standard cost ($8)		112,000
Actual material cost		130,500
Total material cost variance		18,500 (A)
Labour rate planning variance	8,700 (F)	
Labour efficiency planning variance	22,400 (A)	
Labour rate operational variance	0	
Labour efficiency operational variance	4,800 (A)	
Total of variances		18,500 (A)

4.1 Labour planning variances and the learning curve

The learning curve was described in a previous chapter, where it was explained that when a learning curve applies to the manufacture of a new product, it is not possible to establish a standard labour cost. This is because the expected time to make each unit falls with each additional unit that is produced.

A standard labour cost can only be established when a 'steady state' is reached and production of each additional unit should take the same amount of time.

In principle, however, it would be possible to combine standard costing with the learning curve, as follows.

(a) Establish an original standard labour cost per unit, even though a learning effect will apply to production.

(b) At the end of the budget period, revise the standard time per unit. The revised standard time could be calculated using the learning curve formula and applying this to the number of units produced in the period.

(c) With the original standard cost and the revised standard cost, planning and operational variances for labour can be calculated. Because of the learning effect, the labour efficiency planning variance will always be favourable.

5 The value of planning and operational variances

Advantages of a system of planning and operational variances

- The analysis highlights those variances which are **controllable** (operational variances) and those which are **non-controllable** (planning variances).

- **Managers' acceptance** of the use of variances for performance measurement, and their **motivation**, is likely to increase if they know they will not be held responsible for poor planning and faulty standard setting.

- The **planning and standard-setting processes** should improve; standards should be more accurate, relevant and appropriate.

- Operational variances will provide a more realistic and **'fair' reflection of actual performance**.

The limitations of planning and operational variances, which must be overcome if they are to be applied in practice.

- It is difficult to **decide in hindsight** what the **realistic standard** should have been.

- It may become **too easy to justify all the variances as being due to bad planning**, so no operational variances will be highlighted.

- Establishing realistic revised standards and analysing the total variance into planning and operational variances can be a **time consuming** task, even if a spreadsheet package is devised.

- Even though the intention is to provide more meaningful information, **managers may be resistant** to the very idea of variances and refuse to see the virtues of the approach. Careful presentation and explanation will be required until managers are used to the concepts.

Chapter Roundup

- Occasionally, it may be appropriate to **revise a budget or standard cost**. When this happens, variances should be reported in a way that distinguishes between variances caused by the revision to the budget and variances that are the responsibility of operational management.

- A planning and operational approach to variance analysis divides the total variance into those variances which have arisen because of inaccurate planning or faulty standards (**planning variances**) and those variances which have been caused by adverse or favourable operational performance, compared with a standard which has been revised in hindsight (**operational variances**).

- A sales budget may be revised when it is recognised that the original sales budget was based on expectations of the total market size that in retrospect are seen to be inappropriate and unrealistic.

- **When the sales budget is revised**, a **sales volume planning variance** may be reported. This is the difference in profit caused by the difference between the original sales budget and the revised sales budget. This planning variance is called a **market size variance**.

- **When the sales budget is revised,** a **sales volume operational variance** may be reported, for which operational sales managers should be held responsible. This is the difference in profit caused by the difference between actual sales volume and the sales volume in the revised sales budget. This operational variance is called a **market share variance**.

- Planning and operational variances can be reported for direct materials, when the standard cost is revised for the material price, material usage per unit, or both.

- Planning and operational variances can be reported for direct labour, when the standard cost is revised for the labour rate per hour, the standard labour time per unit, or both.

Quick Quiz

1 A planning variance compares what with what?

2 If a planning efficiency variance is valued at an original standard rate, the planning rate variance is valued at the original efficiency level.

   True ☐   False ☐

3 A standard material cost is revised and the standard quantity of material required per unit is reduced in the revised standard, compared with the original standard. At the same time the standard rate per unit of material is increased in the revised standard.

   (a)   The material price planning variance is _____ (favourable/adverse)

   (b)   The material usage planning variance is _____ (favourable/adverse)

4 The standard labour rate per hour in an original standard cost is $10. The standard cost is revised, and the revised labour rate per hour is $12. The labour efficiency variance in hours is 2,000 hours adverse. What is the labour efficiency operational variance in $?

   _____

5 A sales volume operational variance is sometimes called a _____ .

Answers to Quick Quiz

1   A planning variance compares an original standard with a revised standard that should or would have been used if planners had known in advance what was going to happen.

2   False. It is valued at the revised efficiency level.

3   (a)   The material price planning variance is adverse.
     (b)   The material usage planning variance is favourable.

4   2,000 hours (A) × original standard rate $10 per hour = $20,000 (A).

5   Market share variance

Now try the question below from the Practice Question Bank

Number	Level	Marks	Time
Q14	Examination	15	27 mins

13

Performance analysis and behavioural aspects

Topic list	Syllabus reference
1 Using variance analysis	C8 (a) (b)
2 Behavioural implications	C8 (c)
3 Setting the difficulty level for a budget	C8 (d) (e)
4 Participation in budgeting	C8 (f)
5 Variances in a JIT or TQM environment	C8 (g)
6 Standard costs in a rapidly changing environment	C8 (h)

Introduction

In this chapter we discuss the effects of standard costing and variance reporting on management and employee behaviour.

We also discuss the problems of using standard costing in the modern, rapidly changing business environment.

Study guide

		Intellectual level
C8	**Performance analysis and behavioural aspects**	
(a)	Analyse and evaluate past performance using the results of past performance	2
(b)	Use variance analysis to assess how future performance of an organisation or business can be improved	2
(c)	Identify the factors which influence behaviour	2
(d)	Discuss the issues surrounding setting the difficulty level for a budget	2
(e)	Discuss the effect that variances have on staff motivation and action	2
(f)	Explain the benefits and difficulties of the participation of employees in the negotiation of targets	2
(g)	Describe the dysfunctional nature of some variances in the modern environment of JIT and TQM	2
(h)	Discuss the behavioural problems resulting from using standard costs in rapidly changing environments	2

Exam guide

The behavioural aspects of performance analysis and variances may form the discussion part of a Section B question, but you should also be prepared for a tricky Section A multiple choice question on any of the topics in this chapter.

1 Using variance analysis

FAST FORWARD

> Variance analysis is used to analyse and evaluate past performance. It is also used for control purposes: significant variances may indicate that an aspect of performance is out of control and that measures should be taken to improve performance in the future.

1.1 Analysing past performance with variance analysis

Variance analysis compares actual performance with a budget or standard cost. Differences between actual results and the budget or standard are reported in monetary terms as variances, and variances can be used to reconcile budgeted profit and actual profit in an operating statement.The previous chapters have focused mainly on the techniques of calculating variances. For the exam, you also need to show and awareness of what variances tell us, and what control measures management should take when a variance is reported.

Basic principles of variance reporting are that:

(a) the money value that is given to variances should be a **reasonable indication of how much profit has been made or lost** as a result of actual performance differing from the budget or standard

(b) the **managers responsible for variances (adverse or favourable) should be identified**, and they should be expected to account for the variance and, where appropriate, indicate what corrective or control measures they are taking.

1.1.1 Responsibility for planning variances

It was explained in the previous chapter that planning variances arise when a budget or standard cost is revised. 'Errors' in the budget or standard cost are attributable to the managers (planners) who prepared the budget or standard cost. Variances arising because the budget or standard cost was inappropriate should not be attributed to operational management.

In many cases, revisions to a budget or standard cost are due to causes outside the control of the planners. An unexpected increase in the market price for materials, for example, is beyond the control of planners. Similarly an unexpected collapse in market demand for an industry's products, resulting in an adverse sales volume planning variance, cannot usually be 'blamed' on planners.

Even so, planning variances, where they occur, should be identified separately. Operational managers should be held responsible only for variances that may be realistically attributable to differences between actual performance and a realistic budget or standard. In other words, operational managers should be held responsible for operational variances. Unless they were also involved in the budgeting or standard-setting process, operational managers are not responsible for planning variances.

1.1.2 Responsibility for operational variances

Responsibility for operational variances should be traced to the managers who are in a position of authority and control over operations where the variances occur. Operational management responsibility for variances depends on the organisation structure and the division of authority and responsibility between management.

For example, a material price variance is the difference between actual and standard purchase costs of materials. The operational manager responsible for this variance should be the manager who makes the decisions about buying materials. This may be the head of buying in one organisation, and the production manager in a different organisation.

You should be able to identify the managers responsible for operational variances. A general guide is given in the table below.

Variance	Responsibility
Sales price variance	Sales or marketing management
Sales volume variance	Normally sales or marketing management. However if sales are less than budget due to problems with production, the production manager is responsible
Material price variance	The manager responsible for purchasing materials
Material usage variance	Normally the production manager
Labour rate variance	The manager responsible for pay rates. This may be senior management or Human Resources management. However the production manager will be responsible for any adverse rate variances caused by working overtime and paying employees a premium rate per hour
Labour efficiency variance	Normally the production manager
Idle time variance	This depends on the cause of the idle time. It may be caused by lack of sales orders (sales management responsibility), inefficient production management (production management responsibility) or delays in deliveries of key raw material (buying manager responsibility)

1.2 Using variance analysis to improve future performance

Variance analysis is not simply a method of analysing past performance. It should provide guidance to operational management about aspects of performance that need improving. Variances should be a guide to control action and improving future performance.

It is important to understand that a reported variance is a measurement that relates to historical performance. Control action affects the future, not the past. So, for example, if an adverse labour efficiency variance of $10,000 is reported one month, and the production manager takes measures to improve efficiency:

(a) The effect of the control measures should be to improve efficiency, but the value of the efficiency improvement in future months is unlikely to be $10,000. Control measures may result in savings of more or less than $10,000 per month, depending on how effective the measures are.

(b) The effect of control measures should have a reasonably long-term impact, so control measures may result in savings not just in the following control period, but for a reasonably long time into the future.

1.2.1 The significance of variances

Control action to improve future performance should only be taken when a variance seems significant. Some variances are inevitable, because it is most unlikely that actual results will be exactly the same as the budget or standard.

(a) Favourable as well as adverse variances should be investigated, with a view to taking control action, if they seem significant. Control action to improve poor performance may seem an obvious requirement. However control action to reinforce favourable performance should also be expected from management.

(b) Variances need not be investigated if they do not seem significant. For example, variances that are less than, say, 5% of the budget or standard cost amount may be disregarded, because they fall within an acceptable tolerance limit.

(c) Management may not use variances in a single reporting period as a guide to control action, since a variance in one month may be due to a once-only event. Instead of relying on variances reported in a single month, management may monitor cumulative variances over a period of time, and identify those that should be investigated on the basis of performance or trend over a number of months.

1.2.2 The cost of control action

Taking control measures to deal with the cause of a variance takes effort and costs money. Control measures should only be taken if it seems probable that the benefits arising from improved performance are sufficient to justify the cost of investigating the causes of the variance and taking control action.

This is a reason why insignificant variances are not investigated.

1.2.3 Improving performance

An exam question may ask about the nature of control action that an operational manager may take to deal with the cause of an adverse variance and so improve performance. The appropriate control measures will obviously depend on the circumstances and the reasons why a variance occurred, so you may need to use common sense and judgement in dealing with any question on this topic. A few ideas are set out in the following table, to give you an idea of the issues that may be considered.

Variance	Possible control action
Adverse sales volume variance	Consider reducing the sales price in order to increase sales demand, although this will result in an adverse sale price variance

Variance	Possible control action
Adverse material price variance	Search for a supplier who is prepared to offer a lower price. Consider purchasing in bulk quantities in order to obtain large order discounts.
Adverse material usage variance Adverse labour efficiency variance	Consider providing training to the work force, with the objective of improving labour efficiency and reducing wastage of materials

2 Behavioural implications 6/10, 6/12

FAST FORWARD Used correctly, a budgetary control and variance reporting system can **motivate** managers and employees to improve performance, but it may also produce undesirable **negative reactions**.

The purpose of a budgetary control and variance reporting system is to assist management in planning and controlling the resources of their organisation, by providing appropriate control information. The information will only be valuable, however, if it is interpreted correctly and used purposefully by managers *and* employees.

The appropriate use of control information therefore depends not only on the content of the information itself, but also on the behaviour of its recipients. This is because control in business is exercised by people. Their attitude to control information will colour their views on what they should do with it and a number of behavioural problems can arise.

(a) The **managers who set the budget** or standards are **often not the managers** who are then made **responsible for achieving budget targets.**

(b) The **goals of the organisation as a whole**, as expressed in a budget, **may not coincide with the personal aspirations of individual managers**.

(c) **Control is applied at different stages by different people**. A supervisor may get weekly control reports, and act on them; his superior may get monthly control reports, and decide to take different control action. Different managers can get in each other's way, and resent the interference from others.

2.1 Motivation

Motivation is what makes people behave in the way that they do. It comes from individual attitudes, or group attitudes. Individuals will be motivated by personal desires and interests. These may be in line with the objectives of the organisation, and some people 'live for their jobs'. Other individuals see their job as a chore, and their motivations will be unrelated to the objectives of the organisation they work for.

It is therefore vital that the goals of management and the employees harmonise with the goals of the organisation as a whole. This is known as goal congruence. Although obtaining goal congruence is essentially a behavioural problem, **it is possible to design and run a budgetary control system which will go some way towards ensuring that goal congruence is achieved**. Managers and employees must therefore be favourably disposed towards the budgetary control system so that it can operate efficiently.

The management accountant should therefore try to ensure that employees have positive attitudes towards **setting budgets, implementing budgets** (that is, putting the organisation's plans into practice) and feedback of results (**control information**).

2.2 Poor attitudes when setting budgets

Poor attitudes or hostile behaviour towards the budgetary control system can begin at the **planning stage. If managers are involved in preparing a budget** the following may happen.

(a) Managers may **complain that they are too busy** to spend much time on budgeting.

(b) They may **build 'slack' into their expenditure estimates**.

(c) They may argue that **formalising a budget plan on paper is too restricting** and that managers should be allowed flexibility in the decisions they take.

(d) They may set budgets for their budget centre and **not coordinate** their own plans with those of other budget centres.

(e) They may **base future plans on past results**, instead of using the opportunity for formalised planning to look at alternative options and new ideas.

On the other hand, **managers may not be involved in the budgeting process**. Organisational goals may not be communicated to them and they might have their budget decided for them by senior management or administrative decision. It is **hard for people to be motivated to achieve targets set by someone else.**

2.2.1 Poor attitudes when putting plans into action

Poor attitudes also arise **when a budget is implemented**.

(a) Managers may t **put in only just enough effort** to achieve budget targets, without trying to beat targets.

(b) A formal budget may **encourage rigidity and discourage flexibility**.

(c) **Short-term planning** in a budget **can draw attention away from the longer-term consequences** of decisions.

(d) There may be **minimal cooperation and communication** between managers.

(e) Managers will often try to make sure that they **spend up to their full budget allowance, and do not overspend**, so that they will not be accused of having asked for too much spending allowance in the first place.

2.2.2 Poor attitudes and the use of control information

The **attitude of managers towards the accounting control information** they receive **might reduce the information's effectiveness**.

(a) Management accounting control reports could well be seen as having a relatively **low priority** in the list of management tasks. Managers may take the view that they have more pressing jobs on hand than looking at routine control reports.

(b) Managers may **resent control information**; they may see it as **part of a system of trying to find fault with their work**. This resentment is likely to be particularly strong when budgets or standards are imposed on managers without allowing them to participate in the budget-setting process.

(c) If budgets are seen as **pressure devices** to push managers into doing better, control reports will be resented.

(d) Managers **may not understand the information** in the control reports, because they are unfamiliar with accounting terminology or principles.

(e) Managers may have a **false sense of what their objectives should be**. A production manager may consider it more important to maintain quality standards regardless of cost. He would then dismiss adverse expenditure variances as inevitable and unavoidable.

(f) **If there are flaws in the system of recording actual costs**, managers will dismiss control information as unreliable.

(g) **Control information** may be **received weeks after the end of the** period to which it relates, in which case managers may regard it as out-of-date and no longer useful.

(h) Managers may be **held responsible for variances outside their control**.

It is therefore obvious that management accountants and senior management should try to implement systems that are acceptable to budget holders and which produce positive effects.

2.2.3 Pay as a motivator

Many researchers agree that **pay can be an important motivator**, when there is a formal link between higher pay (or other rewards, such as promotion) and achieving budget targets. Individuals are likely to work harder to achieve budget if they know that they will be rewarded for their successful efforts. There are, however, problems with using pay as an incentive.

(a)   A serious problem that can arise is that **formal reward and performance evaluation systems can encourage dysfunctional behaviour**. Many investigations have noted the tendency of managers to pad their budgets either in anticipation of cuts by superiors or to make the subsequent variances more favourable. And there are numerous examples of managers making decisions in response to performance indices, even though the decisions are contrary to the wider purposes of the organisation.

(b)   The targets must be challenging but fair, otherwise individuals will become dissatisfied. **Pay can be a de-motivator as well as a motivator!**

3 Setting the difficulty level for a budget

FAST FORWARD

> **'Aspirations'** budgets can be used as **targets** to motivate higher levels of performance but a budget for **planning and decision making** should be based on **reasonable expectations.**
>
> The level of difficulty in a standard cost may range from very challenging to fairly undemanding: standard costs may be **ideal**, or many establish either a **target** or a **currently attainable** level of performance.

Budgets can motivate managers to achieve a high level of performance. But **how difficult** should budget targets or standard levels of efficiency be? And how might people react to targets of differing degrees of difficulty in achievement?

(a)   There is likely to be a **demotivating** effect where an **ideal standard** of performance is set, because adverse efficiency variances will always be reported.

(b)   A **low standard** of efficiency is also **demotivating**, because there is no sense of achievement in attaining the required standards. If the budgeted level of attainment is too 'loose', targets will be achieved easily, and there will be no impetus for employees to try harder to do better than this.

(c)   A budgeted level of attainment could be the **same** as the level that has been achieved in the past. Arguably, this level will be too low. It might encourage **budgetary slack**.

Academics have argued that each individual has a **personal 'aspiration level'.** This is a level of performance, in a task with which the individual is familiar, which the individual undertakes for himself to reach.

Individual aspirations might be much higher or much lower than the organisation's aspirations, however. The solution might therefore be to have **two budgets**.

(a)   A budget for **planning and decision making** based on **reasonable expectations**
(b)   A budget for **motivational purposes**, with more **difficult targets of performance**

These two budgets might be called an '**expectations budget**' and an '**aspirations budget**' respectively.

Similarly, the level of difficulty in a standard cost may vary.

Type of standard	
Ideal	A standard of performance that assumes the highest possible level of achievement. A desirable target, but not at all achievable at the moment. Reported variances will always be adverse. This can be de-motivating for the managers responsible for performance
Target	This is a standard cost that sets performance targets at a higher level than is currently being achieved. However the targets are not unrealistic. Improvements in performance ewill be needed to turn adverse variances into favourable variances. The value of target standards depends on the strength of motivation of management to improve performance. An incentive scheme may be needed to persuade managers to 'buy in' to the target standard.
Currently attainable	This standard is based on levels of performance that are currently being achieved. They do not provide an incentive to improve performance; although they may encourage management to avoid a deterioration in performance.
Basic standard	This is an original standard that is unchanged over a long period of time. It is used to measure trends and changes in performance standards over time. It is not a useful type of standard for control purposes.

3.1 The effect of reported variances on staff action

Reported variances, if significant and adverse, should prompt managers into taking control action to improve performance. The success of a variance reporting system in achieving this objective will depend on several factors.

(a) The manager who is considered responsible for the variance should agree and accept that the cause of the variance is his responsibility. Variances should be reported to the appropriate manager.

(b) The manager should consider the reported variance to be 'fair'. Variances should be a realistic measure. This is a reason why it is advisable to separate planning variances from operational variances when a budget or standard needs revision. It is also a reason why variances reported using ideal standards may be de-motivating.

(c) The manager should want to do something to deal with the causes of the variance. Incentives and motivation are important factors.

(d) Variance should be reported in a timely manner, as soon as reasonably practical. If a reported variance relates to events that occurred a long time ago, managers will be reluctant to investigate them 'now' because the variance will seem out-of-date.

(e) The manager must believe that the cause of the variance is something that he is in a position to control. If a manager considers the cause of a variance to be outside his sphere of authority, or to be due to a factor that he cannot do anything to change, he will not be motivated to look for control measures.

The control culture within the organisation may also affect the response of managers to variances. If there is a 'blame culture', managers will be blamed for adverse variances and accused of poor performance. This is likely to provoke a defensive reaction, with the manager trying to justify what has gone wrong.

In contrast, if there is an 'improvement culture', variances are considered as useful indicators for control action and improving performance. Managers are not blamed for adverse variances, but encouraged to look for suitable control measures whenever significant adverse variances occur.

4 Participation in budgeting

AST FORWARD

A budget can be set from the **top down** (**imposed** budget) or from the **bottom up** (**participatory** budget). Many writers refer to a third style, the negotiated budget.

4.1 Participation

It has been argued that **participation** in the budgeting process **will improve motivation** and so will improve the quality of budget decisions and the efforts of individuals to achieve their budget targets (although obviously this will depend on the personality of the individual, the nature of the task (narrowly defined or flexible) and the organisational culture).

There are basically two ways in which a budget can be set: from the **top down** (imposed budget) or from the **bottom up** (participatory budget).

4.2 Imposed style of budgeting (top-down budgeting)

In this approach to budgeting, **top management prepare a budget with little or no input from operating personnel** which is then imposed upon the employees who have to work to the budgeted figures.

The times when imposed budgets are effective are as follows.

- In newly-formed organisations
- In very small businesses
- During periods of economic hardship
- When operational managers lack budgeting skills
- When the organisation's different units require precise coordination

They are, of course, advantages and disadvantages to this style of setting budgets.

Advantages

- **Strategic plans** are likely to be incorporated into planned activities
- They **enhance** the **coordination** between the plans and objectives of divisions
- They use **senior management's awareness** of total resource availability
- They **decrease the input from inexperienced or uninformed lower-level employees**
- They **decrease the period of time taken** to draw up the budgets

Disadvantages

- **Dissatisfaction**, **defensiveness** and **low morale** amongst employees
- The **feeling of team spirit** may disappear
- The **acceptance of organisational goals** and **objectives** could be limited
- The feeling of the budget as a **punitive device** could arise
- **Unachievable budgets** for overseas divisions could result if consideration is not given to local operating and political environments
- **Lower-level management initiative** may be **stifled**

4.3 Participative style of budgeting (bottom-up budgeting)

In this approach to budgeting, **budgets are developed by lower-level managers who then submit the budgets to their superiors**. The budgets are based on the lower-level managers' perceptions of what is achievable and the associated necessary resources.

Participative budgets may be effective in the following circumstances.

- In **well-established organisations**
- In **very large** businesses
- During periods of **economic affluence**

- When operational managers have **strong budgeting skills**
- When the organisation's different units act **autonomously**

The **advantages** of participative budgets are as follows.

- They are based on **information from employees** most familiar with the department
- **Knowledge spread** among several levels of management is pulled **together**
- **Morale** and **motivation** is improved: employees feel more involved and that their opinions matter to senior management
- They **increase operational managers' commitment** to organisational objectives
- In general they are **more realistic**
- **Co-ordination** between units is **improved**
- **Specific resource requirements** are **included**
- **Senior managers' overview** is mixed with operational level details

There are, on the other hand, a number of **disadvantages** of participative budgets.

- They **consume more time**
- When individuals are involved in negotiating their budget targets, they may want to set targets that are easily-attainable rather than targets that are challenging. In other words, an ability to negotiate targets may tempt managers to introduce **budgetary slack** into their targets.
- Individuals may not properly understand the strategic and budget objectives of the organisation, and they may argue for targets that are not in the best interests of the organisation as a whole
- **Changes implemented** by senior management may **cause dissatisfaction** if they seem to ignore the opinions of employees who have been involved in negotiating targets
- Budgets may be **unachievable** if managers' are not sufficiently experienced or knowledgeable to contribute usefully
- They can support **'empire building'** by subordinates
- An **earlier start** to the budgeting process will be required, compared with top-down budgeting and target-setting.

4.4 Negotiated style of budgeting

At the two extremes, budgets can be dictated from above or simply emerge from below but, in practice, different levels of management often agree budgets by a process of negotiation. In the imposed budget approach, operational managers will try to negotiate with senior managers the budget targets which they consider to be unreasonable or unrealistic.

Likewise senior management usually review and revise budgets presented to them under a participative approach through a process of negotiation with lower level managers. **Final budgets are therefore most likely to lie between what top management would really like and what junior managers believe is feasible.** The budgeting process is hence a **bargaining process** and it is this bargaining which is of vital importance, **determining whether the budget is an effective management tool or simply a clerical device**.

5 Variances in a JIT or TQM environment 6/12

FAST FORWARD

Standard costing and variance analysis may sometimes be inappropriate in a production environment based on Just-in-Time (JIT) methods or a Total Quality Management (TQM) approach.

The use of standard costs and variance analysis is based on certain assumptions about the way in which operations should be managed. In particular, variance analysis is based on the view that:

(a) all resources should be used as efficiently as possible

(b) a standard cost is a performance target that operational managers should seek to achieve.

However this approach to analysing performance is not always appropriate. Variances indicating adverse performance are sometimes inappropriate in a Just-in-Time (JIT) or Total Quality Management (TQM) environment.

5.1 Variances and a JIT environment

In a JIT manufacturing environment, production is managed on the principle that items should not be produced until they are required to meet sales orders. There should be no accumulation of inventories of work-in-progress and finished goods.

A JIT approach implies that if there are no sales orders, production resources should be kept idle. In addition, as explained in the earlier chapter on the theory of constraints, the volume of production should be restricted to the output capacity of the bottleneck resource, and this means that there will inevitably be idle capacity for all resources that are not the bottleneck resource.

(a) In JIT manufacturing, idle time should therefore be expected.

(b) In a system of standard costing, idle time is an adverse labour efficiency variance, and is undesirable.

If idle time variances are reported for a manufacturing operation that is based on JIT methods, the variances will encourage managers to use idle capacity in a productive way, by producing more and building up inventories. With increases in inventory, there will be a higher reported profit.

This is unacceptable in a JIT environment.

5.2 Variances and a TQM environment   6/12

Total Quality Management (TQM) is an approach to management that originated from different sources, and has a number of different aspects.

(a) One aspect of TQM is the view that work should be 'right first time'. Mistakes that result is wastage and re-working of faulty output should be avoided.

(b) Another aspect of TQM is similar to the JIT principle that items should be produced only when they are needed for the next stage in the production process, and finished goods should not be produced until they are needed for sales orders.

(c) A third aspect of TQM is the principle of continuous improvement or 'kaizen'. This is the view that the organisation should always look for small ways of improving performance standards, and improvements should be made continually. The ideal level of performance will never be reached, because further improvements will always be possible.

Each of these principles of TQM may be inconsistent with standard costing and variance analysis. The inconsistency between standard costing and the view that production resources should be kept idle until required has already been discussed in the context of JIT.

(a) The philosophy in TQM of 'right first time' may be inconsistent with a standard cost that includes an allowance for wastage. TQM is more consistent with environmental cost accounting (material flow cost accounting) than a costing system that allows for normal loss in the standard cost.

(b) The principleof 'kaizen' or continuous improvement is that a steady state of production will never be achieved, because further improvements will always be possible. A standard cost is based on an assumption of a desirable steady state; and this view is inconsistent with the principle of continuous improvement.

5.2.1 Quality and quantity

Standard costing concentrates on **quantity** and ignores other factors contributing to effectiveness. In a **total quality environment**, however, quantity is not the main issue; quality is. Effectiveness in such an environment therefore centres on quality of output, and the cost of failing to achieve the required level of effectiveness is measured not in variances, but in terms of **internal and external failure costs**, neither of which would be identified by a traditional standard costing analysis.

Standard costing systems might measure, say, **labour efficiency** in terms of individual tasks and level of **output.** In a total quality environment, labour is more likely to be viewed as a number of **multi-task** teams who are responsible for the completion of a part of the production process. The effectiveness of such a team is more appropriately measured in terms of **re-working** required, **returns** from customers, **defects** identified in subsequent stages of production and so on.

Traditional feedback control would seek to eliminate an adverse material price variance by requiring managers to source cheaper, possibly lower quality supplies. This may run counter to the aim of maximising quality of output.

5.2.2 Can standard costing and TQM co-exist?

Arguably, there is little point in running both a Total Quality Management programme and a standard costing system simultaneously.

(a) Predetermined standards are at odds with the philosophy of **continual improvement** inherent in a total quality management programme.

(b) Continual improvements are likely to alter methods of working, prices, quantities of inputs and so on, whereas standard costing is most appropriate in a stable, standardised and repetitive environment.

(c) Material standard costs often incorporate a planned level of scrap. This is at odds with the TQM aim of **zero defects** and there is no motivation to 'get it right first time'.

(d) Attainable standards, which make some allowance for wastage and inefficiencies are commonly set. The use of such standards conflicts with the **elimination of waste** which is such a vital ingredient of a TQM programme.

(e) Standard costing control systems make individual managers **responsible** for the variances relating to their part of the organisation's activities. A TQM programme, on the other hand, aims to make **all personnel** aware of, and responsible for, the importance of supplying the customer with a quality product.

Question	TQM and variance analysis

One of the basic tenets of total quality management is 'get it right first time'. Is variance reporting a help or a hindrance in this respect?

Answer

In theory it should not be of any relevance at all, because variances will not occur. In practice an organisation will not get everything right first time and variance reporting may still draw attention to areas for improvement – **if the standard and 'being right' are the same thing.**

6 Standard costs in a rapidly changing environment

FAST FORWARD

The **role of standards and variances** in the rapidly-changing modern business environment is open to question.

It can be argued that standard costs have limited relevance and value in the modern business world, where the environment is continually changing, and the life cycle of products can be very short.

Standard costs are appropriate for a 'steady state' production environment where the manufacturing system produces standard products, often in large quantities, using standard and repetitive production methods and processes.

In many industries today:

(a) **Products are customised** to the individual specifications of the customer. Although there may be a basic product, customers do not buy a standard product. **Standard costing is more suitable for a mass production environment**.

(b) In countries such as the UK, there are **more service industries** than manufacturing industries, and **services are often non-standard in nature** and the way they are delivered.

(c) Standard cost variances focus mainly on material cost and labour cost variances (and overhead variances may be a simple fixed cost expenditure variance). In many manufacturing companies, overhead costs are much more significant than labour costs. Variance reporting therefore fails to focus on the most important costs.

(d) Many of the variances in a standard costing system focus on the control of **short-term variable costs**. In most modern manufacturing environments, the majority of costs, including direct labour costs, tend to be fixed in the short run.

(e) In some industries products have a very short life cycle. In these circumstances, it may not be worthwhile developing a standard cost for new products. Instead costing techniques such as life cycle costing and target costing may be more appropriate for planning and control purposes.

(f) Variance reporting involves regular formal performance reports, typically every four weeks or month. Modern IT systems make it possible for operational managers to monitor performance much more frequently and 'on demand'. Variance reporting is not easily adapted to 'on demand' performance monitoring.

6.1 The role in modern business of standards and variances

However, a survey by Drury *et al* (1993) indicated the **continued widespread use of standard costing systems**. Although this survey is now somewhat out of date, the following points should be noted.

- **Planning**. Even in a TQM environment, budgets will still need to be quantified. For example, the planned level of prevention and appraisal costs needs to be determined. Standards, such as returns of a particular product should not exceed 1% of deliveries during a budget period, can be set.

- **Control**. Cost and mix changes from plan will still be relevant in many processing situations.

- **Decision making**. Existing standards can be used as the starting point in the construction of a cost for a new product.

- **Performance measurement**. If the product mix is relatively stable, performance measurement may be enhanced by the use of a system of planning and operational variances.

- **Product pricing**. Target costs may be compared with current standards, and the resulting 'cost gap' investigated with a view to reducing it or eliminating it using techniques such as value engineering.

- **Improvement and change**. Variance trends can be monitored over time.

- **Accounting valuations**. Although the operation of a JIT system in conjunction with backflush accounting will reduce the need for standard costs and variance analysis, standards may be used to value residual inventory and the transfers to cost of sales account.

Chapter Roundup

- Variance analysis is used to analyse and evaluate past performance. It is also used for control purposes: significant variances may indicate that an aspect of performance is out of control and that measures should be taken to improve performance in the future.

- Used correctly, a budgetary control and variance reporting system can **motivate** managers and employees to improve performance, but it may also produce undesirable **negative reactions**.

- 'Aspirations' budgets can be used as **targets** to motivate higher levels of performance but a budget for **planning and decision making** should be based on **reasonable expectations**.

- The level of difficulty in a standard cost may range from very challenging to fairly undemanding: standard costs may be **ideal**, or many establish either a **target** or a **currently attainable** level of performance.

- A budget can be set from the **top down** (**imposed** budget) or from the **bottom up** (**participatory** budget). Many writers refer to a third style, the negotiated budget.

- Standard costing and variance analysis may sometimes be inappropriate in a production environment based on Just-in-Time (JIT) methods or a Total Quality Management (TQM) approach.

- The **role of standards and variances** in the rapidly-changing modern business environment is open to question.

Quick Quiz

1 Complete the table below to show a possible response to each of the traditional performance measures and a consequence of that response.

Measurement	Response	Consequence of action
Purchase price variance		
Labour efficiency variance		
Cost of scrap		
Scrap factor included in standard costs		

2 What three factors are said to determine the effectiveness of participation in target-setting?

    A   Nature of the task, organisation structure, personality
    B   Personality, technology, organisation structure
    C   Nature of the task, production processes, personality
    D   Personality, leadership style, aspirations

3 A budget for motivational purposes, with fairly difficult targets of performance, is an aspirations budget. **True or false?**

4 Provide five reasons why poor attitudes could arise when a budget is implemented.

BPP
LEARNING MEDIA

5   Match the description to the correct term.

	Term		Description
(a)	Motivation	1	Exists where managers working in their own interests also act in harmony with the interests of the organisation as a whole
(b)	Goal congruence	2	Comes from individual or group attitudes
(c)	Incentive	3	Concerned with getting subordinates to run rather than walk towards desired goals

1

Measurement	Response	Consequence of action
Purchase price variance	Buy in greater bulk to reduce unit price	Excess stocks Higher holding costs Quality and reliability of delivery times ignored
Labour efficiency variance	Encourage greater output	Possibly excess stocks of the wrong products
Cost of scrap	Rework items to reduce scrap	Production flow held up by re-working
Scrap factor included in standard costs	Supervisor aims to achieve actual scrap = standard scrap	No motivation to get it right first time

2   A

3   True

4   (a)   Managers might put in only just enough effort to achieve budget targets, without trying to beat targets.

    (b)   A formal budget might encourage rigidity and discourage flexibility in operational decision making.

    (c)   Short-term planning in a budget can draw attention away from the longer-term consequences of decisions.

    (d)   Cooperation and communication between managers might be minimal.

    (e)   Managers will often try to make sure that they spend up to their full budget allowance, and do not overspend, so that they will not be accused of having asked for too much spending allowance in the first place.

5   (a) 2; (b) 1; (c) 3

Now try the question below from the Practice Question Bank

Number	Level	Marks	Time
Q15	Examination	10	18 mins

PART

D

Performance measurement and control

Performance management information systems

Topic list	Syllabus reference
1 Introduction to planning, control and decision making	D1(a)
2 Management accounting information for strategic planning, control and decision making	D1(a)
3 Management accounting information for management control	D1(a)
4 Management accounting information for operational control	D1(a)
5 Management information systems	D1(b)
6 Open and closed systems	D1(c)

Introduction

Performance management systems, measurement and control is the final section in this Study Text.

This chapter introduces Part E of the syllabus and covers issues relating to **performance management information systems** and their design.

We begin with a look at the **accounting information needs** at all levels of the organisation. Next, we consider the characteristics of a range of management information systems including **transaction processing systems** and **executive information systems.**

The chapter concludes with a short section on **open** and **closed systems**.

Study guide

		Intellectual level
D1	**Performance management information systems**	
(a)	Identify the accounting information requirements and describe the different types of information systems used for strategic planning, management control and operational control and decision making	2
(b)	Define and identify the main characteristics of transaction processing systems; management information systems; executive information systems; and enterprise resource planning systems	2
(c)	Define and discuss the merits of, and potential problems with, open and closed systems with regard to the needs of performance management.	2

Exam guide

Management accounting and information systems are an important part of the F5 syllabus because they play an integral part in producing the information that managers use for performance measurement and performance management.

Performance management information systems provide the information which enables performance measurement to take place.

You could face questions specifically on the topics in this chapter, particularly in a section A multiple choice question, or you may need to use them as a framework for a wider question.

1 Introduction to planning, control and decision making

FAST FORWARD

Strategic planning is the process of deciding on objectives for the organisation, on changes in these objectives, on the resources to attain these objectives, and on the policies that are to govern the acquisition, use and disposition of these resources.

Management control is the process by which managers assure that resources are obtained and used effectively and efficiently in the accomplishment of the organisation's objectives. It is sometimes called **tactics** or **tactical planning**.

Operational control (or **operational planning**) is the process of assuring that specific tasks are carried out effectively and efficiently.

Within, and at all levels of the organisation, **information** is continually flowing back and forth, being used by people to formulate **plans** and take **decisions,** and to draw attention to the need for **control** action, when the plans and decisions don't work as intended.

Key terms

Planning means formulating ways of proceeding. **Decision making** means choosing between various alternatives. These two terms are virtually inseparable: you decide to plan in the first place and the plan you make is a collection of decisions.

Strategic decisions are long-term decisions and are characterised by their wide scope, wide impact, relative uncertainty and complexity.

Control is used in the sense of monitoring something so as to keep it on course, like the 'controls' of a car, not (or not merely) in the sense of imposing restraints or exercising tyrannical power over something. We have more to say about control later in this Study Text.

1.1 Information for planning, control and decision making

Robert **Anthony**, a leading writer on organisational control, suggested what has become a widely used hierarchy, classifying the information used at different management levels for planning, control and decision making into three tiers: **strategic planning**, **management control** and **operational control**.

We consider each tier in turn in sections 2 – 4.

Managerial level

Strategic planning. The process of deciding on objectives of the organisation, on changes in these objectives, on the resources used to attain these objectives, and on the policies that are to govern the acquisition, use and disposition of these resources.

Management (or **tactical**) **control**. The process by which managers assure that resources are obtained and used effectively and efficiently in the accomplishment of the organisation's objectives. It is sometimes called tactics or tactical planning.

Operational control (or **operational planning**). The process of assuring that specific tasks are carried out effectively and efficiently.

2 Management accounting information for strategic planning, control and decision making

FAST FORWARD

Management accounting information can be used to support strategic planning, control and decision making. Strategic management accounting differs from traditional management accounting because it has an **external** orientation and a **future** orientation.

This section identifies the accounting information requirements for strategic planning, control and decision making.

2.1 Future uncertainty

Much strategic planning is uncertain.

(a)   Strategic plans may cover a **long period** into the future, perhaps five to ten years ahead or even longer.

(b)   Many strategic plans involve big changes and **new ventures**, such as capacity expansion decisions, decisions to develop into new product areas and new markets, and so on.

Inevitably, management accounting information for strategic planning will be based on incomplete data and will use **forecasts** and **estimates.**

(a) It follows that management accounting information is unlikely to give clear guidelines for management decisions and should incorporate some **risk and uncertainty analysis** (eg sensitivity analysis).

(b) For longer term plans, **discounted cash flow techniques** ought to be used in financial evaluation.

(c) The management accountant will be involved in the following.

    (i) Project evaluation

    (ii) Managing cash and operational matters

    (iii) Reviewing the outcome of the project (post implementation review)

2.2 External and competitor orientation

Much management accounting information has been devised for internal consumption.

However, it is important to balance this with a consideration of external factors.

(a) Strategic planning and control decisions involve **environmental considerations**.

(b) A strategy is pursued in relation to **competitors.**

2.3 The challenge for management accountants

Traditional accounting systems have had a number of **perceived failings**.

(a) **Direction towards financial reporting**. Historical costs are necessary to report to shareholders, but the classifications of transactions for reporting purposes are not necessarily relevant to decision-making.

(b) **Misleading information** – particularly with regard to overhead absorption.

(c) **Neatness** rather than **usefulness**.

(d) **Internal focus**. Management accounting information has been too inward looking, (for example focusing on achieving internal performance targets, like budgets). However, organisations also need to focus on customers and competition.

(e) **Inflexibility** and an inability to cope with change.

The challenge lies in providing more relevant information for **strategic planning**, **control** and **decision making**. Traditional management accounting systems may not always provide this.

(a) **Historical costs** are not necessarily the best guide to decision making. One of the criticisms of management accounting outlined by *Kaplan, Bromwich and Bhimani* is that management accounting information is biased towards the past rather than the future.

(b) **Strategic issues** are not easily detected by management accounting systems.

(c) **Financial models** of some sophistication are needed to enable management accountants to provide useful information.

2.4 What is strategic management accounting?

The aim of strategic management accounting is to provide information that is relevant to the process of strategic planning and control.

Key term

> **Strategic management accounting** is a form of management accounting in which emphasis is placed on information about factors which are external to the organisation, as well as non-financial and internally-generated information.

2.4.1 External orientation

The important fact, which distinguishes strategic management accounting from other management accounting activities, is its **external orientation**, towards customers and competitors, suppliers and perhaps other stakeholders. For example, whereas a traditional management accountant would report on an organisation's own revenues, the strategic management would report on market share or trends in market size and growth.

(a) **Competitive advantage is relative**. Understanding competitors is therefore of prime importance.

For example, knowledge of competitors' costs, as well as a firm's own costs, could help inform strategic choices: a firm would be unwise to pursue a cost leadership strategy without first analysing its costs in relation to the cost structures of other firms in the industry.

(b) **Customers** determine if a firm has competitive advantage.

2.4.2 Future orientation

A criticism of traditional management accounts is that they are **backward looking**.

(a) Decision making is a forward– and outward-looking process.
(b) Accounts are based on **costs**, whereas decision making is concerned with **values**.

Strategic management accountants will use **relevant costs** (ie **incremental** costs and **opportunity** costs) for decision making. We looked at this topic in Chapter 6.

2.4.3 Goal congruence

Business strategy involves the activities of many different functions, including marketing, production and human resource management. The strategic management accounting system will require **inputs from many areas of the business**.

(a) Strategic management accounting translates the consequences of different strategies into a **common accounting language for comparison**.

(b) It **relates business operations to financial performance**, and therefore helps ensure that **business activities** are **focused on shareholders' needs** for profit. In **not-for-profit organisations** this will not apply as they do not focus on shareholder profitability. (We look at not-for-profit organisations in more detail later in this Study Text.)

It **helps to ensure goal congruence**, again by translating business activities into the common language of finance. Goal congruence is achieved when individuals or groups in an organisation take actions which are in their self-interest and also in the best interest of the organisation as a whole.

2.5 What information could strategic management accounting provide?

Bearing in mind the need for **goal congruence**, **external orientation** and **future orientation**, some **examples** of strategic management accounting are provided below.

Item	Comment
Competitors' costs	What are they? How do they compare with ours? Can we beat them? Are competitors vulnerable because of their cost structure?
Financial effect of competitor response	How might competitors respond to our strategy? How could their responses affect our sales or margins?
Product profitability	A firm should want to know not just what profits or losses are being made by each of its products, but why one product should be making good profits whereas another equally good product might be making a loss
Customer profitability	Some customers or groups of customers are worth more than others
Pricing decisions	Accounting information can help to analyse how profits and cash flows will vary according to price and prospective demand
The **value of market share**	A firm ought to be aware of what it is worth to increase the market share of one of its products

Item	Comment
Capacity expansion	Should the firm expand its capacity, and if so by how much? Should the firm diversify into a new area of operations, or a new market?
Brand values	How much is it worth investing in a brand which customers will choose over competitors' brands?
Shareholder wealth	Future profitability determines the value of a business
Cash flow	A loss-making company can survive if it has adequate cash resources, but a profitable company cannot survive unless it has sufficient liquidity
Effect of **acquisitions** and **mergers**	How will the merger affect levels of competition in the industry?
Decisions to **enter or leave a business area**	What are the barriers to entry or exit? How much investment is required to enter the market?

3 Management accounting information for management control

FAST FORWARD

Management control is at the level below strategic planning in Anthony's decision-making hierarchy and is concerned with decisions about the efficient and effective use of resources to achieve objectives.

Management control, which we briefly touched on in Section 1, is at the level below strategic planning in Anthony's decision-making hierarchy. While strategic planning is concerned with setting objectives and strategic targets, management control is concerned with **decisions about the efficient and effective use of an organisation's resources to achieve these objectives or targets**.

(a) **Resources** (which can be categorised as a series of 'M's): **m**oney, **m**anpower, **m**achinery, **m**ethods, **m**arkets, **m**anagement, and **m**anagement information.

(b) **Efficiency** in the use of resources means that **optimum output is achieved from the input resources used**. It relates to the combinations of men, land and capital (eg how much production work should be automated) and to the productivity of labour, or material usage.

(c) **Effectiveness** in the use of resources means that the **outputs obtained are in line with the intended objectives or targets**.

The time horizon involved in management control will be shorter than at the strategic decisions level, there will be much greater precision and the focus of information will be narrower.

Management control activities are **short-term non-strategic activities**.

3.1 Examples of management control (or tactical) planning activities

(a) Preparing budgets for the next year for sales, production, inventory levels and so on
(b) Establishing measures of performance by which profit centres can be gauged
(c) Developing a product for launching in the market
(d) Planning advertising and marketing campaigns
(e) Establishing a line-of-authority structure for the organisation

3.2 Examples of management control activities

(a) Ensuring that budget targets are reached, or improved upon
(b) Ensuring that other measures of performance are satisfactory, or even better than planned
(c) Where appropriate, changing the budget because circumstances have altered

Management control is an essentially routine affair in that it tends to be carried out in a series of **regular** planning and comparison procedures, that is annually, monthly or weekly, so that all aspects of an organisation's activity are systematically reviewed. For example, a budget is usually prepared annually,

and control reports issued every month or four weeks. Strategic planning, in contrast, might be irregular and occur when opportunities arise or are identified.

3.3 Information requirements

Features of management control information

(a) Primarily generated **internally** (but may have a limited external component)
(b) Embraces the **entire organisation**
(c) **Summarised** at a relatively **low level**
(d) **Routinely** collected and disseminated
(e) Relevant to the **short** and **medium terms**
(f) Often **quantitative** (labour hours, volumes of sales and production)
(g) Collected in a **standard** manner
(h) Commonly expressed in **money terms**

Types of information

(a) Productivity measurements
(b) Budgetary control or variance analysis reports
(c) Cash flow forecasts
(d) Manning levels
(e) Profit results within a particular department of the organisation
(f) Labour revenue statistics within a department
(g) Short-term purchasing requirements

3.4 Source of information

A large proportion of this information will be generated from **within the organisation** (it has an **endogenous source**) and it will often have an accounting emphasis. Tactical information is usually prepared regularly, perhaps weekly, or monthly.

3.5 Management control and strategic planning compared

The dividing line between strategic planning and management control is **not a clear one.** Many decisions include issues ranging from strategic to tactical. Nevertheless, there is a basic distinction between the two levels of decision:

(a) The decision to launch a new brand of calorie-controlled frozen foods is a strategic plan (business strategy), but the choice of ingredients for the frozen meals involves a management control decision.

(b) A decision that the market share for a product should be 25% is a strategic plan (competitive strategy), but the selection of a sales price of $2 per unit, supported by other marketing decisions about sales promotion and direct sales effort to achieve the required market share, would be a series of management control decisions.

Management control tends to be carried out in a series of **regular** planning and comparison procedures (annually, monthly, weekly). For example, a budget is usually prepared annually and control reports issued every month or four weeks. **Strategic planning**, in contrast, might be **irregular** and occur when opportunities arise or are identified.

4 Management accounting information for operational control

FAST FORWARD

Operational control, the lowest tier in Anthony's hierarchy, is concerned with assuring that specific tasks are carried out effectively and efficiently.

The third and lowest tier in Anthony's hierarchy of decision making consists of operational control decisions. Just as 'management control' plans are set within the guidelines of strategic plans, so too are 'operational control' plans set within the guidelines of both strategic planning and management control.

4.1 Example: Link between strategic plans and operational/management control decisions

(a) Senior management may decide that the company should increase sales by 5% per annum for at least five years – **a strategic plan.**

(b) The sales director and senior sales managers will make plans to increase sales by 5% in the next year, with some provisional planning for future years. This involves planning direct sales resources, advertising, sales promotion and so on. Sales quotas are assigned to each sales territory – **a tactical management control decision**.

(c) The manager of a sales territory specifies the weekly sales targets for each sales representative. This is an **operational control decision:** individuals are given tasks which they are expected to achieve.

Operational control decisions are therefore much **more narrowly focused** and have a **shorter time frame** than tactical or strategic decisions.

4.2 Operational control activities

Although we have used an example of selling tasks to describe operational control, it is important to remember that this level of decision making **occurs in all aspects of an organisation's activities**, even when the activities cannot be scheduled nor properly estimated because they are non-standard activities (such as repair work, answering customer complaints).

The scheduling of **unexpected or 'ad hoc' work** must be done at **short notice**, which is a feature of much operational decision making. In the repairs department, for example, routine preventive maintenance can be scheduled, but breakdowns occur unexpectedly and repair work must be scheduled and controlled 'on the spot' by a repairs department supervisor.

Operational control activities can also be described as **short-term non-strategic activities.**

4.3 Information requirements

(a) **Operational information** is information which is **needed for the conduct of day-to-day implementation of plans**.

(b) It will include much **'transaction data'** such as data about customer orders, purchase orders, cash receipts and payments and is likely to have an **endogenous source**.

(c) Operating information must usually be **consolidated into totals** in management reports before it can be used to prepare management control information.

(d) The amount of **detail** provided in information is likely to **vary with the purpose for which it is needed**, and operational information is likely to go into much more detail than tactical information, which in turn will be more detailed than strategic information.

(e) Whereas tactical information for management control is often expressed in money terms, operational information, although quantitative, is more often **expressed in terms of units, hours, quantities of material and so on.**

5 Management information systems

You should be aware of the main characteristics of transaction processing systems, management information systems, executive information systems and enterprise resource planning systems.

5.1 Transaction processing systems

FAST FORWARD

Transaction processing systems (TPS) collect, store, modify and retrieve the transactions of an organisation.

A **transaction** is an event that generates or modifies data that is eventually stored on an information system.

Transaction processing systems (TPS) collect, store, modify and retrieve the transactions of an organisation.

The four important characteristics of a TPS are as follows.

(a) **Controlled processing**. The processing must support an organisation's operations.

(b) **Inflexibility**. A TPS wants every transaction processed in the same way regardless of user or time. If it were flexible there would be too many opportunities for non-standard operations.

(c) **Rapid response**. Fast performance is critical. Input must become output in seconds so customers don't wait.

(d) **Reliability**. Organisations rely heavily on transaction processing systems with failure potentially stopping business. Back-up and recovery procedures must be quick and accurate.

5.1.1 Properties of a TPS

The components of a TPS include hardware, software and people. People in a TPS can be divided into three categories – users, participants and people from the environment.

The **users** are employees of the company who own the TPS. The users will not alter data themselves, but will use the TPS to provide inputs for other information systems such as inventory control.

Participants are direct users of the system. They are the people who enter the data. Participants include data entry operators, customer service staff and people working at checkouts.

People from the environment are people who sometimes require the services of a TPS as they enter transactions and validate data, such as customers withdrawing money from an ATM.

5.1.2 Types of TPS

Batch transaction processing (BTP) collects transaction data as a group and processes it later, after a time delay, as batches of identical data.

An example of BTP is cheque clearance. A cheque is a written order asking the bank to pay an amount of money to the payee. The payee cannot withdraw the money until the cheque is cleared. This involves checking that the payer has enough money in their account to cover the cheque. It usually takes three working days – cheques are cleared in a group during a quiet period of the day.

Real time transaction processing (RTTP) is the immediate processing of data. It involves using a terminal or workstation to enter data and display results and provides instant confirmation. A large number of users can perform transactions simultaneously but access to a central online database is required.

An example of an RTTP system is a reservation system involved in setting aside a service or product for the customer to use at a future time. Such systems are commonly used for flight or train bookings and hotel reservations and require an acceptable response time as transactions are made in the presence of customers.

5.2 Management information systems

Management information systems (MIS) convert data from mainly internal sources into information (eg summary reports, exception reports). This information enables managers to make timely and effective decisions for planning, directing and controlling the activities for which they are responsible.

Key term

Management information systems (MIS) generate information for monitoring performance (eg productivity information) and maintaining co-ordination (eg between purchasing and accounts payable).

MIS extract, process and summarise data from the TPS and provide periodic (weekly, monthly, quarterly) reports to managers.

Today MIS are becoming more flexible by providing access to information whenever needed, rather than pre-specified reports on a periodic basis. Users can often generate more customised reports by selecting subsets of data (such as listing the products with 2 per cent increase in sales over the past month), using different sorting options (by sales region, by salesperson, by highest volume of sales) and different display choices (graphical, tabular).

MIS have the following characteristics:

- Support structured decisions at operational and management control levels.
- Designed to report on existing operations.
- Have little analytical capability.
- Relatively inflexible.
- Have an internal focus.

5.3 Executive information systems

Executive information systems (EIS) draw data from the MIS and allow communication with external sources of information.

Key term

Executive information systems (EIS) provide a generalised computing and communication environment to senior managers to support strategic decisions.

Executive Information Systems draw data from the MIS and allow communication with **external sources** of information. EIS are designed to facilitate senior managers' access to information quickly and effectively. They have

- menu driven user friendly interfaces.
- interactive graphics to help visualisation of the situation.
- communication capabilities linking the executive to external databases.

An EIS summarises and tracks **strategically critical information** from the MIS and includes data from external sources e.g. competitors, legislation and databases such as Reuters.

A good way to think about an EIS is to imagine the senior management team in an aircraft cockpit, with the instrument panel showing them the status of all the key business activities. EIS typically involve lots of data analysis and modelling tools such as **what-if analysis** to help **strategic decision making**.

A model of a typical EIS is shown below:

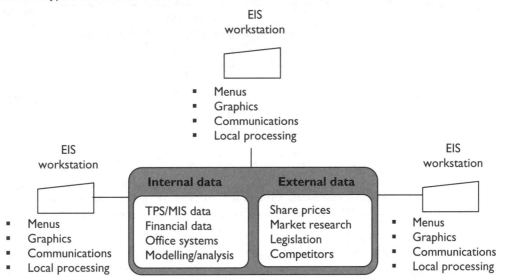

5.4 Enterprise resource planning systems

FAST FORWARD

Executive resource planning systems (ERP systems) are modular software packages designed to integrate the key processes in an orgnanisation so that a single system can serve the information needs of all functional areas.

Most organisations across the world have realised that in a rapidly changing environment, it is impossible to create and maintain a custom-designed software package which will cater to all their requirements and also be completely up-to-date. Realising the requirement of user organisations some of the leading software companies have designed **Enterprise resource planning** software which will offer an integrated software solution to all the functions of an organisation.

ERP systems are large-scale information systems that impact an organisation's accounting information systems . These systems permeate all aspects of the organisation. A key element necessary for the ERP to provide business analysis is the data warehouse. This is a database designed for quick search, retrieval, query, and so on.

Key term

Executive resource planning systems (ERP systems) are modular software packages designed to integrate the key processes in an organisation so that a single system can serve the information needs of all functional areas.

ERP systems primarily support business operations – those activities in an organisation that support the selling process, including order processing, manufacturing, distribution, planning, customer service, human resources, finance and purchasing. ERP systems are function-rich, and typically cover all of these activities – the principal benefit being that the same data can easily be shared between different departments.

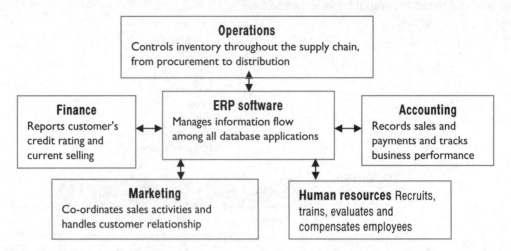

This **integration** is accomplished through a database shared by all the application programs. For example, when a customer service representative takes a sales order it is entered in the common database and it automatically updates the manufacturing backlog, the price, the credit system and the shipping schedule.

ERP systems work in **real-time**, meaning that the **exact status** of everything is always available. Further, many of these systems are global. Since they can be deployed at sites around the world, they can work in **multiple languages and currencies**. When they are, you can immediately see, for example, exactly how much of a particular part is on-hand at the warehouse in Japan and what its value is in yen or dollars.

5.4.1 Example: ERP

Say you are running a bicycle shop. Once you make a sale, you enter the order on the ERP system. The system then updates the inventory of bicycles in the shop, incorporates the sale into the financial ledgers, prints out an invoice, and can prompt you to purchase more bikes to replace the ones that you have sold. The ERP system can also handle repair orders and manage the spare parts inventory. It can also provide automated tools to help you forecast future sales and to plan activities over the next few weeks. There may also be data query tools present to enable sophisticated management reports and graphs to be generated. In addition, the system may handle the return of defective items from unhappy customers, the sending out of regular account statements to customers, and the management of payments to suppliers.

ERP systems can assist with the scheduling and deployment of all sorts of resources, physical, monetary and human. A water company might use their ERP system to schedule a customer repair job, deploy staff to the job, verify that it got done, and subsequently bill the customer. An oil company might use it ensure that their tankers are loaded, that a shipping itinerary is prepared and completed on schedule, and that all the equipment and people required for loading and unloading the cargo in each port are present at the right times. A bus company might use their system to manage customer bookings, record receipts and plan preventative maintenance activities for their fleet.

5.4.2 Benefits of ERP

The benefits that may be realised from a successfully-implemented ERP project include:

(a) Allowing **access** to the system to any individual with a terminal linked to the system's central server.

(b) **Decision support features**, to assist management with decision-making.

(c) In many cases, extranet **links to the major suppliers and customers**, with electronic data interchange facilities for the automated transmission of documentation such as purchase orders and invoices.

(d) A lot of inefficiencies in the way things are done can be removed. The company can adopt so-called **'best practices'** – a cookbook of how similar activities are performed in world-class companies.

(e) A company can **restructure its processes**, so that different functions (such as accounting, shipping and manufacturing) work more closely together to get products produced.

(f)   An organisation can align itself to a single plan, so that all activities, all across the world, are smoothly **co-ordinated**.

(g)   Information and work practices can be **standardised**, so that the terminology used is similar, no matter where you work in the company.

(h)   A company could do a lot more work for a lot more customers without needing to employ so many people.

6 Open and closed systems

FAST FORWARD

Systems can be **open** or **closed**.

The word **system** is impossible to define satisfactorily (the tax 'system', the respiratory 'system', the class 'system'). Basically it means **something that connects things up.**

6.1 Closed systems

Key term

A **closed system** is isolated and shut off from the environment. Information is not received from or provided to the environment.

Closed systems are seldom, if ever, found in naturally occurring situations. A typical example of a closed system would be a chemical reaction that takes place under controlled conditions within a laboratory. Closed systems can be created to **eliminate external factors** and then used to **investigate the relationship between known variables** in an experiment.

All social systems have some interaction with the environment and so cannot be closed systems. A commercial organisation, for example, could not operate as a closed system as it would be unable to react to the external environment and so would not be commercially or economically viable.

6.2 Open systems

Key term

An **open system** is connected to and interacts with the environment and is influenced by it.

An open system **accepts inputs from its surroundings, processes the inputs in some manner and then produces an output.** The **input parameters** can be **foreseen** or be **unpredictable.** Similarly, **outputs** can either be **predicted** or **unforeseen.** For example, consider a metal smelting works. Predictable inputs would include items like the raw materials and coal while the predictable outputs would be ash, smoke and the smelted metal. If the raw material to be smelted became contaminated in some way, it is likely that an undesirable product would be produced. These are examples of unforeseen inputs and outputs.

All social systems, including **business organisations,** are **open systems**. For example, a business is a system where management decisions are influenced by or have an influence on suppliers, customers, competitors, the government and society as a whole. Employees are obviously influenced by what they do in their job, but as members of society at large they are also part of the external environment, just as their views and opinions expressed within the business are often a reflection of their opinions as members of society at large.

6.3 Open and closed systems and performance management

Systems are rarely either open or closed, but open to some influences and closed to others. Organisations must carefully choose the **form of management accounting system** based on the respective scenario.

The chemical laboratory could use a **closed system.** Here, performance is largely influenced by an **internally created environment** and external factors would not affect the output or result of the activity.

However, if an organisation's performance is influenced by **environmental factors**, it should operate an open system that accepts input from the external factors and examines their impact on performance output.

The advantages of an open system are:

(a) It encourages strong **communication**, which helps an organisation to operate efficiently and become effective.

(b) It adapts to the **changing environment** and there is scope for absorbing new pieces of information into the system.

(c) It highlights the **inter-dependencies** of different operations and processes within a business and the environment in which it operates.

(d) It helps business leaders and managers to focus on the **external factors** that shape behaviours and patterns within the organisation.

Management should consider the potential limitations of open systems:

(a) **Non-linear relationships** could exist among variables. A small change in one variable could cause a large change in another and affect the business result in a positive or negative way.

(b) It could prove **difficult to measure** the success of the system, specifically metrics relating to input, processing and output as well as the interrelationship among them.

Question

Open and closed systems

Run-Smart Co manufactures sports clothing for professional athletes. Products are designed to prevent injury and aid the post-exercise recovery process. The company regularly seeks feedback from athletes regarding the effectiveness of products and recommendations to take forward.

Required
Explain which kind of marketing system the organisation has.

Answer

Run-Smart Co operates an open system. The company interacts with its environment. It takes feedback from its customers about the effectiveness of its products and accordingly advises the product design department about customer preferences. Based on customer feedback, the company may decide to alter product design and specification.

Chapter Roundup

- **Strategic planning** is the process of deciding on objectives for the organisation, on changes in these objectives, on the resources to attain these objectives, and on the policies that are to govern the acquisition, use and disposition of these resources.

- **Management control** is the process by which managers assure that resources are obtained and used effectively and efficiently in the accomplishment of the organisation's objectives. It is sometimes called **tactics** or **tactical planning**.

- **Operational control** (or **operational planning**) is the process of assuring that specific tasks are carried out effectively and efficiently.

- **Management accounting information** can be used to support strategic planning, control and decision making. Strategic management accounting differs from traditional management accounting because it has an **external** orientation and a **future** orientation.

- **Management control** is at the level below strategic planning in Anthony's decision-making hierarchy and is concerned with decisions about the efficient and effective use of resources to achieve objectives.

- **Operational control**, the lowest tier in Anthony's hierarchy, is concerned with assuring that specific tasks are carried out effectively and efficiently.

- **Transaction processing systems** (TPS) collect, store, modify and retrieve the transactions of an organisation.

- **Management information systems** (MIS) convert data from mainly internal sources into information (eg summary reports, exception reports). This information enables managers to make timely and effective decisions for planning, directing and controlling the activities for which they are responsible.

- **Executive information systems** (EIS) draw data from the MIS and allow communication with external sources of information.

- **Executive resource planning systems** (ERP systems) are modular software packages designed to integrate the key processes in an organisation so that a single system can serve the information needs of all functional areas.

- Systems can be **open** or **closed**.

1 Which of the following is **not** a feature of strategic management accounting?

    A   External orientation

    B   Historic focus

    C   Non-financial orientation

    D   Inputs from many areas of a business

2 What can strategic management accounting provide information or guidance about to a business?

3 Which of the following are characteristics of a transaction processing system?

    (a)   Reliability

    (b)   Controlled processing

    (c)   Inflexibility

    (d)   Rapid response

4 *Match the terms to the correct definitions*

Terms

    (a)   Transaction processing systems

    (b)   Executive information systems

    (c)   Executive resource planning systems

Definitions

    1   Draw data from the MIS and allow communication with external sources of information

    2   Collect, store modify and retrieve the transactions of an organisation

    3   Modular software packages designed to integrate the key processes in an organisation

5 Open systems are seldom, if ever, found in naturally occurring situations. **True/False?**

6 Interaction with other systems or the outside environment is a feature of open systems. **True/False?**

Answers to Quick Quiz

1   B   Strategic management accounting is forward-looking, by contrast to traditional management accounting which is a backward-looking process.

2   You could list a number of suggestions here. The Study Text gives examples but you may have others. Our list includes:

   (a)   **Competitors' costs**
   (b)   **Financial effect of competitor response**
   (c)   **Product profitability**
   (d)   **Customer profitability**
   (e)   **Pricing decisions**
   (f)   The **value of market share**
   (g)   **Capacity expansion**
   (h)   Decisions to **enter** or **leave** a **business area**
   (i)   **Brand values**
   (j)   **Shareholder wealth**
   (k)   **Cash flow**
   (l)   Effect of **acquisitions** and **mergers**
   (m)   Introduction of **new technology**

3   All of them

4   (a) 2; (b) 1; (c) 3

5   False. It is closed systems that are seldom found.

6   True

Now try the question below from the Practice Question Bank

Number	Level	Marks	Time
Q16	Examination	10	18 mins

Sources of
management
information and
management reports

Topic list	Syllabus reference
1 Sources of management accounting information	D2 (a)
2 Information for control purposes	D2 (b)
3 Costs of information	D2 (c),(d)
4 Costs, benefits and limitations of external information	D2 (e)
5 Controls over generating and distributing internal information	D3 (a)
6 Security and confidential information	D3 (b)

Introduction

In this chapter we look at **internal and external sources of management information** including financial accounting records, government agencies and consumer panels.

We also consider the costs, benefits and limitations of external information and the principal controls and procedures involved in generating and distributing information.

Study guide

		Intellectual level
D2	**Sources of management information**	
(a)	Identify and discuss the principal internal and external sources of management accounting information	2
(b)	Demonstrate how these principal sources of information might be used for control purposes	2
(c)	Identify and discuss the direct data capture and process costs of management accounting information	2
(d)	Identify and discuss the indirect costs of producing information	2
(e)	Discuss the limitations of using externally generated information	2
D3	**Management reports**	
(a)	Discuss the principal controls required in generating and distributing internal information.	2
(b)	Discuss the procedures that may be necessary to ensure security of highly confidential information that is not for external consumption.	2

Exam guide

The topics covered in this chapter could form part of a scenario question in the exam or could feature as a multiple choice question in Section A. Ensure that you are able to **identify** and **discuss** internal and external sources of management accounting information as well as potential controls and security procedures to safeguard data.

One of the competences you require to fulfil performance objective 12 of the PER is collecting and collating data from information systems. This data forms reports to management and is key for control and monitoring performance. In this chapter we look at information sources and procedures that may be necessary to ensure security of highly confidential information.

1 Sources of management accounting information

FAST FORWARD

Internal sources of **information** include the financial accounting records and other systems closely tied to the accounting system.

Capturing data/information from inside the organisation involves the following:

(a) A **system for collecting or measuring transactions data** – eg sales, purchases, inventory, revenue and so on – which sets out procedures for **what** data is collected, **how frequently**, **by whom** and by **what methods,** and how it is **processed,** and **filed** or **communicated.**

(b) **Informal communication** of information between managers and staff (eg, by word-of-mouth or at meetings).

(c) **Communication between managers.**

1.1 Sources of monetary and non-monetary information

1.1.1 The financial accounting records

You are by now very familiar with the idea of a system of sales ledgers and purchase ledgers, general ledgers, cash books and so on. These records provide a **history of an organisation's monetary transactions**.

Some of this information is of great value outside the accounts department – most obviously, for example, sales information for the marketing function. Other information, like cheque numbers, is of purely administrative value within the accounts department.

You will also be aware that to maintain the integrity of its financial accounting records, an organisation of any size will have systems for and **controls over transactions**. These also give rise to valuable information.

An inventory control system is the classic example: besides actually recording the monetary value of purchases and inventory in hand for external financial reporting purposes, the system will include purchase orders, goods received notes, goods returned notes and so on, and these can be analysed to provide management information about **speed** of delivery, say, or the **quality** of supplies.

1.1.2 Other internal sources

Much information that is not strictly part of the financial accounting records nevertheless is closely tied in to the accounting system:

(a) Information about personnel will be linked to the **payroll** system. Additional information may be obtained from this source if, say, a project is being costed and it is necessary to ascertain the availability and rate of pay of different levels of staff.

(b) Much information will be produced by a **production** department about machine capacity, movement of materials and work in progress, set up times, maintenance requirements and so on.

(c) Many service businesses – notably accountants and solicitors – need to keep detailed records of the **time** spent on various activities, both to justify fees to clients and to assess the efficiency of operations.

Staff themselves are one of the primary sources of internal information. Information may be obtained either **informally** in the course of day-to-day business or **formally** through **meetings, interviews** or **questionnaires**.

Question	Sources of information

Think of at least one piece of non-monetary information that a management accountant might obtain from the following sources in order to make a decision about a new product.

(a) Marketing manager
(b) Vehicle fleet supervisor
(c) Premises manager
(d) Public relations officer
(e) Head of research

1.2 External sources of information

FAST FORWARD

External information tends to be more relevant to strategic and tactical decisions than to operational decisions. (Benchmarking is an exception.)

Capturing information from outside the organisation might be carried out formally and entrusted to particular individuals, or might be 'informal'.

1.3 Formal collection of data from outside sources

FAST FORWARD

There are many **sources** of **external information**.

(a)   A company's **tax specialists** will be expected to gather information about changes in tax law and how this will affect the company.

(b)   Obtaining information about any new legislation on health and safety at work, or employment regulations, must be the responsibility of a particular person – for example the company's **legal expert** or **company secretary** – who must then pass on the information to other managers affected by it.

(c)   Research and development work often relies on information about other R & D work being done by another company or by government institutions. An **R & D official** might be made responsible for finding out about R & D work outside the company.

(d)   **Marketing managers** need to know about the opinions and buying attitudes of potential customers. To obtain this information, they might carry out market research exercises.

Informal gathering of information from the environment **goes on all the time, consciously or unconsciously**, because the employees of an organisation learn **what is going on in the world around** them – perhaps from the media, meetings with business associates or the trade press.

Organisations hold external information such as invoices, advertisements and so on **from customers and suppliers**. But there are many occasions when an active search outside the organisation is necessary.

1.4 Specific external sources

FAST FORWARD

Secondary data, such as government statistics or data provided by on-line databases, is not collected by or for the user. **Primary data** – more expensive than secondary data – is more tailored to the user's exact needs. Market research is an example.

1.4.1 Directories

Examples (of business directories) include the following (although there are many others).

(a)   Kompass Register (Kompass)
(b)   Who owns Whom (Dun and Bradstreet)
(c)   Key British Enterprises (Dun and Bradstreet)

1.4.2 Associations

There are associations in almost every field of business and leisure activity, and ACCA itself is an organisation. Associations collect and publish data for their members that can be of great interest to other users. For example, although the services of the Road Haulage Association (RHA) are geared towards transport businesses, their analysis of fuel prices rises could be useful to all motorists.

1.4.3 Government agencies

The government is a major source of economic information and information about industry and population trends. Examples of UK government publications are as follows. Most of these are available online and can be downloaded for free.

(a)   **National Statistics**, divided into 12 separate themes such as economy, health and labour

(b)   The **Digest of UK Energy Statistics** (published annually)

(c) **Housing and Construction Statistics** (published quarterly)

(d) **Financial Statistics** (monthly)

(e) **Economic Trends** now published with **Labour Market Trends** in the **Economic Labour Market Review**

(f) **Public Sector Employment Trends** (annual) gives details of employment in the public sector in the UK

(g) **A variety of publications on the Department for Business, Innovation and Skills website** give data on industrial and commercial trends at home and overseas

(h) **Social Trends** (annual)

Official statistics are also published by other government bodies such as the European Union, the United Nations and local authorities.

1.4.4 Other published sources

This group includes all other publications, including some **digests** and **pocket books** and **periodicals** (often available in the public libraries).

1.4.5 Syndicated services

The sources of secondary data we have looked at so far have generally been **free** because they are **in the public domain**. Inexpensiveness is an advantage that can be offset by the fact that the information is **unspecific** and needs **considerable analysis** before being useable. A middle step between adapting secondary data and commissioning primary research is the **purchase of data collected by market research companies**. The data tend to be expensive but less costly than primary research.

1.4.6 Consumer panels

A form of continuous research which result in secondary data often bought in by marketers is that generated by **consumer panels**. These constitute a representative sample of individuals and households whose buying activity in a defined area is monitored either continuously (every day, with results aggregated) or at regular intervals, **over a period of time**. There are panels set up to monitor purchases of groceries, consumer durables, cars, baby products and many others.

1.5 Information from customers

Customers can provide useful information.

(a) Firms send out satisfaction questionnaires and market research.
(b) Customer comments and complaints sent voluntarily can suggest improvements.

1.6 Information from suppliers

Supplier information comes in several categories.

Information	Comment
'Bid' information	A supplier pitching for a product will detail products, services and prices. This is before a deal is done.
Operational information	If a firm has placed a particular job or contract with a supplier, the supplier may provide details of the stages in the manufacturing process, eg the delivery time.
Pricing information	Component prices vary from industry to industry; some are volatile.
Technology	Technological developments in the supplier's industry can affect the type of input components, their cost and their availability.

1.7 The Internet

FAST FORWARD

The **Internet** increases the richness of external data and reduces the cost of searching for it.

Key term

The **Internet** is a global network connecting millions of computers.

The Internet offers efficient, fast and cost effective **email**, and massive information **search and retrieval facilities**. There is a great deal of financial information available and users can also **access publications** and news releases issued by the Treasury and other Government departments.

Businesses are also using it to **provide information (cheaply) about their own products and services** and to conduct **research** into their competitors' activities.

The Internet offers a **speedy** and **impersonal** way of getting to know the basics (or even the details) of the services that a company provides.

The Internet is commonly used to **access information about suppliers**.

(a) A firm can visit a supplier's website for details of products and services.

(b) The user can search a number of websites through a browser. Note that the Internet may not contain every supplier; arguably it should not be relied upon as the sole source.

(c) A number of business-to-business sites have been opened. Participating members offer their services, and can offer quotes. A lot of the communication search problem is avoided.

 Case Study

papiNet.org is a global community involved in supply chain processes for the paper and printing industries. It supports the use of papiNet.xml, a standard language in which suppliers and customers can exchange information about paper.

Significance

- Printers have a wider opportunity to source paper from suppliers all over the world.
- The lead-time between finding information and obtaining a quote is much reduced, leading to quicker decision making.
- Customers (publishers) can have a better idea of conditions and trends in the market.
- This information is now much cheaper to obtain.

1.8 Database information

A **management information system** or **database** should provide managers with a **useful flow** of **relevant information** which is **easy to use** and **easy to access**. Information is an important corporate resource. Managed and used effectively it can provide considerable competitive advantage and so it is a worthwhile investment.

It is now possible to access large volumes of generally available information through databases held by public bodies and businesses.

(a) Some **newspapers** offer computerised access to old editions, with search facilities looking for information on particular companies or issues. FTPROFILE, for example, provides on-line business information.

(b) **Public databases** are also available for inspection.

Dun and Bradstreet provide general business information. **AC Nielsen** operate on-line information regarding products and market share.

Developments in information technology allow businesses to have access to the databases of **external organisations**. Reuters, for example, provides an on-line information system about money market interest rates and foreign exchange rates to firms involved in money market and foreign exchange dealings, and to the treasury departments of a large number of companies. The growing adoption of technology at **point of sale** provides a potentially invaluable source of data to both retailer and manufacturer.

Case Study

CACI is a company which provides market analysis, information systems and other data products to clients. It advertises itself as 'the winning combination of marketing and technology'.

As an illustration of the information available to the marketing manager through today's technology, here is an overview of some of their products.

Paycheck	This provides income data for all 1.6 million individual post codes across the UK. This enables companies to see how mean income distribution varies from area to area
People* UK	This is a mix of geodemographics, life stage and lifestyle data. It is person rather than household specific and is designed for those companies requiring highly targeted campaigns
iConnect	Allows the marketer to communicate with online potential customers
Channel Choice	Provides a detailed picture of channel preference in the UK. How customers manage and arrange financial services products
StreetValue	A residential property price database based on postcode with over 9 million records
Acorn	This stands for A Classification of Residential Neighbourhoods, and has been used to profile residential neighbourhoods by post code since 1976. It has recently been updated to reflect demographic shifts such as increased car ownership and people working from home. ACORN classifies people in any trading area or on any customer database into 56 types
GreenACORN	Classifies and groups consumers' attitudes and behaviours to green issues
Ocean	This database contains 40 million names and addresses in the UK. It offers actual and modelled lifestyle data, consumer classifications, email addresses and phone numbers

1.8.1 On-line databases

Most external databases are online databases, which are very large computer files of information, supplied by **database providers** and managed by **'host'** companies whose business revenue is generated through charges made to **users**. Access to such databases is open to anyone prepared to pay, and who is equipped with a PC plus internet access and communication software. These days there are an increasing number of companies offering free Internet access. Most databases can be accessed around the clock.

1.9 Data warehouses

A **data warehouse** contains **data from a range of internal** (for instance sales order processing system, nominal ledger) **and external sources**. One reason for including individual transaction data in a data warehouse is that the user can drill-down to access transaction-level detail if necessary. Data is increasingly obtained from newer channels such as customer care systems, outside agencies or Web sites.

The warehouse provides a coherent **set of information** to be **used across the organisation** for management **analysis** and **decision making**. The reporting and query tools available within the warehouse should facilitate management reporting and analysis. This analysis can be enhanced through using **data mining** software to identify trends and patterns in the data.

2 Information for control purposes

Much control is achieved through the **feedback** of internal information.

Control is dependent on the **receipt and processing of information**, both to plan in the first place and to compare actual results against the plan, so as to judge what control measures are needed.

Plans will be based on an **awareness of the environment** (from externally-sourced information) and on the **current performance of the organisation** (based on internal information such as, for example, sales volumes, costs and so on).

Control is achieved through **feedback** – information about actual results produced from within the organisation (that is internal information) such as variance control reports for the purpose of helping management with control decisions.

The sources of information outlined earlier in the chapter are used to supply **management with data for control**.

For instance **payroll records** give information on the total cost of staff and a breakdown into cost by function, role, bonuses, taxes and so on which can show management how different cost areas are performing. As payroll is often a large cost and to some extent discretionary or variable it is important to monitor and control.

Equally, information on **wage payments** will also be relevant to an organisation's cash flow planning. As far as possible, organisations like to keep their cash balances within certain limits. So, by knowing the amount and timing of wages and salary payments the organisation can make any adjustments to ensure cash balances remain within the desire limits.

Information about **inventory** levels can also be instructive. For example, some lines of inventory may be slow moving, but management will need to establish why this is. Has a competitor introduced a rival product, or reduced its prices? Have there been any quality issues with the product which have damaged its reputation in the market place? Is the product in a long-term decline and should production of it be discontinued? In this respect, information about quantities of a product sold compared to quantities produced could also be very useful. For example, if a product is selling very well, production may need to be increased so that demand can be satisfied and any stock-outs avoided.

Customer data is vital in any business that strives to focus on customers. Thus data on buying habits, where customers shop, what they buy and who the main customers are all gives feedback for control purposes.

Equally, data from customer sales accounts can provide useful information on how customer debts are aged. A report on the ageing of debt can provide management with information on how successful its receivables control policy is. Management's response will be different if half of the customer debt has been outstanding for more than say, 60 days, compared with only 5% of the debt being outstanding for more than 60 days.

External data is useful for benchmarking provided the correct or appropriate benchmarks are selected.

3 Costs of information

Be aware of the **cost** of inefficient use of information.

The costs to an organisation of the collection, processing and production of internal information can be divided into three types. These are direct data capture costs, process costs, and indirect costs of producing internal information.

Cost	Examples
Direct data capture	• Use of bar coding and scanners (eg, in retailing and manufacturing) • Employee time spent filling in timesheets • Secretary time spent taking minutes at a meeting
Processing	• Payroll department time spent processing and analysing personnel costs • Time for personnel to input data (eg, in relation to production) on to the MIS
Inefficient use of information	• Information collected but not needed • Information stored long after it is needed • Information disseminated more widely than necessary • Collection of the same information by more than one method • Duplication of information

4 Costs, benefits and limitations of external information

There are specific **costs** not only in obtaining data, but also in maintaining the infrastructure supporting data collection and distribution.

4.1 Costs

Identifying the costs of obtaining external data is not difficult. Effectively there are five types of cost.

Cost	Examples
Direct search costs	• Cost of a marketing research survey (these can be considerable) • Subscriptions to online databases • Subscriptions to magazines, services • Download fees
Indirect access costs	• Management and employee time spent finding useful information • Wasted management and employee time on unsuccessful searches for information • Spurious accuracy / redundancy • Wasted management and employee time on excessive searching • Wasted time on trying to find spurious accuracy
Management costs	• Recording, processing and dissemination of external information • Wasted time due to information overload • Wasted time on excessive processing
Infrastructure costs	• Installation and maintenance of computer networks, servers, landlines etc to facilitate Internet searching and internal electronic communication
Time-theft	• Wasted time caused by abuse of Internet and e-mail access facilities • Lost time • Cost of monitoring and disciplinary procedures • Information overload

As can be seen from the earlier case example, the **Internet** can significantly reduce search time and search cost. More information can be had for less money.

4.2 Benefits and limitations of external data

The benefits can be quantified in the following terms:

(a) The quality of **decisions** that the data has influenced

(b) **Risk / uncertainties** avoided by having the data

(c) The organisation's ability to **respond** appropriately to the environment or to **improve** its performance

One of the principal **limitations** of external data is that its **quality** cannot be guaranteed. Its **quality** will depend on the following characteristics:

(a) The **producers** of the data. (They may have an axe to grind; trade associations may not include data which runs counter to the interests of its members.)

(b) The **reason for the data** being collected in the first place

(c) The **collection method**. (Random samples with a poor response rate are particularly questionable.)

(d) The **age** of the data. (Government statistics and information based on them are often relatively dated, though information technology has speeded up the process.)

(e) **How parameters were defined**. (For instance, the definition of family used by some researchers could well be very different to that used by others.)

Using poor quality external data can have disastrous consequences: projects may proceed on the basis of overstated demand levels; opportunities may not be grasped because data is out of date and does not show the true state of the market.

4.2.1 Advantages arising from the use of secondary (as opposed to primary) data

(a) The data may solve the problem without the need for any primary research: **time and money is thereby saved**.

(b) **Cost savings** can be substantial because secondary data sources are a great deal **cheaper** than those for primary research.

(c) **Secondary data**, while not necessarily fulfilling all the needs of the business, can be of great use:

    (i) **Setting the parameters**, defining a hypothesis, highlighting variables, in other words, helping to focus on the central problem.

    (ii) **Providing guidance**, by showing past methods of research and so on, for primary data collection.

    (iii) **Helping to assimilate the primary research** with past research, highlighting trends and the like.

    (iv) **Defining sampling parameters** (target populations, variables and so on).

4.2.2 Disadvantages to the use of secondary data

(a) **Relevance**. The data may not be relevant to the research objectives in terms of the data content itself, classifications used or units of measurement.

(b) **Cost**. Although secondary data is usually cheaper than primary data, some specialist reports can cost large amounts of money. A cost benefit analysis will determine whether such secondary data should be used or whether primary research would be more economical.

(c) **Availability**. Secondary data may not exist in the specific product or market area.

(d) **Bias**. The secondary data may be biased, depending on who originally carried it out and for what purpose. Attempts should be made to obtain the most original source of the data, to assess it for such bias.

(e) **Accuracy**. The accuracy of the data should be questioned.

The golden rule when using secondary data is **use only meaningful data**. It is obviously sensible to begin with internal sources and a firm with a good management information system should be able to provide a great deal of data. External information should be consulted in order of ease and speed of access.

BPP
LEARNING MEDIA

5 Controls over generating and distributing internal information

FAST FORWARD

> **Controls** need to be in place over the generation of internal information in routine and ad-hoc reports.

One of the competencies you require to fulfil performance objective 6 of the PER is the ability to protect software and data from security risks such as theft, viruses or unauthorised access. You can apply the knowledge you obtain from this section to help to demonstrate this competence.

5.1 Controls over generating internal information in routine reports

(a) Carry out a **cost/benefit analysis.** How **easy** is the report to prepare **compared** with the **usefulness** of the decisions that can be taken as a result of its production? The cost of preparing the report will in part be determined by **who** is preparing it. The cost can be reduced if its preparation can be **delegated** by a director to a junior member of staff.

(b) A **trial** preparation process should be carried out and a **prototype** prepared. Users should be asked to confirm that their requirements will be met.

(c) A **consistent** format and consistent definitions should be used to ensure that reporting is **accurate** and the chance of misinterpretation is minimised. Standard **house styles** will ensure that time is not wasted by managers, staff and report writers on designing alternative layouts.

(d) The **originator** of the report should be clearly identified so that users' queries can be dealt with quickly.

(e) The report should set out clearly **limits to the action** that users **can take as a result** of the information in the report. This will ensure that the organisation's system of responsibilities is maintained.

(f) The **usefulness** of the report should be **assessed** on a periodic basis to ensure that its production is necessary.

5.2 Controls over generating internal information in ad hoc reports

(a) Carry out a **cost/benefit** analysis as above.
(b) Ensure that the required information **does not already exist** in another format.
(c) Brief the report writer so that the **relevant information only** is provided.
(d) Ensure that the **originator** is clearly identified.
(e) Ensure that report writers have access to the **most up-to-date information.**

5.3 Controls over distributing internal information

FAST FORWARD

> A **procedures manual** sets out controls over distributing internal information.

(a) **Procedures manual** (for standard reports)

    (i) Indicates what standard reports should be issued and when (eg budgetary control report for department X on a monthly basis)

    (ii) Sets out the format of standard reports

    (iii) Makes clear who should receive particular standard reports

    (iv) Indicates whether reports should be shredded (if confidential) or just binned

    (v) Makes clear what information should be regarded as highly confidential

(b) **Other controls**

(i) **Payroll and personnel information** should be kept in a **locked** cabinet or be protected by **password** access on a computer system.

(ii) All employees should be **contractually required not to divulge confidential information.**

(iii) The internal mail system should make use of **'private and confidential' stamps**.

(iv) An appropriate **e-mail policy** should be set up.

(1) E-mail is best suited to short messages rather than detailed operational problems.

(2) E-mail provides a relatively permanent means of communication, which may be undesirable for confidential/'off-the-record' exchanges.

(3) Staff may suffer from information overload.

(4) It is uncomfortable to read more than a full screen of information. Longer messages will either not be read properly or will be printed out (in which case they may just as well have been circulated in hard copy form).

(v) **Physical computer security**

Internal security: Management can regulate which staff members have access to different types of data. For instance, access to HR records may be restricted to members of the HR team by keeping these records on a separate server or database. In this way, only certain terminals may access servers with sensitive or confidential data stored on them.

External security: The organisation can also protect its data from external access by using **firewalls.**

A firewall is designed **to restrict access** to a network be selectively allowing or blocking inbound traffic to parts of an organisation's system. It examines message entering and exiting the system and blocks any not conforming to specified criteria. In this way, firewalls can be used to protect data and databases from being access by unauthorised people or terminals. For example, access to key servers could be restricted to a small number of terminals only.

5.4 If information is held on a server

(a) Controls over viruses and hacking

(b) Clearly understood policy on the use of e-mails and corporate IT

(c) Password system to restrict access to particular files

6 Security and confidential information

A number of procedures can be used to ensure the **security of highly confidential information that is not for external consumption:**

- Passwords
- Logical access systems
- Database controls
- Firewalls
- Personnel security planning
- Anti-virus and anti-spyware software

Disaffected employees have potential to do deliberate damage to valuable corporate data or systems, especially if the information system is networked, because they may have access to parts of the system that they are not really authorised to use.

If the organisation is linked to an external network, **people outside** the company (hackers) may also be able to get into the company's internal network, either to steal data or to damage the system.

Sony PlayStation

In April 2011, a hacker breached the security surrounding Sony's PlayStation system.

Reports at the time suggested that up to 77 million PlayStation users could have personal details, email addresses and credit card numbers stolen following the hacker getting into the company's systems and obtaining customer information. There were also suggestions that the breach could lead to the information of every PlayStation user who plays online video games being compromised.

Following the breach, Sony admitted that an 'illegal and unauthorised intrusion' had occurred, which resulted in the loss of a significant amount of personal information, which could potentially be used in identity theft scams.

Following the attack, Sony employed an independent security firm to conduct a thorough investigation into what happened, and it contacted all users to ensure them it had 'taken steps to enhance security and strengthen out network infrastructure by re-building our system to provide you with greater protection of your personal information.'

Various **procedures** are therefore necessary to **ensure the security of highly confidential information that is not for external consumption.**

6.1 Passwords

Passwords are a set of characters allocated to a person, terminal or facility which have to be keyed into the system before further access is permitted.

In order to access a system the user needs first to enter a string of characters. If what is entered matches a password issued to an authorised user or valid for that particular terminal, the system permits access. Otherwise the system **shuts down** and may **record the attempted unauthorised access.**

Keeping track of these attempts can alert managers to repeated efforts to break into the system; in these cases the culprits might be caught, particularly if there is an apparent pattern to their efforts.

The restriction of access to a system with passwords is effective and widely used but the widespread and growing use of PCs and networks is making physical isolation virtually impossible. The wider use of information systems requires that access to the system becomes equally widespread and easy. Requirements for system security must be balanced by the operational requirements for access: rigidly enforced isolation of the system may significantly reduce the value of the system.

6.2 Logical access systems

Whereas **physical access control (doors, locks and so on)** is concerned with the prevention of unauthorised persons **gaining access to the hardware**, **logical access control** is concerned with **preventing those who already have access to a terminal or a computer from gaining access to data or software.**

In a logical access system, data and software, or individual computer systems, will be **classified according to the sensitivity and confidentiality of data:**

(a) Thus payroll data or details of the draft corporate budget for the coming year may be perceived as highly sensitive and made available to identified individuals only.

(b) Other financial information may be made available to certain groups of staff only, for example members of the finance function or a certain grade of management.

(c) Other data may be unrestricted.

A logical access system performs three operations when access is requested:

(a) Identification of the user
(b) Authentication of user identity
(c) Check on user authority

6.3 Database controls

Databases present a particular problem for computer security. In theory, the database can be **accessed by large numbers of people**, and so the possibility of **alteration, unauthorised disclosure or fraud is so much greater than with application-specific files.**

It is possible to construct **complicated password systems**, and the system can be **programmed** to give a limited view of its contents to particular users or restrict the disclosure of certain types of information to particular times of day. It is possible to build a set of **privileges** into the system, so allowing authorised users with a particular password to access more information.

There are problems ensuring that individuals do not circumvent the database by means of **inference**, however. If you ask enough questions, you should be able to infer from the replies the information you are really seeking.

For example, the database forbids you to ask if John is employee Category A. However, if you know there are only three employee categories, A, B, and C, and there is no prohibition on asking about categories B and C, you can work out the members of category A by process of elimination (ie neither B, nor C, therefore A).

These so-called **inference controls** exist to make this difficult by **limiting the number of queries, or by controlling the overlap between questions.**

6.4 Firewalls

Systems can have firewalls to **prevent unauthorised access into company systems**. Firewalls can be implemented in both **hardware and software**, or a combination of both. Firewalls are frequently used to **prevent unauthorised Internet users from accessing private networks connected to the Internet, especially Intranets.** All messages entering or leaving the Intranet pass through the firewall, which examines each message and blocks those that do not meet specified security criteria.

As well as preventing unauthorised access onto company systems, firewalls can also be used to help protect a company's data from corruption by viruses.

6.5 Encryption

Information transmitted from one part of an organisation to another may be intercepted. Data can be encrypted (**scrambled**) in an attempt to make it **unintelligible to eavesdroppers.**

6.6 Other safety measures

Authentication is a technique for making sure that a message has come from an authorised sender.

Dial back security operates by requiring the person wanting access to the network to dial into it and identify themselves first. The system then dials the person back on their authorised number before allowing them access.

All attempted violations of security should be automatically **logged** and the log checked regularly. In a multi-user system, the terminal attempting the violation may be automatically disconnected.

6.7 Personal data

In recent years there has been a growing popular fear that **information about individuals which is stored on computer files** and processed by computer can be **misused**.

In particular, it is felt that an individual could easily be **harmed** by the existence of computerised data about himself which was **inaccurate** or **misleading** and which could be **transferred** to unauthorised third parties at high speed and little cost.

As a result most countries have introduced **legislation** designed to protect the individual. In the UK the current legislation is the Data Protection Act 1998.

6.8 Personnel security planning

Certain employees will always be placed in a position of trust, for example senior systems analysts, the database administrator and the computer security officer. With the growth of networks, almost all employees may be in a position to do damage to a computer system. A recent report claims that 80% of hacking is done by employees.

Although most employees are honest and well intentioned, it may be relatively easy for individuals to **compromise the security** of an organisation if they wish to do so. The following types of measure are therefore necessary.

(a) Careful recruitment
(b) Job rotation
(c) Supervision and observation by a superior
(d) Review of computer usage (eg via systems logs)
(e) Enforced vacations

The key is that **security should depend on the minimum possible number of personnel;** although this is a weakness, it is also a strength.

6.9 Anti-virus and anti-spyware software

The growth of the Internet has led to increased exposure to security risks. Two particular risks derive from exposure to **computer viruses** and to **spyware.**

Computer viruses typically arrive by email and are triggered when the user opens the email and an attachment. **The virus** is a self-replicating computer programme that **infiltrates and then damages a computer system.**

Spyware is a type of programme that **watches** what users do with their computer and then **sends that information** over the Internet to a third party. Customers of online bank accounts have experienced particular problems with spyware when their personal financial data has been captured by keylogging software.

Software has been developed to counteract these risks. **Anti-virus software** works to achieve this by

(a) **Scanning files** to look for known viruses
(b) **Identifying suspicious behaviour** from any computer programme that might indicate infection

Anti-spyware software combats spyware in two ways.

(a) Real-time protection which prevents the installation of spyware by **blocking software** and activities known to represent spyware
(b) **Detection** and **removal** of spyware by scanning software and removing files and entries that match known spyware

Chapter Roundup

- **Internal** sources of **information** include the financial accounting records and other systems closely tied to the accounting system.

- **External information** tends to be more relevant to strategic and tactical decisions than to operational decisions. (Benchmarking is an exception.)

- There are many sources of external information.

- **Secondary data**, such as government statistics or data provided by on-line databases, is not collected by or for the user. **Primary data** – more expensive than secondary data – is more tailored to the user's exact needs. Market research is an example.

- The **Internet** increases the richness of external data and reduces the cost of searching for it.

- Much control is achieved through the **feedback** of internal information.

- Be aware of the **cost** of inefficient use of information.

- There are specific **costs** to obtaining data, but also to maintaining the infrastructure supporting data collection and distribution.

- **Controls** need to be in place over the generation of internal information in routine and ad-hoc reports.

- A **procedures manual** sets out controls over distributing internal information.

- A number of procedures can be used to ensure **the security of highly confidential information that is not for external consumption:**

    - Passwords
    - Logical access systems
    - Database controls
    - Firewalls
    - Personnel security planning
    - Anti-virus and anti-spyware software

Quick Quiz

1   'Published data is always reliable.' **True or false?**

2   *Provide an example for each of the following costs of obtaining external information.*

Direct search costs   …………………………………..

Indirect access costs   …………………………………..

Management costs   …………………………………..

Infrastructure costs   …………………………………..

Time-theft   …………………………………..

3   Organisations have many sources they can use for external data. List six of these.

4   *Choose the correct words from those highlighted.*

Logical/physical access control is concerned with preventing those who **do not have access/already have access** to a terminal or computer from gaining access to **hardware/data or software.**

5   Five measures to control the ability of individuals to compromise the security of an organisation were listed in the chapter. What are they?

1   …………………………………..

2   …………………………………..

3   …………………………………..

4   …………………………………..

5   …………………………………..

6   A number of procedures can be used to make sure confidential data is kept secure. List five of these.

Answers to Quick Quiz

1   False. 'Reliability' of data for a decision is determined by its age, the sample and data definitions. By 'published' data, include the Internet – a source of falsehoods as well as information.

2   See Section 4.1.

3   Directories, Trade associations, Government agencies, periodicals/journals, market research data, and consumer panels

4   Logical
     already have access
     data or software

5   • Careful recruitment
     • Job rotation
     • Supervision and observation by a superior
     • Review of computer usage (for example via systems logs)
     • Enforced vacations

6   Passwords, logical access systems, database controls, firewalls, encryption, personnel security planning, anti-virus and anti-spyware software

     (We list more than five to cover all of the possibilities mentioned in the chapter)

Now try the question below from the Practice Question Bank

Number	Level	Marks	Time
Q17	Examination	15	27 mins

BPP
LEARNING MEDIA

Performance measurement in private sector organisations

Topic list	Syllabus reference
1 Performance measurement	D4
2 Financial performance indicators	D4 (a)
3 Non-financial performance indicators	D4 (b)
4 Short-termism and manipulation	D4 (d)
5 Improving performance	D4 (a) (b) (c)
6 The balanced scorecard	D4 (e)
7 Building Block model	D4 (e)
8 Target setting in qualitative areas	D4 (f)

Introduction

This chapter begins by introducing the term **performance measurement** and then describes various performance measures that are used by private sector organisations (other than variances).

It is important that the performance of an organisation is monitored, and this is most commonly done by calculating a number of ratios.

The chapter concludes by considering alternative views of performance measurement such as the **balanced scorecard** and **building blocks** which offer a contrast to the more **traditional** approaches to performance measurements.

Study guide

		Intellectual level
D4	**Performance analysis in private sector organisations**	
(a)	Describe, calculate and interpret financial performance indicators (FPIs) for profitability, liquidity and risk in both manufacturing and service businesses. Suggest methods to improve these measures	2
(b)	Describe, calculate and interpret non-financial performance indicators (NFPIs) and suggest methods to improve the performance indicated	2
(c)	Analyse past performance and suggest ways for improving financial and non-financial performance	2
(d)	Explain the causes and problems created by short-termism and financial manipulation of results and suggest methods to encourage a long term view	2
(e)	Explain and interpret the Balanced Scorecard, and the Building Block model proposed by Fitzgerald and Moon	2
(f)	Discuss the difficulties of target setting in qualitative areas	2

Exam guide

You must be able to **explain** as well as calculate performance indicators and **apply** your analysis to the organisation in the question. This topic has been a feature of all of the F5 exams so far. The organisations will not necessarily be limited companies.

1 Performance measurement   6/08, 12/10

FAST FORWARD

> **Performance measurement** aims to establish how well something or somebody is doing in relation to a plan.
>
> Performance measures may be divided into two types.
>
> - Financial performance indicators
> - Non-financial performance indicators

Exam focus point

> The July 2010 issue of *Student Accountant* contains an article on **performance management** written by the **examiner**. Ensure that you are familiar with this article. It is available on the ACCA web site.

Performance measurement is a **vital part of** the **planning and control process.** The purpose of performance measurement in relation to a plan or target, which may be short-term or long-term.

1.1 Financial and non-financial performance measures

Measures of performance may be either financial or non-financial.

(a)   Financial measures are typically measures relating to revenues, costs, profits, return on capital, asset values or cash flows. Actual performance is often measured against a financial plan, such as a budget.

(b)   Non-financial measures may relate to a number of different aspects of performance, such as:

- Product or service quality
- Reliability
- Speed of performance
- Risk
- Flexibility

- Customer attitudes
- Innovation
- Capability
- Pollution

It may be asked why organisations in the private sector whose primary objective is to make profits for shareholders should be particularly concerned with non-financial aspects of performance.

The answer is quite simply that non-financial aspects of performance are often a good indicator of future financial performance. Strong financial performance is not achievable over the long term unless non-financial performance is sufficiently strong to sustain the business.

Some performance measurements combine financial and non-financial aspects of performance, especially performance that relates to the efficiency of resource utilisation or capacity utilisation. Measures such as cost per patient day in the hospital service and cost per tonne-mile in the transport and distribution industry are examples.

1.2 Performance measures

The performance measures that are used will vary between organisations. Different measures are appropriate for different businesses. Other factors that influence the design of a performance management system are:

(a) **Measurement needs resources** – people, equipment and time to collect and analyse information. The costs and benefits of providing resources to produce a performance indicator must be carefully weighed up.

(b) **Performance must be measured in relation to something**, otherwise measurement is meaningless. Overall performance should be measured against the **objectives** of the organisation and the **plans** that result from those objectives. If the organisation has no clear objectives, the first step in performance measurement is to set them. The second is to identify the factors that are critical to the success of those objectives.

(c) **Measures must be relevant**. This means finding out what the organisation does and how it does it so that measures reflect what actually occurs.

(d) **Short** and **long-term achievement** should be measured. Short-term targets can be valuable, but exclusive use of them may direct the organisation away from opportunities that will mean success for the business in the long-term.

(e) Measures should be **fair.** They should only include factors which managers can control by their decisions, and for which they can be held **responsible**. Measuring controllable costs, revenues and assets may prove controversial however.

(f) A **variety** of measures should be used. Managers may be able to find ways to distort a single measure, but should not be able to affect a variety of measures. The balanced scorecard (Section 6) provides a method of measuring performance from a number of perspectives.

(g) **Realistic estimates** may be required for measures to be employed. These include estimates of financial items whose value is not certain, such as the cost of capital, and estimates of the impact of non-financial items.

(h) Measurement needs **responses,** above all managers to make decisions in the best interests of the organisation. Managers will only respond to measures that they find useful. The management accountant therefore needs to adopt a modern marketing philosophy to the provision of performance measures: satisfy customer wants, not pile 'em high and sell 'em cheap.

Once suitable performance measures have been selected they must be **monitored on a regular basis** to ensure that they are providing useful information. There is little point in an organisation devoting considerable resources to measuring market share if an increase in market share is not one of the organisation's objectives.

1.3 Quantitative and qualitative performance measures

Quantitative information is information that is expressed in numbers and by measurements. Qualitative information is not numerical, and may relate to issues such as customer loyalty, employee morale and capability. Qualitative information can sometimes be converted into quantitative values through tools such as ranking scales. For example 1 = Good, 2 = Average, 3 = Poor.

(a)   An example of a **quantitative** performance measure is: 1,000 units were produced in 50 hours at a cost of $15 per unit

(b)   An example of a **qualitative** performance measure is 'Market research indicates very strong and positive consume response to the new product.'

Qualitative measures are by nature **subjective** and **judgmental** but they can still be useful. They are especially valuable when they are derived from several **different sources**, as the likelihood of an unreliable judgement is reduced.

Consider the statement.

'Seven out of ten customers think our service is very reliable.'

This is a **quantitative measure** of customer satisfaction (7 out of 10), as well as a **qualitative measure** of the perceived performance of the service (very reliable).

2 Financial performance indicators (FPIs)   12/07, 12/08, 12/09, 12/10, 12/12, 12/13, Specimen paper

FAST FORWARD

Financial performance indicators analyse return on capital, profitability, liquidity and financial risk, often in relation to a plan or budget, or in relation to performance in preceding time periods.

Financial indicators (or **monetary** measures) include:

*   Profit (both gross profit and net profit)
*   Revenue
*   Costs
*   Cash flows
*   Debt and gearing

The two most common ways of using financial measures to assess performance are:

*   Comparing actual results with the **budget** or another financial plan

*   Comparing performance in the most recent time period with performance in a **corresponding previous time period** (or analysing a **trend over time**)

Financial measures may be presented as **ratios**, such as gross profit margin (gross profit/sales), and return on capital employed (net profit/capital employed).

Monetary amounts have meaning only **only in relation to something else**. Financial results should be compared against a **benchmark** such as:

*   Budgeted **sales**, **costs** and **profits**

*   **Standards** in a standard costing system

*   The **trend** over time (last year/this year, say)

*   The results of **other parts of the business**

*   The results of **other businesses**
*   **Future potential** (for example the performance of a new business may be judged in terms of nearness to breaking even).

2.1 Profitability

In private sector organisations, the most important financial performance indicators are measurements of profit.

A company ought of course to be profitable, and there are obvious checks on **profitability**.

(a)   Whether the company has made a profit or a loss on its ordinary activities.
(b)   By how much this year's profit or loss is bigger or smaller than last year's profit or loss.

It is probably better to consider separately the profits or losses on exceptional items if there are any. Such gains or losses should not be expected to occur again, unlike profits or losses on normal trading.

Question
Profitability

A company has the following summarised income statements for two consecutive years.

	Year 1 $	Year 2 $
Turnover	70,000	100,000
Less cost of sales	42,000	55,000
Gross profit	28,000	45,000
Less expenses	21,000	35,000
Net profit	7,000	10,000

Although the net profit margin (net profit/sales) is the same for both years at 10%, the gross profit margin is not.

$$\text{Year 1} \quad \frac{28,000}{70,000} = 40\% \qquad \text{Year 2} \quad \frac{45,000}{100,000} = 45\%$$

Is this good or bad for the business?

Answer

An increased profit margin must be good because this indicates a wider gap between selling price and cost of sales. Given that the net profit ratio has stayed the same in the second year, however, expenses must be rising. In year 1 expenses were 30% of turnover, whereas in year 2 they were 35% of turnover. This indicates that administration, selling and distribution expenses or interest costs require tight control.

Percentage analysis of profit between year 1 and year 2

	Year 1 %	Year 2 %
Cost of sales as a % of sales	60	55
Gross profit as a % of sales	40	45
	100	100
Expenses as a % of sales	30	35
Net profit as a % of sales	10	10
Gross profit as a % of sales	40	45

Profit on ordinary activities before taxation is generally thought to be a **better** figure to use than profit **after** taxation, because there might be unusual variations in the tax charge from year to year which would not affect the underlying profitability of the company's operations.

Another profit figure that should be calculated is **PBIT: profit before interest and tax**. This is the amount of profit which the company earned **before having to pay interest to the providers of loan capital**. PBIT is often the same as 'operating profit'.

PBIT = profit on ordinary activities before taxation + interest charges on long-term loan capital

PBIT is also often Gross profit – Other operating costs.

2.1.1 Sales margin (gross profit margin)

> **Sales margin** is turnover less cost of sales. It is also called gross profit.

Look at the following examples.

(a) **XYZ Printing Company**

	$'000
Turnover	89,844
Cost of sales	(60,769)
Gross profit	29,075
Distribution expenses	(1,523)
Administrative expenses	(13,300)
Goodwill amortisation	(212)
Operating profit (15.6%)	14,040

Cost of sales consists of **direct material** cost, such as paper, and **direct labour**. Distribution and administrative expenses include depreciation. **Sales margin = 32%** (29,075/89,844).

(b) **Fairway Transport, a bus company**

	$m
Turnover	1,534.3
Cost of sales	1,282.6
Gross profit	251.7
Net operating expenses	133.8
Operating profit (7.6%)	117.9

Sales margin = 16% (251.7/1,534.3). The sales margin for the bus company is much lower than for the printing company. Clearly a higher percentage of its costs are operating costs. However, is it useful or meaningful to compare the profitability of the two companies in this way?

(1) Sales margin as a measure is **not really any use in comparing companies in different industries**. Cost structures differ with the nature of business operations.

(2) **Comparisons with similar companies in the same industry** may be of interest. If an organisation has a lower sales margin than a similar business, this suggests problems in controlling costs.

(3) **Trends** in profit margin are also of interest. A falling sales margin suggests an organisation has not been able to pass on input price rises to customers.

(4) A comparison of actual profit with budgeted profit would also be of interest, but this information is not always available to the person who is analysing financial performance.

In short, the value of gross profit margin as a measure of performance depends on the **cost structure** of the industry and the **uses** to which it is put.

2.1.2 Net profit margin

For the purpose of the exam, net profit margin is either profit before interest and tax/sales or operating profit/sales, depending on the information you are given for analysis.

As with gross profit margin, net profit margin only has meaning when compared with performance in the previous period(s) or performance of similar companies in the same industry.

2.1.3 Cost/sales ratios

When there is a significant change in the net profit ratio from one year to the next, it may be useful to identify the main cause of the change. For example if the net profit ratio falls from 8% in one year to 2% in the next year, the fall in the net profit ratio is likely to be due to a fall in the gross profit margin, or an increase in:

(a)   the ratio of sales and distribution costs to sales
(b)   the ratio of administrative costs to sales
(c)   the ratio of another cost to sales, such as R&D costs.

A significant increase in the ratio of costs to sales (with a corresponding fall in profit margin) would need to be investigated.

2.1.4 Earnings per share (EPS)

EPS is a measure that relates profitability to the shareholder. It is the profit after tax (and any preference dividend) divided by the number of shares in issue.

EPS is widely used as a **measure of a company's performance**, especially in **comparing** results over a period **of several years**. A company must be able to sustain its earnings in order to pay dividends and re-invest in the business so as to achieve future growth. Investors also look for **growth in the EPS** from one year to the next.

ey term

> **Earnings per share (EPS)** is defined as the profit attributable to each equity (ordinary) share.

Question   EPS

Walter Wall Carpets made profits before tax in 20X8 of $9,320,000. Tax amounted to $2,800,000.

The company's share capital is as follows.

	$
Ordinary share (10,000,000 shares of $1)	10,000,000
8% preference shares	2,000,000
	12,000,000

Required
Calculate the EPS for 20X8.

Answer

	$
Profits before tax	9,320,000
Less tax	2,800,000
Profits after tax	6,520,000
Less preference dividend (8% of $2,000,000)	160,000
Earnings	6,360,000
Number of ordinary shares	10,000,000
EPS	63.6c

EPS on its own does not really tell us anything. It must be seen **in context**.

(a)   EPS is used for comparing the results of a company **over time**. Is its EPS growing? What is the rate of growth? Is the rate of growth increasing or decreasing?

(b)   EPS should not be used blindly to compare the earnings of one company with another. For example, if A plc has an EPS of 12c for its 10,000,000 10p shares and B plc has an EPS of 24c for its 50,000,000 25c shares, we must take account of the numbers of shares. When **earnings are**

used to compare one company's shares with another, this is done **using** the **P/E ratio or perhaps the earnings yield**.

(c)   If EPS is to be a reliable basis for comparing results, it **must be calculated consistently**. The EPS of one company must be directly comparable with the EPS of others, and the EPS of a company in one year must be directly comparable with its published EPS figures for previous years. Changes in the share capital of a company during the course of a year cause problems of comparability.

(d)   EPS is a figure based on past data, and it is easily manipulated by changes in accounting policies and by mergers or acquisitions. **The use of the measure in calculating management bonuses makes it particularly liable to manipulation.** The attention given to EPS as a performance measure by City analysts is arguably disproportionate to its true worth. Investors should be more concerned with **future earnings**, but of course estimates of these are more difficult to reach than the readily available figure.

2.1.5 Profitability and return: the return on capital employed (ROCE)

It is impossible to assess profits or profit growth properly without relating them to the amount of funds (the capital) employed in making the profits. An important profitability ratio is therefore **return on capital employed (ROCE)**, which states the profit as a **percentage of the amount of capital employed**.

Key terms

> **Return on Capital Employed** $= \dfrac{\text{PBIT}}{\text{Capital employed}}$
>
> **Capital employed** = Shareholders' funds *plus* 'payables: amounts falling due after more than one year' *plus* any long-term provisions for liabilities.
>
> = Total assets less current liabilities.

What does a company's ROCE tell us? What should we be looking for? There are three **comparisons** that can be made.

(a)   The change in ROCE from **one year to the next**

(b)   The ROCE being earned by **other companies**, if this information is available

(c)   A comparison of the ROCE with **current market borrowing rates**

　　(i)   What would be the cost of extra borrowing to the company if it needed more loans, and is it earning an ROCE that suggests it could make high enough profits to make such borrowing worthwhile?

　　(ii)   Is the company making an ROCE which suggests that it is making profitable use of its current borrowing?

2.1.6 Analysing profitability and return in more detail: the secondary ratios

We may analyse the ROCE, to find out why it is high or low, or better or worse than last year. There are two factors that contribute towards a return on capital employed, both related to turnover.

(a)   **Profit margin**. A company might make a high or a low profit margin on its sales. For example, a company that makes a profit of 25c per $1 of sales is making a bigger return on its turnover than another company making a profit of only 10c per $1 of sales.

(b)   **Asset turnover**. Asset turnover is a measure of how well the assets of a business are being used to generate sales. For example, if two companies each have capital employed of $100,000, and company A makes sales of $400,000 a year whereas company B makes sales of only $200,000 a year, company A is making a higher turnover from the same amount of assets and this will help company A to make a higher return on capital employed than company B. Asset turnover is expressed as 'x times' so that assets generate x times their value in annual turnover. Here, company A's asset turnover is 4 times and company B's is 2 times.

Profit margin and asset turnover together explain the ROCE, and if the ROCE is the primary profitability ratio, these other two are the secondary ratios. The relationship between the three ratios is as follows.

Profit margin	×	asset turnover	=	ROCE
$\dfrac{\text{PBIT}}{\text{Sales}}$	×	$\dfrac{\text{Sales}}{\text{Capital employed}}$	=	$\dfrac{\text{PBIT}}{\text{Capital employed}}$

It is also worth commenting on the **change in turnover** from one year to the next. Strong sales growth will usually indicate volume growth as well as turnover increases due to price rises, and volume growth is one sign of a prosperous company.

2.2 Gearing

The assets of a business must be financed somehow, and when a business is growing, the additional assets must be financed by additional capital. **Capital structure** refers to the **way in which an organisation** is **financed**, by a combination of long-term capital (ordinary shares and reserves, preference shares, debentures, bank loans, convertible bonds and so on) and short-term liabilities, such as a bank overdraft and trade payables.

2.2.1 Debts and financial risk

There are two main **reasons why companies should keep their debt burden under control**.

(a)   When a company is heavily in debt, and seems to be getting even more heavily into debt, banks and other would-be lenders are very soon likely to refuse further borrowing and the company might well find itself in trouble.

(b)   When a company is earning only a modest profit before interest and tax, and has a heavy debt burden, there will be very little profit left over for shareholders after the interest charges have been paid. And so if interest rates were to go up or the company were to borrow even more, it might soon be incurring interest charges in excess of PBIT. This might eventually lead to the liquidation of the company.

A high level of debt creates **financial risk**. Financial risk can be seen from different points of view.

(a)   **The company** as a whole. If a company builds up debts that it cannot pay when they fall due, it will be forced into liquidation.

(b)   **Payables**. If a company cannot pay its debts, the company will go into liquidation owing creditors money that they are unlikely to recover in full.

(c)   **Ordinary shareholders**. A company will not make any distributable profits unless it is able to earn enough profit before interest and tax to pay all its interest charges, and then tax. The lower the profits or the higher the interest-bearing debts, the less there will be, if there is anything at all, for shareholders.

When a company has preference shares in its capital structure, ordinary shareholders will not get anything until the preference dividend has been paid.

2.3 Gearing ratios

FAST FORWARD

Gearing ratios measure the financial **risk** of a company's capital structure. Business risk can be measured by calculating a company's operational gearing.

ey term

Financial leverage/gearing is the use of debt finance to increase the return on equity by using borrowed funds in such a way that the return generated is greater than the cost of servicing the debt. If the return on borrowed funds is less than the cost of servicing the debt, the effect of gearing is to reduce the return on equity.

Gearing measures the **relationships between shareholders' capital plus reserves, and debt**. Debt is any loans which pay fixed interest and are secured. In this exam, overdrafts do not form part of debt in a gearing ratio.

The common gearing ratios are:

$$\text{Gearing} = \frac{\text{Debt}}{\text{Debt plus equity}} \quad \text{and} \quad \text{Gearing} = \frac{\text{Debt}}{\text{Equity}}$$

When applying the above ratios, remember **to compare like with like** (apply the same gearing ratio throughout to enable accurate comparisons to be made).

A gearing ratio of over 50% indicates **high** gearing.

There is **no absolute limit** to what a **gearing ratio** ought to be. Many companies are highly geared, but if a highly geared company is increasing its gearing, it is likely to have difficulty in the future when it wants to borrow even more, unless it can also boost its shareholders' capital, either with retained profits or with a new share issue.

2.3.1 The effect of gearing on earnings

The level of gearing has a considerable effect on the earnings attributable to the ordinary shareholders. A **highly geared** company must **earn enough profits to cover its interest charges before anything is available for equity**. On the other hand, if borrowed funds are invested in projects which provide returns in excess of the cost of debt capital, then shareholders will enjoy increased returns on their equity.

Gearing, however, also **increases the probability of financial failure** occurring through a company's inability to meet interest payments in poor trading circumstances.

2.3.2 Example: Gearing

Suppose that two companies are identical in every respect except for their gearing. Both have assets of $20,000 and both make the same operating profits (profit before interest and tax: PBIT). The only difference between the two companies is that Nonlever Co is all-equity financed and Lever Co is partly financed by debt capital, as follows.

	Nonlever Co	Lever Co
	$	$
Assets	20,000	20,000
10% Bonds	0	(10,000)
	20,000	10,000
Ordinary shares of $1	20,000	10,000

Because Lever has $10,000 of 10% bonds it must make a profit before interest of at least $1,000 in order to pay the interest charges. Nonlever, on the other hand, does not have any minimum PBIT requirement because it has no debt capital. A company, which is lower geared, is considered less **risky** than a higher geared company because of the greater likelihood that its PBIT will be high enough to cover interest charges and make a profit for equity shareholders.

2.3.3 Operating gearing

Financial risk, as we have seen, can be measured by financial gearing. **Business risk** refers to the **risk of making only low profits**, or even losses, **due to the nature of the business** that the company is involved in. One way of measuring business risk is by calculating a company's **operating gearing** or 'operational gearing'.

Key term

$$\text{Operating gearing or leverage} = \frac{\text{Contribution}}{\text{Profit before interest and tax (PBIT)}}$$

If contribution is high but PBIT is low, fixed costs will be high, and only just covered by contribution. **Business risk**, as measured by operating gearing, will be **high**. If contribution is not much bigger than

PBIT, fixed costs will be low, and fairly easily covered. Business risk, as measured by operating gearing, will be low.

2.4 Liquidity and cash flow

A company can be profitable but at the same time get into cash flow problems. Liquidity ratios (**current** and **quick**) and **working capital turnover ratios** give some idea of a company's liquidity and ability to generate cash from its business operations.

Profitability is of course an important aspect of a company's performance, and debt or gearing is another. Neither, however, addresses directly the key issue of liquidity. A company needs liquid assets so that it can meet its debts when they fall due.

Key term

Liquidity is the amount of cash a company can obtain quickly to settle its debts (and possibly to meet other unforeseen demands for cash payments too).

2.4.1 Liquid assets

Liquid funds include:

(a)   Cash

(b)   Short-term investments for which there is a ready market, such as investments in shares of other companies (NB **not** subsidiaries or associates)

(c)   Fixed-term deposits with a bank or building society, for example six month deposits with a bank

(d)   Trade receivables

(e)   Bills of exchange receivable

Some assets are more liquid than others. Inventories of goods are fairly liquid in some businesses. Inventories of finished production goods might be sold quickly, and a supermarket will hold consumer goods for resale that could well be sold for cash very soon. Raw materials and components in a manufacturing company have to be used to make a finished product before they can be sold to realise cash, and so they are less liquid than finished goods. Just how liquid they are depends on the speed of inventory turnover and the length of the production cycle.

Non-current assets are not liquid assets. A company can sell off non-current assets, but unless they are no longer needed, or are worn out and about to be replaced, they are necessary to continue the company's operations. Selling non-current assets is certainly not a solution to a company's cash needs, and so although there may be an occasional non-current asset item which is about to be sold off, probably because it is going to be replaced, it is safe to disregard non-current assets when measuring a company's liquidity.

In summary, **liquid assets are current asset items that will or could soon be converted into cash, and cash** itself. Two common definitions of liquid assets are **all current assets** or **all current assets with the exception of inventories.**

The main source of liquid assets for a trading company is sales. A company can obtain cash from sources other than sales, such as the issue of shares for cash, a new loan or the sale of non-current assets. But a company cannot rely on these at all times, and in general, obtaining liquid funds depends on making sales and profits.

2.4.2 The current ratio

The **current ratio** is the standard test of liquidity.

Key term

$$\text{Current ratio} = \frac{\text{Current assets}}{\text{Current liabilities}}$$

A company should have enough current assets that give a promise of 'cash to come' to meet its commitments to pay its current liabilities. Obviously, a ratio in **excess of 1** should be expected. In practice, a ratio comfortably in excess of 1 should be expected, but what is 'comfortable' varies between different types of businesses.

Companies are not able to convert all their current assets into cash very quickly. In particular, some manufacturing companies might hold large quantities of raw material inventories, which must be used in production to create finished goods. Finished goods might be warehoused for a long time, or sold on lengthy credit. In such businesses, where inventory turnover is slow, most inventories are not very liquid assets, because the cash cycle is so long. For these reasons, we calculate an additional liquidity ratio, known as the quick ratio or acid test ratio.

2.4.3 The quick ratio

Key term

$$\text{Quick ratio or acid test ratio} = \frac{\text{Current assets less inventories}}{\text{Current liabilities}}$$

This ratio should ideally be **at least 1** for companies with a **slow inventory turnover**. For companies with a **fast inventory turnover**, a quick ratio can be **less than 1** without suggesting that the company is in cash flow difficulties.

Do not forget the other side of the coin. The current ratio and the quick ratio can be bigger than they should be. A company that has large volumes of inventories and receivables might be over-investing in working capital, and so tying up more funds in the business than it needs to. This would suggest poor management of receivables or inventories by the company.

2.4.4 The accounts receivable payment period

Key term

$$\text{Accounts receivable days or accounts receivable payment period} = \frac{\text{Trade receivables}}{\text{Credit sales turnover}} \times 365 \text{ days}$$

This is a rough measure of the average length of time it takes for a company's accounts receivable to pay what they owe.

The trade accounts receivable are not the *total* figure for accounts receivable in the balance sheet, which includes prepayments and non-trade accounts receivable. The trade accounts receivable figure will be itemised in an analysis of the total accounts receivable, in a note to the accounts.

The estimate of accounts receivable days is only approximate.

(a) The **balance sheet value** of accounts receivable might be **abnormally high** or low compared with the 'normal' level the company usually has. This may apply especially to smaller companies, where the size of year-end accounts receivable may largely depend on whether a few or even a single large customer pay just before or just after the year-end.

(b) Turnover in the income statement excludes sales tax, but the accounts receivable figure in the balance sheet includes sales tax. We are not strictly comparing like with like.

2.4.5 The inventory turnover period

Key term

$$\text{Inventory days} = \frac{\text{Inventory}}{\text{Cost of sales}} \times 365 \text{ days}$$

This indicates the average number of days that items of inventory are held for. As with the average accounts receivable collection period, this is only an approximate figure, but one which should be reliable enough for finding changes over time.

A lengthening inventory turnover period indicates:

(a) A **slowdown** in **trading**, or

(b) A **build-up** in **inventory levels**, perhaps suggesting that the investment in inventories is becoming excessive

If we add together the inventory days and the accounts receivable days, this should give us an indication of how soon inventory is convertible into cash, thereby giving a further indication of the **company's liquidity**.

2.4.6 The accounts payable payment period

term

$$\text{Accounts payable payment period} = \frac{\text{Average trade payables}}{\text{Credit purchases or Cost of sales}} \times 365 \ \text{days}$$

The accounts payable payment period often helps to assess a company's liquidity; an increase in accounts payable days is often a sign of lack of long-term finance or poor management of current assets, resulting in the use of extended credit from suppliers, increased bank overdraft and so on.

All the ratios calculated above will **vary by industry**; hence **comparisons** of ratios calculated with other similar companies in the same industry are important.

One of the competencies you require to fulfil performance objective 12 of the PER is the ability to provide analysis of performance against key financial performance indicators (KPIs). You can apply the knowledge you obtain from this section of the text to help to demonstrate this competence.

| Question | Liquidity and working capital ratios |

Calculate liquidity and working capital ratios from the accounts of a manufacturer of products for the construction industry, and comment on the ratios.

	20X8	20X7
	$m	$m
Turnover	2,065.0	1,788.7
Cost of sales	1,478.6	1,304.0
Gross profit	586.4	484.7
Current assets		
Inventories	119.0	109.0
Receivables (note 1)	400.9	347.4
Short-term investments	4.2	18.8
Cash at bank and in hand	48.2	48.0
	572.3	523.2
Payables: amounts falling due within one year		
Loans and overdrafts	49.1	35.3
Corporation taxes	62.0	46.7
Dividend	19.2	14.3
Payables (note 2)	370.7	324.0
	501.0	420.3
	$m	$m
Net current assets	71.3	102.9
Notes		
1 Trade receivables	329.8	285.4
2 Trade payables	236.2	210.8

	20X8	20X7
Current ratio	572.3/501.0 = 1.14	523.2/420.3 = 1.24
Quick ratio	453.3/501.0 = 0.90	414.2/420.3 = 0.99
Receivables' payment period	$329.8/2,065.0 \times 365 = 58$ days	$285.4/1,788.7 \times 365 = 58$ days
Inventory turnover period	$119.0/1,478.6 \times 365 = 29$ days	$109.0/1,304.0 \times 365 = 31$ days
Payables' turnover period	$236.2/1,478.6 \times 365 = 58$ days	$210.8/1,304.0 \times 365 = 59$ days

As a manufacturing group serving the construction industry, the company would be expected to have a comparatively lengthy receivables' turnover period, because of the relatively poor cash flow in the construction industry. It is clear that the company compensates for this by ensuring that they do not pay for raw materials and other costs before they have sold their inventories of finished goods (hence the similarity of receivables' and payables' turnover periods).

The company's current ratio is a little lower than average but its quick ratio is better than average and very little less than the current ratio. This suggests that inventory levels are strictly controlled, which is reinforced by the low inventory turnover period. It would seem that working capital is tightly managed, to avoid the poor liquidity which could be caused by a high receivables' turnover period and comparatively high payables.

3 Non-financial performance indicators (NFPIs)
12/07, 6/09, 12/10, 12/12, 12/13, Specimen paper

FAST FORWARD

Changes in cost structures, the competitive environment and the manufacturing environment have led to an **increased use of non-financial performance indicators** (NFPIs). Non-financial performance indicators can also be a very useful guide to future financial performance.

There has been a growing emphasis on NFPIs for a number of reasons.

(a) **Concentration on too few variables**. If performance measurement systems focus entirely on those items which can be expressed in monetary terms, managers will concentrate on only those variables and ignore other important variables that cannot be expressed in monetary terms.

(b) **Lack of information on quality.** Traditional responsibility accounting systems fail to provide information on the quality or importance of operations.

(c) **Changes in cost structures.** Modern technology requires massive investment and product life cycles have got shorter. A greater proportion of costs are sunk and a large proportion of costs are planned, engineered or designed into a product/service before production/delivery. At the time the product/service is produced/delivered, it is therefore too late to control costs.

(d) **Changes in competitive environment.** Financial measures do not convey the full picture of a company's performance, especially in a modern business environment.

(e) **Changes in manufacturing environment**. New manufacturing techniques and technologies focus on minimising throughput times, inventory levels and set-up times. But managers can reduce the costs for which they are responsible by increasing inventory levels through maximising output. If a performance measurement system focuses principally on costs, managers may concentrate on cost reduction and ignore other important strategic manufacturing goals.

(f) **NFPIs are a better indicator of future prospects**. Financial performance indicators tend to focus on the short term. They can give a positive impression of what is happening now but problems may be looming. For example, falling quality will ultimately damage profitability.

BPP
LEARNING MEDIA

Unlike traditional variance reports, NFPIs can be provided **quickly** for managers, per shift, daily or even hourly as required. They are likely to be easy to calculate, and easier for non-financial managers to **understand** and therefore to **use effectively**.

3.1 Which NFPIs should be measured?

The most useful NFPIs for measuring aspects of operational performance will vary between different types of business and different business circumstances. Whereas with financial performance measures it is possible to list the most commonly-used measures or ratios, this is not so easy with NFPIs.

Given an exam question in which you are asked to comment on non-financial aspects of performance of an organisation, you will need to use your judgement and try to identify the most suitable measures for the organisation in the question.

As a general guide, NFPIs may be measurements of the following aspects of performance.

(a)   **Quality** of production: wastage rates or percentage of rejects in production

(b)   **Speed** or **efficiency**, such as output per hour; average time taken per unit of activity

(c)   **Delivery**: average time between taking an order and delivery to the customer

(d)   **Reliability**: percentage of calls answered within a given target time; number of equipment failures or amount of 'down time'

(e)   **Customer satisfaction**: number of complaints

(f)   **Innovation**: number of new products developed and launched on to the market

With non-financial indicators, **anything can be measured and compared** if it is **meaningful** to do so. The measures should be **tailored** to the circumstances of the business.

3.2 NFPIs in relation to employees

FAST FORWARD

NFPIs can usefully be applied to **employees** and product/service **quality**.

One of the many criticisms of traditional accounting performance measurement systems is that they **do not measure the skills, morale and training of the workforce**, which can be as **valuable to an organisation as its tangible assets**. For example if employees have not been trained in the manufacturing practices required to achieve the objectives of the new manufacturing environment, an organisation is unlikely to be successful.

Employee attitudes and morale can be measured by **surveying** employees. Education and skills levels, promotion and training, absenteeism and labour turnover for the employees for which each manager is responsible can also be monitored.

3.3 Performance measurement in a TQM environment

Total Quality Management is a highly significant trend in modern business thinking. Because **TQM embraces every activity** of a business, performance measures cannot be confined to the production process but must also cover the work of sales and distribution departments and administration departments, the efforts of external suppliers, and the reaction of external customers.

In many cases the measures used will be non-financial ones. They may be divided into three types.

(a)   **Measuring the quality of incoming supplies.** Quality control should include procedures for acceptance and inspection of goods inwards and measurement of rejects.

(b)   **Monitoring work done as it proceeds.** 'In-process' controls include statistical process controls and random sampling, and measures such as the amount of scrap and reworking in relation to good production. Measurements can be made by product, by worker or work team, by machine or machine type, by department, or whatever is appropriate.

(c)   **Measuring customer satisfaction.** This may be monitored in the form of letters of complaint, returned goods, penalty discounts, claims under guarantee, or requests for visits by service engineers. Some companies adopt a more pro-active approach to monitoring customer satisfaction by surveying their customers on a regular basis. They use the feedback to obtain an index of customer satisfaction which is used to identify quality problems before they affect profits.

3.4 Quality of service

Service quality is measured principally by **qualitative measures**, as you might expect, although some quantitative measures are used by some businesses.

(a)   If it were able to obtain the information, a retailer might use number of lost customers in a period as an indicator of service quality.

(b)   Lawyers use the proportion of time spent with clients.

3.4.1 Measures of customer satisfaction

You have probably filled in **questionnaires** in fast food restaurants or on aeroplanes without realising that you were completing a customer attitude survey for input to the organisation's management information system.

Other possible measures of customer satisfaction include:

(a)   Market research information on customer preferences and customer satisfaction with specific product features

(b)   Number of defective units supplied to customers as a percentage of total units supplied

(c)   Number of customer complaints as a percentage of total sales volume

(d)   Percentage of products which fail early or excessively

(e)   On-time delivery rate

(f)   Average time to deal with customer queries

(g)   New customer accounts opened

(h)   Repeat business from existing customers

4 Short-termism and manipulation   6/08

FAST FORWARD

Short-termism is when there is a bias towards short-term rather than long-term performance. It is often due to the fact that managers' performance is measured on short-term results.

Key term

Short-termism is when there is a bias towards short-term rather than long-term performance.

Organisations often have to make a trade-off between short-term and long-term objectives. Decisions which involve the **sacrifice of longer-term objectives** include the following.

(a)   Postponing or abandoning capital expenditure projects, which would eventually contribute to growth and profits, in order to protect short term cash flow and profits.

(b)   Cutting R&D expenditure to save operating costs, and so reducing the prospects for future product development.

(c)   Reducing quality control, to save operating costs (but also adversely affecting reputation and goodwill).

(d)   Reducing the level of customer service, to save operating costs (but sacrificing goodwill).

(e)   Cutting training costs or recruitment (so the company might be faced with skills shortages).

Managers may also **manipulate** results, especially if rewards are linked to performance. This can be achieved by changing the timing of capital purchases, building up inventories and speeding up or delaying payments and receipts.

BPP
LEARNING MEDIA

4.1 Methods to encourage a long-term view

Steps that could be taken to encourage managers to take a long-term view, so that the 'ideal' decisions are taken, include the following.

(a) **Making short-term targets realistic**. If budget targets are unrealistically tough, a manager will be forced to make trade-offs between the short and long term.

(b) **Providing sufficient management information** to allow managers to see what trade-offs they are making. Managers must be kept aware of long-term aims as well as shorter-term (budget) targets.

(c) **Evaluating managers' performance** in terms of contribution to long-term as well as short-term objectives.

(d) **Link managers' rewards to share price**. This may encourage goal congruence.

(e) **Set quality based targets** as well as financial targets. Multiple targets can be used.

5 Improving performance

Performance is measured to asses show well or badly an organisation has performed over a given period of time. When performance is measured, the objectives should be to:

(a) identify aspects of performance that may be a cause for concern

(b) explain differences between actual performance and the plan or expectation, or deteriorating performance over time

(c) consider ways of taking control measures to improve performance.

In an exam question on performance measurement, it is highly likely that you will be required to do all three of these things in your answer.

5.1 Analyse performance

As explained previously, performance is analysed by comparing actual results with a target (such as a budget) or with performance in previous time periods.

The purpose of analysing performance in this way is to identify whether there are any **aspects of performance that are worse than the target or worse than the previous year, where there may be some cause for concern**.

Where performance is more or less as expected or in line with previous years, there should be no cause for concern, and no reason to investigate this aspect of performance in any detail.

5.2 Identify reasons for unexpected performance or poor performance

Having identified aspects of performance that may be a cause for some concern, the next requirement is to consider possible reasons for actual results, and why for example performance is worse this year than last year.

To identify possible reasons for disappointing performance, you may need to apply your judgement and common sense to the facts in an examination 'case study'.

The table below gives some examples of matters that you may need to consider, but these examples are illustrative and by no means exhaustive.

Aspect of performance	Possible reasons
Increase in rejection rates for faulty products	Using relatively inexperienced staff to do the work Using cheaper materials (to 'save money')
Increase in time between taking a customer order and delivering the product to the customer	Administrative delays in processing customer orders

Aspect of performance	Possible reasons
Increase in frequency of machine breakdowns	Reduction on amount of routine maintenance work
Customer dissatisfaction with on-line sales service	Poor web site design
Longer average time to answer customer calls in a call centre	Reduction in number of call centre staff
Declining labour productivity	Failure to train staff Increase in complexity of the work Use of inexperienced staff

5.3 Improving performance

Having identified reasons for poor performance, whether financial or non-financial performance, the final step is to consider and implement methods of improving performance. **Methods of improving performance should be linked to the possible reasons for the poor performance.**

The aim of corrective measures should be to tackle the problems that are the cause of the poor performance.

Illustrative control measures are shown in the table below.

Aspect of performance	Possible reasons	Possible measures to improve performance
Increase in rejection rates for faulty products	Using relatively inexperienced staff to do the work Using cheaper materials (to 'save money')	Hire more experienced staff Provide training Switch back to better-quality materials
Increase in time between taking a customer order and delivering the product to the customer	Administrative delays in processing customer orders	Set a maximum time limit for processing orders and monitor performance continually
Increase in frequency of machine breakdowns	Reduction on amount of routine maintenance work	Increase routine maintenance of machines
Customer dissatisfaction with on-line sales service	Poor web site design	Re-design the web site. Hire web site design specialists if necessary
Longer average time to answer customer calls in a call centre	Reduction in number of call centre staff	Employ more staff
Declining labour productivity	Failure to train staff Increase in complexity of the work Use of inexperienced staff	Hire more experienced staff Provide training Give the most complex tasks to specialist staff

Some structured approaches to performance measurement have been developed, which combine measurements of financial and non-financial performance. Two of these are described in the next sections.

6 The balanced scorecard

AST FORWARD

> The **balanced scorecard** approach to performance measurement focuses on four different perspectives of performance, and uses both financial and non-financial indicators to set performance targets and monitor performance.

Although business performance may be measured by a single financial performance indicator such as ROI, profit, or cost variances, it is often more suitable to use multiple measures of performance where each measure reflects a **different aspect of achievement**. Where multiple measures are used, several may be **non-financial.**

An important argument in favour of measuring non-financial performance is that current and future financial performance depend largely on non-financial aspects of performance.

If an organisation uses a performance measurement system for monitoring its performance, it seems appropriate that the measurement system should be formally structured, so that:

- all relevant aspects of performance are measured
- targets are set for all key aspects of performance
- actual performance is measured against targets, rather than compared with performance in previous years
- performance targets are consistent with each other.

Perhaps the most widely-used structured approach to performance targeting and measurement is the **'balanced scorecard'.**

A balanced scorecard is a performance measurement system in which:

(a) Objectives and targets are set for **four different aspects or perspectives of performance**: a financial perspective; customer perspective; internal perspective; and innovation and learning perspective. All four perspectives are important for the long-term success of the organisation. Three of these perspectives are non-financial in nature.

(b) There should be a small number of **targets for each of the four perspectives**.

(c) The **different targets for the four perspectives should be consistent with each other**: the four perspectives are sometimes in conflict with each other and it is necessary to establish an acceptable balance between the different perspectives and targets. (Hence, a 'balanced' scorecard.)

(e) **Actual performance is measured regularly and compared with the targets for all of the perspectives**.

(f) Differences between the target and actual performance are investigated, and where appropriate measures are taken to improve performance.

ey term

> The **balanced scorecard** approach emphasises the need to provide management with a set of information which covers all relevant areas of performance in an objective and unbiased fashion. The information provided may be both financial and non-financial and cover areas such as profitability, customer satisfaction, internal efficiency and innovation.

6.1 Perspectives

The balanced scorecard focuses on **four different perspectives**, as follows.

Perspective	Basic question	Identifying performance targets
Customer	What do existing and new customers value from us?	Gives rise to targets that matter to customers: cost, quality, delivery, inspection, handling and so on.
Internal	What processes must we excel at to achieve our financial and customer objectives?	Aims to improve internal processes and decision making.

Perspective	Basic question	Identifying performance targets
Innovation and learning	Can we continue to improve and create future value?	Considers the business's capacity to maintain its competitive position through the acquisition of new skills and the development of new products.
Financial	How do we create value for our shareholders?	Covers traditional measures such as growth, profitability and shareholder value but set through talking to the shareholder or shareholders direct.

Performance targets are set once the key areas for improvement have been identified, and the balanced scorecard is the main monthly report.

The scorecard is **'balanced'** as managers are required to think in terms of **all four** perspectives, to prevent improvements being made in one area at the expense of another.

Important features of this approach are as follows.

(a)   It looks at both **internal and external** matters concerning the organisation.
(b)   It is related to the key elements of a company's **strategy**.
(c)   **Financial and non-financial** measures are linked together.

6.2 Example

An example of how a balanced scorecard might appear is offered below. Arguably, there are too many performance targets here for each of the four perspectives, but this balance scorecard is a good illustration of issues that may be considered as critical for the organisation's success.

Balanced Scorecard

Financial Perspective

GOALS	MEASURES
Survive	Cash flow
Succeed	Monthly sales growth and operating income by division
Prosper	Increase market share and ROI

Customer Perspective

GOALS	MEASURES
New products	Percentage of sales from new products
Responsive supply	On-time delivery (defined by customer)
Preferred supplier	Share of key accounts' purchases
	Ranking by key accounts
Customer partnership	Number of cooperative engineering efforts

Internal Business Perspective

GOALS	MEASURES
Technology capability	Manufacturing configuration vs competition
Manufacturing excellence	Cycle time
	Unit cost
	Yield
Design productivity	Silicon efficiency
	Engineering efficiency
New product introduction	Actual introduction schedule vs plan

Innovation and Learning Perspective

GOALS	MEASURES
Technology leadership	Time to develop next generation of products
Manufacturing learning	Process time to maturity
Product focus	Percentage of products that equal 80% sales
Time to market	New product introduction vs competition

6.3 Example: Balanced scorecard and not-for-profit organisations

Balanced scorecards are used most in private sector organisations, where reward systems may be based on success in achieving targets in each of the four perspectives. It is also possible, however, to use a balanced scorecard in not-for-profit organisations.

Not-for-profit organisations such as charities are likely to have significantly different goals in comparison to profitable businesses. The following are goals that may be relevant to a charity.

Financial perspective

- Increase income from charitable donations
- Improve margins

Internal business perspective

- Reduce overheads
- Claim back tax on gift aid

Customer perspective

- Continued donor support
- Donor involvement in initiatives

Innovation and learning perspective

- More projects supported
- More fundraisers
- More money pledged

Required

Suggest some performance measures for each of the goals outlined above.

Solution

The balanced scorecard for the charity may appear as follows.

Financial perspective	
GOALS	**MEASURES (KPI)**
Income from charitable donations	Donations received
Improved margins	Lower costs and/or increased income from all sources

Customer perspective	
GOALS	**MEASURES (KPI)**
Continued donor support	Pledges given and direct debits set up
Donor involvement in initiatives	Fundraising and charity dinners

Internal business perspective	
GOALS	**MEASURES (KPI)**
Reduce overheads	Lower overheads measured by monitoring and accounts
Claim back tax on gift aid	Improved reclaim times for gift aided donation

Innovation and learning perspective	
GOALS	**MEASURES (KPI)**
More projects supported	Number of projects given support
More fundraisers	Number of fundraisers recruited
More money pledged	Amount of donations promised

Note: KPI = Key Performance Indicator

Spotlight Productions has in the past produced just one fairly successful product. Recently, however, a new version of this product has been launched. Development work continues to add a related product to the product list. Given below are some details of the activities during the month of November.

Units produced	– existing product	25,000
	– new product	5,000
Cost of units produced	– existing product	$375,000
	– new product	$70,000
Sales revenue	– existing product	$550,000
	– new product	$125,000
Hours worked	– existing product	5,000
	– new product	1,250
Development costs		$47,000

Required

(a) Suggest and calculate performance indicators that could be calculated for each of the four perspectives on the balanced scorecard.

(b) Suggest how this information would be interpreted.

Answer

(a) **Customer**

- Percentage of sales represented by new products $= \dfrac{\$125,000}{\$550,000 + \$125,000} \times 100$

$= 18.5\%$

Internal

- Productivity — existing product $= \dfrac{25,000 \text{ units}}{5,000 \text{ units}}$

$= 5$ units per hour

— new product $= \dfrac{5,000 \text{ units}}{1,250 \text{ units}}$

$= 4$ units per hour

- Unit cost — existing product $= \dfrac{\$375,000}{25,000 \text{ units}}$

$= \$15$ per unit

— new product $= \dfrac{\$70,000}{5,000 \text{ units}}$

$= \$14$ per unit

Financial

- Gross profit — existing product $= \dfrac{\$550,000 - 375,000}{\$550,000}$

$= 32\%$

— new product $= \dfrac{\$125,000 - 70,000}{\$125,000}$

$= 44\%$

Innovation and learning

- Development costs as % of sales
$$= \frac{\$47,000}{\$675,000}$$
$$= 7\%$$

(b) Using a range of performance indicators will allow Spotlight Productions to look at the success of the new product in wider terms than just its profitability. For example, productivity is lower for the new product than the existing product, so managers may wish to examine the processes involved in order to make improvements. Sales of the new product look very promising but some additional measure of customer satisfaction could provide a better view of long-term prospects.

7 Building Block model

AST FORWARD

Fitzgerald and Moon's **building blocks** for **dimensions, standards** and **rewards** attempt to overcome the problems associated with performance measurement of service businesses.

Performance measurement in service businesses has sometimes been perceived as more difficult than in manufacturing businesses.

Fitzgerald and Moon (1996) suggested that a performance management system in a service organisation can be analysed as a combination of three building blocks:

- dimensions of performance
- standards
- rewards.

Dimensions of performance	
Profit	
Competitiveness	
Quality	
Resource utilisation	
Flexibility	
Innovation	

Standards	**Rewards**
Ownership	Clarity
Achievability	Motivation
Equity	Controllability

7.1 Dimensions of performance

Dimensions of performance are the aspects of performance that are measured. Fitzgerald and Moon suggested that there are six aspects to performance measurement that link performance to corporate strategy. These are shown in the diagram above.

Some performance measures that might be used for each of these dimensions are as follows.

Dimension of performance	Possible measure of performance
Financial performance	Profitability
	Profits growth
	Gross profit margin, net profit margin
Competitiveness	Growth in sales
	Retention rate for customers
	Success rate in converting enquiries into sales

Dimension of performance	Possible measure of performance
Service quality	Number of complaints
	Customer satisfaction, as revealed by customer opinion surveys
Flexibility	Mix of different types of work done by employees
	Speed in responding to customer requests
Resource utilisation	Efficiency/productivity measures
	Capacity utilisation rates
Innovation	Number of new services offered within the previous year or two years

Fitzgerald and Moon also suggested that the dimensions of performance should also distinguish between the 'results' of actions taken in the past and 'determinants' of future performance.

(a) Financial performance and measures of competitiveness are performance measures that have resulted from measures taken in the past.

(b) Quality, flexibility, resource utilisation and innovation are all aspects of performance that will determine the success (or otherwise) of the organisation in the future.

These six dimensions are measures of competitive success both now and in the future, and so they are appropriate for measuring the performance of current management. Measuring performance in these dimensions 'is an attempt to address the short-termism criticism frequently levelled at financially-focused reports' (Fitzgerald).

7.2 Standards

The second part of Fitzgerald and Moon's framework for performance measurement concerns setting the standards or targets of performance, once the measures for the dimensions of performance have been selected.

There are three aspects to setting standards of performance:

- Individuals need to feel that they 'own' the standards and targets for which they will be made responsible.

- Individuals also need to feel that the targets or standards are realistic and achievable.

- The standards and targets should be seen as 'fair' and equitable for all the managers in the organisation.

7.3 Rewards

The third aspect of Fitzgerald and Moon's performance measurement framework is rewards. This refers to the structure of the rewards system, and how individuals will be rewarded for the successful achievement of performance targets.

There are three aspects to consider in a reward system.

- The system of setting targets and rewarding individuals for achieving the targets should be clear. Clarity will improve the motivation to achieve the targets

- Achievement of performance targets should be suitably rewarded.

- Individuals should be made responsible only for aspects of performance that they are in a position to control.

Question

A service business has collected some figures relating to its year just ended.

		Budget	Actual
Customer enquiries:	New customers	6,000	9,000
	Existing customers	4,000	3,000
Business won:	New customers	2,000	4,000
	Existing customers	1,500	1,500
Types of services performed:	Service A	875	780
	Service B	1,575	1,850
	Service C	1,050	2,870
Employees:	Service A	5	4
	Service B	10	10
	Service C	5	8

Required

Calculate figures that illustrate competitiveness and resource utilisation.

Answer

Competitiveness can only be measured from these figures by looking at how successful the organisation is at converting enquiries into firm orders.

Percentage of enquiries converted into firm orders

	Budget	Actual
New customers (W1)	33%	44%
Existing customers (W1)	37.5%	50%

Resource utilisation can be measured by looking at average services performed per employee.

	Budget	Actual	Rise
Service A (W2)	175	195	+11.4%
Service B (W2)	157.5	185	+17.5%
Service C (W2)	210	358.75	+70.8%

Workings

1   For example 2,000/6,000 = 33%
2   For example 875/5 = 175

What comments would you make about these results? How well is the business doing?

**xam focus
oint**

Be prepared to think up performance measures for different areas of an organisation's business. Remember to make the measures relevant to the organisation in question. There is little point in suggesting measures such as waiting times in queues to assess the quality of the service provided by an educational establishment.

Question

Performance indicators

Suggest two separate performance indicators that could be used to assess each of the following areas of a fast food chain's operations.

(a)   Food preparation department
(b)   Marketing department

Here are some suggestions.

(a)   Material usage per product   (b)   Market share
                Wastage levels   Sales revenue per employee
                Incidences of food poisoning   Growth in sales revenue

8 Target setting in qualitative areas

The balanced scorecard and Fitzgerald& Moon's Building Block model are based on the assumption that performance targets can be set and measured for non-financial aspects of performance. This presumes that all key non-financial aspects of performance can be measured and quantified.

In practice, this is not necessarily the case. Some critical non-financial aspects of performance may be difficult to quantify, or to quantify in a reliable way. There are several problems with qualitative non-financial performance targets.

(a)   There is often a problem with selecting a suitable measure of performance. For example, an important objective for an organisation may be winning and retaining customer loyalty. But how is a reliable target for customer loyalty decided?

         –   Opinion research by a market research firm and setting a 'target score for loyalty'?
         –   The percentage of customers who make a repeat order within x months?

     Similarly, a performance objective may be to deliver a high standard of service to a customer, but how is service quality defined? Having defined service quality, how is it measured?

(b)   By its very nature, qualitative data is not quantified. At best qualitative measures are converted into quantitative measures using a subjective scoring system. When performance is not quantified, it is difficult to target and monitor.

(c)   Data collection and management information systems. An organisation may have a well-established system for measuring quantitative data, especially in the areas of accounting and sales statistics. It is much less likely to have a reliable and comprehensive system for collecting data about qualitative aspects of performance.

Chapter Roundup

- **Performance measurement** aims to establish how well something or somebody is doing in relation to a plan.

  Performance measures may be divided into two types:

  - Financial performance indicators
  - Non-financial performance indicators

- **Financial performance indicators** analyse return on capital, profitability, liquidity and financial risk, often in relation to a plan or budget, or in relation to performance in preceding time periods.

- In private sector organisations, the most important financial performance indicators are measurements of profit.

- **Gearing ratios** measure the financial **risk** of a company's capital structure. Business risk can be measured by calculating a company's operational gearing.

- A company can be profitable but at the same time get into cash flow problems. Liquidity ratios (**current** and **quick**) and **working capital turnover ratios** give some idea of a company's liquidity and ability to generate cash from its business operations.

- Changes in cost structures, the competitive environment and the manufacturing environment have lead to an **increased use of non-financial performance indicators** (NFPIs). Non-financial performance indicators can also be a very useful guide to future financial performance.

- NFPIs can usefully be applied to **employees** and product/service **quality**.

- **Short-termism** is when there is a bias towards short-term rather than long-term performance. It is often due to the fact that managers' performance is measured on short-term results.

- The **balanced scorecard** approach to performance measurement focuses on four different perspectives of performance, and uses both financial and non-financial indicators to set performance targets and monitor performance.

- Fitzgerald and Moon's **building blocks** for **dimensions, standards** and **rewards** attempt to overcome the problems associated with performance measurement of service businesses.

Quick Quiz

1   Give five examples of a financial performance measure.

*   ....   *   ....

*   ....   *   ....

*   ....

2   How do quantitative and qualitative performance measures differ?

3   Choose the correct words from those highlighted.

In general, a current ratio **in excess of 1/less than 1/approximately zero** should be expected.

4   **Service quality** is measured principally by quantitative measures.

True ☐   False ☐

5   *Fill in the blanks.*

NFPIs are less likely to be .... than traditional profit-related measures and they should therefore offer a means of counteracting ....

6   What are the three most important features of the balanced scorecard approach?

7   *Fill in the blanks.*

The five characteristics of a service business are .... , ..., ..., ... and ....

8   Fitzgerald and Moon's standards for performance measurement systems are ownership, achievability and controllability. **True or false?**

9   *Fill in the gaps.*

Fitzgerald and Moon's dimensions of performance can be divided into results (............................... and ....) and determinants (................................. , ..., ... and ....) .

Answers to Quick Quiz

1. - Profit
   - Revenue
   - Costs
   - Share price
   - Cash flow

2. Quantitative measures are expressed in numbers whereas qualitative measures are not.

3. in excess of 1

4. False. Service quality is measured principally by **qualitative** measures.

5. manipulated
   short termism

6. - It looks at both internal and external matters concerning the organisation
   - It is related to the key elements of a company's strategy
   - Financial and non-financial measures are linked together

7. Heterogeneity/variability
   Perishability
   Intangibility

   Simultaneity/inseparability
   No transfer of ownership

8. False. They are ownership, achievability and equity.

9. *Results*

   Financial performance
   Competitive performance

   Determinants

   Quality   Innovation
   Flexibility   Resource utilisation

Now try the question below from the Practice Question Bank

Number	Level	Marks	Time
Q18	Examination	15	27 mins
Q19	Examination	15	27 mins

17

Divisional performance and transfer pricing

Topic list	Syllabus reference
1 Divisionalisation	D5
2 Return on investment (ROI)	D5 (c)
3 Residual income (RI)	D5 (c), (d)
4 Transfer pricing	D5 (a), (b)

Introduction

This chapter looks at **divisional performance** and **transfer pricing** which is a system of charging other divisions of your organisation when you provide them with your division's goods or services.

In a **divisionalised organisation** structure of any kind, if one division does work that is used by another division, transfer pricing may be required. Do not be misled by the term 'price': there is not necessarily any suggestion of **profit** as there usually is with an external selling price. But as we shall see, transfer pricing is particularly appropriate where divisions are designated as **profit centres**.

Study guide

		Intellectual level
D5	**Divisional performance and transfer pricing**	
(a)	Explain and illustrate the basis for setting a transfer price using variable cost, full cost and the principles behind allowing for intermediate markets	2
(b)	Explain how transfer prices can distort the performance assessment of divisions and decisions made	2
(c)	Explain the meaning of, and calculate, Return on Investment (ROI) and Residual Income (RI), and discuss their shortcomings	2
(d)	Compare divisional performance and recognise the problems of doing so	2

Exam guide

You may be required to calculate transfer prices in this exam. You must be able to explain how and why they are used and the problems they can create.

1 Divisionalisation

FAST FORWARD

> Divisionalisation is a term for the division of an organisation into divisions. Each divisional manager is responsible for the performance of the division. A division may be a cost centre (responsible for its costs only), a profit centre (responsible for revenues and profits) or an investment centre or Strategic Business Unit (responsible for costs, revenues and assets).
>
> There are a number of advantages and disadvantages to **divisionalisation**.

In general, a large organisation can be **structured in one of two ways: functionally** (all activities of a similar type within a company, such as production, sales, research, are under the control of the appropriate departmental head) or **divisionally** (split into divisions in accordance with the products or services made or provided).

Divisional managers are therefore responsible for all operations (production, sales and so on) relating to their product, the functional structure being applied to each division. It is possible, of course, that only part of a company is divisionalised and activities such as administration are structured centrally on a functional basis with the responsibility of providing services to *all* divisions.

1.1 Decentralisation

In general, a **divisional structure will lead to decentralisation** of the decision-making process and divisional managers may have the freedom to set selling prices, choose suppliers, make product mix and output decisions and so on. Decentralisation is, however, a matter of degree, depending on how much freedom divisional managers are given.

1.2 Advantages of divisionalisation

(a) Divisionalisation can **improve** the **quality of decisions** made because divisional managers (those taking the decisions) know local conditions and are able to make more informed judgements. Moreover, with the personal incentive to improve the division's performance, they ought to take decisions in the division's best interests.

(b) **Decisions should be taken more quickly** because information does not have to pass along the chain of command to and from top management. Decisions can be made on the spot by those who are familiar with the product lines and production processes and who are able to react to changes in local conditions quickly and efficiently.

(c) The authority to act to improve performance should **motivate divisional managers**.

(d) Divisional organisation **frees top management** from detailed involvement in day-to-day operations and allows them to devote more time to strategic planning.

(e) Divisions provide **valuable training grounds for future members of top management** by giving them experience of managerial skills in a less complex environment than that faced by top management.

(f) In a large business organisation, the **central head office will not have the management resources or skills to direct operations closely enough itself**. Some authority must be delegated to local operational managers.

1.3 Disadvantages of divisionalisation

(a) A danger with divisional accounting is that the business organisation will divide into a number of self-interested segments, each acting at times against the wishes and interests of other segments. Decisions might be taken by a divisional manager in the best interests of his own part of the business, but against the best interest of other divisions and possibly against the interests of the organisation as a whole.

A task of **head office** is therefore to try to **prevent dysfunctional decision making** by individual divisional managers. To do this, head office must reserve some power and authority for itself so that divisional managers cannot be allowed to make entirely independent decisions. A **balance** ought to be kept **between decentralisation** of authority to provide incentives and motivation, **and retaining centralised authority** to ensure that the organisation's divisions are all working towards the same target, the benefit of the organisation as a whole (in other words, **retaining goal congruence** among the organisation's separate divisions).

(b) It is claimed that the **costs of activities that are common** to all divisions such as running the accounting department **may be greater** for a divisionalised structure than for a centralised structure.

(c) **Top management**, by delegating decision making to divisional managers, may **lose control** since they are not aware of what is going on in the organisation as a whole. (With a good system of performance evaluation and appropriate control information, however, top management should be able to control operations just as effectively.)

1.4 Responsibility accounting

FAST FORWARD

Responsibility accounting is the term used to describe decentralisation of authority, with the performance of the decentralised units measured in terms of accounting results.

With a system of responsibility accounting there are five types of **responsibility centre: cost centre; revenue centre; profit centre; contribution centre; investment centre**.

The creation of divisions allows for the operation of a system of **responsibility accounting**. There are a number of types of responsibility accounting unit, or responsibility centre that can be used within a system of responsibility accounting.

In the weakest form of decentralisation a system of **cost centres** might be used. As decentralisation becomes stronger the responsibility accounting framework will be based around **profit centres**. In its strongest form **investment centres** are used.

Type of responsibility centre	Manager has control over ...	Principal performance measures
Cost centre	Controllable costs	Variance analysis Efficiency measures
Revenue centre	Revenues only	Revenues
Profit centre	Controllable costs Sales prices (including transfer prices)	Profit
Contribution centre	As for profit centre except that expenditure is reported on a marginal cost basis	Contribution
Investment centre	Controllable costs Sales prices (including transfer prices) Output volumes Investment in non-current assets and working capital	Return on investment Residual income Other financial ratios

2 Return on investment (ROI)

12/08, 6/11, 6/12, Specimen paper

FAST FORWARD

The performance of an investment centre is usually monitored using either or both of **return on investment (ROI)** and **residual income (RI)**.

ROI is generally regarded as the **key performance measure**. The main reason for its **widespread use** is that it **ties in directly with the accounting process**, and is identifiable from the income statement and balance sheet. However it does have limitations, as we will see later in this chapter.

Key term

Return on investment (ROI) shows how much profit has been made in relation to the amount of capital invested and is calculated as (profit/capital employed) × 100%.

For example, suppose that a company has two investment centres A and B, which show results for the year as follows.

	A $	B $
Profit	60,000	30,000
Capital employed	400,000	120,000
ROI	15%	25%

Investment centre A has made double the profits of investment centre B, and in terms of profits alone has therefore been more 'successful'. However, B has achieved its profits with a much lower capital investment, and so has earned a much higher ROI. This suggests that B has been a more successful investment than A.

2.1 Measuring ROI

FAST FORWARD

There is no generally agreed method of calculating ROI and it can have **behavioural implications** and lead to dysfunctional decision making when used as a guide to investment decisions. It focuses attention on short-run performance whereas investment decisions should be evaluated over their full life.

ROI can be measured in different ways.

2.1.1 Profit after depreciation as a % of net assets employed

This is probably the **most common method**, but it does present a problem. If an investment centre maintains the same annual profit, and keeps the same assets without a policy of regular replacement of

non-current assets, its ROI will increase year by year as the assets get older. This **can give a false impression of improving performance over time**.

For example, the results of investment centre X, with a policy of straight-line depreciation of assets over a 5-year period, might be as follows.

Year	Non-current assets at cost $'000	Depreciation in the year $'000	NBV (mid year) $'000	Working capital $'000	Capital employed $'000	Profit $'000	ROI
0	100			10	110		
1	100	20	90	10	100	10	10.0%
2	100	20	70	10	80	10	12.5%
3	100	20	50	10	60	10	16.7%
4	100	20	30	10	40	10	25.0%
5	100	20	10	10	20	10	50.0%

This table of figures is intended to show that an investment centre can **improve its ROI** year by year, simply **by allowing its non-current assets to depreciate**, and there could be a **disincentive to** investment centre managers to **reinvest in new or replacement assets**, because the centre's ROI would probably fall.

This example has used a mid year NBV but a year end or start of year NBV can also be used.

Question

ROI calculation (1)

A new company has non-current assets of $460,000 which will be depreciated to nil on a straight line basis over 10 years. Net current assets will consistently be $75,000, and annual profit will consistently be $30,000. ROI is measured as return on net assets.

Required

Calculate the company's ROI in years 2 and 6.

Answer

Year 2 – 6.8%
Year 6 – 11.6%

A further disadvantage of measuring ROI as profit divided by net assets is that, for similar reasons, it is not **easy to compare** fairly the **performance of investment centres**.

For example, suppose that we have two investment centres.

	Investment centre P $	Investment centre P $	Investment centre Q $	Investment centre Q $
Working capital		20,000		20,000
Non-current assets at cost	230,000		230,000	
Accumulated depreciation	170,000		10,000	
Net book value		60,000		220,000
Capital employed		80,000		240,000
Profit		$24,000		$24,000
ROI		30%		10%

Investment centres P and Q have the same amount of working capital, the same value of non-current assets at cost, and the same profit. But P's non-current assets have been depreciated by a much bigger amount (presumably P's non-current assets are much older than Q's) and so P's ROI is three times the size of Q's ROI. The conclusion might therefore be that P has performed much better than Q. This comparison, however, would not be 'fair', because the difference in performance might be entirely attributable to the age of their non-current assets.

The arguments for using net book values for calculating ROI

(a)   It is the **'normally accepted'** method of calculating ROI.

(b)   Organisations are continually buying new non-current assets to replace old ones that wear out, and so on the whole, the **total net book value** of all non-current assets together **will remain fairly constant** (assuming nil inflation and nil growth).

2.1.2 Profit after depreciation as a % of gross assets employed

Instead of measuring ROI as return on net assets, we could measure it as return on gross assets ie before depreciation. This would **remove the problem of ROI increasing over time as non-current assets get older**.

If a company acquired a non-current asset costing $40,000, which it intends to depreciate by $10,000 pa for 4 years, and if the asset earns a profit of $8,000 pa after depreciation, ROI might be calculated on net book values or gross values, as follows.

Year	Profit $	NBV(mid-year value) $	ROI based on NBV	Gross value $	ROI based on gross value
1	8,000	35,000	22.9%	40,000	20%
2	8,000	25,000	32.0%	40,000	20%
3	8,000	15,000	53.3%	40,000	20%
4	8,000	5,000	160.0%	40,000	20%

The ROI based on **net book value** shows an **increasing trend over time**, simply because the asset's value is falling as it is depreciated. The ROI based on gross book value suggests that the asset has **performed consistently** in each of the four years, which is probably a more valid conclusion.

Question	ROI calculation (2)

Repeat **Question: ROI calculation (1)**, measuring ROI as return on gross assets.

Answer

Year 2 – 5.6%
Year 6 – 5.6%

However, using gross book values to measure ROI has its **disadvantages**. Most important of these is that measuring ROI as return on gross assets ignores the age factor, and **does not distinguish between old and new assets**.

(a)   **Older non-current assets** usually **cost more to repair and maintain**, to keep them running. An investment centre with old assets may therefore have its profitability reduced by repair costs, and its ROI might fall over time as its assets get older and repair costs get bigger.

(b)   **Inflation** and **technological change alter the cost of non-current assets**. If one investment centre has non-current assets bought ten years ago with a gross cost of $1 million, and another investment centre, in the same area of business operations, has non-current assets bought very recently for $1 million, the quantity and technological character of the non-current assets of the two investment centres are likely to be very different.

2.1.3 Constituent elements of the investment base

Although we have looked at how the investment base should be valued, we need to consider its appropriate constituent elements.

(a) If a **manager's performance is being evaluated**, only those **assets** which can be **traced directly to the division** and are **controllable by the manager should be included**. Head office assets or investment centre assets controlled by head office should not be included. So, for example, only those cash balances actually maintained within an investment centre itself should be included.

(b) If it is the performance of the investment centre that is being appraised, **a proportion of the investment in head office assets would need to be included** because an investment centre could not operate without the support of head office assets and administrative backup.

2.1.4 Profits

We have looked at how to define the asset base used in the calculations but what about profit? If the **performance of the investment centre manager is being assessed** it should seem reasonable to **base profit on the revenues and costs controllable by the manager** and exclude service and head office costs except those costs specifically attributable to the investment centre. If it is the **performance of the investment centre that is being assessed, however, the inclusion of general service and head office costs would seem reasonable**.

Exam focus point

> The profit figure for ROI should always be the amount before any interest is charged.

2.1.5 Massaging the ROI

If a manager's large bonus depends on ROI being met, the manager may feel pressure to massage the measure. The **asset base** of the ratio can be **altered** by increasing/decreasing payables and receivables (by speeding up or delaying payments and receipts).

2.2 ROI and new investments

If investment centre performance is judged by ROI, we should expect that the managers of investment centres will probably decide to undertake new capital investments **only if these new investments are likely to increase the ROI of their centre**.

Suppose that an investment centre, A, currently makes a return of 40% on capital employed. The manager of centre A would probably only want to undertake new investments that promise to yield a return of 40% or more, otherwise the investment centre's overall ROI would fall.

For example, if investment centre A currently has assets of $1,000,000 and expects to earn a profit of $400,000, how would the centre's manager view a new capital investment which would cost $250,000 and yield a profit of $75,000 pa?

	Without the new investment	With the new investment
Profit	$400,000	$475,000
Capital employed	$1,000,000	$1,250,000
ROI	40%	38%

The **new investment** would **reduce the investment centre's ROI** from 40% to 38%, and so the investment centre manager would probably decide **not to undertake** the new investment.

If the group of companies of which investment centre A is a part has a target ROI of, say, 25%, the new investment would presumably be seen as **beneficial for the group as a whole**. But even though it promises to yield a return of 75,000/250,000 = 30%, which is above the group's target ROI, it would still make investment centre A's results look worse. The manager of investment centre A would, in these circumstances, be motivated to do not what is best for the organisation as a whole, but what is **best for his division**.

ROI should not be used to guide investment decisions but there is a difficult **motivational** problem. If management performance is measured in terms of ROI, any decisions which benefit the company in the long term but which reduce the ROI in the immediate short term would reflect badly on the manager's reported performance. In other words, good investment decisions would make a manager's performance seem **worse** than if the wrong investment decision were taken instead.

3 Residual income (RI)   6/11, 6/12, Specimen paper

FAST FORWARD

> RI can sometimes give results that avoid the **behavioural** problem of **dysfunctionality**. Its weakness is that it does not facilitate comparisons between investment centres nor does it relate the size of a centre's income to the size of the investment.

An alternative way of measuring the performance of an investment centre, instead of using ROI, is residual income (RI). **Residual income** is a **measure of the centre's profits after deducting a notional or imputed interest cost**.

(a) The centre's profit is **after deducting depreciation** on capital equipment.

(b) The imputed cost of capital might be the organisation's cost of borrowing or its weighted average cost of capital.

Key term

> **Residual income** is a measure of the centre's profits after deducting a notional or imputed interest cost.

Question   RI

A division with capital employed of $400,000 currently earns an ROI of 22%. It can make an additional investment of $50,000 for a 5 year life with nil residual value. The average net profit from this investment would be $12,000 after depreciation. The division's cost of capital is 14%.

What are the residual incomes before and after the investment?

Answer

	Before investment	*After investment*
	$	$
Divisional profit ($400,000 × 22%)	88,000	100,000
Imputed interest		
(400,000 × 0.14)	56,000	
(450,000 × 0.14)		63,000
Residual income	32,000	37,000

3.1 The advantages and weaknesses of RI compared with ROI

The advantages of using RI

(a) Residual income will **increase** when investments earning above the cost of capital are undertaken and investments earning below the cost of capital are eliminated.

(b) Residual income is **more flexible** since a different cost of capital can be applied to investments with **different risk** characteristics.

The **weakness** of RI is that it **does not facilitate comparisons** between investment centres nor **does it relate the size of a centre's income to the size of the investment**.

3.2 RI versus ROI: marginally profitable investments

Residual income will increase if a new investment is undertaken which earns a profit in excess of the imputed interest charge on the value of the asset acquired. Residual income will go up even if the investment only just exceeds the imputed interest charge, and this means that 'marginally profitable' investments are likely to be undertaken by the investment centre manager.

In contrast, when a manager is judged by ROI, a marginally profitable investment would be less likely to be undertaken because it would reduce the average ROI earned by the centre as a whole.

3.2.1 Example: ROI versus residual income

Suppose that Department H has the following profit, assets employed and an imputed interest charge of 12% on operating assets.

	$	$
Operating profit	30,000	
Operating assets		100,000
Imputed interest (12%)	12,000	
Return on investment		30%
Residual income	18,000	

Suppose now that an additional investment of $10,000 is proposed, which will increase operating income in Department H by $1,400. The effect of the investment would be:

	$	$
Total operating income	31,400	
Total operating assets		110,000
Imputed interest (12%)	13,200	
Return on investment		28.5%
Residual income	18,200	

If the Department H manager is made responsible for the department's performance, he would **resist the new investment if he were to be judged on ROI**, but would **welcome the investment if he were judged according to RI**, since there would be a marginal increase of $200 in residual income from the investment, but a fall of 1.5% in ROI.

The marginal investment offers a return of 14% ($1,400 on an investment of $10,000) which is above the 'cut-off rate' of 12%. Since the original return on investment was 30%, the marginal investment will reduce the overall divisional performance. Indeed, any marginal investment offering an accounting rate of return of less than 30% in the year would reduce the overall performance.

Exam focus point

Examination questions on residual income may focus on the sort of behavioural aspects of investment centre measurement that we have discussed above, for example why it is considered necessary to use residual income to measure performance rather than ROI, and why residual income might influence an investment centre manager's investment decisions differently.

4 Transfer pricing   6/10, 12/11, 12/13

FAST FORWARD

Transfer prices are a way of promoting **divisional autonomy**, ideally without prejudicing the **measurement of divisional performance** or discouraging **overall corporate profit maximisation**.

Transfer prices should be set at a level which ensures that profits for the organisation as a whole are maximised.

Transfer pricing is used when divisions of an organisation need to charge other divisions of the same organisation for goods and services they provide to them. For example, subsidiary A might make a component that is used as part of a product made by subsidiary B of the same company, but that can also

be sold to the external market, including makers of rival products to subsidiary B's product. There will therefore be two sources of revenue for A.

(a) External sales revenue from sales made to other organisations.

(b) Internal sales revenue from sales made to other responsibility centres within the same organisation, valued at the transfer price.

Key term

> A **transfer price** is the price at which goods or services are transferred from one department to another, or from one member of a group to another.

4.1 Problems with transfer pricing

4.1.1 Maintaining the right level of divisional autonomy

Transfer prices are particularly appropriate for **profit centres** because if one profit centre does work for another the size of the transfer price will affect the costs of one profit centre and the revenues of another.

However, as we have seen, a danger with profit centre accounting is that the business organisation will **divide into a number of self-interested segments**, each acting at times against the wishes and interests of other segments. Decisions might be taken by a profit centre manager in the best interests of his own part of the business, but against the best interests of other profit centres and possibly the organisation as a whole.

4.1.2 Ensuring divisional performance is measured fairly

Profit centre managers tend to put their own profit performance above everything else. Since profit centre performance is measured according to the profit they earn, no profit centre will want to do work for another and incur costs without being paid for it. Consequently, profit centre managers are likely to dispute the size of transfer prices with each other, or disagree about whether one profit centre should do work for another or not. Transfer prices **affect behaviour and decisions** by profit centre managers.

4.1.3 Ensuring corporate profits are maximised

When there are disagreements about how much work should be transferred between divisions, and how many sales the division should make to the external market, there is presumably a **profit-maximising level of output and sales for the organisation as a whole**. However, unless each profit centre also maximises its own profit at this same level of output, there will be inter-divisional disagreements about output levels and the profit-maximising output will not be achieved.

4.1.4 The ideal solution

Ideally a transfer price should be set at a level that overcomes these problems.

(a) The transfer price should provide an 'artificial' selling price that enables the **transferring division to earn a return for its efforts**, and the **receiving division to incur a cost for benefits received**.

(b) The transfer price should be set at a level that enables **profit centre performance** to be **measured 'commercially'**. This means that the transfer price should be a fair commercial price.

(c) The transfer price, if possible, should encourage profit centre managers to agree on the amount of goods and services to be transferred, which will also be at a level that is consistent with the aims of the organisation as a whole such as **maximising company profits**.

In practice it is difficult to achieve all three aims.

Question

The transfer pricing system operated by a divisional company has the potential to make a significant contribution towards the achievement of corporate financial objectives.

Required

Explain the potential benefits of operating a transfer pricing system within a divisionalised company.

Answer

Potential benefits of operating a transfer pricing system within a divisionalised company include the following.

(a) It can lead to **goal congruence** by motivating divisional managers to make decisions, which improve divisional profit and improve profit of the organisation as a whole.

(b) It can prevent **dysfunctional decision making** so that decisions taken by a divisional manager are in the best interests of his own part of the business, other divisions and the organisation as a whole.

(c) Transfer prices can be set at a level that enables divisional performance to be measured 'commercially'. A transfer pricing system should therefore report a level of divisional profit that is a **reasonable measure of the managerial performance** of the division.

(d) It should ensure that **divisional autonomy** is not undermined. A well-run transfer pricing system helps to ensure that a balance is kept between divisional autonomy to provide incentives and motivation, and centralised authority to ensure that the divisions are all working towards the same target, the benefit of the organisation as a whole.

4.2 General rules

FAST FORWARD

The **limits within which transfer prices should fall** are as follows.

- **The minimum**. The sum of the supplying division's marginal cost and opportunity cost of the item transferred.
- **The maximum**. The lowest market price at which the receiving division could purchase the goods or services externally, less any internal cost savings in packaging and delivery.

The **minimum** results from the fact that the **supplying division will not agree to transfer if the transfer price is less than the marginal cost + opportunity cost of the item transferred** (because if it were the division would incur a loss).

The **maximum** results from the fact that the **receiving division will buy the item at the cheapest price possible**.

4.2.1 Example: general rules

Division X produces product L at a marginal cost per unit of $100. If a unit is transferred internally to division Y, $25 contribution is foregone on an external sale. The item can be purchased externally for $150.

- **The minimum**. Division X will not agree to a transfer price of less than $(100 + 25) = $125 per unit.
- **The maximum**. Division Y will not agree to a transfer price in excess of $150.

The difference between the two results ($25) represents the savings from producing internally as opposed to buying externally.

4.2.2 Opportunity cost

The **opportunity cost** included in determining the lower limit will be one of the following.

(a)   The maximum contribution forgone by the supplying division **in transferring internally rather than selling goods externally**.

(b)   The contribution forgone by **not using the same facilities** in the producing division **for their next best alternative use**.

If there is **no external market** for the item being transferred, and **no alternative uses for** the division's facilities, the **transfer price = standard variable cost of production**.

If there is an **external market** for the item being transferred and **no alternative, more profitable use** for the facilities in that division, the **transfer price = the market price**.

4.2.3 Example: The transfer price at full and spare capacity

The factors that influence the transfer price charged when divisions are operating at **full capacity** and **spare capacity** are best illustrated using an example.

Until recently, Strike Ltd focused exclusively on making soles for work boots and football boots. It sold these rubber soles to boot manufacturers. Last year the company decided to take advantage of its strong reputation by expanding into the business of making football boots. As a consequence of this expansion, the company is now structured as two independent divisions, the Boot Division and the Sole Division.

The Sole Division continues to make rubber soles for both football boots and work boots and sells these soles to other boot manufacturers. The Boot division manufactures leather uppers for football boots and attaches these uppers to rubber soles. During its first year the Boot Division purchased its rubber soles from outside suppliers so as not to disrupt the operations of the Sole Division.

Strike management now wants the Sole Division to provide at least some of the soles used by the Boot Division. The table below shows the contribution margin for each division when the Boot Division purchases from an outside supplier.

	Boot Division		*Sole Division*
	$		$
Selling price of football boot	100	Selling price of sole	28
Variable cost of making boot (not including sole)	45	Variable cost per sole	21
Cost of sole purchased from outside suppliers	25		
Contribution margin per unit	30	Contribution margin per unit	7

The information above indicates that the total contribution margin per unit is $37 ($30 + $7).

Required

What would be a fair transfer price if the Sole Division sold 10,000 soles to the Boot Division?

Solution

The answer depends on how busy the Sole Division is – that is, whether it has **spare capacity**.

No spare capacity

As indicated above, the Sole Division charges $28 and derives a contribution margin of $7 per sole. The Sole Division has **no spare capacity** and produces and sells 80,000 units (soles) to outside customers. Therefore, the Sole Division must receive from the Boot Division a payment that will at least cover its variable cost per sole **plus** its lost contribution margin per sole (the **opportunity cost**). If the Sole Division can not cover that amount (the **minimum** transfer price), it should not sell soles to the Boot Division. The minimum transfer price that would be acceptable to the Sole Division is$28, as shown below.

$21 (variable cost) + $7 (opportunity cost) = $28

Spare capacity

The minimum transfer price is different if a division has spare capacity. Assume the Sole Division produces 80,000 soles but can only sell 70,000 to the open market. As a result, it has available capacity of 10,000 units. In this situation, the Sole Division does not lose its contribution margin of $7 per unit, and therefore the minimum price it would now accept is $21 as shown below.

$21 (variable cost) + $0 (opportunity cost) = $21

In this case the Boot Division and the Sole Division should **negotiate** a transfer price within the range of $21 and $25 (cost from outside supplier).

4.3 The use of market price as a basis for transfer prices

If an **external market price exists** for transferred goods, profit centre managers will be aware of the price they could obtain or the price they would have to pay for their goods on the external market, and they would inevitably **compare** this price **with the transfer price**.

4.3.1 Example: Transferring goods at market value

A company has two profit centres, A and B. A sells half of its output on the open market and transfers the other half to B. Costs and external revenues in an accounting period are as follows.

	A	B	Total
	$	$	$
External sales	8,000	24,000	32,000
Costs of production	12,000	10,000	22,000
Company profit			10,000

Required

What are the consequences of setting a transfer price at market value?

Solution

If the transfer price is at market price, A would be happy to sell the output to B for $8,000, which is what A would get by selling it externally instead of transferring it.

		A		B	Total
	$	$	$	$	$
Market sales		8,000		24,000	32,000
Transfer sales		8,000		–	
		16,000		24,000	
Transfer costs			8,000		
Own costs	12,000		10,000		22,000
		12,000		18,000	
Profit		4,000		6,000	10,000

The **transfer sales of A are self cancelling with the transfer cost of B**, so that the total profits are unaffected by the transfer items. The transfer price simply spreads the total profit between A and B.

Consequences

(a) A earns the same profit on transfers as on external sales. B must pay a commercial price for transferred goods, and both divisions will have their profit measured in a fair way.

(b) A will be indifferent about selling externally or transferring goods to B because the profit is the same on both types of transaction. B can therefore ask for and obtain as many units as it wants from A.

A **market-based** transfer price therefore seems to be the **ideal** transfer price.

4.4 The merits of market value transfer prices

4.4.1 Divisional autonomy

In a decentralised company, divisional managers should have the **autonomy** to make output, selling and buying **decisions which appear to be in the best interests of the division's performance.** (If every division optimises its performance, the company as a whole must inevitably achieve optimal results.) Thus a **transferor division should be given the freedom to sell output on the open market,** rather than to transfer it within the company.

'Arm's length' transfer prices, which give profit centre managers the freedom to negotiate prices with other profit centres as though they were independent companies, will tend to result in a market-based transfer price.

4.4.2 Corporate profit maximisation

In most cases where the transfer price is at market price, **internal transfers** should be **expected**, because the **buying division** is likely to **benefit** from a better quality of service, greater flexibility, and dependability of supply. **Both divisions** may **benefit** from cheaper costs of administration, selling and transport. A market price as the transfer price would therefore **result in decisions which would be in the best interests of the company or group as a whole**.

4.4.3 Divisional performance measurement

Where a **market price exists**, but the **transfer price is a different amount** (say, at standard cost plus), divisional managers will **argue** about the volume of internal transfers.

For example, if division X is expected to sell output to division Y at a transfer price of $8 per unit when the open market price is $10, its manager will decide to sell all output on the open market. The manager of division Y would resent the loss of his cheap supply from X, and would be reluctant to buy on the open market. A wasteful situation would arise where X sells on the open market at $10, where Y buys at $10, so that administration, selling and distribution costs would have been saved if X had sold directly to Y at $10, the market price.

4.5 The disadvantages of market value transfer prices

Market value as a transfer price does have certain **disadvantages**.

(a) The **market price may be a temporary one**, induced by adverse economic conditions, or dumping, or the market price might depend on the volume of output supplied to the external market by the profit centre.

(b) A transfer price at market value might, under some circumstances, **act as a disincentive to use up any spare capacity** in the divisions. A price based on incremental cost, in contrast, might provide an incentive to use up the spare resources in order to provide a marginal contribution to profit.

(c) Many products **do not have an equivalent market price** so that the price of a similar, but not identical, product might have to be chosen. In such circumstances, the option to sell or buy on the open market does not really exist.

(d) There might be an **imperfect external market** for the transferred item, so that if the transferring division tried to sell more externally, it would have to reduce its selling price.

4.6 Cost-based approaches to transfer pricing

Problems arise with the use of **cost-based** transfer prices because one party or the other is liable to perceive them as unfair.

Cost-based approaches to transfer pricing are often used in practice, because in practice the following conditions are common.

(a) There is **no external market** for the product that is being transferred.

(b) Alternatively, although there is an external market it is an **imperfect** one because the market price is affected by such factors as the amount that the company setting the transfer price supplies to it, or because there is only a limited external demand.

In either case there will not be a suitable market price upon which to base the transfer price.

4.6.1 Transfer prices based on full cost

Under this approach, the **full cost** (including fixed overheads absorbed) incurred by the supplying division in making the 'intermediate' product is charged to the receiving division. The obvious drawback to this is that the division supplying the product **makes no profit** on its work so is not motivated to supply internally. Also, there are a number of alternative ways in which fixed costs can be accounted for. If a **full cost plus** approach is used a **profit margin** is also included in this transfer price. The supplying division will therefore gain some profit at the expense of the buying division.

4.6.2 Example: Transfer prices based on full cost

Suppose a company has two profit centres, A and B. A can only sell half of its maximum output of 800 units externally because of limited demand. It transfers the other half of its output to B which also faces limited demand. Costs and revenues in an accounting period are as follows.

	A	B	Total
	$	$	$
External sales	8,000	24,000	32,000
Costs of production in the division	13,000	10,000	23,000
Profit			9,000

Division A's costs included fixed production overheads of $4,800 and fixed selling and administration costs of $1,000.

There are no opening or closing inventories. It does not matter, for this illustration, whether marginal costing or absorption costing is used. For the moment, we shall ignore the question of whether the current output levels are profit-maximising and congruent with the goals of the company as a whole.

If the transfer price is at full cost, A in our example would have 'sales' to B of $6,000 (($13,000 – 1,000) × 50%). Selling and administration costs are not included as these are not incurred on the internal transfers. This would be a cost to B, as follows.

	A		B		Company as a whole
	$	$	$	$	$
Open market sales		8,000		24,000	32,000
Transfer sales		6,000		–	
Total sales, inc transfers		14,000		24,000	
Transfer costs			6,000		
Own costs	13,000		10,000		23,000
Total costs, inc transfers		13,000		16,000	
Profit		1,000		8,000	9,000

The **transfer sales of A are self-cancelling with the transfer costs of B** so that total profits are **unaffected by the transfer items**. The transfer price simply spreads the total profit of $9,000 between A and B.

The obvious **drawback** to the transfer price at cost is that **A makes no profit** on its work, and the manager of division A would much prefer to sell output on the open market to earn a profit, rather than transfer to B, regardless of whether or not transfers to B would be in the best interests of the company as a whole. Division A needs a profit on its transfers in order to be motivated to supply B; therefore transfer pricing at cost is inconsistent with the use of a profit centre accounting system.

An **intermediate product** is one that is used as a component of another product, for example car headlights or food additives.

4.6.3 Transfer price at variable cost

A variable cost approach entails charging the variable cost (which we assume to be the same as the marginal cost) that has been incurred by the supplying division to the receiving division.

The problem is that with a transfer price at marginal cost the **supplying division does not cover its fixed costs.**

4.7 Identifying the optimal transfer price

Here are some guiding rules for identifying the optimal transfer price.

(a)   The **ideal transfer price** should **reflect the opportunity cost** of sale to the supply division and the opportunity cost to the buying division. Unfortunately, full information about opportunity costs may not be easily obtainable in practice.

(b)   Where a **perfect external market price exists and unit variable costs and unit selling prices are constant**, the **opportunity cost** of transfer will be **external market price** or **external market price less savings in selling costs**.

(c)   In the **absence of a perfect external market price for the transferred item**, but when **unit variable costs are constant**, and the **sales price per unit of the end-product is constant**, the **ideal transfer price** should reflect the opportunity cost of the resources consumed by the supply division to make and supply the item and so should be at **standard variable cost + opportunity cost of making the transfer**.

(d)   When **unit variable costs and/or unit selling prices are not constant,** there will be a **profit-maximising level of output** and the **ideal transfer price** will only be found by sensible **negotiation** and careful **analysis**.

   (i)   Establish the output and sales quantities that will optimise the profits of the company or group as a whole.

   (ii)   Establish the transfer price at which both profit centres would maximise their profits at this company-optimising output level.

   There may be a range of prices within which both profit centres can agree on the output level that would maximise their individual profits and the profits of the company as a whole. Any price within the range would then be 'ideal'.

4.8 Transfer pricing calculations

4.8.1 Sub-optimal decisions

Note that as the level of transfer price increases, its effect on a division within the organisation could lead to sub-optimalisation problems for the organisation as a whole.

4.8.2 Example: Sub-optimal decisions

For example, suppose division B could buy the product from an outside supplier for $10 instead of paying $15 ($6,000/(800/2)) to division A. This transfer price would therefore force division B to buy the product externally at $10 per unit, although it could be manufactured internally for a variable cost of $(13,000 – 4,800 – 1,000)/800 = $9 per unit.

Although division B (the buying division) would save ($15 – $10) = $5 per unit by buying externally, the organisation as a whole would lose $400 as follows.

	Per unit $
Marginal cost of production	9
External purchase cost	10
Loss if buy in	1

The overall loss on transfer/purchase of 400 units is therefore 400 × $1 = $400.

This loss of $1 per unit assumes that any other use for the released capacity would produce a benefit of less than $400. If the 400 units could also be sold externally for $20 per unit, the optimal decision for the organisation as a whole would be to buy in the units for division B at $10 per unit.

	Per unit $
Market price	20
Marginal cost	9
Contribution	11
Loss if buy-in	(1)
Incremental profit	10

The overall incremental profit would therefore be 400 × $10 = $4,000.

4.8.3 Example: Prices based on full cost plus

If the transfers are at cost plus a margin of, say, 10%, A's sales to B would be $6,600 ($13,000 –1,000) × 50% × 1.10).

	A $	A $	B $	B $	Total $
Open market sales		8,000		24,000	32,000
Transfer sales		6,600		–	
		14,600		24,000	
Transfer costs			6,600		
Own costs	13,000		10,000		23,000
		13,000		16,600	
Profit		1,600		7,400	9,000

Compared to a transfer price at cost, **A gains some profit** at the expense of B. However, A makes a bigger profit on external sales in this case because the profit mark-up of 10% is less than the profit mark-up on open market sales. The choice of 10% as a profit mark-up was arbitrary and unrelated to external market conditions.

The transfer price **fails on all three criteria** (divisional autonomy, performance measurement and corporate profit measurement) for judgement.

(a) Arguably, the transfer price does not give A fair revenue or charge B a reasonable cost, and so their profit **performance is distorted**. It would certainly be unfair, for example, to compare A's profit with B's profit.

(b) Given this unfairness it is likely that the **autonomy** of each of the divisional managers is **under threat.** If they cannot agree on what is a fair split of the external profit a decision will have to be imposed from above.

(c) It would seem to give A an incentive to sell more goods externally and transfer less to B. This may or **may not be in the best interests of the company as a whole**.

In fact we can demonstrate that the method is **flawed from the point of view of corporate profit maximisation**. Division A's total production costs of $12,000 include an element of fixed costs. Half of division A's total production costs are transferred to division B. However from the point of view of division B the cost is entirely variable.

The cost per unit to A is $15 ($12,000 ÷ 800) and this includes a fixed element of $6 ($4,800 ÷ 800), while division B's own costs are $25 ($10,000 ÷ 400) per unit, including a fixed element of $10 (say). The **total variable cost is really** $9 + $15 = **$24**, but from division **B's point of view** the **variable cost** is $15 + $(25 − 10) = **$30**. This means that division B will be unwilling to sell the final product for less than $30, whereas any price above $24 would make a contribution to overall costs. Thus, if external prices for the final product fall, B might be tempted to cease production.

4.8.4 Example: Transfer prices based on variable or marginal cost

A variable or marginal cost approach entails charging the variable cost (which we assume to be the same as the marginal cost) that has been incurred by the supplying division to the receiving division. As above, we shall suppose that A's cost per unit is $15, of which $6 is fixed and $9 variable.

	A		B		Company as a whole	
	$	$	$	$	$	$
Market sales		8,000		24,000		32,000
Transfer sales		3,600		–		
		11,600		24,000		
Transfer costs	–		3,600			
Own variable costs	7,200		6,000		13,200	
Own fixed costs	5,800		4,000		9,800	
Total costs and transfers		13,000		13,600		23,000
(Loss)/Profit		(1,400)		10,400		9,000

4.8.5 Divisional autonomy, divisional performance measurement and corporate profit maximisation

(a) This result is **deeply unsatisfactory for the manager of division** A who could make an additional $4,400 ($(8,000 − 3,600)) profit if no goods were transferred to division B, but all were sold externally.

(b) Given that the manager of division A would prefer to transfer externally, **head office** are likely to have to **insist** that internal transfers are made.

(c) For the company overall, external transfers only would cause a large fall in profit, because division B could make no sales at all.

Point to note. Suppose no more than the current $8,000 could be earned from external sales and the production capacity used for production for internal transfer would remain idle if not used. Division A would be indifferent to the transfers at marginal cost as they do not represent any benefit to the division.

If more than the $8,000 of revenue could be earned externally (ie division A could sell more externally than at present), division A would have a strong disincentive to supply B at marginal cost.

Chapter Roundup

- Divisionalisation is a term for the division of an organisation into divisions. Each divisional manager is responsible for the performance of the division. A division may be a cost centre (responsible for its costs only), a profit centre (responsible for revenues and profits) or an investment centre or Strategic Business Unit (responsible for costs, revenues and assets).

  There are a number of advantages and disadvantages to **divisionalisation**.

- **Responsibility accounting** is the term used to describe decentralisation of authority, with the performance of the decentralised units measured in terms of accounting results.

  With a system of responsibility accounting there are five types of **responsibility centre: cost centre; revenue centre; profit centre; contribution centre; investment centre**.

- The performance of an investment centre is usually monitored using either or both of **return on investment (ROI)** and **residual income (RI)**.

- There is no generally agreed method of calculating ROI and it can have **behavioural implications** and lead to dysfunctional decision making when used as a guide to investment decisions. It focuses attention on short-run performance whereas investment decisions should be evaluated over their full life.

- RI can sometimes give results that avoid the **behavioural** problem of **dysfunctionality**. Its weakness is that it does not facilitate comparisons between investment centres nor does it relate the size of a centre's income to the size of the investment.

- Transfer prices are a way of promoting **divisional autonomy**, ideally without prejudicing the **measurement of divisional performance** or discouraging **overall corporate profit maximisation**.

  Transfer prices should be set at a level which ensures that profits for the organisation as a whole are maximised.

- The **limits within which transfer prices should fall** are as follows.

  - **The minimum**. The sum of the supplying division's marginal cost and opportunity cost of the item transferred.

  - **The maximum**. The lowest market price at which the receiving division could purchase the goods or services externally, less any internal cost savings in packaging and delivery.

- Problems arise with the use of **cost-based** transfer prices because one party or the other is liable to perceive them as unfair.

1   *Choose the correct words from those highlighted.*

    ROI based on profits as a % of net assets employed will (a) **increase/decrease** as an asset gets older and its book value (b) **increases/reduces**. This could therefore create an (c) **incentive/disincentive** to investment centre managers to reinvest in new or replacement assets.

2   An investment centre with capital employed of $570,000 is budgeted to earn a profit of $119,700 next year. A proposed fixed asset investment of $50,000, not included in the budget at present, will earn a profit next year of $8,500 after depreciation. The company's cost of capital is 15%. What is the budgeted ROI and residual income for next year, both with and without the investment?

	ROI	Residual income
Without investment	....	....
With investment	....	....

3   'The use of residual income in performance measurement will avoid dysfunctional decision making because it will always lead to the correct decision concerning capital investments.' **True or false?**

4   To prevent dysfunctional transfer price decision making, profit centres must be allowed to make autonomous decisions. **True or false?**

5   Which of the following is not a disadvantage of using market value as a transfer price?

    A   The market price might be a temporary one.
    B   Use of market price might act as a disincentive to use up spare capacity.
    C   Many products do not have an equivalent market price.
    D   The external market might be perfect.

6   *Fill in the blanks.*

    Ideally, a transfer price should be set that enables the individual divisions to maximise their profits at a level of output that maximises ....

    The transfer price which achieves this is unlikely to be a .... transfer price or a .... transfer price.

    If optimum decisions are to be taken, transfer prices should reflect ....

Answers to Quick Quiz

1   (a)   increase
    (b)   reduces
    (c)   disincentive

2 | | ROI | Residual income |
    |---------------------|-------|-----------------|
    | Without investment | 21.0% | $34,200 |
    | With investment | 20.7% | $35,200 |

3   False

4   False. They cannot be allowed to make entirely autonomous decisions.

5   D

6   profit for the company as a whole; market-based; cost-based; opportunity costs

Now try the question below from the Practice Question Bank

Number	Level	Marks	Time
Q20	Examination	20	36 mins

Further aspects of performance management

Topic list	Syllabus reference
1 Not-for-profit organisations	D6 (a), (c)
2 Performance measurement in not-for-profit organisations	D6 (b)
3 Value for money	D6 (d)
4 External considerations	D7 (a), (b), (c)
5 Behaviour aspects of performance management	D7 (d)

Introduction

This final chapter on performance measurement looks at performance analysis in not for profit organisations and the public sector. The problems of having **non-quantifiable** and **multiple** objectives are discussed.

We then go on to consider how **external considerations** are allowed for in performance measurement and finally identify and explain the **behaviour aspects** of performance management.

Study guide

		Intellectual level
D6	**Performance analysis in not for profit organisations and the public sector**	
(a)	Comment on the problems of having non-quantifiable objectives in performance management	2
(b)	Explain how performance could be measured in this sector	2
(c)	Comment on the problems of having multiple objectives in this sector	2
(d)	Outline Value for Money (VFM) as a public sector objective	1
D7	**External considerations and behavioural aspects**	
(a)	Explain the need to allow for external considerations in performance management, including stakeholders, market conditions and allowance for competitors	2
(b)	Suggest ways in which external considerations could be allowed for in performance management	2
(c)	Interpret performance in the light of external considerations	2
(d)	Identify and explain the behaviour aspects of performance management	2

Exam guide

Scenarios in your exam may relate to not-for-profit organisations and the public sector and you need to understand their particular needs and issues. Always **apply** your answers to the specific organisation.

1 Not-for-profit organisations

FAST FORWARD

One possible definition of a **not-for-profit seeking organisation** is that its first objective is to be involved in non-loss operations to cover its costs, profits only being made as a means to an end.

Although most people would 'know one if they saw it', there is a surprising problem in clearly defining what counts as a not-for-profit organisation.

Bois has suggested that not-for-profit organisations are defined by recognising that their first objective is to be involved in **non-loss operations** in order to cover their costs and that profits are only made as a means to an end (such as providing a service, or accomplishing some socially or morally worthy objective).

Key term

A **not-for-profit organisation** is '... an organisation whose attainment of its prime goal is not assessed by economic measures. However, in pursuit of that goal it may undertake profit-making activities.'   (*Bois*)

This may involve a number of different kinds of organisation with, for example, differing legal status – charities, statutory bodies offering public transport or the provision of services such as leisure, health or public utilities such as water or road maintenance.

1.1 Objectives and not-for-profit organisations

FAST FORWARD

Not-for-profit organisations have **multiple objectives** which are **difficult to define**.

A major problem with many not-for-profit organisations, particularly government bodies, is that it is extremely **difficult to define their objectives** at all. In addition they tend to have **multiple objectives**, so that even if they could all be clearly identified it is impossible to say which is the overriding objective.

Question   Objectives

What objectives might the following not-for-profit organisations have?

(a)   An army   (d)   A political party
(b)   A local council   (e)   A college
(c)   A charity

Answer

Here are some suggestions.

(a)   To defend a country
(b)   To provide services for local people (such as the elderly)
(c)   To help others/protect the environment
(d)   To gain power/enact legislation
(e)   To provide education

More general objectives for not-for-profit organisations include:

- Surplus maximisation (equivalent to profit maximisation)
- Revenue maximisation (as for a commercial business)
- Usage maximisation (as in leisure centre swimming pool usage)
- Usage targeting (matching the capacity available, as in the NHS)
- Full/partial cost recovery (minimising subsidy)
- Budget maximisation (maximising what is offered)
- Producer satisfaction maximisation (satisfying the wants of staff and volunteers)
- Client satisfaction maximisation (the police generating the support of the public)

It is difficult to judge whether **non-quantifiable objectives** have been met. For example, assessing whether a charity has improved the situation of those benefiting from its activities is difficult to research. Statistics related to product mix, financial resources, size of budgets, number of employees, number of volunteers, number of customers serviced and number and location of facilities are all useful for this task.

The primary objectives of commercial manufacturing and service organisations are likely to be fairly similar and centre on satisfying shareholders.

Exam focus point

> In an exam, if faced with a question on the public sector, remember that you are likely to have had extensive contact with a variety of public sector organisations and have seen something of how they work. Your greatest contact is likely to have been with the public education system, but you will probably have had contact with some local government authorities which provide a wide variety of services from street cleaning, to leisure facilities, to fire services. You may also have had contact with the health service.
>
> Think now about your experiences and use them in the exam.

2 Performance measurement in not-for-profit organisations

FAST FORWARD

> There are a range of problems in measuring performance of not-for-profit organisations.

Commercial organisations generally have market competition and the profit motive to guide the process of managing resources economically, efficiently and effectively. However, not-for-profit organisations cannot

by definition be **judged by profitability** and do **not** generally have to be **successful against competition,** so other methods of assessing performance have to be used.

As we have already said, a major problem with many not-for-profit organisations, particularly government bodies, is that it is extremely **difficult to define their objectives** at all, let alone find one which can serve a yardstick function in the way that profit does for commercial bodies.

Question

One of the objectives of a local government body could be 'to provide adequate street lighting throughout the area'.

(a) How could the 'adequacy' of street lighting be measured?

(b) Assume that other objectives are to improve road safety in the area and to reduce crime. How much does 'adequate' street lighting contribute to each of these aims?

(c) What is an excessive amount of money to pay for adequately lit streets, improved road safety and reduced crime? How much is too little?

Answer

Mull over these questions and discuss them in class or with colleagues if possible. It is possible to suggest answers, perhaps even in quantitative terms, but the point is that there are no **easy** answers, and no right or wrong answers.

You might consider (partly depending upon your political point of view) that it is therefore not necessary to measure performance in not-for-profit organisations. However, few would argue that such bodies should be given **whatever amount of money** they say they need to pursue their aims, with no **check** on whether it is spent well or badly.

(a) Without information about what is being achieved (outputs) and what it is costing (inputs) it is impossible to make **efficient resource allocations**. These allocation decisions rely on a range of performance measures which, if unavailable, may lead managers to allocate resources based on subjective judgement, personal whim or in response to political pressure.

(b) Without performance measures managers will not know the **extent to which operations are contributing to effectiveness and efficiency;** when diagnostic interventions are necessary; how the performance of their organisation **compares** with similar units elsewhere; and how their performance has **changed** over time.

(c) **Government** may require performance information to decide how much to spend in the public sector and where, within the sector, it should be allocated. In particular they will be interested to know what results may be achieved as a consequence of a particular level of funding, or to decide whether or not a service could be delivered more effectively and efficiently in the private sector. Likewise **people who provide funds for** other kinds of not-for-profit organisations are entitled to know whether their money is being put to good use.

2.1 How can performance be measured?

FAST FORWARD

> Performance is judged in terms of inputs and outputs and hence the **value for money criteria** of **economy, efficiency** and **effectiveness.**

Performance is usually judged in terms of **inputs and outputs** and this ties in with the 'value for money' criteria that are often used to assess not-for-profit organisations (covered in Section 3).

- **Economy** (spending money frugally)
- **Efficiency** (getting out as much as possible for what goes in)
- **Effectiveness** (getting done, by means of the above, what was supposed to be done)

More formal definitions are as follows.

> **Effectiveness** is the relationship between an organisation's outputs and its objectives.
>
> **Efficiency** is the relationship between inputs and outputs.
>
> **Economy** is attaining the appropriate quantity and quality of inputs at lowest cost.

We will look at these concepts in more depth in Section 3.

2.2 Problems with performance measurement of not-for-profit organisations

(a) **Multiple objectives**

As we have said, they tend to have multiple objectives, so that even if they can all be clearly identified it is impossible to say which is the overriding objective.

(b) **Measuring outputs**

Outputs can seldom be measured in a way that is generally agreed to be meaningful. (For example, are good exam results alone an adequate measure of the quality of teaching?) Data collection can be problematic. For example, unreported crimes are not included in data used to measure the performance of a police force.

(c) **Lack of profit measure**

If an organisation is not expected to make a profit, or if it has no sales, indicators such as ROI and RI are meaningless.

(d) **Nature of service provided**

Many not-for-profit organisations provide services for which it is difficult to define a cost unit. For example, what is the cost unit for a local fire service? This problem does exist for commercial service providers but problems of performance measurement are made simple because profit can be used.

(e) **Financial constraints**

Although every organisation operates under financial constraints, these are more pronounced in not-for-profit organisations. For instance, a commercial organisation's borrowing power is effectively limited by managerial prudence and the willingness of lenders to lend, but a local authority's ability to raise finance (whether by borrowing or via local taxes) is subject to strict control by central government.

(f) **Political, social and legal considerations**

(i) Unlike commercial organisations, public sector organisations are subject to strong political influences. Local authorities, for example, have to carry out central government's policies as well as their own (possibly conflicting) policies.

(ii) The public may have higher expectations of public sector organisations than commercial organisations. A decision to close a local hospital in an effort to save costs, for example, is likely to be less acceptable to the public than the closure of a factory for the same reason.

(iii) The performance indicators of public sector organisations are subject to far more onerous legal requirements than those of private sector organisations.

(iv) Whereas profit-seeking organisations are unlikely in the long term to continue services making a negative contribution, not-for-profit organisations may be required to offer a range of services, even if some are uneconomic.

2.3 Solutions

2.3.1 Inputs

Performance can be judged in terms of inputs. This is very common in everyday life. If somebody tells you that their suit cost $750, you would generally conclude that it was an extremely well-designed and good quality suit, even if you did not think so when you first saw it. The drawback is that you might also conclude that the person wearing the suit had been cheated or was a fool, or you may happen to be of the opinion that no piece of clothing is worth $750. So it is with the inputs and outputs of a not-for-profit organisations.

2.3.2 Judgement

A second possibility is to accept that performance measurement must to some extent be subjective. Judgements can be made by **experts** in that particular not-for-profit activity or by the **persons who fund the activity**.

2.3.3 Comparisons

We have said that most not-for-profit organisations do not face competition but this does not mean that all are unique. Bodies like local governments, health services and so on can judge their performance **against each other** and **against the historical results of their predecessors**. And since they are not competing with each other, there is less of a problem with confidentiality and so **benchmarking** is easier.

In practice, **benchmarking** usually encompasses:

- Regularly comparing aspects of performance (functions or processes) with best practitioners
- Identifying gaps in performance
- Seeking fresh approaches to bring about improvements in performance
- Following through with implementing improvements
- Following up by monitoring progress and reviewing the benefits

2.3.4 Quantitative measures

Unit cost measurements like 'cost per patient day' or 'cost of borrowing one library book' can fairly easily be established to allow organisations to assess whether they are doing better or worse than their counterparts.

Efficiency measurement of inputs and outputs is illustrated in three different situations as follows.

(a) **Where input is fixed**

$$\frac{\text{Actual output}}{\text{Maximum output obtainable for a given input}}$$

25/30 miles per gallon = 83.3% efficiency

(b) **Where output is fixed**

$$\frac{\text{Minimum input needed for a given output}}{\text{Actual input}}$$

55/60 hours to erect scaffolding = 91.7% efficiency

(c) **Where input and output are both variable**

Actual output ÷ actual input
compared with
standard output ÷ standard input

$9,030/7,000 meals = $1.29 per meal

$9,600/7,500 meals = $1.28 per meal
Efficiency = 99.2%

As a further illustration, suppose that at a cost of $40,000 and 4,000 hours (inputs) in an average year two policemen travel 8,000 miles and are instrumental in 200 arrests (outputs). A large number of possibly meaningful measures can be derived from these few figures, as the table below shows.

	$40,000	**4,000 hours**	**8,000 miles**	**200 arrests**
Cost $40,000		$40,000/4,000 = $10 per hour	$40,000/8,000 = $5 per mile	$40,000/200 = $200 per arrest
Time 4,000 hours	4,000/$40,000 = 6 minutes patrolling per $1 spent		4,000/8,000 = ½ hour to patrol 1 mile	4,000/200 = 20 hours per arrest
Miles 8,000	8,000/$40,000 = 0.2 of a mile per $1	8,000/4,000 = 2 miles patrolled per hour		8,000/200 = 40 miles per arrest
Arrests 200	200/$40,000 = 1 arrest per $200	200/4,000 = 1 arrest every 20 hours	200/8,000 = 1 arrest every 40 miles	

These measures **do not necessarily identify cause and effect** (do teachers or equipment produce better exam results?) **or personal responsibility and accountability**. Actual performance needs to be compared as follows.

(a) With standards, if there are any
(b) With similar external activities
(c) With similar internal activities
(d) With targets
(e) With indices
(f) Over time, as trends

Not-for-profit organisations are forced to use a **wide range** of indicators and can be considered early users of a **balanced scorecard** approach (covered in Chapter 16).

3 Value for money

FAST FORWARD

Public sector organisations are now under considerable pressure to prove that they operate economically, efficiently and effectively, and are encouraged from many sources to draw up action plans to achieve **value for money** as part of the continuing process of good management.

Although much has been written about value for money (VFM), there is no great mystique about the concept. The term is common in everyday speech and so is the idea.

Key term

Value for money means providing a service in a way which is economical, efficient and effective.

To drive the point home, think of a bottle of Fairy Liquid. If we believe the advertising, Fairy is good 'value for money' because it washes half as many plates again as any other washing up liquid. Bottle for bottle it may be more expensive, but plate for plate it is cheaper. Not only this but Fairy gets plates 'squeaky' clean. To summarise, Fairy gives us VFM because it exhibits the following characteristics.

- **Economy** (more clean plates per pound)
- **Efficiency** (more clean plates per squirt)
- **Effectiveness** (plates as clean as they should be)

The assessment of economy, efficiency and effectiveness should be a part of the normal management process of any organisation, public or private.

(a) Management should carry out **performance reviews** as a regular feature of their control responsibilities.

(b) Independent assessments of management performance can be carried out by 'outsiders', perhaps an internal audit department, as **value for money audits (VFM audits).**

Value for money is important **whatever level of expenditure** is being considered. Negatively it may be seen as an approach to spreading costs in public expenditure fairly across services but positively it is necessary to ensure that the desired impact is achieved with the minimum use of resources.

3.1 Economy

Economy is concerned with the cost of inputs, and it is achieved by **obtaining those inputs at the lowest acceptable cost**. Economy **does not mean straightforward cost-cutting,** because resources must be acquired which are of a suitable **quality** to provide the service to the desired standard. Cost-cutting should not sacrifice quality to the extent that service standards fall to an unacceptable level. Economising by buying poor quality materials, labour or equipment is a 'false economy'.

3.2 Efficiency

Efficiency means the following.

(a) **Maximising output for a given input**, for example maximising the number of transactions handled per employee or per $1 spent.

(b) **Achieving the minimum input for a given output**. For example, a government department may be required to pay unemployment benefit to millions of people. Efficiency will be achieved by making these payments with the minimum labour and computer time.

3.3 Effectiveness

Effectiveness means ensuring that the **outputs** of a service or programme have the **desired impacts**; in other words, finding out whether they **succeed in achieving objectives**, and if so, to what extent.

3.4 Studying and measuring the three Es

Economy, efficiency and effectiveness can be studied and measured with reference to the following.

(a) **Inputs**

  (i)   Money
  (ii) Resources – the labour, materials, time and so on consumed, and their cost

  For example, a VFM audit into state secondary education would look at the efficiency and economy of the use of resources for education (the use of schoolteachers, school buildings, equipment, cash) and whether the resources are being used for their purpose: what is the pupil/teacher ratio and are trained teachers being fully used to teach the subjects they have been trained for?

(b) **Outputs**, in other words the **results of an activity**, measurable as the services actually produced, and the quality of the services.

  In the case of a VFM audit of secondary education, outputs would be measured as the number of pupils taught and the number of subjects taught per pupil; how many examination papers are taken and what is the pass rate; what proportion of students go on to further education at a university or college.

(c) Impacts, which are the effect that the outputs of an activity or programme have in terms of achieving policy objectives.

Policy objectives might be to provide a minimum level of education to all children up to the age of 16, and to make education relevant for the children's future jobs and careers. This might be measured by the ratio of jobs vacant to unemployed school leavers. A VFM audit could assess to what extent this objective is being achieved.

As another example from education, suppose that there is a programme to build a new school in an area. The **inputs** would be the **costs of building** the school, and the resources used up; the **outputs** would be the **school building** itself; and the **impacts** would be the **effect that the new school has on education in the area** it serves.

4 External considerations

AST FORWARD

Performance management needs to allow for **external considerations** including stakeholders, market conditions and allowance for competitiors.

4.1 Stakeholders

ey term

Stakeholders are groups of people or individuals who have a legitimate interest in the activities of an organisation. They include customers, employees, the community, shareholders, suppliers and lenders.

There are three broad types of stakeholder in an organisation.

- **Internal** stakeholders (employees, management)
- **Connected** stakeholders (shareholders, customers, suppliers, financiers)
- **External** stakeholders (the community, government, pressure groups)

The stakeholder approach suggests that **corporate objectives** are, or should be, **shaped** and **influenced** by **those** who have **sufficient involvement or interest** in the organisation's operational activities.

4.1.1 Internal stakeholders: employees and management

Because employees and management are so **intimately connected** with the company, their objectives are likely to have a **strong influence** on how it is run. They are interested in the following issues.

(a) The **organisation's continuation and growth**. Management and employees have a special interest in the organisation's continued existence.

(b) Managers and employees have **individual interests** and goals which can be harnessed to the goals of the organisation.

- Jobs/careers
- Money
- Benefits
- Satisfaction
- Promotion

For managers and employees, an organisation's social obligations will include the provision of safe working conditions and anti-discrimination policies.

4.1.2 Connected stakeholders

Increasing shareholder value should assume a **core role** in the strategic management of a business. If management performance is measured and rewarded by reference to changes in **shareholder value** then shareholders will be happy, because managers are likely to **encourage long-term share price growth**.

Connected stakeholder	Interests to defend	
Shareholders (corporate strategy)	• Increase in shareholder wealth, measured by profitability, P/E ratios, market capitalisation, dividends and yield • Risk	
Bankers (cash flows)	• Security of loan	• Adherence to loan agreements
Suppliers (purchase strategy)	• Profitable sales • Payment for goods	• Long-term relationship
Customers (product market strategy)	• Goods as promised	• Future benefits

Even though **shareholders** are deemed to be interested in return on investment and/or capital appreciation, many want to **invest** in **ethically-sound** organisations.

4.1.3 External stakeholders

External stakeholder groups – the government, local authorities, pressure groups, the community at large, professional bodies – are likely to have quite diverse objectives.

External stakeholder	Interests to defend
Government	• Jobs, training, tax
Interest/pressure groups / charities / 'civil society'	• Pollution • Rights • Other

It is external stakeholders in particular who **induce social and ethical obligations**.

4.1.4 Performance measures

Organisations may need to develop performance measures to ensure that the needs of stakeholders are met.

Stakeholder	Measure
Employees	Morale index
Shareholders	Share price, dividend yield
Government	Percentage of products conforming to environmental regulations
Customers	Warranty cost, percentage of repeat customers

There is a strong link here to the balanced scorecard approach and the need to have a range of non-financial performance indicators as well as financial performance indicators.

4.2 Economic environment

Economic growth

- Has the economy grown or is there a recession?
- How has demand for goods/services been affected?

Local economic trends

- Are local businesses rationalising or expanding?
- Are office/factory rents increasing/falling?
- In what direction are house prices moving?
- Are labour rates on the increase?

Inflation

(a) Is a high rate making it difficult to plan, owing to the uncertainty of future financial returns? Inflation and expectations of it help to explain short termism.
(b) Is the rate depressing consumer demand?
(c) Is the rate encouraging investment in domestic industries?
(d) Is a high rate leading employees to demand higher money wages to compensate for a fall in the value of their wages?

Interest rates

- How do these affect consumer confidence and liquidity, and hence demand?
- Is the cost of borrowing increasing, thereby reducing profitability?

Exchange rates

- What impact do these have on the cost of overseas imports?
- Are prices that can be charged to overseas customers affected?

Government fiscal policy

(a) Are consumers increasing/decreasing the amount they spend due to tax and government spending decisions?

(b) How is the government's corporation tax policy affecting the organisation?

(c) Is VAT affecting demand?

Government spending

Is the organisation a supplier to the government (such as a construction firm) and hence affected by the level of spending?

4.3 Competition

We considered the effects of competitors' behaviour in Chapter 5 when we looked at **pricing strategies**. Performance management must consider information on competitors' prices and cost structures and identify which features of an organisation's products add most value. Management accounting information has to be produced speedily and be up-to-date so that managers can react quickly and effectively to **changing market conditions**.

5 Behaviour aspects of performance management

FAST FORWARD

> It is generally considered to be unreasonable to assess managers' performance in relation to matters that are beyond their control. Therefore **management performance measures** should **only include those items that are directly controllable by the manager** in question.

If people **know** that their performance is being **measured** then this will **affect the standard** of their performance, particularly if they know that they will be **rewarded** for achieving a certain level of performance.

Ideally, performance **measures** will be devised that **reward behaviour** that **maximises the corporate good**. In practice, however, it is not quite so simple.

(a) There is a danger that managers and staff will **concentrate** only upon what they know is **being measured**. This is not a problem if every important issue has a measure attached to it, but such a system is difficult to devise and implement in practice.

(b) **Individuals** have their own goals, but good performance that satisfies their own sense of what is important will not necessarily work towards the **corporate good**. Each individual may face a **conflict** between taking action to ensure organisational goals and action to ensure personal goals.

Point (b) is the problem of **goal congruence.**

5.1 Example: Performance measurement and behaviour

(a) As we saw in Chapter 17, a divisional manager whose performance is assessed on the basis of his division's ROI might reject a proposal that produces an ROI greater than the group's target return if it reduces his division's overall return.

(b) Traditional feedback control would seek to eliminate an adverse material price variance by requiring managers to source cheaper, possibly lower quality, suppliers. This may run counter to an organisational objective to implement a system of TQM with the aim of reducing quality costs.

5.2 Measuring managerial performance

It is difficult to devise performance measures that relate specifically to a manager to judge his or her performance as a manager. It is possible to calculate statistics to assess the manager as an employee like any other employee (days absent, professional qualifications obtained, personability and so on), but this is not the point. As soon as the issue of **ability as a manager** arises it is necessary to **consider him in relation to his area of responsibility**. If we want to know how good a manager is at marketing the only

information there is to go on is the marketing performance of his division (which may or may not be traceable to his own efforts).

5.3 The controllability principle

As we have seen, the **controllability principle** is that managers of responsibility centres should only be held accountable for costs over which they have some influence. From a motivation point of view this is important because it can be very demoralising for managers who feel that their performance is being judged on the basis of something over which they have no influence. It is also important from a control point of view in that control reports should ensure that information on costs is reported to the manager who is able to take action to control them.

5.4 Reward schemes and performance measurement

In many organisations, senior management try to motivate managers and employees by offering organisational rewards (more pay and promotion) for the achievement of certain levels of performance. The conventional theory of reward structures is that if the organisation establishes procedures for formal measurement of performance, and **rewards individuals for good performance**, individuals will be more likely to direct their efforts towards achieving the organisation's goals.

5.4.1 Problems associated with reward schemes

(a)   A serious problem that can arise is that performance-related pay and performance evaluation systems can **encourage dysfunctional behaviour.** Many investigations have noted the tendency of managers to pad their budgets either in anticipation of cuts by superiors or to make subsequent variances more favourable.

(b)   Perhaps of even more concern are the numerous examples of managers making **decisions that are contrary to the wider purposes of the organisation.**

(c)   Schemes designed to **ensure long-term achievements** (that is, to combat short termism) **may not motivate** since efforts and reward are too distant in time from each other (or managers may not think they will be around that long!).

(d)   It is questionable whether any performance measures or set of measures can provide a **comprehensive assessment of what a single person achieves** for an organisation. There will always be the old chestnut of lack of goal congruence, employees being committed to what is measured, rather than the objectives of the organisation.

(e)   **Self-interested performance** may be encouraged at the **expense of team work**.

(f)   High levels of output (whether this is number of calls answered or production of product X) may be achieved at the expense of **quality**.

(g)   In order to make bonuses more accessible, **standards and targets may have to be lowered**, with knock-on effects on quality.

(h)   They **undervalue intrinsic rewards** (which reflect the satisfaction that an individual experiences from doing a job and the opportunity for growth that the job provides) given that they promote extrinsic rewards (bonuses and so on).

Chapter Roundup

- One possible definition of a **not-for-profit seeking organisation** is that its first objective is to be involved in non-loss operations to cover its costs, profits only being made as a means to an end.

- Not-for-profit organisations have **multiple objectives** which are **difficult to define**.

- There are a range of problems in measuring performance of not-for-profit organisations.

- Performance is judged in terms of inputs and outputs and hence the **value for money criteria** of **economy, efficiency** and **effectiveness.**

- Public sector organisations are now under considerable pressure to prove that they operate economically, efficiently and effectively, and are encouraged from many sources to draw up action plans to achieve **value for money** as part of the continuing process of good management.

- Performance management needs to allow for **external considerations** including stakeholders, market conditions and allowance for competitiors.

- It is generally considered to be unreasonable to assess managers' performance in relation to matters that are beyond their control. Therefore **management performance measures** should **only include those items that are directly controllable by the manager** in question.

Quick Quiz

1   What general objectives of non-profit seeking organisations are being described in each of the following?

    (a)   Maximising what is offered
    (b)   Satisfying the wants of staff and volunteers
    (c)   Equivalent to profit maximisation
    (d)   Matching capacity available

2   The public service funding system operates on the basis that performance against non-financial objectives leads to a reduction in the level of funding. **True or false?**

3   *Match the definition to the term.*

Terms		*Definition*	
(a)	Economy	(1)	Ensuring outputs succeed in achieving objectives
(b)	Efficiency	(2)	Getting out as much as possible for what goes in
(c)	Effectiveness	(3)	Spending money frugally

4   Economy means cost cutting. **True or false?**

5   Six problems of measuring performance in non-profit seeking organisations were described in this chapter. Which two are missing from the list below?

    (a)   Multiple objectives   (c)   Lack of profit measure
    (b)   Measuring output   (d)   Nature of service provided

1   (a)   Budget maximisation
    (b)   Producer satisfaction maximisation
    (c)   Surplus maximisation
    (d)   Usage targeting

2   False

3   (a) (3); (b) (2); (c) (1)

4   False

5   Financial constraints
    Political/social/legal considerations

Now try the question below from the Practice Question Bank

Number	Level	Marks	Time
Q21	Examination	15	27 mins

Practice question and answer bank

1 Solo

Solo makes and sells a single product. The following data relate to periods 1 to 4.

	$
Variable cost per unit	30
Selling price per unit	55
Fixed costs per period	6,000

Normal activity is 500 units and production and sales for the four periods are as follows:

	Period 1 units	Period 2 units	Period 3 units	Period 4 units
Sales	500	400	550	450
Production	500	500	450	500

There were no opening inventories at the start of period 1.

The marginal costing operating statement for periods 1 to 4 is shown below.

Marginal costing operating statement

	Period 1 $	Period 1 $	Period 2 $	Period 2 $	Period 3 $	Period 3 $	Period 4 $	Period 4 $
Sales		27,500		22,000		30,250		24,750
Variable production costs	15,000		15,000		13,500		15,000	
Add: Opening inventory b/fwd					3,000			
Less: Closing inventory c/fwd	–		(3,000)		–		(1,500)	
Variable production cost of sales		15,000		12,000		16,500		13,500
Contribution		12,500		10,000		13,750		11,250
Fixed costs		6,000		6,000		6,000		6,000
Profit for period		6,500		4,000		7,750		5,250

Required

(a) Prepare the operating statements for *each* of the periods 1 to 4, based on absorption costing principles. **(5 marks)**

(b) Comment briefly on the results obtained in each period *and* in total by the two systems, marginal costing and absorption costing. **(5 marks)**

(Total = 10 marks)

2 Southcott

Southcott Ltd is a firm of financial consultants which offers short revision courses on taxation and auditing for professional examinations. The firm has budgeted annual overheads totalling $152,625. Until recently the firm has applied overheads on a volume basis, based on the number of course days offered. The firm has no variable costs and the only direct costs are the consultants' own time which they divide equally between their two courses. The firm is considering the possibility of adopting an activity based costing (ABC) system and has identified the overhead costs as shown below.

Details of overheads

	$
Centre hire	62,500
Enquiries administration	27,125
Brochures	63,000
Total	152,625

The following information relates to the past year and is expected to remain the same for the coming year.

Course	No of courses sold	Duration of course	No of enquiries per course	No of brochures printed per course
Auditing	50	2 days	175	300
Taxation	30	3 days	70	200

All courses run with a maximum number of students (30), as it is deemed that beyond this number the learning experience is severely diminished, and the same centre is hired for all courses at a standard daily rate. The firm has the human resources to run only one course at any one time.

Required

(a) Calculate the overhead cost per course for both auditing and taxation using traditional volume based absorption costing.   **(2 marks)**

(b) Recalculate the overhead costs per course using activity based costing and explain your choice of cost driver in your answer.   **(9 marks)**

(c) Discuss the results that you have obtained.   **(4 marks)**

(Total = 15 marks)

3 Abkaber
27 mins

Abkaber assembles three types of motorcycle at the same factory: the 50cc Sunshine; the 250cc Roadster and the 1000cc Fireball. It sells the motorcycles throughout the world. In response to market pressures Abkaber has invested heavily in new manufacturing technology in recent years and, as a result, has significantly reduced the size of its workforce.

Historically, the company has allocated all overhead costs using total direct labour hours, but is now considering introducing Activity Based Costing (ABC). Abkaber's accountant has produced the following analysis.

	Annual output (units)	Annual direct labour Hours	Selling price ($ per unit)	Raw material cost ($ per unit)
Sunshine	2,000	200,000	4,000	400
Roadster	1,600	220,000	6,000	600
Fireball	400	80,000	8,000	900

The three cost drivers that generate overheads are:

Deliveries to retailers   –   the number of deliveries of motorcycles to retail showrooms

Set-ups   –   the number of times the assembly line process is re-set to accommodate a production run of a different type of motorcycle

Purchase orders   –   the number of purchase orders.

The annual cost driver volumes relating to each activity and for each type of motorcycle are as follows:

	Number of deliveries to retailers	Number of set-ups	Number of purchase orders
Sunshine	100	35	400
Roadster	80	40	300
Fireball	70	25	100

The annual overhead costs relating to these activities are as follows:

	$
Deliveries to retailers	2,400,000
Set-up costs	6,000,000
Purchase orders	3,600,000

All direct labour is paid at $5 per hour. The company holds no inventories.

At a board meeting there was some concern over the introduction of activity based costing.

The finance director argued: 'I very much doubt whether selling the Fireball is viable but I am not convinced that activity based costing would tell us any more than the use of labour hours in assessing the viability of each product.'

The marketing director argued: 'I am in the process of negotiating a major new contract with a motorcycle rental company for the Sunshine model. For such a big order they will not pay our normal prices but we need to at least cover our incremental costs. I am not convinced that activity based costing would achieve this as it merely averages costs for our entire production'.

Required

(a) Calculate the total profit on each of Abkaber's three types of product using each of the following methods to attribute overheads:

   (i)   the existing method based upon labour hours; and
   (ii) activity based costing. **(10 marks)**

(b) Write a short report to the directors of Abkaber, as its management accountant. The report should evaluate the issues raised by each of the directors.

   Refer to your calculations in requirement (a) above where appropriate. **(5 marks)**

(Total = 15 marks)

4 Life cycle costing

27 mins

A company manufactures MP3 players. It is planning to introduce a new model and development will begin very soon. It expects the new product to have a life cycle of 3 years and the following costs have been estimated.

	Year 0	Year 1	Year 2	Year 3
Units manufactured and sold		25,000	100,000	75,000
Price per unit		$90	$80	$70
R&D costs	$850,000	$90,000	-	-
Production costs				
Variable cost per unit		$30	$25	$25
Fixed costs		$500,000	$500,000	$500,000
Marketing costs				
Variable cost per unit		$5	$4	$3
Fixed costs		$300,000	$200,000	$200,000
Distribution costs				
Variable cost per unit		$1	$1	$1
Fixed costs		$190,000	$190,000	$190,000
Customer service costs per unit		$3	$2	$2

Required

(a) Explain life cycle costing and state what distinguishes it from more traditional management accounting techniques. **(8 marks)**

(b) Calculate the cost per unit looking at the whole lifecycle and comment on the price to be charged. **(7 marks)**

(Total = 15 marks)

5 Bottlenecks

36 mins

F Co makes and sells two products, A and B, each of which passes through the same automated production operations. The following estimated information is available for period 1.

- **Product unit data**

	A	B
Direct material cost ($)	2	40
Variable production overhead cost ($)	28	4
Overall hours per product unit (hours)	0.25	0.15

- Original estimates of production/sales of products A and B are 120,000 units and 45,000 units respectively. The selling prices per unit for A and B are $60 and $70 respectively.

- Maximum demand for each product is 20% above the estimated sales levels.

- Total fixed production overhead cost is $1,470,000. This is absorbed by products A and B at an average rate per hour based on the estimated production levels.

One of the production operations has a maximum capacity of 3,075 hours which has been identified as a bottleneck which limits the overall estimated production/sales of products A and B. The bottleneck hours required per product unit for products A and B are 0.02 and 0.015 respectively.

Required

(a) Calculate the mix (in units) of products A and B which will maximise net profit and the value (in $) of the maximum net profit. **(6 marks)**

(b) F Co has now decided to determine the profit-maximising mix of products A and B based on the throughput accounting principle of maximising the throughput return per production hour of the bottleneck resource.

Given that the variable overhead cost, based on the value (in $) which applies to the original estimated production/sales mix, is now considered to be fixed for the short/intermediate term:

    (i) Calculate the mix (of units) of products A and B which will maximise net profit and the value of that net profit. **(8 marks)**

    (ii) Calculate the throughput accounting ratio for product B and comment on it. **(3 marks)**

    (iii) It is estimated that the direct material cost per unit of product B may increase by 20% due to shortage of supply. Calculate the revised throughput accounting ratio for product B and comment on it. **(3 marks)**

(Total = 20 marks)

6 BD Company

27 mins

For some time the BD company has sold its entire output of canned goods to supermarket chains which sell them as 'own label' products. One advantage of this arrangement is that BD incurs no marketing costs, but there is continued pressure from the chains on prices, and margins are tight.

As a consequence, BD is considering selling some of its output under the BD brand. Margins will be better but there will be substantial marketing costs.

The following information is available.

	Current year's results – 20X2 (adjusted to 20X3 cost levels)	Forecast for 20X3 (assuming all 'own label' sales)
Sales (millions of cans)	18	19
	$ million	$ million
Sales	5.94	6.27
Manufacturing costs	4.30	4.45
Administration costs	1.20	1.20
Profit	0.44	0.62

For 20X3 the unit contribution on BD brand sales is expected to be $33\frac{1}{3}$% greater than 'own label' sales, but variable marketing costs of 2c per can and fixed marketing costs of $400,000 will be incurred.

Required

(a)   Prepare a contribution breakeven chart for 20X3 assuming that all sales will be 'own label'.

(6 marks)

(b)   Prepare a contribution breakeven chart for 20X3 assuming that 50% of sales are 'own label' and 50% are of the BD brand.   **(6 marks)**

Note. The breakeven points and margins of safety must be shown clearly on the charts.

(c)   Comment on the positions shown by the charts and your calculations.   **(3 marks)**

   Ignore inflation.   **(Total = 15 marks)**

7 RAB Consulting   36 mins

RAB Consulting specialises in two types of consultancy project.

- Each Type A project requires twenty hours of work from qualified researchers and eight hours of work from junior researchers.

- Each Type B project requires twelve hours of work from qualified researchers and fifteen hours of work from junior researchers.

Researchers are paid on an hourly basis at the following rates:

| Qualified researchers | $30/hour |
| Junior researchers | $14/hour |

Other data relating to the projects:

Project type

	A	B
	$	$
Revenue per project	1,700	1,500
Direct project expenses	408	310
Administration*	280	270

* Administration costs are attributed to projects using a rate per project hour. Total administration costs are $28,000 per four-week period.

During the four-week period ending on 30 June 20X0, owing to holidays and other staffing difficulties the number of working hours available are:

| Qualified researchers | 1,344 |
| Junior researchers | 1,120 |

An agreement has already been made for twenty type A projects with XYZ group. RAB Consulting must start and complete these projects in the four-week period ending 30 June 20X0.

A maximum of 60 type B projects may be undertaken during the four-week period ending 30 June 20X0.

RAB Consulting is preparing its detailed budget for the four-week period ending 30 June 20X0 and needs to identify the most profitable use of the resources it has available.

Required

(a)   Calculate the contribution from each type of project.   **(2 marks)**

(b)   Determine the optimal production plan for the four week period ending 30 June 20X0, assuming that RAB is seeking to maximise the profit earned. You should use a linear programming graph, identify the feasible region and the optimal point and accurately calculate the maximum profit that could be earned using whichever equations you need.   **(12 marks)**

(c)   Explain the meaning of a shadow price and calculate the shadow price of qualified researcher time.

(6 marks)

(Total = 20 marks)

8 Plastic tools

27 mins

A small company is engaged in the production of plastic tools for the garden.

Sub-totals on the spreadsheet of budgeted overheads for a year reveal the following.

	Moulding department	Finishing department	General factory overhead
Variable overhead $'000	1,600	500	1,050
Fixed overhead $'000	2,500	850	1,750
Budgeted activity			
Machine hours (000)	800	600	
Practical capacity			
Machine hours (000)	1,200	800	

For the purposes of reallocation of general factory overhead it is agreed that the variable overheads accrue in line with the machine hours worked in each department. General factory fixed overhead is to be reallocated on the basis of the practical machine hour capacity of the two departments.

It has been a long-standing company practice to establish selling prices by applying a mark-up on full manufacturing cost of between 25% and 35%.

A possible price is sought for one new product which is in a final development stage. The total market for this product is estimated at 200,000 units per annum. Market research indicates that the company could expect to obtain and hold about 10% of the market. It is hoped the product will offer some improvement over competitors' products, which are currently marketed at between $90 and $100 each.

The product development department have determined that the direct material content is $9 per unit. Each unit of the product will take two labour hours (four machine hours) in the moulding department and three labour hours (three machine hours) in finishing. Hourly labour rates are $5.00 and $5.50 respectively.

Management estimate that the annual fixed costs which would be specifically incurred in relation to the product are supervision $20,000, depreciation of a recently acquired machine $120,000 and advertising $27,000. It may be assumed that these costs are included in the budget given above. Given the state of development of this new product, management do not consider it necessary to make revisions to the budgeted activity levels given above for any possible extra machine hours involved in its manufacture.

Required

(a) Prepare full cost and marginal cost information which may help with the pricing decision.

(10 marks)

(b) Comment on the cost information and suggest a price range which should be considered.

(5 marks)

(Total = 15 marks)

9 AB

27 mins

AB produces a consumable compound X, used in the preliminary stage of a technical process that it installs in customers' factories worldwide. An overseas competitor, CD, offering an alternative process which uses the same preliminary stage, has developed a new compound, Y, for that stage which is both cheaper in its ingredients and more effective than X.

At present, CD is offering Y only in his own national market, but it is expected that it will not be long before he extends its sales overseas. Both X and Y are also sold separately to users of the technical process as a replacement for the original compound that eventually loses its strength. This replacement demand amounts to 60% of total demand for X and would do so for Y. CD is selling Y at the same price as X ($64.08 per kg).

AB discovers that it would take 20 weeks to set up a production facility to manufacture Y at an incremental capital cost of $3,500 and the comparative manufacturing costs of X and Y would be:

	X	Y
	$ per kg	$ per kg
Direct materials	17.33	4.01
Direct labour	7.36	2.85
	24.69	6.86

AB normally absorbs departmental overhead at 200% of direct labour: 30% of this departmental overhead is variable directly with direct labour cost. Selling and administration overhead is absorbed at one-half of departmental overhead.

The current sales of X average 74 kgs per week and this level (whether of X or of Y if it were produced) is not expected to change over the next year. Because the direct materials for X are highly specialised, AB has always had to keep large inventories in order to obtain supplies. At present, these amount to $44,800 at cost. Its inventory of finished X is $51,900 at full cost. Unfortunately, neither X nor its raw materials have any resale value whatsoever: in fact, it would cost $0.30 per kg to dispose of them.

Over the next three months AB is not normally busy and, in order to avoid laying off staff, has an arrangement with the trade union whereby it pays its factory operators at 65% of their normal rate of pay for the period whilst they do non-production work. AB assesses that it could process all its relevant direct materials into X in that period, if necessary.

There are two main options open to AB:

(a)   to continue to sell X until all its inventories of X (both of direct materials and of finished inventory) are exhausted, and then start sales of Y immediately afterwards;

(b)   to start sales of Y as soon as possible and then to dispose of any remaining inventories of X and/or its raw materials.

Required

(a)   Recommend with supporting calculations, which of the two main courses of action suggested is the more advantageous from a purely cost and financial point of view.   **(9 marks)**

(b)   Identify three major non-financial factors that AB would need to consider in making its eventual decision as to what to do.   **(6 marks)**

(Total = 15 marks)

10 Stow Health Centre   36 mins

Stow Health Centre specialises in the provision of sports/exercise and medical/dietary advice to clients. The service is provided on a residential basis and clients stay for whatever number of days suits their needs.

Budgeted estimates for the year ending 30 June 20X1 are as follows.

(a)   The maximum capacity of the centre is 50 clients per day for 350 days in the year.

(b)   Clients will be invoiced at a fee per day. The budgeted occupancy level will vary with the client fee level per day and is estimated at different percentages of maximum capacity as follows.

Client fee per day	Occupancy level	Occupancy as percentage of maximum capacity
$180	High	90%
$200	Most likely	75%
$220	Low	60%

(c)   Variable costs are also estimated at one of three levels per client day. The high, most likely and low levels per client day are $95, $85 and $70 respectively.

The range of cost levels reflects only the possible effect of the purchase prices of goods and services.

Required

(a)   Prepare a summary which shows the budgeted contribution earned by Stow Health Centre for the year ended 30 June 20X1 for each of nine possible outcomes.   **(6 marks)**

(b)   State the client fee strategy for the year to 30 June 20X1 which will result from the use of each of the following decision rules.

   (i)   Maximax
   (ii)   Maximin
   (iii)   Minimax regret

   Your answer should explain the basis of operation of each rule. Use the information from your answer to (a) as relevant and show any additional working calculations as necessary.   **(10 marks)**

(c)   The probabilities of variable cost levels occurring at the high, most likely and low levels provided in the question are estimated as 0.1, 0.6 and 0.3 respectively.

   Using the information available, determine the client fee strategy which will be chosen where maximisation of expected value of contribution is used as the decision basis.   **(4 marks)**

   (Total = 20 marks)

11 Zero based budgeting   27 mins

You work for a large multinational company which manufactures weedkillers. It has been decided to introduce zero based budgeting in place of the more traditional incremental budgeting. The manager of the research and development department has never heard of zero based budgeting.

Required

Write a report to the manager of the research and development department which explains the following.

(a)   How zero based budgeting techniques differ from traditional budgeting   **(5 marks)**
(b)   How ZBB may assist in planning and controlling discretionary costs   **(5 marks)**
(c)   How ZBB will help to control budgetary slack   **(5 marks)**

   (Total = 15 marks)

12 Dench   18 mins

Dench manufacturing has received a special order from Sands to produce 225 components to be incorporated into Sand's product. The components have a high cost, due to the expertise required for their manufacture. Dench produces the components in batches of 15, and as the ones required are to be custom-made to Sands' specifications, a 'prototype' batch was manufactured with the following costs:

	$
Materials	
4 kg of A, $7.50/kg	30
2 kg of B, $15/kg	30
Labour	
20 hrs skilled, $15/hr	300
5 hrs semi-skilled, $8/hr	40
Variable Overhead	
25 labour hours, $4/hr	100
	500

Additional information with respect to the workforce is noted below:

Skilled   Virtually a permanent workforce that has been employed by Dench for a long period of time. These workers have a great deal of experience in manufacturing components similar to those required by Sands, and turnover is virtually non-existent.

Semi-Skilled   Hired by Dench on an 'as needed' basis. These workers would have had some prior experience, but Dench management believe the level to be relatively insignificant. Past experience shows turnover rate to be quite high, even for short employment periods.

Dench's plans are to exclude the prototype batch from Sands' order. Management believes a 80% learning rate effect is experienced in this manufacturing process, and would like a cost estimate for the 225 components prepared on that basis.

Required

(a)   Prepare the cost estimate, assuming an 80% learning rate is experienced.   **(6 marks)**

(b)   Briefly discuss some of the factors that can limit the use of learning curve theory in practice.

    (4 marks)

    (Total = 10 marks)

13 ACCA-Chem Co   27 mins

ACCA-Chem Co manufacture a single product, product W, and have provided you with the following information which relates to the period which has just ended.

Standard cost per unit of product W

Materials:

Material	Kilos	Price per kilo $	Total $
F	15	4	60
G	12	3	36
H	8	6	48
	35		144

Budgeted sales for the period are 4,500 units at $260 per unit. There were no budgeted opening or closing inventories of product W.

The actual materials used were as follows.

Materials:

Material	Kilos	Price per kilo $	Total $
F	59,800	4.25	254,150
G	53,500	2.80	149,800
H	33,300	6.40	213,120

4,100 units of product W were produced and sold for $1,115,800.

Required

(a)   Calculate the following material variances.

(1)   Price   (3)   Mix
(2)   Usage   (4)   Yield   **(8 marks)**

(b)   Calculate the sales variances.   **(3 marks)**

(c)   Comment on your findings to help explain what has happened to the yield variance.

    (4 marks)

    (Total = 15 marks)

14 Milbao

Milbao manufactures and sells electronic games. Each year it budgets for its profits, including detailed budgets for sales, materials and labour. Departmental managers are allowed to revise their budgets if they believe there have been planning errors.

The managing director has become concerned that recent budget revisions have meant that there are favourable operational variances but less profit than expected.

Two specific situations have recently arisen, for which budget revisions were sought:

Components

A supplier of an essential component was forced into liquidation. Milbao's buyer managed to find another supplier overseas at short notice. This second supplier charged more for the components and also a delivery charge. The buyer has said that he had to agree to the price as the component was needed urgently. Two months later, another, more competitive, local supplier was found.

A budget revision is being sought for the two months where higher prices had to be paid.

Labour

During the early part of the year, Milbao experienced problems with the quality of work being produced by the game designers. The departmental manager had complained in his board report that his team were complacent and had not attempted to keep up with new developments in the industry.

It was therefore decided, after discussion of the board report, that something had to be done. The company changed its policy so as to recruit designers with excellent reputations for innovation on short-term contracts. This has had the effect of pushing up the costs involved but increasing productivity.

The design departmental manager has requested a budget revision to cover the extra costs involved following the change of policy.

Required

(a) Discuss each request for a budget revision, putting what you see as both sides of the argument and conclude whether a budget revision should be allowed. **(7 marks)**

(b) The standard direct material cost of a product was budgeted as $2.50 per unit, consisting of 0.25 litres of raw material at $10 per litre. The standard cost is recalculated once each year. Actual direct material costs during July 20X1 were $29,100 when 11,200 units were made and 3,700 litres of direct materials were used.

The management of Milbao has now accepted that a more realistic standard cost of direct materials, due to a change in the product specification and an unexpected fall in the market price of materials, would have been $2.40 per unit, consisting of 0.3 litres at $8 per litre.

Required

Calculate the planning and operational variances for direct materials in as much detail as possible, and comment on your results. **(8 marks)**

(Total = 15 marks)

15 Budgets and people

In his study of *The Impact of Budgets on People* Argyris reported inter alia the following comment by a financial controller on the practice of participation in the setting of budgets in his company.

'We bring in the supervisors of budget areas, we tell them that we want their frank opinion but most of them just sit there and nod their heads. We know they're not coming out with exactly how they feel. I guess budgets scare them.'

Required

Suggest reasons why managers may be reluctant to participate fully in setting budgets, and suggest also unwanted side effects which may arise from the imposition of budgets by senior management. **(10 marks)**

16 Handra
18 mins

Handra manufactures equipment for metal testing. It also manufactures the electronic chips that go into the manufacture of the testing equipment.

The company has a well-established cost and management accounting system. The cost accounting system records the actual manufacturing costs for the electronic chips and the testing equipment, and also produces standard unit costs for the purposes of budgeting and variance analysis. The management accountant of Handra is pleased with the management information system that is in place within the company, and is particularly proud of the budgetary control reporting system that provides monthly control reports to the board within one week of the end of each month.

The market for metal testing equipment is growing at a reasonable rate, but there are three other competitors in the market. Competition between them is strong and consequently profit margins are fairly low at the moment, although Handra is operating at a profit. Handra's senior management are not sure what any competitor might do next, although they suspect that at least one of them may be in financial difficulty. Handra's sales director is certain that although low prices are one factor in the buying decisions of customers, customers are much more concerned about the quality, reliability and functional features of the equipment that Handra produces.

At a recent board meeting, the board made a decision not to invest in new equipment for manufacturing electronic chips that would significantly reduce the water and energy consumption in the production process. This decision was taken because the discounted cash flow return on investment was considered insufficient.

The board also discussed the current lack of sufficient strategic information within Handra. They were aware that the decision not to invest in the new equipment had not taken into consideration the probability of rising water and energy costs in the future, and they felt they needed more information to help them predict the long term prospects for their industry.

Required

Explain the difference between strategic, tactical and operational information, and give examples of each that should be used by a company such as Handra. **(10 marks)**

17 JM Foods
27 mins

Bill is a marketing manager for JM Foods, a large chain of fast-food restaurants. The directors of the company are considering expanding into a new country.

Bill is responsible for obtaining market data to aid the strategic decision-making process.

Required

(a) Briefly discuss FIVE sources of external information that Bill may wish to consider. **(10 marks)**

(b) Identify and give examples of the different costs involved in obtaining external data. **(5 marks)**

(Total = 15 marks)

18 Spring
27 mins

At a recent board meeting of Spring, there was a heated discussion on the need to improve financial performance. The production director argued that financial performance could be improved if the company replaced its existing absorption costing approach with an activity-based costing system. He argued that this would lead to better cost control and increased profit margins. The managing director agreed that better cost control could lead to increased profitability, but informed the meeting that he believed that

performance needed to be monitored in both financial and non-financial terms. He pointed out that sales could be lost due to poor product quality or a lack of after-sales service just as easily as by asking too high a price for Spring's products. He suggested that while the board should consider introducing activity-based costing, it should also consider ways in which the company could monitor and assess performance on a wide basis.

Required

(a) Discuss the advantages and disadvantages of adopting an activity-based approach to cost accumulation. **(6 marks)**

(b) Explain the need for the measurement of organisational and managerial performance, giving examples of the range of financial and non-financial performance measures that might be used.

(9 marks)

(Total = 15 marks)

19 Animal Farm   27 mins

Animal Farm Company is a company specialising in the veterinary treatment of animals. The services provided by the company are grouped into three categories:

(a) domestic animals
(b) farm animals
(c) 'exotic' animals.

There are several other animal hospitals in the local area, and the owner of Animal Farm, who is also its CEO and chief vet, is very aware of the threat from competitors.

The system used for dealing with customers is as follows. Customers telephone the company's medical centre when they are concerned about their animal. The medical centre receptionist then:

(a) For domestic and exotic animals, suggests whether or not the animal should be brought into the medical centre for examination and treatment

(b) For farm animals, suggests whether a vet should visit the farmer to examine the animal (or animals)

(c) Gives an indicative price of treatment.

Customers cannot bring their animal into the centre without first making an appointment with the receptionist.

Animal Farm has a policy of employing no more than eight veterinary surgeons ('vets'), who work full time on either domestic animals or farm animals. 'Exotic' animals are treated by specialists, who are not full-time employees; these specialists work for the company when required, in response to telephone requests for assistance.

Full time vets are paid a salary of $90,000 each per year. In addition, they receive a bonus of 50% of the amount by which actual fee income exceeds the budgeted fee income for the year. The total bonus is shared equally between the full-time vets.

The full-time vets are also required to deal with complaints from customers about poor treatment or unsuccessful treatments.

The owner and CEO of Animal Farm is committed to keeping staff fully up-to-date with current developments in the treatment of sick and injured animals. Each vet has a personal development programme, and is allowed to attend external training courses and seminars for up to eight days each year.

Animal Farm: statistics for the year ended 31st December 20X4

	Budget	Actual
Number of vets:		
Dealing with domestic animals	5	4
Dealing with farm animals	3	4
Customer enquiries by telephone		
New business	4,000	7,000
Repeat business	15,000	12,000
Number of examinations/treatments		
New business	2,500	3,000
Repeat business	12,700	11,200
Mix of examinations/treatments		
Domestic animals	11,900	9,500
Farm animals	3,200	4,400
'Exotic' animals	100	300
Other statistics:		
Fee income	$2,100,000	$2,250,000
Training costs	$60,000	$80,000
Fees for part-time vets (exotic animals)	$15,000	$48,000
Other operating costs	$1,120,000	$1,390,000
Number of complaints	300	410

'Repeat business' refers to customers who have used the services of the Animal Farm medical centre before.

Required

Using the Fitzgerald and Moon framework for the analysis of performance systems, select a performance indicator for ANY FIVE of the six dimensions of performance in the framework, and use this to measure the performance of Animal Farm in 20X4. **(15 marks)**

20 Divisional performance measures

36 mins

(a) Compare and contrast the use of residual income and return on investment in divisional performance measurement, stating the advantages and disadvantages of each. **(7 marks)**

(b) Division Y of Chardonnay currently has capital employed of $100,000 and earns an annual profit after depreciation of $18,000. The divisional manager is considering an investment of $10,000 in an asset which will have a ten-year life with no residual value and will earn a constant annual profit after depreciation of $1,600. The cost of capital is 15%.

Calculate the following and comment on the results.

(i) The return on divisional investment, before and after the new investment
(ii) The divisional residual income before and after the new investment **(8 marks)**

(c) Explain the potential benefits of operating a transfer pricing system within a divisionalised company. **(5 marks)**

(Total = 20 marks)

21 Non-profit seeking organisations

27 mins

(a) The absence of the profit measure in non-profit seeking organisations causes problems for the measurement of their efficiency and effectiveness.

Required

Explain why the absence of the profit measure should be a cause of the problems referred to. **(7 marks)**

(b)   A public health clinic is the subject of a scheme to measure its efficiency and effectiveness. Amongst a number of factors, the 'quality of care provided' has been included as an aspect of the clinic's service to be measured. Three features of 'quality of care provided' have been listed.

(i)   Clinic's adherence to appointment times
(ii)   Patients' ability to contact the clinic and make appointment without difficulty
(iii)   The provision of a comprehensive patient health monitoring programme

Required

(i)   Suggest a set of quantitative measures which can be used to identify the effective level of achievement of each of the features listed.   **(6 marks)**

(ii)   Indicate how these measures could be combined into a single 'quality of care' measure.

(2 marks)

(Total = 15 marks)

Part A Multiple Choice Questions

All questions are worth 2 marks each

1   The following statements have been made about Activity Based Costing (ABC):

(1)   In a system of ABC, there is no under- or over-absorption of overheads.

(2)   In a system of ABC, a larger proportion of overheads is attributed to low volume products than in a traditional absorption costing system.

Which of the above statements is/are true?

A   1 only
B   2 only
C   Neither 1 nor 2
D   Both 1 and 2

2   The following statements have been made about target costing:

(1)   When applying target costing to a product in the design stage of development, the production specification may be changed in order to achieve the target cost.

(2)   Target costing must take into consideration all the expected lifetime costs of the product.

Which of the above statements is/are true?

A   1 only
B   2 only
C   Neither 1 nor 2
D   Both 1 and 2

3   Which one of the following is NOT a way of maximising return over a product life cycle?

A   Design costs out of the product
B   Minimise the time to market
C   Maximise the break even time
D   Maximise the length of the life span

4   The following production budget is for a company that makes two products, A and B. The company's budgeted output and sales are restricted by a maximum available of 3,500 direct labour hours in the budget period.

	Product A	Product B
Output and sales	2,000 units	10,000 units
Direct labour hours per unit	0.5	0.25
	$ per unit	$ per unit
Budgeted direct material cost per unit	8.00	5.0
Budgeted direct labour cost per unit	8.00	4.0
Budgeted production overhead cost per unit	19.50	8.0
Budgeted sale price per unit	40.00	25.0

If the company were to use a throughput accounting system, what would be the throughput accounting (TA) ratio for Product B?

A   1.60
B   2.00
C   2.35
D   2.50

5   In flow cost accounting (also called Material Flow Cost Accounting), the cost of waste is called:

A   system costs
B   environment-related costs
C   delivery and disposal costs
D   the cost of negative products

6   A company makes and sells two products, X and Y. The following budget has been prepared.

	Product X	Product Y
Budgeted units of production and sale	8,000	10,000
	$	$
Sales price per unit	18.00	21.60
Variable cost per unit	7.75	10.00
Fixed cost per unit	6.00	6.00

What is the breakeven point in sales revenue, to the nearest $100?

A $147,700
B $195,700
C $196,400
D $201,100

7   The following draft annual budget has been prepared for the machining room of a production centre. The machining room makes four components which are then transferred to an assembly and fitting department.

	Component			
	W	X	Y	Z
Variable cost per unit	$20	$15	$8	$15
Fixed cost per unit	$25	$20	$16	$30
Hours per unit	3 hours	2 hours	1 hour	1.5 hours
Cost of buying from external supplier	$60	$46	$24	$48
Budgeted production (units)	4,000	3,000	6,000	2,000

The machining room has a maximum capacity of 24,000 hours per year, but any quantity of any of the components can be purchased from an external supplier if required. It is considered essential that the budgeted quantities of all four components must be delivered to the assembly and fitting department. This means that some the budgeted requirement for components will have to be purchased externally.

In order to optimise the financial return, which component should be purchased externally?

A   Component W
B   Component X
C   Component Y
D   Component Z

8   A company makes two products X and Y, with the same machines and the same direct labour work force. The following information is available for the next budget period.

	Labour hours per unit	Machine hours per unit
Product X	0.6 hours	0.3 hours
Product Y	0.5 hours	0.2 hours

During the period there will be a maximum of 20,000 machine hours and 48,000 direct labour hours available, and these resources could be limiting factors on output and sales. If linear programming is used to determine the optimum production quantities of Product X and Product Y, which one of the following would be a constraint in the linear programming model?

A $0.3x + 0.2y \le 48{,}000$
B $0.5x + 0.2y \le 20{,}000$
C $0.6x + 0.3y \le 20{,}000$
D $0.6x + 0.5y \le 48{,}000$

9   A company currently sells a product for $40 and at this price demand is 16,000 units per month. It has been estimated that for every $3 increase or reduction in the price, monthly demand will fall or increase by 2,000 units.

What is the formula for the demand curve for this product?

A $48 - 0.0001875Q$
B $64 - 0.0015Q$
C $64 - 0.003Q$
D $64 - 0.015Q$

10   Which one of the following pricing policies is most likely to be the most appropriate for a new product for which the price elasticity of demand is expected to be inelastic?

A   Marginal cost plus
B   Market skimming
C   Penetration pricing
D   Price discrimination

11   A company uses its direct labour work force to make a product for which the sales price and unit cost are as follows.

	$
Direct materials	10
Direct labour (2 hours)	20
Variable overheads (2 hours)	4
Fixed overheads (2 hours)	30
Selling price	80

The work force is operating at full capacity and it is not possible to obtain any additional labour hours in the near future. A customer has asked the company to perform a special job that would require 20 hours of direct labour time.

What would be the relevant cost of diverting labour from its existing work to perform the special job for the customer?

A $400
B $500
C $700
D $740

12 The following pay-off table shows the monthly contribution that would be earned from each of four mutually exclusive options (options 1 – 4) given three different outcome situations. It is not possible to predict or estimate the probability of each outcome scenario.

If the choice of option is made on the basis of the minimax regret criterion, which option will be selected?

Outcome situation	Option A	Option B	Option C	Option D
Outcome 1	32,000	40,000	25,000	22,000
Outcome 2	50,000	40,000	80,000	60,000
Outcome 3	75,000	38,000	50,000	52,000

13 The following statements have been made about budgeting:

(1)   An incremental budget is a budget that remains unchanged throughout the budget period, regardless of any change in the actual level of activity.

(2)   Zero based budgeting is used to compare the incremental cost and related benefits of activities.

Which of the above statements is/are true?

A   1 only
B   2 only
C   Neither 1 nor 2
D   Both 1 and 2

14 The first unit of an entirely new product took 160 labour hours to make and the labour cost was $3,200. Four units have now been produced and it is thought that a 75% learning curve applies to the work.

What will be the expected labour cost of the fifth unit to be produced?

A $1,004
B $1,231
C $1,641
D $1,800

15 Which one of the following is generally regarded as a benefit of using spreadsheets for budgeting?

A   Audit trail
B   Complexity of modelling
C   Greater participation in budgeting process
D   Use of sensitivity analysis

16 In which of the following production environments is the use of standard costs most appropriate?

A   For mass produced products
B   In a JIT production environment
C   In a target costing environment
D   In a TQM production environment

17 A standard unit of product contains two materials, P and Q. The standard direct materials cost is:

		$
Material P	0.1 kg at $8 per kg	0.8
Material Q	0.3 kg at $4 per kg	1.2
Total direct material cost		2.0

Management can control the mix of the materials and so in standard costing variance reports, direct materials variances are reported as mix and yield variances.

In the period just ended, 45,000 units of finished products were made. They used 6,900 kg of Material P, which cost $7 per kg, and 12,600 kg of Material Q, which cost $5 per kg.

What was the direct materials yield variance?

A $7,500 (A)
B $8,100 (A)
C $12,300 (A)
D $15,600 (A)

18 A company sells a single product. Budgeted and actual sales data for the period just ended are as follows.

	Sales	Sales price per unit	Cost per unit
Budget	20,000 units	$50	$40
Actual results	17,000 units	$48	$42

The budget was based on an expectation that the company would maintain its 20% share of the market. It was subsequently recognised that the actual market size, due to unforeseen changes in customer buying behaviour, was only 90,000 units. It was therefore decided to report sales volume variances as a market share variance ad a market size variance.

What was the market share variance, and should this be controllable by operational sales managers?

A $6,000 (A): controllable by operational managers
B $10,000 (A): controllable by operational managers
C $18,000 (A): not controllable by operational managers
D $20,000 (A): not controllable by operational managers

19 In the budget period just ended, a very large adverse direct materials usage variance has been reported. Control action should be taken. Which one of the following actions might help to improve materials usage rates?

A   Alter the mix of materials to a cheaper mix
B   Reduce the sale price of the company's products
C   Switch to a cheaper materials supplier
D   Give production staff some training

20 The following statements have been made about management information:

(1)   Budgetary control information comes mainly from sources outside the organisation.
(2)   An EIS provides an integrated database system for the management of operations.

Which of the above statements is/are true?

A   1 only
B   2 only
C   Neither 1 nor 2
D   Both 1 and 2

21 Which one of the following is a characteristic of feedback?

A   It is used mainly for planning purposes
B   It is secondary data
C   It comes from internal sources within the organisation
D   It consists entirely of financial information

22 The following statements have been made about a balanced scorecard (BSC) performance reporting system

(1)   There must be just one Key Performance Indicator for each of the four perspectives of performance.

(2)   A performance target to reduce the amount of wastage in production would relate to the innovation and learning perspective of the BSC.

Which of the above statements is/are true?

A   1 only
B   2 only
C   Neither 1 nor 2
D   Both 1 and 2

23 Which one of the following elements in the Building Block model of performance management (Fitzgerald & Moon) relates to setting standards of performance?

A   Achievability
B   Competitiveness
C   Controllability
D   Motivation

24 The following information relates to an investment centre, which is a separate product division in a large company.

	$
Net current assets	60,000
Non-current assets	240,000
Profit before depreciation	50,000
Depreciation	10,000

The company's cost of capital is 10%. What is the most appropriate measure of the centre's Return on Investment (ROI)?

A   3.3%
B   13.3%
C   16.7%
D   20.8%

25 There are two profit centres A and B. Profit centre A transfers a product to profit centre B, but could also sell the product in an external market at a price of $30. The marginal cost of making the product in profit centre A is $8 per unit and the full cost is $14 per unit. There would be a variable cost of $1 per unit for sales and distribution to customers in the external market, but no such costs for internal transfers.

To avoid disputes between the profit centre managers, what should be the transfer price for the product?

A $22
B $29
C $30
D $37

26   For a not-for-profit organisation with multiple objectives, which aspect of performance is the most difficult to assess?

A   Financial
B   Economy
C   Efficiency
D   Effectiveness

1 Solo

> **Top tips**. Remember that when inventory levels **increase**, absorption costing reports the **higher** profit figure because some of the fixed production overhead will be carried forward in closing inventory (which reduces the cost of sales and hence increases the profit).

Marking scheme

		Marks
(a)	Operating statement	5
(b)	Calculation of differences	1
	Comments for each period	3
	Comments on total difference	1
		5
		10

(a)   Absorption costing operating statement

	Period 1		Period 2		Period 3		Period 4	
	$	$	$	$	$	$	$	$
Sales		27,500		22,000		30,250		24,750
Production costs								
Variable	15,000		15,000		13,500		15,000	
Fixed	6,000		6,000		5,400		6,000	
	21,000		21,000		18,900		21,000	
Add: Opening inventory b/fwd	–		–		4,200		–	
Less: Closing inventory c/fwd	–		*(4,200)		–		**(2,100)	
Production cost of sales	21,000		16,800		23,100		18,900	
Under-absorbed overhead	–		–		600		–	
Total production costs		21,000		16,800		23,700		18,900
Profit for period		6,500		5,200		6,550		5,850

The absorption rate for fixed costs is $\dfrac{\$6,000}{500\,\text{units}} = \$12$ per unit

Inventory is valued at $30 + $12 = $42 per unit
* 100 units at $42 per unit = $4,200
** 50 units at $42 per unit = $2,100

(b)

	Period 1	Period 2	Period 3	Period 4	Total
	$	$	$	$	$
Marginal costing profit	6,500	4,000	7,750	5,250	23,500
Absorption costing Profit	6,500	5,200	6,550	5,850	24,100
Difference (Absorption costing less marginal costing profits)	–	1,200	(1,200)	600	600

Period 1

Profits based on marginal costing and absorption costing principles are the same for period 1. This is because there is no change in inventory levels during this period.

Period 2

Profits based on absorption costing principles are $1,200 higher than those based on marginal costing principles. Inventory levels have increased by 100 units during this period, and the 100 units of closing inventory include absorbed fixed overheads of $1,200 (100 units × $12 per unit).

Period 3

During this period, inventory levels have fallen by 100 units. When inventory levels fall in a period, absorption costing profits are less than marginal costing profits by $1,200 (100 units × $12 per unit).

Period 4

The difference in profit in this period = change in inventory levels × fixed overhead absorbed per unit

= (opening inventory + production − sales) × $12
= (0 + 500 − 450) × $12
= 50 × $12
= $600

Since opening inventory is nil, and closing inventory is 50 units (0 + 500 − 450) then inventory levels have increased by 50 units. Absorption costing principles report higher profits than marginal costing principles when inventory levels increase in a period, therefore absorption costing profits are $600 greater than marginal costing profits during this period.

Total

Total absorption costing profits are $600 greater than total marginal costing profits in periods 1 − 4. This is because at the beginning of period 1, opening inventory was nil, and at the end of period 4, closing inventory was 50 units. The reasoning behind this is the same as for period 4 above.

2 Southcott

> **Top tips.** Because ABC is new to you, this first ABC question in the bank is **not exam standard**. Nevertheless, you need to be able to provide a good answer as it tests the key skills you need for the topic.
>
> Part (a) should have caused you no problems. The original absorption basis was course days and so you simply needed to calculate the number of course days (number of courses × duration of course) for each course and total the results. Dividing total overheads by this figure gives an overhead cost per course day. Overheads are included in the cost of a course on the basis of the course duration.
>
> Part (b) provides an example of the application of ABC to a **service organisation.** The **principles** to apply are the **same** as those you would apply when dealing with a manufacturing organisation.
>
> Step 1   Determine the cost driver for each category of overhead.
> Step 2   Calculate a cost per cost driver (cost/number of cost drivers)
> Step 3   Include overhead in the cost of a course on the basis of the number of cost drivers generated by a course.
>
> Don't forget to provide **reasons** for your choice of cost drivers. A 'tag-on' requirement like this might be worth the three marks that can make the difference between a pass and a fail.

(a)

	Auditing	Taxation	Total
No of courses sold	50	30	
Duration of course (days)	2	3	
No of course days	100	90	190

Overhead cost per course day = $\dfrac{\$152,625}{190}$ = $803.29

Overhead cost per course

Auditing $803.29 × 2 days = $1,606.58
Taxation $803.29 × 3 days = $2,409.87

(b) **Overhead costs per course using activity based costing**

		Auditing $ per course		Taxation $ per course
Centre hire at $328.95 per day	(× 2)	657.90	(× 3)	986.85
Enquiries administration at $2.50 per enquiry	(× 175)	437.50	(× 70)	175.00
Brochures at $3 per brochure	(× 300)	900.00	(× 200)	600.00
Overhead cost per course		1,995.40		1,761.85

Workings

1   Centre hire cost per course day = $\dfrac{\$62,500}{190}$ = $328.95

2   Enquiries administration cost per enquiry = $\dfrac{\$27,125}{(50 \times 175)+(30 \times 70)}$ = $2.50

3   Brochure cost per brochure printed = $\dfrac{\$63,000}{(50 \times 300)+(30 \times 200)}$ = $3 per brochure

Reasons for the choice of cost drivers

(i)   The cost driver for centre hire costs is the number of course days, since the centre is hired at a standard daily rate.

(ii)   The cost driver for enquiries administration is the number of enquiries, since more enquiries would result in an increase in the cost of enquiries administration.

(iii)   The cost driver for brochure costs is the number of brochures printed, since an increase in the number of brochures printed would lead to a higher cost.

(c)   Using traditional absorption costing, taxation has a higher overhead cost per course. This is because the courses are longer so more overhead is absorbed on a cost per course day basis.

Using ABC, however, the results are reversed and taxation courses have a lower overhead cost per course. This is mainly due to the high number of enquiries for auditing courses which do not necessarily result in course bookings. This highlights the need for the firm to analyse the reasons for this and take action if possible.

3 Abkaber

> **Top tips.** Part (a) is fairly straightforward requiring the calculation of profit for the three products under both absorption costing and ABC. Under ABC make sure you calculate the costs per cost driver.
>
> Part (b) requires a discussion of the impact of ABC and an analysis of each of the directors' comments. It is important that you apply your understanding of ABC to each of these comments.

(a)   (i)   **Existing method**

	Sunshine $	Roadster $	Fireball $
Direct labour ($5 per hr) (W1)	1,000,000	1,100,000	400,000
Materials (W2)	800,000	960,000	360,000
Overheads (at $24) (W3)	4,800,000	5,280,000	1,920,000
Total costs	6,600,000	7,340,000	2,680,000
Output (Units)	2,000	1,600	400

	Sunshine	Roadster	Fireball
	$	$	$
Selling price	4,000	6,000	8,000
Cost per unit (W4)	3,300	4,587.5	6,700
	700	1,412.5	1,300
Total profit	$	$	$
(output in units × profit/unit)	1,400,000	2,260,000	520,000

Total profit = $4,180,000

Workings

1 Labour cost

Sunshine	200,000 hrs × $5 per hour =	1,000,000
Roadster	220,000 hrs × $5 per hour =	1,100,000
Fireball	80,000 hrs × $5 per hour =	400,000

2 Material cost

Sunshine	2,000 × 400 =	800,000
Roadster	1,600 × 600 =	960,000
Fireball	400 × 900 =	360,000

3 Overhead per labour hour

	$
Total overhead cost =	12,000,000
Total labour hours =	500,000 hrs

Overhead per labour hour = $\dfrac{\$12,000,000}{500,000} = \$24$

4 Cost per unit

Sunshine: $\dfrac{\text{Total costs}}{\text{Units produced}} = \dfrac{6,600,000}{2,000} = \$3,300$

Roadster: $\dfrac{\text{Total costs}}{\text{Units produced}} = \dfrac{7,340,000}{1,600} = \$4,587.50$

Fireball: $\dfrac{\text{Total costs}}{\text{Units produced}} = \dfrac{2,680,000}{400} = \$6,700$

(ii) Activity based costing

	Sunshine	Roadster	Fireball
	$	$	$
Direct labour ($5 per hr) (as (W1) above)	1,000,000	1,100,000	400,000
Materials (as (W2) above)	800,000	960,000	360,000
Overheads			
Deliveries (W5(a))	960,000	768,000	672,000
Set up costs (W5(b))	2,100,000	2,400,000	1,500,000
Purchase orders (W5(c))	1,800,000	1,350,000	450,000
	6,660,000	6,578,000	3,382,000
Output units	2,000	1,600	400
	$	$	$
Selling price	4,000	6,000	8,000
Cost per unit (W4)	3,330	4,111.25	8,455
Profit/(loss) per unit	670	1,888.75	(455)
Total profit/(loss)	$1,340,000	$3,022,000	($182,000)

Total profit = $4,180,000

Workings

5   Overheads

$$\frac{\text{Overhead cost of deliveries to retailers}}{\text{Total number of deliveries}} = \frac{2,400,000}{250} = \$9,600$$

$$\frac{\text{Overhead cost of set-ups}}{\text{Total number of set-ups}} = \frac{6,000,000}{100} = \$60,000$$

$$\frac{\text{Overhead cost of purchase orders}}{\text{Total number of purchase orders}} = \frac{3,600,000}{800} = \$4,500$$

5(a)   Deliveries overheads

Sunshine	$9,600 × 100 =	$960,000
Roadster	$9,600 × 80 =	$768,000
Fireball	$9,600 × 70 =	$672,000

5(b)   Set-up cost overheads

Sunshine	$60,000 × 35 =	$2,100,000
Roadster	$60,000 × 40 =	$2,400,000
Fireball	$60,000 × 25 =	$1,500,000

5(c)   Purchase order overheads

Sunshine	$4,500 × 400 =	$1,800,000
Roadster	$4,500 × 300 =	$1,350,000
Fireball	$4,500 × 100 =	$450,000

(b)   REPORT

To:	Directors, Abkaber
From:	Management accountant
Subject:	The implications of activity based costing
Date:	12.12.X2

Labour hours and activity based costing allocation

Labour hours

For the allocation of overheads on the basis of labour hours to be appropriate, there would need to be a direct relationship between overheads and labour hours. From the information available, this does not appear to be the case.

Abkaber has invested in new technology and as a result has significantly reduced the size of its workforce. Direct labour costs now account for a relatively smaller proportion of total costs with overheads making up the highest single cost item. Allocation of overheads on the basis of labour costs would tend to allocate too great a proportion of overheads to the higher volume Sunshine than the lower volume Fireball, ignoring the fact that the lower volume product may require relatively more support services. It therefore seems likely that attributing overheads on the basis of labour hours may lead to inappropriate decisions.

Activity based costing

Activity based costing attempts to overcome this problem by identifying the factors which cause the costs of an organisation's major activities.

The idea behind activity based costing is that activities such as ordering, materials handling, deliveries and set up cause costs. Producing goods creates demand for activities. Costs are assigned to a product on the basis of the product's consumption of activities.

Supporters of ABC argue that it is activities that generate costs, not labour hours.

The accuracy of any ABC system will depend on the appropriateness of the activities as cost drivers. Each cost driver selected should be appropriate to the overheads to which it relates. There should be a direct and proportionate relationship between the relevant overhead costs and the cost driver selected.

The labour hours costing system and ABC result in markedly different profit figures, especially with respect to the Fireball which appears profitable under the first system but loss making under ABC.

The reason for this is that, although the Fireball uses twice as many hours per unit as the Sunshine, its low output volume of only 400 units (compared with 2,000 units of Sunshine) means that a proportionately lower amount of overheads is absorbed.

Under activity based costing, the Fireball shows a loss because ABC recognises the relatively high set-up costs, deliveries and purchase orders.

Finance director's comments

The finance director is questioning the viability of the Fireball, but doubts whether ABC provides more information than the labour hours costing method.

ABC helps the company focus on the fact that the low volumes of Fireball involve a disproportionate amount of set-up costs, deliveries and purchase orders, resulting in a relatively higher allocation of overheads.

It may be the case that a review of current activities relating to Fireball may reduce costs. There are also other, non-financial, considerations for continuing to produce the Fireball. As the more expensive of the three products, it may have brand value and help raise the reputation of the company as well as that of the other models.

4 Life cycle costing

Top tips. You can expect calculations to be combined with discussion in an exam question. Make sure you show your workings clearly and write full answers to the discussion parts.

(a) **Life cycle costs**

Life cycle costs are the **costs incurred on products and services from their design stage, through development to market launch, production and sales, and their eventual withdrawal from the market**. A product's life cycle costs might therefore be classified as follows.

(i)   Acquisition costs (costs of research, design, testing, production and construction)

(ii)   Product distribution costs (transportation and handling)

(iii)   Maintenance costs (customer service, field maintenance and 'in-factory' maintenance)

(iv)   Operation costs (the costs incurred in operations, such as energy costs, and various facility and other utility costs)

(v)   Training costs (operator and maintenance training)

(vi)   Inventory costs (the cost of holding spare parts, warehousing and so on)

(vii)   Technical data costs (cost of purchasing any technical data)

(viii) Retirement and disposal costs (costs occurring at the end of the product's life)

Life cycle costing versus traditional management accounting systems

Traditional management accounting practice

This is, in general, to report costs at the physical production stage of the life cycle of a product; costs are not accumulated over the entire life cycle. Such practice does not, therefore, assess a product's profitability over its entire life but rather on a **periodic basis**. Costs tend to be accumulated according to function; research, design, development and customer service costs incurred on all products during a period are totalled and recorded as a period expense.

Life cycle costing

(i) Using **life cycle costing**, on the other hand, such costs are traced to individual products over **complete life cycles**. These accumulated costs are compared with the revenues attributable to each product and hence the **total profitability** of any given product can be **determined**. Moreover, by gathering costs for each product, the relationship between the choice of design adopted and the resulting marketing and production costs becomes clear.

(ii) The **control function** of life cycle costing lies in the **comparison of actual and budgeted life cycle costs for a product**. Such comparisons allow for the refinement of future decisions about product design, lead to more effective resource allocation and show whether expected savings from using new production methods or technology have been realised.

Life cycle costing and AMT environments

Research has shown that, for organisations operating within an **advanced manufacturing technology environment**, approximately **90%** of a product's life-cycle cost is determined by decisions made **early** within the life cycle. In such an environment there is therefore a need to ensure that the tightest cost controls are at the **design stage**, because the majority of costs are committed at this point. This necessitates the need for a management accounting system that assists in the planning and control of a product's life cycle costs, which monitors spending and commitments to spend during the early stages of a product's life cycle and which recognises the reduced life cycle and the subsequent challenge to profitability of products produced in an AMT environment. Life cycle costing is such a system.

Summary

Life cycle costing **increases the visibility of costs** such as those associated with research, design, development and customer service, and also enables **individual product profitability** to be more fully understood by attributing all costs to products. As a consequence, more **accurate feedback** information is available on the organisation's success or failure in **developing new products**. In today's **competitive environment**, where the ability to produce new and updated versions of products is of paramount importance to the survival of the organisation, this information is vital.

(b) **Lifecycle costs**

			$'000
R&D (850 + 90)			940
Production	–	variable (750 + 2,500 + 1,875)	5,125
	–	fixed (500 × 3)	1,500
Marketing	–	variable (125 + 400 + 225)	750
	–	fixed (300 + 200 + 200)	700
Distribution	–	variable (25 + 100 + 75)	200
	–	fixed (190 × 3)	570
Customer service (75 + 200 + 150)			425
Total life cycle costs			10,210
Production ('000 units) (25 + 100 + 75)			÷ 200
Cost per unit			$51.05

The suggested price will therefore provide a profit over the complete lifecycle.

5 Bottlenecks

Top tips. This question will have given you useful practice of limiting factor analysis.

As you will see in the layout of our workings to part (b)(i), you can adopt the same approach as taken in (a) when dealing with a TA environment. You had to remember to deduct the 'variable' costs from the total throughput contribution, but otherwise there were some very easy marks available for part (b)(i).

Exam questions in F5 will tend to have more marks for interpretation than this question.

(a)   We need to carry out **limiting factor analysis**.

Step 1   Establish scarce resources, if any

We are told that one of the production operations is the bottleneck, limiting production/sales.

Step 2   Rank products on the basis of contribution per unit of the limiting factor

	A	B
	$	$
Direct material cost	2	40
Variable production overhead cost	28	4
	30	44
Selling price	60	70
Contribution per unit	30	26
Bottleneck hours per unit	0.02	0.015
Contribution per bottleneck hour	$1,500	$1,733
Ranking	2	1

Step 3   Determine profit-maximising product mix

Product	Demand		Hours required	Hours available		Units of production
B	45,000 × 1.2 = 54,000	(× 0.015)	810	810	(÷ 0.015)	54,000
A	120,000 × 1.2 = 144,000	(× 0.02)	2,880	2,265	(÷ 0.02)	113,250
			3,690	3,075		

Maximum profit calculation

Product	Units	Contribution per unit	Total contribution
			$
A	113,250	× $30	3,397,500
B	54,000	× $26	1,404,000
			4,801,500
Less: fixed production overhead			1,470,000
Maximum net profit			3,331,500

(b)   (i)   Throughput return per production hour of the bottleneck resource = (selling price – material cost)/hours on the bottleneck resource

Step 1   Rank products on the basis of throughput return per bottleneck hour

	A	B
	$	$
Selling price	60	70
Material cost	2	40
Throughput return	58	30
Bottleneck hours per unit	0.02	0.015
Return per bottleneck hour	$2,900	$2,000
Ranking	1	2

Step 2   Determine profit-maximising product mix

Product	Demand	Hours required	Hours available			Units of production
A	144,000	2,880	2,880	(÷ 0.02)		144,000
B	54,000	810	195 (bal)	(÷ 0.015)		13,000
		3,690	3,075			

Maximum profit calculation

Product	Units	Throughput return per unit	Total return $
A	144,000	× $58	8,352,000
B	13,000	× $30	390,000
Total throughput return			8,742,000
Less: overhead costs			
shown as variable in (a) ((120,000 × $28) + (45,000 × $4))			(3,540,000)
fixed			(1,470,000)
Maximum net profit			3,732,000

(ii)   TA ratio = throughput return per hour/conversion cost per hour

Conversion cost per hour = overhead costs/bottleneck hours
                                = $(3,540,000 + 1,470,000)/3,075
                                = $1,629.27

∴ TA ratio for B = $2,000/ $1,629.27 = 1.2275

Efforts should be made to improve the size of the TA ratio as follows.

(1)   Improving throughput ($) per unit by increasing selling price or reducing material cost per unit. Product B has a very high material cost element ($40).

(2)   Improving the throughput return per hour by reducing the time spent on the bottleneck resource. If product B spent 0.012 hours instead of 0.015 hours on the bottleneck resource, say, its TA ratio would improve.

The organisation's overall position can be improved by reducing conversion costs and/or by reducing or eliminating the impact of any bottlenecks.

Product B's TA ratio, at 1.2275, is greater than 1 and so the product is worth producing. Product A's ratio is 1.780 ($2,900/$1,629.27), however, and hence priority should be given to product A.

(iii)   If the direct material cost of B increases by 20%, its throughput return becomes $(70 – (40 × 120%)) = $22.

Its return per bottleneck hour is then $22 ÷ 0.015 = $1,467.

Its TA ratio becomes $1,467/$1,629.27 = 0.900.

The return from B is now less than the associated production cost through the bottleneck resource and so production of B is not worthwhile in a TA environment.

Product A is being produced to maximum demand, however, and the residual capacity used by product B has no incremental cost since all overhead cost is fixed in the short and intermediate term. In these circumstances, product B is still generating a positive cash flow of $1,467 per hour (or $22 per unit).

6 BD Company

Assumption. Manufacturing costs for the BD brand will be the same as for own label brands.

Initial workings

Manufacturing costs

We need to analyse the cost behaviour patterns by separating the manufacturing costs into their fixed and variable elements, using the high-low method.

	Sales Millions	Costs $ million
20X3	19	4.45
20X2	18	4.30
	1	0.15

Variable manufacturing cost per can = $0.15

Fixed manufacturing cost = $4.45 million − (19 million × $0.15)

= $1.6 million

Selling prices

Selling price per can in 20X3	= 6.27/19	= $0.33
∴ Unit contribution per can	= $0.33 − $0.15	= $0.18
∴ Contribution per can of BD brand	= $0.18 × 133 1/3%	= $0.24
Variable cost per can of BD brand	= $0.15 + $0.02	= $0.17
∴ Selling price per can of BD brand	= $0.17 + $0.24	= $0.41

(a) **Data for chart**

		$ million	$ million
Variable costs	(19 million × $0.15)		2.85
Fixed costs:	manufacturing	1.60	
	administration	1.20	
			2.80
Total costs			5.65

Breakeven point $= \dfrac{\text{fixed costs}}{\text{contribution}} = \dfrac{\$2.8m}{\$0.18}$

$= 15.55$ million cans

$= \$5.13$ million sales

Margin of safety $= 19m - 15.55m = 3.45$ million cans $= \$1.14$ million sales

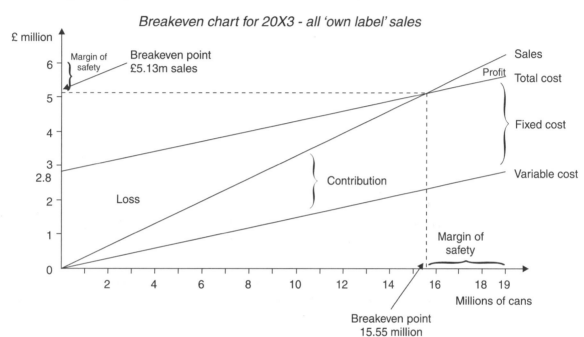

Breakeven chart for 20X3 - all 'own label' sales

(b) **Data for chart**

		$ million	$ million
Variable costs:	own label (9.5m × $0.15)		1.425
	BD brand (9.5m × $0.17)		1.615
			3.040
Fixed costs:	manufacturing	1.600	
	administration	1.200	
	marketing	0.400	
			3.200
Total costs:			6.240
Sales value:	own label (9.5m × $0.33)		3.135
	BD brand (9.5m × $0.41)		3.895
			7.030

Our standard mix is 1 own label, 1 BD brand.

Breakeven point $= \dfrac{\text{fixed costs}}{\text{contribution per mix}} = \dfrac{\$3.2m}{\$(0.18+0.24)} = \dfrac{\$3.2m}{\$0.42}$

$= 7.62$ million mixes $= 15.24$ million cans

$$= 7.62 \times (\$(0.33 + 0.41)) \text{ million sales} = \$5.64 \text{ million sales}$$

Margin of safety $= 19m - 15.24$ million $= 3.76$ million cans $= 1.88$ million mixes

$$= 1.88 \times (\$(0.33 + 0.41)) \text{ million sales}$$

$$= \$1.39 \text{ million sales}$$

Profit $= \$7.03$ million $- \$6.24$ million $= \$790,000$

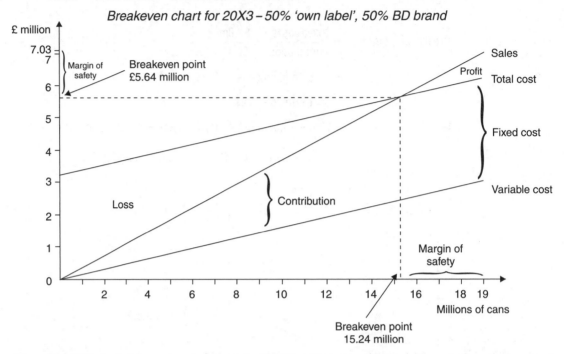

Breakeven chart for 20X3 – 50% 'own label', 50% BD brand

(c) The **first chart** shows a breakeven point of 15.55 million cans ($5.13m sales value) and a margin of safety of 3.45 million cans ($1.14m sales value). Forecast profit for sales of 19 million cans is $620,000.

The **second chart** shows a breakeven point of 15.24 million cans ($5.64m sales value) and a margin of safety of 3.76 million cans ($1.39m sales value). Forecast profit for sales of 19 million cans is $790,000.

Option 2 therefore results in a higher profit figure, as well as a lower breakeven point and increased margin of safety. On this basis it is the better of the two options.

Other factors which management should consider before making a decision

(i) The supermarket chains may put the same pressure on margins and prices of the BD brand as they do on the own label brands.

(ii) Customers may realise that the BD brand is the same product as the own label brand and may not be willing to pay the premium price.

(iii) If the mix of sales can be changed in favour of the BD brand then profits will improve still further.

7 RAB Consulting

> **Top tips.** This is a straightforward linear programming question. The best way to approach graphical linear programming questions is to work through the **six steps** we recommend in the text.
>
> - Define variables
> - Establish objective function
> - Establish constraints
>
> - Graph the problem
> - Define feasible region
> - Determine optimal solution
>
> Notice the approach we have taken to choosing our sample **iso-contribution line**. This is something that students often find difficult, so choose easy **numbers (related to the coefficients of the variables)**, making sure that the line then falls within the feasible region.

(a)

		Type A $ per project		Type B $ per project
Revenue		1,700		1,500
Variable costs				
Labour				
– qualified researchers	(20 hrs × $30)	600	(12 hrs × $30)	360
– junior researchers	(8 hrs × $14)	112	(15 hrs × $14)	210
Direct project expenses		408		310
		1,120		880
Contribution		580		620

(b) **Step 1** **Define variables**

Let a = number of type A projects
Let b = number of type B projects

Step 2 **Establish objective function**

Maximise contribution (C) = 580a + 620b, subject to the constraints below.

Step 3 **Establish constraints**

Qualified researchers time: $20a + 12b \leq 1,344$
Junior researchers time: $8a + 15b \leq 1,120$
Agreement for type A: $a \geq 20$
Maximum for type B: $b \leq 60$
Non-negativity: $b \geq 0$

Step 4 **Graphing the problem**

Constraints

Qualified researcher time: if a = 0, b = 112
if b = 0, a = 67.2

Junior researcher time: if a = 0, b = 74.67
if b = 0, a = 140

Agreement for type A: graph the line a = 20

Maximum for type B: graph the line b = 60

Step 5   Define feasible region

Iso-contribution line

$580a + 620b = 35{,}960$ (where $35{,}960 = 58 \times 62 \times 10$) goes through the points (62, 0) and (0, 58)

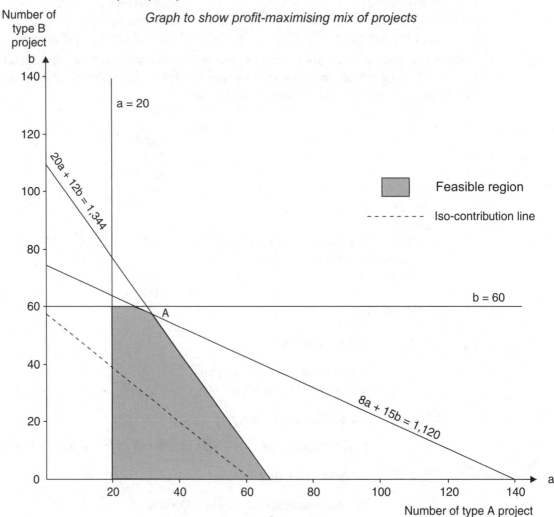

Graph to show profit-maximising mix of projects

Moving the iso-contribution line away from the origin, we see that it leaves the feasible area at the intersection of the two time constraints (point A).

Step 6   Determine optimal solution

Find the coordinates of A

$20a + 12b$	$= 1{,}344$	(1)	
$8a + 15b$	$= 1{,}120$	(2)	
$20a + 37.5b$	$= 2{,}800$	(3)	(2) × 2.5
$25.5b$	$= 1{,}456$		(3) − (1)
b	$= 57.10$		
$20a + 685.20$	$= 1{,}344$		substitute into (1)
a	$= 32.94$		

The profit-maximising mix of projects is 32.94 of type A and 57.10 of type B.

Profit for profit-maximising mix

		$
Contribution from type A:	32.94 × $580	19,105
Contribution from type B:	57.10 × $620	35,402
Total contribution		54,507
Less: fixed costs		(28,000)
		26,507

(c)   **Shadow price**

The shadow price is the **extra contribution** or profit that may be earned if one more unit of a **binding resource** or **limiting factor** becomes available.

It can be used to inform managers of the **maximum price** that should be paid for more of a scarce resource over and above the basic rate. The shadow price of a constraint that is not binding at the optimal solution is zero.

Calculation of shadow prices

At the optimal solution, A = 32.94 and B = 57.10
Contribution = $54,507

Qualified researchers

(32.94 × 20) + (57.10 × 12) = 1,344 = availability

The constraint is **binding**. If one more hour of labour was available, the new optimal product mix would be at the intersection of the lines:

$$20a + 12b = 1,345 \ (1)$$
$$8a + 15b = 1,120 \ (2)$$

(2) × 2.5

$$20a + 37.5b = 2,800 \ (3)$$

(3) − (1)

$$25.5b = 1,455$$
$$b = 57.06$$

Substitute into (1)

$$20a + 684.72 = 1,345$$
$$a = 33.01$$

Contribution = (580 × 33.01) + (620 × 57.06) = $54,523

The **shadow price** of one hour of qualified researcher's time is the extra contribution generated which is $16.

8 Plastic tools

Top tips. The techniques required in part (a) are extremely **straightforward** (calculation of overhead absorption rates for example) so beware of making a silly arithmetical error.

In part (b), there is a lot of information that you can use when suggesting a suitable price range. Your **higher-level skills** are required, however. Make sensible comments on the various possible prices.

The most important point to make in (c) is that **cost is not the only factor to consider** when setting prices, although of course it must be considered.

(a) **Calculation of overhead absorption rates**

	Moulding dept $'000	Finishing dept $'000	General factory overhead $'000
Variable overhead			
Initial allocation	1,600	500	1,050
Reapportion general overhead (800:600)	600	450	(1,050)
Total variable overhead	2,200	950	–
Budgeted machine hours	800	600	
Variable overhead rate per hour	$2.75	$1.58	

	$'000	$'000	$'000
Fixed overhead			
Initial allocation	2,500	850	1,750
Reapportion general overhead (1,200:800)	1,050	700	(1,750)
Total fixed overhead	3,550	1,550	–
Budgeted machine hours	800	600	
Fixed overhead rate per hour	$4.44	$2.58	

Information to assist with the pricing decision

	$ per unit	$ per unit
Direct material		9.00
Direct labour: moulding dept (2 × $5)	10.00	
finishing dept (3 × $5.50)	16.50	
		26.50
Variable overhead: moulding dept (4 × $2.75)	11.00	
finishing dept (3 × $1.58)	4.74	
		15.74
Variable manufacturing cost		51.24
Fixed overhead: moulding dept (4 × $4.44)	17.76	
finishing dept (3 × $2.58)	7.74	
		25.50
Full manufacturing cost		76.74

A **full-cost plus price** will be **based on this cost** of $76.74 **plus a mark-up** of between 25% and 35%. Taking a high, low and average mark-up, the potential prices are as follows.

	25% mark-up $ per unit	30% mark-up $ per unit	35% mark-up $ per unit
Full manufacturing cost	76.74	76.74	76.74
Mark-up	19.19	23.02	26.86
Full cost-plus price	95.93	99.76	103.60

Certain incremental or specific fixed costs have been identified, however, and these should be borne in mind for a well-informed pricing decision.

Product cost based on incremental fixed costs

	$'000	$ per unit
Variable manufacturing cost		51.24
Incremental fixed costs: supervision	20	
depreciation	120	
advertising	27	
	167	
Incremental fixed cost per unit (÷ 20,000 (W))		8.35
Incremental total cost per unit		59.59

Working

Total market = 200,000 units per annum

Ten per cent market share = 20,000 units per annum

(b) The cost information provides a range of bases for a pricing decision.

Variable manufacturing cost

The variable manufacturing cost is $51.24 per unit. At a price below this level there would be no contribution to fixed overheads. Since the prevailing market price is between $90 and $100 each, such a low price might suggest that the product is of inferior quality.

Incremental total cost

The incremental total cost per unit is $59.59. Management must select a price above this level to be sure of covering all costs associated with this product. This unit rate depends on achieving an annual volume of 20,000 units.

Full manufacturing cost

The full manufacturing cost per unit is $76.74. A price based on this cost will ensure that all costs are covered in the long run, if the annual volume of 20,000 units is achieved. Since competitors' prices range between $90 and $100 it seems possible that the company can compete with a price calculated on a full cost-plus basis.

The range of prices suggested, using the company's usual mark-up of between 25 per cent and 35 per cent, is $95.93 to $103.60 per unit.

Given the current price range of the competitors' products and the fact that the product is expected to offer some improvement over competitors' products, a price towards the upper end of the suggested range would be appropriate.

9 AB

> **Top tips.** This question has four ingredients of a good and testing problem on decision making.
>
> - It tests your ability to grasp the **nature of a decision problem**, and think about the assumptions you may have to make. It is assumed that inventory in hand of finished X, valued at $51,900 at full cost, is valued at the full cost of production and not at the full cost of sale.
> - It tests your knowledge of **relevant costs**. For example, the $3,500 capital cost of Y will be incurred whatever course of action is taken, although with the alternative recommendation we have made the spending could be deferred by 33 weeks. Selling and administration overhead has been assumed to be a fixed cost and so is irrelevant to the decision.
> - It includes a consideration of **non-financial factors**. We looked at the workforce, customers' interests and competition – you may have focused on different areas.

(a) **Full cost of production per kg of X**

	$
Direct materials	17.33
Direct labour	7.36
Production overhead (200% of labour)	14.72
	39.41

The quantity of inventory-in-hand is therefore $51,900/$39.41 = 1,317 kg

At a weekly sales volume of 74 kg, this represents 1,317/74 = about 18 weeks of sales

It will take 20 weeks to set up the production facility for Y, and so inventory in hand of finished X can be sold before any Y can be produced. This **finished inventory** is therefore **irrelevant** to the decision under review; it will be sold whatever decision is taken.

The problem therefore centres on the inventory in hand of direct materials. Assuming that there is no loss or wastage in manufacture and so 1 kg of direct material is needed to produce 1 kg of X then inventory in hand is $44,800/$17.33 = 2,585 kg.

This would be converted into 2,585 kg of X, which would represent sales volume for 2,585/74 = 35 weeks.

If AB sells its existing inventories of finished X (in 18 weeks) there are **two options**.

(i) To produce enough X from raw materials for 2 more weeks, until production of Y can start, and then dispose of all other quantities of direct material – ie 33 weeks' supply.

(ii) To produce enough X from raw materials to use up the existing inventory of raw materials, and so delay the introduction of Y by 33 weeks.

The relevant costs of these two options

(i) **Direct materials**. The relevant cost of existing inventories of raw materials is $(0.30). In other words the 'cost' is a benefit. By using the direct materials to make more X, the company would save $0.30 per kg used.

(ii) **Direct labour**. It is assumed that if labour is switched to production work from non-production work in the next three months, they must be paid at the full rate of pay, and not at 65% of normal rate. The *incremental* cost of labour would be 35% of the normal rate (35% of $7.36 = $2.58 per kg produced).

Relevant cost of production of X

	$
Direct materials	(0.30)
Direct labour	2.58
Variable overhead (30% of full overhead cost of $14.72)	4.42
Cost per kg of X	6.70

Relevant cost per kg of Y

	$
Direct materials	4.01
Direct labour	2.85
Variable overhead (30% of 200% of $2.85)	1.71
	8.57

(*Note.* Y cannot be made for 20 weeks, and so the company cannot make use of spare labour capacity to produce any units of Y.)

It is cheaper to use up the direct material inventories and make X ($6.70 per kg) than to introduce Y as soon as possible, because there would be a saving of ($8.57 – $6.70) = $1.87 per kg made.

AB must sell X for at least 20 weeks until Y could be produced anyway, but the introduction of Y could be delayed by a further 33 weeks until all inventories of direct material for X are used up. The saving in total would be about $1.87 per kg × 74 kg per week × 33 weeks = $4,567.

(b) **Non-financial factors that must be considered in reaching the decision**

(i) **The workforce**. If the recommended course of action is undertaken, the workforce will produce enough units of X in the next 13 weeks to satisfy sales demand over the next year, (with 18 weeks' supply of existing finished goods inventories and a further 35 weeks' supply obtainable from direct materials inventories). When production of Y begins, the direct labour content of production will fall to $2.85 per kg – less than 40% of the current effort per kg produced – but sales demand will not rise. The changeover will therefore mean a big drop in labour requirements in production. Redundancies seem inevitable, and might be costly. By switching to producing Y as soon as possible, the redundancies might be less immediate, and could be justified more easily to employees and their union representatives than a decision to produce enough X in the next 3 months to eliminate further production needs for about 9 months.

(ii) **Customers' interests**. Product Y is a superior and 'more effective' compound than X. It would be in customers' interests to provide them with this improved product as soon as possible, instead of delaying its introduction until existing inventories of direct materials for X have been used up.

(iii) **Competition**. CD is expected to start selling Y overseas, and quite possibly in direct competition with AB. CD has the advantage of having developed Y itself, and appears to use it in the preliminary stage of an alternative technical process. The competitive threat to AB is two-fold:

(1) CD might take away some of the replacement demand for Y from AB so that AB's sales of X or Y would fall.

(2) CD might compete with AB to install its total technical process into customers' factories, and so the competition would be wider than the market for compound Y.

10 Stow Health Centre

Top tips. Did you get confused in part (a)? The occupancy level will vary with the client fee per day, while the variable cost per client day is independent. In other words, at each of the **three different levels of client fee** per day, there are **three possible levels of variable cost** per client and so 3 × 3 = **9 possible levels of contribution per client day.**

The most tricky aspect of part (b) was dealing with the **minimax regret decision rule**. This rule involves choosing the strategy which will **minimise the maximum regret** (ie drop in contribution) from choosing one option instead of the best option. This requires you to draw up an **opportunity loss table**. This will show the **drop in contribution** at **each level of variable cost** from **choosing a level of client fee which is not the best option**. For example, at a variable cost of $95 per day, the best strategy would be a client fee of $200 per day. The opportunity loss from using a fee of $180 would be the difference between the contributions at the two fee levels.

For part (c) you simply need to **calculate an EV of variable cost per day**. You are then faced with a situation of one level of client fee per day and one level of variable cost per day at each level of 'demand'.

(a) We need to calculate budgeted contribution and so the summary will need to show the various income (fee) and variable cost levels.

	Client fee per day		
Variable cost per day	$180	$200	$220
$	$	$	$
95	1,338,750	1,378,125	1,312,500
85	1,496,250	1,509,375	1,417,500
70	1,732,500	1,706,250	1,575,000

Workings

Number of client days:
Maximum capacity = 50 × 350 = 17,500
High occupancy level = 90% × 17,500 = 15,750
Most likely occupancy level = 75% × 17,500 = 13,125
Low occupancy level = 60% × 17,500 = 10,500

Number of client days × contribution per client day (fee − variable cost) = contribution

(b) (i) The **maximax** decision rule involves choosing the outcome with the **best possible result**, in this instance choosing the outcome which **maximises contribution**. The decision maker would therefore choose a **client fee of $180 per day**, which could result in a contribution of $1,732,500.

(ii) The **maximin** decision rule involves choosing the outcome that offers the **least unattractive worst outcome,** in this instance choosing the outcome which **maximises the minimum contribution**. The decision maker would therefore choose a **client fee of $200 per day**, which has a lowest possible contribution of $1,378,125. This is better than the worst possible outcomes from client fees per day of $180 and $220, which would provide contributions of $1,338,750 and $1,312,500 respectively.

(iii) The **minimax regret** decision rule involves choosing the **outcome that minimises the maximum regret** from making the wrong decision, in this instance choosing the outcome which minimises the opportunity lost from making the wrong decision.

We can use the calculations performed in (a) to draw up an **opportunity loss table.**

	Variable cost per day			Maximum regret
Client fee per day	$95	$85	$70	
$	$	$	$	$
180	39,375 (W1)	13,125 (W4)	0 (W7)	39,375
200	0 (W2)	0 (W5)	26,250 (W8)	26,250
220	65,625 (W3)	91,875 (W6)	157,500 (W9)	157,500

The minimax regret decision strategy would be to **choose a client fee of $200** to minimise the maximum regret at $26,250.

Workings

1. At a variable cost of $95 per day, the best strategy would be a client fee of $200 per day. The opportunity loss from using a fee of $180 would be $(1,378,125 – 1,338,750) = $39,375.
2. The opportunity loss in this case is $(1,378,125 – 1,378,125) = $0.
3. The opportunity loss in this case is $(1,378,125 – 1,312,500) = $65,625.
4. At a variable cost of $85 per day, the best strategy would be a client fee of $200 per day. The opportunity loss from using a fee of $180 would be $(1,509,375 – 1,496,250)= $13,125.
5. The opportunity loss in this case is $(1,509,375 – 1,509,375) = 0.
6. The opportunity loss in this case is $(1,509,375 – 1,417,500) = $91,875.
7. At a variable cost of $70 per day, the best strategy would be client fee of $180 per day. The opportunity loss from using a fee of $180 would be $(1,732,500 – 1,732,500) = $0.
8. The opportunity loss in this case is $(1,732,500 – 1,706,250) = $26,250.
9. The opportunity loss in this case is $(1,732,500 – 1,575,000) = $157,500.

(c) **Expected value of variable costs** = $(0.1 \times \$95) + (0.6 \times \$85) + (0.3 \times \$70) = \$81.50$.

We can now calculate an expected value of budgeted contribution at each client fee per day level.

		Client fee per day	
Variable cost	$180	$200	$220
$81.50	1,551,375	1,553,312.50	1,454,250

If **maximisation of EV of contribution is used as the decision basis**, a **client fee of $200 per day** will be selected, with an EV of contribution of $1,555,312.50 (although this is *very* close to the EV of contribution which results from a client fee of $180).

11 Zero based budgeting

REPORT

To: R&D manager
From: Management accountant
Date: 01.01.X3
Subject: Zero based budgeting

(a) **Zero based budgeting and traditional budgeting**

The traditional approach to budgeting works from the premise that last year's activities will continue at the same level or volume, and that next year's budget can be based on last year's costs plus an extra amount to allow for expansion and inflation. The term 'incremental' budgeting is often used to describe this approach.

Zero based budgeting (ZBB) quite literally works from a zero base. The approach recognises that every activity has a cost and insists that there must be quantifiable benefits to justify the spending. ZBB expects managers to choose the best method of achieving each task by comparing costs and benefits. Activities must be ranked in order of priority.

(b) A **discretionary cost** is not vital to the continued existence of an organisation in the way that, say, raw materials are to a manufacturing business. ZBB was developed originally to help management with the difficult task of allocating resources in precisely such areas. **Research and development** is a frequently cited example; others are **advertising** and **training**.

Within a research and development department ZBB will establish priorities by ranking the projects that are planned and in progress. Project managers will be forced to consider the benefit obtainable from their work in relation to the costs involved. The result may be an overall increase in R&D expenditure, but only if it is justified.

(c) **Budgetary slack** may be defined as the difference between the minimum necessary costs and the costs built into the budget or actually incurred. One of the reasons why, under traditional budgeting, an extra amount is added to last year's budget may be because managers are overestimating costs to avoid being blamed in the future for overspending and to make targets easier to achieve. Slack is a protective device and it is self-fulfilling because managers will subsequently ensure that their actual spending rises to meet the (overestimated) budget, in case they are blamed for careless budgeting.

In an R&D department a further incentive to include slack is the nature of the work. Managers may well have 'pet' projects in which their personal interest is so strong that they tend to ignore the benefit or lack of benefit to the organisation which is funding them.

The **ZBB approach**, as described in (a) above, clearly will not accept this approach: all expenditure has (in theory) to be justified in cost-benefit terms in its entirety in order to be included in next year's budget. In practice it is more likely that managers will start from their current level of expenditure as usual, but ZBB requires them to work **downwards**, asking what would happen if any particular element of current expenditure and current operations were removed from the budget.

12 Dench

(a) **Cost estimate for 225 components is based upon the following assumptions:**

(1) The first batch of 15 is excluded from the order (and total cost for first batch is likewise excluded); and

(2) The 80% learning rate only applies to the skilled workforce, (and related variable overhead) due to their high level of expertise/low turnover rate.

Cumulative Batches	Cumulative Batches	Total Time Hours	Cum ave time/batch Hours
1	15	20	20
2	30	32	16
4	60	51.2	12.8
8	120	81.92	10.24
16	240	131.072	8.192

Total cost for 16 batches (240 components)

		$
Material A:	$30 batch	480
Material B:	$30/batch	480
Labour:	Skilled 131.072 hr @ $15/hr	1,966
	Semi-skilled $40/batch	640
Variable OH:	131.072 hr @ $4/hr	524
	5 hr/batch at $4/hr	320
		4,410
Less: Cost for 1st batch (15 components)		(500)
∴ cost for 225 components		3,910

(b) The limited use of learning curve theory is due to several factors:

(i) The learning curve phenomenon is not always present.

(ii) It assumes stable conditions at work (eg of the labour force and labour mix) which will enable learning to take place. This is not always practicable (eg because of labour turnover).

(iii) It must also assume a certain degree of motivation amongst employees.

(iv) Extensive breaks between production of items must not be too long, or workers will 'forget' and the learning process would have to begin all over again.

(v) It is difficult to obtain enough accurate data to decide what the learning curve is.

13 ACCA-Chem Co

> **Top tips.** There are quite a lot of calculations in this question. Whilst it's easy to say that you should split your time so that you spend enough time on the written elements, written element (a) (iv) is dependent upon your answer to the earlier calculations.
>
> Work through (a) (iv) carefully, and make sure you understand the link between the different variances.

(a)   (1)   **Price variances**

	$	$
Material F		
59,800 kgs should have cost (× $4)	239,200	
but did cost (× $4.25)	254,150	
		14,950 (A)
Material G		
53,500 kgs should have cost (× $3)	160,500	
but did cost (× $2.80)	149,800	
		10,700 (F)
Material H		
33,300 kgs should have cost (× $6)	199,800	
but did cost (× $6.40)	213,120	
		13,320 (A)
Total material price variance		17,570 (A)

(2)   **Usage variances**

	F	G	H
4,100 units of output of			
product W should need	61,500 kgs	49,200 kgs	32,800 kgs
but did need	59,800 kgs	53,500 kgs	33,300 kgs
Usage variance in kgs	1,700 kgs(F)	4,300 kgs (A)	500 kgs (A)
× standard price per kg	× $4	× $3	× $6
Usage variance in $	$6,800 (F)	$12,900 (A)	$3,000 (A)

Total material usage variance = $9,100 (A)

(3)   **Mix variances**

Total kgs used = 146,600 kgs

Standard mix for actual use

		kgs
F	$^{15}/_{35}$ × 146,600 =	62,829
G	$^{12}/_{35}$ × 146,600 =	50,263
H	$^{8}/_{35}$ × 146,600 =	33,508
		146,600

	Actual quantity standard mix	*Actual quantity actual mix*	*Variance*	*Standard cost per kg*	*Variance*
	Kgs	Kgs	Kgs	$	$
F	62,829	59,800	3,029 (F)	4	12,116 (F)
G	50,263	53,500	3,237 (A)	3	9,711 (A)
H	33,508	33,300	208 (F)	6	1,248 (F)
	146,600	146,600	–		3,653 (F)

Total mix variance = $3,653 (F)

(4) Yield variance

The yield variance can be calculated in total or for each material input.

In total

146,600 kg input should yield (/35)	4188.57 units
146,600 kg input did yield	4100.00 units
	88.57 (A)
@ $144 per unit	$12,754 (A)

	Standard quantity standard mix	Actual quantity standard mix	Variance	Standard cost per kg	Variance
	Kgs	Kgs	Kgs	$	$
F	61,500	62,829	1,329 (A)	4	5,316 (A)
G	49,200	50,263	1,063 (A)	3	3,189 (A)
H	32,800	33,508	708 (A)	6	4,248 (A)
	143,500	146,600	442 (A)		12,753 (A)

(b)

	$
4,100 units should have sold for (× $260)	1,066,000
but did sell for	1,115,800
Selling price variance	49,800 (F)

Budgeted sales for period	44,500 units
Actual sales volume	4,100 units
Volume variance in kgs	400 units (A)
× standard profit per kg ($(260 − 196))	× $64
Sales volume profit variance	$25,600 (A)

(c) **Adverse yield variance**

An analysis of the materials mix variance (see (a)(i)(3)) shows that 3,029 kgs of F and 208 kgs of H (the more expensive materials) were replaced by 3,237 kgs of G (the cheapest material). This **substitution of cheaper material** could have led to the adverse yield variance. It is **also** possible that the yield variance was because the material G that was used was of a **lower than standard quality** since it was purchased at a price below its standard price.

Adverse efficiency variance

The adverse labour efficiency variance may have been due to Material G taking longer to process than normal because it was of a poor quality. Alternatively, the fact that in Department Q the actual rate was less than the standard rate could mean that less skilled labour was used than provided for in the standard, and that this then lowered productivity with the result that the yield was lower than expected.

14 Milbao

Top tips. Part (a) does not require detailed technical knowledge but should be based on your knowledge of how budgets and control systems can operate effectively.

You need to be able to calculate planning and operational variances with confidence. The question in (b) should provide useful practice.

(a) **Components**

Arguments for a revision

The problem arose due to a liquidation of a supplier which is **outside the control** of the buyer who is unlikely to have been aware it was going to happen.

The buyer will expect this revision to be allowed as it is outside his control and is likely to be demoralised and demotivated if it is refused.

Arguments against a revision

The buyer accepted the deal with the new supplier **without attempting to negotiate**. This may have been a panicked reaction to the immediate problem which has increased Milbao's costs.

The buyer is responsible for sourcing the cheapest materials and this could have been achieved with an alternative local supplier. A more **considered, careful approach** would have achieved a better deal.

A buyer should also have a good knowledge of his supplier's circumstances and it could be argued that some advance knowledge of liquidity problems could have been expected.

Conclusion

The budget revision should not be allowed. Although the liquidation was outside the control of the buyer, he could have achieved a better price.

Labour

Arguments for a revision

The Board made the decision to change the recruitment policy and this decision was outside the **control** of the departmental manager. The departmental manager is therefore not responsible for the extra cost.

Arguments against a revision

The **organisation as a whole** is in control of this decision so the cost is controllable.

The departmental manager **requested** a change in recruitment so is responsible for the extra cost involved.

The **productivity increases** have benefited the department involved so it should also be charged with the costs involved.

Conclusion

This was an **operational decision** that the departmental manager requested and agreed to. It has had the desired effects so no budget revision should be allowed.

(b) The original standard cost was 0.25 litres × $10 = $2.50. The revised standard cost is 3 litres × $8 = $2.40.

Material price planning variance

	$ per litre
Original standard price	10.00
Revised standard price	8.00
Material price planning variance	2.00 (F)

The planning variance is favourable because the change in the standard price reduces the material cost.

Materials actually used 3,700 litres

Material price planning variance = 3,700 litres × $2 (F) = $7,400 (F).

Material price operational variance

	$
3,700 litres of material should cost (revised standard $8)	29,600
They did cost	29,100
Material price operational variance	500 (F)

Material usage planning variance

	litres
Original standard usage per unit	0.25
Revised standard usage per unit	0.30
Material usage planning variance	0.05 (A)

Number of units produced: 11,200

Original standard price per litre: $10

Material usage planning variance = 11,200 × 0.05 (A) × $10 = $5,600 (A)

Material usage operational variance

	litres
11,200 units should use (revised standard: × 0.3)	3,360
They did use	3,700
Material usage operational variance in litres	340 (A)
Original standard price per litre	$10
Material usage operational variance in $	$3,400 (A)

Tutorial check: The variances may be summarised as follows.

	$	$
11,200 units of product at original std cost ($2.5)		28,000
Actual material cost		29,100
Total material cost variance		1,100 (A)
Material price planning variance	7,400 (F)	
Material price operational variance	500 (F)	
Material usage planning variance	5,600 (A)	
Material usage operational variance	3,400 (A)	
Total of variances		1,100 (A)

Comments on variances

Planning variances are outside the area of responsibility of operational managers.

The material price operational variance was $500 favourable, indicating that the purchasing manager was able to obtain prices for the raw materials that were slightly below the market price of $8.

The material usage operational variance shows that although the standard cost was revised to include a bigger standard usage of materials, actual usage was nevertheless greater than the revised standard. Actual usage was about 0.33 litres per unit (3,700/11,200) rather than the standard 0.3 litres.

15 Budgets and people

> **Top tips.** You are **unlikely to get a full question on the behavioural aspects of budgeting**. The issue is more likely to be examined in the context of a wider question on budgeting.
>
> It is well worth attempting this question, however, as it covers a wide range of the possible issues that you could encounter. Make sure that you **deal with both parts** of the question (the reasons for reluctance and the side effects of imposed budgets). Beware, however, of writing down everything you can possibly think of which is remotely related to the behavioural aspects of management accounting.

There is one major **reason why managers may be reluctant to participate** fully in setting up budgets and that is a **lack of education in the purposes of the budgeting process**. The budget's major role is to communicate the various motivations that exist among management so that everybody sees, understands and co-ordinates the goals of the organisation.

Specific reasons for the reluctance of managers to participate are as follows.

(a) Managers view budgets as **too rigid a constraint on their decision making.** For example, a manager may be unable to sanction an item of expenditure if it has not been budgeted for. The natural reaction to this supposed restriction of their autonomy is resistance and self defence.

(b) Managers feel that the top management **goals expressed by the budget will interfere with their personal goals** (for example their desire to 'build an empire' with substantial resources under their control, large personal income and so on). A successful budgetary system will harmonise the budget goals with the managers' personal goals, but it is by no means easy to achieve a successful system.

(c) Managers imagine that the purpose of budgets is to provide senior management with a **rod** with which to chastise those who do not stay within budget. They will be unwilling to help in the construction of such a rod.

(d) Managers view the budgeting process as one in which they must **fight for a fair share** of the organisation's **resources** in competition with colleagues with other responsibilities.

(e) Managers misinterpret the **control function** of the budgeting system to be a method whereby **blame** can be **attached**. By not participating in the budget setting process, they are able to blame an 'unattainable' or 'unrealistic' budget for any poor results they may have.

As a reaction to these uneducated notions, the behaviour of managers involved in budget preparation can conflict with the desires of senior management. Such behaviour is often described as **dysfunctional**; it is counter-productive because it is **not goal congruent.**

The **unwanted side effects** which may arise from the **imposition of budgets** by senior management (for example under an authoritative rather than a participative budgetary system) are examples of **dysfunctional behaviour** and include the following.

(a) There may be a **reluctance to reduce costs** for fear that future budget allowances may be reduced as a consequence of successful cost cutting.

(b) Managers may **spend up to their budget** in order to justify levels of expenditure. This is particularly the case in local government circles where there is a tendency to spend any available cash at the end of a financial year.

(c) There may be **padding**, whereby managers request inflated allowances. In turn senior management may cut budgets where they suspect padding exists. Padding is sometimes called slack and represents the difference between the budget allowance requested and the realistic costs necessary to accomplish the objective.

(d) In extreme cases of authoritative budgeting, the **'emotional' responses** of managers can be highly detrimental to the goals of the organisation, for example non-cooperation.

16 Handra

> **Top tips.** At first glance this question may appear straightforward. Do not forget to provide sensible examples of the different types of information that may apply to Handra.

Strategic, tactical and management information are **classifications of information** that distinguish the purposes for which that information is used. It can also be used to distinguish the type of information that is used at different levels in the management hierarchy of an organisation with a hierarchical management structure.

Strategic information

Strategic information is used for strategic decision-making. It often relates to **long-term objectives** and performance, and to matters that are **external** to the organisation.

For Handra, relevant strategic information would include information about **competitors** in the market. It appears that a competitor may be in financial difficulty; it may be useful for Handra to know more about this and the reasons why the competitor may be in difficulty. It would also be useful to have information about how rival organisations may respond to any competitive initiative by Handra.

The management of Handra would also benefit from strategic information about **technological developments** in the industry, the possibility of rising water and energy prices, or even the possibility of government action to discourage excessive energy use by business organisations.

Tactical information

Tactical information is generally associated with **planning and control activities** within the framework of annual budgets or plans. It is information to help management make decisions for planning, or for monitoring actual performance against the budget expectation, and also to manage spending and efficiency within the organisation.

Tactical information can include both **non-financial and financial information**. Examples of tactical information include budgets, variance reports for control purposes, efficiency and capacity ratios, and summary information about quality failures (re-working of faulty items and items returned under warranty) and on-time deliveries.

Operational information

Operational information is information provided to management, supervisors and other employees at a **day-to-day operational level**. It is usually detailed information and much of it is non-financial in nature. It is needed to help individuals to do their day-to-day work.

Examples of operational information include detailed information about throughput times, machine failures and downtime, bottlenecks, complaints, quantities of rejected items and so on.

Information systems should provide **sufficient relevant information** for decision-making at all levels and for all management and operational purposes within the organisation. When information is not sufficient, there is a much greater risk of inappropriate decision-making by management.

17 JM foods

> **Top tips.** Ensure that you refer back to the scenario throughout your answer to part (a) to maximise your score.

(a)   There are many sources of external information available to Bill.

Business directories

Business directories are a form of **secondary data**.

Bill could use business directories to compile a list of competing fast-food restaurants currently operating in the new country.

Government agencies

The government is a major source of **economic information** and information about industries and popular trends. Many government publications are available online and can be downloaded for free.

Official government statistics on **consumer tastes and trends** as well as **socio-demographic data** could help to indicate whether the proposed expansion is commercially viable. The data could also influence the food that the company chooses to offer to the new market.

Information from customers

Bill should encourage the company to send out **customer satisfaction surveys** and conduct **market research**.

Customer **comments** and **complaints** in existing markets could influence the ingredients used and the food offered in the new country.

Information from suppliers

Bill could research and contract a range of potential suppliers in the new country.

This would provide valuable **cost data** to feed into **budgets** and any **investment appraisal techniques** that the directors may wish to use as part of the decision-making process.

The internet

The internet can be used to provided information about **suppliers** and **competitors**.

For example, Bill could visit the websites of competitors already operating in the proposed country to obtain details of the products/services they offer.

Such data will give the directors an idea of the prices they can expect to charge in the new country and the **margins** they can expect to earn on each product.

(b)   **Direct search costs** are directly attributable to the activities performed to obtain external data. For example, download fees or the costs of a market research survey.

Indirect access costs include management and employee time spent finding useful information. They also include costs incurred as a result of wasted management and employee time on unsuccessful and excessive searches.

Management costs are the costs incurred in the recording, processing and dissemination of external information. The also include costs attributable to time wasted on excessive processing due to information overload.

Infrastructure costs are costs attributable to the tools and equipment used to obtain external data. For example, installation and maintenance of computer networks and internal electronic communications.

Time-theft costs include lost time, the cost of monitoring and wasted time caused by the abuse of internet and email facilities.

18 Spring

> **Top tips.** This is a wholly written question but it has specific requirements. Stick to these as they guide your answer. Make sure you provide in-depth discussion not just lists of points.
>
> **Easy marks.** The pros and cons of activity based costing in part (a), provided you know these.

(a)   **Advantages of ABC**

The complexity of manufacturing has increased, with wider product ranges, shorter product life cycles and more complex production processes. ABC recognises this complexity with its multiple cost drivers.

In a more competitive environment, companies must be able to assess product profitability realistically. ABC facilitates a good understanding of what drives overhead costs.

In modern manufacturing systems, overhead functions include a lot of non-factory-floor activities such as product design, quality control, production planning and customer services. ABC is concerned with all overhead costs and so goes beyond 'traditional' factory floor boundaries.

Disadvantages of ABC

It has however been suggested by critics that activity based costing has some serious flaws. Some measure of (arbitrary) cost apportionment may still be required at the cost pooling stage for items like rent, rates and building depreciation.

Unless costs are caused by an activity that is measurable in quantitative terms and which can be related to production output, cost drivers will not be usable. What drives the cost of the annual external audit, for example?

ABC is sometimes introduced because it is fashionable, not because it will be used by management to provide meaningful product costs or extra information. If Spring's management is not going to use ABC information, an absorption costing system may be simpler to operate. Put another way, the cost of implementing and maintaining an ABC system can exceed the benefits of improved accuracy.

Implementing ABC is often problematic. Recent journal articles have highlighted the following issues.

(i) An incorrect belief that ABC can solve all an organisation's problems
(ii) Lack of the correct type of data
(iii) Difficulty in determining appropriate cost drivers

(b) **Performance measurement** is a part of the system of financial control of an enterprise, as well as being important to investors. Managerial performance and organisational performance are linked, since the decisions that managers make will influence how well or otherwise the organisation performs. This performance needs to be measured as part of the **control process**. The key elements of such a process are as follows.

Step 1   **Plans and targets are set for the future**. These could be long-, medium- or short-term plans. Examples include budgets, profit targets and standard costs.

Step 2   **Plans are put into operation**. As a consequence, materials and labour are used, and other expenses are incurred.

Step 3   **Actual results are recorded and analysed**.

Step 4   **Information about actual results is fed back** to the management concerned, often in the form of accounting reports.

Step 5   **The feedback is used by management to compare** actual results with the plan or targets.

Step 6   By comparing actual and planned results, management can then do one of three things, depending on how they see the situation.

(a) **They can take control action**. By identifying what has gone wrong, and then finding out why, corrective measures can be taken.

(b) **They can decide to do nothing**. This could be the decision when actual results are going better than planned, or when poor results were caused by something which is unlikely to happen again in the future.

(c) **They can alter the plan or target** if actual results are different from the plan or target, and there is nothing that management can do (or nothing, perhaps, that they want to do) to correct the situation.

The usual assumption in financial management for the private sector is that the primary financial objective of the company is to maximise shareholders' wealth. Financial targets may include targets for earnings; earnings per share; dividend per share; gearing levels; profit retention and operating profitability.

There are a variety of ways that such performance can be measured. As part of the system of financial control in an organisation, it will be necessary to have ways of measuring the progress of the enterprise, so that managers know how well the company is doing. A common means of doing this is through ratio analysis, which is concerned with comparing and quantifying relationships between financial variables, such as those variables found in the balance sheet and profit and loss account of the enterprise.

Ratios can be grouped into the following four categories: profitability and return; debt and gearing; liquidity: control of cash and other working capital items; shareholders' investment ratios ('stock market ratios'). The ratios can be seen to be interrelated.

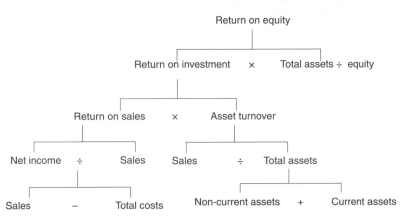

Such ratios help in providing for an overall management plan to achieve profitability, and allow the interrelationships between ratios to be checked.

There is a danger, however, in focusing excessively on financial performance measures which can be easily quantified, thus placing an undue emphasis on maximising short-term performance even if this conflicts with maximising long-term performance. Non-financial objectives may include employee welfare; management welfare; the welfare of society; service provision objectives and the fulfilment of responsibilities to customers and suppliers.

It is therefore important that a range of non-financial indicators be developed to provide better predictors for the attainment of long-term profitability goals. Here are some examples.

- Quality
- Number of customer complaints
- Lead times
- Delivery to time
- Non-productive hours
- System (machine) down time

Unlike traditional variance reports, measures such as these can be provided quickly for managers, per shift or on a daily or hourly basis. They are likely to be easy to calculate, and easier for non-financial managers to understand and therefore to use effectively.

A popular approach in current management thinking to performance measurement (for service and non-service organisations) is the use of what is called a 'balanced scorecard'. The balanced scorecard approach aims to provide management with information covering all relevant areas of performance. The information provided may include both financial and non-financial elements. The scorecard is 'balanced' in the sense that managers are required to think in terms of all four perspectives (customer perception, innovation capability, internal processes and financial measures), to prevent improvements being made in one area at the expense of another. The method had the advantages of looking at both internal and external matters concerning the organisation and of linking together financial and non-financial measures.

19 Animal Farm

Profit

The actual profit of the company can be compared with the budgeted profit. (Profitability could also be compared with profits in the previous year, but data for making this comparison is not available.)

	Budget		Actual	
	$	$	$	$
Revenue		2,100,000		2,250,000
Salaries, full-time vets	720,000		720,000	
(8 × $90,000)				
Bonus	–		75,000	
50% × (2,250,000 – 2,100,000)				
Part-time vets	15,000		48,000	
Other costs	1,120,000		1,390,000	
Total costs		1,855,000		2,233,000
Profit		245,000		17,000

Actual profit is a long way below the budgeted profit.

Competitiveness

A measure of competitiveness may be the success rate in turning customer enquiries by telephone into actual examinations and treatments. (Note: There could be other and better measures of competitiveness, such as growth in share of the local market. Data is not available here to make this measurement.)

In the table below, 'success rate' is the percentage of customer enquiries by telephone that result in an actual examination or treatment.

	Budget	Actual
New business		
Enquiries	4,000	7,000
Examinations/treatments	2,500	3,000
Success rate	63%	43%
Repeat business		
Enquiries	15,000	12,000
Examinations/treatments	12,700	11,200
Success rate	85%	93%

The company has not been as successful as expected (budgeted) in converting enquiries from new customers into 'sales', but it has been more successful than expected in converting calls from 'repeat' customers into sales.

Quality

Quality of service can be measured by complaints. A useful measure is the number of complaints as a percentage of examinations and treatments.

	Budget	Actual
Complaints	300	410
Examinations/treatments	15,200	14,200
Percentage rate of complaints	2.0%	2.9%

It would be useful to analyse complaints according to the type of animals treated in each case, but the data is not available.

The rate of complaints is higher than expected, suggesting that the quality of service is not up to the expected standard.

Resource utilisation

The key resource in the company is probably the time of the full-time vets. Useful measures of performance would therefore be average revenue per full-time vet and average number of treatments given per full time vet. Ideally, income from the treatment of exotic animals should be excluded from revenue, but we do not know how much income was earned from treating exotic animals.

	Budget	Actual
Revenue	£2,100,000	$2,250,000
Number of full-time vets	8	8
Average revenue per vet	$262,500	$281,250
Number of treatments, excluding exotic animals	15,100	13,900
Average number of treatments per full-time vet	1,875	1,737.5

Average revenue per vet was $18,750 (about 7%) above budget, although some of this increase must be due to the higher-than-budgeted quantity of treatments of exotic animals. The average number of treatments by full time vets was7.3% lower than budgeted This suggests that either treatments were longer than budgeted or vets had more 'non-contact time' than expected.

Flexibility

An aspect of flexibility is probably the ability of the centre to respond to requests for treatment of exotic animals. A suitable measure of performance might therefore be the percentage of revenue that comes from treating exotic animals. The budget might state the minimum required percentage.

	Budget	Actual
Total number of treatments	15,200	14,200
Treatments of exotic animals	100	300
	0.7%	2.1%

The company has possibly demonstrated its flexibility by treating more exotic animals than provided for in the budget. However, this still remains a low proportion of the total annual number of treatments.

Innovation

There is no data for measuring innovation in a satisfactory way, although the amount spent on training (per vet) might be used as an indication of 'new learning' and so an ability to innovate and provide new methods of treatment.

	Budget	Actual
Spending on training	$60,000	$80,000
Full-time vets	8	8
Training costs per vet	$7,500	$10,000

By spending more than budgeted on training, the Centre might demonstrate its ability to innovate and offer new treatments for animals.

20 Divisional performance measures

> **Top tips**. Parts (a) and (b) require you to demonstrate knowledge you should have picked up directly from the text. No application skills are required at all in this instance.
>
> That being said, it is vital that you do not learn the advantages and disadvantages of ROI and RI in a parrot fashion as they underlie the very core of the chapter. You **must understand how and why ROI affects managerial behaviour**, for example. You are just as likely to get a written question on this area as a calculation-based one.
>
> The calculations required in (b) should not have caused you any problems.
>
> Part (c) is **basic book knowledge** and so you should have been able to score quite a few of the marks available.

(a)   The **residual income (RI)** for a division is calculated by deducting from the divisional profit an imputed interest charge, based on the investment in the division.

The **return on investment (ROI)** is the divisional profit expressed as a percentage of the investment in the division.

Both methods use the **same basic figure for profit and investment**, but **residual income** produces an **absolute** measure whereas the **return on investment** is expressed as a **percentage**.

Both methods suffer from **disadvantages** in measuring the profit and the investment in a division which include the following.

(i)   Assets must be valued consistently at historical cost or at replacement cost. Neither valuation basis is ideal.

(ii)   Divisions might use different bases to value inventory and to calculate depreciation.

(iii)   Any charges made for the use of head office services or allocations of head office assets to divisions are likely to be arbitrary.

In addition, **return on investment** suffers from the following **disadvantages**.

(i)   Rigid adherence to the need to maintain ROI in the short term can discourage managers from investing in new assets, since average divisional ROI tends to fall in the early stages of a new investment. Residual income can overcome this problem by highlighting projects which return more than the cost of capital.

(ii) It can be difficult to compare the percentage ROI results of divisions if their activities are very different: residual income can overcome this problem through the use of different interest rates for different divisions.

(b) (i) **Return on divisional investment (ROI)**

	Before investment	After investment
Divisional profit	$18,000	$19,600
Divisional investment	$100,000	$110,000
Divisional ROI	18.0%	17.8%

The ROI will fall in the short term if the new investment is undertaken. This is a problem which often arises with ROI, as noted in part (a) of this solution.

(ii) **Divisional residual income**

		Before investment	After investment
		$	$
Divisional profit		18,000	19,600
Less imputed interest:	$100,000 × 15%	15,000	
	$110,000 × 15%		16,500
Residual income		3,000	3,100

The residual income will increase if the new investment is undertaken. The use of residual income has highlighted the fact that the new project returns more than the cost of capital (16% compared with 15%).

(c) **Potential benefits of operating a transfer pricing system within a divisionalised company**

(i) It can lead to **goal congruence** by motivating divisional managers to make decisions, which improve divisional profit and improve profit of the organisation as a whole.

(ii) It can prevent **dysfunctional decision making** so that decisions taken by a divisional manager are in the best interests of his own part of the business, other divisions and the organisation as a whole.

(iii) Transfer prices can be set at a level that enables divisional performance to be measured 'commercially'. A transfer pricing system should therefore report a level of divisional profit that is a **reasonable measure of the managerial performance** of the division.

(iv) It should ensure that **divisional autonomy** is not undermined. A well-run transfer pricing system helps to ensure that a balance is kept between divisional autonomy to provide incentives and motivation, and centralised authority to ensure that the divisions are all working towards the same target, the benefit of the organisation as a whole.

21 Non-profit seeking organisations

Top tips. Like many examination questions, part (a) can be answered by taking a **logical, structured approach** that is offered to you by the wording of the question itself. You can take (1) **efficiency** and (2) **effectiveness** in turn (this solution opts to deal with effectiveness first) and explain for each why the absence of a profit measure causes problems. This suggest that you need to explain why the **presence of a profit measure** helps with the assessment of efficiency and effectiveness.

Take note of the **examples about objectives** we have provided in part (a) – they may prove **useful in your exam** as this requirement is perhaps one of the more likely to appear on the subject of non-profit seeking organisations.

For part (b), remember that indicators need to be **compared against a yardstick** to be of any use for performance measurement purposes. The fact that 8% of appointments were cancelled is useless information. When considered in conjunction with a target of 5%, it becomes useful!

(a) **Effectiveness** refers to the use of resources so as to achieve desired ends or objectives or outputs.

In a profit-making organisation, objectives can be expressed financially in terms of a target profit or return. The organisation, or profit centres within the organisation, can be judged to have operated effectively if they have achieved a target profit within a given period.

In non-profit seeking organisations, effectiveness cannot be measured in this way. The organisation's objectives cannot be expressed in financial terms at all, and non-financial objectives need to be established. The effectiveness of performance could be measured in terms of whether targeted non-financial objectives have been achieved, but there are several **problems** involved in trying to do this.

(1) The organisation might have several **different objectives** which are difficult to reconcile with each other. Achieving one objective might only be possible at the expense of failing to achieve another. For example, schools have the objective of providing education. They teach a certain curriculum, but by opting to educate students in some subjects, there is no time available to provide education in other subjects.

(2) A non-profit seeking organisation will invariably be **restricted in what it can achieve by the availability of funds**. The health service, for example, has the objective of providing health care, but since funds are restricted there is a limit to the amount of care that can be provided, and there will be competition for funds between different parts of the service.

(3) The objectives of non-profit seeking organisations are also difficult to establish because the **quality** of the service provided will be a significant feature of their service. For example, a local authority has, amongst its various different objectives, the objective of providing a rubbish collection service. The effectiveness of this service can only be judged by establishing what standard or quality of service is required.

(4) With differing objectives, none of them directly comparable, and none that can be expressed in profit terms, **human judgement** is likely to be involved in deciding whether an organisation has been effective or not. This is most clearly seen in government organisations where political views cloud opinion about the government's performance.

Efficiency refers to the rate at which resources are consumed to achieve desired ends. Efficiency measurements compare the output produced by the organisation with the resources employed or used up to achieve the output. They are used to control the consumption of resources, so that the maximum output is achieved by a given amount of input resources, or a certain volume of output is produced within the minimum resources being used up.

In profit-making organisations, the efficiency of the organisation as a whole can be measured in terms of return on capital employed. Individual profit centres or operating units within the organisation can also have efficiency measured by relating the quantity of output produced, which has a **market value** and therefore a quantifiable financial value, to the resources (and their costs) required to make the output.

In non-profit seeking organisations, output does not usually have a market value, and it is therefore more difficult to measure efficiency. This difficulty is compounded by the fact that since these organisations often have **several different objectives**, it is difficult to compare the efficiency of one operation with the efficiency of another. For example, with the police force, it might be difficult to compare the efficiency of a serious crimes squad with the efficiency of the traffic police, because each has its own 'outputs' that are not easily comparable in terms of 'value achieved'.

In spite of the difficulties of measuring effectiveness and efficiency, control over the performance of non-profit seeking organisations can only be satisfactorily achieved by assessments of **'value for money'** (economy, efficiency and effectiveness).

(b) (i) To measure effectiveness, we need to establish objectives or targets for performance. Since these cannot be expressed financially, **non-financial targets** must be used. The effective level of achievement could be measured by comparing actual performance against target.

Adherence to appointment times

(1) Percentage of appointments kept on time
(2) Percentage of appointments no more than 10 minutes late
(3) Percentage of appointments kept within 30 minutes of schedule
(4) Percentage of cancelled appointments
(5) Average delay in appointments

A **problem** with these measures is that there is an implied assumption that all patients will be at the clinic by their appointed time. In practice, this will not always be the case.

Patients' ability to contact the clinic and make appointments

(1) Percentage of patients who can make an appointment at their first preferred time, or at the first date offered to them
(2) Average time from making an appointment to the appointment date
(3) Number of complaints about failure to contact the clinic, as a percentage of total patients seen
(4) If the telephone answering system provides for queuing of calls, the average waiting-for-answer times for callers and the percentage of abandoned calls

Comprehensive monitoring programme

Measures might be based on the definition of each element or step within a monitoring programme for a patient, It would then be possible to measure the following.

(1) Percentage of patients receiving every stage of the programme (and percentage receiving every stage but one, every stage but two, and so on)
(2) If each stage has a scheduled date for completion, the average delay for patients in the completion of each stage

(ii) A **single quality of care** measure would call for subjective judgements about the following.

(1) The key **objective**/objectives for each of the three features of service
(2) The relative **weighting** that should be given to each

The objectives would have to be measured on comparable terms, and since money values are inappropriate, an index based on percentage or a points-scoring system of measurement might be used. A target index or points score for achievement could then be set, and actual results compared against the target.

Solutions to Part A Multiple Choice Questions

1 B ABC is a system of absorption costing and if overheads are charged on the basis of a budgeted rate, there will be under- or over-absorption. In a system of ABC, a larger proportion of overheads is charged to low volume products.

2 A The product specification may be changed, for example by using more standard components or changing the materials content of the product; however, changes should not reduce the value of the product to the customer, because this will affect the price the customer will be prepared to pay. Target costing may be combined with life cycle costing, but this is not necessary.

3 C Return will be increased if the break even time is shortened, not maximised.

4 A Total factory costs: [2,000 units × $(8 + 19.50)] + [10,000 × $(4 + 8)] = $175,000
Factory cost per unit of bottleneck resource = $175,000/3,500 hours = $50
Product B throughput per unit = $25 - $5 = $20
Product B throughput per unit of bottleneck resource = $20/0.25 = $80
TA ratio = $80/$50 = 1.60

5 D In flow cost accounting, a distinction is made between positive and negative products, but a cost is attributed to each. Cost consists of materials system costs and delivery and disposal costs.

6 C

	Product X	Product Y	Total
	$	$	$
Sales revenue	144,000	216,000	360,000
Variable costs	62,000	100,000	162,000
Contribution			198,000
Fixed costs	48,000	60,000	108,000

Contribution/Sales ratio = 198,000/360,000 = 0.55
Breakeven point = $108,000/0.55 = $196,364

7 A

	Component			
	W	X	Y	Z
Additional cost of external purchase	$40	$31	$16	$33
Hours saved	3	2	1	1.5
Extra cost per hour saved	$13.3	$15.5	$16	$22
Ranking for external purchase	1st	2nd	3rd	4th

8 D The two maximum constraints would be 0.6x + 0.5y ≤ 48,000 and 0.3x + 0.2y ≤ 20,000

9 B Price at which demand is 0 = $40 + (16,000/2,000) × $3 = $64

When P = a – bQ, b = 3/2,000 = 0.0015

10 B If demand is expected to be inelastic with regard to price, low prices are not going to affect market demand significantly, so market skimming will almost certainly result in profit maximisation. Price discrimination will not offer any benefit, even if it is possible, when demand is price inelastic.

11 C

	$ per hour
Labour cost	10
Variable overhead cost	2
Lost contribution (80 – 34)/2	23
Relevant cost per hour	35

Total relevant cost = 20 hours × $35 = $700

12 D Regret table

Outcome situation	Option 1	Option 2	Option 3	Option 4
	$	$	$	$
Outcome 1	8,000	0	15,000	18,000
Outcome 2	30,000	40,000	0	20,000
Outcome 3	0	37,000	25,000	23,000
Max. regret	30,000	40,000	25,000	23,000

13 B The definition in statement 1 is a definition of a fixed budget. Incremental decision packages in ZBB are used to measure the incremental cost of an activity or incremental activity, and to assess the benefits that this will provide. Incremental decision packages can be ranked according to the net benefit they will provide.

14 A Average time for first 4 units = 160 × 75% × 75% = 90 hours
Total time b in learning curve formula = log 0.75/log 2 = - 0.1249387/0.30103 = - 0.4150374
Average time for first 5 units = 160 × 5$^{- 0.4150374}$ = 1,600 × 0.5127449 = 82.03918 hours
Total time for first 5 units = 5 × 82.03918 hours = 410.196 hours
Cost per hour = $3,200/160= $20 per hour
Cost for 5th unit = (410.for first 4 units = 360 hours
Value of 196 – 360) hours × $20 = $1,003.92

15 D There is a poor or non-existent audit trail with spreadsheets. Spreadsheets and participation in budgeting are unrelated. Models can be complex, but there is a greater risk of errors in formulae in the model. The use of spreadsheets does, however, greatly assist risk and uncertainty analysis.

16 A Standard costing is most appropriate when the products manufactured are identical. This occurs in a mass production environment.

17 A

	kg
45,000 units of output should use (× 0.4)	18,000
They did use (6,900 + 12,600)	19,500
Yield variance in kg	1,500 (A)
Weighted average standard cost per kg ($2/0.4kg = $5)	$5
Yield variance in $	$7,500 (A)

18 B In retrospect the market size was 90,000 units and if the company maintained a 20% market share it would have sold 18,000 units.

Market share variance:

	units
Expected sales to maintain market share	18,000
Actual sales	17,000
Market share variance in sales units	1,000 (A)
Standard profit per unit	$10
Market share variance in $ profit	$10,000 (A)

19 D Adverse materials usage may be caused partly by inefficiencies or errors by production staff. Training may improve their ability to do the work, an improve materials usage rates.

20 C Budgetary control information comes mainly from sources inside the organisation.

An Enterprise Resource Planning (ERP) system provides an integrated database system for the management of operations.

21 C Feedback is used mainly for control reporting purposes. It is primary data. It comes from internal sources within the organisation. It may consist of both financial and non-financial information.

22	C	There can be (and usually are) several Key Performance Indicators for each of the four perspectives of performance. A performance target to reduce the amount of wastage in production would relate to the internal perspective of the BSC.
23	A	There are three aspects to setting standards in the Building Block model: ownership, achievability and equity (fairness).
24	B	($40,000/$300,000) × 100% = 13.3%
25	C	The transfer price should be the opportunity cost for Profit Centre B of not being able to sell the product in the external market. This is the external market price minus the variable selling and distribution cost: $30 - $1 = $29.
26	D	When an organisation has multiple objectives, especially when these are not ranked in order of importance, it is difficult to assess performance. Some objectives may be met, but performance with regard to other objectives may be very poor and disappointing.

Index

BPP
LEARNING MEDIA

Notes

Review Form – Paper F5 Performance Management (6/14)

Please help us to ensure that the ACCA learning materials we produce remain as accurate and user-friendly as possible. We cannot promise to answer every submission we receive, but we do promise that it will be read and taken into account when we update this Study Text.

Name: _____ Address: _____

_____

_____

How have you used this Text?
(Tick one box only)

☐ Home study (book only)

☐ On a course: college _____

☐ With 'correspondence' package

☐ Other _____

Why did you decide to purchase this Text? *(Tick one box only)*

☐ Have used BPP Texts in the past

☐ Recommendation by friend/colleague

☐ Recommendation by a lecturer at college

☐ Saw information of BPP website

☐ Saw advertising

☐ Other _____

During the past six months do you recall seeing/receiving any of the following?
(Tick as many boxes as are relevant)

☐ Our advertisement in *ACCA Student Accountant*

☐ Our advertisement in *PQ*

☐ Our brochure with a letter through the post

☐ Our website www.bpp.com

Which (if any) aspects of our advertising do you find useful?
(Tick as many boxes as are relevant)

☐ Prices and publication dates of new editions

☐ Information on Text content

☐ Facility to order books off-the-page

☐ None of the above

Which BPP products have you used?

Text	☑	Home Study Package	☐
Kit	☐	i-Pass	☐
Passcards	☐		

Your ratings, comments and suggestions would be appreciated on the following areas.

	Very useful	Useful	Not useful
Introductory section	☐	☐	☐
Chapter introductions	☐	☐	☐
Key terms	☐	☐	☐
Quality of explanations	☐	☐	☐
Case studies and other examples	☐	☐	☐
Exam focus points	☐	☐	☐
Questions and answers in each chapter	☐	☐	☐
Fast forwards and chapter roundups	☐	☐	☐
Quick quizzes	☐	☐	☐
Question Bank	☐	☐	☐
Answer Bank	☐	☐	☐
Index	☐	☐	☐

Overall opinion of this Study Text	Excellent ☐	Good ☐	Adequate ☐	Poor ☐

Do you intend to continue using BPP products?   Yes ☐   No ☐

On the reverse of this page is space for you to write your comments about our Study Text. We welcome your feedback.

The BPP Learning Media ACCA Range Manager of this edition can be e-mailed at: pippariley@bpp.com

Please return this form to: Pippa Riley, ACCA Range Manager, BPP Learning Media Ltd, FREEPOST, London, W12 8AA

TELL US WHAT YOU THINK

Please note any further comments and suggestions/errors below. For example, was the text accurate, readable, concise, user-friendly and comprehensive?